Tom Horn
in
Life and Legend

Also by Larry D. Ball

The United States Marshals of New Mexico and Arizona Territories, 1846–1912
    (Albuquerque, 1978)

Desert Lawmen: The High Sheriffs of New Mexico and Arizona, 1846–1912
    (Albuquerque, 1992)

Elfego Baca in Life and Legend (El Paso, 1992)

*Ambush at Bloody Run: The Wham Paymaster Robbery of 1889; a Story of Politics,
    Religion, Race, and Banditry in Arizona Territory* (Tucson, 2000)

Tom Horn
in
Life and Legend

Larry D. Ball

University of Oklahoma Press : Norman

Publication of this book is made possible through the generosity
of Edith Kinney Gaylord.

Library of Congress Cataloging-in-Publication Data

Ball, Larry D., 1940–
   Tom Horn in life and legend / Larry D. Ball.
   pages cm
   Includes bibliographical references and index.
   ISBN 978-0-8061-4425-2 (cloth)
   ISBN 978-0-8061-5175-5 (paper)
1. Horn, Tom, 1860–1903. 2. Apache Indians—Wars, 1883–1886.
3. Detectives—West (U.S.)—Biography. 4. Frontier and pioneer life—
West (U.S.) 5. Frontier and pioneer life—Wyoming. 6. Trials (Murder)—
Wyoming—Cheyenne. 7. West (U.S.)—Biography. I. Title.
   E83.88.H67B35 2014
   979'.03092—dc23
   [B]
                         2013043109

2 3 4 5 6 7 8 9 10

Contents

List of Illustrations

FIGURES

MAPS

Preface

On Monday morning, 13 January 1902, two men walked into the lobby of the Inter Ocean Hotel in Cheyenne, Wyoming. Both men wore badges, and they were obviously there on business. Edwin J. Smalley, sheriff of Laramie County, and Undersheriff Richard A. Proctor spied the man they were looking for, a well-known livestock detective named Tom Horn, talking with another individual. Smalley recalled this tense moment:

> We found him sitting on one of the leather settees in the lobby and talking to a Union Pacific Special Agent by the name of [Frank] Wheeler. Tom usually wore his coat and his vest unbuttoned and carried his gun thrust into his trousers, fastened, of course, to the trouser belt. The butt of his gun rested right at the pit of his stomach which made it easy for him to draw in quick time. I called "Hello Tom," and he got to his feet and put his hand out to greet me and said, "Hello Tommy." He called me Tommy. I shook hands with him with my right hand and at the same time grabbed his gun with my left. He was mildly surprised at my taking his gun but showed no inclination to fight. I said, "Tom, I have a warrant for your arrest." 'The h—— you have! What for?" he demanded. I then read the warrant to him and said, "You'll have to come along to the jail with me Tom." "All right," he said. . . . I didn't even put the cuffs on him. As we were walking along I asked, "How much do you weigh Tom?" "I weigh about two-hundred and one pounds," he said.

"How old are you Tom and what is your height?" I asked. "I'm forty-four years, forty-four months, forty-four days, forty-four hours, and forty-four seconds, and I'm six foot one inch tall," he answered with his usual joking manner.[1]

The arrest of Tom Horn on that January morning in 1902 brought to an abrupt end the active life of one of the most notable frontier personalities in the post–Civil War era. Although Horn lived nearly two more years, he spent that time in the Laramie County Jail (with the exception of a few minutes of freedom in an abortive escape attempt). On 20 November 1903, Horn was hanged for the murder of a fourteen-year-old boy. Even before his death, the legend of Tom Horn had begun to emerge. This legend continues to flourish, and Horn still occupies a prominent place in the pantheon of Wild West personalities. He contributed to his own legend through his *Life of Tom Horn, Government Scout and Interpreter*, written while he awaited execution. In spite of the author's wild exaggerations and inaccuracies, this volume has had remarkable endurance and has been reprinted many times. Like many other legendary frontier characters, Tom Horn attracted new attention with the growth of popular interest in the Wild West in the 1920s and 1930s. Since that time, his story has attracted writers of both fiction and nonfiction, who have produced numerous books and countless articles. Movies, radio, and television have added to the lore. Some aficionados of the Wild West place Tom Horn among the top frontier gun wielders—alongside such men as Wyatt Earp and Wild Bill Hickok—but the dark cloud of his criminal conviction marred his reputation. Had he died in a shoot-out or even from a bullet in the back, Tom Horn might have earned a place among the most admired frontier notables. This Missouri farm boy's early years were filled with creditable activities—civilian packer and chief of scouts in the Apache wars of the 1880s, pioneer rodeo star, deputy sheriff, deputy United States marshal, Pinkerton detective, and chief packer in the Cuban campaign of 1898. Not until he entered into the service of Wyoming cattle barons as a range detective in the 1890s did allegations of wrongdoing—including work as a hired killer—cloud his reputation. His association with livestock magnates, to whom Horn was loyal in spite of the risk to himself, eventually led to his death.

Since the appearance of Jay Monaghan's *Last of the Bad Men: The Legend of Tom Horn* in 1946, some writers have explored the factual side of Tom Horn's life. Monaghan's volume remains a standard treatment, since he had access to people who were personally acquainted with his subject. Most of the serious research in recent years concerns the last decade of Horn's life, when he served as a range detective and hired assassin. The work of Dean Krakel, Mark Dugan, Doyce Nunis, and Chip Carlson represents the best of this research. Yet Tom Horn remains a shadowy and elusive figure, especially in regard to his activities in Arizona Territory. The present work—to some degree built upon the work of other writers—is an effort to document and bring into sharper relief the story of Tom Horn from beginning to end. Any attempt to recount the life of Tom Horn is fraught with difficulties, and I have concluded that I was naïve to rush into such a controversial subject, one that wiser scholars had avoided. There were at least three Tom Horns, I now know: first, the Tom Horn in the documents; second, the hero of his own wildly exaggerated autobiography; and finally, the Tom Horn of legend. My aim is to recover the historical Tom Horn.

In making this effort, I have received the assistance of so many individuals and institutions that any attempt to list them will inevitably lead to inadvertent omissions. I apologize in advance for any such oversights. Nor does the order in which the following names appear indicate the relative value of this assistance. First and foremost, I am grateful to Chip Carlson of Cheyenne. Not only has he provided encouragement and helpful material, but he and his wife, Karen—an authority on Wyoming history in her own right—took the time away from busy schedules to introduce my wife and me to geographic sites, including the infamous fence gap, associated with Tom Horn's activities. In addition, Chip's website—http://www.tom-horn.com/forum—is an ongoing repository of new information. Allan Radbourne of Bridgwater, Somerset, England, has not only been generous with the fruits of his research into the Apache campaigns but has provided helpful advice and important photographs. Bruce J. Dinges, director of publications for the Arizona Historical Society, in Tucson, has also provided assistance in too many ways to enumerate.

Many others have assisted with this project. They include (in no particular order of importance): William Clements, professor of folklore, Arkansas State University; Stanley C. Brown, Prescott, Arizona; Richard Pierce, Chandler, Arizona; Britt Wilson, Redlands, California; Edwin R. Sweeney, Saint Charles, Missouri; Charles Herner, Tucson, Arizona; Robert DeArment, Sylvania, Ohio; John and Karen Tanner, Fallbrook, California; Nancy Coggeshall, Reserve, New Mexico; John P. Wilson,

Las Cruces, New Mexico; Richard Proctor, San Clemente, California; Allan Ferg and Keith Basso, Arizona State Museum, University of Arizona, Tucson; Bud Shapard, Pisgah Forest, North Carolina; Ron Lacy (aka Tom Horn), Newcastle on Tyne, England; Bill O'Neal, Carthage, Texas; Linda Langham, Salem, Oregon; Lori Davisson, Tucson, Arizona; Ben Traywick, Tombstone, Arizona; Wendy John, Safford, Arizona; James Moore, Tallahassee, Florida; George Gause and Jerry Thompson, Laredo, Texas; Rick Miller, Harker Heights, Texas; Karen Williams, Safford, Arizona; Irvin Van Enwyck, Morristown, Arizona; Douglas Hamilton, Tucson, Arizona; Chuck Parsons, Luling, Texas; Bob Everett, former director, Jim Gatchell Museum, Buffalo, Wyoming; John Boessenecker, San Francisco, California; Bob McCubbin, Santa Fe, New Mexico; Paul Hutton, Distinguished Professor of History, University of New Mexico (Albuquerque); and Bob Mattoon, San Jose, California.

Numerous libraries and archives have been of much assistance: Scotland County Memorial Library, Memphis, Missouri; Kansas State Historical Society (Topeka); State Historical Society of Missouri, Columbia; Nebraska State Historical Society, Lincoln; Union Pacific Railroad Archives (Omaha); Special Collections Department, Marriott Library, University of Utah, Salt Lake City; L. Tom Perry Special Collections Department, Harold B. Lee Library, Brigham Young University, Provo, Utah; Wyoming State Archives, Cheyenne; American Heritage Center, University of Wyoming, Laramie; Special Collections Department, University of California, Santa Barbara; Colorado State Historical Society and Denver Public Library, Denver, Colorado; Pueblo Public Library (Colorado); Arizona Historical Society (Tucson), and the Special Collections Department, University of Arizona Library, Tucson; Arizona History and Archives Division, Arizona State Library (Phoenix); Special Collections Department, Hayden Library and Arizona Historical Foundation, both of Arizona State University; Sharlot Hall Museum and Library, Prescott, Arizona; National Archives and Records Administration (Washington, D. C.) and its facilities at College Park, Maryland, and Denver, Colorado; the Center for Southwest Research, University of New Mexico (Albuquerque); New Mexico State Historical Society, Santa Fe; Western History Collections, University of Oklahoma (Norman); Manuscripts Division, Library of Congress, Washington, D. C.; the Tampa Bay History Center (Florida); Special Collections Department, Northern Arizona University, Flagstaff; White

Mountain Apache Cultural Center, Fort Apache Historic Site, Whiteriver, Arizona; U.S. Army War College Library, Carlisle, Pennsylvania; Public Library, Canon City, Colorado; Marion County Historical Society, Salem, Oregon; Multnomah County Public Library, Troutdale, Oregon; Museum of Northwest Colorado, Craig, Colorado; Rutherford B. Hayes Presidential Center Library, Fremont, Ohio; Nita Stewart Haley Memorial Library, Midland, Texas; Special Collections Department, New Mexico State University, Las Cruces; Jim Gatchell Museum, Buffalo, Wyo.; the Ray and Pat Browne Library for Popular Culture Studies, Bowling Green State University (Ohio); San Antonio Public Library (Texas); Nevada Historical Society, Reno; Department of Special Collections, University of Nevada Library, Reno; and the Silver City Museum, New Mexico.

The staff of the Interlibrary Loan Department of the Dean B. Ellis Library at Arkansas State University deserves special mention. Two supervisors, Margaret Daniels (ret.) and Linda Keller, present supervisor, with her assistant, Michael Sheppard, have gone far beyond the call of duty to find books, articles, and other materials relevant to this work.

The author also wishes to express his appreciation for the assistance of B. Byron Price, Director of the University of Oklahoma Press. Charles E. Rankin, Editor-in-Chief, and Steven Baker, Managing Editor, deserve special praise for their patience and understanding in guiding the author through the publication process.

Material from the author's previous articles in *Colorado Heritage, the Journal of Arizona History,* and the *Journal of the Wild West History Association* have been incorporated into this volume; see the Bibliography for details. Finally, I extend my thanks and gratitude to my son, Durwood Ball, associate professor of history at the University of New Mexico, Albuquerque. His experience as an editor and historian has been of much benefit. Most especially, my wife, Ruth, deserves much credit for the successful completion of this work. Not only has she listened patiently to the endless saga of Tom Horn, but she has endured a constant clutter of notes and volumes on her dining room table for the past decade. In addition, she assisted with research, and read, reread, and corrected the manuscript. Her patience and forbearance is much appreciated.

Jonesboro, Arkansas
January 2014

Tom Horn
in
Life and Legend

CHAPTER 1

Missouri Roots

The family of Tom Horn was typical of thousands who sought a new life on the American frontier in the eighteenth and nineteenth centuries. While there is some uncertainty about Tom Horn's ancestry, it appears that Jacob John Horn, born about 1721 to English parents, possibly in Philadelphia, was an early progenitor. Jacob married Duschea van Natta, who bore him four children. Their last child, Hartman, was born in Virginia in 1747. Subsequently, Jacob Horn relocated his family to the frontier village of Washington, twenty-five miles southwest of Pittsburgh, Pennsylvania. Duschea Horn, who was apparently born in Germany, insisted that only her native language be spoken in the household; hence the erroneous story that the Horn family was from Germany. In 1771 Hartman married Elizabeth Hough and settled in Buffalo, a few miles west of Washington. Among their children were Martin, born 1772, and C. Hartman, in 1794. After the younger Hartman Horn married, his wife gave birth to a son, Martin C., in 1813. Hartman then moved his family to Mt. Vernon, in Knox County, northeast of Columbus, Ohio. In their new surroundings, Hartman's wife gave birth to Thomas H. Horn, on 15 January 1825. In 1833 Martin Horn, elder brother of Hartman, joined him in Knox County.[1]

On 12 December 1850, Thomas H. Horn married Mary Ann Maricha Miller. Mary Ann, born on 22 January 1831, came from a locally influential family. Her father received a 4,000-acre land grant on the Muskingum River (later Coshocton County) for honorable service in the War of 1812 and eventually served in the Ohio legislature. On Mary Ann's maternal side, one ancestor, Abraham Clark, as a representative of New Jersey, was a signer of the Declaration of Independence. Her maternal grandfather fought in the bloody Shawnee Indian Wars in the Ohio country in the 1780s and '90s.[2]

Thomas and Mary Ann Horn began married life on the Horn family farm in Coshocton County. Their first child, Charles, was born on 1 January 1852. (A second child, who may have been a twin of Charles, died in 1854.) While Thomas Horn was hardworking, he was something of a gambler, and, like many frontiersmen, given to speculation. When he and his father, Hartman, joined three Knox County farmers in a cattle venture, Thomas Horn was designated to manage the money. Rather than paying off the initial debt, the Horns invested the proceeds in a second venture, apparently with the complicity of some of the partners. When the other partners, as well as their creditors, filed suit in 1851, an Ohio judge ordered Thomas Horn to pay his indebtedness of more than $800. Horn indicated that he was bankrupt. The next year Thomas Horn, his father, C. Hartman, and other family members departed Ohio at night. Angry creditors pursued the Horns through the courts for many years.[3]

The Horn family settled in Scotland County, Missouri, in 1853, in the northeastern corner of the state on the Iowa border. Thomas Horn and his brother, Martin, as well as their father, C. Hartman, purchased property near Etna, in Harrison Township, southeast of the county seat of Memphis. Founded in 1834, Etna was situated on an important east–west roadway and soon boasted stores, churches, and a newspaper. With typical frontier optimism, the inhabitants expected a railroad to come their way.[4]

The family of Thomas Horn soon began to grow into a frontier brood. In addition to Charles and the deceased twin, who were born in Ohio, Mary Ann Horn gave birth to ten more children. William, or "Willie," who was born in 1856, died at the age of eight. Nancy "Nannie" Belle arrived in 1858, and Thomas H., Jr., was delivered on 21 November 1860. Martin Isaac Horn followed two years later, while Mary Ann was visiting relatives in Coshocton County, Ohio. The remaining children were all born in Scotland County, Missouri: Hannah May, 1865; Austin H., called "Oss," 1866, and Mary "Maude" Ambrosian, 1869. A set of twins, Ima and Ina, were born in 1871, but died the following year. The twelfth and last child, Bertha ("Alice"), was born four years later.[5]

Thomas Horn, Sr., built a substantial home and barn a few miles northeast of Etna and was soon the largest landholder in the county, with title to 1700 acres. In addition to raising cattle, horses, and sheep, according to one newspaper, the elder Horn speculated in farm products. Before railroads arrived in northeastern Missouri, he purchased large herds of animals, drove them to Alexandria, on the Mississippi River, and sold them. In September 1874, Thomas, Sr., purchased ten shares of stock in the newly established Citizens' Bank of Memphis at ten dollars per share. He and a partner, W. W. Purmort, who owned a hardware store in the county seat, began to introduce improved breeds of cattle. The editor of the *Memphis Reveille* praised the Horn-Purmort herd as "some of the finest cattle in the world." In May 1885, Purmort & Horn advertised short-horned cattle for sale, all "well bred and registered."[6]

In later years Thomas Horn, Jr., remembered his father as an active and energetic man, always on the go. It was not uncommon to see his father ride off "to an election or a public sale" of livestock. Although Thomas Horn, Sr., "had only a common school education," according to another informant, he "wrote a good hand, [and] was a natural mathematician and persistent reader." The elder Horn did not shy away from the rough-and-tumble aspects of frontier life. He enjoyed horse races, Tom, Jr., recalled, and was a man of "nerve." Thomas, Sr., had the reputation of being the best man with his fists in Scotland County and was regarded as "the most prominent man in his section of Missouri."[7]

In spite of his seeming success, Thomas Horn, Sr.'s creditors pursued him all the way from Ohio. In 1867 one former partner filed a damage suit against him for $1,650. When Scotland County Sheriff H. H. Byrne attached the property necessary to fulfill the monetary terms of the suit, Tom, Sr., took steps to put his land out of all suitors' reach. He placed some property in the name of Mary Ann Horn and "sold" other pieces of real estate to his sons, Charles and Martin.[8]

Thomas Horn, Sr., took a keen interest in community affairs. He and his brother, Martin, were strong supporters of Andrew Jackson and the recently created Democratic Party. Indeed, Martin cast his first presidential vote for Jackson in 1828. In February 1872, Thomas Horn, Sr., presided at a Democratic gathering in his precinct. Two years later, he was an unsuccessful nominee for delegate to the county convention.

The brothers also answered the call to jury duty and served as road supervisors and as members of Scotland County fair committees. At one
fair, Tom Horn, Sr., won prizes for best bull and best cow.[9]

Tom Horn, Jr., was born in a border state just before the Civil War,
during the highly charged atmosphere of sectional conflict. Since Dem-
ocrats throughout the border region were suspected of being Confederate sympathizers, many migrated to the Colorado and Montana mining
country in order to avoid the secessionist stigma. However, Thomas
Horn, Sr., and his family stayed put in spite of such problems. While
some skirmishes took place between Union and Confederate forces in
and around Scotland County, and the Horns may have given aid and
comfort to the latter, there is no indication that the Civil War seriously
disrupted the Horns' everyday lives. But many years later, Tom Horn,
Jr., recalled that he was born in "a troublesome time." "Anyone born
in Missouri is bound to see trouble," he wrote, citing Bill Nye (Edgar
Wilson), the noted nineteenth-century humorist. [10]

Tom Horn, Sr., and his wife imposed a stern religious discipline at
home. The Horns, including Tom, Jr.'s Uncle Martin and Aunt Drusilla
Horn, were devout Disciples of Christ (the forerunner of the present-
day Christian Church). This protestant sect, considered radical in the
early nineteenth century, was founded by Thomas Campbell in Washington County, Pennsylvania, the Horn family's ancestral home. The
Campbellites, as they were called, emphasized a simple gospel, democratic church polity, and the unity of the Christian community. Their
call for a stern piety in daily life fitted the hardships of frontier life. As
their children grew up, Tom, Sr., and Mary Ann Horn employed the
rod liberally in an effort to enforce order in the home. They were very
disappointed that none of their children showed a keen interest in the
church.[11]

Instead of religious services, the forest and its wildlife exercised a relentless pull upon young Tom. "We had Sunday schools and church,"
he recalled,

> and as my mother was a good, old-fashioned Campbellite, I was
> supposed to go to church and Sunday school, as did most of the
> boys and girls in the neighborhood. . . . I had nothing particular
> against going, if it hadn't been for the 'coons, turkeys, quail. . . .
> [Hunting] kept me busy most every Sunday. . . . I would steal
> out the [family] gun and take the dog and hunt all day Sunday

and many a night through the week, knowing full well that . . . I would get a whipping or a scolding from my mother or a regular thumping from father.[12]

Tom's education also suffered. "My mother was always anxious to have all the children go to school during the winter months," he wrote, "and I always had to go, or to start anyway." Unfortunately, "all the natural influences of the country were against my acquiring much of an education," he admitted. Since the summer months were taken up with "hard and long hours putting in crops and tending to them," he "had little legitimate time to fish and hunt bee trees." With the arrival of winter (and school), all the adventuresome Tom, Jr., wanted to do was "to go look after the game." Nonetheless, "I was ordered to go to school," he wrote, and "I had to go." Whether he matriculated the full six grades of elementary school is not known. Yet Tom Horn, Jr., later demonstrated some basic writing talent.[13]

Although the school was located only a mile from the Horn farm, Tom, Jr., found many distractions in that short walk. With winter snows on the ground, "I would always be finding fresh rabbit or 'coon or cat tracks crossing the trail to school," he said, and "I never could cross a fresh track" without following it up. "I would then go on a little farther," he recollected, "and then I would say to myself, 'I will be late for school and get licked.'" But the desire to see where the animal trail led was "overpowering." "I would go back in the orchard behind the house," admitted the truant boy, whistle for his hunting dog, Shedrick, and "school was all off." "'Shed' and I would go hunting." "I could climb any tree in Missouri, and dig frozen ground with a pick [for animal burrows], and follow cold tracks in the mud or snow," he recalled proudly. Had the school building "been nearer," he protested, "I could have gotten there a great deal oftener" (a doubtful statement in view of Horn's having spent much of his adult life outdoors). In spite of Mary Horn's concern about her son's "Indian ways," she took some pride in his hunting ability. "When our neighbors would complain of losing a chicken," he recalled "mother would tell them that whenever any varmint bothered her hen-roosts, she would just send out Tom and 'Shedrick.'"[14]

In spite of such distractions, young Tom not only obtained the rudiments of an elementary education at Etna, but continued to read throughout his life. As one Scotland County resident recalled, the boy was "an enthusiastic reader of dime novels." Many years later, when Tom Horn faced the hangman's noose in Cheyenne, Wyoming, he informed the *Denver Post* that army officers in Arizona helped him with his education: "The very creditable education he has now, he explains by the interesting story that the officers of the post took a fancy to him as a bright, ambitious lad, gave him the rudiments of the ordinary public school training, and loaned him books which he took out on the hills and studied industriously while he herded sheep. And from that time on he has been a self-made man."[15]

While he complained about work on the farm, young Tom also learned things from such drudgery that stood him in good stead later in life. The Horn farm was a typical nineteenth-century agricultural enterprise, involving orchards and livestock as well as raising other crops. He learned much about the care of livestock and developed a special affinity for horses that remained with him throughout his life. While he was reluctant to acknowledge his father's teaching, there is little doubt that the elder Horn schooled his son in the care of animals.[16]

Young Tom had a reputation as a mischief maker around Etna. He organized playmates into a band of "outlaws," with himself as the leader, and made "frequent raids . . . on chicken coops and orchards," according to an old resident. On one occasion, Tom and a friend lifted "a large quantity of shot" from a general store in Etna. As they walked out of the store, the loot began to escape through a hole in Tom's pocket, spilling across the floor and giving them away. "The lads were arrested for the theft but were not prosecuted."[17]

Fighting was part of such young boys' lives. Little Sammy Griggs, one of Tom's hunting companions, proved a challenging opponent. On one occasion, Tom and Sammy, both of whom took great pride in their hunting dogs, quarreled over whose animal was the best. Tom admitted that he "went home pretty badly used up" after this fracas.[18]

The same Scotland County resident who recalled Tom's fondness for the penny dreadfuls also remembered that, like many local boys, he "was inordinately fond of firearms." Anxious to impress his comrades, young Tom secretly slipped "an old fashion[ed] revolver" from the family home and carried it on one of their escapades. In a bit of horseplay, he "accidentally discharged" the weapon, wounding nine-year-old Charles Harris in the shoulder. A story circulated later in Horn's life that he killed Harris, but fortunately, Harris recovered.[19]

The Horn household was a busy place "known far and wide for its hospitality." Mary Ann Horn, a woman with a big heart, "was famous for her charity." "There was never a neighbor who did not send for her in time of need," according to one informant. In addition to Tom, Jr., his siblings, and parents, the Horn household contained one grandfather as well as "an orphan nephew of Mrs. Horn, a girl who lived with them for many years and many hired hands." The latter increased in number during planting and harvesting time. With so much work required around the house, Mary Ann Horn kept extra help busy. Eva Horn Whitehead, a niece of Tom, Jr., recalled that her mother worked in the Horn household in 1879.[20]

One of the many guests in the Horn household was Benjamin S. Markley, a nephew of Mary Ann. Bennie, whose family owned a farm in St. Francis County, in eastern Arkansas, came to live with the Horns in the 1870s. Tom, Jr., took an instant dislike to cousin Bennie, who was two years older. A poor marksman and hunter, Bennie ran to the womenfolk for protection from young Tom and his friends, who considered him a "sissy." Eventually, Tom picked a fight with Bennie. "I had him whipped before my mother and the rest of the family could get me off him," he recalled proudly. "Dad was there but he did not try to help the women pull me off," he continued, "for I do think Ben was a little too good [even] for him."[21]

By the time of Bennie Markley's arrival, the relationship between Tom and his father had become strained. At the age of fourteen, the young boy simply quit school and informed the elder Horn that he was going to help full time on the farm. It was not long before "things [at home] were beginning to get rather binding on me," he wrote later, and his father's resort to frequent "thumpings" began to wear thin. Nor did Tom exhibit any particular affection for the women in the household, although he evidently had some feelings for his mother. This apparent disdain for females continued throughout his life, although he was known to associate with them occasionally for recreational purposes. While he admitted that tormenting cousin Bennie Markley "made me no favorite with the women folks," he went on to admit that their disapproval "was of little importance to me."[22]

Aside from his hunting rifle, Tom Horn's most prized possession was his dog, Shedrick. Any mistreatment of this much-loved pet was a mistreatment of its master. One day when Tom was fourteen, he got into a scuffle with two boys from a passing immigrant train. The older of the pair carried a shotgun. In a moment of youthful bravado, Tom, who favored a rifle for hunting—it required more skilled marksmanship—blurted out "that a man who shot game with a shotgun was no good." In reply, the wielder of the shotgun "asked me if I called myself a man," recalled Horn. This challenge set off a "scrap" between Tom and the older boy. Soon the younger of the immigrant boys, as well as Shedrick, joined in the scuffle. Not only did the younger of the migrant boys give Tom a good bruising, but the older boy shot and killed "Shed."[23]

Tom, Sr., was outraged at this insult to his household and rode furiously to overtake these malicious travelers. Tom, Jr., never learned just what transpired when his father caught up with them, but he recalled the elder Horn "was pretty badly done up" when he returned. To see his father in such a bruised condition was unusual, since the neighbors considered him "the hardest man to whip" in that part of the state. The death of young Tom's pet hound was "the first . . . real sorrow of my life," he wrote later.[24]

Since the Horn farm was within eyeshot of this popular immigrant road, wagonloads of pioneers were a common sight. The *Reveille* and the *Conservative,* both published in the county seat of Memphis, frequently reprinted letters from former Scotland County residents who had made new homes in the distant wilderness. On 16 March 1876, the *Reveille* reported that eighteen local citizens had just left for the West and another ten were about to depart.[25]

Members of the Horn family were not immune to this contagion. In November 1874, Tom's older brother, Charles, decided to seek his fortune in California. On 29 November Charley married nineteen-year-old Elizabeth (Lizzie) Blattner in neighboring Clark County, Missouri, and, observed the *Memphis Reveille*, the "happy pair started for the golden shores of California soon after the nuptial knot was tied." Another Scotland County resident, D. F. Burch, may have accompanied the newlyweds on their long journey.[26]

The travels of the older brother, as well as local newspaper coverage of frontier settlement, inspired Tom, Jr., to think about going west. "One day Charles . . . came back from the west for a visit," wrote Tom Horn's biographer, Jay Monaghan, who had an opportunity to interview the elder brother in 1930. To young Tom, the older sibling appeared "full of success." "As is usual with sons who have come from a long way off," continued Monaghan, "Charles gave proof to the hope that Tom had seen shining in the eyes of all immigrants." This visit, which probably took place in 1876 or 1877, loomed large in the life of Tom, Jr., who was growing up and becoming restless.[27]

In his autobiography, Tom Horn maintained that a "disagreement" with his father precipitated his departure. "When I saw I was in for a daisy [of a whipping]," he wrote, "I told him . . . it was his last time, for I was going to leave home." After a week of his mother's nursing, Tom had healed enough to take to the road. "As soon as I could get around," he recalled, "I sold my rifle for $11.00, kissed my mother for the last time in my life, went out and took a look at old 'Shedrick's' grave, got a lunch and started west."[28]

In spite of their disagreements, Tom, Jr., was still his father's son and even admired the elder Horn, although the two were never close after Tom, Jr., left home. "The nerve which the son displayed throughout the trying times through which he [later] passed," a friend later remarked, "were inherited from his father and grandfather or his father's side, while what tenderness he may have possessed came from his mother."[29]

The date of Tom Horn's departure for the West remains a question. While he maintained that he was "about fourteen years old" when he departed Scotland County, the dates he provided in *Life of Tom Horn, Government Scout and Interpreter* are almost uniformly wrong. Family tradition suggests that he left home at the age of sixteen or seventeen. "I had . . . heard of the West—California, Texas and Kansas," he wrote later, "but from all the geography I had picked up at school I could not form any idea as to the location . . . of these places." Nonetheless, he followed the setting sun and "walked and walked day after day, stopping at farmhouses to get my grub; and many a good woman would give me a lunch to take with me."[30]

In Kansas City, Missouri, an employment agent suggested that Horn might find work on the Atchison, Topeka and Santa Fe Railroad. In Newton, Kansas, where the Santa Fe maintained a division headquarters, he got his first job. Always anxious to inform readers of the wages he earned, Horn recalled that he "worked on the tracks at Newton about twenty-six days and got $21.00 for it."[31]

Tom, Jr., was not the only Horn to be bitten by the western bug. In 1877 Tom Horn, Sr., filed on land near Grinnell, Kansas, in present-day

Gove County, and began a new farming venture. Many years later, in 1902, Tom, Jr., admitted that he helped his father on the Grinnell homestead and boasted untruthfully that he helped the elder Horn fight off an Indian attack. While there was no fight with Indians, drought turned Tom, Sr.'s, endeavor into a bust, and he returned to Missouri after only two years.[32]

Tom, Jr.'s, older brother, Charles, was also drawn to Kansas. Apparently, he and Lizzie soured on California and returned to Scotland County, Missouri, where their first child, Laura, was born in January 1876. Charles soon bundled up Lizzie and Laura and settled in the Flint Hills of eastern Kansas. Tom, Jr., may have assisted his older brother there in a cattle venture. However, the brothers quickly concluded this was a mistake and joined their father in an effort to make a new start in Burrton, a booming village on the Atchison, Topeka and Santa Fe Railroad, eighteen miles west of Newton. Tom Horn, Sr., was evidently attracted to Burrton, since several of his old Scotland County friends, including B. F. Shacklett and D. F. Burch, had settled there. (Like Charles Horn, Burch had also given up on the West Coast.) Although the town was only four years old in 1877, Burrton's 365 residents were showing "some degree of energy," according to one journalist. They were building a grain elevator, bridging the Arkansas River, and making a play for the trade of neighboring counties. Tom Horn, Sr.'s, contribution to Burrton's boom was a livery stable.[33]

In January 1878, the *Harvey County News* of Newton noted that Charles Horn and his family were among the "latest arrivals" in Burrton. Tom, Jr., who may have drifted into this vicinity already, recalled that he worked as a mule skinner for a freighter named Blades. John W. Blades, who resided in Burrton, may have been Tom's new employer. When Tom Horn, Sr., asked Charles to manage the livery stable, the older brother persuaded Tom, Jr., to join him. The brothers soon proudly hung a shingle—Horn & Horn Livery—in front of their establishment.[34]

Charles and Lizzie Horn began to put down roots. In addition to the livery business, Charles started a farming and ranching venture. The couple built a new house, which much "improved the neighborhood," said the *Burrton Telephone*. Charley played on the local baseball team and was elected a precinct constable. Like many other hardworking men in the late nineteenth century, Charles Horn deplored the efforts of reformers to improve mankind. He considered the temperance movement a particular nuisance. However, he made the best of a bad situation and developed a taste for the newfangled carbonated drinks. In June 1881, the *Burrton Monitor* noted with amazement that "Charley Horn can drink more soda-pop than any man in Kansas." At the same time, Charles and Lizzie continued to add to their growing family. In October 1882, Lizzie gave birth to a twelve-pound baby girl, Elizabeth. From time to time, Thomas, Sr., and Mary Horn visited Burrton. On one occasion, the senior Horn, with four local farmers, formed a committee to test the effectiveness of two competing plows, the Hapgood Sulky Plow and the Grand DeTour Walking Plow, in breaking the tough Kansas buffalo grass. The committee concluded that the Hapgood Plow did "better work." Charles Horn signed as a witness to this demonstration.[35]

In spite of their promising livery business, Tom, Jr., failed to stick with his brother. When a trail-herd crew passed through Burrton on its way back to Texas, Tom jumped at the chance to join up. Many years later, Charles Horn informed writer Jay Monaghan that Tom made two drives from Texas to Dodge City (possibly in 1878 and '79). He was a good horseman and showed some feeling for animals, but he did not exhibit the same sensitivity toward fellow drovers. One old-time cowhand who rode with Horn on these dangerous drives recalled that he was not only "big f'r his age," but he had an ego to match his frame. "He figgered he was better mentally, physically, yes, and by God, morally, than the rest of us boys," said this old cowboy; "damned if I know whether he was or not." Not only had Tom Horn grown into an impressive physical specimen, but Charles Horn recalled that "Tom had better eyes than most Indians." Charles Wells, a Wyoming stockman who met Tom Horn in Dodge City in the late 1870s, recalled that he was "a well built, fine looking chap," and "highly intelligent."[36]

Intelligent or not, Tom Horn enjoyed the free-for-all existence of the cowhands on the drives from Texas to the Kansas cattle towns. While Horn apparently did not drink heavily in his youth, he and fellow herders still engaged in antics that could lead to gunplay. One story has Horn and other rowdies getting revenge on Dodge City prostitutes who were fleecing them. These angry cowhands entered the girls' cribs after they had gone to sleep, tying ropes around furniture, including bedsteads, and whipping their horses into a headlong dash down the street. "Furniture came jerking out through doors and windows," according to one writer, with the unfortunate women plunging "headlong into the dust." Jay Monaghan reported an even more serious escapade when Tom Horn and "a skylarking companion" carelessly fired their revolvers into a freshly painted outhouse near San Antonio, Texas, and unwittingly shot and killed a woman, "Ma Hawthorne," and her daughter. If this incident occurred, the San Antonio newspapers failed to report it.[37]

After his second trail drive in late 1879, Tom Horn showed up at Charles Horn's doorstep with infected tonsils, a dangerous medical problem in that day. With urging from Charles, Tom returned to Scotland County, where Dr. D. B. Fowler, a former Confederate Army surgeon, removed the infected tissue on Christmas Eve. With such a happy Christmas gift, he was soon back on his feet and looking westward again.[38]

His health restored, Tom Horn set his sights on the silver boomtown of Leadville, Colorado. Many of his old friends in Scotland County, as well as in Burrton, Kansas, were bitten by this same bug. In March 1880, the *Memphis Conservative* announced that ten local residents, including Doctor Fowler, were leaving for the Colorado mines. The *Burrton Telephone* reported a similar exodus. After recovering from the tonsillectomy, Tom made his way to Burrton in order to urge brother Charles to accompany him to Leadville. When Charles countered with the suggestion that they should buy out their father's interest in the livery stable, Tom was not interested. "Tom was always like that," recalled Charles, who believed this journey set him off on a tragic course. "Our life back in Kansas was too tame for Tom," who "wasn't content to cultivate a hundred and sixty acres . . . drink a little whisky, pitch horseshoes on a Sunday, marry a brood woman and raise his own baseball nine." After Tom's departure for Colorado in 1880, the family rarely heard from him. Charles didn't see him again for twenty years.[39]

The citizens of Burrton took little notice of Tom Horn's departure. Only when his name began to appear in the newspapers as a scout in the Apache wars and as a gun for hire in Wyoming did they recall that he had once resided in their midst. They "still couldn't credit all they heard about him," said Ernest Dewey, a Kansas writer. "'A little stupid, maybe,' they figured him, but 'not hardly a dangerous fellow.'" "Burrton, apparently, was the only place Tom Horn ever lived that people . . . were not afraid of him," concluded Dewey. Old-time Burrtonites remembered Tom as a "sullen-eyed, sour-faced 17-year-old," who obviously detested the drudgery of the livery stable business. This distaste for routine labor never left him.[40]

Just making his way to Leadville was an adventure. On the last leg of his journey, Tom Horn took a stagecoach from South Park, Colorado. Many years later the driver, Fay Gorham, recalled the young Missourian because he insisted on riding topside. This particular Leadville run was also memorable, according to Gorham, because another passenger, a hefty, heavily painted prostitute, nearly caused the coach to tip over on a steep grade. When Horn finally reached Leadville, he found that many friends and acquaintances had preceded him. In a letter to the *Memphis Reveille* in April 1880, a former Scotland County resident described Leadville as a "truly a wonderful city" of thirty-five thousand people. Calling himself Zeke, this anonymous writer was surprised at the number of "our old [Scotland] county men" residing in Leadville, among them "Dr. Fowler, D. F. Burch, Tom Horn, Jr., Bartlett, Shacklett and others." A few weeks later, the census enumerator listed "Thomas Horn, age 19, single, miner" residing in the satellite community of Gunnison City.[41]

Like thousands of other treasure seekers, Tom Horn soon found that the fabled riches were elusive. Apparently, he went to work as a mucker in the mines just to make a prospector's stake. In a bit of irony, Doctor Fowler, whose skilled hands saved Tom's life, struck pay dirt on his Jennie Boone claim. Unfortunately, Fowler soon died and did not get to enjoy his newfound wealth. Tom Horn quickly tired of the dangerous mine shafts, according to Jay Monaghan, and sought other employment. Two railroad companies—the Denver and Rio Grande, and the Atchison, Topeka and Santa Fe—were vying for the right to serve this isolated mining region. To gain access to Leadville, tracks had to be laid through the narrow Royal Gorge of the Arkansas River, which could accommodate only one set of rails. Both companies employed gunmen to gain control of this valuable right-of-way. If Tom Horn, who was only twenty years of age, did hire out his gun to one of these companies, it was perhaps his first experience in a line of work that eventually became his stock-in-trade.[42]

Like thousands of others in the Leadville region, Tom Horn was on the lookout for more promising diggings. When Horn "heard talk of a twenty-seven-hundred-pound nugget of pure silver that had been found in Arizona," according to Jay Monaghan, he could not resist. Apparently, this was a reference to a remarkable discovery by William Munson, a freighter, who stumbled upon an enormous piece of quartz near Globe, Arizona. "Munson's chunk," as it was called, reportedly produced thirty-five hundred dollars' worth of silver.[43]

In order to make his way to Arizona, Horn worked at various jobs along the way. One report has him driving a stagecoach between Las Vegas and Santa Fe, New Mexico (and meeting Billy the Kid as well). In the *Life of Tom Horn*, he wrote that a man named Murray hired him to drive a mail hack on the route between Santa Fe and Prescott, Arizona. His first assignment was the route to Crane's Station, near Fort Wingate, in western New Mexico. The first postmaster for Crane's Station was appointed in May 1881, which suggests that Horn probably reached Arizona a short time later. Soon thereafter, Murray dispatched him and another man to herd mules to Beaverhead Station, on the Verde River, in Arizona Territory, where Indians had depleted the herd.[44]

Horn neglected to mention the name of the man who assisted him in this drive to Beaverhead Crossing. (Horn did not like to share the spotlight.) One story holds that his companion was Frank Stilwell, a brother of Comanche Jack Stilwell, a noted scout in Indian Territory. Frank Stilwell soon became a well-known gunman and associate of the Clanton gang around Tombstone, Arizona, and was killed by Wyatt Earp and his followers in 1882. There is no evidence for the association of Horn and Stilwell. A more likely candidate for Horn's associate on this mission was Jim Payne (Paine). Henry W. Daly, who served with Tom Horn in the army packtrains and who knew both men, said that Horn and Payne traveled to Arizona together.[45]

After delivering the mules, Horn left Murray's employ and made his way down the Verde River to Camp Verde. Camp Verde was an important military post guarding the road from New Mexico to the Prescott mining region as well as the western flank of the Apaches' homeland. At this army installation, Tom Horn found work as a night herder for a civilian contractor serving the post. While Horn referred to his new employer as George Hansen, he was actually George W. Hance. George Hance and his brother, John, were influential local entrepreneurs. They owned a farm, raised cattle, ran a freighting outfit, and contracted various services to the army. George Hance was also post sutler at Camp Verde. (When Tom Horn had a chance encounter with him many years later, in the 1890s, Hance praised him as "the best night herder he ever saw.") A short time after Horn worked for the Hance brothers, John Hance relocated to the northern part of the territory and became widely known as a pioneer promoter of tourism to the Grand Canyon.[46]

After three months, Tom Horn left the Hance brothers and made his way to Prescott, the territorial capital, a mining center, and the location of the territory's major military post, Whipple Barracks. "Broke and hungry," according to one writer, Horn used "his last two-bits" to purchase "a beer and free lunch at Dan Thorne's saloon on Whisky Row," where he heard that Brevet Maj. Gen. Orlando B. Willcox, commander of the Military Department of Arizona, was in the market for civilian workers to deal with an outbreak of hostilities with the Apaches. The army needed teamsters, herders, packers, and blacksmiths. Much to Tom Horn's surprise and gratification, First Lt. William Wallace Wotherspoon, the regimental and depot quartermaster at Whipple Barracks, put him on the payroll. Wotherspoon's "Report of Persons and Articles Employed and Hired" showed Horn hired as a teamster on 7 September 1881, at $30 per month. In the *Life of Tom Horn*, Horn accorded himself what he considered the more respectable position of herder and boasted that since his co-workers were Mexicans, Wotherspoon made him "boss of the Quartermaster's herd."[47]

By the time Tom Horn arrived in Arizona, in 1881, the army had effectively broken the Apache nation as a military threat. Yet small groups of renegades, especially the rebellious Chiricahuas and Warm Springs peoples, continued to cause alarm for much of the following decade. The majority of the Western Apaches—some 5,000—were concentrated on the White Mountain Apache Reservation (usually called the San Carlos Reservation). Situated in eastern Arizona, south of the Salt River and north of the Gila, this reservation encompassed a largely inhospitable region, sixty by ninety miles. The agent resided at San Carlos, a small settlement situated where the San Carlos River flowed into the Gila River, fifteen miles east of the mining camp of Globe.[48]

Strangely enough, Tom Horn's introduction to Apache warfare did not come from the warlike Chiricahuas, but from the more peaceable White Mountain Apaches who resided near Fort Apache. When Colonel Eugene Asa Carr, commander of Fort Apache, attempted to arrest

Noch-ay-del-klinne, a popular medicine man, on Cibecue Creek, on 30 August 1881, his followers killed eight soldiers and wounded others. In turn, the bluecoats killed Noch-ay-del-klinne and several of his followers. In the absence of a leader, the uprising quickly fizzled out. While Tom Horn was not present at the encounter on the Cibecue, as he later claimed, he had a peripheral part in the army's mop-up operations. In September 1881, General Willcox, the departmental commander, dispatched several columns into the Apache homeland from the Tonto Basin southward to the Gila River. Lieutenant Wotherspoon's records showed that Tom Horn was "in the field" as a teamster during this roundup.[49]

During the military operations against the Cibecue rebels in September and October 1881, Tom Horn became acquainted with a man who would exercise much influence in his life. Albert (Al) Sieber, a civilian chief of scouts, was legendary in the annals of the Apache campaigns. In Horn's autobiography, he praised Sieber as the supreme exemplar of the Indian fighter. Sieber was born in the Rhineland in 1845. In the aftermath of the Revolutions of 1848 in Europe, his mother moved the family to Minnesota. After serving in the Union Army, Al Sieber sought his fortune in the West and was soon prospecting around Prescott. During Brig. Gen. George Crook's campaign against the Western Apaches in 1872–73, Sieber served as a civilian scout and continued in this capacity for nearly two decades. In his recollections, Tom Horn credited Sieber with employing him as a scout and interpreter and training him for the position of chief of scouts. "Al Sieber, Chief of Scouts, came into Whipple [Barracks] from Tonto Basin and stayed a couple of weeks," Horn wrote. "He asked me how I would like to go with him as Mexican [Spanish] interpreter at $75.00 a month. He told me I would be with Him all the time."[50]

Actually, the facts of Tom Horn's initial association with Al Sieber were very different. While Sieber may have helped him find employment with the army, it was not as a scout and interpreter. Writing in 1904, Sieber recalled that he first met Tom Horn in 1882 and that Horn "went to work for me in the government pack train." As Quartermaster Lieutenant Wotherspoon's employment records indicate, he (not Sieber) signed Horn on as a packer, on 1 December 1881. Since Sieber did not possess the authority to hire for the army, he probably recommended Horn for the position. Horn's first assignment was at Fort

McDowell, a military post southeast of Prescott, on the western margin of the Apache homeland.[51]

Tom Horn's new boss was not Al Sieber, but a veteran packmaster, James R. Cook. Born in Ireland, in 1852, Cook immigrated to the United States after the Civil War. By 1871 he was serving as a packmaster in General Crook's command in Arizona Territory. Cook's comrades nicknamed him Long Jim or Tall Jim, not only because he was six feet, eight inches tall, but because another of Crook's packmasters was also named James Cook. This latter Cook, a former Fifth Cavalry trooper, shorter in stature, became "Short Jim." When the two Cooks appeared on the same quartermaster's roster, Short Jim was listed as "James Cook, 2nd." When not in the army packtrain, Long Jim Cook often joined Al Sieber and other scouts and packers in prospecting expeditions. It is unfortunate that Tom Horn did not see fit to admit in his autobiography that he served his apprenticeship under the tutelage of Long Jim Cook. He continued to work in Cook's train at various times until 1885.[52]

Although assigned to Fort McDowell, Long Jim Cook's packtrain was on duty in the field when Tom Horn signed on, on 1 December 1881, and was transferred from officer to officer as the campaign continued against Apache renegades:

> 1–9 January 1882   "Transferred Jan. 9, 1882, to Lieut.
>   F[rederick] Von Schrader, 12 Inf AAQM in the field"
> 10–31 January 1882   "Transferred to Lt. Frank West, 6th
>   Cav., Cmdg. Co. 'E,' Indian Scouts"
> 31 January 1882   "Respectfully transferred to Lt. M[illard]
>   F[illlmore] Waltz, 12th Inf, AAQM, Fort McDowell, A. T."
> 1 September 1882   First Lieutenant G. L. Scott, 6th Cav.,
>   Asst. Adj.[53]

The packtrain service was a small and highly skilled fraternity when Tom Horn entered its ranks. While the army provided enlisted men for a few trains in Arizona, most of the packers were civilian employees. These men were "a picked or chosen crew," recalled Henry W. Daly, a veteran packmaster and eventually the chief packer of the army. They were "ready to undergo all manner of hardship and danger," he added, and "always maintained an esprit-de-corps for the pack service."

This was largely due to the efforts of General Crook, who nurtured the packtrains in his campaigns against Native Americans in the Pacific Northwest and in Arizona Territory. Tom Horn began at the lowest rank in the packtrain, "packer second class"—or, in informal lingo, as a "scrub" or "plebe" packer. The first thing the "scrubs" learned was that pack mules played a critical part in the army's efforts to suppress the Apaches. These warriors sought refuge in the most impenetrable, trackless mountain ranges, where army wagons could not go. Only the surefooted mules—"a cross between a male donkey (jack) and a female horse"—were able to carry the essential supplies that soldiers needed to maintain a relentless pursuit. "All the noted [Apache] chiefs with whom we talked later on," recalled Thomas Cruse, a veteran officer in these campaigns, declared that only the mule trains enabled soldiers "to hold on to the trail as long as the Indians left one." Jason Betzinez, a follower of Geronimo, echoed this sentiment when he remarked that the packtrains made it impossible for the renegades to remain "out of reach" of the pursuing troops.[54]

The army packtrain consisted of a standard complement of men and animals—a packmaster, cargador (assistant packmaster), cook, blacksmith, and ten packers, to manage a train of fifty loaded mules. A bell mare (usually white) led the train. The mules, each with a fixed place in the column, were trained to follow her bell. The cook rode the bell mare, and each packer was mounted on his own mule. Young untrained mules had their tails roached or shaved and were called shavetails. (Hence, a new second lieutenant, fresh from West Point, became a "shavetail.") Wherever the packers ventured in support of units of bluecoats or Apache scouts, they normally camped separately "in dignified seclusion," observed C. H. Ward, a writer for Cosmopolitan, "as becomes members of that ancient and honorable guild." In emergencies, the army also hired entire civilian trains or formed additional packtrains using enlisted men.[55]

While the army did not consider civilian packers to be combatants, Apache renegades disregarded such niceties and targeted the trains carrying ammunition. The mule skinners had to defend themselves, and many packers voluntarily joined troops on the firing line against the Apaches. Packtrain personnel possessed talents beyond mule skinning. They were often experienced "Indian men," who lived with Indian women and were well acquainted with Apache customs. Many packers were also prospectors and cattle raisers who knew the southwestern border country better than soldiers and could guide army columns through difficult terrain. Always masters at manipulating paperwork and funds, army quartermasters routinely hired persons in one category, such as packers, but intended them for additional jobs, such as scouting, courier duty, and interpreting. When the need arose, Long Jim Cook, Tom Horn's boss, was called from his train for scouting duty. In such instances, the assistant packmaster (cargador), or another member of the train, assumed the duties of his superior. A common subterfuge of army quartermasters in Arizona Territory was to hire a highly valued civilian scout or interpreter as a master (or superintendent) of transportation—with supervisory authority over several packtrains—in order to keep this person on the payroll between campaigns. In this way, the quarter-masters could tap the military transportation fund, which supported the packtrains, in order to hire men for other duties.[56]

Tom Horn had crammed many experiences into the five or so years since he left Scotland County, Missouri. While he had knocked about from job to job, Horn had the capacity to learn fast and work hard. Not only did he demonstrate an ability to manage animals, but his fondness for weapons since childhood had enabled him to hire out his gun in Leadville. As Jay Monaghan observed, Tom Horn was ambitious and had a "singleness of purpose" with the ambition to make good. Thus far, his labors on the frontier had provided few visible returns, but in looking back on his arrival in Arizona Territory, Horn rightly considered this time as an important milestone in his life. "My feelings were so different and my life was so different from what it was at home [Missouri] that it seemed to me then as though I had been all my life on a stage line," he wrote later. "I was not traveling on foot any more, for I had a good horse, saddle, bridle, and a Winchester rifle."[57]

CHAPTER 2

Scrub Packer

When Tom Horn chose Arizona Territory as a likely place to seek his fortune in 1881, he could hardly anticipate what this desert land had in store. If he traveled there to prospect for mineral wealth, that aim was quickly overshadowed, as he was immediately caught up in the conflict with the Apaches. When Horn signed on with Long Jim Cook's packtrain in December 1881, he also signed on for difficult and hazardous duty, since the army expected the packers and their sturdy animals to stick with the soldiers in pursuit of fugitive Indians. No sooner had Quartermaster Lt. Millard Waltz entered Horn's name on his roster than Gen. Orlando Willcox, the department commander, ordered Cook's train to San Carlos, the headquarters for the White Mountain Apache Reservation. San Carlos would be Tom Horn's base of operations for several years to come.[1]

The discontent among the Apaches, which had erupted the previous August at Cibecue Creek, continued to fester. A few weeks after the fighting at Cibecue, several Chiricahua Apache chiefs, including Chatto, Chihuahua, and Nachez (Naiche), who feared military reprisals for alleged complicity in this uprising, fled to Mexico. In April 1882, shortly after Tom Horn settled in at San Carlos, they returned secretly to the reservation to persuade Chief Loco and his Warm Springs (Ojo Caliente) followers to return with them to Sonora. On the night of 18 April, after threats and cajoling, Loco reluctantly agreed. When Albert D. Sterling, agency chief of police, rode out to investigate, the renegades shot him to death and proceeded to mutilate the corpse. Although a packer with Cook's train, Horn may have been staying temporarily at a camp of Chief Pedro's Coyotero Apaches near Chief Loco's rancheria when the excitement erupted. While Horn's recollections have to be used with care, historian Bud Shapard concludes that he provides some "colorful insights" about Loco's breakout. "At daylight, or a very little after, I heard a lot of firing at the Chiricahua camp," Horn wrote. "There were [friendly] Indians camped all around me," he continued, "and they began to arm themselves and in about ten minutes word came in that the Chiricahuas were leaving for the war path." Since the "bronks" (broncos), as the whites called the renegades, were too numerous for the packers and the friendly Coyoteros to fight, Horn and his companions took refuge across the Gila River among some rocks known locally as the Triplets.[2]

From this position they had a ringside view of the renegades' escape. Tom Horn left a vivid description of the spectacle of this Apache exodus: "Great droves of horses and mules were strung out for about a mile and a half. There must have been five thousand head of them. Squaws and Indian children everywhere, driving the stock. Of course they had their camp outfits. The squaws were all yelling at the children, and the children [were] yelling at the loose stock. A small bunch of perhaps twenty warriors was in front, and behind was the main band of warriors." Actually, the fugitives, including perhaps four hundred men, women, and children, were driving only a few hundred animals, some of which the renegades had stolen from beef contractor Daniel Houston Ming. At one point, some warriors "stopped and looked at us," wrote Horn, but they decided to forgo an attack on such a well-fortified position. In about thirty minutes, this colorful parade passed from view up the Gila River Valley.[3]

With Chief of Police Sterling out of the picture, and Agent Joseph C. Tiffany away in the East, leadership of the pursuit fell to the inexperienced chief clerk and post trader, Charles T. Connell. When he and his police sergeant followed the retiring hostiles too closely, the Chiricahuas turned and killed the sergeant in a hail of gunfire. A group of fifty friendly Apache scouts then managed to catch up with the renegades, killing one and wounding others. "Several Americans who were in the cattle [or packers?] camp on the river, among them Tom Horn," Connell recalled, "saw several [hostile] Chiricahuas bleeding from wounds

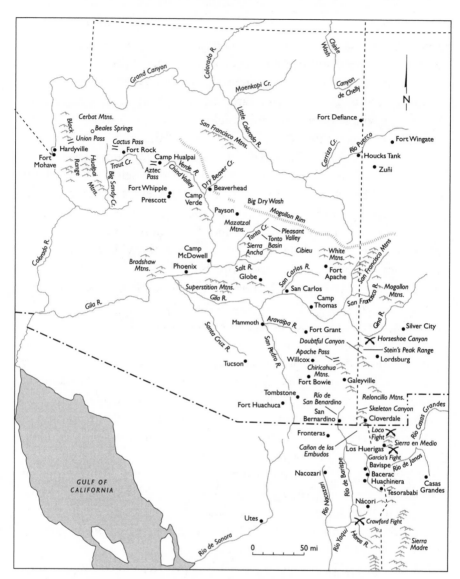

Apachería. Copyright © 2014 by the University of Oklahoma Press.

received in the fight." "A very confused state of affairs" prevailed at
the agency headquarters, with the "tenderfoot" chief clerk in charge,
recalled Horn. The panicky Connell issued arms to "every [friendly]
Indian," observed Horn, even though the hostilities were confined to
a only a few Chiricahuas and Warm Springs Apaches. The reservation
residents readily took advantage of this largess. In the excitement, "the

chief clerk kept no accounts of the guns," wrote Horn, "and very few of them did he ever get back." Since the fugitives cut the telegraph line to Fort Thomas, Tom Horn agreed to ride to the fort, eighteen miles up the Gila River, with news of the outbreak. While he made the ride in two hours, according to his account, friendly Apaches at San Carlos had already alerted the post commandant with smoke signals that something was amiss.[4]

As the renegades turned south toward the protection of the Sierra Madres in Mexico, Capt. Tullius Cicero Tupper, Sixth Cavalry, who commanded regulars at Willcox, assumed command of a combined force of Indian scouts and cavalrymen. At least four packtrains, including Long Jim Cook's, supported this force, while several civilian scouts led search parties in advance of Tupper's men. One of these trackers was Al Sieber, who obtained a detachment of packers from Cook's train, including Tom Horn, to support his scouts. While Sieber failed to mention that Horn was with him in this particular foray, he did recall that the young Missourian assisted him on "numbers of scouting expeditions" between 1882 and 1885.[5]

Civilian scouts like Sieber and the Indian scouts whom they led occupied an anomalous place in the regular army. In Arizona Territory, Apaches were enlisted into the regular army, paid the same wages as white soldiers, and subject to the same military discipline. However, they could not advance beyond the rank of sergeant major. White officers who commanded such scout companies often served only a short time before being transferred, leaving the civilian chiefs of scouts to maintain a permanent connection between the Indian enlisted men and the professional officers. This placed a heavy burden on the civilian scouts. "The only way to get to know Indians is to live with them," wrote Henry W. Daly, veteran packmaster and friend of Tom Horn. This meant that "most scout leaders had Indian wives," continued Daly, and they could speak, "either officially or unofficially," the language of the spouse's people. The chief of scouts had not only "to know Indians," added Daly, but, more importantly, "to know what to watch for" when they were at work. "This greatly limited the field from which [civilian] scout chiefs were picked," he noted, "and guaranteed a good man fairly continuous employment." It was not uncommon for the army to retain such persons "on the pay rolls between campaigns so as to have them when trouble started," wrote Daly. This job, he observed, was difficult and dangerous, with none of the glamour associated with scouting in dime novels. "A chief of scouts rode a mule," he wrote, since "that was the only way they could keep up with their [Indian] scouts," who usually "traveled on foot," easily covering fifty miles a day.[6]

The civilian chief of scouts (*nan-tan* in the Apache language) performed a wide array of duties. Will C. Barnes, a sergeant at Fort Apache in the 1880s, said the scout "was supposed to know intimately the Indians and the country—its trails and water-holes; and was used as a guide." One of the chief of scout's primary duties was to ensure the loyalty of the Apaches. If an Apache scout proved disloyal in the field, noted Dan R. Williamson, Al Sieber would tolerate no such breach of discipline and "was often known to shoot them" in front of their companions. Not only did the chief of scouts keep order in the Apache scouts' camp, but he was responsible for issuing their rations and ammunition. The Apaches were notorious for consuming several days' rations at one sitting if they were not watched closely, according to Lt. William Shipp, who served with Tom Horn in 1885–86. Ammunition was issued to Apache scouts sparingly, since they were known to wager precious cartridges in card games. According to Charles Lummis, who covered the Apache campaigns for the *Los Angeles Times,* Apache men loved "toying with the seductive pasteboards." When gambling was combined with whiskey, quarrels often erupted. "The big thing we always had to watch out for was the Indians getting drunk," recalled Henry Daly, who maintained that the only way to deal with an inebriated Apache was to knock him out.[7]

Tom Horn's boast that Al Sieber gave him responsibilities as a scout and interpreter from their first meeting was inaccurate. Horn was a "scrub" in Long Jim's packtrain, and Sieber gave him only menial tasks at first. "Sieber just wanted me because I was young and active and could travel with him all day and herd the horses at night," recalled Horn, "and do the cooking and tend to the packs [mules] and clean his gun every night." Horn contended that this "was fun for me," but he admitted that Sieber could be a tough taskmaster. When he became upset with his young packer the veteran scout voiced his anger in terms "more forceful than elegant."[8]

In the meantime, Captain Tupper pursued the Chiricahua and Warm Springs fugitives into Chihuahua. Al Sieber, with Tom Horn and some Apache scouts, trailed one party of renegades into the vicinity of Cloverdale, in the bootheel of New Mexico. Although Sieber's party overtook the hostiles, Horn recalled that "the whole place was alive with Indians." All they could do was "stay close" and monitor the escapees' movements. When the renegades crossed into Chihuahua, Tupper resolved to follow, even though he was violating Mexican Territory. If Tom Horn is to be believed, Tupper was not only anxious for a fight but wanted "to capture a pony for his little girl." Tupper overtook the hostiles at a lone mountain called Sierra Enmedio (Middle Mountain) about twenty miles south of the border. "Sieber took out a telescope he had borrowed from Tupper," recalled Tom Horn, and "there were the Indians and horses as natural as could be." At daybreak the following morning, 28 April 1882, Tupper attacked the startled Apaches. While Horn admitted that he "did not get to see much"—an uncharacteristically modest admission on his part—he saw enough to describe the bedlam at the battle at Middle Mountain: "Well, there were 'things doin' all right just then. Braves were yelling and squaws were yelling. There must have been a thousand dogs barking, and horses were running every which way. There were probably three thousand horses [actually, about 250] there, and it was not very light yet." Reverting to type, Horn then made the wild claim that he saved a wounded soldier by carrying him to safety through Apache gunfire.[9]

Even though Loco's warriors were poorly armed, they still outgunned Captain Tupper's modest company-sized force, which soon ran short of ammunition. Tupper was soon forced to withdraw. Fortunately, Col. George Alexander Forsyth, Fourth Cavalry, joined him that day with 450 additional men. On 29 April, the following day, Forsyth, now commanding the entire force, pursued Loco deeper into Chihuahua, where he encountered Col. Lorenzo García with 250 Mexican cavalrymen. García had just surprised and severely mauled Loco and his band. The fugitives, still reeling from Tupper's attack, had let down their guard. The Mexicans killed at least 78 Apaches, while losing 22 men. After enduring a pro forma scolding from García for illegally crossing the international boundary, Forsyth shared his rations with the Mexicans and then withdrew to American soil.[10]

The Loco campaign was Tom Horn's baptism by fire, although his account is not entirely reliable. Even Dan L. Thrapp, who (rightly) used Horn's recollections with caution, admitted that Horn's description of the Tupper-Loco battle in his autobiography revealed "some personal knowledge of certain phases of the operation." But whenever the opportunity arose, Horn consistently exaggerated his role. In an interview with a reporter in 1898, he boasted that he was a chief of scouts in command of a hundred Apaches under Captain Tupper, though in fact he was a packer.[11]

As soon as Horn returned with Long Jim Cook's train to Fort McDowell—its official duty station—the packers were ordered into the field again. A White Mountain Apache warrior, Na-ti-o-tish, who had refused to surrender after the Cibecue Creek encounter, defied agency authorities. On 6 July, these renegades killed Charley Colvig, the agency chief of police, and three policemen, and fled northward. They briefly menaced the mining camp of McMillenville, north of Globe, and crossed the Salt River into the Tonto Basin, where they raided the ranches of John Tewksbury, Al Rose, and Will Sigsbee, killing Sigsbee and one ranch hand. In the meantime, General Willcox dispatched several military columns into the Tonto Basin, with Major Adna Chaffee and some Sixth Cavalry troopers from Fort McDowell in the lead. After arriving in the basin, Chaffee, who needed additional packers, sent out an appeal for volunteers. On 13 July, Abram Henson (Charles) Meadows, whose family ranched in Diamond Valley, and Frank Prothero, a family friend, rode to Chaffee's camp on Pine Creek to sign on. There Meadows met Tom Horn, whom he recalled was a "scrub scout" at the time. (Sieber had probably pulled Horn, a scrub packer, from the packtrain for other duties.) Meadows and Horn became friends. They were destined to meet later under very different circumstances.[12]

While Meadows and Prothero were at Chaffee's camp, the renegades descended upon the Meadows ranch in Diamond Valley, killing Charlie's father and a brother, John, Jr. Henry Meadows, another brother, was badly wounded in the leg and eventually lost the limb. The Meadows womenfolk, a sturdy bunch armed with rifles, held out until Chaffee could send a relief party. Among this party was Tom Horn, probably serving as a packer on this occasion. Like all packers, he performed a wide variety of duties in the field.[13]

Major Chaffee refused to permit Na-ti-o-tish and his followers any rest. His force, consisting of Troop I, Sixth Cavalry and Company E, Indian Scouts, with Al Sieber as civilian chief of scouts, and Long Jim Cook's packtrain in support, continued to pursue the fugitives toward the Mogollon Rim on the northern extremity of the Tonto Basin. Tom

Horn later made the ridiculous claim that he led a separate party of White Mountain Apache volunteers—his "war dogs"—in this chase. While an inexperienced twenty-two-year-old would never be accorded such an important command, the San Carlos agent did make an effort to mobilize such a force. Dan Ming, a former San Carlos chief of police and subsequently a good friend of Tom Horn, was in charge of this volunteer company. Apparently, Horn saw nothing wrong in substituting himself for Ming in his account of the pursuit.[14]

On 17 July 1882, Adna Chaffee overtook Na-ti-o-tish and his followers at Chevelon Forks (Big Dry Wash), a tributary of the Little Colorado River. At this point, the trail, which led to the Navajo lands farther north, entered a thousand-foot-deep gorge and exited by another gully on the north side. The distance from rim to rim varied from four hundred to seven hundred yards. The last of the renegades were just making their way up the far side as Chaffee's men took up positions on the south rim. Na-ti-o-tish, who underestimated the size of the pursuing force, decided to make a stand. Second Lt. George H. Morgan, who commanded the Indian scout company, recalled that about 3:00 P.M. the two sides began to exchange rifle fire before all the renegades had gained the far side. "Sieber and I lay behind a large rock in front of one another," recalled Morgan. When "Sieber played the old trick of exposing his hat on the end of a stick . . . Indian marksmen made quite good practice on it." "Whenever a shot would spatter on the rock behind us," he continued, "the [Apache] Sergeant and scouts would unite in the one English word I ever heard them get off—'Damn!'"[15]

Major Chaffee ordered the pack mules held well behind the firing line, but some of the packers, including Tom Horn, were determined to join the Apache scouts and cavalrymen at the rim. Horn, whose recollections accorded well with Morgan's, wrote later, "As we came to the banks of the cañon the renegades were starting up on the opposite side. We opened fire on them, of course. About halfway up the side of the cañon, the trail ran on a wide bench. Then there would be a place on the bench leading straight away from us. The distance was just about six hundred yards, and when they came to that place, it made fine shooting." While the riflemen on the south rim pinned down the fugitives on the opposite side, Chaffee sent out two separate parties to work around the hostiles' flanks. When these two units suddenly emerged on the north rim, they achieved complete surprise, killing many renegades and driving the remainder away. Horn, who was near Major Chaffee, heard him bellowing oaths with a voice that was legendary in military circles. "He swears by ear," recalled Horn, "and by note in a common way, and by everything else in a general way." At the height of the battle, Mother Nature suddenly interrupted with what Horn called "the heaviest hail and rain storm that I ever saw in my life." "It got so very dark that we could not see across the cañon," he wrote. Both sides soon gave up the fight.[16]

The encounter at Chevelon Forks was costly. At least twenty-two Apaches were killed, including Na-ti-o-tish. Chaffee lost two men, with several wounded. Another casualty was an Apache scout who attempted to desert to the renegades; his brother was on the other side. Al Sieber shot him on the spot. Lieutenants George Morgan and Frank West won Medals of Honor for bravery in the fight. The Battle of Chevelon Forks, or Big Dry Wash, was the last major battle with Apaches inside the United States. While skirmishes with hostile Apaches continued for several more years in New Mexico and Arizona, major campaigns would take place in northern Mexico. Aside from a small hard core of warlike Chiricahuas and Warm Springs people, the other groups of Apaches remained sullenly at peace on the San Carlos Reservation.[17]

With Na-ti-o-tish's followers subdued, Long Jim Cook's packtrain returned to the reservation, where new troubles were brewing. American and Mexican outlaws who lurked around its borders considered the Apache herds a prize for the picking. In the spring of 1882, a band of Hispano rustlers from eastern Arizona raided a reservation horse herd and made off with several animals. When Apache policemen prepared to pursue the outlaws, at the suggestion of Al Sieber, Tom Horn joined them. The posse overtook the thieves at a water hole on the Fort Thomas–Fort Apache road, and a fight ensued in which three desperadoes were killed. General Willcox, with his twelve-year-old son, Charles McAlister Willcox, and a small escort, happened along as the pursuers discussed what to do with the dead outlaws. Some wanted to leave the corpses where they fell as a warning to other miscreants. When Horn presented this plan to the commander, Willcox heatedly overruled him, threatening to put him in irons and pointing out that such callousness had the effect of encouraging "turbulence on the Reservation." "Oh, what a raking he did give me!" recalled Horn, who later boasted that he refused to take this scolding lying down but instead stood up to the officer and, following Al Sieber's practice of turning the air blue with invective when in an uncomfortable spot, "swore and tore along at a pretty fair rate." As in so many instances in the *Life of Tom Horn,* the author was blowing smoke. When asked many years later if this encounter at the water hole actually took place, Charles Willcox recalled it well, but he said that Horn did not swear at his father. In spite of Horn's impertinence, Charles Willcox said, his father "took a liking" to the brash young Missourian. Horn even taught young Charles how to ride a horse.[18]

Tom Horn's stay at San Carlos later in the summer of 1882 coincided with a change in the command of the Military Department of Arizona. On 4 September, Brig. Gen. George Crook replaced Orlando Willcox. Crook, who had waged a memorable campaign against the Apaches a decade earlier, lost no time in establishing his authority. After listening sympathetically to Apaches' complaints, he sternly informed them that any new disturbance would be met with force. To impress the Apaches with his determination, Crook established a subpost of Camp Thomas at the reservation headquarters and placed in command a veteran Indian fighter, Capt. Emmett Crawford, Third Cavalry, with Second Lt. Britton Davis as second-in-command. Crook assigned Second Lt. Charles B. Gatewood, another experienced officer, the task of monitoring the White Mountain Apaches who resided farther east, near Fort Apache. Five fresh companies of Apache scouts were enlisted into the army to better police the reservation.[19]

In his many years as an Indian fighter, George Crook had come to regard the packtrains as a key to any successful campaign. "The General's hobby, if he had one, was pack trains," recalled Britton Davis. Crook, who "insisted on the best in men, mules, and equipment," assigned Thomas Moore, the army's chief packer, the duty of putting the trains in tip-top shape. The responsibility for hiring civilian packers at San Carlos and seeing that the trains were ready for action fell to Quartermaster Lt. Britton Davis, whom the Apaches called Nal-soos-Nantan, or "writing captain," since his duties required the use of pen and paper. Among Davis's five fully equipped packtrains was that of Long Jim Cook and his veteran crew. Tom Horn was transferred with Long Jim's train from Fort McDowell to San Carlos on 1 October 1882.[20]

Horn's stay at San Carlos afforded him an opportunity to make acquaintances that would later stand him in good stead. Henry W. Daly, an Irish immigrant who had served as a packer in the Nez Perce campaign before transferring to Crook's packtrains in the Southwest in the early 1880s, recalled that he met Horn "in 1880 or 1881 at San Carlos Agency." Horn was often seen in the company of another packer, Billy Harrison, who became his "side kick," added Daly, who continued to encounter Horn in packtrain duties until Geronimo's surrender in 1886. Another person whom Horn soon called a friend was Mickey Free, a part-Mexican-part-Apache scout and interpreter with Al Sieber.[21]

Although Horn now had enough experience to graduate from the rank of "scrub" packer, he suddenly quit the packtrain on 29 October 1882. Seeking employment around Fort Thomas, he became acquainted with William D. Ganzhorn, a merchant and justice of the peace, and Anton Mazzanovich, a Sixth Cavalry trooper. Mazzanovich recalled that Horn worked as a cowhand for Bernard (Barney) and John H. Norton, a pair of enterprising brothers who owned the NN brand at nearby Cedar Springs. The Norton brothers were also partners with Madison W. Stewart in a freighting and contracting firm in Tucson. Horn drove a freight wagon for Norton & Stewart between Globe and Willcox. Elias A. Jones, who became a good friend of Horn, managed the line at this time.[22]

Horn's fortunes took a turn for the better when Tully, Ochoa and Company, a Tucson firm, employed him as foreman of its herds contracted to the San Carlos Apache reservation. He signed a twelve-month contract for $150 a month, a considerable increase over his packer's wages. While Pinckney Randolph Tully and Estevan Ochoa were the primary contractors, they subcontracted the management of their beef contract to two enterprising brothers, Eugene O. and Matthew F. Shaw. Eugene Shaw was the beef agent at San Carlos. Tom Horn answered directly to him. Through his new duties, Horn soon became well-known to ranchers in the region, among them Dan Ming, the former reservation chief of police, who owned a ranch in Aravaipa Canyon, a few miles south of the agency, and Burt and Horace Dunlap, two brothers from Ohio, who established the Western Reserve Ranch in the eastern end of Aravaipa Canyon in 1882.[23]

As foreman of Tully and Ochoa's contract herds, Tom Horn soon had his hands full. In addition to holding and protecting the cattle against bad weather, predators, and rustlers, his duties including hiring cowhands, driving herds to the reservation, and delivering the weekly quota of beeves to the agency. Finding men who would work as cow-hands under such dangerous conditions was not easy. He was fortunate to find one reliable herder in Ben R. Clark, who worked with Horn in 1883 and 1884 and later served as sheriff of Graham County in the 1890s.[24]

The San Carlos Apache Reservation was a large and complex opera-tion in the 1880s. Charles Pinckney Elliott, a second lieutenant in the Fourth Cavalry assigned to the army's subpost in July 1884, recalled that the agency consisted of a helter-skelter collection of adobe build-ings, corrals, and Apache wickiups situated on "an open space" ("the flats") where the San Carlos emptied into the Gila River. "Above the flats," he added, "stood the school buildings occupied as store rooms, officers [quarters], and living rooms by the Commanding Officer and his assistants. Still further to the west down the Gila River on the same bench stood the Agency buildings, storehouse, and traders [sutler] store. Below the Agency building on the flats near the river were the corrals and slaughter house for Indian [contract] cattle."[25]

As herd foreman, Tom Horn followed a weekly routine. "Once a week the required number were cut out of the herd," recalled Britton Davis, and "driven to the Agency, weighed on a stock scale, and turned into the corral." With an army officer standing by to see that each steer met government standards, the animal was then prepared for slaughter. "An Indian policeman with a rifle stood on the adobe wall of the cor-ral and shot the beeves down," added Davis, and the agency butcher immediately cut up the beef and issued the meat to the reservation inhabitants.[26]

Driving newly purchased cattle from outlying ranches to replenish the contract herd was a routine chore for the young foreman. On sev-eral occasions, he picked up cattle at the Murphy brothers' ranch near Mammoth, a mining camp fifty-five miles south of the reservation, on the San Pedro River. The brothers—Daniel, John, William and Le-muel—employed John Rhodes to manage their Arizona holdings. "A powerful young fellow, as honest as the day is long, [and] not afraid of the Devil himself," according to one newspaperman, Rhodes became a good friend of Tom Horn and was destined to play an important part in the young herder's life.[27]

On one such drive from an outlying ranch, Tom Horn heard that hostile Apaches were on the prowl. In a panic, he made a decision that he later regretted. William (Bill) Walker, a cowhand who had just helped deliver a herd to the reservation for the Erie Cattle Company, recalled hearing about Horn's dilemma. The young foreman "was scared to cross trails" with the renegades, said Walker, and "got spooked and turned them [beeves] loose about ten miles from San Carlos." Rather than voluntarily delivering themselves to the reservation, the animals broke in all directions and became ripe pickings for any greedy person—white or Apache—in the vicinity. In his recollections, Tom Horn admitted to turning a herd of 2,000 steers loose and justified this decision by claiming that Chief Loco and his followers "were running the whole country." In subsequently pleading his case with Agent Philip P. Wilcox, Horn claimed that he "could not get any cowboys to stay at the camp to look after the cattle." Since the damage had already been done, Wilcox decided to take no disciplinary action and merely instructed Horn to try to assemble a record of the number of animals killed by the Apaches. When Walker encountered Horn later in Wyoming and reminded him of this embarrassing incident, he "acted peeved, and growled at me." "'I reckon *you* wouldn't have no trouble a-tall gittin' in an' out o' that [Apache] rattlers den,'" remarked Horn, 'with them scalp hunters on the prod!'"[28]

Reservation officials often complained about the poor quality of beeves that contractors supplied. Britton Davis alleged that in order to make contracted cattle appear at specified weights, herders watered them in the Gila River immediately before delivery. He joked that some cattle were so emaciated that herders carried individual beeves to the reservation scales "on their ponies!" In 1884 Capt. Emmet Crawford charged Eugene O. Shaw, Tom Horn's employer, with failing to live up to his contract and ordered him to remove his herd from the reservation by 1 July. As a consequence Horn, who neglected to mention this embarrassing situation in his autobiography, lost his job.[29]

But while he was still the foreman on the reservation, in the spring of 1883, Tom Horn took temporary leave from his job to participate in General Crook's pursuit of Apache renegades into the Sierra Madre of northern Mexico. He claimed that he accompanied Al Sieber as a scout, but apparently he went with Long Jim Cook's packtrain. Sieber noted that "Horn was with me when I went into Mexico with General Crook" in 1883, but he provided no details. Sieber probably took Horn out of the packtrain for incidental tasks. In early May 1883, Crook's

expedition crossed the international boundary near present-day Douglas, Arizona, with Capt. Adna Chaffee's company of the Sixth Cavalry
(42 men) and Capt. Emmet Crawford's Apache scouts (193). Second Lt.
Charles B. Gatewood, Sixth Cavalry, and Second Lt. James O. Mackay,
Third Cavalry, assisted Crawford. Capt. John Gregory Bourke and First
Lt. Gustav Joseph Fiebeger served as aides-de-camp. Al Sieber was civilian chief of scouts, and Mickey Free and Gracias Severiano were interpreters. Nashville "Buckskin Frank" Leslie, a Tombstone gunman and
friend of Tom Horn, was a courier. Canadian-born Archie McIntosh
(son of a Scotsman and Chippewa mother) went along as a guide, while
an Apache, Pa-nayo-tish ("Peaches" to the whites), assisted. A *New
York Herald* correspondent, A. Frank Randall, lugged his photographic
equipment along, eventually losing it in an accident on the trail.[30]

To keep the expedition supplied, Crook mobilized five trains comprising 350 mules and eighty packers. Lieutenant Gatewood signed on
thirty-one packers at Fort Apache; Lt. Britton Davis enrolled forty-
eight at San Carlos. Sam Bowman from Indian Territory, part white,
part Choctaw, served as superintendent of trains. A veteran packmaster
was in charge of each train: Frank Monach, Charles Hopkins, Frank
Stanfield, Long Jim Cook, and Short Jim Cook. It is unfortunate that
Horn's description of this campaign, one of the army's most memorable
expeditions in the post–Civil War Era, is one of the poorest in his autobiography. Luckily Capt. John Gregory Bourke, General Crook's aide,
kept a diary and later published a classic account of the expedition.[31]

In spite of Horn's refusal to admit in his autobiography that he served
with the lowly packers, he betrayed some awareness of their activities when he described the assembly of the expeditionary force at San
Bernardino ranch on the Mexican border. "The packers were laughing," he reported, because it appeared at first that Crook was taking
only a small force, which meant that the mules would "have scarcely a
load" to carry. However, "on the evening before we were to pull out
[30 April 1883]," wrote Horn, "the Quartermaster sent along enough
extra flour and sugar to load the pack mules down to the ground." (The
typical army mule carried 250–300 pounds.) As the disappointed packers soon learned, Crook intended using these extra rations to feed the
renegade Apaches whom he expected to bring back.[32]

On 1 May, the long column proceeded down the banks of the San
Bernardino River into Sonora, passing through the villages of Bavispe

and Baserac (Vasaraca), both on the Bavispe River. Near Nácori the expedition turned eastward and began to climb into the Sierra Madre proper. In a rare instance of the convergence Horn's recollections with those of John G. Bourke and Gustav Fiebeger, all three recalled the presence of prehistoric structures and wild fruit trees along the trail. Horn remembered it as "a lovely country," where "limes grew wild and for miles up and down the creek were peach trees by the thousand." Peaches, the guide (a mere coincidence of name!), informed Horn that "there were ripe peaches there five months in the year." John Rope, one of Crook's Apache scouts, recalled that he had never seen peaches before and mistook them for "some kind of walnuts." In addition to peaches, Bourke saw other wild fruit, including pomegranates.[33]

On 10 May Crook set up a base camp and sent Al Sieber and Capt. Emmet Crawford with 150 scouts ahead to locate the fugitives Apaches' rancheria. In an interview with a Denver journalist several years later, Tom Horn substituted himself for Al Sieber, boasting that he was "at the head of the scouts under Gen. George Crook" in the 1883 incursion. Al Sieber only remarked that Horn "proved himself a very valuable man to me on many occasions" during the campaign. Actually, Horn's duties were probably confined to Crook's base camp. His autobiography makes no mention of Captain Crawford's surprise raid on the Apache fugitives' rancheria on 15 May, in which they lost much of their camp equipage. Had Horn been present, he would surely have highlighted this adventure. Within a few days, Chihuahua, perhaps the most respected Chiricahua chief, rode into the American camp with Bonito and Geronimo to talk with General Crook. In one of the most outlandish passages in the *Life of Tom Horn*, the author claimed that in these discussions Geronimo, who distrusted Crook's official interpreters (they were Mexicans), demanded that Horn translate. According to Horn, Geronimo had taken a liking to him at an earlier meeting and "preferred that I be the one to do the interpreting." Horn, who admitted that such attention caused him to feel "puffed up," went so far as to tell a Denver newsman some years later of going into the Sierra Madres and arranging a treaty with the renegades, so that they voluntarily returned to San Carlos.[34]

After giving himself a central place in the talks, Tom Horn proceeded to present his version of behind-the-scenes discussions between himself, Al Sieber, and Mickey Free, all of whom feared that some of the more hardened renegades secretly planned to massacre the American force if Geronimo agreed to surrender. As a consequence, according to Horn, Sieber instructed him always to carry a concealed knife when they entered the hostile camp. When Crook learned that the renegades planned a dance, which might lead to further problems, he ordered Sieber to see that this event was cancelled. Many years later, John Rope affirmed that the renegades did, indeed, plan a massacre. After protracted discussions, 52 warriors and 273 women and children agreed to return to San Carlos. Geronimo, who insisted upon remaining behind allegedly to gather up his scattered followers, promised to return to Arizona in the near future.[35]

If Horn performed any duties other than those of a packer, they probably involved distributing rations to the large number of fugitives entering the American camp. Crook assigned Lieutenant Gatewood to supervise "the issue of rations to all renegades," recalled Tom Horn, "and to count them each day." Since Horn expressed familiarity with this task, it was probably one of his jobs as a packer. When Geronimo was informed that he and his followers could "draw their rations," recalled Horn, the "old wolf" was ecstatic. The "ration business . . . is the joy of every renegade's heart," Horn astutely observed. "Flour and sugar cut a big figure in all they do when once they conclude to accept it [peace]." Horn could have added tobacco to the list.[36]

On 30 May 1883, General Crook ordered the expedition to strike for Arizona by way of the eastern slope of the Sierra Madre. However, a complication arose when the expedition reached the Arizona border. Mexican ranchers, angered that Crook permitted the renegades to bring stolen livestock with them, made an official complaint to the U.S. government. "Every bunch of them [renegades] had a great drove of horses," recalled Tom Horn, and "refused to give it up," even though Mexican attorneys met them at the boundary and attempted to take possession. Anton Mazzanovich, who was present with a packtrain of army personnel, recalled that the expedition was stalled at the border for two weeks "on account of . . . stock the Indians stole from Mexican ranchers in Sonora." The War Department eventually made an effort to right this wrong by ordering Crook to confiscate the renegades' animals, auction them off, and send the proceeds to Mexico City. Far from the thousand animals that Horn asserted were in this stolen herd, the figure was closer to a hundred.[37]

The arrival of the Apache renegades at San Carlos in late June set off a heated dispute as to their disposition on the reservation. To Agent Philip P. Wilcox and his peaceable wards, as well as the public at large, the repatriation of these fugitives set the stage for the renewal of Indian atrocities. When Wilcox recommended that they be sent to some distant place in the East, Crook was astonished and did not know how to react. In the interim, the general forbade any public discussion of the subject of the Chiricahuas' return. He then traveled to Washington where he worked out an arrangement permitting the Chiricahuas to reside on the reservation under army jurisdiction as prisoners of war. The army was given the additional duty of "keeping the peace, administering justice, and punishing refractory Indians" over the entire reservation. Agent Wilcox's duties were reduced to feeding his wards and a few other routine matters.[38]

To put this new arrangement into effect, George Crook assigned his most experienced officer, Capt. Emmet Crawford, to supervise the reservation. Second Lt. Britton Davis served as Crawford's assistant at San Carlos, while Second Lt. Charles Gatewood presided over the White Mountain Apaches at Fort Apache. As might be expected, in his autobiography Tom Horn gave himself a significant role in the management of the Chiricahua prisoners of war. He asserted that Al Sieber, who was suffering from rheumatism and complications arising from "old wounds," was unavailable to assist Crawford. Only he, Tom Horn, could pick up where Sieber left off. Accordingly, "Captain Crawford, Gatewood and I were left with the Indian problem," boasted Horn. In this untruthful account, Horn made himself a chief of scouts and aide to Crawford and Gatewood, with Mickey Free as his first sergeant. Horn claimed that Crawford ordered him and Free to monitor the activities of Geronimo and the other prisoners of war at their camp on Turkey Creek, near Fort Apache. The old shaman often complained when Crawford employed friendly Apaches as "secret police" to spy on the Chiricahuas, wrote Horn, and protested, perhaps accurately, that "his people did not want to be herded like goats."[39]

Upon returning to San Carlos in June 1883, Tom Horn resumed his old job as foreman of Eugene O. Shaw's contract herd and continued in this capacity until Shaw was expelled from the reservation on 1 July 1884. However, Horn did not suffer the fate of his employer. Instead, he simply moved from the employ of the contractor to the pay of the

Apache agency. On the day that Shaw departed, Agent Wilcox hired Horn as an assistant reservation farmer to replace Shaw's brother, Matthew. Two such positions—head farmer and assistant farmer—were authorized to help the Apaches learn Euro-American agricultural techniques. Both positions paid an annual salary of $900. Horn had no interest in farming and did not have to perform any actual farm work. Wilcox asked Commissioner of Indian Affairs Hiram Price for authorization to keep Horn in the farming slot on official records but to use him as a clerk in the sutler's store. Apparently, Price consented. Horn's appointment took place (on paper) on 9 September 1884, although he had begun work in the store on 1 July.[40]

This sleight of hand on the employment roster caused a bureaucratic tempest in a teapot for Wilcox's successor, Charles D. Ford, who became the Indian agent in November 1884. Apparently, Wilcox failed to explain Tom Horn's unusual status to his successor, who found the agency employee records in a shambles. Ford, who wanted employees he knew and could trust, asked Horn to resign (or fired him?) effective 31 December 1884 and appointed J. A. Mercer to the position of assistant farmer and J. M. Winnerick to the storekeeper's position. Only later, in January 1885, did Ford become aware that Horn had served as the sutler's clerk. In a letter of 6 January 1885, Commissioner Price pointed out that someone already occupied the position of storekeeper. According to federal regulations, two persons—Horn and Winnerick—could not occupy same slot. Ford explained that the termination of Tom Horn was not a disciplinary measure but was "necessary in order to give me the use among the Indians of the services of the Asst Farmer [Horn]," since Horn was formerly "in charge of the agency cattle." Apparently, Agent Ford hired Tom Horn as an agency herder on 1 January 1885.[41]

In the meantime, tensions were mounting on the reservation. Not only did Agent Ford complain about Captain Crawford's encroachment upon his authority, but the federal government persisted in its efforts to reform and "uplift" the Apaches for eventual citizenship. While the reservation inhabitants might grudgingly submit to the government's promotion of education and economic self-sufficiency, Washington's attempts to suppress other offenses—the brutalization of women and the illegal manufacture of native moonshine, tizwin—provoked many Apache men. A tizwin binge near the agency headquarters on 7 May

1884 led to two deaths. One of Crawford's highest priorities was to prepare the Apaches to form their own courts and abandon justice by vendetta. Ironically, Crawford himself sometimes bypassed the courts and inflicted summary justice upon troublesome Apaches. In one instance, an Apache jury convicted Charlie, a San Carlos Apache scout, for the murder of his wife and sentenced him to death. Rather than permit members of the victim's family to inflict the death penalty, Britton Davis, Crawford's second-in-command, recalled that the captain insisted that they should "attend to it ourselves." Even though Crawford made the decision to execute the murderer, he wanted no part in carrying out such a grisly exercise. Instead, he assigned the task to Davis. In turn, Davis passed the duty on to Chief of Scouts Al Sieber who had performed such duties before. Assisted by Bill Duclin, another veteran packmaster, Sieber summarily shot the prisoner and buried his body in a sand bar in the Gila River.[42]

Such callousness was not lost on Tom Horn, who had occasion to accompany Al Sieber on his periodic patrols into the remote corners of the reservation. On one trip, which probably took place in 1883 or 1884, Sieber and Horn rode from Fort Apache across the Tonto Basin and reported to Whipple Barracks. Their assignment was to travel "in a leisurely manner and to keep a good lookout among the settlers of the Tonto Basin," wrote Horn, "to see if any of them had been molested by the Indians." Throughout the journey, he recalled, everything was "lovely": "we were treated to everything they [settlers] had to give us, and we lived fat and enjoyed the junket as I never enjoyed a visit before nor since." "Sieber was a great favorite with all the settlers," he added, "and I was called 'Sieber's boy.'" (To Tom Horn, who was writing in a jail cell awaiting the hangman's noose, such a "junket" must have seemed light years away, in some distant golden age.)[43]

On another patrol, Al Sieber demonstrated the vicious streak for which he was noted among the Apaches. Although the precise date of this incident is not known, it may have taken place in 1882 or 1883, when the agency police were especially active in breaking up tizwin parties. With Tom Horn and some scouts, the Sieber party came upon an old Apache named Chu-ga-de-slon-a ("Centipede") who was brewing his tizwin. When ordered to cease, Centipede angrily accused the reservation gendarme of being a "jon-a-chay" ("Jon-a-cha"), meaning "an old meddlesome squaw." (The term can also mean "devil" or "curly horned one.") When Centipede made a threatening move toward his gun, Horn observed Sieber spring toward the offender. "I guess he must have pulled his knife as he did so," added Horn, "for he caught that Indian by the hair and made one swipe at him with his knife which nearly cut his head off." In a fit of uncontrollable rage, the veteran Indian fighter picked up Centipede, threw his body into his own brewing pot, and ordered Apache women standing nearby to spread the word "'that they had better leave off making that stuff.'" In spite of his familiarity with violence on the frontier, Horn admitted that Sieber's attack upon Centipede gave him "a very queer feeling."[44]

Such disregard for human life may well have had a deleterious effect upon Tom Horn's subsequent conduct. Jay Monaghan, Horn's biographer, went so far as to assert that Horn and Al Sieber "killed renegades for fun or for their women." In relating some of his experiences to fellow Pinkerton operative Charles Siringo a few years later, Tom Horn recalled one fight with renegades in which a squaw was killed. When soldiers informed him that the dead woman had a baby, still alive, in her arms, Horn informed the bluecoats "that he would fix the brat." He "put a bullet into the urchin's brain," added Siringo. Admittedly, Charlie Siringo was not always a reliable source, and Tom Horn was a noted braggart, but it is also true that callousness and brutality were common features of life in Apacheria in the 1880s.[45]

In spite of exposure to such brutality, Tom Horn made some effort to settle down on the reservation, and he may have taken an Apache girl as his common-law wife. While Horn avoided admitting that he was a "squaw man" in his recollections about living with Chief Pedro (Hacke-yanil-tli-din) and the White Mountain Apaches, he hinted at such a relationship. Although a Carrizo Creek Apache, Pedro led his people in a union with the White Mountain Apaches in the 1850s and strived to reach an accommodation with the white man. By the time Tom Horn became acquainted with Pedro, the chief was nearly deaf and used an ear trumpet. According to Horn, Pedro took a liking to him and instructed his son, Ramon (Chi-kis-in), "to treat me as a brother." "There are many fine girls here," said Pedro, "and I know several that are waiting now to get a chance to throw a stick at you." (If an Apache girl tossed a stick at a man, he was free to court her.) While the chief urged him and Ramon "to buy each of us a wife and set up a house of our own," wrote Horn, he insisted that he and Ramon only went so far as to hire one of the latter's sisters as "housekeeper." Her name was Sawn, and her husband had been killed recently in a quarrel with another Apache, leaving her alone with three children to support. "In a week's time we had a fine lodge," admitted Horn, "and were the proudest 'Injins' in camp." To show off their horses and finery newly purchased from Mexican smugglers, added Horn, the two young bravos paraded through Fort Apache. It may be significant that the meaning of the word "Sawn" in the Apache language is "my wife" or "the old lady."[46]

While Horn was careful to refer to Sawn as his "housekeeper," he may have lived with her or another White Mountain girl. Alonzo Kinney Griffith, who claimed to have talked with older Apaches on the reservation in the 1920s, asserted that Horn became "somewhat Indianized." Horn took "unto himself a young widow, who did his washing, mending and cooking," wrote Griffith, implying that they lived as husband and wife. Charles B. Gatewood, Jr., son of Lt. Charles B. Gatewood, Sr., who was Tom Horn's boss in the last Geronimo campaign, agreed. "Although Horn lived at one time with a woman of Pedro's band," wrote Gatewood, "it was not with either official or conventional sanction." Indeed, Donald McCarthy, a miner who became acquainted with Horn at San Carlos, may have been referring to his association with an Apache girl when he characterized the young Missourian as a "a moral degenerate." Irvin Van Enwyck, who is part Apache and fluent in this tongue, also finds some support for this assertion in Apache tradition:

> The older Apache folks . . . said the stories were [that] Horn & a young Apache man lived w[ith] the young man's young widowed sister & her two children one summer somewhere north of San Carlos. There was the rumor she was pregnant w[ith] Horn's child when they went their separate ways. It was also said she might have either been ½ Mexican or a Mexican adopted by the Apaches as a child. At any rate she's supposed to have gone back to Mexico and faded into obscurity, possibly with "The Lost Ones" [Apaches who refused to surrender and continued to reside in the Sierra Madre after the deportations in 1886].

Horn is said to have named his first child, a daughter, Tomasita, after himself. A second child, possibly a boy, may have been born after Horn left Arizona in 1890. If these stories are true, Tom Horn could have descendants in Arizona and the Republic of Mexico today.[47]

The extent of Tom Horn's immersion in Apache culture is difficult to determine, although he claimed that the White Mountain Apaches gave him an Indian name, "Talking Boy," and that Mickey Free was the first to call him by that name. While Horn asserted that he received this sobriquet because he learned the Apache language so quickly, Apaches who knew Horn maintained that he was so-called because he was "a talker." Irvin Van Enwyck agrees and says that the Chiricahuas called Tom Horn, "Idaa-yadafti", which means "he talks about himself," hence "Talking Boy." Van Enwyck adds that they gave him this name "because of his inability to shut up." A chatterbox would stand out among the Apaches, who could be notably reticent. All in all, Henry Daly's assertion that "most scout leaders had Indian wives, either officially or unofficially," probably held true for Tom Horn.[48]

In spite of Tom Horn's tendency to exaggerate his association with the Apaches, there is evidence in one particular area of their lifelong influence upon him. Horn learned the art of braiding with horsehair from the Apaches and practiced it enthusiastically for the rest of his life. "It is something that takes years of practice to become perfect in" he recalled. "Before I left the Apache and Mexican country, I, myself had become an expert in all work of that kind." He was not exaggerating. Today, examples of his handiwork are in both private hands and many museums. Horn also reportedly practiced herbal medicine that he learned from the Apaches.[49]

Tom Horn's claim that he was fluent in the Apache language and served the army as an interpreter in that tongue remains one of his most controversial assertions. "Sieber spoke Apache and Mexican both," wrote Horn, "and as there were always Indians with us, I began to learn the language very rapidly." There is no evidence to support his contention. The army selected Apache interpreters very carefully. Many were Mexicans whom the Apaches had captured and raised as their own. At best, Tom Horn learned a few words and phrases and managed a form of "pidgin" Apache—a mixture of Spanish, English, and Apache—that enabled him to communicate with the Apache scouts while on campaign. Charles B. Gatewood, Jr., whose father took Tom Horn with him to negotiate the surrender of Geronimo in 1886, declared emphatically that the scout "could *not* speak much Apache." Yet Horn did become proficient enough in Spanish to interpret for the army in the field. Even this was "border Spanish," a lingo that he learned while working with Mexicans in the packtrains. Billy Harrison, Horn's fellow packer, learned Spanish the same way. Both men spoke Spanish "fairly well," according to Henry Daly.[50]

With time, Arizona Territory became a home of sorts to this roving adventurer. Tom Horn was generally well liked, although he tended to be boastful and somewhat full of himself. Donald McCarthy, the mining man, recalled Horn fondly "for his nice free and openhanded ways." "He was reckoned then by everyone who knew him as a clean cut and promising young man of about 23 or 24 years of age," continued McCarthy. "He was strikingly well built and handsome, and about six feet tall, and might have weighed around 180 pounds." Al Sieber remembered Horn as "jolly, jovial, honorable and whole-souled." Even Anton Mazzanovich, who was critical of Horn's boastfulness, admitted that he had good qualities. He was "a fine looking chap," recalled Mazzanovich, although he could be "somewhat loud and wonderful [boastful] . . . , when he had several jolts of cowboy's delight [whiskey] under his belt."[51]

As the Apache threat began to decline in the mid-1880s, Horn sought to exploit new opportunities in the vicinity of the reservation. Aravaipa Canyon, a few miles south of the reservation in northern Graham County, provided attractive opportunities as both a ranching and mining area. Horn was encouraged to venture into ranching by the success of friends—Welford C. Bridwell (Clay Beauford), Dan Ming, Elias A. Jones, and Burt and Horace Dunlap—all of whom ran cattle in Aravaipa Canyon. While working on the reservation, Horn began a start-up herd, possibly by purchasing cattle and horses from border bandits. One of his first purchases consisted of eight horses from a Mexican smuggler. Horn took in a partner in his first ranching effort. Although he neglected to mention this partner's name, it may have been Billy Harrison, with whom he had worked as a packer. By the spring of 1885, their efforts had begun to pay off. "I had about 100 head of cattle and 26 good horses," he wrote his father in January of the following year. Since they did not own grazing land, these budding entrepreneurs probably arranged to run their livestock on the land of friends in Aravaipa Canyon, which Horn began to call home.[52]

Since Tom Horn's purpose in traveling to Arizona was to follow the mining booms, he spent some time prospecting. This came naturally, since Al Sieber and Long Jim Cook took him on their prospecting trips. These men were always on the lookout for "color" even while on military operations. Another civilian scout, Jack Dunn, became legendary as the discoverer, in 1877, of a valuable silver lode that led to the founding of Bisbee, Arizona. By 1885 Tom Horn also held claims in the Deer Creek Mining District, which lay along the southern margin of the San Carlos Reservation and spilled over into Aravaipa Canyon. While the heart of this district was the camp at Mammoth, on the San Pedro River, mining operations stretched eastward to Klondyke camp, at the eastern end of Aravaipa Canyon, near the Dunlap brothers' ranch. Another mining camp lay a few miles north of the Ming and Dunlap ranches at the townsite of Aravaipa. One of Tom Horn's diggings in this area was known as the Ore Hanna. As was typical of small promoters, Horn took in partners, including John P. Harr, a fellow Missourian, Wid Childress, a Texan, and his ranching friends, the Dunlap brothers, Dan Ming, and W. C. Bridwell, all of whom pooled their resources to erect the first smelter at the Aravaipa townsite.[53]

One of Horn's most ridiculous claims in his autobiography was that he, Sieber, Cook, and other packers were with Edward Schieffelin when the latter made the silver discovery that led to the founding of the Tombstone Mining District. Horn asserted that he and Sieber also made a minor discovery in that region and sold it to a mining promoter named Leach for $2,800. While Charles Leach was a prominent mining man and the manager of the Grand Central Mining Company in Tombstone, there is no evidence of such a purchase.[54]

By 1885 Tom Horn had been a resident of Arizona Territory for four years—the longest period he had spent in one place since leaving Missouri. Whether he anticipated such an exciting introduction to the territory is not clear. He participated in three campaigns against the Apaches in his first year in the territory. As he worked at various jobs on the San Carlos Reservation, he not only made friends among the local whites, but he established close contacts with the Apache people—and possibly had a common-law relationship with an Apache woman. While he made some attempts at cattle raising and mining, he could be easily lured away by the promise of adventure. When Chief of Scouts Al Sieber selected him as an assistant scout on General Crook's Sierra Madre Expedition in 1883, Tom Horn was excited at the prospect.

Sieber, who applauded his "valuable services" in this Mexican adventure, continued to use the young Missourian on policing missions on the reservation. By 1885 Horn had "won considerable notoriety" in southern Arizona, Donald McCarthy recalled, and "his star had then risen to a considerable eminence."[55]

CHAPTER 3

Chief of Scouts

By the spring of 1885, Tom Horn had spent nearly four years in Arizona Territory, his longest stay in one place since leaving home. For much of this time, Horn was on the payroll of the United States government, working in civilian capacities for either the army or the San Carlos Apache Reservation. He made some gesture toward a settled existence but never a serious commitment. As a packer and sometime assistant to Chief of Scouts Al Sieber, he seemed to thrive in the ambiguous border, or war zone, that extended from the reservation to the international boundary and beyond. In this wild out-of-doors environment, Horn could occupy himself with horses, guns, and armed conflict. As he explained in a letter to his father in February 1886, he could never return to the farm life of his boyhood. While Horn was not yet widely known in Arizona Territory, he was soon to begin a yearlong adventure that would be a turning point in his life and attract the attention of the national press. After two years of unsteady peace at San Carlos, Geronimo, the Chiricahua medicine man and war leader, bolted the reservation with a few followers on the night of 17 May 1885 and made for Mexico.[1]

At this time, Tom Horn was probably on the reservation payroll as a herder, although he and a partner were attempting to start a herd of their own. However, their efforts were in vain. "I had about 100 head of cattle and 26 good horses," Tom informed his parents, "but the Indians and Mexicans cleaned me out . . . and left me dead broke." He and his partner attempted to run down the thieves, who killed his associate and left Horn "slightly wounded." (Horn made no reference to this incident in the *Life of Tom Horn*.)[2]

Apparently, Horn decided to return to what he knew best, the trade of a packer. Within a few days of Geronimo's breakout, Horn had rejoined Long Jim Cook's packtrain. General Crook had five well-prepared packtrains scattered around the Apache reservation. Three were at San Carlos: Number 1, with Long Jim Cook as packmaster; Patrick M. Keogh's Number 2 train; and Number 3, with William (Billy) Duclin. Number 4 was stationed at Fort Apache, with Frank Houston (Huston) in charge, and Number 5, Henry Daly's headquarters train, was assigned to Whipple Barracks. (Each train was known informally by the name of the packmaster—that is, Daly's train, Duclin's train, and so on.) At this time, Cook's train included twelve men: Silvaria Laguna, cargador; Jim Pyle, cook; Ed Arhelger, blacksmith; and packers Bob Jackson, Jim Gibbons, Anastacio Sota, Antonio Salazar, Antonio Díaz, Antonio Lujan, Fred Nelson, Billy Harrison, and Tom Horn. As in past Apache disturbances, Chief of Scouts Al Sieber drafted young Horn from Cook's train and put him to work. "When the Chiricahuas broke away from their White Mountain Reservation [in May 1885]," Sieber recalled, "I took Tom Horn along with me." Edward Arhelger, another member of Long Jim's packtrain, also asserted that Horn was present. Horn was soon in the thick of the chase. The Chiricahuas, who fled east into the Mogollon Mountains, split up into twos and threes in order to make pursuit more difficult. Horn and an Apache scout named Spike chased one group, reportedly led by the elderly Warm Springs chief Nana, but lost the trail along the New Mexico–Arizona border. On 22 May, Capt. Allen Smith and First Lt. Charles B. Gatewood encountered Geronimo in western New Mexico, but came out second best in the fight, with two men killed and others wounded. Geronimo slipped through the army dragnet and reached Mexico in the first week of June.[3]

To exercise close control, Crook established his headquarters in the field at Fort Bowie and organized two separate columns for the pursuit into Mexico. Capt. Emmet Crawford, whom Crook had recalled from Texas, led two troops of cavalry, with Second Lts. Britton Davis and Charles P. Elliott in charge of Indian scouts. To reinforce the packtrains of Henry Daly and Long Jim Cook, Crook summoned Tom Moore, the army chief packer, with three additional trains from Camp Carlin, Wyoming. While Tom Horn betrayed considerable knowledge of these packtrain movements in his autobiography, he never admitted that he was a packer. He may have been justified in this instance, since Sieber pulled him out of Long Jim's train to serve as an assistant scout. Mickey Free, who was listed as Apache interpreter, also assisted Sieber. While General Crook ordered Crawford to scour the western slope of the Sierra Madres, in Sonora, Capt. Wirt Davis (not to be confused with Britton Davis) led a comparable force along the eastern (Chihuahuan) slope of this same range.[4]

When Crawford's troops crossed into Sonora on 11 June 1885, they were the largest American force to enter Mexico since Crook's campaign two years earlier. Unfortunately, Tom Horn failed to describe this dramatic moment in his book. "Things sure did look like war," he recalled cryptically, "and in June we pulled into Mexico." From the start, Crawford was beset with difficulties. Ironically, one of the problems was his chief of scouts. Sieber, a notorious practical joker, spooked the entire packtrain by showing the mules the skin of a bear that Apache scouts had just killed. Suddenly, "the plain was full of bawling, crazed mules, running in every direction," Britton Davis recalled; it took hours to round them up. South of Oputo, Sonora, a local resident (an American) mistook Britton Davis's scouts for hostiles, killing one and wounding another. While Davis and Al Sieber managed with difficulty to dissuade the comrades of the dead man from seeking vengeance against the American, several scouts killed twenty head of cattle at a nearby hacienda. Crawford charged them with mutiny, sent them to Fort Bowie for trial, and compensated the victim.[5]

On 19 June, Captain Crawford was informed of a renegade rancheria near Oputo and began to plan an attack. In a questionable move, he decided against sending any white officers or white scouts. Instead, he dispatched Chatto with some Apache scouts, who attacked the renegades' camp four days later. Unfortunately, the renegades, who proved to be followers of Chief Chihuahua, discovered the scouts before they could surround the village. Nevertheless Chatto and his men succeeded in killing one renegade and captured eleven women and children. "Both Sieber and I felt," wrote Britton Davis, "and Crawford now agreed with us, that had either of us been with the scouts we would have bagged the entire [hostile] camp."[6]

In August 1885, Emmet Crawford made a decision that directly affected Tom Horn's future as a scout. In order to cooperate more closely
with Wirt Davis's column in Chihuahua, Crawford led his command
over the Sierra Madre. It was a very difficult crossing, recalled Henry
Daly, whose train was in support. On the trackless and precipitous
slopes, many "mules fell and rolled down the mountain slopes." Unbeknownst to Crawford, Wirt Davis's scouts had already had two encounters with the fugitives, killing several warriors and capturing some
women and children. Once on the eastern slope, Crawford ordered
Britton Davis to take Al Sieber, Chatto, Mickey Free, and thirty-two
scouts, with supporting pack animals, and follow the trail of one group
of renegades whose trail led toward New Mexico. By sending Sieber
away, Crawford had, in effect, left his immediate command without a
chief of scouts. Since Tom Horn had been assisting Al Sieber, he became an acting "chief of scouts" by default and assumed responsibility
for the scouts remaining with Crawford.[7]

Apparently, Al Sieber had no qualms about recommending Tom
Horn to Emmet Crawford for this responsible job. Sieber sometimes
left the main column on what he called "side-scouts" or "side-trips." In
such instances, he assigned young Tom Horn to assume important duties. Sometimes, Sieber took Horn with him. At other times, he placed
Horn in charge of a separate party of scouts with orders to meet him at
particular place or left him in charge of the remaining scouts in camp. "I
ever found Tom true to the last letter of the law to any and every trust
confided to his care," wrote Sieber. By the summer of 1885, he was
ready to give Tom even more responsibilities.[8]

It was not long before the Apache scouts presented their acting chief
with problems. When some of the scouts, who were inveterate gamblers and drinkers, got into a dangerous scuffle, Horn had to handle the
situation. The altercation quickly escalated into a brawl when friends of
the scufflers began "to take sides and fight." At this point both Horn
and Captain Crawford "walked in the middle of the fighting parties and
disarmed them," according to Ed Arhelger, who witnessed this ticklish
moment, and "no further harm was done." Horn had passed an important test. After three years of experience in dealing with the Apaches
under various conditions, he had gained the confidence of his commander and the respect of the scouts.[9]

On one side trip, Horn and his scouts had an entertaining encounter with a Sergeant Nolan, who was escorting Chiricahua women and

children prisoners back to Fort Bowie. When this tough Irish sergeant spied Horn and his scouts approaching, Nolan mistook them for hostiles and ordered his charges to take cover. Preparing to protect the prisoners with his life, Nolan exclaimed, according to Horn,

> Ladies, there are people approaching that are your friends and are enemies of mine and the United States Government. Now, I, Sergeant Nolan, do order you to get behind that reef of rocks, and I want you to be d——d quick about it, and not stand there gaping like a lot of low-down shanty Irish! Here, you little black-haired imp of the devil, let that pack horse go and come along here! To h——l wid yer d——n talk, and do ye moind! You think that you will be rescued, do ye? Not while Nolan is at the wheel; you won't lose your course. I will order a court-martial and hang every mother's son of ye to the yardarm!

When a member of Nolan's party finally convinced him that these would-be assailants were actually scouts, he exclaimed, "God be praised! I was afraid I would have to take a life, and I was using my best judgment to conduct myself as a gentleman before ladies."[10]

In late July 1885, the renegades slipped back into Arizona by way of Guadalupe Canyon, with Crawford, Tom Horn, and the Apache scouts still in pursuit. When the fugitives managed to steal fresh horses from some shaky and irresolute cowhands north of Tombstone, a disgusted Crawford called off the chase. Since the scouts' enlistments were nearing an end anyway, Crawford set a course for the reservation. While en route, Crawford encountered Maj. Frederick Van Vliet, Tenth Cavalry, who was on a scouting mission from Fort Grant. Among Van Vliet's force was William T. Corbusier, an army surgeon. Many years later, Corbusier recalled this meeting because a young scout named Tom Horn performed rope tricks for their amusement.[11]

In order to keep constant pressure upon Geronimo and his followers, General Crook resolved to send Emmet Crawford and Wirt Davis back into Mexico with new scout companies on a winter campaign. Davis enlisted the First Battalion, Indian Scouts (100 men), at San Carlos. Crawford, with First Lt. Marion Perry Maus (pronounced Maws), Tenth Cavalry, Second Lt. William E. Shipp, and Tom Horn, traveled to Fort Apache to recruit the Second Battalion, Indian Scouts (also 100

men). Crawford sent Horn to the nearby cattle camp of the beef contractor to purchase hide for moccasins (which would be needed in the
Sierra Madre). The man in charge turned out to be the young scout's
friend Horace Dunlap. On 11 November, Crawford, Horn, and the
new scout battalion set out on the 159-mile journey to Fort Bowie, arriving fifteen days later.[12]

When Tom Horn joined Captain Crawford's command for the winter campaign, he was no longer a mere packer. Now he was a chief of
scouts. On 13 October 1885, Lieutenant John (Jack) Mitchell Neall, the
acting assistant quartermaster at Fort Bowie, signed Horn on as a superintendent of trains. While a superintendent was technically in charge of
two or more trains, this title could also mean chief of scouts. William
Harrison, Horn's longtime sidekick, was also appointed a superintendent of trains and assigned to Crawford's expedition as a chief of scouts.
A few days later, the Tucson *Arizona Weekly Star* announced Horn's
employment: "Mr. Thomas Horn is appointed superintendent of pack
trains, to date the 11th instant, at monthly compensation of one hundred
dollars, and will at once report for duty with scouts and pack trains
under command of Captain Emmet Crawford, 3d Cavalry, relieving
James Allsop, this day discharged." Apparently, army officers had lost
confidence in Allsop. Leonard Wood, a young contract surgeon who
had recently arrived at Fort Huachuca, characterized Allsop as a mere
"frontier bummer."[13]

Since Al Sieber was expected to guide this winter expedition, the
appointment of Tom Horn was cause for some surprise. Various explanations were given for Horn's selection. Horn said Sieber "was crippled
up and too old for such hard work," while Henry Daly alleged that
Crawford "had some trouble with Sieber" and the old scout "refused
to go with him." Sieber gave a third explanation, asserting that when
the Apaches "became very unruly" on the reservation General Crook
sent him back to deal with the problem. "When I left to obey orders,"
continued the former chief of scouts, "I placed Horn in charge of my
scouts with Captain Crawford." A short time later, a Prescott newspaper announced that Sieber had, indeed, been sent to the reservation
in anticipation of some trouble there. Even if Sieber had accompanied
the expedition, Crawford would have had to choose a second chief of
scouts, since a civilian scout was usually assigned to each scout company.
In the absence of Sieber, Crawford's two choices, Horn and Harrison,

"were transferred from Long Jim's pack train for that purpose," recalled Henry Daly. Both men were also chosen for "their knowledge of Spanish." Much to Daly's dismay, he learned later that he might have received one of the scout slots had Crawford known that this veteran packmaster was to be assigned to him. While Daly did not mention it, he might have also been miffed that Tom Horn was jumped from the position of a mere packer to that of superintendent of trains, never having served as a cargador or packmaster.[14]

When the *Life of Tom Horn* was published in 1904, old pioneers and veteran soldiers were outraged at the author's exaggerated claims and overreacted, denying that Horn ever held the position of a chief of scouts. Thomas N. Wills, who punched cattle with Horn in 1883 and '84, attributed such denials to "rank conscious" army officers who did not want civilian scouts to have any of the credit for suppressing the Apaches. In their estimation, according to Wills, a civilian scout "ranked lower than a private." Horn's ability to act as a Spanish interpreter may have had some bearing on Crawford's decision to take him along in the 1885–86 campaign. William Shipp, who commanded one scout battalion, recalled that Horn "interpreted from Spanish to English" while Concepción Aguirre, who had lived with the Apaches, served as Apache interpreter. "The two interpreters were necessary," added Shipp, "because no one could be found to interpret directly from Apache [to English]." However, Captain Crawford and Lieutenant Maus, the expedition's second-in-command, could also speak Spanish.[15]

Crawford continued to rely primarily on enlisted Apache scouts rather than American regulars. The Second Battalion, Indian Scouts, consisted of four companies. First Lieutenant Maus, an 1874 West Point graduate, commanded companies A and B; Second Lieutenant William E. Shipp, Tenth Cavalry, led companies C and D. Maus's "reputation was that of a rugged individual who could sustain nearly any hardship necessary to complete his mission," according to one writer. Charles F. Lummis, who met Shipp at Fort Bowie, described him as "a bright and pleasant West Pointer, with the figure of an Apollo." Second Lt. Samuel Lane Faison, First Infantry, served as battalion adjutant and supervisor of packtrains for Crawford. Thomas B. Davis was surgeon, and Private Frank Nemeck served as hospital steward (medic). Horn, of course, served as Maus's chief of scouts, and Billy Harrison held this position under Shipp.[16]

By now Horn had earned the scouts' respect. Sam Noche, a Chiricahua with the rank of Sergeant Major, served as "leading guide and
scout" of the battalion, according to William Shipp, and had no "superior for these duties." Other members of the scouting companies
included: Cooney, Cuso, Dutchy, Wassil [Massai], Kat-e-kahn, and
Chi-kiz-in. While Cooney and Cuso were "honest, and loyal," continued Shipp, "Dutchy was a known murderer . . . , but in many respects
a valuable scout." Chi-kiz-in, Chief Pedro's son, was Tom Horn's
Apache "brother," whom he called Ramón. One of the scouts, Sam
Noche, became a favorite of Tom Horn.[17]

When Chief of Scouts Tom Horn rode out of Fort Bowie with Captain Crawford's command in November 1885, he realized that he was
on his own. "How I did miss Sieber," he confessed with uncharacteris-
tic humility, "for he knew everything!" (Horn never acknowledged the
presence of the other chief of scouts, Billy Harrison, in his autobiography.) The sudden appearance in late November of Chiricahua raiders
led by Josanie (Ulzana), a brother of Chief Chihuahua, added a sense
of urgency to Crawford's duties. Apparently angry because the White
Mountain people refused to join the fugitives, the raiders senselessly
slaughtered a dozen White Mountain Apache women and murdered
Will Harrison (not to be confused with the chief of scouts) and William
Waldo, who were tending the Dunlap brothers' contract herd near Fort
Apache. On their return to Mexico, Josanie and his followers ambushed
an Eighth Cavalry troop in southwestern New Mexico, killing five and
wounding two. While Captain Crawford, with Horn and Harrison as
scouts, searched the Whetstone and Dragoon Mountains in southeastern Arizona, this murderous band reached Mexico in safety, leaving as
many as forty-five people dead.[18]

When Crawford led his column across the international boundary
on 11 December 1885, he immediately began to encounter problems.
The presence of the Apache scouts in Crawford's command, as well
as that of Wirt Davis, aroused the fears of Sonorans and Chihuahuans,
who made no distinction between Apache scouts and renegades. When
clashes occurred between Crawford's scouts and Mexican policemen,
General Crook expressed "deep regret" at these offenses but took no
further action. Unfortunately, Crawford contributed to this problem
by permitting his scouts to leave the main column in order to hunt
wild game. While "the officers and chiefs of scouts," meaning Horn or

Harrison, were supposed to accompany such parties and "see that no depredations were committed," recalled William Shipp, there were too few white men available to watch the scouts.[19]

As if Crawford did not have enough on his mind, a deputy U.S. marshal arrived with a warrant for scout Dutchy, who was wanted for murder. Crawford managed to convince the lawman that he would hand Dutchy over when the column returned to Arizona. To add to Crawford's worries, some of his subordinates, including Henry Daly, began to express grave doubts about the reliability of the Chiricahua scouts. "From signs and actions of the scouts," Daly recalled, "I became convinced that they knew more about the movements of Geronimo than they were reporting to Captain Crawford." Horn agreed. After expressing his concern to Sergeant Major Noche, Daly confronted his commander. Just what followed is not clear, although Crawford apparently ordered Nosey, a medicine man, to carry out a religious ritual featuring a medicine bag. After all the scouts kissed the medicine bag and testified to their loyalty, Daly and the other white men present were finally "convinced of their sincerity" in pursuing the renegades.[20]

After receiving a report that the renegades were south of Nácori Chico, on Christmas Day, 1885, Crawford ordered Tom Horn with Noche, who knew the country well, and nine additional scouts to push ahead in an effort to cut the hostiles' trail. In the meantime, Crawford established a base camp and set up a temporary camp fifteen miles to the south. On 3 January 1886, the captain led seventy-five scouts, with supporting pack mules, in the direction of the Aros River, hoping that Tom Horn and his party were hot on the trail of Geronimo. Sure enough, on 7 January, Horn sent couriers to Crawford with news that they had cut the hostiles' trail. Crawford immediately ordered the main force to take one blanket and 100 rounds of ammunition each and follow the Horn-Noche party. The Americans "were ordered to provide themselves with moccasins," added Henry Daly, "as their heavy boots would make too much noise . . ." on the rocky trail.[21]

The column crossed the swollen Aros River, a tributary of the Yaqui, and was soon in extremely rough country. "The march was now conducted wholly at night and no fires allowed," recalled Maus, who never forgot the terrible conditions they endured. Sleep was impossible. "We made our coffee and cooked our food in the daytime," he wrote, in order to minimize smoke from their fires. Their moccasins soon wore thin as they made their way through "deep and dark canyons" and clambered from boulder to boulder. Although still ahead of the main force, Tom Horn had similar memories of their harrowing march. The burden of their cartridge belts and rifles was almost unbearable. "A hundred rounds of 45–70 cartridges weighs eleven pounds when you first put them on," wrote Horn, "and at the end of twenty days, they weigh about as much as a small locomotive." Horn declared, however, that he "never did make any calculations on getting killed." After messaging Crawford on 7 January, Horn's party entered a "fearfully broken" region along the Sonora-Chihuahua border known as Espinosa del Diablo (the Devil's Backbone). When they spotted the renegades' camp two days later, Horn immediately informed Crawford, who led his seventy-five scouts in an eighteen-hour march to catch up with Horn's men. Early on the morning of 10 January, the two detachments met about a mile and a half from the renegade camp, which was located on the north bank of the Aros River, about forty miles southeast of Nácori in an area known locally as Teópar (after a nearby abandoned Spanish mission).[22]

To surround the Apache camp, Captain Crawford assigned a scout detachment each to Lieutenants Maus and Shipp and Chiefs of Scouts Horn and Harrison. In spite of the scouts' efforts to move quietly, the renegades detected their presence and gave the alarm. "The hostiles, like so many quail," said Maus, "disappeared among the rocks." The scouts gave chase, but Geronimo's warriors eluded them, and Crawford called off the pursuit. Yet this surprise attack was not a complete failure. The scouts captured the fugitives' food, camping gear, and animals, a setback for the hostiles. With his penchant for braggadocio, Tom Horn later boasted that after *he* located the enemy rancheria, Crawford gave him leave "to go on and finish the job," telling him, "You have made a fine hunt of it, so far, and you must take command now."[23]

In the *Life of Tom Horn*, the author went on to place himself in Crawford's position:

> I broke the command up into four bunches. I took the east side, and sent Shipp to the west side. The east side was close to the mountains and the west side was nearly a mile from the Aros River. I placed Maus on the south side, and left Captain Crawford on the north side. We were approaching the camp

from the north. I wanted Lieutenant Shipp to start the fight on his side, next to the river, and make the Indians come towards me. . . . I knew that the way the Indians would break would be towards the rough country [mountains], and I had seen to it that rough country was on my side.

When Shipp's men killed several women and children, Horn reported, he stepped in to stop the slaughter, employing the Al Sieber method—a swearing tirade.[24]

In the afternoon, one of the women traveling with Geronimo arrived with word that the renegades wanted to surrender. Since Concepción Aguirre, Captain Crawford's Apache interpreter, was several miles in the rear with Daly's packtrain, the captain could not meet with the renegade chieftains that afternoon. He conferred with his officers and Chiefs of Scouts Horn and Harrison, and all agreed that Crawford should meet Geronimo, Nachez, and the other chiefs the following day (11 January). Crawford also instructed "the [Spanish] interpreter, Mr. Horn, and myself . . . to be present" at these talks, wrote Marion Maus. The indications were that the renegades were in a bad way and would probably surrender since they "were without any food or camp outfit and had no animals."[25]

On the evening of 10 January, the men in Crawford's party made camp near the remains of the fugitives' rancheria on the left bank of the Aros River. "The ridge on which it [the camp] was located fell off abruptly to the river side in a high, rocky bluff, along the edge of which ran a line of big rocks," recalled William Shipp. "Outside of these rocks was an open space containing a few scrubby trees." The night was cold and rainy, according to Horn, and "we were all tired and worn out." While some scouts slept near their fires, others rolled up in their blankets in an open area between the rocks and the riverbank. Since Crawford anticipated no danger from Geronimo's camp across the river, he failed to post sentinels. Even "the scouts relaxed their usual vigilance," recalled Shipp. For an experienced Indian fighter like Emmet Crawford, such carelessness was very much out of character.[26]

As dawn began to break on the morning of Monday, 11 January 1886, rain continued to fall and a heavy mist made visibility difficult. Since all personnel had had such fatiguing duties in the last several days, Crawford permitted them to sleep late. Everyone, including the officers

and white scouts, remained wrapped in their blankets, blissfully unaware that a second, and unanticipated, enemy was approaching from
the north. Suddenly, about 7:00 A.M., "loud cries of alarm came from
some of the scouts who were lying down [below] among the rocks,"
recalled Marion Maus. Seeking the reason for this outcry, "Lieutenant Shipp, Mr. Horn and I ran forward at once to ascertain the cause
of the alarm," continued Maus, "when a severe fire of musketry was
opened on our camp." As the scouts realized they were under attack,
they vacated the area as fast as they could. "Our scouts called out [to the
attackers] that we were American troops," Horn later informed newsman Charles Fletcher Lummis, "and yelled to Capt. Crawford and me
that the assailants were Mexicans." Assuming their attackers were Wirt
Davis's Apache scouts who had strayed too far west, Crawford and the
other white men took some time to realize that these aggressors were
Mexicans. In a most unfortunate oversight, Harvey Nashkín and other
Apache scouts had spied these soldiers in the vicinity the day before, but
failed to inform their commander.[27]

The assailants were loud and full of bravado, shouting "Viva México"
and "Viva Guerrero." One officer yelled, "'Follow me, *valientes!*' Tom
Horn recalled, "and straight at us they came on a run." Another Mexican "was telling his men that the hair of us scouts was good and long,"
recalled Sergeant Harvey Nashkín, "and . . . the best thing to make hair
ropes of." As the scouts returned fire from positions in the rocks, Tom
Horn rushed out into the open in an effort to stop the Mexican gunfire.
Hospital Steward Nemeck "heard Mr. Horn speaking and thought the
Mexicans understood who we were." Feeling the danger had passed,
Crawford ran forward to join Horn and waved a white handkerchief
as a signal to the aggressors. Nemeck, who had to stop and extinguish
a fire caused by enemy bullets, then heard both Crawford and Horn
shouting in Spanish, "*soldados Americanos!*" (American soldiers). Lieutenant Shipp observed that Tom Horn was the first American in Crawford's command to attempt to gain the attackers' attention. In an official
deposition some weeks later, Tom Horn stated that "Captain Crawford
hollowed [*sic*] to me to go ahead and speak" to the aggressors when
they were about three hundred feet away. In a subsequent interview
with Charles Lummis, the chief of scouts added that in obedience to
Crawford, he "went out and got upon a rock, probably thirty-five yards
from him [Crawford]. Most of the Mexicans stopped on the ridge but

several came up close to where we were. Three of them passed me within thirty yards, going toward Capt. Crawford. I called out to them in Spanish: 'We are American soldiers, and the Indians here are soldiers, too.'"[28]

Emmet Crawford saw an international incident looming unless he could stop the firing. At the same time, his scouts posed a serious threat, since the Mexicans thought the scouts were renegades. As the Mexicans continued to attack, Crawford shouted to Horn, "My God, Chief, can't you stop them?" Otherwise, he added, "these scouts will kill them all!" Harvey Nashkín, who heard Crawford shouting to the scouts, "Don't shoot," also observed the captain standing out in front of the scouts' position waving "a white piece of cloth." After perhaps fifteen or twenty minutes of Horn's continuous appeals to them in Spanish, said Shipp, "a small party appeared in the open space near us," only about seventy-five feet away. These aggressors, whom Crawford was now able to identify as the Chihuahuan militiamen known as Seguridad Públicos (Public Security or "SPs"), comprised 128 volunteers under the command of Second Lt. Santa Ana Pérez. They were guided by the Tarahumara Indian scouts of Don Mauricio Corredor, reputed to be the man who shot Victorio.[29]

By this time dawn was breaking, and Lieutenant Maus, who could see Chief of Scouts Horn talking with the Mexicans, "felt sure that the trouble was over." Crawford and Maus then approached them. "I told them distinctly [in Spanish] who we were," declared Maus, and pointed out that he and other officers were in uniform. When four Mexicans approached Horn, "the first three passed me without stopping," he wrote, while "the fourth stopped . . . [and] drew a bead on me. . . . I called to him in Spanish: 'Lower your rifle! We are American soldiers!' He lowered his rifle about a second, and smiled."[30]

Since Mauricio Corredor and his scouts led the attack, he and nine or ten men were among the first to approach Horn and Crawford. When Corredor saw the heads of numerous Apaches protruding above the rocks, he suddenly realized this was no ragtag body of Apache renegades, and, according to Maus, began to shout, *"no tiras, no tiras"* (don't fire, don't fire). At the same time, the Mexican officer began to edge toward a nearby hill with his men. Observing this maneuver, the Apache scouts shouted the alarm and moved to protect both their flanks. Even as the scouts were taking these precautions, Captain Crawford was determined to prevent his scouts from shooting and ordered Maus to go among them and see that they held their fire.[31]

In spite of the Americans' efforts, the confrontation continued to spiral out of control. After the Mexicans ceased fire, wrote William Shipp, he saw his commanding officer "standing on a rock about five feet high where everyone could see his whole body." "None of our white people had their weapons," continued Shipp, although "there were about ten Mexicans close in front of us." "Lieutenant Maus and Mr. Horn kept calling to them in Spanish: 'Don't shoot! We are American soldiers!'" "'(Yes, yes)' [the Mexicans replied]," continued Shipp, "but were all the time edging around till they got behind a tree." Suddenly, from about twenty-five yards away, "they opened fire without warning. Mr. Horn jumped down off his rock and grabbed his left arm. I asked him if he was hurt. He said yes. (The ball passed through the fleshy part of his arm.)" Horn later said the Mexican who shot him was the man who had first lowered his rifle and smiled. "Suddenly, he changed his mind: then he took a quick aim at me and fired, hitting me in the left arm."[32]

While Horn's injury was not life threatening, Captain Crawford received a wound to his head that ultimately proved fatal. In describing this incident in the *Life of Tom Horn,* the author added some details that were not included in official reports. Horn recalled that Crawford jumped up on a large rock and held a white handkerchief. "He could not speak Spanish," continued Horn, "but he could swear in a moderately clever way, not like [Al] Sieber or [Adna] Chaffee, but still he was doing very well." Even as Horn urged his scouts to hold their fire, Lieutenant Maus "heard a single shot behind me, instantly followed by a heavy volley." This shot, which struck Crawford, "seemed like a death knell," added Maus. The fatal bullet "was fired by one of the party of nine Mexicans with whom we had been talking," wrote Maus. Harvey Nashkín, another Apache scout, said that "a Mexican behind a bush shot and hit Captain Crawford in the head." "One of my scouts yelled to me to come back, that Crawford was killed," wrote Tom Horn. At the time, "I was half way down [into the basin] meeting the Mexicans," he continued, "and . . . wondering why they had not yet hit me." By this time, the attackers were only fifty feet away from the chief of scouts. Suddenly, "I need wonder no more, for I was struck in the arm." When Horn's scouts saw that he had been hit, they shouted, "Come back!" Shipp described Horn's wound as a very painful and "ugly flesh wound"—inflicted by none other than Don Mauricio Corredor.[33]

With the expedition commander unable to carry on, Marion Maus assumed command and ordered the scouts to protect both flanks against the Chihuahuans. In one of the most fanciful passages in his recollections, Tom Horn claimed that he took charge of the situation and placed "Shipp out on one side to stop their [Mexican] flankers, and Maus on the other side to do the same." "I . . . told each of them to start the game [open fire] when they were compelled to for their own protection," continued Horn. While Maus no doubt relied upon Horn for assistance in this emergency, the lieutenant was certainly in charge.[34]

The Apache scouts, who hated all Mexicans passionately, opened fire upon Corredor and his scouts, who were still out in the open. Four were killed instantly, including Corredor, and four or five were wounded. The firing then became general, and the Americans ran for cover. William Shipp saw a Chiricahua scout named Bender drop Corredor. The unidentified Chihuahuan who shot Crawford was also killed, not twenty-five yards away from Crawford's body. Subsequently the Mexicans accused Horn of firing the bullet that killed Mauricio Corredor, but Horn was unarmed at the time. In the *Life of Tom Horn,* the author felt free to exaggerate his role, alleging that he ordered his scouts "to give it to them!" "All my scouts seemed to shoot at once," he continued, and "they went down in groups and bunches!" "Some of my scouts wanted to be down where I was . . . ," he added, "and Chikis-in [Ramón] and about a dozen came down and kept on shooting at some of the wounded Mexicans who were trying to crawl away." Chief of Scouts Horn, whom the Apaches called, Nan-t-an tle-ha-des-aadn, recalled Harvey Nashkín, "told us to stop shooting at the Mexicans. If he had not told us to do that, we should have killed them all."[35]

During this second exchange of gunfire, which lasted at least an hour, the Mexicans were forced to withdraw to some rocks about two hundred yards away—close enough to shout taunts at the scouts. "Several Mexicans said if we had not had enough to come out and fight again," said Tom Horn in his deposition. However, he ignored this derision and continued to try to convince the Mexicans that the Americans' purpose was "to kill hostile Indians, not Mexicans." In his autobiography, Horn admitted that he used less formal language, asking the Mexicans "how they liked the entertainment?" When a Chihuahuan asked their identity, "I told him we were a bunch of sportsmen down from the United States, looking for some game, and thanked him for the time we were having." Horn invited this man "to get his 'valientes' [brave ones] together again, and try another charge." When the Mexicans asked, "What do you want?" Horn replied, "Everything you have." Harvey Nashkín was close enough to hear these shouted challenges. When a Chihuahuan asked "our officer [Maus?] to give him twelve of us scouts to kill," recalled Nashkín, Horn replied, "You think these scouts are like boys, but they can fight."[36]

"The fight was going on again quite briskly," Horn recalled. Anyone who left the cover of the rocks was in danger of losing his life. "It was not worth my while to try to stop it," Horn frankly admitted. The Americans, Horn among them, were still mystified at the persistence of the Mexican attack. "I thought Mexico and the United States were at war, and that we were in it," he recalled. The scouts were eager to take the battle to the assailants. Horn recalled that Chi-kis-in, his White Mountain brother, "came to me and wanted to scatter our men and go after the Mexicans and kill them all," but the chief of scouts "told them not to do so until I ordered them." Actually, Maus, whose first object was to open talks with Geronimo, had ordered Horn to restrain his scouts and to continue to try to gain the attention of the aggressors.[37]

The Chihuahuans only grudgingly replied to the appeals of the chief of scouts. "After we had driven them all away from us they [finally] answered," Horn recalled. A Chihuahuan shouted, "Oh, you white man that talks Mexican, I want to talk to you." "What do you want?" replied Horn; "I spoke to you many times and you would not answer." "Now we want to talk," came the reply. "I told them to stop firing a minute, and I'd come over and tell them what we wanted," Horn later explained to correspondent Charles Lummis. The Mexicans answered, "All right. Put down your arms and come over." "I took off my cartridge belt, laid down the gun I had picked up [after being wounded]," said Horn, "and went over." In a very arrogant tone, one of the Chihuahuans asked, "What have you been doing here?" to which the chief of scouts replied, "I came over to tell you that we are American troops." When they asked for his commander, Horn informed them that he was severely wounded and would probably die. Then one of the Mexicans, an old man, said, "Our captain is killed, too. Here is his gun [shaking a Winchester in his hand] and *I'd like to kill a Gringo with the same gun.*"[38]

As the young chief of scouts walked, unarmed, up to the nearest Mexicans, Lieutenant Maus feared for his safety and had to resist an urge "to call the courageous fellow back." Yet he was impressed with Horn's command of the Spanish language and knew that communications had to be opened. When Horn finally beckoned to his commander to join him, Maus "followed him over to where some of them [Mexicans] were lying." While these aggressors protested that the entire incident was "all a mistake"—they were "very sorry," "what a great pity" [que lástima] and so on"—and that they thought the Americans were renegades, Maus did not believe them. Nor did Horn. "I asked them if they did not know an American from a *broncho* [Apache warrior] at twenty-five yards," he recalled, "and they . . . said they saw the Indian heads in the rocks, taking them for hostiles." "All six of us white men were in full view of them when they shot Crawford," wrote William Shipp, and were wearing either uniforms or civilian dress that clearly distinguished them from Apaches. Crawford sported "a large moustache and chin beard," while "Mr. Horn had plain clothing, but he was standing on a rock in full view, with his hat in his hand," continued Shipp. Horn's "hair is very light and short and his complexion very light." Even some of the Apache scouts "had on their army blouses and chevrons," Shipp asserted. While he listened to the Mexican explanation incredulously, Lieutenant Maus was so happy "to have the murderous affair" ended that, for the moment, he "accepted their explanations."[39]

Tom Horn had demonstrated courage in confronting the Chihuahuans. He later claimed that he had also tried to move the wounded Crawford to safety, but his arm wound made this difficult. The Apache scouts would not help because of their superstitious fear of handling "a wounded man." "I had to drag him with one hand," wrote Horn, although the enemy gunfire was intense. This was nonsense, of course. When Dr. Thomas Davis, the expedition's surgeon, arrived later in the day with Henry Daly's packtrain, the surgeon found Crawford lying behind the rock from which he had fallen.[40]

With communications now open between the two sides, Lieutenant Pérez began to make demands. As Tom Horn later informed Charles Lummis:

> The Mexicans demanded all the horses and burros we had captured from the hostiles. They claimed that the Indians had stolen

the stock from them. Lieut. Maus told them they couldn't have the animals, which belonged [as booty] to the scouts, who had captured them from the broncos in the fight of the day before. Then the Mexicans said *part* of the stock was theirs; and wanted all rounded up, so that they could pick out theirs. They said they needed five or six [animals] to take their wounded home on. Lieut. Maus told them he'd think the matter over.

Even though the Americans in Maus's party were very suspicious of the Mexicans, and opposed assisting them, the lieutenant insisted that they cooperate.[41]

When Maus failed to respond quickly, the Mexicans began to get "pretty badly worked up," recalled Tom Horn, who was summoned to their camp for the second time. Before leaving, Horn instructed his scouts "to be sure to kill all the Mexicans if they killed me." When Maus learned of the "dreadful condition" in the Mexican camp, he sent Surgeon Davis to their assistance. Late in the day, Horn again accompanied Maus to the Mexican camp, where the officers exchanged notes explaining their respective positions in writing. Lieutenant Pérez explained their actions as "accidental," having encountered an armed forced in the dark, believing them to be hostile Apache renegades. Both Horn and Maus were surprised at the Mexicans' continued belligerence. The Chihuahuans asked, said Horn, "What's the matter with your scouts, that they don't come around to see us?" When Maus explained that his Apaches disliked the Mexicans, continued the chief of scouts, "They said: '*If your Indians want to fight let them come out in this little flat, and we'll give them some more of it.*'" Maus tried to explain that the Americans "didn't come down there to fight Mexicans," added Horn. As Maus and Horn left the militiamen's camp, Pérez assured the lieutenant that "he wanted to be friends," but Maus remained very suspicious. He was "anxious to get rid" of the Mexicans, and gave them some rations, but they showed no signs of departing. Maus's primary task was to fulfill Captain Crawford's assignment—talks with Geronimo, who refused to venture forth until the Chihuahuans left.[42]

On Tuesday, 12 January, Lieutenant Maus decided to move his camp up the trail toward Nácori, hoping this would encourage Geronimo to agree to a meeting. However, the Chihuahuans interrupted these plans by again asking for horses to transport their dead and wounded to Chihuahua City. Maus agreed to supply the animals and ordered Tom Horn and Sergeant Concepción Aguirre, the Apache interpreter, to deliver the animals. Distrustful of the Mexicans, Horn and Aguirre stopped a hundred yards short of the militia camp and shouted to the Chihuahuans to come and get the mounts. The Mexicans reacted indignantly and sat tight. Horn, whose wound was causing him much pain, shouted that "he was no servant for them," Aguirre later testified, "and if they would not [come out and] take [the horses] they would have to arrange [differently] with the lieutenant [Maus]." When the Mexicans stubbornly refused to fetch the animals, added Aguirre, "we went back to camp with the horses."[43]

About noon Apache scouts informed Maus that some of the ponies captured in Geronimo's camp had strayed close to the Mexicans. Not anticipating any problems, Maus sent Aguirre to retrieve them. However, the Chihuahuans, still stinging from the imagined affront by Horn and the interpreter, "stopped him and asked why he hadn't brought the horses to them." "Why didn't you come and take them when we brought them?" Aguirre answered testily. "I'm going after my horses— you go and talk to Lieut. Maus," he insisted. Suddenly, "the Mexican sergeant turned to his men and said; 'Keep this interpreter, and don't let him escape. . . . He shall die here with us.'" In the course of browbeating Aguirre, the Chihuahuans became so enraged at the hapless interpreter that scout Harvey Nashkín saw them throw rocks at him. The Mexicans then went one step further and accused Chief of Scouts Horn of killing Mauricio Corredor. In denying this charge, Horn pointed out (correctly) that it proved "that they recognized me [as an American] at the time" of the initial engagement. Through subsequent diplomatic exchanges, this accusation eventually reached government circles in Washington. (Later, Horn took credit for killing the Mexican officer.)[44]

Sergeant Aguirre's dilemma was going from bad to worse. The Mexicans forced him to climb up on a rock and call for Lieutenant Maus to come over. "We only want to arrange [for] the horses," they declared. While Tom Horn urged his lieutenant "not to go," Maus insisted that he had to. (Maus later said that he intended to send Horn, but his wound was causing him so much pain that he could not perform this duty.) "I was the only one left who could converse in Spanish," explained Maus. No sooner had he arrived than the Chihuahuans surrounded the American officer, who joined Aguirre as a hostage. A few minutes later, Maus "sent over a note saying he was held prisoner," recalled Horn, and that his captors now demanded not only the mules but additional food as well. Furthermore, the Chihuahuans complained that the first six ponies offered to them were "worthless." Maus, who later admitted that his captors "acted very menacingly," tried to act "in an off-hand way." He assured them that he would provide the animals as soon as he returned to his camp. When they insisted that Maus stay, he instructed Aguirre to fetch six horses from Lieutenant Shipp, who was in command of the American camp in Maus's absence. At this point, Aguirre trudged to the American camp and returned with five horses—not the mules that the Chihuahuans demanded. "We won't have these—they're no use," they grumbled.[45]

Unless Lieutenant Maus found a way out, things were at an impasse. When he offered to return to his camp and select "six serviceable horses that you *will* take,'" his captors said he could not leave. They insisted that the American expedition was in their country illegally and should accompany them to Chihuahua City. While Captain Crawford had left his official portfolio at base camp in Nácori, by a stroke of good fortune Lieutenant Shipp had in his possession a letter from the *presidente* of the Sonoran town of Sahuaripa. Maus sent the much traveled Concepción Aguirre to fetch this missive. Unknown to the interpreter, his mission may have ultimately resulted in the release of his commanding officer. When Aguirre informed Shipp, Horn, and the scouts that their commander was a prisoner, they reacted angrily. "Our scouts got mad," Maus remarked, and began "to strip for a fight" and shouted insults at the Mexicans, who suddenly expressed alarm to their hostage. When Maus protested that he could not restrain his scouts while being held hostage, the Mexicans reluctantly agreed to release him if he agreed to provide them with six army mules (but only after they agreed to sign a receipt).[46]

In the *Life of Tom Horn,* the author boasted that he devised a clever ruse to gain his commander's release. When Aguirre delivered the Mexicans' demands to Lieutenant Shipp, Horn informed them that they could have "the mules and grub," but Lieutenant Pérez would have to send some of his men to claim these items. When they arrived, Horn berated them for their insulting behavior toward an American army officer, to which one Chihuahuan replied defiantly that the Americans "had better not make any trouble." "I told him if that was their game," recalled the chief of scouts, "they should see how it was going to work

[out]." At this point, he informed the Chihuahuans that they were his prisoners. He ordered them to climb upon a nearby rock and "to call over to their comrades and tell them just the kind of a fix they were in." Horn then demanded that the Mexicans release Lieutenant Maus "in one minute or the Apaches would shoot them." Fortunately, with the threat of more deaths looming, the Mexicans released Maus. With "the row" ended, according to Horn, "I told the Mexicans to come over and get some of the extra horses [sic; actually they were mules]." Unfortunately, Horn's claim that he engineered Maus's release is impossible to substantiate, since the only other reference to such a hostage episode is in John Heard, Jr.'s, fictional account of the Crawford incident, "The Killing of the Captain," which appeared in *Cosmopolitan Magazine* in 1894. To further diminish his credibility, Horn also asserted that he obtained the assistance of Geronimo and his warriors in the confrontation with the Mexicans! It is too bad that Tom Horn exaggerated his role in the Crawford incident, since it marked the emergence of his name as a well-known figure in the Apache campaigns. Had he been more honest and restrained, Horn would have earned a respectable place in Southwestern history.[47]

For Lieutenant Marion Maus, the sudden responsibility for two hundred Apache scouts presented many difficulties. While Maus had won the applause of Colonel Nelson Miles for bravery in the Nez Perce campaign, in 1878, managing the rough-and-ready Apache scouts was another matter, and the experience of Chief of Scouts Horn was most welcome. According to John Rope, one of Maus's scouts, only a day or two after assuming command the lieutenant made the mistake of offending the scouts. Experienced army officers usually permitted the Apache scouts to keep any booty they secured on campaign, such as camp gear and animals. During their time in Mexico, the scouts had collected various items not only from the Sonorans but from the renegades, all of which they were soon gambling away. Maus, who wanted to return the plunder to the rightful Mexican owners, asked Tom Horn and Concepción Aguirre to help him recover these ill-gotten goods. The startled scouts glared at him so defiantly that Maus "turned pale," according to scout John Rope, and stalked off. Tom Horn eased the tension by producing a bottle of rum and passing it around. Soon, he and several scouts "were squatted in a circle near one of the campfires," wrote Alonzo Kinney Griffith, and "dealing four-card monte." When "Nantan" Horn won some of their spoils, the scouts were not offended. They liked the big, jovial Missourian, who was on a first-name basis with many of them. Some of the White Mountain Apache scouts may even have been "related" through Horn's Apache "wife," or through his "brother," Chi-kis-in, who was one of the expedition's scouts.[48]

After the departure of the Chihuahuan militiamen, Marion Maus relocated his camp farther up the Nácori trail in the hope of persuading Geronimo to talk and sent runners ahead to Fort Bowie with the news of the confrontation at Teópar and Crawford's severe injury. This news caused a public outcry in the United States, but Tom Horn received an indirect benefit from the widespread newspaper coverage since his name was associated in print with Emmet Crawford.[49]

Much to Marion Maus's credit, he continued to focus on arranging talks with Geronimo and the Chiricahua chiefs, who finally agreed to meet Maus, Tom Horn, and Concepción Aguirre on 14 January. Much to Maus's dismay, only a few minor warriors showed up for the meeting. The following day, however, Geronimo and Chief Nachez put in a belated appearance. Maus, Horn, and Aguirre listened patiently as Geronimo presented a long litany of grievances, which Maus considered "purely imaginary or assumed." When Maus assured the grumpy shaman that he would present these complaints to General Crook, the renegades promised to meet him at the Arizona border "in about two moons." Since the renegades were "tired of being out," Lieutenant Maus informed Crook, he was confident that they would surrender.[50]

With fantastic brashness, Tom Horn later claimed the credit for making these arrangements. Shrugging off the presence of Lieutenant Maus, Horn declared that he informed his superior that the renegades "wanted to see me." In another memory failure, Horn said he met Chief Chihuahua, not Geronimo, who asked Horn to "make arrangements for him to meet General Crook." "I did all I could in a talk," Horn asserted, "and made arrangements to bring General Crook to meet him in the full of the March moon at the San Bernardino Peak." At least Horn got the location right. The renegades did provide Maus with a few hostages, including the aging Warm Springs chief Nana.[51]

When Lieutenant Maus and his command set off from the meeting with Geronimo on 16 January, they faced a sad and dangerous two-hundred-mile trek to the international border. Two days into the march, Captain Crawford died. The trail was rough, and the men were demoralized by the death of Captain Crawford. Bad luck continued to beset the expedition, as Sonoran citizens renewed their complaints of depredations by the Apache scouts. Riding in advance of the column were Maus and Tom Horn, serving as Spanish interpreter. On 21 January residents of Temosache, a village near Nácori, complained that the scouts were firing their weapons and otherwise causing disturbances. Cristóbal Valencia, the local police commissioner, and his assistant, Casimiro Grajeda, rode out to confront the Americans. When Grajeda asked Lieutenant Maus to order the Indians to put away their weapons, the American officer quickly complied. Horn then accompanied Valencia and Grajeda into Nácori, where he obtained official written permission for Captain Crawford's remains to be placed in a temporary grave.[52]

During the ride into Nácori, Commissioner Valencia found Horn eager to talk about the recent encounter at Teópar. Apparently unaware that one of Valencia's duties was to gather intelligence about the movements of the Americans, the naïve chief of scouts rattled on about the death of Crawford. After the attack on Geronimo's camp and the subsequent arrangements to talk with the renegades, Horn reported, according to Valencia:

> At daybreak of the 11th a party of national troops from Chihuahua, which was following the trail of the same hostile Apaches, . . . misled by this confused state of affairs, opened fire upon them, both sides engaging in the conflict; that as Captain Crawford noticed the mistake by the national troops, he got upon a large rock and endeavored, by raising a white handkerchief, to make himself known, the interpreter [Horn] imitating his action; but that the firing was fierce at the time, and that Captain Crawford received a shot in the forehead and fell mortally wounded; that the interpreter, also wounded in the arm, ran and called out to make himself known; and that thereupon the nationals discovered that they were attacking the American force of tame Apaches, suspended their firing, and approached to explain their mistake.

While Horn rambled on, he was unwittingly placing officials in Washington, D.C., in an embarrassing position. By interpreting the Chihuahuans' attack as accidental—which Maus and others denied—Horn weakened the subsequent arguments of American diplomats. In later discussions, Mexico City was able to use Tom Horn's garrulousness against American diplomats.[53]

As the American force continued its trek north, Mexican citizens resumed complaints of depredations by the Apache scouts as well as the Apache hostages. Apparently, Maus had assigned Tom Horn the duty of watching the hostages, but the chief of scouts did not take this assignment seriously. Although he admitted that the hostages "would do as they pleased" when away from Geronimo, Horn saw no reason to put them under a close guard on the long journey to Arizona. If the other Americans in the column were as irresponsible as the chief of scouts, the complaints of the Mexicans were only to be expected. Charges against the scouts continued to mount up. On 28 January a resident of Bavispe, Sonora, charged them with stealing four mules from him on the march southward the previous month. When Maus attempted to reclaim these mules from the scouts, who still had the animals in their possession, the Apaches berated the officer with "opprobrious epithets, wherefore he abstained." The embarrassed officer assured the claimant that he would take care of the matter upon returning to Arizona, "where he could make himself respected." When the command reached Bacerac, on the Bavispe River, a local official announced that he intended to provide a Mexican escort for the Apache scouts to the international boundary (whether Maus liked it or not). While the lieutenant initially objected, a stroke of good fortune came the American's way when Major Emilio Kosterlitzky, a Mexican officer, interceded on behalf of the Americans. Kosterlitzky, a Russian émigré who had worked his way up in Mexico's regular army, managed to dissuade this local official.[54]

In spite of anti-American demonstrations in various villages, Marion Maus managed to keep his troublesome scouts out of harm's way, all the while blaming unscrupulous liquor dealers for selling mescal to his scouts. On 30 January, Maus reached Capt. Wirt Davis's camp on Carretas Creek, in northern Chihuahua. The following day, the command reached the supply base at G. W. Lang's ranch, just inside the New Mexico border. Maus's stay on American soil was short, however, since General Crook ordered him and his scouts back into Sonora to await the arrival of Geronimo. Maus set up a temporary camp on the San Bernardino River, a few miles south of the international boundary, and awaited the renegades' signal.[55]

The successful withdrawal of the Crawford expedition from Mexico was a historic event, and Tom Horn, as a chief of scouts, could take some pride in having contributed to its success. Although only twenty-five years of age, he had won applause from both Americans and Mexicans for his bravery at Teópar. In spite of Horn's failure to restrain his scouts on the journey north from Mexico, Lieutenant Maus characterized him as "a courageous fellow" for exposing himself to Mexican rifle fire, while Lieutenant Shipp praised him for "bravery and coolness" when he walked unarmed into the Mexican camp. Even Lieutenant Santa Ana Pérez, commander of the Chihuahuan militia, added his applause. After Mauricio Corredor and several of his scouts fell to the Apache scouts' rifle fire, Pérez testified, "a beardless American [Tom Horn] came forth and gave us to understand that his party . . . were not hostile Indians." In a subsequent dispatch from Chihuahua City, Mexico, Pérez reiterated his admiration for Tom Horn, referring to him as "an American boy [who] jumped up and told them that they were American troops," even though his "arm was shattered to pieces."[56]

CHAPTER 4

"A Good Indian Man"

When Tom Horn returned to the Arizona border with First Lt. Marion Maus and the Apache scouts in February 1886, the young chief of scouts was ready for a rest, not to mention a payday. As a superintendent of trains—his formal title on Fort Bowie quartermaster Jack Neall's payroll—Horn earned a monthly wage of $100, a handsome income for the average frontiersman. In the *Life of Tom Horn*, he tried to impress readers with his earnings at various jobs, and he was particularly fussy if the army failed to pay him on time. After some correspondence between Lieutenant Maus and General Crook's adjutant, the army paymaster eventually arrived by buggy with pay for Horn and fellow scout Billy Harrison.[1]

While awaiting the arrival of Geronimo and his followers, Tom Horn accompanied Lieutenant Maus and some Apache scouts to Fort Bowie for a meeting with General Crook. There Horn had an opportunity to talk with Capt. John Gregory Bourke, Crook's scholarly aide-de-camp, who visited Maus's camp to gather ethnological data from the Apache scouts. Horn also used this visit to Bowie as an occasion to boast about his exploits in the fight with the Chihuahuan militia. Thomas Jacob Cleary, a first lieutenant in the Tenth Infantry, recalled how Horn proudly pointed to a bullet hole in his red flannel shirt and "seemed prone to impress one with his own importance."[2]

While at Fort Bowie, Horn also took the time to write to his parents in Memphis, Missouri, and let them know about his recent adventure.

Unknown to the young chief of scouts, the *Memphis Reveille* had already informed its readers that one of their own had been a part of the tragic Crawford incident. When Tom, Jr.'s, letter arrived, his father permitted the paper to reprint part of it. After apologizing for not keeping them informed of his activities, Tom wrote:

> I am, as you doubtless are aware, employed by the government as Chief of Scouts for Arizona and New Mexico, and interpreter of the Mexican and Apache languages. Am well and hearty and get good pay for my services. I was wounded in the fight in which Capt. Crawford was killed, but it is not a serious wound. [I] was shot through the arm above the elbow, but it is nearly well now. I used to run a great many risks in this country (Mexico) and the United States, but it is getting so there is no danger any more. The last of the Apache's [sic] will surrender in six weeks, I am sure. We have them killed off until there is only about 30 remaining. After these Indians come in, I promise you I will write oftener, will get a good job and be stationed [at an army] post. Don't think I am a hard [man?] because I am a scout. I try to be [good?] and am always sober. I speak the Spanish language as fluently as a Mexican.

Horn exaggerated, of course, when he said he was an Apache interpreter. He promised his father that he would send him copies of Lieutenant Maus's reports "so you can see what they say about me."[3]

Tom Horn's tendency to embellish and talk too much had the unfortunate consequence of spreading unfair rumors about his boss, Marion Maus. Soon after Maus returned to the border with the Crawford column, gossip spread that he had acted cowardly at Teópar. While the ultimate source of this tale is unknown, William Edwardy, a newspaper correspondent, later informed Capt. John G. Bourke that Horn and others had told him that in the fight with Geronimo, Maus "had burst out crying" and "had hidden behind a rock during the firing." Furthermore, Maus "didn't know what to do when the Mexicans came," continued Edwardy, "and allowed them to take just what property they wanted." After this alleged exhibition of cowardice, added Edwardy, Lieutenant William Shipp was so angry that he wouldn't speak to Maus. "It was said in jest that he [Maus] was swapped for a mule," according to Edwardy. Hence, soldiers jokingly referred to Maus as the army's "mule man."[4]

In the meantime, the U.S. government demanded satisfaction from Mexico City for the death of Emmet Crawford. In his *Annual Report for 1886*, George Crook pulled no punches, characterizing Crawford's death as "an assassination" by Chihuahuan outlaws who were out for "scalp-money." (The Mexican government paid for the scalps of dead hostiles.) To assemble evidence for his position, Crook ordered Lieutenant Maus to collect official depositions from Lieutenant Shipp, Tom Horn, Billy Harrison, and others involved. Mexico responded with similar statements from Lt. Santa Ana Pérez and others in his command. On 15 February 1886, Henry L. Jackson, the American ambassador to Mexico, filed a formal complaint with Mexican Foreign Minister Ignacio Mariscal, followed a few weeks later with a copy of Lieutenant Maus's official report and depositions. While President Porfirio Díaz expressed regret at Captain Crawford's death, he excused the Chihuahuan militiamen's actions and published Lieutenant Pérez's report in the *Estado de Chihuahua*, the official government newspaper. In May Matías Romero, Mexican ambassador to the United States, presented his government's official position: the killing of Captain Crawford was accidental. Among the pieces of evidence cited in this report were the (indiscreet) remarks of "the interpreter Tomás" characterizing the death of Crawford as an accident. Ironically, some Chihuahuan deponents quoted in the Mexican report praised this "beardless young man" (Tom Horn), who risked his life to stop the gunfire. President Grover Cleveland desired good relations with the southern neighbor, as Shelley Bowen Hatfield has pointed out, to defeat their common enemy, the hostile Chiricahuas. So in spite of evidence of Chihuahuan treachery at Teópar, the matter of Crawford's death was quietly dropped.[5]

While the two governments exchanged testy missives, Lieutenant Maus, Tom Horn, and his scouts waited impatiently for the arrival of Geronimo, Nachez, Chihuahua, and their followers. At long last, on 15 March 1886, "smoke signals were seen at several points" in the vicinity of Fronteras, recalled Packmaster Henry Daly, "and Lieutenant Maus at once proceeded with a party of scouts to . . . investigate." Not content with merely being a member of Maus's party, Horn later claimed that he (alone) "started out right away to go and find the [Indian] messenger." The messenger, a nephew of Chief Chihuahua, said they were ready to meet General Crook, "when I [Horn] said the word." Horn maintained that he sent a heliograph message to General Crook, and the conference was arranged. Of course, Horn erred on several counts: he did not operate alone and there was no heliograph in the region at this time.[6]

To reduce the fears of the renegades that the Mexicans might interrupt the talks, General Crook agreed to meet the hostiles farther north at Cañon de los Embudos (Canyon of Funnels), but still in Sonora. The talks took place on two separate days, 25 and 27 March 1886. In spite of Tom Horn's insistence in the *Life of Tom Horn* that Geronimo would agree to Horn, and Horn only, as his Apache interpreter, his name does not appear in the list of interpreters. Yet Horn was definitely nearby. As a chief of scouts, he had the duty to stay close to his scouts and ensure that Geronimo did not woo away any of them. Geronimo "was such a great talker," remarked Horn, "that he could make wrong seem right" to the scouts. That Horn was present in the background of this conference is confirmed by the photographs of Camillus S. Fly, the enterprising Tombstone photographer. On 25 March 1886, he snapped two images that included Horn.[7]

As the talks progressed, the renegade leaders, especially Chief Chihuahua, expressed a sincere desire to surrender. "While I was giving the scouts orders to keep away from Geronimo's camp," recalled Tom Horn, Chihuahua "said to put him and all the people with him under a close guard." Apparently, Chihuahua desired that he and his more than seventy followers should be isolated from Geronimo. In spite of the best efforts of Crook and his subordinates, Geronimo and his immediate following of twenty warriors purchased whiskey from Charles Tribolet, a Tombstone moonshiner who had set up a temporary grog shop nearby. As Geronimo quaffed generous helpings of spirits, he became more anxious about surrendering. If Tom Horn is to be believed, he encouraged Geronimo to take flight. Should the Chiricahuas return to San Carlos, said Horn, "they would only go to the guardhouse." This may be the usual Tom Horn bluster. While Horn does not betray in the *Life of Tom Horn* the average Arizonan's overweening hatred of the Chiricahuas, at the same time, he does not exhibit any disloyalty to the army. Indeed, Tom Rynning, a sergeant in Crook's personal packtrain at this time, credited Horn with attempting to alert General Crook to the danger of Tribolet's moonshine "skullduggery." Unfortunately, Crook "didn't get the information in time to prevent the mischief" that ensued.[8]

Historian Dan Thrapp has asked the question, Would someone more experienced than Tom Horn, such as Al Sieber, have been able to prevent Geronimo from bolting again? In spite of Sieber's "immense personal influence" over the Chiricahuas at this time, Thrapp (answering his own question) concluded that he could have done no more than Tom Horn. The result was that, as Lieutenant Maus and his scouts escorted the Chiricahuas toward Fort Bowie (and eventual imprisonment), Geronimo, with twenty warriors and a few women and children, deserted the column on 30 March and escaped back into Sonora. Chief Chihuahua and seventy-nine followers—the majority of the renegades—continued on to Fort Bowie. On 7 April Crook placed them on a special train and sent the renegades into exile in Florida. In the meantime, Lieutenant Maus, with Tom Horn's scouts, and supported by Henry Daly's packtrain, undertook a futile pursuit of Geronimo, losing the trail near Fronteras.[9]

By this time Tom Horn had actively participated in several campaigns against the Apaches, as a packer and scout. He had received the praises of General Crook, Al Sieber, and Lieutenant Maus. When, in 1891, the army adjutant general called for recommendations of persons who merited recognition for services in the Indian campaigns, Marion Maus, now a captain, recommended that Tom Horn be recognized "for gallant conduct . . . in the Apache campaign of 1885–86." "I cannot commend too highly Mr. Horn, my chief of scouts," wrote Maus. "His gallant services deserve a reward which he has never received." Unfortunately, the adjutant general rejected Maus's recommendation on the grounds that Horn "was neither an officer nor enlisted man" (an erroneous argument). The fact that Maus received the Congressional Medal of Honor for "most distinguished gallantry" in the Crawford incident was probably small comfort to Tom Horn.[10]

By the time Maus, Horn, and Henry Daly returned to Fort Bowie, on 3 April 1886, a change in command of the Military Department of Arizona was in the making. The escape of Geronimo had irretrievably harmed George Crook's reputation, even though his unrelenting campaign had reduced the Chiricahua menace to Geronimo and a mere twenty warriors. As a consequence, Brig. Gen. Nelson A. Miles replaced Crook, who transferred to the Department of the Platte. "Things in an Indian way were at a standstill for a couple of months," recalled Tom Horn. Bowing to the demands of southwesterners that he abandon Crook's reliance upon friendly Apaches to hunt their own kind, Miles tried to reassure Arizonans that his regulars were fully capable of running down the renegades. At best, he said he would enlist only a few Apaches as guides (no more than five per cavalry troop or infantry company). In selecting officers to lead the search for Geronimo, Miles sought men who possessed what was later called "the right stuff." Capt. Henry W. Lawton, a six-foot-six-inch Fourth Cavalry officer, fit Miles's bill. The new departmental commander ordered Lawton to get on the fugitives' trail and stick to it until they were killed or captured. In addition to stationing troops along the southern border of the San Carlos Reservation to prevent any renegade intrusions, Miles expanded the modest network of army heliograph stations then in service in Arizona and southwestern New Mexico. At some point in the late spring Tom Horn may have assisted with the location of some sites.[11]

There is some uncertainty as to Tom Horn's movements in late April and early May. Henry Daly, the veteran packmaster, said that Horn served as chief of scouts for Lawton's expedition, which constituted Nelson Miles's primary effort to run down the renegades. Lawton departed Fort Huachuca on 5 May 1886. If Horn was present, he was probably assigned to Lt. Leighton Finley, who commanded twenty Apache scouts. Going by way of Nogales, Lawton entered Sonora with orders "to follow Geronimo's trail even though it takes him to the City of Mexico," according to the *Los Angeles Times*. Even as Lawton took the field, Geronimo and Nachez were committing mayhem in southeastern Arizona and northern Mexico. In this free-for-all atmosphere, the Chiricahuas ambushed Capt. Thomas C. Lebo just south of the international boundary on 5 May, killing one soldier and wounding a second. A few days later, the hostiles ambushed Capt. Charles Albert Phelps Hatfield, killing two troopers and wounding two.[12]

If Horn did accompany Lawton, he soon quit the expedition. In the *Life of Tom Horn,* he gave the ridiculous excuse that a San Francisco newspaper accused him of being too close to the Chiricahua renegades and of having "more influence with the hostiles than Geronimo himself." In other words, General Miles had a "traitor in his command," continued Horn, who decided to withdraw for the good of the army. Horn also said that Lieutenant Jack Neall, the Fort Bowie quartermaster, informed him that owing to Miles's reduction of the number of Apache scouts, there would be no need for civilian scouts. Fortunately,

Capt. William A. Thompson, Miles's adjutant, came to Horn's rescue. Thompson, who was "one of my best friends," recalled Horn, reassigned him to Fort Apache and ordered him to "remain there till General Miles looked around and saw the lay of the land." Thompson was sure that Miles would still need a few Apache scouts and that there would still be a place for civilian scouts such as Horn. While Horn was thin-skinned and could get his feelings hurt very easily, the likeliest explanation for his behavior was some concern over wages.[13]

In spite of his grousing, Horn dutifully showed up at Fort Apache. His name remained on Quartermaster Neall's payroll continuously from October 1885 through October 1886 as a superintendent of trains. Rather than accompanying Captain Lawton's column into Mexico in early May, it appears that Horn traveled with Maus to Fort Apache, where they disbanded the Second Battalion, Indian Scouts. Maus's party left Fort Bowie on 12 April, which would preclude Horn's service with Lawton. Horn remained at Fort Apache for several weeks, per Captain Thompson's orders. On 11 May Thompson ordered Maj. James F. Wade, the Fort Apache commandant, to instruct Horn, interpreter Concepción Aguirre and Joseph Felmer (another civilian scout) to return forthwith to Fort Bowie. All three men had taken riding mules from Fort Bowie that belonged on Quartermaster Neall's inventory. Since under army regulations Neall was personally responsible for these animals and their accoutrements, he wanted everything returned immediately. Whether Horn was able to comply with this order is not clear. At this time, he was in the field with Lt. Everett E. Benjamin, who was searching for renegades northeast of Bowie Station, in the Stein's Peak Range.[14]

Mules aside, Captain Thompson, who considered Horn "one of the most experienced Indian trailers and fighters in the country," was determined to put Horn to good use in Henry Lawton's pursuit of the renegades in Sonora. On 18 June, Lieutenant Neall informed Thompson that Horn had just departed Fort Bowie for Fort Huachuca, where Nelson Miles maintained a nerve center for Sonoran operations. There Horn received orders to join Lawton in Mexico immediately. In his version of these events, Horn added his usual bit of self-inflation. "General [Miles] told me . . . that he wanted me to go to Mexico and find Captain Lawton," wrote Horn, "and act as chief of scouts with him and see what we could do" about running down the renegades. Miles also sent along William M. Edwardy, a freelance newspaper correspondent, to assist Lawton however he could.[15]

On 18 June, Tom Horn, with William Edwardy, Billy Long (a scout), and a few soldiers, departed Fort Huachuca for Lawton's camp in Sonora. In a dispatch to the *San Francisco Chronicle* from Cumpas, Sonora, on 2 July, Edwardy related an incident that reflected Tom Horn's standing among the Apache scouts. On the first day out of Fort Huachuca, Horn's party overtook Second Lt. Harry C. Benson:

> It was nearly midnight when we struck Lieutenant Benson's camp, and I then had, for the first time, an opportunity of witnessing the remarkable vigilance and stealth for which the Apache is noted. As we approached the camp a deathlike silence reigned; it seemed that the whole camp was wrapped in heavy slumber, but suddenly a dark figure rose noiselessly beside us, and an Indian sentinel called out, "Hello, Tom," showing that he had not only noted our approach, but had been able to distinguish in the darkness the form of Tom Horn, the noted scout, who was one of our party.

Benson had with him nineteen enlisted men of the Eighth Infantry, Second Lt. Robert A. Brown and his thirty Apache scouts, a wagon, and a packtrain, all destined to join Lawton. Tom Horn and Lieutenant Brown would soon become well acquainted, as Horn became his chief of scouts.[16]

As Horn and his small party rode into the Cananea Mountains on the following day, William Edwardy witnessed firsthand the skills required of experienced scouts such as Tom Horn. As they approached Jaralitos Canõn, a particularly narrow and dangerous defile, Horn immediately placed everyone on alert and rode ahead to search for signs of Apaches. He immediately spotted "a fresh Indian trail." After examining the tracks, he concluded that as many as twenty warriors were present and that they were almost certainly observing the American party. Knowing that his "little band" was in danger, recalled Edwardy, the experienced Indian fighter instructed them

> to carefully examine their weapons to see if they were properly loaded and in good working order. The saddles were cinched

up, and the lariats thrown loose and allowed to drag on the ground, so that the animals could be easily secured in case it became necessary to dismount. The party, with rifles thrown across the horns of their saddles, then entered the canõn, one at a time, allowing the distance of about one hundred yards to intervene between the riders. In this way the line stretched out . . . a thousand yards, making it impossible for the Indians to fire upon more than one man at a time. The party passed through the canõn in safety.

Strangely enough, when Geronimo surrendered a few weeks later, Horn and Edwardy learned that the hostiles were prepared to ambush their party had not Horn's precautions been taken.[17]

While Horn and his party managed to avoid a fight on this occasion, the renegades lingered in the vicinity and remained a threat. After spending the night at an abandoned rancho, they continued on to the Bacauchi area, where the widow of Ignacio Pesqueira, the deceased governor of Sonora, offered them hospitality and permitted them to pasture their animals with the hacienda's livestock. Assuming that their horses and mules were secure, Horn and his companions went blissfully to sleep on the night of 20 June without posting sentinels. An experienced chief of scouts should have known better than to underestimate Chiricahua renegades or Mexican rustlers. "It never occurred to any one that [renegade] Indians were in the vicinity," Edwardy wrote, "and [we] awoke in the morning to find that all of our animals were gone." Horn, Long, and Edwardy, with some Pesqueira vaqueros, took up the thieves' trail, but soon gave up the chase. Señora Pesqueira kindly loaned the American party mounts for the remainder of their journey.[18]

Horn's party rode into Captain Lawton's camp at Saracachi Ranch on 22 June. Lawton, who was answerable to the government for the stolen animals, was upset. "Of course, I was in a *good humor* when I heard it," he wrote to his wife, obviously fighting to control himself. "Now of course the papers will say *Lawton* has lost his horses," he added.[19]

For an experienced scout such as Tom Horn to be caught literally napping was very embarrassing. In recalling this journey in his autobiography, he made only an oblique reference to the theft and assumed no responsibility for the loss:

> I went down and struck Lawton's camp . . . in Sonora. . . . I crossed a trail of Indians in the Heiralitas [Jarralitos] Mountains as I went down, and, after I reported to Lawton, I told him what I had seen, and he asked me what to do. He had twenty-five Apache scouts and two troops of cavalry and four or five white scouts. I told him to leave all the outfit except the scouts and to go and take up the trail I had just left. This we did, and as we were all in light traveling order, we went at a good lively gait.

Among this group of picked pursuers, according to Horn, was Surgeon Leonard Wood, who boasted, "We will run them off the earth!" In a remarkable burst of prevarication, Horn boasted that they killed seventy-five renegades on this fictitious manhunt.[20]

While Captain Thompson thought he was doing Lawton a favor by sending him experienced scouts such as Tom Horn and Billy Long, the commander was not impressed. On 2 July he wrote Thompson that since "Horn and Long lost the mules they were riding on their way down, I have nothing to mount them on here." Lawton was not pleased with any reinforcements, white or Apache, that he had received, complaining that they only made trouble. He sent Horn and Long back to Fort Huachuca on 3 July, with William Edwardy accompanying them as a courier. When Lawton complained about the Apache scouts, he was probably recalling their recent drunken binge in Sinoquipe, Sonora, which, according to Leonard Wood, resulted in several knifings and many bruises. By this time, Lawton was in the vicinity of Teópar, where Crawford was killed and Horn wounded the previous January.[21]

Captain Lawton made one exception in his assessment of the reinforcements that General Miles had provided. Leonard Wood, an assistant surgeon, soon turned into a fighting man. Wood had made the difficult journey to the Sierra Madre with a packtrain guided by Zebina (Casimiro) Streeter, an old border ruffian who had lived and raided with the Apaches before entering army service as a civilian scout at five dollars a day. When Henry Lawton, who was desperate for supplies, learned of Wood's approach, he sent Sgt. Archibald Atkinson Cabaniss, Troop B, Fourth Cavalry, to meet the supply train and ensure that the food and ammunition arrived safely. Cabaniss, the son of another assistant army surgeon, would play an important part in Tom Horn's career some years later. On 26 June, Second Lt. Robert A. Brown arrived at Lawton's camp with fresh Apache scouts and nineteen infantrymen. Since they were malingerers and jailbirds from the Fort Huachuca guardhouse, Lawton feared they would simply cause him more problems. However, Wood, who was anxious for a line officer's job, volunteered to assume command. Wood, who also held the rank of lieutenant, soon whipped them into shape.[22]

Tom Horn, with no immediate assignment after reporting back to Captain Thompson at Fort Huachuca, took some time off to visit friends. William D. (Bill) Ganzhorn, whom Horn had known at Fort Thomas in 1882, was running a saloon in Tombstone. John D. (Jack) Ganzhorn, son of the saloon man, recalled years later that "several old civilian scouts," among them Tom Horn, visited his father that summer of 1886. Young Jack, only five years of age at the time, "listened big-eyed" to the noted scout's "exciting tales of chasing Geronimo." Horn may also have visited Michael Gray, who had a ranch near old Camp John A. Rucker in the Chiricahua Mountains, a few miles north of the international boundary. Although Rucker had been abandoned some time earlier, the army temporarily reopened this camp in the summer of 1886. John Plesent Gray, son of the owner, recalled that Tom Horn sometimes visited the ranch with his Apache scouts. One of Horn's purposes was to give his scouts an opportunity to hunt wild game, which was plentiful in the vicinity. Horn was also well acquainted with John Slaughter, owner of the famous San Bernardino Ranch, situated on Arizona's border with Mexico (near present-day Douglas). Slaughter, always a genial host, provided Horn with food, a comfortable bed, and any horses that he might need.[23]

In the meantime, Nelson Miles, becoming concerned at Lawton's lack of success, began to seek an alternative means to bring in the renegades. When Miles received a report that the hostiles were very tired and might be persuaded to surrender, he decided to supplement his military efforts with a more diplomatic approach. Miles asked Sgt. Maj. Sam Noche, an Apache scout who had been with Emmet Crawford at Teópar, to suggest the names of some Chiricahuas who might agree to make the dangerous journey to Sonora and broach the subject of surrender directly to Geronimo. Noche suggested Kayitah (Ki-e-ta) and Martine, both of whom had ties to Geronimo's band. To serve as an escort for these "peace commissioners," he selected a veteran Sixth Cavalry first lieutenant, Charles B. Gatewood. Miles gave a very reluctant Gatewood, suffering from a bladder infection, his orders in Albuquerque, New Mexico, on 13 July. Gatewood hired twenty-one-year-old George Medhurst Wratten as his Apache interpreter. Wratten, who had clerked in the same San Carlos sutler's store where Tom Horn had worked, possessed a remarkable ear and learned Apache quickly. Wratten married into the tribe and became a lifelong advocate for the Apaches. Tom Horn, doubtless envious of this young man's language skills, mentioned him (snidely) only once in the *Life of Tom Horn*.[24]

As Lieutenant Gatewood, George Wratten, Kayitah, and Martine made their way from Fort Bowie toward Sonora, they had a passing encounter with Tom Horn. On their way south, Gatewood's party spent the night of 15 July at the ranch of Theodore F. White, headquarters of the Chiricahua Cattle Company, twenty-five miles south of the post. The next day George Whitwell Parsons, a Tombstone mining man, encountered the Gatewood party there and noted in his diary that Tom Horn was there too. While Gatewood continued toward the international boundary, Horn proceeded to Fort Huachuca. On 16 July, Col. William B. Royall, the Fort Huachuca commandant, informed Captain Thompson that "the scouts of Capt. Lawton's command, Edwardy, Horn and Long are still at this post" and that he intended to dispatch them, along with Henry Daly's packtrain, to Captain Lawton. Daly had just been released from the post hospital, where he was treated for an attack of sciatic rheumatism. After depositing supplies at Oposura, Sonora, the Daly-Horn party continued on to Lawton's camp, fifteen miles south of Nácori, arriving on 29 July 1886.[25]

Daly and Horn found Henry Lawton very discouraged. Even though his scouts surprised the Chiricahuas on 13 July, killing three and seizing their camp equipage, the majority of the hostiles were still at large. Apparently, Lawton was pleased to receive any fresh reinforcements, even Horn, Edwardy, and Long, all of whom he had previously sent back to Arizona, and he immediately assigned Horn as chief of scouts to Lt. Robert A. Brown's Apache scouts. In another surprise, Lawton "sent for Tom Horn, chief of scouts, and myself to come to his camp," recalled Henry Daly, who "found him with a map spread out on his bed." Lawton "asked our views as to where the hostiles were then located." While Horn and Daly agreed that "they were somewhere within forty or fifty miles south of his [Lawton's] camp," the two veteran Indian fighters disagreed as to the direction they had taken. Lawton decided to follow Horn's suggestion and went south toward the Aros River. As Daly later admitted, both he and Horn were wrong.[26]

On 2 August 1886, Captain Lawton reached the Aros. When William Edwardy and Jack Wilson (a civilian courier) found the tracks of two unidentified riders who were also heading for the river, Lawton ordered his command to cross the swollen stream. Lieutenant Brown's Apache scouts refused to attempt such a dangerous crossing, but "Lawton, Horn and I stripped off to try it," wrote Leonard Wood. Although Lawton quickly abandoned the idea, Wood and Horn persisted in trying to swim across. While Wood succeeded in crossing after "an exceedingly hard swim," continued the surgeon, "Horn came very near going under, as although a big strong chap he had not done much swimming in rough water." Wood and Horn finally reached the opposite bank, while Lawton wisely ordered his men to build a raft. In the meantime, Lieutenant Brown took his scouts upstream and found a safer crossing.[27]

While Lawton's men were still crossing the river the following day, Lieutenant Gatewood and his "peace commissioners," Kayitah and Martine, rode up with Lt. James Parker as escort. Much to Leonard Wood's surprise, Gatewood, who was still suffering from a bladder infection, admitted to the surgeon that he had "no faith" in General Miles's plan and wanted "to go home." A few hours after Gatewood's arrival, Leonard Wood took Tom Horn and twenty-five Apache scouts up to the crest of the Sierra Madre in an effort to determine if Geronimo had slipped around the Americans' flank and escaped to the north. William Edwardy and Billy Long went along as couriers. "Each man carried two belts of ammunition, and an extra pair of moccasins," wrote Wood. While they were sleeping in a cave on Nácori Creek, heavy rains sent the stream over its backs and flooded their cave. The next day Wood, Horn, and their men trekked twenty-two miles toward the mountain crest in what Wood admitted "was the hardest climb I have had this summer." On the return trip, Wood proceeded down the Aros with part of his command, while "Horn took some of the Indians and bore rather to the right and attempted to reach [Lawton's] camp by crossing the country near the river." Wood returned without difficulty, but Horn and his followers encountered "frightfully rough" terrain, straggling into Lawton's camp three hours later. The Wood-Horn re-connaissance party had covered seventy-five miles, but found no sign of the fugitives.[28]

On 11 August the restless surgeon, with Tom Horn at his side, set off on a second side trip, this time in a search for wild game. While the two were making their way up a canyon, "suddenly a couple of bullets struck so near us that we were both covered with dirt," wrote Wood. The two remained "under cover for some time." Their assailants, who must have been Chiricahua rear guards, eventually withdrew without trying to finish them off. This encounter, Wood concluded, indicated that Lawton was "sometimes very near them [renegades] without see-ing them." Such encounters led Tom Horn to believe that Lawton's remorseless pursuit was tiring the hostiles out. As long as the packtrains kept Lawton adequately supplied, Horn wrote, "we would make them run till they got tired of running." For much of July and early August, "Geronimo was from ten hours to four days ahead of us," continued Horn. After the renegades' subsequent surrender, they informed the chief of scouts that their "rear guard saw us many times." "It was a great race," added Horn, "and I knew the renegades could not stand it much longer."[29]

Since departing Fort Huachuca in early May, Henry Lawton had encountered nothing but problems. On 12 August, the captain fell ter-ribly ill with food poisoning and was near death. Fortunately, Doctor Wood managed to pull him through with a purgative. Three days later, several of Lieutenant Brown's Apache scouts got drunk in the village of Bacadéhuachi and began to terrorize the townspeople. Among the revelers were Kayitah and Martine, the peace commissioners! As Law-ton attempted to coax his command out of town, Leonard Wood ob-served that some scouts in the rear were still causing trouble. Fearing further violence, he sent Tom Horn forward to inform Lawton. In the meantime, the drunken scouts confronted Wood and "proposed that we should all go off and kill some Mexicans!" Finally, Wood and Chief Packer Willis Brown formed a "police brigade" from the few remaining sober scouts, struck a few troublemakers over the head, and disarmed them. The result was "a rather damaged looking lot of drunks," de-clared Wood.[30]

By 17 August, Lawton was camped just north of Oputo, Sonora. Taking Leonard Wood and Tom Horn with him, he backtracked to this "sleeping little town" in an effort to gain intelligence about the renegades. While the visit yielded no new information, upon returning to camp the captain received the first reliable news of the hostiles from Mexican packers, who reported them near Fronteras. Geronimo was cleverly seeking information in regard to surrender terms from Jesús Aguirre, prefect of Arispe District (where Fronteras was located), in order to have a bargaining chip when he talked with the Americans. Fortunately, Lt. Wilber E. Wilder, who had just arrived in Fronteras, learned that Geronimo, who was holed up east of this village in the Terras Mountains, had sent two women into town to spread the word that he was willing to discuss surrender terms. Wilder sought out these two women and urged them to caution Geronimo against an arrangement with the Mexicans, who would almost certainly kill them all. When Lieutenant Gatewood reached Fronteras later this same morning, he went directly to Prefect Aguirre. Just what transpired is not clear, although Gatewood probably tried to determine the extent, if any, of Aguirre's negotiations with Geronimo. In the meantime, Chief of Scouts Horn and Lt. Abiel L. Smith arrived in Fronteras just as Lieutenant Gatewood was preparing to seek out Geronimo's Terras Mountain sanctuary.[31]

That afternoon Gatewood rode into Lieutenant Wilder's camp three miles south of Fronteras, where he talked with Col. George A. Forsyth, Fourth Cavalry, who had just arrived with more troops from Arizona. Prefect Aguirre forbade Gatewood to follow the Apache women when they departed for Geronimo's camp, but the American officer was determined to trail them. He was still suffering from a kidney ailment and remained in camp all day on 21 August, but he did send Kayitah and Martine out to search for signs of the renegade camp. Captain Lawton arrived in Fronteras the next day and flew into a rage when he learned that Gatewood was still dawdling. Leonard Wood and Lt. Thomas Clay, who feared "a big row," managed to dissuade the angry officer from confronting the ailing Gatewood. Later in the day, Prefect Aguirre treated Lawton to drinks at a local bar, whereupon Lawton became so inebriated that Wood had to put him to bed in a back room of the cantina. At the first opportunity, Wood conveyed to Gatewood Lawton's order that he "take his Indians and immediately go out on the trail." In describing the captain's drunken binge later to Captain John G. Bourke, William Edwardy referred to it as Henry Lawton's "grand 'bat' in Fronteras."[32]

Still ailing, Lieutenant Gatewood prepared to seek out Geronimo, although not fast enough for Henry Lawton. While Lieutenant Wilder agreed to provide him with a small escort of Apache scouts, Gatewood's biggest concern was an adequate team of interpreters. While Gatewood could speak a "pidgin English-Spanish-Apache," according to writer Louis Kraft, this lingo (which Tom Horn probably spoke as well) was much too imprecise for formal negotiations. The army's usual procedure in formal talks with the Apaches was to have one interpreter translate from English to Spanish and a second from Spanish to Apache, and vice versa. In such delicate circumstances, the presence of at least two interpreters for each language (four in all) was considered essential. One would translate while the second person served as a witness. Gatewood already had one Apache interpreter, George Wratten, and Lt. Robert A. Brown agreed to loan him a second one, Jesús María Yestes, a personal acquaintance of Geronimo. Since Gatewood also desired a second Spanish interpreter, Brown was willing to loan him his chief of scouts, Tom Horn. Horn and Yestes were taken along, recalled Robert A. Brown, because George Wratten, Gatewood's interpreter, "was not fully qualified to carry on negotiations."[33]

Correspondent William Edwardy gave a different explanation for the presence of Tom Horn in Gatewood's party. While Edwardy was not a member of this group and reflected the civilian bias against army officers, he was in a position to be familiar with the events leading up to Gatewood's meeting with Geronimo. In conversation with John G. Bourke in April 1889, Edwardy declared that he and Tom Horn were scouting in the field when Henry Lawton led his command to Fronteras, went on his drunken binge, and, according to Edwardy, did not fully recover for several days. While still suffering from a hangover, Lawton "went out on a wild goose chase to hunt Geronimo" and "lost part of his command and all his pack train." At the same time, Edwardy continued, he and Tom Horn, who were serving as Lawton's guides on this inauspicious foray, became "separated from him, and had nothing to eat for (3) three days." Luckily they stumbled upon on Gatewood, Wratten, and the two Apache "peace commissioners," who "gave them food." Given Edwardy's distrust of army officers, he may have exaggerated in this instance. While Lawton did get lost, there is no indication that he strayed as far as Edwardy alleged, nor is there evidence to support the correspondent's story about him and Tom Horn fortuitously finding Gatewood's party.[34]

It is unfortunate that Tom Horn failed to present a reliable account of the events surrounding Geronimo's surrender in the *Life of Tom Horn*. In a book replete with errors, embellishments, and outright prevarications, the dozen pages that he devoted to this episode—one of the high points of his career—are the most muddled and preposterous in the entire autobiography. While his own contributions to bringing about Geronimo's surrender were respectable enough, Horn had the gall to claim that he alone was responsible for the medicine man's decision to give up. According to Horn, Lieutenant Gatewood did not select him to accompany the mission to Geronimo. Instead, Horn insisted that *he* had selected the lieutenant. Gatewood and his two Chiricahua peace commissioners went alone into the mountains to find Geronimo's camp, but they returned unsuccessful after four days. When Gatewood complained "that he could not get his two friendly Indians to approach the Chiricahuas," alleged Horn, "Lawton asked me if I could do anything," and "I told him frankly that I was the only one who could do anything." While he and Gatewood were waiting for a heliograph reply from General Miles as to how to proceed (heliography was not available in Mexico), wrote Horn, Geronimo sent an Apache woman with word that he "wanted to see me." "I was very much put out at the way I was being treated," added Horn, "and would not tell Lawton [what the messenger said], but told him to call George Wratten, a boy who was with Gatewood, and let him do the interpreting. This he did."[35]

This impasse was finally broken, according to Tom Horn, when General Miles directed Lawton (by heliograph) "to send Gatewood and myself to see what we could do [with Geronimo]." Horn alleged that he refused to undertake such a hazardous mission unless Miles agreed to meet later with the renegade leader. (Miles wanted to avoid the embarrassment that Crook had recently experienced.) Horn informed Lawton that "I could never tell Geronimo but one lie for he would find out . . . and then he would kill me." Finally, Miles "said for me to fix a date and he would keep it." As Horn prepared to ride to Geronimo's camp, he wrote, "Gatewood said he would take his chances if I would let him go." Horn assured him he would not be taking any chances and urged Gatewood to "come on."[36]

The actual events leading to the opening of negotiations with Geronimo differed radically from Tom Horn's version. On the evening of 22 August, Lieutenant Gatewood and his party, including Horn, set out from Lieutenant Brown's campsite near Fronteras. When they found one of Geronimo's abandoned camps the next morning, Gatewood sent a courier back to update Captain Lawton and continued on the trail of the four Chiricahuas (two women and two men) some fifteen miles farther into the Terras range. "We proceeded slowly & cautiously," recalled Gatewood, "with a piece of flour sack to the fore as a white flag." The following day, "the trail was decidedly hot." By noon, they were safely camped in a canebrake on the Bavispe River, about thirty miles directly south of the international boundary and John Slaughter's San Bernardino Ranch. About 2:00 P.M. on 25 August, Kayitah and Martine, following the trail alone, came upon the hostile camp and presented General Miles's surrender terms. Geronimo agreed to talk, but only to Gatewood. Nachez, who was the hereditary chief and superior to Geronimo, "sent word that we would be perfectly safe so long as we behaved ourselves," recalled Gatewood. As a precaution, the renegades insisted that Kayitah remain with them as a hostage, while Martine carried the renegades' invitation to Gatewood.[37]

Gatewood's party took the lead, but Henry Lawton's regulars, with Brown's scouts, followed closely. Correspondent William Edwardy, who was traveling with the scouts, described their movements for the *San Francisco Chronicle*:

> Lieutenant Gatewood, with two Chiricahua Indians and a small escort, first took the trail. . . . Horn, with his Indian scouts, next followed, and Captain Lawton, with the [dismounted] cavalry, came in close upon their heels. The trail led through the roughest portion of the Torres [Terras] mountains and the route had evidently been selected [by Geronimo] with the view to render pursuit next to impossible. Gatewood and Horn, with his Indian scouts, pressed forward as rapidly as possible upon the trail.

In the meantime, Captain Lawton attempted to lead his men and pack animals directly from Fronteras to the Bavispe River but encountered such rough terrain that he had to search for another route. On the afternoon of 24 August, Brown and thirty Apache scouts arrived at Gatewood's camp, followed by Captain Lawton and the main body of troops later that day. Through Martine, who returned to Gatewood's camp at sundown, Geronimo conveyed assurances that he and Nachez desired to "talk peace." Given the source of such promises, interpreter George Wratten recalled that everyone felt very insecure. We "lay on our rifles all night," he wrote.[38]

In his *San Francisco Chronicle* dispatch, William Edwardy captured the dramatic moment when Lieutenant Gatewood and his official party—Horn, Wratten, Yestes, and five soldiers—began talks with the renegades:

> On . . . the 25th, the entire American column, with Lieutenant Brown's scouts, moved to a point within a mile of Geronimo's camp, where three representatives of Nachez suggested that they talk in a more hospitable area on the nearby river bank. Soon, the entire band of twenty-four hostile warriors were gathered around Gatewood, who shared a special tobacco supply. When Geronimo requested whiskey, the lieutenant refused. In a two-hour meeting, Geronimo regaled the group with his usual long list of grievances, but eventually said they would surrender, on two conditions: if they could live on the reservation; and avoid any punishment. Gatewood replied that he was not authorized to offer terms, but cautioned Geronimo that this was the last opportunity for him and his companions to surrender.

Geronimo and his followers remained extremely wary, as Private Lawrence Jerome, one of Lawton's men, recalled. The fugitives "had rifle pits dug and fortifications thrown up" around their camp.[39]

Geronimo was especially sensitive to the presence of any Apache scouts in the vicinity of the talks. "Gatewood started on this trip [to Geronimo's camp] from my own camp," recalled Robert Brown, "and I started with him, with Tom Horn and Jesús Maria Yestes and my thirty scouts." However, "one of Geronimo's band came out . . . and stated that the Scouts must go back." While "Horn and Yestes were needed by Gatewood for the conference," continued the former scout commander, "I had to turn back." Many years later, in April 1929, Brown recalled the final negotiations with Geronimo and attempted to place the role of Horn and Yestes in perspective:

> As for myself I was necessarily kept close to my command of Indians scouts. Tom Horn was my Chief of Scouts and Jose [*sic*, Jesús] Maria Yestes was my Indian interpreter. These two men were the only members of the command capable of translating

the Indian language into English. Yestes translated from Indian to Mexican and Horn made the translation from Mexican to English, and vice versa. These two men were used at all the conferences.

Apparently Brown forgot that George Wratten was present. It appears that Gatewood used this young man as a witness.[40]

When Lieutenant Gatewood presented General Miles's surrender terms, the old medicine man and his followers withdrew to confer among themselves. Eventually, they returned to restate their position: "the reservation or fight." Gatewood continued to press Geronimo and Nachez, pointing out that the U.S. government had recently moved many Chiricahuas, including Chief Chihuahua's band, far to the east. If Geronimo and his comrades wanted to see their family and friends again, they should surrender and submit to this same relocation. This was the first Geronimo had heard of the fate of Chief Chihuahua. The news was so unexpected that the hostiles again withdrew for "another private council." When Geronimo returned again, he expressed a desire to continue to fight but also proposed a feast and a continuation of discussions.[41]

The discussions continued late on 25 August. When Geronimo suggested that Gatewood return to Arizona and ask General Miles for more lenient terms, Gatewood replied firmly that the commander had made up his mind. After shaking hands, the two leaders parted. The following morning, Gatewood and his interpreters "met our handsome friend [Geronimo] & four or five bucks a few hundred yards from camp," he recalled. In a surprising overnight change of position, Geronimo informed Gatewood that "the whole party, 24 bucks & 14 women & children, would meet the General at some point in the United States, [and] talk the matter over with him," adding that he would "surrender to him [Miles] in person, provided the American commander [Lawton] would . . . protect them from Mexican & other American troops that might be met on the way." With Lawton's concurrence, a courier set off to General Miles and prepared to lead the entire assemblage to Skeleton Canyon (Cañon Bonito), just inside the Arizona border.[42]

In spite of various eyewitness accounts of these meetings, Lieutenant Gatewood's actual procedure is not always clear. It appears that Gatewood, who spoke the Apache language, sometimes talked directly with the renegades and used his Spanish interpreters (Yestes and Horn) only as witnesses. In other instances Gatewood let the talks progress, with "George Wratten interpreting and two others confirming his words," according to Robert Utley, Geronimo's biographer. In the first meeting with the hostiles, Gatewood recalled:

> I used interpreters because of the importance of the occasion . . . although I could carry on an ordinary conversation with them in their own dialect, I was too liable to make mistakes that might occasion misunderstanding & it was a poor time to risk anything. It took but a few minutes to deliver my message [through interpreters], which was, "Surrender, & you will be sent to join the rest of your people in Florida, there to await the decision of the President of the United States as to your final disposition. Accept these terms, or fight it out to the bitter end."

Louis Kraft, a close student of these events, also concluded that Gatewood used his interpreters. Tom Horn, who was in a good position to inform us of the mechanics of the negotiations, failed to describe (or even admit to) his role as Spanish interpreter. When Gatewood felt confident of his language skills at certain moments in the negotiations, the participation of the interpreters, including Tom Horn, could have merely consisted of a nod, indicating they concurred with his choice of words.[43]

On 28 August, Henry Lawton began the northward trek with the Chiricahuas, who warily kept their distance (but stayed close enough for protection). No sooner had the expedition gotten under way than Prefect Jesús Aguirre, with 180 Sonoran militiamen, overtook them and demanded custody of the Chiricahuas. Lieutenant Gatewood, who had immediate responsibility for the Chiricahuas, decided to ride on ahead with Geronimo and his followers, while Lawton fell back and stalled for time. "I happened to be the nearest [officer] ready [to meet the Mexicans] and started off at once on a mule," recalled Leonard Wood, while "Lieutenant [Abiel L.] Smith and Tom Horn, chief of scouts, jumped on their mules and rode down to meet them [Mexicans] in a dense canebrake." The Mexicans were "extremely hostile," recalled Wood, and they threatened "to attack the Indian camp in spite of the fact that we assured them that the Indians were our prisoners." With Horn interpreting, "Wood told the prefect that the Americans and Apaches had joined forces and were ready to attack if he and his army proceeded." Wood and Horn did their best to keep the Mexicans "busy talking until finally Lawton came," added Wood. As a concession to the Mexican official, Lawton arranged for Aguirre and several of his party to have a face-to-face talk with Geronimo. It was an extremely tense moment; everyone present had his hand on his weapon. To save face, Aguirre insisted that one of his men accompany the Americans to witness the formal surrender in Arizona. Lawton consented.[44]

Each day on the trail brought unexpected stresses. Geronimo and Chief Nachez grew more nervous as they picked up rumors that some of Lawton's subordinates were discussing the possibility of killing all of the hostiles if they did not surrender to General Miles. Tensions mounted when the column reached Guadalupe Canyon, on 31 August, where the renegades had recently killed four soldiers. Lt. Abiel L. Smith, who assumed command of the column when Lawton was briefly called away, "expressed a desire to pitch in with the troop & have it out right there," averring "I haven't promised them anything." Even Leonard Wood, who had opposed such treacherous talk earlier, now reportedly joined Smith's side. Geronimo and Nachez, who observed Smith's angry outburst, quickly rode a good distance away. Only with the greatest difficulty did Gatewood dissuade the soldiers from assassinating Geronimo. Ironically, Smith later received a brevet for meritorious service with Lawton.[45]

Unknown to Geronimo, an even more outrageous act of treachery was being contemplated at a higher level. Nelson Miles was desperate to end the war with Geronimo and, of course, advance his own career. When southwesterners learned through newspaper reports that the renegades were not actual prisoners and that surrender terms would not be negotiated until a meeting with Miles, the public called even more shrilly for Geronimo's demise. Miles, who was haunted by the specter of Geronimo again taking flight as he had the previous March, dropped ominous hints to Lawton that he could use *any* means to prevent Geronimo from escaping. To Lawton's credit he resisted the temptation to employ such perfidy. "I didn't like to do it," recalled Lawton. He was "afraid it wouldn't do."[46]

Apparently, Tom Horn had a part to play in Nelson Miles's plan to assassinate Geronimo and his followers. On 28 August 1886, William Edwardy delivered a Lawton dispatch to Miles at Fort Bowie. While awaiting orders to return to Lawton, who was still in Sonora, Capt. William A. Thompson, Miles's adjutant, presented Edwardy with a sealed document for delivery to the expedition commander. This letter instructed Lawton that "under no circumstances" should he permit Geronimo to escape, "whether he agreed to surrender or not." If Geronimo should reject surrender terms, "Edwardy, Horn and 'Billy Long' . . . were to shoot him (Geronimo) and Natchez dead." Just as Edwardy was about to leave Miles's office, the department commander had second thoughts and expressed the fear that his written instructions "might fall into the wrong hands." "Miles tore the paper into little pieces," Edwardy recalled, and instructed him to commit these orders to memory "and deliver [them] verbally to Lawton." In a letter to Lawton, on 1 September 1886, Miles referred to these instructions when he ordered the captain to "tell Edwardy not to repeat any conversation he heard here except to you." Others were privy to the plot, however. "It was arranged that in case of any ugly spirit breaking out during the conference or the Indians refusing to be reasonable," Leonard Wood recalled, "each [white] man should kill the Indian next to him." Presumably, Tom Horn was expected to shoot either Geronimo or Nachez. As events transpired, there was no necessity to take such measures.[47]

While we cannot know whether Tom Horn would have participated willingly in such a perfidious act, he was always loyal to his employers, even to the point of committing criminal acts on their behalf. Unfortunately, he did not mention this conspiracy in the *Life of Tom Horn*. This is not surprising, since General Miles liked Horn and came to his aid in the future. As a "Miles man" in his later years, Tom Horn could not (and would not) violate a trust.

On 2 September, Captain Lawton and Lieutenant Gatewood led their weary column into Skeleton Canyon. When Miles finally put in an appearance the next afternoon, "Geronimo lost no time in being presented [to Miles]." In only a few words, Miles bluntly informed him that "they would be sent to Florida & there await the final action of the President of the United States." In spite of the general's insulting abruptness, Geronimo turned to Gatewood and said, "Good, you told the truth." Geronimo shook hands with Miles and, as if attaching himself to his protector, "followed our commander wherever he went," recalled Gatewood. Nachez, grieving for a brother who was missing in Mexico, put in a belated appearance and surrendered the following day."[48]

After the formal surrender, Nelson Miles condescended to personally convey Geronimo and Nachez to Fort Bowie in an army ambulance, arriving the night of 5 September. Henry Lawton, with the remainder of his force, including Tom Horn, followed with the rest of the Chiricahua warriors and women and children. It was an especially unnerving journey, since a large crowd of local residents "rode on each side, front, and rear," recalled John Hand, who was present. This civilian party, which constituted a sort of vigilante force, was hopeful that Geronimo and his men would make "a break," thus giving all present an opportunity to shoot them down. Indeed, Chief Mangus, with three warriors and three women, successfully escaped into the mountains. With bluecoats standing at attention on the parade ground, recalled Tom Horn, "Geronimo and his outfit rode in and laid down their arms" on the morning of 8 September. The ever-vigilant Tombstone photographer Camillus Fly was there with his camera. When Fly "showed Geronimo a portrait taken during the interview with Crook [the previous March]," according to the San Francisco Chronicle, "Geronimo pulled a pair of spectacles out of his pocket, examined the views critically and grunted his satisfaction." Although illiterate, the infamous Apache warrior had reading glasses for close-up work.[49]

Later in the day, Nelson Miles issued his captives fresh clothing, and then Captain Henry Lawton prepared to hustle them off to Bowie Station, where a special Southern Pacific train waited to transport them into exile. Even now, however, Geronimo had the capacity to create drama. George Dunn, a civilian employee at this time, recalled that Lieutenant Jack Neall, the long-suffering quartermaster, instructed him "to drive the four-mule buckboard" that would carry Geronimo, with two additional prisoners and Tom Horn as escort, to the railroad station. When Dunn replied that he had no experience with a "four-up," the quartermaster replied offhandedly, "'oh, you can herd them.'" Somehow, Dunn managed to wrestle the mule team into line with several other ambulances that were to form the cavalcade. However, as soon as his team "smelled the Indians," recalled Dunn, the animals panicked and "tied up in a knot." After some soldiers helped Dunn manhandle the rebellious mules back into position, Tom Horn, Geronimo, and two other Chiricahuas climbed aboard. But the old medicine man had one last game to play. As Dunn prepared to get under way, he looked back "to see if all were seated." Geronimo had disappeared![50]

George Dunn, already wrestling with a pesky mule team, was beside himself. "I asked Tom Horn where he had gone," recalled Dunn. The chief of scouts replied reassuringly, "He is playing fox." The wary medicine man had sought a safer place. When Horn finally found the fearsome warrior, who had created public hysteria for years, he was hunkered down "in the bottom of an escort wagon among the squaws." After soldiers returned Geronimo to the buckboard, General Miles's ambulance and a squad of cavalry led the procession out of the gate as the band played "Auld Lang Syne." Dunn's buckboard was second to the general's conveyance in the line. Even then, the trip to Bowie Station was not without incident. While negotiating a steep decline out of the fort, Dunn's brakes failed. "We went down on the gallop and scattered the squad of soldiers . . . in all directions," recalled Dunn, narrowly avoiding a collision with Miles's ambulance. By the time he reached the station, Dunn's "fingers were blistered from trying to hold those mules." Without any delay or fanfare, Miles placed the prisoners on the train and sent them to San Antonio, Texas, and eventually to Florida.[51]

In the *Life of Tom Horn* the author made no mention of the fact that he escorted Geronimo to Bowie Station, although he did recognize that this moment was a historic one. When the "dreaded Chiricahuas" were placed on the special train, wrote Horn, "the terror of Mexico and all the Southwest, were gone . . . and Arizona was left in a more peaceful condition than it had ever enjoyed before." In spite of his role in bringing about the defeat of the Chiricahuas, Horn did not betray an intense hatred of these tough warriors. While he had ties with the army and enjoyed the support of Nelson Miles and other officers, he also had ties with the Apache people (possibly including an Apache wife). Their exile may have caused him some problem, especially when Miles treacherously included the loyal Apache scouts in this exiled group. Horn and other civilian employees demonstrated "their contempt for the white man's inhumanity to the red man," Alonzo Kinney Griffith wrote, by withdrawing to the Fort Bowie post sutler's store for a drink.[52]

Although Horn left readers of his autobiography with the impression that he was finished with the army, such was not the case. Within days, he was on the trail of Chief Mangus, who had escaped during the trek to Fort Bowie. On 10 September, Maj. William Thompson wired General Miles that Mangus, a son of the famous chieftain, Mangas Coloradas, was attempting to slip through the army cordon along the boundary in order to retrieve loot that he had stashed in Sonora. Brevet Col. Eugene Beauharnais Beaumont, commander of the Fort Bowie Military District, who hoped to trap the fugitives in the Chiricahua Mountains, complained to Thompson in his reply on 16 September that the dilatory behavior of his subordinates had permitted the renegades to escape. "It would appear that Capt. [Otho] Budd, personally never left his camp in Bonito Canon for twenty-four hours," said Beaumont, "but sent Horn with Indians [scouts] miles away instead of giving personal attention to scouting." Then, inexplicably, Budd shifted his camp to a point near Fort Bowie and messaged Thompson: "Gave [Lieutenant Henry?] Johnson Pima scouts and sent others to [Fort] Bowie under Chief of Scouts Horn. [We] found no Indians in Chiricahuas . . . [but] cooperated with [Captain Theodore A.] Baldwin." "It is difficult to conceive what these officers were endeavoring to do," Beaumont moaned. If Tom Horn was aware of Beaumont's anguish, he made no mention of it. On 15 September, Baldwin trailed Mangus to a point near the mining camp of Galeyville. When heavy rains obliterated the trail, "I mounted four Indians and sent them with Mr. Horn to see if they could find the trail," Baldwin reported. Later, "Mr. Horn returned with information that the hostiles had been seen at Skeleton Canon," which placed them near the Mexican border. Only in October did Capt. Charles L. Cooper, Tenth Cavalry, capture Mangus and his few followers in Chihuahua. Mangus and his people were quickly shipped off to Florida.[53]

Even though Tom Horn was not in on the capture of Mangus, General Miles was pleased with his performance and contemplated a new assignment for him. In late October 1886, the department commander ordered Assistant Surgeon Leonard Wood to take a few men and retrace Captain Henry Lawton's route through Sonora. While Wood's instructions were to round up livestock that had strayed from Lawton's column, his secret assignment was to gather geographic data for military maps. On 23 October, Miles instructed Second Lt. John A. Dapray at Fort Bowie to send "scouts and interpreters Horn, Edwardy, and Montoya to report to Dr. Wood at once." Unknown to Miles, however, Tom Horn had quit the service on the last day of September. Leonard

Wood carried out the assignment without mishap and returned to Arizona in January.[54]

Tom Horn's reason for leaving the service is not clear, although he gave the excuse that his mining property in Aravaipa Canyon needed attention. An unconfirmed report held that he quit because of a dispute with Nelson Miles over back wages. "Tom Horn swore he would not sign up [again] until he had been given his back pay and restored to his previous rank of Chief of Scouts," according to an old Apache scout at Fort Apache. "After a stormy session between the blunt, trail-begrimed scout and the spit-and-polish general," this story continues, "Talking Boy won and was paid in full to date." Upon receiving his pay, Tom Horn refused to sign up again. In the *Life of Tom Horn,* he was very cryptic about his departure. "I took my scouts back to the reservation, [and] discharged them," he wrote, "and was then discharged myself." Of course, he did not quit over wages. Nor did the army fire him; Horn left of his own volition.[55]

If Nelson Miles was upset with Tom Horn in any way, he did not betray it. Indeed, the general liked Horn and characterized him as "an industrious, intelligent scout and guide." Miles kept in touch with Horn after the Apache campaign and later commented on Horn's "very excellent reputation among all the officers and men who knew him." Horn "was trusted with important duties, and responsibilities where integrity and truthfulness were important and in fact indispensable." In the highly partisan officer corps, riven by factions, Horn became a "Miles man" and relied upon this ambitious general for future references. Donald F. McCarthy, who knew Horn at San Carlos and followed his career, was aware of Miles's support. While Horn was merely "a packer, and a would-be Chief of Scouts" during the Crook years, McCarthy observed (incorrectly), "with the coming of Miles . . ., his star rose high." In spite of Tom Horn's braggadocio, Second Lt. Robert A. Brown, Horn's immediate superior in the Geronimo campaign, praised him as "a capable Chief of Scouts" who "rendered the Government faithful service." Even Packmaster Henry Daly, who may have envied Horn's successes, admitted that he served "ably" as chief of scouts.[56]

Thomas H. Horn, Sr. (1825–91), a strict disciplinarian in the home, eventually became alienated from his son, Thomas, Jr. (*Life of Tom Horn, Government Scout and Interpreter* [1904], p. 41).

Mary Ann Horn (1831–1908), a typical frontier mother, raised a large brood of children. It was her misfortune to live long enough to be aware of Tom Jr.'s unfortunate fate. Courtesy Arizona Historical Society, Tucson (#7694).

Albert (Al) Sieber, noted civilian scout in Arizona's Apache campaigns, trained Tom
Horn to follow in his footsteps. Unfortunately, this training included a significant
degree of callousness and cruelty which Horn carried throughout his subsequent
career. Courtesy Western History Collections, University of Oklahoma (#663).

Tom Horn spent much of his time in Arizona Territory as a civilian packer for the U.S. Army. This photograph is believed to be that of James "Long Jim" Cook (standing right), Horn's boss in the packtrain. Courtesy Arizona Historical Society, Tucson (#19850).

For several years in the 1880s, Tom Horn resided at or near San Carlos, the headquarters of the White Mountain Apache Reservation. Courtesy Special Collections Department, University of Arizona, Tucson (N-12, 489).

Camp at San Carlos
west half looking south

Tom Horn appeared twice in Camillus S. Fly's photographs of Gen. George Crook's negotiations with Geronimo and the Chiricahua renegades in March 1886. Among those identified: front row, fifth from left, Tom Horn in white shirt; sixth, First Lt. Marion Maus; seventh, Capt. Cyrus Roberts; eighth, Charles D. Roberts (son of Captain Roberts); ninth, George Crook (seated); tenth, interpreter Antonio Besias; eleventh, interpreter Jesús María Yestes; twelfth, interpreter Antonio Díaz; thirteenth, interpreter Concepción Aguirre. Second row, seventh from left, Charles M. Strauss, mayor of Tucson; tenth, Second Lt. William Shipp; eleventh, Second Lt. Samson Faison; twelfth, Capt. John G. Bourke; thirteenth, interpreter Ramón Montoya; fourteenth, Al Sieber; eighteenth, Packmaster Henry Daly; twenty-second, packer Tommy Blair. Courtesy Arizona Historical Society, Tucson (#78158).

In Fly's second image, Tom Horn, still in a white shirt, is leaning on a rock with his Apache scouts around him. Lt. Marion Maus is seated at Horn's right foot. Alchesay (scout) is seated at Maus's left. Lt. Samson Faison is fourth to the left of Horn. Horn, whose weight fluctuated greatly during periods of intense scouting activities, is very trim and clean-shaven. Courtesy Arizona Historical Society, Tucson (#78155).

Capt. Emmet Crawford, who selected Tom Horn as one of his chiefs of scouts for the winter 1885–86 campaign against Apache renegades in Mexico. Horn was only a few feet away from Crawford when Chihuahuan militia inflicted a mortal wound on the captain and shot Horn in the arm. Courtesy Arizona Historical Society, Tucson (#1181).

First Lt. Marion Maus, who assumed command after Crawford was incapacitated, later complimented Tom Horn for his services on Crawford's ill-fated expedition. Courtesy Arizona Historical Society, Tucson (#16010).

CHAPTER 5

"A Restive Soul"

Since arriving in Arizona Territory in 1881, Tom Horn had spent much of his time in the employ of the federal government, as an employee of the army or the White Mountain Apache Reservation at San Carlos. Until he left his position as superintendent of trains (chief of scouts) at Fort Bowie, on 30 September 1886, Horn had been in the field for seventeen months in active pursuit of renegade Apaches. With the deportation of the Chiricahuas, however, Horn left his civilian job with the military and returned to Aravaipa Canyon, which he thought of as home. Not only did he have mining property in the area, but several close friends in the canyon were always ready to offer him hospitality, and employment, among them Burt and Horace Dunlap, Dan Ming, and Elias A. Jones. In fact, he went directly into the employ of the Ming-Jones outfit in October 1886 and remained with them until early 1888, at which time he became foreman for the neighboring Dunlap spread, where he spent most of 1888 and part of the year 1889. Since work as a cowhand was often seasonal, Horn also worked roundups on other ranches, including the Chiricahua Cattle Company in the Sulphur Springs Valley. Indeed, Horn's "standing as a cow hand," recalled Horace Dunlap, was such that "he had a choice of employment" on any spread.[1]

The pursuit of "color" had been one of Tom Horn's primary goals when he arrived in Arizona Territory, and he undertook various mining ventures, both alone and with partners. Most of his prospecting took place in the Deer Creek Mining District, which lay along the southern margin of the San Carlos Reservation, in the Santa Teresa Mountains, and further south, in the Aravaipa Mining District. Initially, prospectors were enthusiastic about the Deer Creek District. In July 1888, the *Tucson Weekly Star* reported that the "veins of mineral ore" in this district were very promising. In one mining venture, Tom Horn partnered with John P. Harr, a Willcox barber; Wid Childress, a cowhand; and Burt and Horace Dunlap in developing a mine near present-day Winkelman. When Horn needed ready cash for this venture, he worked as a mucker in the Aravaipa Mine or the Grand Reef Mine. The result was a valuable digging that the investors named the Ore Hanna Mine.[2]

In the midst of these endeavors, Horn received a visit from friends who resided in Pleasant Valley, in the northeastern corner of the Tonto Basin. These friends believed that his scouting and Indian fighting experiences would be of use in suppressing an outbreak of violence in their region—the Tewksbury-Graham Feud or Pleasant Valley War. This conflict began as a vendetta. On one side stood the family of James D. Tewksbury, Sr., and his followers; on the other, Thomas H. Graham and his followers. This was not a typical range war such as the struggle between big ranching companies and small homesteaders in Wyoming in which Tom Horn would later become involved. The feuding factions in Pleasant Valley were modest settlers running small herds. As in many feuds, the starting point of the conflict was soon forgotten in the ongoing bloodshed.

While there had been minor shooting incidents between members of the two families in the early 1880s, the Tewksburys prompted an outcry in 1885 when they introduced a large flock of sheep onto traditional cattle ranges in Tonto Basin. (The owners of these sheep, Peru P., William A., and John F. Daggs, who resided in Flagstaff, had been near neighbors of the Horn family in Scotland County, Missouri, and one can only wonder if the Daggs brothers had something to do with Tom Horn's invitation to Pleasant Valley.) The Grahams were not blameless in the Pleasant Valley War, being accused of participating in a far-flung rustling enterprise that extended from the Navajo lands in the north to Mexico in the south. These grievances erupted into open warfare in 1887, forcing the residents of Pleasant Valley and vicinity to choose sides. The killing began in February when one of the Daggses' shepherds was mysteriously shot. In July, Martin "Old Mart" Blevins, a

Graham partisan, disappeared without a trace. In the course of the next six months at least twenty people died violent deaths. "Although the feud is often described as a conflict between cattlemen and sheepmen," historian Gary L. Roberts rightly concludes, "prejudice and irrational hatred . . . kept the war alive."[3]

In the *Life of Tom Horn,* the author's cryptic remarks about his participation in the Pleasant Valley War left only questions and no answers:

> Early in April of 1887, some of the boys came down from the Pleasant Valley, where there was a big rustler war going on and the rustlers were getting the best of the game. I was tired of the mine and willing to go. . . . Things were in a pretty bad condition. It was war to the knife between cowboys and rustlers, and there was a battle every time the two outfits ran together. A great many men were killed in the war. . . . I was the mediator, and was deputy sheriff.

While the identity of this Pleasant Valley delegation is not known, Horace Dunlap declared that John Rhodes "sent for Horn." Rhodes, who had worked with Horn at San Carlos, was now foreman for John C. Shields's PK Ranch in Pleasant Valley. He would soon marry the widow of John Tewksbury, who was a victim of the feud. Edwin (Ed) Tewksbury, who became acquainted with Tom Horn during the 1882 Apache campaign, could well have been a member of the delegation.[4]

There is some question about the date—April 1887—that Tom Horn said he traveled to the Tonto Basin. Some writers, including Dan L. Thrapp, believe him. Thrapp has speculated that Horn may have been responsible for the disappearance of Martin Blevins, who vanished in July of that year. Thrapp based this theory upon Horn's remark to a Wyoming deputy U.S. marshal in 1902 that he killed his first man at the age of twenty-six and that his victim was "a coarse old sonofabitch." However, the testimony of Elias Jones, Horace Dunlap, and other Aravaipa cattlemen indicates that Horn was working there throughout 1887. Burt Dunlap recalled that Horn "was absent for a few months" on business in the Tonto Basin in 1888, and William Clay Colcord, a Pleasant Valley rancher who also knew Horn, declared that he arrived there that year.[5]

That Tom Horn went to Pleasant Valley as a "mediator" is also highly questionable, although some of his friends believed him. Al Sieber, who was aware of Horn's residence in Pleasant Valley, declared that he refused to align with either of the feuding factions "although every inducement was offered him." Horace Dunlap asserted that Horn kept "clear of any connection with either faction" and that his purpose was to assist John Rhodes in maintaining "an armed neutrality and protect his employer's interests," as well those of Mrs. Al Rose, whose husband had also been killed. The truth was that Tom Horn, as a close friend of John Rhodes and Ed Tewksbury, could not avoid taking sides. Walter Tewksbury, a grandson of James Tewksbury, Sr., insisted that Horn "positively took an active part in the war." However, by the time Horn arrived, most of the Graham faction had been killed or expelled, and enough of the Tewksbury faction remained alive to dominate Pleasant Valley. Bill Colcord's assertion that Horn's purpose was to assist in the "clean up [of] the Valley after Graham & Tewksbury had quit" fighting makes sense.[6]

Just what official credentials, if any, Tom Horn carried to Pleasant Valley is also uncertain. He boasted that he represented three sheriffs simultaneously—William "Buckey" O'Neill of Yavapai County, Commodore Owens of Apache County, and Glenn Reynolds of Gila County—which was impossible. Owens was in office in 1887 and 1888, O'Neill in 1889 and 1890, and Reynolds in 1889. Crossdeputization among frontier lawmen was common, however, and it is possible, as Horace Dunlap later asserted, that Horn carried two deputy sheriffs' badges, representing Sheriff George E. Shute of Gila County (1887–88) and Sheriff William J. Mulvenon of Yavapai County (1887–88). These two districts had primary responsibility for law enforcement in the Tonto Basin. Horn may also have carried another appointment that he did not care to mention, that of range detective. In researching the Tewksbury-Graham Feud, Earle R. Forrest encountered old-timers who insisted that Horn "was employed as a detective or spy by someone." Some years later, Tom Horn's brother, Charles, informed the *Denver Times* that Tom was "employed as a detective by prominent cattle and sheep men in Arizona." Tom Horn later admitted to a Denver newspaper that he had killed men in various venues in Arizona: as an army scout, as a detective, and as a "regulator" in a campaign against cattle thieves. However, he insisted that these killings were "always in the interest of somebody else," presumably meaning prominent cattle-and sheepmen (or an association) in the Tonto Basin.[7]

Conditions in the Tonto Basin were certainly ripe for a range detective in the late 1880s. The rustling problem extended beyond the basin, as wielders of "the sticky rope" plied their trade throughout eastern Arizona. To the east, in Apache County, ranchers formed the Apache County Stock Growers' Association, with a view to launching a concerted effort against these desperadoes. Will C. Barnes, a former soldier and an acquaintance of Tom Horn, served as secretary of this organization. In November 1886, association members were instrumental in getting their "law and order" candidate, Commodore Perry Owens, elected sheriff of Apache County. This same organization also employed an especially aggressive detective, Jonas V. Brighton. In 1887, Brighton killed two rustlers, one of whom was Isaac (Ike) Clanton, of the notorious Cochise County band of outlaws. While there is no indication that Horn and Brighton were acquainted or worked in concert, their areas of responsibility were so close together that local residents sometimes confused the two. The two men were much alike—noisy and boastful—according to one writer, and "some gossips said that Brighton was actually the loud-mouthed Tom Horn," though the writer points out that a self-promoter like Horn would not have wanted to be confused with anyone else.[8]

Upon arriving in Pleasant Valley in 1888, Tom Horn conducted himself much as a range detective might be expected to operate. He adopted the guise of a cowboy and horsebreaker, a strategy he would later employ in Colorado and Wyoming. Indeed, Al Sieber, who may not have been aware of Horn's real mission, understood that he "went to work in Pleasant Valley as a ranch hand." Bill Colcord, a common cowhand at this time, worked roundups with Horn and Ed Tewksbury. One especially difficult job that Horn undertook was a horsebreaking stint for Silas W. Young, who had taken over the ranch of feud leader Tom Graham when he left the basin. These were wild Oregon horses, according to Bill Young, son of Silas. Horn "put on quite a show as he 'took the rough' out of them," recalled Bill. The stalwart Horn, who was able to break "the big rank Oregon broncs with ease," added Young, broke a "big, beautiful bay" especially for the youngster.[9]

By the time Tom Horn arrived in the Tonto Basin, livestock men had formed a vigilante organization, the Committee of Fifty. Jesse W.

(Bud) Ellison, owner of the Q Ranch near Payson, and his foreman, Glenn Reynolds, were reportedly the leaders. Many years later, Ellison justified his action by observing that "where you have these wars, always there's got to be a cleaning-up process [afterwards]"—Tom Horn's alleged purpose in the basin. If suspected thieves failed to leave on the vigilantes' first warning, according to a St. Johns newspaper, "then comes the Regulators' hideous carnival—the dangle of death." While the vigilantes claimed that they belonged to neither of the feuding factions, several members of the Tewksbury faction, including John Rhodes and Ed Tewksbury, were members of the Committee of Fifty. Tom Horn was soon a member, not only because his friends belonged, but because he had grown close to Glenn Reynolds, a vigilante leader. Some Tonto Basin residents, who feared Reynolds as a dangerous type, soon grew to fear Tom Horn as well. John Henry "Rim Rock" Thompson, a Pleasant Valley rancher and fellow deputy sheriff with Horn at this time, recalled that many people considered Horn and Reynolds "killers." On 11 August 1888, vigilantes hanged three suspected rustlers—James Stott, James Scott, and Jeff Wilson—just inside the Apache County border. According to Joseph Fish, a local historian, Reynolds and Horn were unquestionably among these regulators.[10]

The survivors of this grisly vendetta were very wary of outsiders, as Leonard Wood found out. When Wood and a detachment of Fort Apache scouts entered the Tonto Basin to locate heliograph stations in August 1888, "a bunch of mounted men . . . came into camp and were rather on the fight," he noted in his diary. Wood began to talk with the leader, who turned out to be John Rhodes, "a great friend of Tom Horn." Once Rhodes learned of Wood's connection to Horn, he graciously permitted Wood to continue on his way.[11]

In spite of his law enforcement (and extralegal) duties in Tonto Basin, Tom Horn found time for recreational activities. In November 1888, he entered the steer-tying event at a cowboy tournament, as rodeos were then called, in Payson. While many other capable cowhands competed, "Charlie Meadows, of Payson, and Mr. Horne [sic], of Pleasant Valley" stood out for their dexterity with the rope, according to the *Prescott Hoof and Horn*. Much to Horn's dismay, Meadows, better known as "Arizona Charlie," took the first prize of fifty dollars; Horn had to settle for the second-place prize of $25. The following year, Horn won the steer-tying event in Globe's Fourth of July celebration with the remarkable time of only fifty-eight seconds. "The almost electric flash of Tom Horne [sic]," said the Silver Belt, left all other competitors in the shade. When asked what attributes made a good steer tyer, Horn replied that in addition to chance, dexterity with a rope, and a good horse, "coolness, [and] a steady hand" were necessary. While Horn lost out in the footrace, his friends urged him to consider entering the steer-tying contest at the territorial fair in Phoenix.[12]

In the meantime, important changes were taking place in the Tonto Basin, where Deputy Sheriff Horn continued to reside. In November 1888, Glenn Reynolds was elected sheriff of Gila County. When Reynolds took office in January 1889, he persuaded Horn to stay on as his deputy in the far northern precincts. In February, the Arizona Territorial Assembly annexed to Glenn Reynolds's jurisdiction that portion of Yavapai County in Tonto Basin that was affected by the recent vendetta, thereby increasing the responsibilities of Reynolds's deputies in this region, Tom Horn and "Rim Rock" Henry Thompson.[13]

In October 1889, Tom Horn entered the steer-tying event at the annual territorial fair in Phoenix. Rivalry was keen "among the cowboys all over the Territory," recalled Horn, and "Charley Meadows . . . was making a big talk that he could beat me." Apparently, the "boys" in the sheriff's office in Globe, who were anxious to wager on Horn, persuaded Sheriff Reynolds to give him time off to attend. When the two cowboys squared off against each other before "a huge crowd" on 17 October , Tom Horn won handily, with the remarkable time of one minute, nineteen seconds; Arizona Charlie followed with a distant two minutes, six seconds. The following day Horn and Thomas Rice, another well-known cowhand, put on an exhibition of bronco riding that was "appreciated by the large crowd," said one observer. The following March, in a show of cockiness while visiting Tucson, the new territorial steer-tying champion issued a public challenge to all comers. Horn offered to put up $500, according to the Daily Star, "that he could throw and tie any steer in less time than any cowboy in Arizona, New Mexico, or Texas." Horn's supporters among the sporting crowd put up an additional $1,000, but there were no takers.[14]

News of the performances of Tom Horn and Charlie Meadows at Phoenix soon reached William F. Cody, better known as Buffalo Bill. Cody, who was organizing a new Wild West show for a European tour, asked both men to accompany him. While Horn "flatly dismissed the idea," according to one writer, his name soon circulated nationwide as a winner in cowboy tournaments. Even Arizona Charlie, who eventually joined Cody's show, publicized Horn's name. While visiting the office of the *New York National Police Gazette* in December 1892, Meadows boasted that among the cowboys he had "met and defeated" was Tom Horn. In January 1895, the *Philadelphia Times* praised Tom Horn's remarkable defeat of Charlie Meadows and several other "well-known vaqueros of the Mexican-American border."[15]

While Tom Horn competed in Phoenix, Sheriff Reynolds was preparing for the fall term of District Court in Globe. Among the defendants were five former Apache scouts. These scouts, led by Haskay-bay-nay-ntayl, better known as Apache Kid, had murdered another Apache, named Rip, in May 1887. The Kid and his followers then shot former scout Al Sieber, giving him a painful foot wound. As they fled the reservation, the Apaches crossed Aravaipa Canyon and stole Tom Horn's best horse. After the murderers eventually surrendered, a lengthy jurisdictional squabble took place between the federal and territorial courts. When the U.S. Supreme Court overturned their first conviction and returned them to Gila County, Sheriff Reynolds had them rearrested. While Tom Horn was in Phoenix, in October 1889, the Apache Kid and three associates were convicted of the assault on Al Sieber and sentenced to seven years in the territorial prison in Yuma. In recalling these events, Tom Horn claimed that Reynolds originally intended for him to serve as Apache interpreter at these court proceedings, but instead permitted him to attend the Territorial Fair. On 1 November 1889, Reynolds, with Deputy William D. "Hunkydory" Holmes, set off with the prisoners for the railroad at Casa Grande, ninety miles away. En route the following day, the Apache Kid and his fellow prisoners, speaking in their native tongue, which the lawmen could not understand, concocted an escape plot that resulted in the deaths of Reynolds and Holmes.[16]

Tom Horn expressed great regret at not being present with Reynolds and Holmes. He believed that his knowledge of the Apache language would have enabled him to prevent this tragedy. "I won the prize roping at the fair," he continued, "but it was at a very heavy cost." However, there was something amiss in Horn's assertion. The steer-tying event took place on Thursday, 17 October 1889; the lawmen were killed on 2 November, two weeks after the contest. Horn could have easily traveled to Globe in time to accompany Reynolds, had the sheriff requested his assistance. With the death of Glenn Reynolds, Undersheriff Jerry Ryan assumed the helm, and Tom Horn's deputyship came to end. "In the winter [1889–90] I again went home" to Aravaipa Canyon, he recalled.[17]

Although his duties as a deputy sheriff (and possibly as a cattle detective) in Pleasant Valley occupied only parts of two years, these experiences were important in setting the stage for his subsequent career as a Pinkerton operative and a range detective in Wyoming. These activities also marked the beginning of a change in the former scout's conduct— from warring against hostile Apaches on behalf of the U.S. Government to hunting down white livestock thieves on behalf of the big cattle companies. In other words, he was now hunting his own kind.

By 1889 Tom Horn had resided eight years in Arizona Territory and was generally well liked. Horace Dunlap said he was "invariably good-natured and obliging, not given to profanity or vulgarity, loyal to his employer and friends." Dunlap added that Horn was "honorable" and "a general favorite." One of Horn's acquaintances said, according to Dunlap, that "he had never heard of anyone's having so many friends in this state." Ben Clark, who worked with Horn at San Carlos, said that he "seldom engaged in boisterous conduct and had the good will and respect of all who knew him." He was, according to Clark, "a whole-souled, honest fellow." He "could do more work than two ordinary men" around a mine, a Solomonville journalist remarked, "and never betrayed a buyer in order to dispose of his claim." If Tom Horn had an eccentricity in this roughhewn environment, it was his desire to present a clean-cut appearance. In the days when cowpunchers "smelled of horse, whisky and sweat," recalled Thomas N. Wills, "Tom scrubbed religiously." As another old-timer complained, according to Wills, "'Thar he is a scrapin' of his nails but I dunno what fer. Why he takes a bath even when he aint a goin' floozeyin'." While he was not a dandy, added Wills, Horn preferred the clean-shaven look and was always recognizable by his large ears and his preference for tucking his pants legs inside his boots.[18]

Although not considered a gunfighter or badman, Tom Horn was regarded as a man not to be toyed with. Horn was "a wonderful shot," recalled Frank Murphy, a fellow cowhand. He would climb upon "the ridge pole of a corral and drop on the back of a bronco," continued

Murphy, and then reach down from the animal's back, pick up a can, throw it in the air, and shoot holes in it while at full tilt. Because of this proficiency, friends cautioned Horn to beware. An enemy would shoot him in the back rather than face him in "a fair fight." In 1888 Wid Childress, one of Tom Horn's mining partners, had some sort of grievance against him and threatened his life. Childress rode all the way to Silas Young's ranch in the Tonto Basin, where Horn was breaking horses, to confront him. Bill Young, who recalled this incident, feared the ex-scout would kill Childress in a fight. Fortunately, Young was able to dissuade Childress from his mission and convinced him that "Horn was cunning as an Apache yet very brave and mean." Bill Young always believed "he had saved his [Wid's] life."[19]

In spite of his size and strength, Tom Horn was surprisingly inept in saloon brawls and street fights. Donald F. McCarthy, who knew Horn at San Carlos, concluded that "there was no fight in Tom Horn, in the sense of mortal combat." Horn invariably came out second best in such encounters. In a squabble, a Globe baker hit Horn over the head with a heavy object and gave him an ugly scalp wound; Horn did not manage to land any blows. After taking a sound beating from a prospector on a Solomonville street, the veteran packer struggled to his feet, acknowledged that he had been beaten "fair and square," and walked away with no apparent desire for revenge.[20]

Even though he generally held females in low regard, Horn could be swayed by an attractive young woman. When Horn learned that a café waitress he was fond of in Solomonville was seeing someone else, he became so angry that he threw hot coffee in her face! Yet Ryder Ridgway, who talked with old Graham County residents about Horn, reported that he "shunned the ladies as he did the smallpox."[21]

Horn could always be counted on to assist law enforcement officers. In part, his cooperative attitude stemmed from the loss of his startup herd to rustlers a few years earlier. Indeed, Burt Dunlap described Horn as "more down on thieves, and thievery than any man I have ever known." "I have a natural hatred for men that steal and follow a crooked life," Horn once remarked. In January 1890, a new opportunity in law enforcement came Tom Horn's way. Cyrus Wells "Doc" Shores, the sheriff of Gunnison County, Colorado, and a part-time Pinkerton detective, traced two horse thieves, Joe and Will Kirkpatrick, to Aravaipa Canyon. Shores contacted rancher Burt Dunlap, who was also the local postmaster, and asked for assistance. Dunlap asked Tom Horn, "Well, Tom, what shall I tell the sheriff?" Without hesitating, he replied, "Why, tell him his [wanted] men are here and we'll help him get them." Wearing a temporary deputy's badge, Horn met Shores at Willcox in mid-January. Shores was very impressed with Horn, whom he described as "a tall, dark-complected man with a black mustache." (Apparently Horn's skin had darkened since 1886, probably owing to continued exposure to the sun.) "He was around thirty years of age," continued Shores, "and presented an imposing figure of a man—deep chested, lean loined, and arrow straight." Only one negative trait marred this favorable impression, recalled Shores: Horn's "black, shifty eyes." Since Horn knew the two Colorado fugitives personally, their arrests were almost anticlimactic in Doc Shores's eyes. Upon their arrival in Aravaipa Canyon, Tom Horn took Shores to "an old shack that Horn used as a [mining] headquarters." From there, Horn led Shores to a nearby cook shack (apparently on the Dunlap spread), where one of the fugitives, going by the alias James Wylie, took his meals. Leaving Shores outside, Horn strolled into the building, grabbed Wylie's gun and holster from a chair, and ordered him to step outside. "Horn was not the type of man one liked to argue with," recalled Shores. When Horn placed the other fugitive, who was using the alias Jack Smith, under arrest at a neighboring ranch, he exclaimed, "God damn you, Tom, I thought you were a friend of mine." Not Tom Horn, who despised thieves! Shores and Horn brought the fugitives into Willcox on Sunday, 19 January 1890. While Shores paid Horn fifty dollars for his trouble, a Gunnison, Colorado, news dispatch credited Sheriff Shores alone for "a piece of good work."[22]

Doc Shores was so impressed with this former scout's fearless behavior that he suggested that Horn go into law enforcement. "You sure have done a good job for me, and with your background as an Indian scout and understanding of the Mexican lingo, I believe I could get you a job with the Pinkerton National Detective Agency." Horn was receptive, and Shores informed James McParland, Superintendent of the Pinkerton National Detective Agency's branch office in Denver, "that Tom Horn would make them a good man to work out of their Western Office, as he spoke good Mexican and was a good smart officer." When McParland passed this recommendation on to the agency's headquarters in Chicago, William Pinkerton obtained numerous references from Horn's Arizona friends and from army officers, including a letter from Gen. Nelson Miles. All in all, Pinkerton characterized the quality of Horn's application package as "impeccable". In recalling McParland's letter requesting that he "go to work for them," Horn had little to say except that he thought "it would be a good thing to do."[23]

Tom Horn's friends were disappointed to see him leave. "I regretted to lose his services," recalled Burt Dunlap, whose ranch was Horn's to look after when Dunlap was away. "When Horn was there I felt that every thing was just as safe as though I was present." Dan Ming and Elias Jones were also saddened at Horn's departure. Horn had resided under the same roof with Jones for a full year. In reflecting upon Horn's decision to join the Pinkertons, Thaddeus (Bud) Ming, Dan Ming's son, concluded that this decision led ultimately to Horn's regrettable end. But, as Bud Ming observed, Tom Horn was "a restive soul." By a stroke of luck, Horn and his partners in the Ore Hanna Mine and several other properties in Aravaipa Canyon were in the process of selling out to eastern investors. Concluded in late January, the sale netted the partners some $40,000. Among the new owners was John Heard, Jr., a Boston mining engineer and popular author who met Tom Horn during the negotiations and would later write about him. W. J. Parks, who had mining claims in the same area, concluded that Horn had extracted "several thousand dollars worth of high grade silver ore" from his claims before selling "for a good price." After selling his mining interests and leaving his power of attorney with a Solomonville lawyer, Horn rode down to Willcox to catch a Southern Pacific train to Denver.

"Mr. Tom Horn, one of the best and most expert all-around cow hands in the country, has, after a residence of fourteen years [sic; actually it was nine] in Arizona, tired of cowboy life," D. A. Hunsaker of the Willcox Southwestern Stockman reported. Horn "came up from Aravaipa Thursday [19 April 1890] and is going to Denver, Colorado, where he expects to reside in the future."[24]

As Tom Horn boarded the Southern Pacific train for Denver, he had high hopes for a more prosperous future. He had gained a reputation as a scout, tracker, and lawman and made some money from mining but hoped to do better. The Pinkerton National Detective Agency, founded in Chicago in 1850 by Allan Pinkerton, was a well-established firm with a national reputation. They served private individuals and pursued bank and train robbers, but the Pinkertons were most notable for their ties to the rising corporate interests in Gilded Age America. Unfortunately, the agency's close relationship with the great corporations placed it in opposition to smaller fry, such as labor unions. In the rapidly growing West, the Pinkerton Agency, which had established a branch office in Denver in the 1880s, pursued this same policy. Not only did the Pinkertons earn a reputation as a defender of the mining companies against labor organizers, but the agency took the side of the big livestock companies in a bitter struggle with homesteaders and small ranchers for control of the region's vast grazing lands.[25]

Upon arriving in Denver, Tom Horn made his way to the Pinkerton branch office at 220 Opera House Block (the Tabor House block). Company policy dictated that "each operative served a trial period," reports historian Frank Morn, "while his character and work habits were scrupulously checked." The novice had to become familiar with the company handbook, *General Principles of Pinkerton's National Police Agency,* and such things as keeping an expense account and writing reports (sometimes in cipher). "Some of the rules were stern," according to historian Howard R. Lamar, and the agency maintained that "the end justified the means if the ends were 'for the accomplishment of justice.'" Since the agency intended Horn to become its second "cowboy detective"—the first was Charles Angelo Siringo—he had to learn the investigative procedure known as "making the rounds," which required the operative to move from saloon to saloon and drink and gamble "at all hours of the night and day." Operative Charlie Siringo reportedly had a wonderful capacity "to drink and hold a great deal of whiskey," according to Raymond W. Thorp, a Wyoming Stock Growers Association official who knew him well. "A man posing as an outlaw who couldn't drink plenty of whiskey would have been dead before he got started," observed Thorp. The one cardinal rule that all operatives had to abide by, according to Superintendent McParland, was that they must "never consent to talk" about their work.[26]

Since leaving Kansas in 1879, Tom Horn had maintained only tenuous contact with family members. However, his arrival in the Mile High City brought him closer to some of them. After experiencing severe financial problems in Missouri, Thomas Horn, Sr., and his wife, Mary, disposed of their property and left Scotland County in 1888. With daughter Bertha "Alice" Horn, they settled in British Columbia. Austin H. ("Oss"), a younger brother of Tom, Jr., joined them there. Hannah May Horn, five years younger than Tom, married William Allen Williams in 1885, and settled in northern Washington near the Canadian border. Charles Horn, who was probably the closest of all family members to Tom, Jr., gave up farming in Kansas and settled in Boulder, Colorado. Another sister, Mary Ambrosian Horn, or "Maude," who was nine years younger than Tom, was single and working as a dressmaker in Denver. Upon his arrival there, Tom moved in with Maude, who agreed to be his housekeeper. When Tom was away on assignment, he authorized Maude to hold onto his wages. Maude eventually joined the Horn family in British Columbia, where she married Matthew Simpson in 1897.[27]

After a period of training, Tom Horn became a full-time operative in August 1890. His first assignment was as an undercover agent for the railroad. All operatives were instructed to be on the lookout for railroad employees who were stealing from their employer. In November Superintendent McParland assigned the novice detective to his first real case. On 12 November 1890, the Southern Pacific Railroad's Overland Pacific passenger train plunged through a trestle over Lake Labish, just north of Salem, Oregon, killing five people and injuring many more. Railroad officials, who suspected foul play, asked the Pinkerton Agency to investigate. The railroad suspected that an itinerant worker, James McCabe, and a second unnamed man had sabotaged the train in order to rob it. On 3 December, Tom Horn departed by train for Salem, Oregon. Using the undercover name Thomas H. Hale, he worked on a railroad construction gang where he hoped to get a lead on the whereabouts of McCabe and his partner. It was dangerous work, as they were "all ex-convicts," Horn explained in a subsequent report. Not only did he sleep and eat with them, but he toiled "right along with men in order to gain their confidence." From Salem, Horn/Hale trailed Jim McCabe and his partner to Truckee, California, and finally to Reno, Nevada. Horn "made the rounds" of "all the saloons and gambling places," he reported, and "played at a number of places and lost money." To facilitate his movement among Reno's underworld, he hired Max C. Sweeney, a local gambler, to accompany him. After staking Sweeney at several gambling establishments, Horn became dissatisfied with him because "he always lost." When the detective finally realized he was frittering away his expense money on a deadbeat and getting no closer to his quarry, he became "tired of it." He dismissed Sweeney.[28]

While pursuing leads in Reno, Horn was suddenly stopped dead in his tracks. In a bizarre turn of events that forever clouded Horn's reputation, Reno authorities arrested him for armed robbery. On the night of 9 April 1891, a masked man entered the Palace Hotel, climbed the stairs to its second-floor casino, pointed a revolver at faro dealer James Conroy, and took $800 in cash. The bandit wore "a black silk handkerchief with eye holes over his face," according to Conroy, and was "the coolest man in the room." Within only a few minutes, Reno policemen arrested a suspect who had just boarded a westbound train. He had $270 in cash on his person. Although the suspect, Thomas Hale, protested that he was a Pinkerton detective, the *Nevada State Journal* insisted that "there is reason to believe that he is the robber":

He is known to have been bucking at the tiger [gambling] in the afternoon previous to the robbery. In one place he represented himself as being a cowboy and in another place said he was a gambler. The mask, which was made of black sateen, from the back of a vest, was found yesterday by the officers, and a pistol found in Hale's valise—a 38 calibre, 5-inch barrel, Smith & Wesson, nickel-plated—was identified as that which the robber had in his hand, when he took the money.

Although a grand jury indicted Horn for the casino robbery, the Pinkerton Agency arranged for his bond, and he was permitted to return to Denver. Horn's trial was set for Monday, 13 July. Pinkerton officials were not unduly alarmed, since the agency's enemies often harassed the company by means of legal actions.[29]

No sooner had Horn returned to Denver than McParland sent him on a new assignment to New Mexico Territory. Atlantic and Pacific Railroad officials suspected that some of its employees were in league with thieves at Coolidge Station, a whistle-stop 130 miles west of Albuquerque, and asked the Pinkerton Agency to investigate. Tom Horn was familiar with this area, having delivered mail there when it was known as Cranes Station (or Bacon Springs) ten years earlier. Horn went undercover. Attempting to play the part of a thief, he gambled and caroused with the suspects but failed to gain their confidence. As Horn's trial date in Reno was approaching, McParland sent Charlie Siringo to take his place. When Siringo arrived in Coolidge, he found his fellow operative hard up for expense money—"on the hog," in the parlance of the day. With a stake from Siringo, Horn bribed a brakeman to permit him to hitch a ride to Albuquerque. His ride turned out to be a livestock car, according to Siringo:

> the "brakey" opened the trap door on top of the car, through which the hay is put into the racks which hang on the inside of the car. Horn being a big six-footer it was a tight squeeze for the "brakey" to shove him through the small hole. When inside, the trap door was fastened by the "brakey" and poor Horn couldn't get out if he wanted to. He was a Horn among horns, as he had to lie in the hay rack above the clashing steer horns.

After Horn's departure, a "redheaded hobo" approached Siringo and said, "Say, Cully, did you see de 'brakey' shove dat tall guy in [with] de steers?" When Siringo replied affirmatively, this rover added, "Dat guy is a fly cop for de Dickensons [Pinkertons]." Had Horn not left when he did, the hobo confided to Siringo, "De gang was going to do him up [rob him] tonight and get his big gun and watch."[30]

Pinkerton officials took pride in standing by their operatives. Since Horn had no criminal record, his attorneys asked Burt and Horace Dunlap, the operative's good friends, to gather depositions affirming Horn's good character in Arizona Territory. As Horace Dunlap recalled, people "were happy to attest to Tom's good character." Burt Dunlap "rode over two thousand miles in securing these sworn testimonials," recalled his brother, and obtained them from "territorial and county officials, army officers, prominent cattlemen, [and] judges." In Chicago, William Pinkerton went to the trouble to visit Nelson Miles, whose office was also in that city, and personally obtained a deposition. In a letter to Horace Dunlap, on 24 June 1891, Horn expressed appreciation for Miles's "big send-off to Billy Pinkerton. . . . I guess Miles satisfied him that I was not that kind of a man."[31]

On Saturday evening, 11 July 1891, Tom Horn arrived in Reno with Assistant Superintendent John C. Fraser and Doc Shores. The trial got under way before District Judge A. B. Cheyney on the following Monday. District Attorney Thomas V. Julien and William Woodburn, a former U.S. Congressman, prosecuted; J. L. Wines and J. W. Dorsey defended. While the prosecution repeated substantially the same case as at the preliminary hearing, the defense had mustered four witnesses, a sizable sheaf of depositions on the defendant's behalf, and certified copies of Tom Horn's accounts from his investigation of the Lake Labish train wreck. The atmosphere in the courtroom was far from stuffy, as each juror sported "a large sunflower in his button-hole." In recalling these events, Doc Shores believed that the defense attorneys weakened Tom Horn's case when they introduced his notebook, which revealed that "he had been checking [up on] conductors on both freight and passenger trains" as he traveled. In other words, Horn had been spying on them. In spite of this setback, the jury announced on 17 July that it "stood six for conviction and six for acquittal." The presiding judge had to declare a mistrial and set a new trial date—Tuesday, 29 September 1891. Apparently, some members of the panel concluded that there were grounds for believing Horn's case was one of mistaken identity. The robber had his pants legs tucked inside his boots. Tom Horn had the same habit, which could have confused the identification.[32]

Now out on bail again, Tom Horn set out on his most famous case as a Pinkerton operative. On the evening of 31 August 1891, bandits robbed a Denver and Rio Grande Western passenger train near Cotopaxi, in Fremont County, Colorado, twenty-five miles west of Cañon City. The bandits attacked the mail and express cars and escaped with $3,600 in cash and gold bars. Sheriff Robert C. Stewart had suspects in mind immediately: Richard "Old Dick" McCoy and his sons Joseph, Charles, Thomas, and Streeter, whose ranch lay within view of the robbery site. The McCoy ranch was a gathering place for a loose aggregation of thugs and petty thieves referred to as the Wet Mountain Gang. Old Dick and his eldest son, Joseph ("Little Joe"), were already in trouble, charged with a recent murder. However, Old Dick was out on bail and awaiting trial when the Cotopaxi robbery took place. Little Joe was also at liberty, having recently escaped from the Cañon City jail. Local authorities also suspected other, more experienced criminals who were loitering around the McCoy ranch, among them Frank Elliott, alias Bert Curtis, alias Daniel Breckinridge; Robert Eldridge, alias Thomas R. Watson, alias Peg Leg; William Parry; and George Boyd.[33]

Sheriff Stewart dispatched a deputy and posse to Cotopaxi the morning after the robbery, and a host of other agencies quickly descended on the crime scene, including railroad detectives, deputy U.S. marshals and Pinkerton operatives. The D & RG had a contract with the Pinkerton

Agency. Superintendent McParland sent Tom Horn and Gunnison County Sheriff Doc Shores, who also worked occasionally for the agency. Since Shores arrived first, he examined the scene for evidence, questioned Old Dick McCoy, and headed for the Sangre de Cristo Mountains to track the fugitives, accompanied by Huerfano County Sheriff Edward Farr. Who should they meet in the mountains but Tom Horn? At the same time, Sheriff Stewart's posse was searching this same area. In the absence of one overall director of the manhunt, the various posses were stumbling all over each other. Tom Horn complained that he had been arrested "twice in two days and . . . taken in to Salida to be identified!" A few days later, Shores and Horn, who had joined forces, got on the wrong track and trailed four heavily armed suspects to Taos, New Mexico, only to find that they were legitimate cattlemen.[34]

Working alone, Horn followed a lead to Moffat, a newly constructed village on the Denver and Rio Grande Railroad forty miles south of Salida. Archie A. McDonald and his son, John Angus McDonald, were among the carpenters at work on new buildings. Many years later, John McDonald recalled that shortly after the Cotopaxi train robbery "a tall, good looking fellow" rode into town, gave his name as Tom Horn, and expressed an interest in buying cattle. A short time later, McDonald observed him with five other men in a poker game in John Gish's saloon. Since young McDonald "neither drank nor gambled," the saloon owner asked him to "look after the game, as all of them were drinking some." Suddenly, someone laid a revolver on the table, recalled McDonald, whereupon Horn "pulled his gun, and laid it on the table in front of him." Someone at the table "had attempted some shenagin [sic] with the cards," concluded McDonald, "and the gun pulling was merely to let them know that . . . no crooked work would be countenaced [sic]." While generally good sports, added McDonald, these men, including Tom Horn, would stop anyone attempting to cheat "quicker than you could bat your eye."[35]

After a week of random searching, the hunters gave up the chase. As events transpired, their withdrawal was part of a calculated plan to lull the McCoy band "into a feeling of security." The detectives now began a "still hunt" for the highwaymen, a term used in the late nineteenth century to describe a low-key search with a few detectives working undercover. Sooner or later, the robbers, who had gone to ground in the Sangre de Cristos, would become impatient and emerge from their mountain hideaway.[36]

In the meantime, Tom Horn's second trial in Reno was scheduled for Tuesday, 29 September 1891. Assistant Superintendent Fraser arrived early to mobilize forces on behalf of his subordinate, and even William Pinkerton put in an appearance. Pinkerton characterized Tom Horn as one of his "most trusted operatives," informing the press that the robbery charges resulted from a "case of mistaken identity." Selecting jurors proved difficult, which the *Nevada State Journal* attributed to "the great publicity" accorded the case of the hapless Pinkerton detective. When jury selection was finally completed on 30 September, Prosecutor Julien began his case with the testimony of Henry Bergstein, a physician who had encountered the bandit on the hotel staircase leading to the upstairs casino. The robber "was in the act of pulling a mask over his face with his right hand and had a pistol in his left," according to Bergstein. "He motioned me into the back part of the room," continued the witness, and then "walked up to the faro table and took a stack of money." When James Conroy, the faro dealer, asked, "What are you doing?" the robber replied "Ugh." The physician described the bandit as "a tall man, [with] prominent cheek bones, deep eyes, [and a] peculiar walk, as if one shoulder was higher than the other." Because the thief's mask had "a large hole" for his eyes, added Bergstein, "I could see his cheek bone; and part of his face." In spite of this witness's close proximity to the highwayman, he could not make a positive identification. Tim Pollard, who also testified at the first trial, admitted that he could not positively identify the accused man.[37]

James Conroy, who had seen the defendant several times in the Palace Hotel prior to the robbery, testified that he had just piled the day's earnings on his gaming table when Dr. Henry Bergstein appeared with "a man with a mask on and a pistol in his hand" behind him. "I asked him what he wanted, and he simply replied 'ugh,' 'ugh'; he took a pile of money, put it in his pocket, and then took the stack of $400 and did likewise, at the same time making a polite bow." After withdrawing down the stairs, continued Conroy, the bandit "turned back slightly and looked back and raised the mask so that I could see a part of his face, one side from the eye down." When Prosecutor Julien asked Conroy if he recognized the robber, the witness replied, "Mr. Horn." In the course of defense counsel's cross-examination, Conroy asserted that he recognized the defendant "by the fact that he had seen him before [the robbery], and not from any thing he recognized about the robber [during the holdup]." William Crews, who dealt faro at another casino, testified that Horn lost $48 at one sitting at his table, but won $8 on another occasion. The prosecution also entered in evidence the revolver, mask, and $272.20 taken from Tom Horn at the time of his arrest.[38]

Since Prosecutor Julien had apparently made little effort to gather additional evidence after the first trial, Horn's attorneys went on the attack. Their first efforts were to establish Tom Horn's prior good record by again presenting the depositions introduced at the first trial and to present witnesses whose testimony supported the defense's contention that Horn was a victim of mistaken identity. Two army officers, Lt. John Neall and Capt. Mason Maxon, who happened to be accessible for the trial, testified to Horn's good reputation in Arizona. J. S. Miller, a railroad night watchman, said he observed six suspicious men "down by the engine house" on the night of the casino holdup. Miller concluded that "they were scheming and plotting to do somebody up (rob them)," said the *State Journal*. Miller also overheard the tallest of the six men, "who resembled the defendant," say that "he had to get out of town." This suspect said to his comrades that "he would commit the deed whether the rest helped him or not." Miller, who followed this menacing group to an alley behind the Palace Saloon, did not see any of them enter the hotel, but saw them board a train after the robbery. When the prosecution failed to break down Miller's testimony, a local newsman was impressed with his "straightforward" statement of facts. The *San Francisco Chronicle,* which followed Horn's case with some interest, credited the appearance of this new witness with helping to swing the jury to the defendant's favor.[39]

On Thursday, 1 October, the defense presented the report that Tom Horn mailed to his home office the night of the robbery. A witness confusingly named Thomas Thomas testified that he saw Tom Horn, who was wearing a brown coat, in Chase's Saloon twenty minutes before the robbery of the Palace Casino. William Pinkerton testified that Horn came to his agency with strong recommendations and had been "an honest and efficient employee." Tom Horn then took the stand. When the defense attorney asked him to briefly relate his past work experiences, Horn probably came nearer telling the truth about his past than on any other occasion:

> I have worked on ranches and broke [*sic*] horses; have been
> a foreman on a cattle ranch; have been in the employ of the

Government as an interpreter and scout and finally chief of scouts. Have spent most of my life in Arizona and Old Mexico. I worked for the Chiracaua [sic] Cattle Company, Ming & Jones, Bert Dunlop [sic] and at the San Carlos reservation, for the Government. As a scout I was under General Crook and afterward under General Miles. I was in the Apache war and was present at the time of and assisted in the capture of Geronimo. I acted as interpreter during the surrender of Geronimo. I had charge of 100 scouts.[40]

The defendant then explained his movements on the evening of the Palace Hotel robbery: "I went around town, playing at the games and visiting the saloons. I went down to Chase's [saloon] to see if I could find the man [suspect] McCabe. [I] went up to my room and wrote my customary daily report . . . , and then went down to mail it. . . . I heard the train whistle blow and concluded I would have to get a move on me. I hurried to my room, packed my things, went to the train and boarded it."

After he was arrested, an officer suggested that he turn over the remainder of the money he had stolen and "say who my pal [accomplice] was." "I told them I had no money but my own and had not committed any crime." On cross, Prosecutor Woodburn attempted to discredit the defendant by characterizing him as a mere "railroad spotter," a low-level detective who spied on railroad employees. In his defense, Horn said that all Pinkerton operatives were instructed "to note any irregularities" that they observed on any railroad that retained the Pinkerton Agency. Not only did Woodburn fail to provide "sufficient foundation" for his allegations, according to one observer, but Horn went on to "explain clearly and fully the meaning of the cipher" in his notebook. The rest of the trial was uneventful. Assistant Superintendent Fraser and Doc Shores followed Horn to the stand to present routine information. The presiding judge delivered his instructions to the jury, which then withdrew. In "only ten minutes," according to the *San Francisco Chronicle,* the panel returned with a Not Guilty verdict. "Thus ends a remarkable case," said the *Nevada State Journal,* noting that the holdup was "one of the most daring and well executed robberies ever perpetrated on the coast."[41]

The acquittal of the Pinkerton operative did not sit well with Reno residents, who were convinced of his guilt. When Horn died on the gallows in 1903, the *Nevada State Journal* recalled that many Nevadans were convinced that he robbed the Palace Hotel, and, furthermore, that "the Pinkerton agency did everything in its power to clear him and succeeded." When William Pinkerton showed up for Horn's trial, Reno residents concluded that his purpose was to spread agency money around. A *San Francisco Chronicle* reporter disagreed. While acknowledging that Pinkerton played a key role in Horn's acquittal, this correspondent opined that he did so by locating key witnesses "who proved it was a clear case of mistaken identity." In a subsequent interview with a *Chronicle* reporter, Pinkerton declared "that he would travel 20,000 miles to get one of his men out of trouble, if he knew he was innocent." He later asserted that another notorious highway robber, Frank Shercliffe, confessed to the robbery of the Reno faro game.[42]

In later years, Charlie Siringo declared that Tom Horn told him "all about the affair" in Reno and admitted to the robbery. Horn boasted that not only did the agency continue to pay him "while on trial," but "he was paid for his time while turning the trick and while laying in jail." Siringo alleged that even William Pinkerton personally admitted to him "that Tom Horn was guilty of the crime" but that the agency "could not afford to let him go to the penitentiary while in their employ."

Tom Horn's many friends in Arizona greeted his acquittal with much satisfaction. "Tom H. Horn, the boss cattle tyer, and knight of the lariat, was recently acquitted . . . in Reno, Nevada," said A. H. Hackney in the *Arizona Silver Belt*. It was "clearly a case of mistaken identity," he continued, as "another fellow about as tall as Tom who encases the nether part of his pantaloons in the legs of his boots . . . was the guilty wretch." Likewise, a Solomonville newsman expressed the opinion that Horn's "many friends here will be glad to hear of his acquittal." Naturally, Tom Horn made no mention of this embarrassing incident in his autobiography.[43]

In a strange twist to the already unusual story, the trial became the basis for a painting that was later famous in police circles. According to Joseph E. Rogers, a police superintendent in Toronto, Canada, in the early 1900s, a cowboy-artist named Ludcke was a spectator at Horn's trial in Reno. After listening to several witnesses testify that one lone bandit held up a dozen tough gamblers (of course, this was not true), Ludcke was inspired to paint a picture of an imaginary bandit.

He completed this painting upon his return to Spokane, Washington, and entitled it *Hands Up!* This piece of frontier art was unusual in that the highwayman's pistol seemed to be pointing at the viewer no matter where the viewer stood. It happened that William Pinkerton spied this painting while on business in Spokane. He liked it and had Ludcke paint a life-size copy. Pinkerton displayed this painting in his office and had additional copies made. He gave one to Superintendent Rogers.[44]

Tom Horn returned to Denver just in time to resume work on the Cotopaxi train robbery. Old Dick McCoy, the suspected ringleader, was abruptly removed from the picture in October, when he was sentenced to eighteen years for an earlier murder. In the meantime, two suspects were spotted near Trinidad and word was relayed to Superintendent McParland, who again sought the assistance of Doc Shores. "Well, Pag [Peg Leg Watson]," said McParland in his Irish brogue, has "gone out of the mountains," meaning he had come out of hiding. While Shores agreed to resume the chase, he did so with the request that Tom Horn accompany him. McParland agreed. After a night's rest at the Brunswick Hotel, Horn and Shores arose early the next morning and prepared to catch a train for Trinidad. As they were walking down Larimer Street to a streetcar stop, Horn decided to save time by catching a moving car. "Oh, we can jump on right here," he insisted. The car, which "was going like fury," recalled Shores, threw his partner "a long ways on to the paved street, his Winchester going one way, the roll of blankets another and his six shooter another way." Horn, who fell on his head, was stunned and unable get to his feet. When Shores placed Horn's revolver back in its holster, the detective, still addled, jerked it out and would have fired it at some imaginary enemy had not Shores taken the weapon away from him. Finally on board their train, Tom Horn obtained ice for his aching head, and the two sleuths made their way to Trinidad.[45]

In Trinidad, they met Deputy Sheriff Francis Marion (Frank) Ownbey, who had relayed information about the bandits to McParland. The three men then proceeded to Walsenburg, where they were joined by Ed "Black Bill" Kelly, a part-time deputy sheriff, who was the original source of this tip. Kelly had seen the suspects and said he could lead the lawmen to their abandoned camp. While subsequent events are difficult to unravel, apparently one or all of the lawmen concluded that Kelly was misleading them and threatened to kill the hapless deputy sheriff.

In describing this incident some years later, Frank Ownbey recalled that Kelly "went back on . . . his first statements and endeavored to throw us off the trail." Doc Shores said that Ownbey and Horn were the ones who threatened to shoot Kelly. However, Ownbey, who implied that Doc Shores may have been the man who suggested that they kill Kelly, credited Horn with saving him. "Well if you are going to kill him," Horn reportedly remarked, "we will have to fix up a job and show that we had to kill him in self defense." At this point Shores interjected that Kelly "is nothing but an old horse thief any way, and . . . [killing him] would only make trouble for us." "I was disappointed in his [Horn's] willingness to shoot down Black Bill in cold blood," Shores wrote later, and "was beginning to think that perhaps I had been wrong in recommending him" to the Pinkerton Agency. The officers ultimately decided against killing Black Bill.[46]

No sooner had Shores and Horn returned to Denver than they learned that Kelly's tip was correct after all. The two suspects that Kelly had spotted were Peg Leg Watson and Bert Curtis, who had emerged from hiding and were fleeing in the direction of New Mexico. Shores and Horn, whom McParland instructed to take up the chase again, traveled by train to Rocky Ford, Colorado, and purchased horses for the overland pursuit. When one of their new animals threw Tom Horn into a thicket and scratched him up, some local cowhands had a good laugh. However, Shores was quick to inform them that his partner was a rodeo champion who could "teach you all how to ride broncos." Taking this tumble hard on the heels of his dangerous fall in Denver, Horn must have wondered if the detective gods were against him![47]

As the two detectives pursued the two fugitives through northeastern New Mexico and into the Oklahoma Panhandle, Doc Shores's doubts about Tom Horn's reliability seemed to be confirmed. There was an unsettling side to his personality. Shores had gotten a hint when Horn and Frank Ownbey had threatened to kill "Black Bill" Kelly. When Shores informed him that he had brought only "light handcuffs" to secure any prisoners that they captured, Horn replied testily, "I had better be taking my coffin." Horn insisted that since he weighed more than Shores he should ride the best horses. When they stopped at a saloon in an effort to gather information about the fugitives, "Horn tried to drink about all the whiskey they had," recalled Shores. A helpful minister who had encountered the outlaws cautioned the detectives

that Peg Leg and Curtis were "pretty hard men," to which Horn replied, "We are hard men too." All in all, "Tom was more and more
showing a side to his character that I had never seen before," wrote
Shores. "On comparatively short trips he had been cooperative, full of
stories, and a pleasant companion," he added. "On a long trail he was
moody, insisted on his own way, and wanted the best of everything."
He would ride for many miles and "never speak a word," as though
he was "brooding over something." "This experience ended my close
friendship with Tom," concluded Shores, "and I made it a point of
never working with him again."[48]

On Monday, 26 October, Shores and Horn rode into the village of
Washita, seventy-five miles south of Oklahoma City, where a boardinghouse owner informed them that two men answering the description of Peg Leg and Curtis were staying nearby with a farmer named
Polk. With the assistance of a deputy U.S. marshal named Henderson
and the boardinghouse owner, the detectives approached the Polk place
just before sunrise the following morning. Much to the lawmen's surprise, Bert Curtis was sleeping on the front porch. When Shores and
Horn pointed their rifles at the amazed fugitive, he meekly surrendered.
When Shores asked Curtis why he did not shoot, he replied, "Why
didn't you come in the day time?"[49]

At this moment, Bert Curtis, who continued to utter threats after his
arrest, was risking death. The man hunters were weary and fed up with
the threats of the desperadoes, who left warnings along their trail that
they would kill the lawmen at the first opportunity. When Shores asked
Horn how he would feel if they killed Curtis, Horn replied that he was
tired of Curtis's "cheap threats" and told Curtis he would prefer "to
leave you wherever I found you." Only the supplications of a woman
in the house, presumably Mrs. Polk, dissuaded the officers from shooting Curtis. (Whether Shores was serious about shooting Curtis is not
clear.) Since Peg Leg Watson was visiting a brother across the border in
Texas and not expected back for several days, the detectives took their
prisoner to Gainesville, Texas, where Shores, with Curtis in chains,
caught a train for Fort Worth. Arriving there in the evening, Shores arranged for local lawmen to hold Curtis in their jail. When a *Fort Worth
Gazette* reporter asked for the name of his prisoner, Shores lied, saying
he was a horse thief named George Hines. Then Shores boarded a train
and delivered Bert Curtis to Denver.[50]

In the meantime, Tom Horn and Deputy Marshal Henderson returned to the farmhouse and lay in wait for Peg Leg Watson's return.
On the evening of 29 October 1891, the unsuspecting Watson rode up.
Horn sprang from hiding, rifle in hand, and ordered Watson "to throw
up his hands." When the outlaw attempted to turn his horse and make
his getaway, the Pinkerton man ran up to the outlaw and "shoved the
rifle into his stomach," according to one report. In recalling this dangerous moment, Tom Horn dismissed it offhandedly, remarking, "I had
no trouble with him." When Horn arrived with Peg Leg at the Denver
depot on the evening of 1 November, a *Denver Times* newsman noted
that the outlaw "was guarded by a Pinkerton man [Horn], one of the
best in the service."[51]

If Doc Shores had grown tired of Tom Horn's temperamental behavior, he must have chaffed even more when Horn boasted to the *Denver
Republican* that he was responsible for capturing the train robbers. "One
advantage the pursuers had lay in the fact that the Pinkerton operative
[Horn] was an ex-scout in the United States army," said the reporter,
and "thoroughly up in his work and familiar with the topography of the
country through which they were passing." Horn "was able to calculate
almost exactly the number of days that the fugitives were ahead of their
pursuers," the article said, enabling the two pursuers to make "three
days' travel to their one."[52]

On the morning of 3 November, Doc Shores, Tom Horn, and an
operative named Rose returned to Dick McCoy's ranch and arrested
sixteen-year-old Tom "Kid" McCoy and John Price on federal coun-
terfeiting charges. While en route to the Cotopaxi railroad station,
young McCoy made a break for a nearby patch of timber. When Horn
scolded Shores for not taking a shot at the escaping figure, Shores replied in obvious anger, "Damn you, I think you are about brave enough
to shoot the boy." McCoy was recaptured ten days later. Other arrests
in the train robbery case soon followed, including Frank Price, Frank
Hallock, and William Parry.[53]

In late December 1891, Tom Horn and Fremont County Sheriff
Stewart trailed one of Dick McCoy's sons, Joseph, to Vernal, Utah. On
the morning of the 30th, Horn and Stewart surprised the fugitive while
he was eating breakfast at a boardinghouse. Observing "a big Colt's pistol" in the outlaw's waistband, Tom Horn grabbed the weapon before
he could react. "Well, you have come up with me at last," exclaimed

McCoy. While Horn had to agree, he pointed out that Joe McCoy would have been dead by now if he had reached for his own gun. Horn received much praise for his capture of Joe McCoy, which represented the pinnacle of his career as a Pinkerton operative. Superintendent McParland characterized it as "the most important arrest made for a long time in this part of the country," and the *Rocky Mountain News* was equally complimentary.[54]

In January 1892 the Cotopaxi robbers were tried in U.S. District Court in Denver. Among the defendants were Robert Eldridge, alias Peg Leg Watson, Bert Curtis, and William Parry. William Parry, who turned state's evidence—"peached," in frontier slang—was the key government witness. The federal prosecutor sprang a surprise when he brought Old Dick McCoy—"a surly fellow"—from the state prison to testify for the government. Doc Shores and Tom Horn took turns on the witness stand and described their capture of Peg Leg Watson and Bert Curtis. On one occasion, Watson caused "quite a sensation" when he casually walked out of the courtroom. Realizing that something was amiss, Tom Horn sprang from his chair and "started madly after 'Pegleg,'" only to find the defendant "unconcernedly walking up and down the corridor." When Horn asked the bandit what "he meant by leaving so unceremoniously," Watson replied offhandedly that "the proceedings were dry and uninteresting to him." Peg Leg and Curtis were found guilty of mail robbery and sentenced to life in prison. On 15 February Horn and Shores testified in the cases of several minor players who were either discharged or found not guilty, and so this infamous train robbery case finally came to a close.[55]

Since joining the Pinkerton Agency in April 1890, Horn had traveled much of the West and undertaken difficult and risky assignments. Robert and William Pinkerton, the company principals, considered him a reliable man. "We used him principally to follow up rustlers, cattle and horse thieves, [and] stage and holdup men," wrote Robert Pinkerton in 1906. "We found in Horn a most thorough plainsman and trailer; a man of unquestionable courage and good judgment in all that pertained to his class of work."[56]

In studying Tom Horn's life, some writers have detected an abrupt change in his behavior when he left the government to join the Pinkerton Agency. In Arizona he was a respected citizen; later, he became a suspected hired killer in Wyoming. This change of personality may not have been as abrupt as some writers believe, however. Nearly a decade of exposure to the violence and mayhem of the Apache campaigns had undoubtedly brought about a profound, if unconscious, change in him. Apacheria was, in effect, a war zone, although the U.S. government refused to designate it as such. In many ways, Tom Horn had hardened in this hard land. Jim King, who punched cattle with Horn in Arizona and who later, as a rancher in southwestern Wyoming, was able to observe his activities there, recalled that "it was everybody's business to kill at a price" in southern Arizona. "Raiding bands of Indians, soldiers and Mexicans was the daily occupation along the line between Arizona and Mexico for years," he continued, and "these raids all meant killings by ambush, and at a price." Tom Horn "seldom saw or heard anything except to scheme, skulk, trail and kill," declared Jim King. "He, by custom and habit, had the idea . . . baked into his very soul," added this Wyoming rancher, "that there was nothing wrong in killing renegade thieves when their depredations couldn't be stopped in any other way." Men "had grown habituated to violence" on the southwestern border, notes historian Edward H. Peplow, Jr., leaving "every man . . . [with] a burning desire to kill an Apache." If the dangerous work of a lawman and detective in the Pleasant Valley War suggested that he was already pursuing a new course in his life, his decision to join the Pinkerton Agency set him firmly on a course from which he never turned back.[57]

CHAPTER 6

Range Detective in Wyoming

With the conviction of the Cotopaxi train robbers in February 1892, Tom Horn was free for a new assignment. As one of only two Pinkerton "cowboy detectives" posted in Denver, he would have plenty of work. Charlie Siringo, Denver's senior Pinkerton agent, was already on assignment at Coeur d'Alene, Idaho, where a violent mine workers' strike was under way. A new task for Horn was soon to come, as Superintendent James McParland had work for him in neighboring Wyoming. Unfortunately for students of his career, Horn abruptly ended his autobiography, the *Life of Tom Horn,* at this point, remarking only that in 1892 he "came to Wyoming." Writing from his jail cell in Cheyenne in 1902–1903, with the hangman's noose looming, he must have realized that his association with Wyoming over the past decade had been a serious mistake.[1]

For many years, an explosive situation had existed on the Wyoming cattle ranges, as large cattle companies vied with small livestock men and homesteaders for control of the state's grazing lands. While Wyoming's vast grasslands were a part of the U.S. government's public domain and theoretically open to any legitimate settler, the wealthy cattlemen and livestock companies arbitrarily took possession of these grazing lands so unscrupulously that observers compared their brazen conduct to that of the feudal lords of Europe's Middle Ages. They controlled or influenced state agencies through the Wyoming Stock Growers Association (WSGA) and the Republican Party. Many owners and investors resided in the eastern states or in the United Kingdom. Foremen and managers who failed to keep their employers fully informed of local conditions contributed to misunderstandings. Homesteaders and small ranchers who filed legally for their modest parcels found it difficult to survive against this powerful economic force. By the late 1880s, the big livestock companies were facing serious problems: poor management practices, overgrazing, extremely harsh winters, foreign competition, predatory animals, and thieves. The federal government began to take measures to prevent illegal grazing, and this also caused the barons some concern. Rather than admit that impersonal forces contributed to the reduction of their herds, cattle company officials in Wyoming tended to blame human hands, wielders of "the long rope." Charles B. Penrose, a Pennsylvania physician who spent some time in Wyoming, observed that as profits declined, "stealing became relatively of more account" as an explanation for the cattle barons' problems. In seeking out the culprits, the livestock men pointed to small ranchers and homesteaders, or "nesters," as the worst offenders. "The epithet 'rustler' often referred to no more serious a transgressor," writes historian David M. Emmons, "than one who would homestead on a cattleman's grazing land." As the cattle companies lost confidence in the willingness of local juries—filled, of course, with homesteaders and small ranchers—to convict accused rustlers, they took to circumventing the rule of law. In 1889 vigilantes hanged two alleged thieves, one of whom was a woman, Ella "Cattle Kate" Watson. This lawless act was followed by the assassination of two men in Johnson County in the fall of 1891 and the lynching of a third suspect in neighboring Crook County.[2]

A short time after Tom Horn finished his train robbery assignment, in February 1892, the Pinkerton Agency sent him into the midst of this range war, where the cattle companies were determined to eradicate the Wyoming rustler problem with one direct blow. Inspired by the recent efforts of vigilante cattlemen to suppress rustling in Montana, two influential livestock men—William C. Irvine, manager of the Ogallala Land and Cattle Company, and Hiram B. Ijams, secretary of the Wyoming Stock Growers Association—assumed the responsibility for organizing a similar effort in Wyoming. However, there was a difference. While the Montana vigilantes operated in secrecy, the Irvine-Ijams plan called for open actions. As the primary target of this aggressive plan, the leaders singled out Johnson and several neighboring counties. In the spring of

1892 they hired an "army" consisting of some forty local cattlemen and hired Texas gunmen, supplied with a list of seventy rustlers, to kill off their rustler problem. Given the Pinkerton National Detective Agency's reputation for recruiting armies to suppress labor agitators in the East, Tom Horn's superiors at the agency's Denver branch are suspected of assisting the livestock companies in planning and executing this lawless enterprise. Jay Monaghan, Tom Horn's biographer, declared that some Wyoming cattle barons actually traveled to Denver to discuss "their problem" with Superintendent McParland. Since Tom Horn had experience in an Arizona range war, the agency superintendent suggested that the stockmen talk with their "cowboy" operative. If such a meeting took place, just what transpired is not known.[3]

There is some evidence that Pinkerton operative Tom Horn carried out recruiting duties for the cattlemen. Bruce Sieberts, a rancher in South Dakota, recalled that Horn visited him for this purpose. Not only did the Pinkerton man try to persuade Sieberts to join the cattlemen's reckless venture, but Horn asked Sieberts's neighbor, a man named Fleming, as well. Horn offered "$150 per month [and] all expense extra if you *killed* a rustler or *nester*," Sieberts asserted. While discussing Horn's offer, the three men shared a jug of whiskey and proceeded to get "pretty *tight*." When "Fleming told him [Horn] he sided with the rustlers and small ranchers," Sieberts continued, Horn became so angry that Sieberts feared the detective and Fleming "might shoot it out." Fortunately, the recruiter thought better of it and cooled down. Although Horn had no success in South Dakota, the Wyoming cattle barons succeeded in signing on one man in Idaho and twenty-one in Texas.[4]

On 4 April 1892, Frank Canton, second-in-command of the mercenaries, met the Texans' train in Denver and led them to Cheyenne, where they joined the Wyoming contingent. The entire party consisted of forty-six fighting men and six noncombatants: three teamsters, two newspapermen, and a surgeon, Charles Bingham Penrose. Frank Wolcott, a Union Army veteran and manager of the VR ranch in Converse County, Wyoming, commanded the entire force. From Cheyenne, the "invaders" traveled by train to Casper and then overland to Johnson County. On 9 April they killed two alleged rustlers, Nate Champion and Nick Ray, in a grisly siege at the KC Ranch. When Johnson County Sheriff William "Red" Angus received word of these killings

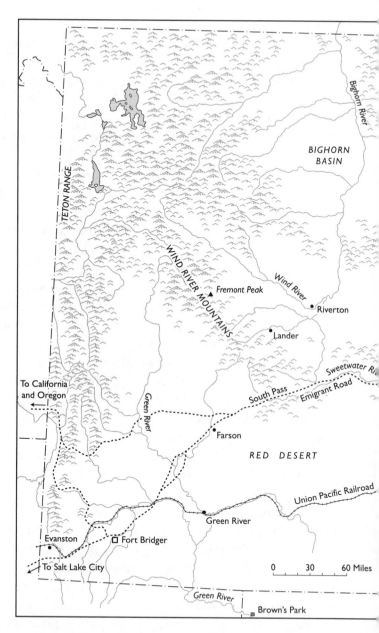

Wyoming rangelands. Copyright © 2014 by the University of
Oklahoma Press.

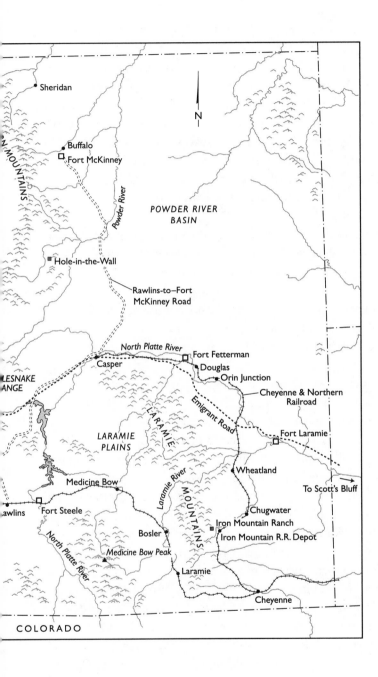

Sheridan

Buffalo
Fort McKinney

N MOUNTAINS

Powder River

POWDER RIVER
BASIN

Hole-in-the-Wall

Rawlins-to–Fort
McKinney Road

North Platte River
Casper
Fort Fetterman
Douglas
Orin Junction

ESNAKE
ANGE

Cheyenne & Northern
Railroad

Emigrant Road

LARAMIE

LARAMIE
PLAINS

Fort Laramie

Wheatland

To Scott's Bluff

Medicine Bow

Laramie River

awlins
Fort Steele

MOUNTAINS

Chugwater
Iron Mountain Ranch
Iron Mountain R.R. Depot

Bosler

North Platte River

Medicine Bow Peak

Laramie

Cheyenne

COLORADO

at his office in Buffalo, he issued a call for a posse. Some three hundred men responded. This unusually large force, which had the color of a popular uprising, laid siege to the mercenaries at the TA Ranch, fourteen miles south of Buffalo. Upon receiving word of the siege, Acting Governor Amos Barber, a physician with little political experience, asked President Benjamin Harrison to send troops to defend the beleaguered mercenary army. On 13 April, troops from Fort McKinney (near Buffalo) took charge of the regulators and escorted them to Fort D. A. Russell, in Cheyenne, to await court action. After much legal maneuvering, the cattlemen's attorneys got the entire body of invaders set free in January 1893.[5]

Newspapers accused the Pinkerton Agency of active involvement in the Johnson County debacle, but if the agency provided assistance and advice to the cattlemen, there is little evidence that it went beyond Operative Tom Horn's recruiting services. Furthermore, Assistant Superintendent John Fraser, McParland's second-in-command, deplored the misinformation circulated by the newspapers and declared that, within his memory, "the [Wyoming] cattlemen have never employed one of our men."

William Walker, who was detained by the mercenaries at the KC ranch, asserted late in life that Tom Horn was a member of the invading force and was present when Champion and Ray were killed. However, Walker is the only firsthand source to place Horn there. Walker's memory probably failed him in this instance. Since Horn subsequently became a widely publicized fixture in the efforts of big cattlemen to dominate the Wyoming range, it was easy to assume that the former scout was present in April 1892. In 1914, William Irvine, one of the ringleaders of the invasion, insisted that "Tom Horn had nothing to do with the Invasion proper, nor was he even in the employ of our crowd." Doc Shores, who was familiar with Horn's movements at this time, was of the same opinion. "I don't think Tom Horn was in the Johnson County War at all," Shores informed Jay Monaghan in 1930. If Horn did accompany the cattlemen's mercenaries to the KC ranch on 9 April, he made a very hasty withdrawal. Four days later, he was back in Denver, where newspapers reported him assisting in the arrest of two Wisconsin fugitives.[6]

As the full extent of the cattlemen's plans for Johnson County, which included the overthrow of the local government, became known, public outrage burgeoned. Newspapers editorialized pro and con. A heated exchange took place between the *Cheyenne Daily Sun,* the mouthpiece of the Republican Party (and the Cheyenne Ring), and the *Daily Leader,* which took a middle-of-the-road position. The Denver *Rocky Mountain News* characterized the "invasion of the Wyoming cattle range as an outrage without precedent in the history of the West." This newspaper went on to become one of the most vocal critics of the Wyoming cattle barons and one of the staunchest supporters of the homesteaders.

Within days of the arrest of their mercenary force, the range lords had put in place a fallback plan to cleanse the range of thieves—a plan that involved the U.S. District Court of Wyoming, its United States marshal, and ultimately, the U.S. Army. If the president could be convinced that an "insurrectionary condition" existed in Johnson and surrounding counties, he might be persuaded to impose martial law. If the chief executive sent the army into this rebellious region, the civil government of Johnson County (which the cattle barons alleged was controlled by rustlers) would be nullified. In the barons' plan, U.S. Marshal Joseph P. Rankin and his deputies were key players. If the rustler element—a large part, if not all, of the population, in the cattlemen's estimation—resisted the marshal's efforts to serve the process of the U.S. Court, the constitution gave the president authority to dispatch troops into the troubled region. The barons were assured that Acting Governor Amos W. Barber and Wyoming's U.S. senators, Joseph M. Carey and Francis E. Warren, also desired the imposition of martial law.[7]

Marshal Joseph Rankin, a staunch Republican famous for his heroism in the 1879 Ute rebellion in Colorado, was in an unenviable position. Many small ranchers and homesteaders believed that Rankin, a big livestock man, was in the cattle barons' camp. While Rankin denied that he had prior knowledge of the invasion of Johnson County, the fact that Frank Canton, a leader of the mercenaries, was a Rankin deputy suggested otherwise. The test of Rankin's allegiance came very soon, when the small ranchers and homesteaders in Johnson County announced through their organization, the Northern Wyoming Farmers and Livestock Association, that they intended to hold their own cattle roundup on 11 May 1892. On 3 May the big cattlemen, who maintained that only the Wyoming Stock Growers Association had the right to schedule roundups for the state, persuaded U.S. District Judge John Riner to issue an injunction—*Henry Blair et al. v. O[scar]. H. Flagg et al.*—forbidding thirty-three residents of Johnson County from "conducting or participating in round-ups other than those authorized by state officers."[8]

Marshal Rankin, who anticipated a violent reception in Johnson County, obtained the approval of U.S. Attorney General William H. H. Miller to incur the expense of a posse comitatus. In early May, Rankin recruited six men for this dangerous undertaking. In spite of the federal lawman's efforts at secrecy, word of these appointments spread quickly. Unfortunately, three of the new deputies—George A. Wellman, Robert L. Gibson, and James G. Craig—were either ranch owners or cattle company employees. As Frank B. Crossthwait, a Department of Justice examiner, pointed out in a subsequent report, these new deputies were "the objects of the enmity and hatred of the rustlers." As the new foreman of Henry Blair's Hoe Ranch in Johnson County, Deputy George Wellman had another mark against him. "There is much feeling against the foremen" of the cattle companies in Johnson County, according to a news dispatch of 19 April. The small ranchers and homesteaders expected the foremen, the on-site representatives of absentee ranch owners, to be more sympathetic to their cause and keep them informed of the owners' machinations. But they were disappointed. The foremen "are believed to have known of the movement [invasion] and kept still," the smaller fry complained.[9]

Among Marshal Rankin's six new deputies was a complete stranger, Thomas H. Hale. Hale seemed to appear out of nowhere. Of course, Thomas H. Hale, commissioned on 5 May 1892, was none other than Pinkerton operative Thomas H. Horn. Although the precise nature of Horn's assignment in Wyoming is unclear, many years later, in October 1939, Russell Thorp, secretary of the Wyoming Stock Growers Association, admitted that "Tom Horn was brought up to this country by our Association" in 1892. Thorp went on to say that Horn "was not particularly successful as a livestock detective from the Association's angle," and that the organization let him go in "a comparatively short time." A few months after Horn's arrival in Wyoming, U.S. Marshal Rankin admitted to Attorney General Miller that he deputized Hale/Horn to serve in Johnson County "at the request of the cattlemen." The stockmen had acquired him "from the Pinkerton Agency in Denver," said Rankin, who went on to explain that Horn was selected "because of his peculiar fitness for the work." Apparently, Rankin was referring to

Horn's training as a "cowboy detective," since the marshal declared that the detective "was to remain in Johnson county and watch for the [rustler] parties against whom warrants were to be sworn out." Rankin's arrangement with Superintendent McParland in regard to Horn's commission as a deputy U.S. marshal is not clear, except that Horn was first a Pinkerton operative and second a federal lawman. If Horn's duties for the cattlemen in Johnson County coincided with Rankin's tasks, there would be no trouble. If a conflict arose between the two missions, Horn would fulfill his Pinkerton assignment first. As the *Cheyenne Daily Sun* observed, the new deputy marshal held an unusual (and independent) status in the federal posse. He was "a special man."[10]

Rankin's new deputies provoked immediate public outrage. When Deputy George Wellman, who had punched cattle for the sprawling Hoe Ranch for more than a decade, returned to Johnson County on 9 May, he had just been appointed to the prestigious position of foreman, a job that the rustling element held in particular contempt. The next day, as Wellman and Thomas J. Hathaway, a Hoe cook, were riding to Buffalo to meet with Marshal Rankin, assassins shot and killed Wellman about thirty miles south of the county seat. Hathaway, who fled the scene, maintained he was unarmed at the time and could not resist. Since Wellman was not a member of the cattlemen's mercenary force and was well liked in Johnson County, there was some question as to why the outlaws targeted him alone among ranch foremen. According to one report, the rustlers believed Wellman knew in advance about the invasion plans and "should have told men with whom he had lived peaceably for eleven years" of these plans. Robert Gibson, another of Rankin's new appointees, may have inadvertently contributed to Wellman's demise by divulging some of Marshal Rankin's instructions "in a public bar," news that spread quickly through the grapevine and reached the rustlers before Wellman arrived at the Hoe Ranch.[11]

The day after Wellman's murder, Marshal Rankin, with Chief Deputy Thomas Jefferson Carr and Deputy Tom Hale (Horn), arrived in Buffalo, where they found the inhabitants in a highly agitated state. In a subsequent report, Rankin said the people fully believed a rumor that he and his two subordinates were the vanguard of fifty more possemen, a second cattlemen's "invasion" force. Sheriff "Red" Angus went to so far as to openly accuse Rankin of planning "to assume government of the county at any moment." "The very night I arrived," Rankin recalled, "I got word that I would be killed if I went a foot out of town." These threats were made by a hard core of "local thugs," according to historian John W. Davis. They were not necessarily associated with rustling in Johnson County and had nothing to do with the legitimate homesteader–small rancher element. These outlaws, known locally as the Red Sash Gang because of the colorful sash that many wore around their waists, cleverly played upon public fears of martial law and paraded the streets of Buffalo "loaded down with artillery," said Marshal Rankin. Led by Charles "Wild Charlie" Taylor, a Colorado fugitive, this band included several unsavory characters—among them Johnson Long, Frank Smith, Clayton Cruse (Crewes), Ed Starr, Henry ("Black Henry") Smith, and Charles Denby. The marshal, who remarked that he had seen "some pretty tough districts" in his day, characterized Buffalo as "about the 'chilliest' place he ever struck." Even Sheriff Angus appeared to be allied with the Red Sashes. Angus was "about the worst of the gang in this kind of attack upon me," Rankin opined. Angus even admitted that he knew the rustlers "were stealing and killing cattle right along," continued the U.S. marshal, but he made no effort to stop the thievery. Rather than being in league with the Red Sashes, Angus was probably resentful at the interference of the federal lawmen in his bailiwick. Just when Angus became aware of the presence of the Pinkerton detective Tom Hale is not known. The sheriff could not have been happy about it.[12]

In spite of Sheriff Angus's seeming hesitancy, his sympathies lay with the legitimate homesteaders and small ranchers, not with the handful of outlaws who plagued his county. As a result, Angus grudgingly agreed to cooperate with Rankin and his federal interlopers. When the Red Sash Gang's threats drove two of the U.S. marshal's new deputies, Craig and Gibson, out of the state, Angus obligingly permitted Rankin to pin federal badges on two deputy sheriffs, Howard Roles and Thomas G. Smith. While Roles had a reputation as a solid lawman, Smith, who was also a WSGA range detective, was suspected of having participated in the lynching of a suspected rustler the previous year. With this small force, which included Deputy Thomas H. Hale (Horn), Marshal Rankin began to serve the writs of injunction against the members of the Northern Wyoming Farmers and Livestock Association. This was not as difficult as Rankin expected, since the organization had voluntarily abandoned its plans for the unauthorized roundup. Within a short time, Rankin's force served eighteen writs, although the threats of the rustlers were such that these efforts were confined to the county seat. Nonetheless, Rankin felt confident that his deputies could complete the assignment without him. On 19 May, he and Chief Deputy Carr left for Cheyenne, although they had to slip out of Buffalo "quietly and unexpectedly" in the night.[13]

Marshal Rankin was sufficiently impressed with the ability of Pinkerton Operative Hale to vest him with leadership of the remaining deputies in Johnson County. Furthermore, Rankin believed that Deputy Sheriff Thomas Smith, who had a longstanding association with the local inhabitants, would be able to "slip through" any obstructions that the rustlers might throw up as the federal lawmen attempted to serve the remaining writs. When a reporter for the *Cheyenne Daily Sun* learned of Hale's new assignment, he recalled the fate of George Wellman and expressed doubt that another report would ever be "received from the special man [Hale]." Sure enough, when Deputies Hale, Smith, and Roles attempted to arrest three of the Red Sash band, Wild Charlie Taylor, Black Henry Smith, and Johnson (Jack) Long, these toughs trained their rifles on the lawmen and "compelled them to dismount, disarm, and approach . . . with hands up." "When the deputy marshals made known the object of their visit," Marshal Rankin reported, "they were . . . driven away." But except for this setback, Horn and his associates had no difficulty serving the remaining writs. Apparently, the pressure of recent events had begun to separate the majority of Johnson County residents, who were basically law-abiding, from the dozen or so bona fide desperadoes who made up the Red Sash Gang.[14]

In spite of Marshal Rankin's expression of confidence in Thomas Hale (Horn), it quickly became apparent that Hale's first loyalty was to his employer, the Pinkerton Agency. As a consequence, Rankin passed the leadership of his posse on to Deputy Marshal Smith. Not only was Smith the chief deputy sheriff of Johnson County, but he had already worked on the George Wellman murder case. Yet Rankin retained Hale as a member of the posse. The arrest of the Red Sash Gang, the primary suspects in Wellman's death, now became Marshal Rankin's top priority. The murder of a deputy U.S. marshal was a federal crime. In plotting Wellman's death, Wild Charlie Taylor and his associates reportedly drew straws to decide who would commit the deed. Ed Starr drew the short straw. The outlaws' motive for this vicious deed

was vague, according to historian John W. Davis. It appears that they
wanted Deputy Marshal Wellman dead "for no other reason than a vicious streak and a general anger toward men wearing stars who were
associated with big cattlemen."[15]

Violations of the federal laws in Johnson County kept Marshal
Rankin and his subordinates scrambling throughout the summer of
1892. (Neighboring counties, which the cattle companies had originally
targeted, were apparently ignored in this mop-up operation—hence the
name Johnson County War.) On the night of 18 May, members of the
Red Sash Gang set fire to several buildings at Fort McKinney, two miles
from Buffalo. When First Lt. Charles B. Gatewood and two enlisted
men attempted to blow up an adjacent building to prevent the fire
from spreading, all three were injured in a premature explosion. The
audacious firebrands made a second attempt on this federal installation
the following night. U.S. Judge Riner issued warrants for Charles Taylor, Black Henry Smith, and Johnson Long, charging them with arson
against public property. As in the Wellman killing, the motive for this
attack was never clear, except that the arsonists harbored "a deep bitterness against the military" for its interference in Johnson County affairs.
Two days later, Deputy Marshal Hale paid a visit to Fort McKinney.
The circumstances of Hale's decision to call on the fort were puzzling.
Hale, who was assisting his fellow deputy marshals in serving the remaining writs, simply "quit the work" without an explanation, according to one report, and rode off in the direction of the fort. However,
the Pinkerton detective may have had both personal and official reasons
for this visit. Since arson on an army post was a federal crime, the U.S.
Marshal's Office had the duty of investigating the fire. Hale may also
have wanted simply to renew his acquaintance with "Beak" Gatewood,
his old boss in the Geronimo campaign.[16]

Deputy Marshal Hale/Horn and his fellow possemen often had to
rub shoulders with members of the Red Sash Gang on the streets of
Buffalo. The arrogant outlaws verbally and physically abused the marshals, going so far on one occasion as to throw limburger cheese at
the officers. In late May 1892, Hale had a bizarre encounter with the
notorious Black Henry Smith, a prime suspect in the George Wellman
murder and noted for his bullying and obnoxious behavior. This outlaw
leader threw a fit when the proprietor of a local hardware store refused
to sell him a revolver. (Another customer had already purchased the
weapon, but had not yet picked it up.) Black Henry grabbed the pistol,

walked outside, and drawing his own weapon, proceeded to "tree the town." At this point Deputy Hale stepped into the picture. On 21 May, a Buffalo correspondent of the *Rocky Mountain News* reported an incident involving Hale/Horn that could possibly be connected to Smith's menacing behavior. The deputy marshal "bought a $27 six-shooter and gave it to Henry Smith," according to this newsman, "one of the most noted of the alleged rustlers." Needless to say, the citizens of Buffalo were mystified at the federal officer's odd behavior. Did Hale give the outlaw a pistol in order to salve his hurt feelings? Whether or not these two events were connected, Hale's conduct was strange indeed, and the *News* noted that the deputy was acquiring "quite a reputation for eccentricity" in Buffalo.[17]

It was also becoming apparent that Tom Hale was an agent for an organization other than the federal court, and that he merely wore the deputy marshal's badge as a cover. In his dispatch reporting Hale's gift to Black Henry Smith, the *Rocky Mountain News* Buffalo correspondent remarked:

> Hale [Horn] says he is not under United States Marshal Rankin's authority at all, but that he is in this section for the purpose of making a full report to someone or somebody, whose name, title or position does not seem very clear on the cattle war and [its] causes. Hale has been making a close investigation of large tracts of fenced land, remarking of the immense inclosure [sic] possessed by Hard Winter Davis . . . that he, Hale, would bet a $60 suit of clothes that Davis would not have such an amount of land fenced this time next year.

(Henry W. Davis, known locally as "Hard Winter," owned the Flying A Ranch on Salt Creek, a tributary of the Powder River.) Such remarks by the outspoken deputy marshal prompted much speculation as to the identity of his employers. If he was investigating cases of illegal fencing of public domain, Hale was serving a government agency. If he was in the employ of the Wyoming Stock Growers Association (through the Pinkerton Detective Agency), Hale was not working in the best interests of the big cattlemen, all of whom were squatting on public land.[18]

Deputy Marshal Hale's snooping around Hard Winter Davis's spread may have provoked a dangerous confrontation with Flying A cowhands in a Buffalo saloon. Walter Shelley Phillips, an employee of the Chicago,

Burlington and Quincy Railroad, which was building through northern Wyoming at this time, recalled this incident. Writing some years later under the pseudonym El Comancho, Phillips recalled that Dell Stover, Davis's foreman, and some cowpunchers cornered Horn and his fellow deputies in a Buffalo saloon on the night of 10 June. Gunplay appeared imminent, wrote Phillips:

> [Stover] walks over t' where Horn's standin' that night, grabs him by th' shoulder an' jerks him to his feet. Man! There's a glare in Stover's eyes like a flame that flares an' flickers in the wind. 'Stand up on yore hin' laigs, yo' polecat, ontil I tell yore fortune,' says Stover, all choked up with mad hate. 'Horn,' he says, 'this goes for yo' an' yore whole damn outfit. It's my Christ convicted opinion that the hull caboodle o' yo' is what no white man c'd call another an' live in the same world with him. What are yo' going t' do about it?

Even though Stover made menacing gestures toward his revolver, Horn refused to be provoked and "never batted an eye," said Phillips. When it became apparent that neither Horn nor the other federal deputies were going to risk a gunfight, tensions eased. "Our outfit turns our back on the Horn gang an' files out slow," said one of Stover's cowhands. While the author added dialogue and may have confused some details, this story may reflect an actual event during those tense times.[19]

The livestock barons, still hoping to persuade President Benjamin Harrison to proclaim martial law, induced a United States commissioner in Cheyenne to issue new arrest warrants in the Wellman case. The fact that there were more than twenty names on this new list indicated that the big cattlemen were trying to provoke a violent response in Johnson County. On 10 June, William Irvine of the Ogallala Land and Cattle Company persuaded U.S. Judge Riner to issue a second injunction against twenty-seven more residents of Johnson County. Apparently Irvine mistakenly believed the small ranchers and nesters—the "rustler element"—still intended to hold an unauthorized roundup.

Fresh military movements suggested to many Wyoming citizens that martial law was in the offing. In early June, troops were stationed temporarily at Camp P. A. Bettens, near Suggs (present-day Arvada), in Sheridan County. Suggs was a tough end-of-track community on the

Burlington Railroad, which was being constructed into Montana. A second camp was set up near old Fort Fetterman, in Converse County, on the southern border of Johnson County. No sooner had the regulars—buffalo soldiers of the Ninth Cavalry Regiment—settled into their temporary camps than local residents clashed with the black soldiers in Suggs on 17 June. One trooper was killed, two wounded, and one citizen was also wounded.[20]

Deputy Marshal Hale/Horn continued to be in the middle of the federal lawmen's activities in Johnson County. As the newspaper debate over the likelihood of martial law heated up in June, the Pinkerton operative was as talkative as usual. When the editor of the *Buffalo Bulletin* asked Horn for his opinion about the necessity for martial law, he belittled the big cattlemen's demands, remarking sarcastically, "There is as much necessity for martial law in this county as there is in heaven." At the same time, rumor had it that Horn and the other deputies were about to collide with the rustler element. On 15 June, Charles Henry Burritt, a Buffalo attorney and spokesman for the big cattlemen, reported that Deputy Marshals Hale and Thomas Smith were in Buffalo, and that a group of Red Sashes had fortified themselves a few miles to the south, declaring that "they would just as soon die resisting arrest as to be arrested by the U.S. Deputy Marshals and taken to Cheyenne to be murdered."[21]

In the face of growing public criticism in the northern counties, U.S. Marshal Rankin faced the task of serving another batch of twenty-three new murder warrants in Johnson County. This assignment would require a larger posse. Even though Benjamin Fowler, U.S. District Attorney for Wyoming, struck off thirteen of these new names on 19 July, Rankin still had to serve ten more murder warrants in Johnson County with only three deputies—Thomas Smith, Howard Roles, and Tom Hale, who was not always willing to do the marshal's bidding. When Charles Burritt informed the marshal on 22 July that citizens of Johnson County could not be "depended on at all" for posse duty, Rankin had to go further afield in his search for prospective deputies. Among the men he sought was Utah's most notable man hunter, Joe Bush, but to no avail. As a stopgap measure, the chief federal lawman finally found deputies in an unlikely place—the U.S. Army. While federal law forbade the use of regular enlisted troops as a marshal's posse (because a posse was a civilian body), the army's civilian employees, such as scouts, were not subject to such restrictions. In late June, General John R. Brooke, commander of the Department of the Platte, agreed to the use of two veteran civilian scouts—Frank Grouard and Baptiste "Little Bat" Garnier—as deputy marshals.[22]

On the evening of 22 July, Deputy Marshal Thomas Smith led his posse out of Buffalo. In addition to Grouard and Garnier, the two civilian scouts, this force included Tom Horn, a former scout. The following day, when the deputies came upon fugitives Ed Starr and Johnson Long near Suggs, shots were exchanged. Although accounts of this encounter are conflicting, it is clear that Starr spotted the posse through binoculars and attempted to get away. When Deputy Marshal Smith managed to overtake him, the cagey badman suddenly turned and got the drop on Smith. Starr sternly "advised him to return to his companions," according to one newsman, "which he reluctantly did." In the meantime, Horn, Grouard, and Garnier chased Long into Suggs and, after an exchange of gunshots, took him into custody and placed him under guard at nearby Camp Bettens.[23]

No sooner had the federal lawmen arrived at Camp Bettens than Ed Starr and some forty heavily armed men rode up and began to taunt them. Although U.S. District Attorney Fowler, who reported this incident, praised the possemen as "brave & efficient," a mere four men were much "too weak" to stand up to forty rustlers. In the confusion, Johnson Long made his escape. The confrontation with Starr and Long was Tom Horn's first serious fracas in Wyoming. It would not be his last.[24]

In spite of the efforts of Deputy Marshals Smith, Hale/Horn, and others, the Red Sash Gang—estimated from twenty-five to forty men though it was probably smaller—continued to defy the federal posse. To add to Marshal Rankin's difficulties, the press persisted in agitating the public with reports that he planned to recruit a new posse of forty men, invade turbulent Johnson County, and arrest George Wellman's murderers "at all hazards." The fact that Hugo Donzelman, a Cheyenne attorney in the employ of livestock company interests, was assisting Rankin in the search for new possemen convinced homesteaders and small stockmen in the affected area that the chief federal lawman was still a flunky of the cattle barons. When a reporter for the *Cheyenne Daily Leader* asked Rankin if he intended to recruit such a large posse, he "threw up both hands in perfect horror." "Don't know anything

about it," he protested, and "stalked off on his dignity." With Donzelman's assistance, Rankin managed to recruit six additional possemen
on 29 July, even though the marshal told Attorney General Miller that
only "two of them [were] of any value for work of this kind." When he
dispatched this new force to Buffalo, Rankin announced that he would
follow them in a few days. In the eyes of the cattle barons, who had
counted on him as their tool, this was a sign that the federal lawman
was no longer responsive to their interests. They believed he should
have personally led the new deputies to Buffalo. With these new reinforcements, Deputy Thomas Smith boasted on 11 August that "he
intended to go out after" the four primary suspects in the Wellman
murder: Black Henry Smith, Ed Starr, Charlie Taylor, and Jack Long.
Tom Horn (Hale) was still part of this posse.[25]

In spite of Joseph Rankin's best efforts to enforce federal law in
Johnson County, newspapers continued to criticize his deputies' conduct. Deputy Thomas Smith and his subordinates, including Tom
Horn, "have been . . . lying around playing billiards, reading novels,
[and] gambling," said the *Rocky Mountain News* of Denver. When confronted, Smith gave the excuse that the outlaws had stolen their horses
and threatened to kill the federal officers if they attempted an arrest.
"Eight men [outlaws] are banded together and will resist [the posse],"
said Smith, "and . . . there is sure to be a fight." A few days later, the
same reporter noted that the federal possemen had now been in town
a week and "had done nothing toward solving the Wellman murder."
Strangely, "all but Hale [Horn] and Smith have laid away their firearms,
being apparently ashamed to carry them." In order to intimidate the
newly arrived federal deputies, said one observer, "a lot of 'rounders'
[troublemakers] about town procured and wore red sashes" in imitation
of the outlaws. When Marshal Rankin visited Johnson County a few
days later, he was so disappointed in his new subordinates that he immediately sent them back to Cheyenne.[26]

In spite of their disappointment in Marshal Rankin, the cattle barons
won what looked at first like a victory in their effort to bring about
martial law. On 30 July 1892, President Harrison issued a proclamation against lawlessness in Johnson and neighboring counties. While
this proclamation did not place the region under martial law, it threatened such action if the troublesome element failed to "retire peaceably to their abodes." If civil lawmen and the courts were permitted

to function unhindered, of course, there would be no need for martial law. In spite of much skepticism, the proclamation had a salutary effect. When Marshal Rankin paid another visit to Johnson County in mid-August, he was pleased to observe a remarkable change of affairs. Sympathizers with the rustlers had withdrawn "to their homes or dispersed," he informed Attorney Miller, and the members of the Red Sash outlaw band had "left the Country in various directions." Since the Wellman murder, a slow, almost imperceptible change had taken place in the attitudes of Johnson County residents as the true colors of Charlie Taylor and his Red Sash bullies emerged more clearly. A new solidarity among law-abiding citizens from all walks of life began to emerge. A Buffalo dispatch reported that there was "no sympathy" for the outlaws and that "the men desired by the marshals have been warned and have fled the country." Charlie Taylor, the outlaw chieftain, "was last seen 150 miles from here a month ago," said Buffalo newspaperman Jack Flagg, "and was still traveling." A mere piece of paper from Washington, D.C., had done what a federal posse was unable to accomplish. In spite of the cattle barons' propaganda campaign against the "nesters," there had never been a close association between the small ranchers and the rustlers.[27]

Even though the rustler threat had diminished, Marshal Rankin left four deputies in Johnson County to prevent "any reorganized defiance of the United States authority." He left instructions with Thomas G. Smith, Tom Hale (Horn), Frank Grouard, and James Huff to patrol against the return of any of the Red Sash band. The chief federal lawman was confident that these deputies "would now be able, since the President's proclamation, to make . . . arrests." And indeed, after weeks of disappointment, the chief federal lawman and his deputies began to make arrests in the George Wellman case. On 22 August, Tom Horn and Thomas Smith arrested Kid Donnelly as an accessory in this case. Rankin, who escorted the prisoner to Cheyenne, was very put out when a journalist snidely remarked that the marshal arrived in the state capital "wearing a white Stetson and the air of [a] conquering hero." On 25 August, Deputies Smith, Hale/Horn, and Grouard took up an unrelated case—that of an army deserter, Henry E. Johnson. The lawmen found the fugitive hiding in a haystack and coaxed him out. Although the federal officers arrested the ranch owner for harboring a deserter, he was eventually released.[28]

The urgings of the big cattle companies and the "Cheyenne ring," an alleged cabal of state officials and wealthy cattlemen, failed to persuade

U.S. Marshal Rankin to cooperate in their efforts to bring about martial law in Johnson County. "There was a point beyond which he could not go," said one newsman. "His duty as an officer and his manhood as a man [*sic*] restrained him," added this writer. By September 1892, the cattle barons were determined to see the head of Joseph Rankin tumble "into the official basket." As editorialists assessed Rankin's performance as marshal, one newsman suggested that one of his deputies, Thomas H. Hale (Horn), had done considerable harm to the federal lawman's reputation. Hale's eccentric conduct, coupled with public doubts about his mission in Johnson County, said this writer, may have helped bring about the marshal's "downfall." The presence of this maverick deputy, a Pinkerton answerable to a Pinkerton superior, and in such a critical area, could only cause problems for Marshal Rankin. Clearly, many citizens believed that Rankin was not the master of his own house. The presence of a subordinate with an agenda that differed from the mission of his superior had the effect of discrediting him.[29]

In a letter of 31 October 1892, Rankin tried to explain to Attorney General Miller the problems presented by Deputy Hale/Horn. Rankin said that during his most recent visit to Buffalo, in September, he "rather complained" to his troublesome subordinate for failing to make any further progress in the Wellman murder case. In a near act of insubordination, Rankin reported, "He [Hale] said, 'I will be frank with you and state [that] I am instructed, through my [Pinkerton] office in Denver, to take no instructions from you whatever; that the cattlemen are our clients, and we are working for their best interests. My instructions . . . were to try to drive these men out of the country and not arrest them." Clearly, Rankin and Horn were operating at cross-purposes. Horn declared that the cattle companies believed any rustlers arrested and taken to Cheyenne for trial would be freed by sympathetic juries. If the evidence was not overwhelming against these felons, and a clear-cut conviction won, "the cattlemen would be in a worse fix than ever,'" asserted Horn. "'I have carried out my instructions from the Denver [Pinkerton] office," he continued, "'and have rather tried to drive these men out of the country . . . [and not] arrest them.'" It appears that Horn was already pursuing the tactics that he would employ for the next decade in the interest of the big livestock owners. It was more expedient to terrorize and drive suspected rustlers out of Wyoming than to go to the expense of attempting legal action. (There is no indication that he yet contemplated the ultimate

solution—assassination.) In spite of efforts to have Joseph Rankin removed, the president permitted him to remain in office, completing his
term on 8 August 1894.[30]

Because of Marshal Rankin's growing dissatisfaction with Tom Hale,
his days in Johnson County were numbered. After assisting Sheriff
"Red" Angus in the pursuit of two thieves in mid-October, the *Buffalo Bulletin* reported, "U.S. Marshal Hale left Buffalo on Monday last
[24 October] to the regret of the many friends that he has made during
his stay." In spite of his sometimes erratic and inexplicable behavior,
Hale had been a common sight around Buffalo since the previous May.
After he left Johnson County, Horn's next Pinkerton assignment is not
clear. In the meantime, U.S. District Attorney Benjamin Fowler, who
had responsibility for the Wellman case, continued to press the pursuit of the primary suspects. To bring about the arrest of Black Henry
Smith, Fowler employed Samuel N. Moses, a well-known range detective and presently a lawman in South Dakota. After a long chase over
much of the Southwest, Moses caught up with Smith in Indian Territory and returned him to Cheyenne on 7 March 1893. Two days earlier, Clayton Cruse, another suspect in the Wellman case, surrendered
to Johnson County authorities.[31]

Although still in Pinkerton employ, Tom Horn continued to serve
as Joseph Rankin's deputy and to assist in the Wellman investigation.
In January 1893, while Sam Moses pursued Black Henry Smith, Deputy
Marshal Hale/Horn traveled to the West Coast. Although the nature
of his mission is not known, Horn was on official business. To add to
the mystery surrounding Horn's trip, Johnson County Sheriff "Red"
Angus and Deputy Sheriff Howard Roles, whom the *Sun* characterized as "former friends" of the deputy marshal, met Horn at the Cheyenne railroad depot when he returned in February. As late as July 1893,
Hale/Horn's name remained on Rankin's roster of deputies, although
his official duties after the California trip are not known.[32]

In the meantime, District Attorney Benjamin Fowler made a futile
attempt to prosecute the suspects in the assassination of Deputy U.S.
Marshal George Wellman. Among the persons Fowler subpoenaed as
witnesses was Tom Horn, who gave his mailing address as Chugwater,
headquarters of the Swan Land and Cattle Company. "The trial is at-
tracting a great crowd to the United States court," said the *Cheyenne
Daily Sun,* "and every step is being contested . . . by able attorneys

on both sides." When Fowler failed to make an adequate case against Henry Smith in November 1893, Judge John Riner instructed the jury "to bring a verdict of not guilty." Realizing he would no longer need Tom Horn as a witness, Fowler excused him from further service. The case against Clayton Cruse was also dismissed, while Ed Starr, the suspected triggerman in the Wellman assassination, fled to Montana. He was shot to death in a personal squabble in September 1898.[33]

By the time Tom Horn left Johnson County in October 1892, he was probably considering severing ties with the Pinkerton National Detective Agency. At the same time, agency officials were thinking the same thing. In the *Life of Tom Horn,* he admitted that he "never did like the work." While the date of his separation from the agency and the circumstances of his departure are not known, Charlie Siringo, who eventually turned against the Pinkertons (and Tom Horn), asserted that the agency "discharged" Horn because he "was too rough." However, Doc Shores, who was working as a Denver and Rio Grande Railroad detective in Utah at the time Horn quit, insisted that he resigned because he disliked the duty of spying on railroad employees:

> He was checking conductors on the Oregon Short Line and turned one in [for thievery]. This conductor claimed he was framed and that no such man as Horn had ever ridden with him, and to prove it he dared Horn to pick him out of a crowd. The railroad management asked Pinkerton's [*sic*] to send the operative to Ogden to prove whether he could pick the conductor out of a crowd of railroad men in a room. Horn went into the room, walked up to the conductor and said HOW ARE YOU. The conductor shook hands with Tom Horn. Then they all went out and got drunk together. That is when Horn quit Pinkerton's.[34]

In an interview with the *San Francisco Call,* William Pinkerton provided a different explanation for Horn's departure: "Unfortunately, Horn got to drinking and I was forced to threaten him with Dismissal if he did not quit. The last time I saw him we were bound westward on a train, he for Ogden and I for this city [San Francisco]. He was drinking then and I told him that it was his last chance and that instructions had been left by me in Denver to dismiss him if he showed up drunk again." It appears that Tom Horn, who seldom took a drink stronger than beer before he left Arizona, had succumbed to a bad habit. While Horn said he left the company in 1894, his departure more than likely took place in late 1892 or 1893.[35]

In reflecting on his time as a Pinkerton operative in a letter to Doc Shores in March 1896, Horn expressed disappointment at the paltry income of fifteen dollars a week. "Fame wont [sic] fill a hungry Belley [sic]," he remarked. "I never had any ambition to be a great Detective but was always ambitious to accomplish anything I was put at," he continued, "and I liked the work for the simple reason that I have a natural hatred for men that Steal and follow a crooked life." While Horn admitted that "the excitement of the life is all right," he complained that the "Red Tape [would] drive a [common] Indian like myself wild." In spite of his complaints, Horn had demonstrated bravery and nerve during his six months in Johnson County, indicating that he was not without some talent (and luck).[36]

Yet Wyoming livestock barons must have been impressed with Tom Horn's abilities, since he was soon serving as a range detective for the Swan Land and Cattle Company at Chugwater. At its greatest extent in the 1880s, this company encompassed 600,000 acres. From his headquarters ranch, the Two Bar, at Chugwater, thirty miles north of Cheyenne, manager John Clay, Jr., ran 40,000 head of cattle and 500 horses. While Clay was aware that impersonal forces had been hard on Swan herds in recent years, he considered rustlers a special menace and had joined with other local cattlemen in forming the Laramie County Protective Association. Clay's obsession with rustlers is somewhat puzzling. When he became president of the Wyoming Stock Growers Association in 1894, he presented a rosier picture than had his predecessors. Public "sentiment . . . as to stealing . . . has changed for the better," he declared, adding that for the first time, juries were "giving us some protection." Apparently, however, this was not enough for the tough-minded Scotsman, who desired to suppress thievery completely.[37]

Unfortunately, we know very little about what brought Tom Horn to Chugwater. According to Doc Shores, Edward Ivinson, a Laramie banker and investor in the Swan Company, referred Horn to manager John Clay. Lawrence Woods, Clay's biographer, suggests that the Laramie County Protective Association may have been Horn's actual employer, although this is not clear. His wages were probably one hundred dollars per month, the going rate for range detectives at the time. Clay probably assigned him a specific geographic area to patrol, with instructions to monitor the activities of small ranchers and homesteaders suspected of livestock theft. At his murder trial, in 1902, Horn's testimony gave the impression that he had great latitude on the range: "I go where I please and when I please, and come back when I get ready. All I do is show up home once in a while and report how things are going on [on the range]. Nobody asks me any questions about where I am going next or what I am going to do until it is done." Whatever the terms of his employment, Tom Horn began his assignment at Chugwater under cover as a horsebreaker.[38]

Horn had considerable freedom to devise his own methods. His purpose, he testified at his trial, was "to keep track of the cattle in the country in a general way and . . . shove [reclaim] all the cows and calves that I found . . . belonging to the company in anyone else's pasture." Of course, his primary purpose was to "keep as good track of the people in the country as I can that are [illegally] killing and marketing beef." "To protect the interests of the company," the detective boasted, "I have got out there [on the range] where the stealing was going on and remained continuously." "I associate myself so directly with the neighborhood that stealing cannot go on without my being present," continued Horn. "If they steal I will catch them in the act." While Horn later gained the reputation of an assassin for hire in the cattlemen's war on rustlers on the Wyoming ranges, there is no indication at this early date that John Clay expected him to do more than collect evidence and bring about the legal arrest of suspected thieves. It was the company's obligation to see to a conviction. In the most extreme cases, Clay may have authorized his detective to harass or run suspected rustlers out of the region. This had been one of Horn's goals in Johnson County in the summer of 1892.[39]

When testifying before the coroner's jury in the Willie Nickell murder case in August 1901, Tom Horn indicated that one of his aims was to keep potential rustlers off guard by carrying out night patrols. "I rode those pastures [in the Sybille Creek region, west of Chugwater] three or four years," he informed the jury. "If they [rustlers] didn't see me they would see some signs of me." His equipment was limited to what he could carry. He did not take a slicker or overcoat with him, he added, but had "a government blanket for a saddle blanket is all." "I do not use coffee when I am out; I take a little bread and a pound of bacon. Whenever I get hungry I shoot a jack rabbit and broil it. The living is not very good; [but] the working months are short." Contrary to Horn's testimony, the Swan Company sometimes made arrangements with various ranchers to provide him with food and lodging while on his rounds.[40]

John Clay, Jr., was impressed with his new range detective. Clay, who wrote an autobiography and some fiction about the cattle industry, included Horn in one of his short stories, "The Fate of a Cattle Rustler" (1910). Tom Horn "was a natural-born sleuth," wrote Clay.

> Though I knew him well and spent many days with him, I never fathomed his character. His movements were catlike; he could crawl like a snake or stand up in a fight and take his medicine with others. He had hunted Apaches with Miles, he had run train robbers to the ground . . . and now his headquarters were by the banks of the Chug[water] and Sybille Creek. He seemed to have an innate hatred of a house, and a road was of little use to him. Like the Boer behind his kopje [fortified hill], he kept under cover, shunning the divides, slipping up ravines, diving into canyons, reaching his point by tracks known only to himself. You never knew his movements, and yet he always turned up at the right moment. A strange, incomprehensible being, with sinews of steel, nerves of iron, the cunning of a fox, the pertinacity of a hound.

If one added "the craft of the red man" to Tom Horn's makeup, continued Clay, "you have a dangerous combination either in love or war."[41]

When Horn took up his duties, in 1893, John Clay was concerned about cattle losses along Sybille Creek, in the Laramie Mountains west of Chugwater. Several small ranchers and nesters lived along the creek and just across the county line, in Albany County. Among these settlers, John Clay and other big ranchers, regarded Ferdinand "Fred" Albert Langhoff as the leader of a cattle theft ring. In Clay's eyes, the Two Bar was "a solitary ship surrounded by rocks and quicksand in the form of small ranchmen, sheepmen, and dry farmers," wrote Lawrence Woods. Efforts to prosecute Langhoff and his associates had failed. Fred Langhoff had skipped the country, and his wife, Evangeline (Eva), was reportedly butchering Two Bar calves and selling the meat in Laramie.

At the beginning of September, Detective Horn was ready to undertake his first mission on behalf of John Clay. Alexander (Al) Bowie, the Two Bar foreman, had persuaded Ira S. Fredendall, the Laramie County sheriff, to make Horn a temporary deputy. To keep a watch on Eva Langhoff's movements, Horn arranged to stay with her neighbors Charles and Minnie Rietz. "None of us knew what he was working on," Minnie later declared. In recalling the investigation, Horn said he secretly examined the Langhoff barn, where he "found sufficient evidence to convince him" that Two Bar cattle were being killed there. He also saw Eva and her associates "load three calves in a wagon and bring them to town [Laramie] . . . where the calves were delivered at Balch's market."[42]

After two months of observing the suspects, Detective Horn and Al Bowie were ready to move against them. On 12 November 1893 they approached the Langhoff barn with two local residents, Gustav W. Rosentreter and Otto Plaga, as possemen and witnesses. When Rosentreter, a German immigrant, said he would prefer not to go along, a friend told him "you had about as well make up your mind to go as Tom Horn will deputize you anyway." Horn, Bowie, and their posse arrived at the Langhoff barn about 7:00 P.M. The lawmen "found Mrs. [James] Cleve was holding a lamp and Mrs. Langhoff and three men were butchering and skinning the stock," Horn later testified. Since he had inspected these same calves earlier and determined that they were Two Bar animals, Horn insisted that he had the necessary evidence for a conviction. When one suspect, knife in hand, said threateningly, "I have a notion to cut the buttons off your vest," Horn leveled his revolver at the man and shouted, "Drop that knife or I'll put a bullet in your head." "The knife dropped and the show was over," recalled Rosentreter. Young Otto Plaga was so impressed with Horn's nerve that he soon took it into his head to become a range detective himself. Suddenly Horn and Bowie had five prisoners on their hands, Eva Langhoff, James Cleve and his wife, Nellie (Nettie), Louis Bath, and Samuel (William) Taylor.[43]

Since Horn made the arrests in Albany County and had no warrants in hand, Eva Langhoff and her associates insisted that he had no jurisdiction. However, Horn refused to take no for an answer and took them to Cheyenne by way of Iron Mountain and the Cheyenne and Northern Railroad. For a few hours, Deputy Sheriff Horn and Eva Langhoff and her "gang" were a newsworthy event. The *Cheyenne Daily Sun*

noted the presence of this "Woman Rustler" in the capital city and
touted Eva Langhoff as "one of the characters of the west." She "has
no superior among all the men of the state" as a cattle thief, the *Sun*
declared. This "magnificently built and proportioned woman," who
had taken up with Louis Bath after her husband fled the state, according to the *Sun*, "can easily lift 200 pounds and carry it away." (John
Clay characterized her as an "Amazon.") "She is said to be the leader
of the gang that has infested the Sybille country for a long time," added
the reporter, and "is familiar with all the ways and means to disguise
a brand." While this story did not openly compare her with "Cattle
Kate" Watson, the unfortunate woman whom cattlemen lynched four
year earlier, readers must have noted the similarities.[44]

To ensure that his arrests were legal, Horn took his prisoners before Justice of the Peace Herman Glafcke for a hearing on 14 November. While Al Bowie signed a formal complaint, Tom Horn, as deputy
sheriff, signed the return on an arrest warrant. Later that day, he and
Bowie delivered their prisoners by rail to the Albany County sheriff
in Laramie. The Langhoff case "created a great deal of interest," according to the Laramie *Daily Boomerang*, which headlined one article
"Story of Deputy Horn. How He Waited for Weeks in the Hills" (in
order to gather evidence against the thieves). The next day at the preliminary hearing Defense Attorney Charles W. Bramel made much of
Tom Horn's decision to transport his prisoners in a roundabout way,
via Cheyenne, rather than overland directly to Laramie. The citizens
of Cheyenne held "malice" against the defendants, Bramel alleged, and
knowing this, Horn took this route "for the purpose of parading them
in the streets of Cheyenne." The detective's decision "was a piece of
spite work," Bramel insisted. Furthermore, the calves that Eva Langhoff
butchered were not Swan livestock, continued the defense attorney,
but belonged to Louis Bath and his family. In spite of Bramel's clever
plea, the justice of the peace bound the defendants over for trial at the
next district court session.[45]

After these proceedings, a *Laramie Republican* reporter sought out
Deputy Sheriff Horn in an effort to size him up. Horn's gifts as a racon-
teur worked their magic on the gullible reporter:

Mr. Horn fitted himself out as a cowboy and commenced to
ride the range. He was not unfamiliar with the methods of the

rustlers, having lived on the range in Texas on a similar mission. He put in two months on the range and at last became to all intents and purposes one of the thieves. He gained the confidence of the five people he arrested. On the sly he made love to Mrs. Langhoff and at last saw some of the cattle slaughtered and followed the meat and hides to the place where they were sold.

While Horn insisted that he was only a "cow puncher," this newsman was not taken in. He concluded that this detective "is a very well posted man and . . . able to speak several languages."[46]

In spite of Tom Horn's assertion that he had the "dead wood" on the thieves, Eva Langhoff and her companions were among friends. The trial, which began on Friday, 12 January 1894, did not go smoothly for the prosecution. Defense attorneys challenged so many potential jurors that a new pool had to be brought in. When the taking of testimony finally began, only four defendants faced the bar: Eva Langhoff, Louis Bath, William Taylor, and James Cleve. (Nettie Cleve was released.) Taylor and Cleve were granted separate trials, leaving Louis Bath and Eva Langhoff to be tried together. In spite of the testimony of Horn, Bowie, and other eyewitnesses, the jury acquitted Eva Langhoff, while Louis Bath was found guilty and sentenced to eighteen months in the state penitentiary. The district attorney chose not to prosecute the cases against Cleve and Taylor. While a local journalist characterized this trial as the most important one at this court session, Tom Horn was very disappointed. Yet he maintained that his investigation had some positive effect. The publicity surrounding the discovery of "the Langhoff gang" discouraged these suspects from continuing their nefarious activities.[47]

Since his employment as a range detective was seasonal, Tom Horn pursued other trades in his off time, and he soon earned a reputation as a top cowhand and horsebreaker. In 1894 David Morris, foreman of one of the Swan ranches, purchased a two-year-old Oregon cutting horse named Muggins. Muggins was run in with a hundred other horses for breaking. When Morris asked for the best horsebreaker in the region, someone suggested Horn. According to Charles Camp, a subsequent owner of Muggins, Horn found this "fine neck-reined colt" a very "apt pupil . . . in his skillful hands." "Tom Horn knew a horse," continued Camp, "and his great strength and size and panther-like agility made all bronchos look like playthings to him." As "a master reinsman and

horseman" Horn was fortunate enough to break the single most famous cutting horse in Wyoming history. Although Horn shared Muggins with fellow cowhands, John Clay recalled that the range detective
delighted in riding this horse "a great deal" on the Two Bar range.[48]

Tom Horn was involved in another horsebreaking endeavor about
this same time with Robert Ellsworth (Bud) Cowan, a cowhand for
John Cuthbert Coble, manager and part owner of the Iron Mountain
Cattle Company. Coble sent Cowan with six hands up to the Powder
River country to fetch a horse herd that Coble had left there earlier.
Horn accompanied this drive as one of the crew. According to Cowan,
Horn was actually a Wyoming Stock Growers Association detective at
the time, which is plausible since Charles Wells, a rancher in the Big
Horn Basin, also encountered Horn working as a detective in 1894.
Wells, who had met Horn in Kansas in the 1870s, said they "recognized
each other at once." "Chuck, . . . I would consider it a personal favor if
you would just forget about our having met here today," said Horn as
they departed, "as I am working for the Wyoming Livestock Assn. and
am going down into the [Big Horn] basin on business." Horn did not
confide his "business" to Wells.[49]

By November 1894, Tom Horn was back in Laramie County. Horn
returned to the Two Bar on Sunday, 11 November, said a Chugwater
gossip columnist, "just in time for dinner, of course." Horn "remained
'till after dinner Monday, when he again sought rural recreation." A few
days later, a Chugwater correspondent calling himself "A Prevaricator"
remarked that "Thos. Horn has opened night school for the benefit of
cow punchers." While this writer's joke is not clear, he was probably
referring to the detective's night patrols in search of rustlers. Since cold
weather was setting in, Horn's duties soon ended. Bud Cowan recalled
the he and Horn "went into winter camp" in a line shack on John
Coble's Iron Mountain Ranch. To pass the time, recalled Cowan, they
engaged in Tom Horn's favorite recreations, breaking horses and making "rawhide ropes, quirts, and hackamores all that winter [1894–95]."[50]

CHAPTER 7

Murder on Horse Creek

Range Detective Tom Horn was deeply angered at the failure of the Laramie jury to send Eva Langhoff and her entire gang to jail for cattle theft. The conviction of only one of the five thieves was a turning point in Horn's career. When Horn found that "nester" juries in Albany and Laramie counties were just as soft on livestock thieves as their counterparts in the north, he resolved to abandon the court system. Instead, he adopted more direct means of suppressing rustling, including threats, intimidation, harassment, and expulsion from his patrol area. If the ultimate punishment—assassination—was necessary, so be it, although he would inflict it only if compensated appropriately. In reflecting upon this change in Horn's approach, the *Wyoming State Tribune* recalled later that he "caused the rumor to be circulated . . . that he was through trying to protect the interests of his employers through the medium of the law, and would thereafter take things into his own hands."[1]

While the Langhoff case may have soured Tom Horn on Wyoming's justice system, this setback has been overemphasized as the primary reason for his adoption of the methods of a regulator. For one thing, more than a year elapsed between the Langhoff trial in early 1893 and Horn's first suspected assassination, in July 1895. To embark on a regulator campaign, Tom Horn would have needed the approval (and pay) of his employers. When the cattlemen's invasion of Johnson County in 1892 proved to be too conspicuous, a few barons, determined to carry on the "war" against livestock thieves at all costs, decided on a lower-profile campaign. This decision ultimately led them to support Horn's proposal of selective assassination. "After the failure of the 'invasion,'" wrote Charles Penrose, the invaders' physician, "some effort was made to eliminate the rustlers by means of secret individual killing." The identity of the range barons who hired Horn has never been made public. According to biographer Jay Monaghan, Horn and an anonymous rancher "talked it over" and concluded that "there was no use going to the expense of a trial when a conviction was impossible."[2]

Tom Horn's adoption of regulator tactics did not represent an abrupt change from his past activities. This choice followed from his earlier successes: chief of scouts in the apprehension of Geronimo; the capture of the Cotopaxi train robbers; and the very dangerous work in Johnson County in 1892. Horn came to Wyoming after exposure to a period of unbridled government- sanctioned violence against the Apaches followed by violent experiences in the Pleasant Valley War. In the *Life of Tom Horn,* he is such a good storyteller that readers often mistake the book for a lighthearted tale. Behind the fast-paced narrative, though, is a story of brutality and callousness that even today can have a chilling effect on the reader. As writer John Rolfe Burroughs observed, "Throughout his formative years his principal business in life—in fact, the way he earned his living—was tracking down (and sometimes killing) other men (albeit 'red' men) for pay." His hatred of thieves—of all races—remained undiminished. William C. Irvine, the prominent Wyoming cattleman and acquaintance of Tom Horn, recalled that "he classed thieves with wolves and coyotes and looked upon himself as a benefactor of society in destroying them." With that deep-seated, even obsessive hostility toward thieves, Irvine concluded, Horn could kill "without feeling or compunction when certain he was after a guilty man."[3]

It was not long before word of Tom Horn's willingness to assassinate rustlers for a price reached prospective employers, probably in 1894 or early 1895. At this time, he was still on the Wyoming Stock Growers Association payroll, according to a subsequent president, Russell Thorp. U.S. Senator Joseph M. Carey, who chaired a secret Wyoming Stock Growers Association committee for the purpose of combating rustling after the 1892 debacle, was responsible for hiring Horn. Carey reportedly believed that the former scout was peculiarly suited for this task, since similarities existed between hunting Apache renegades and white livestock thieves. However, when the senator learned that Horn was "ready to kill cattle thieves at $500 a head," Carey was reportedly "horrified" and expressed a desire to fire him immediately. Instead, WSGA officials instructed Horn to forgo making arrests—presumably fearing he might kill someone—and confine his activities to gathering evidence in writing against suspects. According to Dean Krakel, a respected student of Horn's Wyoming career, Horn presented a report to a WSGA meeting in Cheyenne, where "Rustlers and Grangers were discussed in terms defined as uncomplimentary." After talking over the subject, and concluding that "the law would do nothing," the members still faced the question, "What final action should be taken?"[4]

Sensing a moment of uncertainty, Tom Horn walked "to the center of the floor, cigar in hand, [and] . . . surveyed the group," according to Krakel. "In a cool voice [he] said, 'Men, I have a system that never fails, when everything else has. Yours has!'" Even though some men present were well acquainted with range violence, many were stunned by Horn's nonchalant discussion of exterminating thieves. As the meeting became hotter, the association officials quickly nixed any plans that involved bloodshed. "Collecting evidence is one thing, assassination is another," exclaimed the president. A minority of those present, however, pointed out that there was nothing to prevent individual ranchmen or cattle companies—even though still members of the association—from contracting privately for the services of Tom Horn or any other such person. This small element, sometimes referred to as "professional agitators" or "radicals," "wanted the maximum penalty inflicted on the beef-stealing thieves." The association let Horn go after this meeting, and from this point on, he "made private arrangements" with individual cattlemen.[5]

As Tom Horn's reputation spread among the range barons in 1894 and 1895, Wyoming governor William A. Richards sought a meeting with him. Richards, whose Great Basin ranch was troubled by thieves, arranged through Will Irvine, a member of the State Livestock Commission, to talk with Horn. Richards was reluctant to see Horn in the governor's office, so Irvine had the detective meet the governor at the State Livestock Commission office, which was also in the capitol. At this meeting, which probably took place in September 1895, Irvine informed Tom Horn that Richards wanted to discuss "the best way of stopping the stealing" in the Great Basin. Said Irvine, "The Governor was quite nervous, so was I, Horn perfectly cool. He talked generally, was careful of his ground, told the Governor he would either drive every rustler out of Big Horn County, or take no pay other than $350 advance to buy two horses and a pack outfit. " After outlining in a general way his method of suppressing rustling, Irvine recalled, Horn said that upon completion of his task he should receive $5,000. "'Whenever everything else fails,'" he added, "'I have a system which never does.'" The governor, who was "stunned" at the detective's coolness, ended the meeting as quickly as possible. Since Horn "was an intelligent fellow" and sensed the governor's discomfort, continued Irvine, he got up from his chair and remarked, "I presume that is about all you wanted to know sir." He added that he would be happy to "be of service" as he bid them goodbye.[6]

After the detective had departed, Richards remarked to Irvine, "So that is Tom Horn. A very different man from what I expected to meet." "Why, he is not bad-looking," added the governor, "and is quite intelligent; but a cool devil, ain't he?" In spite of the governor's efforts at secrecy, word of the Richards-Horn parley was soon on the streets. In an editorial on two recent assassinations of alleged cattle thieves in the southern part of the state, Jack Flagg of the *Buffalo Voice* made an oblique reference to this meeting. "Such murdering could not be done in any other state of the Union as is done here," remarked Flagg. "The perpetrators go scott [*sic*] free, and then come right into the capitol and hold conferences with the men who are hiring them to do the work.[7]

One of the most prominent of the barons who endorsed extreme measures against rustlers was John Cuthbert Coble, manager of the Iron Mountain Ranch Company, in Laramie County. Coble was born in Carlisle, Pennsylvania, in 1858, and educated at Dickinson College. In 1877 he and an older brother, Alexander C. (Bob) Coble, started a cattle business in Custer County, Nebraska. In the early 1880s, the Cobles moved their herd to Johnson County, Wyoming, where they went into partnership with Sir Horace Plunkett, a British aristocrat. In 1888 John Coble began a new ranching venture near Iron Mountain, about thirty miles northwest of Cheyenne. In addition to his brother, John Coble had various partners in the 1890s, including William E. Lawrence, a Laramie businessman (and co-manager for a time), as well as two Omaha entrepreneurs, Dr. C. J. Coffman and realtor Harry J. Windsor. This extensive enterprise, which eventually included four separate spreads, grazed as many as 6,000 cattle. At the same time, John Coble also raised prize horses and often entered them in competition. The company's first headquarters was about five miles west of the Iron Mountain railroad depot. Eventually, Coble moved the headquarters to Bosler, a whistle-stop thirteen miles west on the Union Pacific Railroad in Albany County.[8]

As manager of this ambitious ranching enterprise, John Coble became widely known as a person with "hundreds of warm personal friends," according to one observer. This Iron Mountain rancher, who enjoyed any festivity, has "a dome-shaped head, which is quite bald on the top," said the *Denver Post,* "but sports a soft fringe of silky black hair at the sides and back; has a long, oval face, a round, aggressive chin, a black mustache worn in the military fashion, with pointed ends, which he continually twists; well defined brows, [and] a straight nose." (Strangely, the newspaper mentioned Coble's "slate-colored eyes," curiously like Horn's.) Coble maintained an active social life and enjoyed fine clothing and expensive buggies. He was a member of the Protective Order of Elks, the Masonic Lodge, and the cattlemen's exclusive Cheyenne Club in Cheyenne. Indeed, Bob Coble deplored his younger brother's "high stepping ideas." While Coble "entertains [on] . . . a most lavish scale," according to one observer, he "doesn't go in for women's society." In September 1895, John Coble, while in his cups, scandalized members of the Cheyenne Club by shooting up Thomas Mesker's painting *The Young Bull.* Although it was only a copy of a more famous painting by Paulus Potter, Coble maintained that this rendering of a bull was a "travesty on pure bred stock." Coble's employees at the Iron Mountain ranch were "the most hilarious lot of cowboys that section ever produced," according to the *Rocky Mountain News.* "The tales of the doings at the old Coble ranch would make interesting reading in a yellow backed novel."[9]

In some ways, John Coble represented the avant-garde of Wyoming's cattle barons. He believed the era of the range cattle industry was drawing to a close. As he and his co-manager, W. E. Lawrence, explained to a potential investor, Franklin Bosler, in July 1896, the future lay in smaller herds of no more than 5,000 to 6,000 head of pastured livestock. The herds were to be well cared for in the winter and fed on hay, rather than fending for themselves on the open range. Indeed, one of Coble's primary concerns was storing up sufficient hay to winter his herds. In August 1898, he informed Franklin Bosler that his cowhands were at work "in the hay field." "I think that is pretty good considering that most of the men are *Cow* punchers," he wrote. Losses were indeed greatly reduced, and a healthier (and hence, more profitable) herd was ready for the spring roundup. Coble and his partners guarded the company's interests closely. In another effort to induce Bosler to join the company, Coble assured him that "so long as I have the management of this ranch & business I will stake my life & all, that you will have fair treatment & consideration at all times. Everything will be open & above board," he promised. Relations between Coble and his partners were not always cordial. In 1898 W. E. Lawrence sold his interest to Franklin Bosler, attributing his decision to the "ill feeling" that had grown up between him and John Coble.[10]

Coble's bête noire were the one-man ranching operations and small homesteads that were moving into western Laramie County and eastern Albany County, the domain of the Iron Mountain Ranch Company. "Settlers are rapidly filling up the country," reported a Cheyenne dispatch in November 1895. "At the rate of this year's settlement, very few acres of vacant land will be left." These hardy souls were filing on key streams and fencing off their parcels, making the free movement of cattle more difficult. The fact that nesters were filtering into land between the four separate ranches that constituted the Iron Mountain Ranch Company was particularly galling to Coble. "This section of Wyo is becoming so fenced up by small owners," W. E. Lawrence (Coble's co-manager) complained to Franklin Bosler, in May 1898, "that there is not room enough to handle a herd the size of ours properly." Like most range barons, Coble, who was convinced that the small fry built their herds by stealing from the big companies, wanted these nesters driven out. Among the big ranches that adjoined Coble's domain, officials of the Swan Land and Cattle Company's Two Bar spread and Ora Haley, the largest cattleman in southern Wyoming, were radicals who endorsed the use of stern (and even lethal) measures against rustlers. On one occasion, Coble went so far as to fight off three would-be thieves with a rifle when they attempted to raid his herd.[11]

Among the small ranchers in Coble's immediate neighborhood, he regarded Kelsey (Kels) P. Nickell as a major problem. Nickell, known as a most contentious man, had to audacity not only to settle "in the middle of the Iron Mountain range," according to one report, but then proceeded to fence it off. Even though the range was still federal land, and Nickell proved up his parcel legally, John Coble subscribed to the cattlemen's dictum, "possession is nine points [of the law], and the [big] cattlemen got there first." Kels Nickell was "stubborn, red-headed, quarrelsome," according to one writer; another described him as "of middle height, with nervous, reddish-brown eyes, drooping red mustache and a firmly set mouth." "It wasn't his way to bend his back under adversity," recalled Edwin Smalley, who became Laramie County sheriff in 1901, "but to flail in with both fists." Needless to say, he often collided with his neighbors. A veteran of the Sioux campaigns, Nickell was reportedly one of the first bluecoats to arrive on the Little Big Horn battlefield after the Sioux and Cheyenne warriors dispatched George Armstrong Custer and his command in 1876. Kels and his wife, Mary, raised eight children.[12]

John Coble and Kels Nickell often quarreled. When Coble's cattle trespassed on Nickell land, the latter reacted in typically emotional fash-ion by threatening to poison his own land with Paris green in order to destroy Coble's intruding livestock. "You will not have a head of stock left," Nickell informed Charles Irwin, a Coble employee. In July 1890 Nickell confronted Coble and his foreman, George Cross, at the Iron Mountain railway depot and complained about trespassing cattle. When the foreman's explanation failed to satisfy Nickell, he pulled "a big knife," according to the *Daily Leader*. Cross picked up a stone to defend himself. As Cross tried to walk away, Nickell "made a pretty strong threat." Coble then reportedly tried "to talk the matter over quietly," according to this report, but "Nickells [*sic*], without a word, dashed at Coble with the knife and made two effective slashes . . . in the abdomen." Nickell denied this report, saying that he tried to walk away before the altercation led to violence. However, Coble and Cross followed him and continued to make threats, whereupon he had to defend himself. Coble filed assault charges against Nickell, who was incarcerated in Cheyenne. For several days, John Coble's condition was critical. His abdominal wounds were so deep that his entrails were ex-posed. Although the doctor feared peritonitis might set in, Coble even-tually recovered.[13]

This encounter, in which a homesteader inflicted a dangerous wound on a prominent cattle baron, attracted a great deal of atten-tion. When Kels Nickell's trial took place, one newsman described it grandiosely as "one of the most sensational criminal cases in the history of the county." Newspapers were clearly sympathetic with Coble, who could have died, and they characterized Nickell as a "ruffian" with "no standing whatever" who "bears a bad character in his neighborhood." Not only had he been in other fights, but when he sold meat in Cheyenne, he "never shows the hides" (implying that he was a thief). Nickell complained of inhumane treatment in jail, but he received very little sympathy. A notable aspect of the trial was the novel argument that Nickell's attorney, John C. Thompson, employed in his defense. Thompson argued that his client "was an arrant coward!" Nickell "cut Coble without knowing what he was doing," Thompson declared, "and while trying to escape." Although Nickell was eventually released, Coble, who was thin-skinned and sensitive to any affront to his dignity, never forgot this attack.[14]

In 1892 several of the big ranchers in the Iron Mountain area decided to take stern action against Kels Nickell and one of his neighbors, James Miller, both of whom were suspected of cattle theft. Harry J. Windsor, a sometime partner of John Coble, called for a meeting to discuss this problem. The gathering, which took place at the Andrew F. Whitman ranch on a Sunday afternoon, discussed measures that might "induce Nickell and Miller to leave the country." When no suitable suggestion was forthcoming, someone proposed that they should lynch Nickell. When this idea was voted down, the meeting broke up without a plan of action. However, one of those present, a man named Parker, "rode over to Nickell's alone and found him sitting inside his cabin door with his rifle on his knee." The wary granger, who had somehow learned about this meeting, was "waiting for the adjournment of that Sunday conclave" to learn his fate, according to the *Rocky Mountain News*. With such increasingly contentious animosities abounding in the Iron Mountain country, a tough detective like Tom Horn was bound to show up sooner or later.[15]

When Horn went to work for John Coble, apparently in 1895, it did not take long for the two men to realize that they shared a strong mutual hatred for livestock thieves. Coble later admitted that "a great personal friendship grew up between them," and when Horn faced the hangman's noose, in November 1903, he wrote his former employer: "if ever a man had a true friend, you have proven yourself one to me." In spite of their unequal wealth and social position, Horn soon referred to his employer as "Johnny" and had free run of the ranch. Bob Coble explained his brother's dependence upon Tom Horn by saying that John Coble had lost confidence in range detectives until he met Horn. The other detectives he had hired were shifty, unreliable, ineffectual in detecting rustlers, and yet demanded their pay. Coble regarded his introduction to Horn as a stroke of good fortune. "We got to have someone to ride the ranges [against rustlers]," Bob Coble observed, "and it must be a man who can do the work without bringing the matters into court." Horn was that man. Of course neither John Coble nor Tom Horn could foresee where their association would lead. When Horn stood trial for murder, in October 1902, the *Denver Post* reflected on Horn's lethal acquaintance with "a cattleman from Pennsylvania who believed that ranching in Wyoming could be conduc[t]ed on a strictly Western basis, without regard to the fact that the state had well defined limits and a duly established representative of law and order in the capital at Cheyenne." Unfortunately, Tom Horn did not realize the depth of the animosities in the Iron Mountain Region when he signed on with Coble, observed Dean Krakel. Tom Horn "was asking for trouble."[16]

By the time Tom Horn arrived in Wyoming, the cattle companies no longer dominated the economy. Whether his employer was the Wyoming Live Stock Association or an individual cattle company, the various forces working against the industry in the 1880s and '90s— natural, human, and economic—had reduced the herds of the "beef bonanza" kings in Wyoming from a peak figure of 1.5 million head to a mere 300,000. As many cattle companies disbanded or reduced their scale of operations, or even added sheep to their inventory, the number of the WSGA's dues-paying members also declined from 400 members in the early 1880s to 96 (only 81 had paid their dues) in 1893. The funds available to pay range detectives and brand inspectors were reduced commensurately. Yet a few diehard radicals clung to their advocacy of direct action toward nesters and small ranchers—hence the employment of Tom Horn. Unfortunately, this unwary former scout went into the service of a declining institution and lacked the perspective to understand the fragility of the cattlemen's position. Tom Horn was, in effect, attaching himself to an anachronism.[17]

When Horn began to patrol the Iron Mountain Ranch Company's range in 1895, there were signs that extreme measures against suspected rustlers were passé and that county sheriffs and local juries were becoming more responsive to the barons' complaints. Even John Clay, Jr., a

fervent enemy of the homestead element, admitted in his presidential
address to the WSGA in 1896 that the local law enforcement system
was protecting their herds much better than before. Yet Clay believed
things could be better. In his semifictional piece "The Fate of a Cattle
Rustler," written in 1910, Clay has Al Bowie, the Two Bar foreman,
remark to Tom Horn, "Those Cheyenne juries are not worth the powder to blow them into ———." And even though the WSGA refused
to endorse extreme measures like assassination as a means to suppress
livestock theft, some individual cattlemen continued to believe in taking the law into their own hands. In a surprisingly candid letter to Doc
Shores in July 1897, James McParland, superintendent of the Denver
branch of the Pinkerton Agency, raised the possibility of detectives
joining livestock men in a campaign against Wyoming cattle thieves.
"The Southern and North Western counties of Wyoming are pretty
badly in the hands of outlaws," he wrote. "I will say to you 'confidentially' that they [ranchers] have come to me time and again asking if I
would send a good killer up there," he continued, but "I told them that
we were not in that kind of business."[18]

While Johnson County and its immediate neighbors received the
most publicity for rustling problems, some southern counties experienced similar problems. Cattlemen in these latter counties were among
the ranchers who asked McParland for "a good killer." No doubt
McParland's letter referred to Laramie and Albany counties, where officials of the Swan Land and Cattle Company and the Iron Mountain
Ranch Company, among others, were still experiencing some frustra-
tion in the prosecution of livestock thieves. Some suspects, for example,
were repeat offenders. In September 1895, the Swan Land and Cattle
Company charged James Cleve with stealing a calf. Cleve, whom Tom
Horn had arrested along with Eva Langhoff in 1893, was released by a
friendly judge. William Lewis, a British immigrant who owned a one-
man spread on Horse Creek a few miles south of Iron Mountain, was
another problem. Lewis, who had been suspected of cattle theft for
some time, and who was regarded as "a very disagreeable neighbor,"
according to the Cheyenne *Sun-Leader,* apparently exhausted the patience of the big cattlemen—the "radicals"—in the region. He probably should have taken heed when both John Coble and John Clay filed
charges against him in 1893 and again in 1894 and 1895. However, "the
general feeling of the population toward the large livestock owners was

antagonistic and defiant," according to one historian, and local juries routinely refused to convict people like William Lewis. When Lewis filed damage suits totaling $15,000 against the Swan, Coble, and Laramie County Sheriff Ira L. Fredendall for false arrest, it was his last act of defiance. The cattle barons had reached the end of their tether and felt compelled to employ more direct means against this nettlesome problem.[19]

Since his last appearance in the Laramie County court, two unsuccessful attempts had been made on Lewis's life, and he "often expressed himself as fearing for his life," said the Laramie *Boomerang*. Yet when arsonists torched his house, he rented a neighboring ranch building and continued to run a small herd. On Saturday, 3 August 1895, John Whittaker, a neighboring rancher, with his foreman, George Shanton, discovered Lewis's lifeless body in his corral. Whittaker summoned Sheriff Ira Fredendall and Coroner Edwin P. Rohrbaugh from Cheyenne. Shanton examined the area but found no solid evidence. Lewis was shot three times. From the degree of decomposition, Rohrbaugh placed the death on 31 July or 1 August. A coroner's jury, convened at the scene, issued the usual verdict that the deceased had died at the hands of "some person or persons unknown." Governor William Alford Richards offered a $500 reward.[20]

Sheriff Fredendall faced an uphill battle as he sought evidence in the Lewis murder. It was not difficult to find motives for this assassination. Not only did the cattle companies want to be rid of him, but Lewis's nester neighbors did not like the cantankerous Englishman either. "All the people within a radius of fifteen miles of Lewis' place say that they are glad that he is dead," said the *Daily Sun*. Yet no one, wrote Mark Dugan, had a better motive "than the Swan Land and Cattle Company, John Coble, and the others Lewis had sued." Furthermore, Fredendall found hides from stolen cattle at Lewis's ranch. Given the general disdain for the dead man, newsmen predicted (rightly) that the $500 reward would not "stir his former neighbors up to action in hunting his murderers." After making a good faith effort, Sheriff Fredendall had to admit that he had "not the slightest clue" as to the identity of the murderer.

This brutal assassination was an ominous sign that the cattle interests were bent on escalating the "war" against rustlers. In recalling that only three years had passed since the cattlemen's invasion of Johnson

County, the *Rocky Mountain News* asked, "Does this murder of Lewis indicate that the men employed in that raid [in Johnson County] are again coming to the surface [?]" Obviously fearing the worst, the *News* urged Wyoming Governor Richards to "bring the whole executive power of the state" to bear in the Lewis case before another large-scale disturbance materialized. The *Carbon County Journal,* in Rawlins, suggested that Billy Lewis "was killed either by one of the cattlemen" in the Iron Mountain region or, more probably, "the killing was done at the suggestion of one of the large [cattle] companies." Whatever the motive for this brutal slaying, another observer remarked, "the assertion is made openly [in Cheyenne] that no one will ever be punished for the crime"—a prescient observation.[21]

On 10 September 1895, Frederick U. Powell was shot to death in the same area as Billy Lewis. Powell, who had lost an arm in a railroad accident, lived with his wife and small son, William, on Horse Creek, just inside Albany County. Like Lewis, the big cattlemen suspected Powell of livestock theft. When a rancher caught Powell with "nine of my beeves killed and ready for shipping" and informed Albany County Sheriff Mortimer N. Grant, this officer replied "that there was nothing we could do." "I was only one of those who suffered" from Powell's nefarious acts, the anonymous stockman added. Also like Billy Lewis, Fred Powell feuded with his neighbors and even served a jail sentence for setting fire to the property of a neighbor. Shortly before his death, Powell received a threatening letter: "Mr. Powell—This is your third and last warning. There are three things for you to do—quit killing other people's cattle or be killed yourself, or leave the country yourself at once." Even though Powell resided in Albany County, Laramie County Sheriff Fredendall, who was familiar with these Iron Mountain squabbles, personally urged Powell to move away. Unfortunately, he moved too slowly. Unlike the Lewis murder, there was a witness to the assassination of Fred Powell. Andrew Ross, who was helping Powell put up hay, heard the fatal shot and attempted to assist the mortally wounded man. However, there was nothing that Ross could do except inform a passing mail carrier, who carried the news to Sheriff Grant.[22]

In examining the murder scene, the sheriff found evidence that the killer fired shots from a rise about 250 feet from his victim. After Andrew Ross departed the scene to talk with the postal worker, the assassin evidently "walked down to examine the body," inadvertently leaving a size 8 boot print. (The killer might have also fired a pistol shot into Powell's body at close range.) The sheriff was unable to identify the owner of the boot print but noted that the assassin's "foot prints were also well sunken into the sand," according to one reporter, indicating that the killer "was a rather heavy man." "The work of killing Powell was an excellent piece of nerve and marksmanship," added this newsman, as the victim "was shot in the heart." A coroner's jury returned the standard verdict. Even though Sheriff Grant had "an idea" as to the killer's identity, the Laramie *Daily Boomerang* concluded that it was unlikely that the murderer would ever be apprehended. Speculation was widespread that the killer was "a man hired for the purpose"—a man who killed for money—and the men who hired the assassin had five more names on their list. On 11 September, the day after the murder, this same newspaper reported that "the men who furnished the money for the killing are having trouble with the man hired to do the work." The hit man demanded $1,000 each for the murders of Lewis and Powell, according to this report, "while the employers claim that they contracted for the work at $500." "The man who acted directly as the employer of the assassin," added the *Boomerang,* "is heartily sick of the entire transaction." Something good could come from this squabble, the reporter concluded: "there will probably not be any more killing."[23]

While it was clear that no arrests would be forthcoming in either case, speculation abounded on the streets of Laramie and Cheyenne. Even more disconcerting, "the names of parties implicated are freely spoken of on the streets," the *Daily Sun-Leader* remarked. (This information was either withheld from lawmen, or they lacked solid evidence to act.) On 16 September 1895, a Cheyenne dispatch to the *Rocky Mountain News* reported that "a prominent ranchman" had boasted openly in a Cheyenne bar immediately after the Lewis killing that he knew the murderer, and this anonymous cattleman predicted that Fred Powell would also be shot. A few days later, William Green, a small rancher northwest of Cheyenne, was found dead from a gunshot wound. Local cattlemen had accused him of cattle theft, ransacked his cabin, and threatened his life. When a coroner's jury ruled that Green had taken his own life, the investigation ended.[24]

While the facts of the Lewis and Powell killings did not fully emerge until Tom Horn's trial for murder seven years later, rumors on the streets of Cheyenne and Laramie in September 1895 held that John C.

Coble was the money man and Tom Horn the assassin. "This precious pair of a Pennsylvania cattleman and a professional killer are said to have planned an active campaign against . . . undesirable neighbors" in the Iron Mountain area, remarked the *Denver Post* in October 1902. Coble and Horn embarked on this campaign "on account of a propensity of cattle stealing or taking up of land that other people [cattle barons] wanted," added the *Post*. Somehow, the small fry "must be persuaded to make way for their betters." If the big ranchers' purpose was to frighten settlers out of the Iron Mountain region, they succeeded to some degree. "Several people have left the Horse Creek region," according to one report, "fearing that they might be . . . on the death list."[25]

Tom Horn's intimidation tactics were not subtle. He wanted people to see him. Mary Powell, widow of the murdered man, recalled that they had observed him at a distance in the fall of 1893, evidently when he was working on the Eva Langhoff case. Later, the Powells encountered the detective face-to-face while they were rounding up cattle on Horse Creek. Mary observed Horn stealthily trailing Fred "a short distance" behind. Just a few weeks before Fred Powell was murdered, someone shot at him. While Powell suspected this same man as the shooter, a second suspicious character soon entered the picture. Shortly before Fred Powell was gunned down, his nine-year-old son, William, happened upon a stranger lying on the bank of Horse Creek. Running to his parents, the boy said excitedly that this mysterious man, who was riding a Two-Bar horse, was "quite large and clean shaven." If this stranger was Tom Horn, perhaps his purpose in moving about so openly was to terrorize people whom his employers wanted to leave the region. When Fred Powell did not scare, Horn may have felt compelled to kill him.[26]

The *Rocky Mountain News,* which took the side of the homesteaders and encouraged Democratic Party affairs in Wyoming, made a significant move that would enable it to better cover these Wyoming problems. On 4 October 1895, the *News* announced the establishment of a permanent news bureau in Cheyenne. This liberal, reformist paper, which had been the first to report the cattlemen's invasion of Johnson County in 1892, exercised a great influence on public opinion in the central Rocky Mountain region. With veteran journalist George R. Caldwell in charge of the Cheyenne bureau, the *News* declared that its purpose was to fight "public corruptionists irrespective of their personality or party affiliation" in Wyoming and be "a fearless exponent of the rights of the people." This newspaper had long maintained a paternalistic attitude toward its youthful northern neighbor and steadfastly opposed the mendacity of the cattle barons. Furthermore, Denver— "The Hub of the West"—had outdistanced all competitors in the central Rocky Mountain region in economic growth and was pulling Cheyenne and surrounding communities into its orbit. By helping to mold public opinion in southern Wyoming, the *Rocky Mountain News* was making the Cowboy State susceptible to public scrutiny. Later the *Denver Post,* a major competitor of the *News,* established its own news bureau in Cheyenne.[27]

In the meantime, Judge Richard H. Scott of the First Judicial District summoned a special grand jury to meet in Cheyenne on Tuesday, 1 October, to investigate the Lewis and Powell murders. (Even though Fred Powell was killed in Albany County, the two killings were presumed to be connected.) When John A. Baird, the Laramie County prosecutor, promised as "thorough an examination as possible," the *Daily Boomerang* in neighboring Albany County predicted "startling developments" would result. When Sheriff Fredendall began to serve subpoenas for witnesses in the Iron Mountain community, one important witness, range detective Tom Horn, could not be found. He had reportedly "fled for parts unknown," according to the *Boomerang.* Nor could the lawman find rancher William L. Clay, who was known to be close to the detective. When the sheriff finally located Horn and Clay in Bates Hole, near Casper, he sent Deputy F. C. Thomasson to retrieve them. Thomasson found Clay, but he had to leave a summons for Horn with the Natrona County sheriff, who was able to serve the document. Not since Horn brought the Langhoff gang to Cheyenne in November 1893 had he attracted such attention. As events transpired, Horn soon wired Fredendall from Glenrock, Wyoming, promising to answer the summons. "Tom Horn and W. L. Clay Present from Bates' Hole" was the *Wyoming Tribune* headline on 3 October. Tom Horn's employer, John C. Coble, was also among those summoned.[28]

When grand jurors took their seats on 1 October, Judge Scott, who was obviously anxious to forestall further range wars, reminded the jurors that "the standard of a community is always measured by its respect for and enforcement of the law." He assured them that not only were their deliberations secret, but that they were free to "express . . .

opinions and ideas as to the crime in this jurisdiction." After examining sixteen witnesses in the first two days, the grand jury adjourned until the following Saturday, in order to summon "important witnesses." At the same time, the *Rocky Mountain News* broke a startling story concerning the Lewis case. Mary Powell recalled that her husband, Fred, sent their son, Billy, on an errand to William Lewis's ranch shortly before he was killed. As Billy Powell approached the Lewis residence, two men armed with rifles "leaped from a clump of brush." When they realized Billy Powell was not the person they were after, they quickly retreated. Lewis was murdered a short time later. Within a few days, "the Powell boy saw one of the same men lurking near his father's ranch." Soon thereafter, Fred Powell was killed.[29]

Billy Powell was the subject of an even more dramatic moment during the grand jury hearings. While he and his mother were standing outside the courthouse, the nine-year-old suddenly "shrank behind his mother's skirts and pointing to one of a [group?] near at hand cried out: 'Oh, mama, there is one of the men who was [there?] with guns.'" When he regained his composure, the boy added, according to the *Rocky Mountain News,* "and he is the man who hid close to our ranch when father was killed." While the newspaper refrained from naming him, it was later said that Tom Horn was that man. Young Billy's outburst created quite a stir among bystanders and prompted the jury to question both Mary Powell and her son on the morning of Saturday 5 October. "Public indignation is rapidly approaching a white heat" continued the *News,* "and nothing short of the finding of a true bill against these assassins of the brush covert and the midnight hour will satisfy the people."[30]

Tom Horn had another tense moment during the grand jury session when Kels Nickell, the Iron Mountain homesteader, confronted him about his activities in the Iron Mountain community. Nickell, who may have suspected that Horn had assassinated his neighbors, Lewis and Powell, recalled this confrontation six years later while testifying before the coroner's jury that investigated the murder of his son, Willie Nickell. Kels Nickell testified:

I said, "Tom, if you got any business in my vicinity, I am going to tell you now, you keep [to] the road because I have heard a whole lot. I know there is a whole lot of [criminal] things done; I don't know for sure whether you are doing this business [assassination]." I said, "If you have any business about my place come like a man. . . . After knowing what I know if it would be possible to kill you I would kill you." I said, "If I didn't have a rifle I would make a sneak [attack] on you." He [Horn] said, "I am perfectly satisfied; I will tell you now, I will never make no sneaks; if I have business at your place I will come there [openly]."

When asked on the witness stand if Kels Nickell said these things, Horn denied the incident. "No, sir, I wouldn't allow fifteen of the worst men in the world to tell me that," he remarked defiantly. "He wouldn't tell me half before I would have got him to stop." The truth was that this "hick" of a homesteader, who had nearly killed the detective's employer, John C. Coble, had also forced the veteran range detective to back down.[31]

During the grand jury proceedings, the *Daily Boomerang* printed a story that it believed would be "of great assistance in running the murderer of F. U. Powell and William Lewis to earth." Although the reporter refrained from mentioning Tom Horn by name, the reader was clearly free to make the connection. While riding through the Horse Creek area, an unnamed Laramie resident overheard two locals talking about a mysterious man who was observing their movements with field glasses from a nearby hill:

> "Say, did you see him [Horn] on duty up there," remarked one to the other.
> "No I did not see him," was the response.
> "Well, you can bet that he saw us and knew us," replied the speaker.

"It is supposed that reference was made to the murderer of Powell," continued the *Boomerang*, "and the fact that he had seen and known them shows that he was known by these men to be equipped with a field glass." Furthermore, the person who reported this conversation to the Laramie newspaper "recalled that he had seen a [mounted] man in the vicinity of Powell's house with a gun."[32]

In spite of questioning numerous witnesses, the grand jury managed to gather only "hearsay" evidence in the Lewis case. Thus far, witnesses "have received their information from someone else," according to the

Boomerang, "and the someone else has got his from Mr. So and So, and so on." People who boasted that they knew the "facts," the *Cheyenne Daily Sun-Leader* observed, "have declined to testify." Apparently, the big cattlemen in the Iron Mountain area had succeeded in so intimidating potential witnesses that they refused to talk. In spite of growing public doubt as to the aggressiveness of the grand jury's investigation, some still believed that "one or more indictments will be found."

Cattleman Will Irvine, who was a passenger on the same train that carried Horn to Cheyenne for the grand jury proceedings, recalled that the detective "talked freely to me." "They are trying to implicate me in this recent killing," he said to Irvine, "but they will find I know what constitutes evidence." The following morning, Irvine observed Tom Horn at the courthouse nonchalantly "pitching at a crack in the floor for a dollar a throw [!]" Evidently, he was "not in the slightest worried [while] waiting his turn to be called by the Grand Jury." Horn protested that he was a hundred miles away in Bates Hole when Billy Lewis was killed. But reports that Tom Horn had "left the jurisdiction" of Sheriff Fredendall at the very moment the officer had a subpoena for him are not suggestive of innocence.[33]

During the grand jury's deliberations, the *Rocky Mountain News* tried to impress upon the panel members that this was a critical moment in the maturity of their state. An editorial urged the jurors to ask themselves "in whose instance and for whose behoof [*sic*] they are being financially victimized at home and held up to execration abroad." The answer was obvious, continued the editorial: "Is it not written in letters of blood upon the records of cattle barons . . . [who] have ever been a law unto themselves and consequently lawless to others[?]" The writer reminded the people of Wyoming of "the mercenary adventurer, the ready Winchester and the prepared torch" with which the "lords of the Wyoming ranges have guided themselves" for many years. Declaring, like Louis XIV of France, "I am the state," continued this newsman, "the cattle baron has said that the small stockman and ranchers must go, and go he must, even if it is feet foremost." The *News* advocated "a prompt and merciless enforcement of the laws" in Wyoming and "the formation of a popular political sentiment" that would vote responsible men into governmental office. "In the Lewis and Powell assassination cases the people expect first, indictment, and second, conviction." Unfortunately, this Denver editorialist was a few years ahead of his time.[34]

When the grand jury reconvened on Saturday 12 October, there was still some hope for an indictment in the Lewis case. As many as thirty witnesses were present for questioning, although not all were interrogated. Even though the panel remained in session until late Saturday evening, no indictments were found. When it became clear to Judge Scott that the jury would take no action, he adjourned the panel sine die (with no future date for reconvening), according to the *Daily Sun-Leader.* "While the grand jury labored earnestly in the effort to arrive at the facts of the murder of William Lewis," said the panel's report, "we are unable to discover sufficient evidence upon which to find an indictment."[35]

Although Tom Horn was in Cheyenne twice during the grand jury's proceedings, there is no indication that the jury actually questioned him. In recalling his subpoena some years later, Horn said he "reported to Col. Baird" and that he "just simply told where I was" at the time of Lewis's assassination, alleging that he was at Bates Hole. Apparently, Horn meant that he talked with the prosecuting attorney, rather than going before the grand jury. In reporting these deliberations, George Caldwell, the *Rocky Mountain News* Cheyenne bureau chief, confirmed this, stating that neither Coble nor Horn nor the younger Whittaker was called before the jury. This was an especially glaring omission, he added indignantly, since "no three persons were more recently connected with the [Lewis] case than these." Unfortunately, Caldwell failed to elaborate on this statement. Apparently, this was the only time during the grand jury proceedings that a newspaper suggested in print that Tom Horn was a prominent suspect in the Lewis murder (the first newspaper mention of Horn in this case was simply a report of a summons to appear before the grand jury). It was also the first time that the names of Horn and Coble were associated in print. (The Whittaker referred to could have been one of two brothers, Dugald R. and John Whittaker, who were ranchers in the Iron Mountain area.)[36]

An inquisitive citizen did not have to go far to find an explanation for the grand jury's failure to return an indictment. "The cattle barons of Laramie county and their henchmen" have a right to be "jubilant," exclaimed the *Rocky Mountain News,* since they had succeeded in terrorizing both jurors and witnesses. Laramie County District Attorney Baird "says that grand jury witnesses . . . personally told him they were afraid to tell what they knew," added the *News.* Some jurors were so afraid that they asked witnesses only "the most cursory questions." Furthermore, Laramie county officials "were afraid to do their full duty," continued the *News* accusingly. They feared "the political vengeance of the state gang—a gang which has ever been in close, interested and natural allegiance with range combinations." Even if the jurors did not question Horn, a rumor circulated that a number of the grand jurors were "satisfied in their own minds as to who caused the death of Lewis"—presumably meaning Tom Horn. Apparently, they voted on a true bill against Tom Horn, although this fact did not come out at the time. Some years later, when Horn faced the hangman's noose for another crime, the *Laramie Republican* said that the grand jury in the Lewis case "came within two votes of bringing an indictment against Horn." Since an indictment required a minimum of nine of the twelve jurors, at least seven must have voted for a true bill against the range detective. Another report also held "that Horn's friends came to his rescue with their money," implying that the range barons employed bribery in some fashion.[37]

Since a grand jury normally accompanied all district court sessions, the forthcoming Albany County court term in Laramie would presumably investigate the murder of Fred Powell. The *Rocky Mountain News,* still hopeful that the people of Wyoming would rise to the occasion, reminded them that "there is another chance of these secret slayings being brought home to their cowardly perpetrators." Unfortunately, this was not to be the case. On 23 October, the *Daily Boomerang* made the startling announcement that "there is no truth in the report that a grand jury will be summoned at this place." Since some sort of explanation was called for, this newsman declared that a delegation of Albany County officials had visited Cheyenne during its recent grand jury session "to learn from the officials there whether they had any information that could be used here [in the Powell case]." Unfortunately, the authorities in the state capital "knew of no clue regarding the killing of Powell." Consequently, the search for Powell's killer "is practically abandoned," concluded the *Boomerang,* "if, indeed, anything has ever been done."[38]

No doubt Albany County Sheriff Mortimer N. Grant took offense at this criticism of his office. Well over six feet tall, Mortimer Grant, a cousin of Ulysses Grant, who had been a delegate to Wyoming's state constitutional convention, took pride in doing his duty. In investigating both the Lewis and Powell murders, he recalled, "I had enough circum-stantial evidence to convince me that Horn had killed those ranchmen. . . . I did all in my power to run the murderer down." In the Powell case, he continued, "I found tracks plainly made where the murderer went down to see if his victim was dead." Grant insisted that he measured these footprints and later, when an opportunity (fortuitously) arose, "I measured his [Horn's] feet while he was asleep and they fit the measurements exactly." If his recollections are to be believed, Grant managed to slip into Horn's hotel room in Cheyenne or Laramie and, while the detective was passed out after a drunken binge, examine his feet—a bizarre event that would have been very embarrassing to the supposedly vigilant ex-scout had he known about it. In regard to the Billy Lewis assassination, Mortimer Grant declared that he was able to detect signs of Tom Horn's movements "in and out" of Billy Lewis's corral. The Albany County sheriff went so far as "to get a detective and special assistance" in Denver, but this effort was apparently unsuccessful. Unfortunately, Grant was defeated at the next election, a loss he attributed to having been "too active in the pursuit of the murderer [of Powell] for my own good."[39]

Inexplicably, Tom Horn boasted about his assassination of Billy Lewis and Fred Powell in Cheyenne and Laramie saloons. Will Irvine, who was among the cattlemen's inner circle, concluded from Horn's conduct that the detective "undoubtedly" murdered both Lewis and Powell. In a letter to Charles Penrose, in 1914, Irvine remarked that Horn "would kill without the slightest compunction or feeling when he was certain he [the victim] was a guilty man." The range detective had "been laying for [Lewis] . . . for some time," continued Irvine. After observing Lewis "kill a beef not his own," Horn "deliberately followed him into his own corrall [sic], shook hands with him, [and] killed him." By leaving his victim "dead with his own [stolen] beef," added Irvine, Horn was leaving a warning to other thieves. Horn reportedly boasted later that as he pointed his revolver at Lewis, who realized he was about to die, terror swept across his face and he let out a terrible scream. In conversation with Deputy U.S. Marshal Joe LeFors in 1902, Horn remarked callously that Lewis "'was the scaredest [sic] S.O.B. you ever saw.'" Shortly after the Lewis and Powell assassinations, Horn encountered Doc Shores, his old Pinkerton associate; told Shores "what he was doing," meaning killing for money; and even went so far as to explain how he had killed the two men. When Shores realized that his old friend felt no remorse, Shores "quit corresponding with him." With such rumors circulating in Wyoming, no wonder the public harbored such disdain for Tom Horn. From the time of the Lewis and Powell murders, he remained what would today be called "a person of interest" to Wyoming lawmen.[40]

That fear and intimidation interfered with the Lewis and Powell murder investigations was readily apparent. The inhabitants of the Iron Mountain country had "a wholesome fear of the fate which might overtake anyone who gave evidence tending to incriminate" Tom Horn, observed the *Denver Times*. Robert Ellsworth "Bud" Cowan, the Coble cowhand who broke horses with Tom Horn, admitted to the existence of such fear. Cowan and George R. Shanton, John Coble's foreman in 1895, had the unpleasant distinction of having arrived at both the Lewis and Powell murder scenes shortly after these tragic events. In regard to the Lewis killing, Horn "left tracks in that corral, too!" insisted Cowan. "You could see where he got off his horse and walked up facing Lewis." Although Horn shot Lewis "near the heart," he added, "he lived to drag himself halfway to the house, leaving a trail of blood."[41]

Cowan and Shanton happened to be working cattle near the Powell ranch on the day of Powell's death. Many years later, in 1926, Cowan declared: "Now I positively know that Tom Horn was on Horse Creek, not more than three miles from Powell's ranch, two or three hours before the killing." "George Shanton and I met him there and talked with him for a while," continued Cowan. After leaving Horn, the two cowhands continued their work and eventually arrived at Powell's ranch "about thirty minutes after the killing of Powell." Cowan and Shanton, who examined the murder scene, detected clear indications that Tom Horn lay in wait "behind some rocks across the creek." "Tom always had a habit of sitting down on his heels while he talked or killed time," wrote Cowan, "and would break up little sticks or twigs—pine needles, dry leaves, anything within reach that he could snap in his fingers." Afterward the detective "would leave the pieces in a little pile in front of him." If Horn was killing time in a cabin, said Cowan, "he would whittle or break up splinters." Cowan and Shanton found not only a sizable pile of twigs at the ambush site, but boot prints as well, indicating that Horn "had waited there for some time."[42]

In his autobiography, *Range Rider,* which appeared in 1930, Bud Cowan slightly revised his version of the Powell killing. Cowan said he and Shanton saw the range detective "riding like a wild Indian" away from the Powell ranch. "We both waved at him," said Cowan, "but he never stopped." When the two cowpunchers rode up to the Powell ranch, they came upon Mary Powell and her son, William. Both of them were crying. When the two men reached the hayfield and spied Powell's body, continued Cowan, "we both understood why Tom Horn was in such a hurry." They carried Powell's body up to the ranch house, Cowan recalled, and "then we went to Laramie and got the sheriff and coroner." While there is no reason to doubt that Cowan and Shanton saw Tom Horn near the Powell ranch, Cowan's memory may have failed him in some details. Cowan said he and Shanton were not summoned to testify before the grand jury in the Lewis murder, but the *Daily Boomerang* listed George Shanton as one of the men called to testify on 12 October 1895. A Tom Shanton, perhaps George's brother, was also summoned. In a separate letter to *The Frontier*, in 1925, George Shanton said that he and his fellow cowhands were convinced in the fall of 1895 that "the whisperings against Tom Horn were more or less confirmed." The range detective would disappear "at unexpected moments for five, six and ten days at a time," Shanton remarked, and he would always take the best horses—the "rimrockers"—"that had won reputations for their ability to cover the longest distances in the shortest possible time."[43]

If Cowan and Shanton knew so much about these murders, one wonders why they did not present their observations to the grand jury in Cheyenne. Fear and intimidation had much to do with it, not to mention the frontier code against ratting on a friend. "You don't betray a friend if you can help it," protested Cowan, "no matter what he does." And finally, the two cowhands "pledged ourselves to secrecy about meeting Tom on the road," Cowan admitted, "because it wasn't healthy for anyone to know too much in that country." Yet "nearly everyone around . . . knew in their hearts that Tom Horn killed Powell," admitted Cowan. Apparently, Tom Horn was not concerned about his encounter with Cowan and Shanton and had already made elaborate plans to establish that he was a hundred miles away. In 1902 the *Cheyenne Daily Leader* reported that "a man familiar with the circumstances" of Powell's death insisted that Horn shot him early in the morning and then rode frantically to Bates Hole. Horn, "a marvelous rider," according to this anonymous informant, "dashed off to the ranch of a friend twelve or fifteen miles away" and from there had a series of relay horses every fifteen miles, arriving in Bates Hole about 7 P.M. This ride was "not such a remarkable feat"; a good rider could average eight miles an hour.[44]

Tom Horn reportedly demanded payment of $600 each for the Lewis and Powell murders. In both cases, John C. Coble of the Iron Mountain Cattle Company and John Clay, Jr., manager of the Swan Land and Cattle Company, were suspected of being the moneymen. Presumably, the report of a "falling out" between the gunman and his employers that followed upon the heels of the Lewis killing referred to these wealthy cattlemen. In his subsequent investigation of Horn's crimes, in 1901, Deputy U.S. Marshal Joseph LeFors talked with a man named George Prentice, an employee of the Swan Land and Cattle Company, who admitted serving as a payoff man for Horn's "jobs." "Prentice paid Horn on the train between Cheyenne and Denver," according to LeFors. In Horn's confession to LeFors in January 1902, he also admitted receiving his pay "on the train between Cheyenne and Denver." This may have been only a partial payment, since Walter Stoll, who prosecuted Horn for murder in 1902, informed the *Daily Leader* that a Cheyenne resident had met Horn in a local hotel and turned over part of the money due him for these 1895 assassinations. While Laramie County officers "knew the name of the cattleman who made this money available," said this Cheyenne journal, "they refused to divulge it."[45]

The belief that Tom Horn murdered William Lewis and Fred Powell was widespread but not unanimous. Even Mary Powell, widow of the murdered man, eventually concluded that Horn was not responsible for her husband's death. She believed Etherton P. Baker, a neighbor with whom Fred Powell often quarreled, was the guilty party. Mark Dugan, who researched both murders, concluded that the big ranchers hired Horn to kill Lewis, a known thief, but that the barons had no evidence of rustling against Powell. This is puzzling since Powell was earlier suspected of cattle theft. However, Powell also squabbled with other homesteaders in his neighborhood, as did Billy Lewis. Chip Carlson, a keen student of Tom Horn's Wyoming years, maintains that Horn was not guilty of either murder. Carlson concludes that Horn's "brash proposals, his heavy-handed methods, and his braggadocio concerning the Langhoff incident contributed to his reputation as an intimidating, fearsome detective." In any case, Horn was a logical suspect in both assassinations, and the observations of Bud Cowan and George Shanton, as well as the suspicions of the Laramie County grand jury, strongly suggest his guilt.[46]

Apparently, the livestock barons who supported Tom Horn were surprised at the intense outburst of public feeling that the Lewis and Powell murders provoked. Indeed, the degree of outrage was so great, Will Irvine recalled, that "it was necessary to stop it." While Irvine maintained that he made no monetary contribution to the "kitty" for Tom Horn's murderous deeds, he boasted that he played a part in preventing further killings. It happened that "the go between, between Horn and his principal" was recuperating from an illness at the Cheyenne Club. This unnamed cattleman knew Irvine well and confided in him. After the murder of Powell, "there was such a Devil of a stink that I went to him and advised him to pull Horn off," said Irvine. At that moment, he added, Horn was then "up in Bates Hole laying for a third [victim].". This intermediary "took my advice," said Irvine, and the killing stopped.[47]

Even though the killing stopped, the citizens of Wyoming refused to forget the two brutal slayings and were often reminded of them by subsequent events. When a Mrs. Wurl, wife of a rancher near Tie Siding, Wyoming, was brutally murdered in December 1896, investigators reportedly concluded that she "was killed through the same instrumentality that caused the death of Powell and Lewis." Since Mr. Wurl was not "in any way . . . identified with the cattle rustling element," this line of investigation was soon dropped. It remained possible that future grand juries would resurrect the Lewis and Powell cases. In February 1897, an Albany County grand jury in Laramie took up the Fred Powell case and made "a diligent investigation," according to one report, but failed to muster evidence "strong enough to warrant action by the jury."[48]

Such extreme measures were simply not necessary, in the view of James McParland, the Pinkerton official in Denver. In a letter to Doc Shores, in July 1897, McParland expressed the opinion that the barons' effort "to kill off these fellows [rustlers] has not been successful." His suggestion for a remedy was simple enough. "If these Cattle and Sheep men who have made fortunes would have only thrown Politics aside and invested a little money in electing the proper county officers who would inforce [sic] the Law," McParland remarked, "they could soon have rid the country of these outlaws." If they had followed his advice, continued the Pinkerton man, he would have sent "a couple of men into their country who would co-operate with the gang for a while until we were able to jump them." However, the cattle barons considered this procedure too expensive, and as a result, McParland believed, "these Rustlers will soon have [control of] the whole country."[49]

While the livestock interests who had hired Tom Horn might not agree with McParland's recommendation, they were sufficiently alarmed at the degree of public outcry following the Lewis and Powell assassinations to abandon such extreme measures for a while. Whether Tom Horn's employer, John Coble, made the decision to send the detective out of the state or not, he suddenly disappeared from his old range in late November 1895. As Cheyenne journalist John Charles Thompson later recalled after the Lewis and Powell killings, "the finger of suspicion pointed so accusingly at Horn that there was a lull in assassinations." On 28 November 1895, the *Denver Post* announced that "Tom Horn, the Wyoming detective, is in town." "It was he who captured the Rio Grande train robbers in 1891," added the reporter, "and who recently broke up a gang of Wyoming cattle thieves." (It is tempting to conclude that Horn met George Prentice for his payoff on this train trip to Denver.) Whatever his reason for traveling to Denver, Tom Horn soon left Wyoming, presumably for good.[50]

CHAPTER 8

Adventurer

When Tom Horn left Wyoming, it was only natural that he would return to the area that he called home, Aravaipa Canyon, in Graham County, Arizona. In mid-December 1895, Horn wrote to his old friend and former employer, Burt Dunlap, informing him that he would arrive about the first of January. The return of the former scout and "boss cattle tyer" was a locally newsworthy event, and Burt Dunlap and his brother, Horace, were happy to have his services again. Burt, who was active in Republican Party politics and often away from his ranch, put Horn to work immediately. In March 1896, the Willcox *Sulphur Valley News* reported that Tom Horn—than whom "no cowboy is better known in southern Arizona"—was now foreman of the Dunlaps' Western Reserve Ranch.[1]

Tom Horn returned to Arizona with plans to try once more to go into ranching. At thirty-five years of age, and perhaps with some money in his pocket (however ill-gotten), he probably thought this second effort had a good chance of success. Yet he needed additional funds to make a go of it. Apparently, some "prominent people" in Graham County urged him to enter the Graham County sheriff's race, but his candidacy did not fly. In another effort to obtain financial backing, Horn wrote Henry Miller Porter, a Denver banker and entrepreneur, with a proposal for assistance. While Horn's proposal is lost, Porter's reply of 16 January 1896 provides some hints about Tom Horn's plan. "Your scheme is a good one," said Porter, "but at present I have . . . other obligations." Yet Horn refused to give up. "I am going to buy

200 cows in a short time," he informed Doc Shores, "and in three years I will have a good herd of cattle." In reflecting back on the tragic course of Tom Horn's life, Shores admitted that he felt "a sort of responsibility" for his former Pinkerton partner's problems. If he had not persuaded Horn to go to work for the agency, Shores continued, "chances are that he would have built up a cattle business in Arizona and ended his career honorably."[2]

While attempting to get his feet on the ground, Horn could always work in law enforcement. In March 1896, a Solomonville newspaper reported that "Detective Horn" had arrested two "strolling thespians" wanted for burglary in Geronimo, a village a few miles north of Fort Thomas. Since there is no indication that Horn had hung out his shingle as a private detective, Graham County authorities probably hired him for this special assignment. When William P. (Billy) Birchfield was elected sheriff in November, he appointed Horn as deputy sheriff for the Aravaipa area.[3]

In spite of his attempts to settle down, Tom Horn continued to betray signs of wanderlust. Coincidentally, his return to Arizona took place just as the United States Army planned what would be its last formal campaign against Apache renegades. Since the deportation of the Chiricahuas in 1886, a few Apache fugitives continued to raid and murder, while others—"The Lost Ones"—made the Sierra Madre in Sonora their home. The most notorious of these outlaws were Adelneitze, Na-shult-pi-e ("Little Brown Lizard"), Massai, and the Apache Kid. Of these fugitives, the Apache Kid, who murdered Gila County Sheriff Glenn Reynolds in 1889, was the most notorious. At one time, there was a $5,000 reward on his head. As a result of several murders in southern Arizona about the time of Tom Horn's return to Graham County, Colonel Edwin Vose Sumner, commander of the Seventh Cavalry Regiment at Fort Grant, began preparations for a campaign against these elusive raiders. While officials in Washington renewed the "hot pursuit" convention with the Republic of Mexico, Sumner established a temporary base at the San Bernardino ranch of former Cochise County Sheriff John H. Slaughter on the international boundary. Additional Indian scouts were recruited and packtrains refurbished.[4]

When Tom Horn learned of Colonel Sumner's preparations, he quickly offered his services. Sumner recalled the means by which General Nelson Miles brought in Geronimo and his followers a decade earlier: while Miles sent troops and Apache scouts in relentless pursuit of the renegades, he dispatched a separate "peace delegation" into Sonora in an effort to persuade the fugitives to surrender peacefully. On 25 April 1896, Sumner asked General Frank Wheaton, his superior in Denver, for authorization to employ two Chiricahua Apache prisoners from Fort Sill, Oklahoma, to help locate the renegades in Mexico and to try to persuade them to surrender. With the two Chiricahuas and a five-hundred-dollar appropriation, Sumner remarked confidently, he could "get hold of those renegades and save further trouble and expense." While Wheaton did not reject this plan out of hand, he doubted that Arizonans, who remembered prior Chiricahua atrocities, would agree to such a move. Instead, Wheaton suggested that the colonel use some of his own Indian scouts and, to ensure their reliability, that some dependable American should be placed in charge of these "peace commissioners." To assure his superior that he intended to place an American in charge, in a letter of 4 May, Sumner declared that he intended "to employ Mr. Thomas Horn" as leader of this delegation. As far as the cost was concerned, Sumner merely wanted "money enough to pay well for success or at least enough to pay Mr. Horn for the attempt, be it successful or not."[5]

In an effort to impress Colonel Sumner, Tom Horn fed this unsuspecting officer a very inflated version of his accomplishments. Horn was "the man who went into Geronimo's camp alone and persuaded him to see and talk to Lieut. Gatewood," Sumner informed Wheaton, and he "is supposed to be the only white man with whom the renegade Masse [Massai] will hold any communication." While "this may or may not be true," continued Sumner, who was obviously becoming suspicious, Horn "is willing to risk it, and may meet with success a second time." The colonel requested a prompt response from Wheaton, since Horn "intends leaving the country" (probably for Mexico) very soon. "If the plan is approved I shall of course want instructions as to what promises I can authorize Mr. Horn to make the renegades in case of surrender," he added. In spite of Wheaton's doubts that the War Department would approve this plan, he passed it on through Army Adj. Gen. George D. Ruggles to the commanding general, Nelson Miles. While Miles, who knew Tom Horn well, objected to the use of prisoners of war as peace commissioners, he agreed to the employment of locally available Apache scouts. Sumner and Horn put their heads together again and reduced their request. On 12 May, Sumner sent a wire (in cipher) to General Wheaton: "Horn asks for only one Indian from

[Fort] Sill, Nochi by name," and Wheaton forwarded Horn's request to Washington. Sam Noche had worked closely with Horn in the Crawford expedition of 1885–86.[6]

There was a striking resemblance between the Sumner-Horn plan and Gatewood's Geronimo mission a decade earlier. The two Chiricahuas that Sumner requested from Fort Sill would be, in effect, latter-day counterparts to Kayitah and Martine, Gatewood's "peace commissioners." Tom Horn's projected role was analogous to that of Gatewood, which would certainly have pleased Horn. The $5,000 reward on the Apache Kid's head was attractive as well. Colonel Sumner's outrageous claim—he had been taken in by Horn—that the former scout had gone alone into Geronimo's camp indicates that Horn had a part in initiating the scheme. Sumner would not have intentionally made such ridiculous statements to higher-ups who knew the facts of the Gatewood mission. Horn's outlandish claims show that he had already begun to exaggerate his role, and thus his legend, in the Apache campaigns.

The Sumner-Horn plan was not the only proposal on General Miles's desk. William Morris Stewart, U.S. senator from Nevada, presented a separate scheme on behalf of H. G. Howe, U.S. deputy mineral surveyor in Tombstone. (Stewart had mining investments in southern Arizona.) Since the renegades were always alert to any troop movements, Howe suggested going after the fugitives without using soldiers. A black man in Tombstone known as Jim, said Howe, could be of assistance in running these fugitives down. This man, who had been Senator Stewart's driver, claimed to be "well acquainted with these Indian trails," wrote Howe, "and has . . . watched the Kid come down to a spring and water his horse." Howe believed that Jim and "a few selected Indians" could capture this outlaw.[7]

Faced with rival proposals, Nelson Miles produced his own plan. Massai and the Apache Kid would never surrender to Tom Horn's peace delegation, the general asserted, but would have to be "hunted down." In Miles's scheme, which combined elements of both proposals, Horn would still play a part. While refusing the use of Chiricahua prisoners of war, he ordered that Horn and Jim be employed as scouts and guides for four months—from approximately 1 June through 30 September 1896—at a wage of seventy-five dollars per month. On 21 May Secretary of War Daniel S. Lamont signed off on Miles's recommendation and made available the necessary $500 (with the caveat that, if possible, the plan be carried out for less). Two days later, Miles sent the approved plan to General Wheaton, with copies of Senator Stewart's correspondence about Jim attached.[8] In presenting his modified plan, Miles made an effort to correct Horn's exaggerations. While he complimented Horn as "an industrious, intelligent scout and guide" in the Geronimo campaign, the general declared that he was not the first man to enter Geronimo's camp and convince him "to see and talk to Lieutenant Gatewood."

General Wheaton and his adjutant, Col. William Jefferson Volkmar, were surprised at General Miles's changes to Colonel Sumner's plan to suppress the renegades. Not only was Tom Horn's proposal to use a Chiricahua prisoner of war scratched, but there were other changes. They did not understand how Jim came to be selected in place of Sam Noche. Furthermore, Colonel Sumner had authorized wages of one hundred dollars per month, for "Thomas Horn, as scout, guide and interpreter," but General Miles reduced it to seventy-five. These arbitrary changes gave Horn some pause, but the allure of scouting was too much to ignore. On 11 June, First Lt. William H. Baldwin, the Fort Grant quartermaster, added Horn's name to his "Report of Persons and Articles Employed and Hired." Horn was to serve as a "scout, guide & [Spanish] interpreter."[9]

Sumner had already begun to send Seventh Cavalry troopers into Mexico. In late April, First Lt. Edwin Connor Bullock met with Lt. Col. Emilio Kosterlitzky, the veteran Mexican lawman, at John Slaughter's San Bernardino ranch and agreed to cooperate against the renegades. The following month, Second Lt. Nathan King Averill, accompanied by John Slaughter and several cowhands, surprised a fugitive camp in the New Mexico bootheel. They killed one warrior, wounded one woman, and captured an Apache girl. A few days later, Averill combined forces with First Lt. Sedgwick Rice and came upon another camp in Cochise County, near the international boundary. William H. Eckhorst, who was with a supporting packtrain, recalled that one of the Apache scouts deliberately gave their position away and thus spoiled the surprise. Nonetheless, the troops killed one warrior, Adelneitze, who had escaped from American troops at the time of Geronimo's surrender. Massai, however, managed to escape. In congratulating Averill and Rice, the Arizona *Silver Belt* remarked that this was the army's "greatest success in Indian warfare" in Arizona in a decade.[10]

By the time the U.S. government renewed the "hot pursuit" convention with Mexico, on 4 June 1896, Tom Horn had arrived for duty.

Eight days later, the *Sulphur Valley News* observed him passing through Willcox with First Lt. William J. Nicholson and a Seventh Cavalry detachment en route to San Bernardino ranch. Apparently, Horn had time to regale the editor with his exploits in the 1886 Crawford expedition. Not only did Horn have "charge of the scouts" during this tragic campaign, he told the editor, but "it was largely through his efforts that Crawford's troop got out of Mexico." Not only was Horn "one of the best known Indian fighters in Arizona," but the army was presently paying him "a very fancy salary to give the officers of the 7th [Cavalry] the benefit of his experience." (There was nothing fancy about wages of seventy-five dollars per month.)[11]

Shortly after the arrival of Nicholson, Horn, and the Apache scouts at Slaughter's ranch, Second Lt. William Yates, with a separate detachment, surprised the camp of Na-shult-pi-e sixty miles farther south. Yates captured an Apache girl and camp equipment, but the chief, three warriors, four women, and one child made their escape. Fearing that Yates's men were tiring out, Colonel Sumner sent Lieutenant Nicholson and his troops to replace Yates. On 1 July, Nicholson and Horn departed San Bernardino with five enlisted men, two Indian scouts, and three civilian packers, with orders to try to locate Na-shult-pie-'s trail. Seven days later, they met Colonel Kosterlitsky, with Mexican troops, on the western slope of the Terras Mountains. (Horn had not seen Kosterlitsky since 1886.) The two forces scoured the area as far south as the Bavispe River, and then Nicholson proceeded south with his detachment, but torrential rains and flooding forced him to turn back. Near Batipeta, Nicholson and Horn talked with a Mexican "who claimed he had seen these [renegade] Indians," the lieutenant informed Colonel Sumner. However, the Americans quickly sized up this informant, whose real purpose was to "sell a few quarts of mescal." After rejoining the troops at Batipeta, they returned to the Bavispe River, where Nicholson, Tom Horn, and two Apache scouts continued their search but failed to find any sign of the fugitives. "Most of the work had to be on foot," Nicholson added, as the country was "rough beyond description." On one occasion, six pack mules "rolled down the mountain at one time." Nicholson, Horn, and the command returned to San Bernardino on 22 July, after a difficult and unsuccessful patrol.[12]

By mid-August Horn was back at Fort Grant. The *Sulphur Valley News,* now under the editorship of the scout's good friend, Horace

Dunlap, reported that "Thos. Horn, the well known scout, has been at the post for a short time but is expecting to be ordered to the Mexican border again. Tom has just the right temperament for a chief of scouts, and we believe he really enjoys the dangers and hardships of field service." Dunlap was correct. On 18 August, First Lt. Selah P. H. "Tommy" Tompkins led a detachment including Tom Horn, four Indian trailers, and Assistant Surgeon Powell C. Fauntleroy into the Stein's Peak range along the Arizona–New Mexico border. Although Tompkins's primary assignment was to track the renegades, he was also instructed to be on the lookout for other troublemakers, including Yaqui raiders from Mexico and a band of American outlaws known as the High Fives who had recently robbed a Nogales bank and killed a pursuing posseman.[13]

In a strange turn of events, Tom Horn and Doctor Fauntleroy, who had separated from their detachment, stumbled onto the trail of the American outlaws just below New Mexico's border with Chihuahua. Believing they had found the trail of renegade Apaches, the two men followed it until they came upon the remains of a cow just recently killed. Horn concluded that the men who left this trail were the highwaymen. These three High Fives, Bob Hayes, Bob Christian and Code Young, were attempting to make their way to New Mexico. Other members of the band had fled into Mexico with ex-Sheriff John Slaughter and a posse hard on their heels. When Horn and Fauntleroy rejoined the detachment, Tompkins returned to Fort Grant on 29 August, where the sighting of the bandits was reported to law enforcement officials.[14]

No sooner had Tom Horn arrived at Fort Grant than Colonel Sumner sent him to Tombstone with orders to look into U.S. Mineral Surveyor Howe's claim that a black man, Jim, could find the Apache Kid. Using the letterhead of John Montgomery, a Tombstone livery stable owner, Horn reported his findings on 4 September. He said he believed Howe was honest and well intentioned but gullible for having swallowed Jim's story. The detective then looked up Jim, whose full name was apparently James Young. Jim "give me a great game of talk," wrote Horn, but "when I pin[n]ed him down he acknowledged to me that he had seen the Kid only once." In fact the black man "knew nothing at all about the Kid or any other hostile Indian," concluded Horn, who sized up his informant as "a liar of the first water." In an effort to pick up sign of the renegades on his return journey to Fort Grant, Tom Horn rode a wide circuit by way of San Bernardino ranch, the Animas Valley, and Steins Peak range, reaching Grant in mid September.[15]

Although Horn was scheduled to work only until the end of September, Colonel Sumner asked Adjutant General Volkmar "for information relative to [the] further employment of Mr. Horn as guide and scout." Volkmar reiterated that he had funds to pay Horn for four months only and that Horn "should be discharged . . . at the expiration of that time," or 30 September. While Tom Horn could claim no successes in his recent Sonoran excursions, he was soon treating listeners to tall tales of his imaginary exploits. With his tour of duty terminated, he traveled to Tucson, where his old friend Bill Ganzhorn, the former Tombstone hotel man, was driving a hack. Jack Ganzhorn, Bill's teenage son, recalled that Horn "dropped into town from a scouting trip after the Apache Kid" and regaled them with his recent exploits. In recalling this campaign for a *Denver Republican* reporter two years later, Horn invented a tale about his pursuit of Apaches who stole army horses from Fort Grant. The intrepid scout "set off alone on the trail of the marauders," said the *Republican,* and returned eight days later with "the strangest procession the eyes of man ever rested upon." "Across the back of each of the first seven horses was lashed the body of a dead Indian!" As for the Apache Kid, whom Tom Horn never sighted, numerous reports of the outlaw's movements continued to circulate, but proof of his death was never documented. The reward was never paid. Presumably, the Kid, whom Tom Horn had worked with as a scout in the 1880s and whom he later pursued, died in the Sierra Madre of natural causes.[16]

No sooner did Tom Horn return to the employ of Elias Jones in Aravaipa Canyon than William Kidder Meade, U.S. marshal of Arizona Territory, requested his assistance in the pursuit of the High Fives outlaw band. When Meade asked Horn to meet him at Willcox on 7 November, Horn was unable to comply, since the fall roundup was under way. In his letter, Horn betrayed a side of his personality that tended to confirm the suspicions Wyoming officers already held about him:

> If the business [manhunt] is not too pressing and you write and explain it to me I will give you any assistance I can. If it concerns the *Outlaws on the Border* and you are going out with a posse I could not go as I know that with any posse you could

get you could not accomplish any thing as no one knows as well as myself the way in which the posse would be handicapped. I can stand a better show to get them by going alone and will go and get some of them at least and drive the rest out of the country *if there is any thing in it for me.*

Horn assured the federal officer that "*No cure no pay* is my mottoe [*sic*]." "So if I dont [*sic*] get them it costs no one a cent." Horn was obviously contemptuous of the average posseman. In a postscript, he cautioned Meade that any posse that he could muster from the saloon crowd would "only find fresh sign," meaning that the High Fives could easily elude such amateur lawmen. Whether Marshal Meade made a second appeal for Horn's assistance is not known.[17]

In addition to ranch work, Horn resumed prospecting in the Deer Creek mining district. Touted as one of "best mining properties" in Arizona, this district spilled over into the Apache Reservation. Although Congress passed legislation in June 1896 to segregate this mineral-bearing area from the reservation, a government survey was required before the field could be opened to official claims. In the meantime, many prospectors, among them Tom Horn and his friend Dan Ming, staked out illegal claims; they would make them official when the time arrived. In February 1897, Horn made a special trip to Willcox to confer with a mineral expert. A short time later, a Globe newspaper remarked that Horn had "promising copper claims" on the reservation lands. But misfortune continued to dog Tom Horn's footsteps. When surveyors finally separated the Deer Creek strip from the San Carlos Reservation, the official line still "placed his claims inside of the reservation," according to the *Arizona Bulletin,* "and he was compelled to abandon them."[18]

With his various efforts to make a new start in Arizona ending in disappointment, Tom Horn resolved to return to Wyoming. After saying his goodbyes to his employers, Dan Ming and Elias Jones in late 1897 or early 1898, he packed his gear and set out for John Coble's Iron Mountain Ranch near Bosler, Wyoming, about twenty miles north of Laramie. Bud Cowan, who had worked cattle and horses with Horn earlier, soon found himself working with him again. Cowan recalled that he and Horn broke polo ponies for Coble and then hired out to the PO Ranch, near Cheyenne, in a similar capacity. The two cowhands were still at the PO when the War with Spain erupted. For a man with such a restless nature, the war offered an unexpected opportunity. Several days

before the U.S. Congress voted for war on 25 April 1898, Commanding Gen. Nelson A. Miles and his staff were already laying plans for war.
Recalling Horn's services in the Apache campaigns, Miles resolved to
put him to use, not as a scout but in the packtrain service. Anticipating
a campaign in Cuba, where there were few roads, Miles believed that
packtrains were "about the only means available for the transportation
of supplies to an army." While Lt. Col. Gilbert Cole Smith, chief of
the Quartermaster Depot at Jefferson Barracks, near St. Louis, sent out
a general call across the West for packers, Tom Horn's summons had
a more personal touch. Capt. Marion Maus, Horn's former boss and
now General Miles's aide, found Horn in Wyoming. Maus asked him
to report to Lt. Col. Edwin Byron Atwood, chief quartermaster of the
Department of the Colorado, in Denver. On the morning of 9 April,
a Cheyenne newsman observed Horn boarding a train for Denver. A
few days later, Colonel Atwood informed Army Quartermaster General
Marshall Ludington that "Tom Horn, a strong healthy looking man
who has been in Government Service for more than fifteen years," had
appeared at his office asking for employment. Horn, who gave Miles
and Maus as his references, was soon on his way to Jefferson Barracks.[19]

Clearly flattered by Miles's summons, Horn took full advantage of
this opportunity to recount his exploits to any newspaperman willing to
listen. The *Casper Derrick* reported that Horn had been appointed chief
packer for the U.S. Army. In announcing that General Miles intended
for Horn "to direct the movements of the pack train in Cuba," the
Denver Republican added (in a fantastic misinterpretation) that Horn, "a
big, broad-shouldered man with muscles firm as steel," was "as modest as if he had never followed a trail of Indian moccasins." Not only
did Horn claim to have eighteen years of experience in Indian fighting,
but he claimed that Apaches had killed his father, who had also been
a scout! To avenge his father's death, Horn said, he killed dozens of
Indians and commanded 100 Indian scouts in the 1882 Tupper expedition into Mexico. Now on a roll, the windy Horn made himself chief
of scouts and Apache interpreter for General Crook in the Sierra Madre
Campaign of 1883, even alleging that he "arranged a treaty with the
renegades." Somewhat nearer the truth, Horn also claimed to have performed heroic deeds in the battle with Mexican troops when Captain
Emmet Crawford was killed in 1886. In the space of a few lines, Tom
Horn presented what was, in effect, a summary of his subsequent highly
exaggerated autobiography.[20]

Whatever the precise nature of Miles's job offer, Tom Horn immediately spun his new position into a colonelcy. As William Muir, a veteran packer, departed Wyoming for Jefferson Barracks, he informed the *Cheyenne Tribune* that he was going to "join Colonel Tom Horne's [*sic*] pack trains." Likewise, when William Hall and several other Wyoming cowboys announced that they were going to join Horn's "mule brigade," they declared that he "possesses the title of director of pack trains." (After the war, Horn told Glendolene Kimmell, an impressionable young schoolteacher, that General Miles designated him "chief pack master for Shafter's army, with the rank and pay of colonel" and that he was soon made "master of transportation.") While Horn would eventually be promoted to the civilian position of chief packer of all packtrains in Gen. William Shafter's Fifth U.S. Army Corps, he began as packmaster of Packtrain No. 3, according to Henry Daly, who met him at Jefferson Barracks. Furthermore, to equate his position with that of a colonel in the regular army was stretching a point. Even as corps chief packer, Horn actually answered to a first lieutenant, who was in overall command of packtrains in the assault on Santiago, Cuba. In an unusually modest (and more truthful) moment after the war, Horn admitted to the *Rocky Mountain News* that he "received the [equivalent] pay of a first lieutenant."[21]

Surprisingly, John Coble, Horn's former employer in Wyoming, reacted negatively when he heard that his friend was joining the packtrain service. In a letter to Franklin Bosler, who was considering an investment in the Iron Mountain Ranch Company, Coble expressed astonishment that Horn desired to go to Cuba. "What a fool he is," continued the rancher. "He will only be a stepping stone for some officer to rise on." On Saturday, 23 April, Capt. Frederick von Schrader, assistant quartermaster at Jefferson Barracks, entered Horn's name as a packmaster on the monthly "Report of Persons and Articles Employed and Hired" and issued his contract at a monthly wage of $100. On 25 April, a reporter for the *St. Louis Globe-Democrat* observed Tom Horn and his fellow packers putting their untrained mules through their paces for the benefit of onlookers. In a lengthy article, the reporter observed that "Boss Packer Tom Horn and Assistants Have Lots of Fun and Hard Work in Teaching 'Green' Mules." He wrote:

> Who is Tom Horn? He is a robust, stalwart 6-footer, who has been an army packer for Uncle Sam for fifteen years in Arizona,

New Mexico and along the Mexican border. He is one of the few men in the world who can play a game of tag with a mule's hind feet and not come out second best in the score. He ought to be admirably qualified to hold office under a Democratic administration, because he can stand more kicks than Gov. [Lon V.] Stephens [of Missouri] ever dreamt of.[22]

As Maj. Gen. William Shafter assembled the Fifth Army Corps at Tampa, Florida, for the invasion of Cuba, Quartermaster General Marshall Ludington pressured his subordinates at Jefferson Barracks to ship packtrains to Tampa Bay as quickly as possible. On 27 April, Captain Von Schrader transferred the trains of Tom Horn and G. S. Green, with twenty-four additional personnel, to Maj. James Worden Pope, assistant quartermaster at Tampa. As these and additional trains made their way by rail to Florida, the *St. Louis Post-Dispatch* was moved to remark, "this looks like 'business.'" On 1 May 1898, Horn and his trains were transferred to Captain John Bellinger, chief quartermaster at Tampa. Apparently, Nelson Miles intended from the start for Horn to occupy a responsible position in the packtrain service, since Horn later maintained that he was "acting chief packmaster" for the Fifth Corps and in charge of 520 mules and 133 packers.

As in the Apache campaigns in Arizona, an officer, not a civilian, was in overall command of the packtrains. Major General Shafter placed First Lt. Archibald Atkinson Cabaniss, Twenty-fourth Infantry, in this position. Cabaniss, who entered the army as an enlisted man in 1885, served as a sergeant with Captain Henry Lawton's expedition in Sonora the following year, where he probably became acquainted with Tom Horn. Two years later, Cabaniss received a direct commission as a second lieutenant and was promoted to first lieutenant, Twenty-Fourth Infantry, in 1895. At Tampa, Shafter placed Cabaniss in command of sixteen trains. While nothing is known about the relationship between Tom Horn and Archibald Cabaniss, Horn's prior experience must have been helpful to Cabaniss at Tampa Bay and in Cuba.[23]

As the loading of the Cuban Expeditionary Force (CEF) got under way in early June, General Shafter ordered Cabaniss to select "six of the best trains" for initial shipment. Additional trains would follow later. The majority of the pack mules and packers were placed aboard the *Gussie,* a creaky old side-wheeler (75 men, 325 pack mules and 6 bell mares in train numbers 1, 3, 8, 9, and 13). Train No. 16 (65 mules and a bell mare) was assigned to the transport *Clinton*. Presumably, Cabaniss and Horn were aboard the *Gussie*. On 1 June, all packtrain personnel, including Tom Horn, as acting corps chief packer, were transferred to Lt. Colonel Joshua West Jacobs, the Fifth Corps chief quartermaster for the trip to Cuba. At long last, Tom Horn's promotion to the position of chief packer of the Fifth Corps came through on 13 June, the day before the force departed for Cuba. A pay increase to $133.33 per month accompanied this promotion. Henry Daly, who was also in Tampa at this time, said Horn went to Cuba "with 6 packmasters" under his command. Since Horn's new responsibilities required much paperwork, he had two clerks, P. E. Butler and D. D. Grimes. Horn later praised Grimes as his "leading assistant" in Cuba. Another last-minute promotion had some bearing on Horn's position. "About midnight of June 13th," Lt. Col. Charles Frederic Humphrey, the superior of Archibald Cabaniss (and hence of Tom Horn), was elevated to the position of chief quartermaster of the CEF.[24]

About 10:00 A.M. on 22 June 1898, Fifth Corps troops began to go ashore at Daiquiri, on the south coast of Cuba, heading for the nearby port city of Santiago. Although the surf was high and beat heavily against the shore, the navy's small boats managed to land 6,000 fighting men by nightfall. By morning, Brig. Gen. Henry Lawton's Second Infantry Division had secured Siboney, a coastal village seven miles west of Daiquiri. Shafter designated this place as a second landing site. The unloading of mules and equipment began that day and continued through the following day, 24 June, In the absence of specially designed boats to transport the horses and mules to shore, General Shafter and his staff had long since agreed that the animals would have to swim. After the war, Tom Horn spread the tale that swimming the mules to the beach was his idea. His friends helped spread this myth.[25]

While Horn did not originate the idea of swimming the mules ashore, he may have improved upon the methods used to get the mules to the beach. After all, he and his fellow packers had experience in swimming their animals across swollen streams in the Southwest. The first step was to put the poor beasts in the water. "With the help of other Arizona buckaroos he led the mules up the open deck way," recalled Rough Rider Oscar Wager, "pushed them overboard, and they'd swam [*sic*] ashore." Tom Rynning, a Rough Rider sergeant, said the packers "let the gangplank down till it was floating in the water." They would then place "a rope across the animal's caboose and heave him into the ocean" An *Army and Navy Journal* correspondent who observed this process, said that "a rope is passed over their heads fastened to the halter, another is passed behind two [mules] together and they are forced overboard." This procedure sounds dangerous to the mules but since many were pushed through a side hatch which was closer to the water, it may have been relatively harmless. As this process was improved upon, the mules were led onto floating wooden platforms before being pushed into the water.[26]

Once the animals were in the water, "the high surf and rough sea" made moving them to the beach very "difficult and tedious," wrote Quartermaster Humphrey. The packers "worked through the days, and as late into the nights as was possible, until all had been landed," he added. When some mules became panicky in the high water, Tom Horn and his packers put a halter and rope on each animal and several of them were "tethered and towed ashore" behind small boats. Calling on his past experiences, Horn realized that the animals slavishly followed the bell mare. Therefore, he "directed that the [small] boats be formed in a semi-circle to provide a makeshift breakwater," according to Kirk Knox, a Wyoming newspaperman, "and then [he] asked for a small boat and a bell-mare." The chief packer then tied the bell mare to his boat and signaled the release of the mules, which "followed the boat and the mare ashore." To further assist the mules, William Shafter recalled that some packers "adopted the trick of walking up and down the beach, ringing a bell." Mistaking this sound for a bell mare, the mules obediently swam ashore. Inevitably, a few animals became disoriented and swam out to sea. Henry L. Marcotte, an *Army and Navy Journal* correspondent, was perturbed at this loss of valuable animals. When he "asked a man in charge of landing the animals why he did not have boats to turn the frightened animals to shore," this individual replied offhandedly, "Oh, hell, we've got all we can do to land those headed for shore."[27]

Overall, General Shafter was pleased with the landing. On 23 June, he reported that he had "lost less than 50 animals" since leaving Tampa. We "lost more putting them through the surf to land," he continued, than on the journey to Cuba. Shafter was also pleased with the performance of his packers and characterized their success in swimming the mules ashore as "wonderful". In a newspaper interview after the war, Tom Horn boasted, exaggerating as usual, that "we didn't lose one [mule] in unloading" the animals. While "we had to throw them into the sea from the transport ships and swim and wade with them ashore through the devil's own surf," he continued, "It didn't look then as though they could be killed at all." In spite of many difficulties in landing the livestock, a *St. Louis Globe-Democrat* correspondent observed that "to-night [23 June] General Shafter has the satisfaction of knowing that all the men, guns, mules and supplies . . . are safely on land." None of this would have gone so smoothly if the Spanish had tried to prevent the landing.[28]

While rounding up his mules along the beach at Daiquiri, Chief Packer Horn spied Col. Leonard Wood, an acquaintance from the Apache campaigns. Although busily organizing his regiment, the First Volunteer Cavalry (Rough Riders), Wood stopped, shook hands with Horn and said, "So you're in the pack train! That's fine." "'Yes,' Horn replied, 'I'm pack master but I'm acting chief [packer].'" For a moment, the two fighting men reminisced about their experiences in the Sierra Madre in the summer of 1886. "Do you remember when we were climbing up that canyon together after deer in Sonora and the renegades shot so close that it sprinkled dirt into our mouths?" "You bet I do," replied Horn. That was the end of the conversation. The colonel went about his business, and so did Tom Horn.[29]

Although Lieutenant Cabaniss and Chief Packer Horn succeeded in landing their mules, there were additional delays in getting equipment to the beach owing to the haphazard loading of the transports. The mules were especially finicky: each would accept only its personal aparejo (pack saddle). Cabaniss and Horn spent the night frantically searching for these items in order to have trains ready on the morning of 24 June. The packers had all six trains "completely fitted out" by the following day, but Cabaniss, who soon learned that the civilian packtrains ranked very low in the army's supply system, was concerned that his trains lacked supplies necessary for the long term. On 28 June, he presented General Shafter a long list of essentials, reminding him that some of these items had been requested before the ships left Tampa."[30]

As the lead elements of the Fifth Corps under General Lawton moved inland from Siboney, they were confined to a single dirt track, generously named El Camino Real. This "road" ran westward from Daiquiri to Siboney, seven miles away, and then turned north toward Santiago, twelve miles farther north. "The wagon road . . . was not passable for anything but pack-trains when the troops first began to use it," recalled John D. Miley. In some places, "the banks of the trail were three or four feet high," according to correspondent Richard Harding Davis, "and when it rained it was converted into a huge gutter, with sides of mud, and with liquid mud a foot deep between them." Mosquitoes and other tropical pests were plentiful. In spite of these handicaps, Brig. Gen. Adna Chaffee's Third Brigade, part of Henry Lawton Second Division, occupied Siboney on 23 June. Henceforth Tom Horn's pack-trains would work from supply dumps at both Daiquiri and Siboney. In spite of Shafter's desire to build up his supply dump before advancing inland, the field commander, Maj. Gen. Joe Wheeler, Shafter's second-in-command, sensed that the Spanish were putting up only token resistance. Wheeler ordered Chaffee's brigade and Colonel Wood's Rough Riders to continue their advance toward Santiago. In a sharp fight on 24 June, the Americans overwhelmed an enemy delaying force at Las Guásimas, three miles north of Siboney. While Wheeler's unanticipated advance kept Spanish troops off balance, according to historian David Trask, the aggressiveness of this former Confederate officer not only upset Shafter's plans "and led to serious logistical complications" but placed greater stress upon the packtrains.[31]

Other than the human foot, the primary means of moving supplies to the front were the pack mules. Since Quartermaster Humphrey had assured General Lawton that he would "have a pack train loaded and on its way by daylight" on 24 June, the packers and mules were under pressure to perform. As the Americans assaulted the enemy fortification at Las Guásimas that day, they needed the immediate assistance of the ammunition packtrains. During this brief but intense firefight, an order was passed back, "Machine guns to the front!" "Almost immediately . . . a shrill 'yip yip' was heard from the rear," according to correspondent Kennett F. Harris, "and four mules packed with the barrels and tripods of the Colts came on a quick trot." Caspar Whitney of *Harper's Magazine* also observed a "mule-train . . . doing its utmost . . . to keep the troops supplied with hardtack and bacon and coffee." "The First and Tenth regulars could not have won honors at La Quasima [sic]," Tom Horn later boasted, "had it not been for the regular supplies of ammunition" that his men delivered.[32]

To his credit, General Shafter quickly grasped the importance of Tom Horn's lowly mules. They were so critical that Shafter withdrew all transportation resources from individual units and placed them under the immediate control of his corps headquarters. With Capt. Edward H. Plummer serving as acting transportation officer, each of the three divisions—Wheeler's, Lawton's, and Kent's—at the front was allotted one packtrain and twenty-five wagons. (Most of the wagons had not yet been assembled, so few were actually available.) When two new packtrains arrived from Tampa two days later—making eight in all— the CEF commander held them in reserve in case of an emergency. When Shafter authorized one train for each division he cautioned General Wheeler that "these pack trains must not be diverted to any other purpose" than for rations and forage. While some subordinates criticized Shafter for devoting "too much time in attending to details" concerning transportation, Wheeler agreed that careful "management of his pack-trains" was necessary. Only the lowly mule could be relied upon to ensure the timely delivery of food and ammunition to the front line.[33]

In spite of General Shafter's hasty reorganization of transportation re-sources, Tom Horn's packers and their mules were spread thin. Shafter still hoped that the mules could keep the front adequately supplied "until the greater part of the commissary, quartermaster, and hospital stores could be disembarked," wrote correspondent Herbert Sargent; and then, when improvements were made on the El Camino Real, wagon transport could assume some of this workload. After observing firsthand the burdens imposed on the packtrains from his headquarters at El Pozo, eight miles north of Siborney, Shafter made a second change to his transportation policy. He assigned two packtrains to each division and held all other trains and wagons at his headquarters. While Captain Plummer continued to supervise transportation, wrote Sargent, General Shafter insisted on being "constantly informed as to where the transpor-tation was most needed." Since packtrains could not pass one another on the narrowest parts of El Camino Real, Shafter ordered the trains to carry supplies to the front at night and return to base the following day. Tropical rains soon turned the sunken parts of the road into a slough, and the mules moved forward slowly and laboriously.[34]

In spite of this difficulty, Horn and Cabaniss somehow kept the frontline forces supplied at a subsistence level. Writing on 27 June from the village of San Juan, a short distance above El Pozo, a *Boston Herald* reporter observed that "it taxes the quartermaster's department to the utmost to get provisions and ammunition [to the front]. Last night one pack train arrived with supplies sufficient to last until tonight, and as this dispatch is being written another train of ammunition is coming in." In the meantime, another train lugged "a battery of Gatling guns and dynamite guns" to the front. So desperate was General Shafter to build up sufficient supplies for the forthcoming assault on his next objective, San Juan Heights, according to one reporter, that "all transportation personnel, even the higher-ups, were called on to lend a hand and personally lead a train." Tom Horn, the corps chief packer, was among them, according to Rough Rider Sergeant Tom Rynning. Rynning recalled how he and his comrades, who had been living on mangoes for several days, were overjoyed when Tom Horn "brought us up a pack-train of grub." D. D. Grimes, Horn's clerk, later recalled that this grueling routine kept them "on the road night and day," as Shafter built up a supply dump for the coming battle.[35]

In spite of General Shafter's strict instructions about the use of mules, Chief Packer Horn did not always comply. As Horn was leading a pack-train up to the front, he encountered Col. Leonard Wood and Lt. Col. Theodore Roosevelt. Both officers were on foot. Complaining that their horses "were worn out," they asked if Horn could provide them with fresh ones. Apparently they were willing to settle for mules. Since the chief packer "had received . . . orders to supply no one mules;" he later recalled, he was running a risk if he disobeyed. Yet, "having served with Wood in Arizona and esteeming him highly, he made an exception" and provided both officers with mules.[36]

The diligence of Tom Horn and his fellow packers impressed correspondents on the scene. John C. Hemment characterized the mules as intelligent animals and the packers as "interesting and picturesque." The "mule packers . . . came from the wild and woolly West," wrote Hemment, "and were whole-souled, jolly." "The feature which these men most glory in is their capacity for cursing," he added, "and it seems as though the mules understand every blessed word they say." The packers announced their approach on the El Camino Real with a "sonorous 'Whoopla!,'" and a "shrill whistle brings the mule to time in every instance." "With ropes dangling around them in the fashion most affected by the cowboy," concluded Hemment, their most conspicuous piece of equipment was "a large black snake whip, which they use with great dexterity." Hemment described a couple of packers galloping up in advance "warning everybody in sight to clear the road," followed by the mules, "all frothing and foaming from the extra exertion." When one mule suddenly left the train in order to grab a bunch of nearby grass, a packer, whip in hand, shouted, "What you doin' thar, mule?" Knowing he would soon feel "the tip of [a] . . . snake whip," the errant animal returned to his place in line.[37]

As the Fifth Corps chief packer, Tom Horn had important responsibilities. While he personally led some pack trains to the front, he had paperwork to do as well. Horn's immediate boss, Lieutenant Cabaniss, dealt with superior officers who determined the type and amount of supplies to be carried to the front. The chief packer saw that the supplies were loaded and moved to the front. Since General Shafter relied so heavily upon the pack trains—wagons still played a minor part—Tom Horn's men and mules were in an "emergency mode" from the start. After the war, Capt. Marion Maus applauded Horn for his services." Horn "deserves the highest commendation and praise," wrote Maus, as he "was indefatigable in all his hard work and exceptionally correct in his [written] reports of what had been done."[38]

On 1 July, the Americans assaulted well-dug-in Spanish defenders on the San Juan Heights, a low-lying ridgeline that shielded the southern approach to Santiago de Cuba. With Gatling guns providing suppressing fire, the Americans seized the heights, although with significant casualties. In the meantime, General Lawton's men devoted the entire day to overcoming enemy resistance at nearby El Caney, which guarded the eastern flank of Spanish defenses.

As Shafter's forces prepared for the assault on San Juan Heights, Tom Horn was an eyewitness to an embarrassing and controversial moment for the Americans. As Brig. Gen. Hamilton Hawkins's Seventy-first New York Volunteers approached their jumping-off position at the base of San Juan Hill, the Mauser rifles of the Spanish soldiers, firing high-velocity smokeless powder cartridges, panicked the poorly trained Americans, who fled back in disarray among the trailing units, causing great confusion. Tom Horn, who happened to be leading an ammunition train to the front, was following a path that took him directly through the Seventy-first. The New Yorkers "got so badly rattled," he recalled, "that they didn't know a Spaniard from an albino."

In recounting this incident to Glendolene Kimmell, Horn said that he "saw one officer use every means to stop the retreat—stampede rather—of his men, pleading, commanding, threatening, even striking at them with his sword." When this officer realized that "his efforts were unavailing," continued Horn, "he broke his sword and stamped upon the pieces." Fortunately, Brig. Gen. Jacob Kent, who happened to be nearby, persuaded the men to lie down in some tall grass. The rattled soldiers threatened to disrupt Horn's train as they dodged "among and under the feet of the pack mules." Horn and his packers eventually regained control of their animals, but only with "oaths and lashes." In the end, the train ran "clean over a battalion that lay in the grass and woods," continued Horn, who admitted that "we must have crippled quite a few."[39]

Horn was also an eyewitness to much bravery at San Juan Heights. He praised both the Rough Riders and the "colored men of the Ninth and Tenth cavalry." The blacks "are wonders," he added. They "are strong as bulls" and "the strongest and best runners." As these African Americans clambered up the heights in the face of heavy fire, Horn observed that the poorly trained men of the volunteer regiments did not measure up to the regulars. Like most Americans, the chief packer had no love for the Cuban rebels who were supposed to assist them. Horn observed one native lift the canteen of a Rough Rider sergeant who was prostrate with exhaustion at the foot of San Juan Hill. "The sergeant was so blamed tired," said Horn, "that he didn't have the energy to shoot the thief."[40]

As the exhausted Americans worked desperately in a torrential downpour to improve their trench defenses on San Juan Heights on the afternoon of 1 July, ammunition and rations were nearly exhausted. The packers and mules were at their best in these trying moments. Cabaniss recalled how thankful he was that he had set aside three trains exclusively as "ammunition trains." Royal A. Prentice, a Rough Rider from New Mexico, remembered how happy they were to see the trains "bringing up boxes of rifle ammunition" on this momentous afternoon. Eventually "a train arrived loaded with great slabs of salt pork interspersed with sacks of sugar." Although the packers were noncombatants, the enemy did not spare them. As the Spaniards kept up heavy rifle fire, their rounds arced over the American troops and fell in the rear, endangering the packers and their mules. "One does not expect gallantry in a pack train," a *St. Louis Post Dispatch* correspondent declared, but after seeing a train arrive in the midst of enemy gunfire, this reporter concluded that "this charge, led by the usual bell mare, was one of the sights of the day." "The soldiers in the field had all the hardtack, bacon, beans and canned tomatoes they wanted," boasted D. D. Grimes, Tom Horn's assistant, although "no delicacies" were delivered.[41]

After the war, critics accused General Shafter of failing to provide his men with basic rations on San Juan Heights. Such accusations reflected directly upon Tom Horn and his packers. Referring to this controversy as the "cracker [hardtack] problem," correspondent and artist Frederic Remington observed that "the gallant Cabanais [*sic*] pushed his mules day and night." "I thought they would go to pieces under the strain," continued Remington. "Too much credit cannot be given them," he added, "and I think every 'packer' who worked on the Santiago line will never forget it." If the men on San Juan Heights suffered any privations, said Remington, it was the fault of the Fifth Corps commander, who sent his force into the field "without its proper ratio of pack-mules." As Cabaniss and Horn were well aware, the civilian packtrains were at the bottom of the pecking order in the Santiago campaign. While the soldiers would have done without if the packers had not delivered supplies, Caspar Whitney of *Harper's Magazine* asserted that the professional soldiers looked down upon these civilian employees. "The only reward I heard of their receiving was curses from head quarters," added Whitney, "and fever from exposure and over-exertion." After the war, packer John Clark echoed Whitney's observation, remarking that their status in Cuba was comparable to that of "stokers on board a warship." Yet the packers' work "is the most important of any that is done" in a military campaign. "Should their work stop," Clark asserted, "the whole force would stop."[42]

Even with the seizure of San Juan Heights, the battle for Santiago was far from over. As the fighting men slowly extended their siege line around Santiago, Tom Horn's packtrains were called upon to carry supplies even greater distances in order to support units on the far side of the city. While a few wagons were now contributing to the supply effort, the four- and six-mule teams could not negotiate the muddy ridge line where the trenches lay. Only the most surefooted mules could climb the heights. The Americans expended huge quantities of rifle and machine gun ammunition to suppress enemy fire. Clerk D. D. Grimes recalled that the Colt rapid-fire guns (an early machine gun) were a particular burden. "The way they ate up ammunition was a caution," he remarked. In a subsequent interview with a Cheyenne newsman, Tom Horn agreed with Grimes, pointing out that these new weapons posed a new problem: "how ammunition was to be furnished them." One packtrain of forty mules, he recalled, carried 80,000 rounds. Yet "we kept the guns supplied and always had a surplus, he boasted. "I am proud of the service of the pack trains," he added. Their performance was "a revelation to the world."[43]

The dangers to the packers and their mules continued for several days as they resupplied San Juan Heights, prompting Tom Horn to conclude that "the duties of a packer in time of battle are as dangerous as those of a soldier." Joseph Lee (Leery), a member of a packtrain carrying ammunition up to San Juan Heights, blundered into an ambush one evening. Lee received a bullet through his hat, and another round ricocheted off his saddle and killed his mule. Fortunately, he managed to jump behind a fellow packer as they escaped "through a shower of bullets." Both Lieutenant Cabaniss and Tom Horn considered themselves lucky to have lost no packers to enemy gunfire. "I didn't have a man killed in the whole campaign," Horn recalled, although "we were constantly passing from the rear to the front while the bullets were flying thicker than falling leaves in autumn." "Those Mauser bullets! They never quit going, once they were let loose," he added, "but seemed to carom like billiard balls on the trees and hills in the rear of us. I never saw anything like it, and I never want to again." "But Lord!" he said, "when a Mauser bullet came zipping along and struck a mule," the poor animal went down on his back "with his feet kicking in the air." It was "just as though a pile driver had hit him."[44]

Although General Shafter anticipated much more fighting before the capture of Santiago, his position was greatly enhanced on Sunday, 3 July, when Rear Adm. William Sampson and the American fleet destroyed the Spanish squadron of Vice Admiral Pascual Cervera y Topete, which was attempting to escape the blockade of Santiago Harbor. But troop strength in the siege lines was deteriorating at an alarming rate in the first two weeks of July. Not only did disease begin to ravage the Fifth Corps, but some 20,000 refugees fled into the American lines from Santiago, all of them expecting the Americans to feed them. As Tom Horn and his packtrains worked even harder to deliver the necessary supplies, more packers were prostrated by yellow fever, malaria, and dysentery.

Even Tom Horn, who was unusually hardy, contracted yellow fever. While he later complained about the "daily allowance of twenty to ninety grains of quinine" that he and his packers had to take, this medication probably saved his life. In a letter to a friend at Fort Thomas, Arizona, packer Surrill L. Sweeter complained that he was "d——n near dead and wore out": "Well, I have been where the bullets were thick; seen lots of men killed and many others are sick. . . . I don't think I will live to get back; it is a long ways to walk [to Arizona]. Every day I have had a hard time of it. . . . I get $50 per month and think we will get $75 soon. . . . We have to work day and night and I have not been dry since I landed here." Yet Sweeter was proud of the fact that he and his fellow packers, against great odds, had "carried ammunition" to the front at a critical time.

In late July, Lieutenant Cabaniss obtained a "surgeon's certificate of disability" and requested six months' medical leave. "Hard work is telling on teamsters and packers," Shafter informed Secretary of War Russell Alger on 10 July. At least fifty percent were incapacitated. Yet Chief Packer Tom Horn, who was now forty pounds underweight, managed to continue leading trains to the siege lines.[45]

In spite of these hardships, Tom Horn found time to assist ailing soldiers. After the war, a former Rough Rider informed William McLeod Raine, a popular western writer, that Horn cared for him and a comrade when they fell ill in Cuba. "A friend and he were lying out on a pile of brush, both of them very sick men," wrote Raine, "when a big brown-faced Westerner stopped to ask them where they were from?" When one of them replied, "Arizona," continued Raine, "that was enough for this 'brown-faced' frontiersman," who turned out to be Tom Horn. "He took them into his own tent, waited on them, fed them, and nursed them back to health." One of Horn's packers, P. E. Butler, a member of Packtrain No. 3, found a way to use the packers' medical problems to his advantage by endorsing a patent medicine in stateside newspapers, Chamberlain's Colic, Cholera and Diarrhoea remedy." "We [packers] all had diarrhea in more or less violent form," declared Butler. Having to "rush and rush night and day to keep the troops supplied," he continued, Chamberlain's tonic enabled the packers to continue their rigorous schedule.[46]

Much to the relief of Tom Horn and his packers, General José Toral, commander of Spanish forces in Santiago, surrendered on 14 July 1898. American troops marched into the city three days later. The occupation of Santiago came none too soon for Horn and his men. They were ready to go home. "I got about all I wanted of that kind of service," he later informed a Denver reporter. "If anybody imagines we had a snap [in Cuba], he is mightily mistaken." Horn called it "the toughest job I ever tackled, and I have been upon many an Indian campaign through deserts and over rugged mountains." In a burst of patriotic feeling, he admitted that he "would go again if our country should get into trouble and need my services." Likewise D. D. Grimes, who returned with Horn to Denver, declared that he "didn't care to stay after the war was over." When Colonel Jacobs, the chief quartermaster in Santiago, tried to persuade them to continue on as packers, both men refused. "If we had stayed there another month, we would have been planted [dead]," Grimes added. "A man can't live forever on quinine."[47]

Tom Horn's last few days in Santiago were apparently the only restful ones he had experienced since arriving on the island on 23 June. While Lieutenant Cabaniss returned to his regular unit, quartermaster records indicate that Horn and many other civilian employees were "employed in general work in the Quarter Masters Department, Army of Occupation of Cuba." On 6 September 1898, Colonel Jacobs released him and D. D. Grimes at the same time. Both men immediately boarded a ship for Montauk Point, on Long Island, New York, where Horn was admitted to a hospital for treatment of yellow fever. Somehow, Robert Pinkerton, who supervised the detective agency's affairs in the East, learned of this former employee's situation, obtained Horn's release, and provided him with railroad fare. Accompanied by D. D. Grimes, Horn immediately departed for the West.[48]

The two packers arrived in Denver on Friday, 23 September. After registering at the Albany Hotel and indulging in the luxury of a bath, Horn paid a visit to the headquarters of the Military Department of Colorado, now commanded by Col. Edwin Sumner, his former boss in Arizona. Apparently, Horn's reason for traveling directly to Denver was to request government assistance for his medical problems. When Lt. Col. Edwin Byron Atwood, the military department quartermaster, said he was not authorized to provide such assistance, Horn turned to Army Quartermaster General Marshal I. Ludington, in Washington. In a letter to Ludington on 30 September, Horn asked if he was eligible for "pay & commutation of rations from the time he left Santiago, Sept. 6, till Sept. 23 when he reported to Col. Atwood." Although puzzled by this request, Ludington asked Lieutenant Colonel Jacobs, who was still in Santiago, what benefits the packers were entitled to. As might be expected, Ludington replied in the negative, even though Colonel Jacobs, Horn's boss in Cuba, complimented him for his services. The request was rejected in a letter stating that there was no evidence that pay was due Horn. Civilian employees were not entitled to the benefits accorded military personnel.[49]

While in Denver the ex-chief packer had an opportunity to talk with newspapermen. Stretching the truth as usual, Horn told the *Rocky Mountain News* that "Only Nine of His Force of 123 Sturdy Men Survived the Awful Ordeal" in Cuba. "I saw twenty-three of my boys buried and others died on board ship and were dropped in the ocean. Only nine men out of the entire force which packed ammunition and provisions for the soldiers at Santiago were able to return," he said mournfully. "The remainder are dead, wounded, sick with fever or disabled from traveling by the terrible inroads of the climate." While Horn was exaggerating, many of his men had suffered the same debilitating illnesses as the soldiers in the Santiago Campaign. At least one, Richard M. Stevens, packer second class in Charles McLaughlin's train, was buried at sea. Three days later, a *Denver Republican* reporter found Horn "tossing and rolling in a fever" in his room at the Albany Hotel. "I guess the Old Man's got me on his list at last," he moaned. "I thought I was getting out pretty lucky, but maybe I spoke too soon."[50]

Rather than return to Arizona, Horn made his way to the ranch of John C. Coble in Wyoming. Coble had a new partner, Franklin Bosler, and had moved the headquarters of the Iron Mountain Ranch Company to Bosler, eighteen miles north of Laramie. Coble had not had an easy time of it since this move. He was still recovering from a serious fall from his horse. Horn's reason for seeking the hospitality of John Coble is not known. His illness may have demanded immediate care, or he may have desired to remain near Denver, hoping to receive further military benefits. Whatever the reason, on 26 September he was en route to Cheyenne on a passenger train in the company of none other than George Prentice, who allegedly served as the payoff man in the Billy Lewis and Fred U. Powell assassinations in 1895.[51]

Tom Horn's association with the campaign in Cuba was not quite over. When Congress launched an investigation into the conduct of the campaign, the former chief packer received notice that he might

be called to testify before a committee that was looking into the quality of the food provided the CEF. Nicknamed the Beef Court because
of allegations that the army had issued tainted canned beef, this committee deposed numerous campaign veterans (among them Horn's old
boss Marion Maus). On 12 April 1899, Horn received a subpoena to
appear before the committee. Informing the *Denver Evening Post* of this
summons, he launched into a scathing indictment of General Shafter,
alleging that he knew about the poor quality of the beef rations but did
nothing about it. Horn declared that the cans of beef that his packtrains
carried to the front "frequently exploded" in the hot sun. Reflecting
the disdain of many civilian employees for professional soldiers, Horn
remarked that "Shafter was about as unpopular a man among his men
and officers as it was possible to be," calling him "a brute of the first
water." "In my opinion his place is as a hog driver at the stock yards."
It was probably best for all concerned that Tom Horn did not testify.
The committee concluded its work before he could make the trip to
Washington.[52]

Horn could look back on his service as chief packer for the Fifth Corps
as one of the high points of his life. He served capably and endured the
same privations and debilitating diseases that his comrades suffered. In
addition to his supervisory role, Horn personally undertook the hazardous duty of leading packtrains to the front lines. Veterans of the Santiago Campaign remembered his efforts to deliver desperately needed
food and ammunition to San Juan Heights with much appreciation.
Indeed, Major General Shafter credited the packers and their animals
with the victory in the Santiago Campaign. "The pack trains saved us,"
admitted the Fifth Corps commander. "They were invaluable."[52]

CHAPTER 9

The Wild Bunch

When Tom Horn arrived at John Coble's ranch at Bosler, Wyoming, in late September 1898, he was seriously ill with yellow fever. Having lost forty pounds, he presented a "sallow complexion" and was "a mere skeleton of his former self," according to a friend. Coble immediately put him to bed. Hugh McPhee, a Coble employee at this time, recalled that a string was tied from Horn's wrist to a bell in the cook shack so he could call the cook if he needed attention. On one occasion, the cook found him on the floor "with the sweat just pouring off him." Eventually, Coble sent Horn to Cheyenne, where Nannie Clay Steele, a boardinghouse operator, nursed him back to "a semblance of health." When a *Sun-Leader* reporter spotted Horn on the street, he was surprised at how "thin and emaciated" he was. Nonetheless, Horn insisted that he was "getting better" and now able to take walks. When he was finally able to leave the boardinghouse in February 1899, his first act was to go on "a big drunk," according to McPhee.[1]

While Horn was convalescing, a new job possibility came his way. In October 1898, the War Department began to form new packtrains for a campaign against Emilio Aguinaldo's rebel movement in the newly conquered Philippine Islands. Initially, these trains were to be organized at Camp Carlin, near Cheyenne, as well as at Jefferson Barracks, near St. Louis. On 5 October Horn wrote Quartermaster General Marshall I. Ludington asking for a position as packmaster. "I think for the services that I rendered in Cuba as Chief Packer of the 5th Army Corp[s]," he wrote, "that I should be intitled [*sic*] to pack mastership of one of the trains organized here as this [Wyoming] is my home." Horn pointed out that not only had Col. Joshua West Jacobs, his superior in Santiago, given him high marks, but "I am well and personaly [sic] known by nearly all the generals in the army." Horn also got a glowing reference from Lt. Col. Marion Maus, who described him as "one of the bravest men I ever saw." Unfortunately, the Quartermaster Department soon canceled its Camp Carlin recruitment plans, leaving a large group of applicants, including Tom Horn, high and dry in Cheyenne. They still had the option of paying their own travel expenses to St. Louis, and a few did so, but not Tom Horn. What would have happened had he gone to the Philippines? Would he have remained in military service and eventually retired with dignity and public applause? It is impossible to say. His old comrade Henry Daly stuck with the packtrain service, received the rank of major in the regular army, and retired after World War I. Unfortunately, stick-to-it-iveness was not Tom Horn's forte.[2]

But Horn had other employment options. John C. Coble and Swan Land and Cattle Company officials, who continued to distrust their nester neighbors in the Iron Mountain region, were always ready to employ him as a range detective. No doubt there was a groan or a shudder within the granger element when this menacing figure suddenly resumed patrols on the Laramie plains after three years' absence. And John Coble and Tom Horn were again walking side by side on the streets of Cheyenne as though suspicions of their collaboration in the Lewis and Powell assassinations four years earlier had vanished. "J. C. Coble, [of] Iron Mountain, and Tom Horn are at the Inter Ocean [Hotel]," the *Cheyenne Daily Sun-Leader* announced in March 1899. At this time, Coble and Franklin Bosler, who had recently invested in the Iron Mountain Ranch Company, were reportedly trying to persuade several small ranchers and homesteaders to sell out,—possibly as a way to reduce the threat of cattle rustling.[3]

In spite of his disappointments, Tom Horn's career soon took a significant turn. He became involved in the pursuit of a band of highwaymen led by George Sutherland Currie, alias "Flat Nose George." Among his associates were Harvey Logan, alias Kid Curry; Harvey Logan's brother, Lonnie; and a cousin, Robert E. Lee, alias Robert Curry. These men were part of a loosely organized gang reportedly led by Robert LeRoy Parker, alias Butch Cassidy. After a series of small-time store and mail robberies in Montana and Wyoming, Flat Nose

George and the Logan brothers murdered a Johnson County deputy sheriff in April 1897, and followed up with an unsuccessful raid on a bank in Belle Fourche, South Dakota. On 2 June 1899, the Currie band—including Harvey Logan, Harry Longabaugh, alias Sundance Kid, and three others—held up the Union Pacific's Overland Flyer at Wilcox station, forty miles north of Laramie, Wyoming. The highwaymen took as much as $50,000 in coin, unsigned bank bills, and jewelry. After separating into threes, Currie, Harvey Logan, and Longabaugh fled northward in the direction of the Hole-in-the-Wall, an infamous outlaw lair in southern Johnson County. The second trio, who have not been identified, rode toward Brown's Park, in northwestern Colorado. Within hours, Union Pacific detectives, U.S. Marshal Frank Hadsell of Wyoming, and several county sheriffs, were in pursuit. When rewards of $3,000 were posted for each robber, as many as 100 men joined various posses in a helter-skelter chase. Three days later, Flat Nose George and his two comrades ambushed a posse north of Casper, killing Converse County Sheriff Josiah Hazen. The outlaws continued their flight into the Big Horn Basin, where sympathetic ranchers, including Billy Hill and William A. (Billy) Speck, provided them with food and fresh horses. Eventually, they escaped into the Wind River Range, where the posses abandoned the chase.[4]

Still resolved to continue the manhunt, Union Pacific officials, with the cooperation of Marshal Hadsell and the Pinkerton Detective Agency, decided on a less visible pursuit—in frontier parlance, a "still hunt." Instead of large, noisy posses, a few detectives using stealth and undercover methods would infiltrate areas where the bandits were believed to be hiding. Even though Flat Nose George Currie had at most only five men with him in the Wilcox robbery, U.P. detectives believed Butch Cassidy and other Wild Bunch members were also involved behind the scenes. By late June, however, the outlaw band had split up and scattered throughout the Rocky Mountains. Flat Nose George remained in Wyoming, Cassidy and several companions were hiding out near Alma, New Mexico, others sought sanctuary in Brown's Park, Colorado, and Lonnie Logan and his cousin Bob Lee returned to their home in Harlem, Montana. To seek these fugitives out, the man hunters would have to cover a vast amount of territory.[5]

Experienced detectives were deemed necessary for this widespread still hunt, which would be divided into northern and southern searches.

The two men selected to head up these endeavors were Tom Horn and Charlie Siringo. Siringo, who was still a Pinkerton operative, was assigned the southern Rockies; Horn was assigned the northern region. "Several still hunts have taken the trail," said a Cheyenne dispatch to the *Salt Lake Herald* on 19 June. "Among these is Colonel Tom Horn, who was chief of scouts under General Miles." "Horn is a dead shot," added the reporter, "and should he come upon the robbers they will never live to tell of the meeting" (a prescient observation). The dispatch failed to mention Horn's employer, which could have been the U.P. Railroad or U.S. Marshal Hadsell or both. On 7 July, Hadsell, who heartily endorsed the still hunt as the only reasonable means of "effecting the capture of these outlaws," informed his superior, Attorney General John W. Griggs, that he had employed a detective without prior authorization. The marshal defended this decision as an "urgent necessity" to keep pressure on the train robbers. Apparently, Hadsell's new hire was Tom Horn, although he proposed to employ additional men who were familiar with the Wild Bunch's haunts and their friends "to act as detectives or scouts." Whatever the source of Horn's paychecks, he served both as a U.P. detective and a deputy U.S. marshal.[6]

In preparation for their missions, Tom Horn and Charlie Siringo each operated with a partner. Siringo took along a Pinkerton colleague, W. B. Sayers, while Tom Horn went further afield and called on his old Arizona friend Edwin Tewksbury. If all the detectives were "as competent" as Tewksbury, wrote the *Globe Times,* the train robbers would "soon be run to earth." Tewksbury had recently been tried for the murder of Tom Graham in 1892 but released. (Legend has it that Tom Horn was with Tewksbury when he ambushed Graham and that Horn fired the first shot.) When Tewksbury joined Tom Horn in Cheyenne, another old Arizona friend, Burt Dunlap, was also present. Dunlap was vacationing with his wife in Denver. On 14 July, Dunlap, Horn, and Tewksbury got together at the Inter Ocean Hotel. While this must have been an enjoyable occasion for Horn, it is doubtful that either Dunlap or Tewksbury knew the full scope of their friend's activities in Wyoming. Tewksbury would soon get a good taste.[7]

While Charlie Siringo and W. B. Sayers tracked members of the Wild Bunch in Utah, Colorado, and New Mexico, Tom Horn and Ed Tewksbury began their search in Johnson County, Wyoming. In an interview with the *Rocky Mountain News* some months later, Horn declared that Flat Nose George Currie and his comrades returned to the Hole-in-the-Wall from the Wind River Range after the posses gave up the chase in June. "Detectives have been watching the rendezvous ever since," he added. At first, Horn and Tewksbury may have tried to work under cover. Horn used his old moniker, Thomas H. Hale. Since Tewksbury was a stranger to this region, he used his own name. Other detectives may have also been at work in northern Wyoming. Nonetheless, residents of the Powder River area were soon aware of the presence of Horn and Tewksbury.[8]

Although the detectives' primary task was to search for the train robbers, Horn was always on the lookout for livestock thieves. In this instance, he probably made no distinction between the bandits and the local residents who gave them aid and comfort. Flat Nose George Currie began his career in Crook and Johnson counties as a livestock thief, and Horn considered the small ranchers thieves as well. The locals assumed that the detectives were looking for rustlers. The authorities believed that Bill Speck and his employer, rancher Billy Hill, had helped the Flat Nose George band escape two months earlier, so Speck and Hill were especially concerned when the detectives appeared. The presence of Tom Horn and Ed Tewksbury immediately "aroused speculation as to the nature of their business," Speck recalled many years later. He and his neighbors believed "Horn was a 'killer' for the stock associations." Sure enough, "Johnny Nolan [Nolen] received an anonymous letter . . . saying that Horn was headed that way," added Speck, "and that himself, Billy Hill, and Alex Ghent were slated for execution." John "Shorty" Wheelwright also recalled seeing Horn and his companion. "We didn't know who he was when he was here," recalled Wheelwright, since "he went by the name of Tom Hale and always had an Indian boy with him." (Tewksbury's mother was Native American.) The two were very skittish, he added, and "never stayed two nights in the same place." Yet Horn put in an appearance at the Grigg Post Office, a few miles west of present Kaycee, on the Middle Powder River. Not only did Horn have to mail his reports, as well as receive mail, but rural post offices were "information booths," according to writer Thelma Condit, for intelligence in regard to outlaw movements as they were for all sorts of gossip.[9]

One day J. Elmer Brock, whose father owned a ranch near Mayoworth in Johnson County, encountered a very frightened Billy Hill, who insisted that Tom Horn "was after him." As a means to get at Hill, Horn and his partner, "reputed to be part negro" (Tewksbury was sometimes mistaken for a black man) started a range fire. Horn's strategy worked. In checking out the blaze, Hill unwittingly wandered near the detectives' campsite, giving Horn his opportunity. "I am going to shoot him right where his suspenders cross," Horn allegedly said to Tewksbury, who suddenly had second thoughts. "Something tells me that if you kill this man," he warned Horn, "we will both be killed." Horn hesitated. Thus, Tewksbury "saved the rancher's life." While Brock's source for this story is not known, he reports that Tewksbury wrote to Billy Hill later and explained how he narrowly escaped death. Tewksbury's letter contained such detail of this event, said Hill, that he "could only conclude it was the truth." Alex Ghent, whom the authorities considered another Wild Bunch associate, also had a harrowing encounter with Horn about this time. In an effort to intimidate Ghent, Horn lurked in the vicinity of Ghent's cabin in the Hole-in-the-Wall. After training his rifle on the cabin for a few minutes, the detective rode menacingly around the shack and departed. Apparently, Horn intended to convey the message that Ghent should avoid assisting outlaws and leave the country.[10]

In August 1899, Flat Nose George Currie and the Logan brothers left the Hole-in-the-Wall, heading for Chadron, Nebraska, where Currie's two sisters lived. The outlaw leader's girl friend, called "Black Mot," also planned to meet him in Chadron. Before taking up the outlaws' trail, Horn and Tewksbury were joined by railroad detectives and representatives of the Wyoming Stock Growers Association. (Apparently, the bandits were riding stolen horses that the association desired to reclaim.) As Ed Tewksbury recalled, the detectives trailed the train robbers down the Powder River Valley into southeastern Montana, then into South Dakota, and finally into Nebraska. Since the outlaws were well mounted, they cleanly outdistanced their pursuers. Upon arriving in Chadron, the Wyoming possemen (presumably including Horn and Tewksbury) found railroad detectives already on the scene. They "swarm in and out on every train," according to one reporter, in search of the bandits. While Flat Nose George secretly visited his sisters, Kid Curry and Lonnie Logan holed up at a place called Twenty-Mile Ranch near Crawford, Nebraska. Even though the highwaymen tried to keep a low profile, they betrayed their presence by indiscreetly passing bank notes from the Wilcox train robbery in a Chadron haberdashery.[11]

In spite of the presence of so many officers, the bandits made a successful getaway back into Wyoming. In addition to having family in Chadron, George Currie, who as a boy worked as a "meek and humble grocery clerk" in a local store, had friends in the vicinity. Even "good deacons of the church offer excuses for him," one newsman grumbled. The lawmen complained that the outlaws were tipped off by a report in the *Omaha World-Herald,* which forced the detectives to move prematurely. "The Union Pacific detectives, United States deputies and the sheriff [Charles Dargan] . . . left town hurriedly today," according to a Chadron dispatch of 18 August. The posse rode to Twenty-Mile Ranch as quickly as possible, but their quarry had fled back into Wyoming. Flat Nose George also managed to escape. As the unhappy detectives went their separate ways, they continued to complain that "the newspapers . . . exposed their operations."[12]

Back on the train robbers' trail, the Horn-Tewksbury team traced them to the Hole-in-the-Wall, and then farther west into the remote Jackson Hole country. In early September the man hunters overtook two suspects and shot it out with them. Horn gave his version of these events later to the *Rocky Mountain News:*

> After following the trail of the two men for nearly a month, they came upon them in camp just as they were getting supper. One was engaged in frying bacon and the other at some distance from the fire, getting their traps together. He [Horn] and his companion at once opened fire on them, the man who was cooking being first hit. The other man sprang behind a tree and began shooting rapidly, one of his shots hitting the half-breed [Tewksbury] in the leg. Horn advanced and finally got the other man as he was endeavoring to escape.

Horn left the outlaws, whom he called Smith and Montgomery, "dead on the ground" and took his wounded partner to the railroad station at Opal, Wyoming, on the Oregon Short Line. There was "no question as to their being members of the gang that robbed the Union Pacific train at Wilcox," insisted Horn, "as their trail was struck shortly after the affair [Wilcox robbery] and has been followed all the time, although occasionally lost, and taken up again."[13]

After this event Ed Tewksbury, who had had enough of Wyoming and of Tom Horn, returned to Arizona. Apparently, the two men had been quarreling for some time, although the reason for their disagreement is not known. Shorty Wheelwright, a resident of the Hole-in-the-Wall, saw Horn and an "Indian boy" (presumably Tewksbury) arguing in a Buffalo saloon about this time. When the "Indian boy" disappeared, Wheelwright and his friends "figured Tom Horn had shot him in the back." Of course, Tewksbury was very much alive. Dan R. Williamson, the sheriff of Gila County under whom Tewksbury had served as a deputy, recalled Ed's return to Globe, reporting that his former deputy said very little about his experiences with Tom Horn except that the "Wyoming layout was too tough for him." In an apparent reference to Horn's involvement in the state's range difficulties, Tewksbury "predicted disaster for Horn," added Williamson. According to Jimmy Anderson, another Globe resident, Tewksbury remarked that "what Tom wanted from him was to kill some criminals, from ambush." While Tewksbury did not object to killing someone if that person deserved it, continued Anderson, he was not in favor of ambushing people.[14]

In October 1899, an important break occurred in the Wilcox robbery case when Lonnie Logan and Bob Lee attempted to pass stolen bills through their saloon business in Harlem, Montana. With this new information in hand, the Union Pacific Railroad and Pinkerton Agency sent Tom Horn and Charlie Siringo back into the field. While Siringo investigated the Logan brothers' old haunts in northern Montana, Horn returned to the Hole-in-the-Wall country, where Lonnie Logan and Bob Lee had reportedly again taken refuge. When questioned about his latest activities some weeks later, Horn asserted that he had been "on the trail of the robbers alone and single handed ever since the expose in the little town in Montana." From the Hole-in-the-Wall, Horn traveled to southern Wyoming. Apparently, he was still combining livestock work with the search for the train robbers (the outlaws combined rustling and train robbery as well). In October, Ora Haley, the Laramie cattle baron, hired Horn. Haley, a friend and neighbor of John C. Coble, controlled a vast range that stretched from the Union Pacific tracks south into northwestern Colorado. Since some of the Wilcox robbers were thought to be hiding in this region, Horn was able to perform double duty without difficulty. Haley arranged for Horn to board with Fred and Catherine Bell, who owned a small spread near Laramie City. In his typical boastful fashion, the detective informed the

Bells that he was searching for the Wilcox robbers and asserted that "he was the only man who could track them successfully." When Horn left on patrol, Catherine Bell assumed that the outlaws would probably kill him. However, he returned a few days later. In December, Thomas Jefferson Carr, a Union Pacific detective, informed Frank Canton, a former Johnson County sheriff, that "'Tom Hale or Horn' and two other detectives had been looking for the robbers." (Carr had served as a deputy U.S. marshal with Horn in Johnson County in 1892.)[15]

By late December 1899, Tom Horn was back in the Hole-in-the-Wall country, still on the trail of Flat Nose George Currie. On 2 January 1900, Horn called on Bill Speck, who was suspected of withholding information about the Wilcox robbers. Apparently still using the undercover name of Tom Hale, the detective was, at first, very disarming. Horn "was very entertaining when he wanted to be," recalled Speck. The following morning, however, Horn suddenly revealed that he was a U.P. officer and began to question his host about neighboring ranchers, including Speck's employer, Billy Hill. Horn declared bluntly that Speck and Hill "knew altogether too much as to the whereabouts of the train robbers," and he threatened to take Speck back to Cheyenne for further questioning. When Speck expressed surprise, Horn declared that "there was considerable suspicion in that neck of the woods about a 'homely, ungainly, lantern-jawed, long-nosed cuss' named 'Old Speck' who was always hanging around Billy Hill." "Well, I never heard before that a feller could be hung on his looks," protested Speck, "but if that's the law, I guess I'll get the limit, cause I can't transmogrify my looks." Much to Bill Speck's relief, Tom Horn departed on the second day, leaving Speck with visions of ending his days "in some secluded draw or else hanging from a convenient cottonwood tree."[16]

In his subsequent report to Edmund C. Harris, chief of the Union Pacific's Secret Service Department, Tom Horn frankly admitted threatening Bill Speck. "I told him that he had some information that I wanted and he must give it to me," said Horn, "or I would kill him." When Speck "commenced to cry and said the . . . rustlers would kill him if he told," the detective reminded his host that he "was worse" than the outlaws. Speck said the three Wilcox bandits who visited him the previous June were George Currie, Harvey Ray (possibly an alias of Harvey Logan), and a third unidentified man. As this outlaw trio left Speck's dugout, Currie said they were going to Canada. Since Speck had finally given him some helpful information, Tom Horn graciously decided "it best not to kill him." Speck "will tell me if any of them ever writes to [Billy] Hill or [Alex] Ghent," Horn informed Harris confidently. After leaving Speck's dugout, Horn made his way to Casper. In mid-January, a Casper news dispatch reported that "Deputy United States Marshal Tom Horn has been here for the last ten days . . . on the trail of the Wilcox robbers." When asked about the Currie band, Horn declared confidently that these men would "surely be captured sooner or later."[17]

On 27 January 1900, Tom Horn arrived in the state capital. The purpose of this visit was "business," he declared, meaning his search for Flat Nose George Currie. On this occasion he revealed for the first time that he and Ed Tewksbury had killed two suspected train robbers in Jackson Hole, news that was revealed the following day by the *Rocky Mountain News* bureau in Cheyenne. When Horn was seen conferring with U.P. detectives, one observer concluded that their purpose was "to make up the official report of the transaction [shooting]" in order for Horn to file for the reward. At this point, what began as a straightforward report of a shooting quickly degenerated into an embarrassing controversy—one that had long-term adverse consequences for Tom Horn's already questionable reputation. The problem began when the *Cheyenne Sun-Leader* declared on 29 January that the *News's* "sensational report" of these killings the previous day was untrue. In fact, said the *Sun-Leader,* one posseman (presumably Tewksbury) was wounded, but "none of the robbers were shot." On this same day another Cheyenne dispatch denounced the story as "a fake" and went on to assert that Tom Horn, "the veteran scout and Indian fighter," also denied it. However, a day later, the detective again changed his story. "Tom Horn, who was unwilling to make any definite statement," said the *Sun-Leader,* "now claims the reward of the Union Pacific for the capture [killing] of two of the robbers."[18]

A writer for the *Rocky Mountain News* pointedly asked Horn if the story was true. He replied in the affirmative, but added that the encounter took place "about forty miles west of Jackson's Hole" and that it had happened only three weeks earlier. (His reason for placing this incident four months after it happened is not known.) Horn then volunteered additional details of the encounter, including the wounding of Ed Tewksbury, and leaving the dead suspects unburied. After a flying trip to Denver—presumably connected with his claim of the reward—the much-sought-after detective returned to Cheyenne, where a *Sun-Leader* newsman confronted him again. "'Mr. Horn, the newspapers are having a great fight over you," said this reporter. "It was maintained by one side and denied by the other," continued this writer, "that you killed two men a few weeks since in the Jackson-Hole country." "You newspaper men are pretty tough customers," Horn grumbled, adding that he did not believe "those matters should be given [to] the papers anyhow." Although discomfited, Horn admitted that "Ed. Taxbury [*sic*] and myself were compelled to kill two men a few weeks since." Their victims "were notorious horse and cattle thieves and criminal raiders named Monte and Blair," he continued, but "they were not the Wilcox train robbers." Apparently working from information received from Bill Speck, Horn added that the train robbers were hiding in British Columbia and he planned to look for them there. "We know who they are," he declared, "and the Union Pacific will pursue them to the end." Horn ended his interview with the remark that "my companion, Taxbury, was wounded in the stomach" in this encounter. (Tewksbury was presumably shot in the leg, not the stomach.)[19]

The controversy surrounding Tom Horn's story continued as the *Wyoming Tribune,* the mouthpiece of former U.S. Senator Joseph M. Carey, saw an opportunity to embarrass its chief competitor, Edward A. Slack, editor of the *Sun-Leader.* Even after Slack attempted to correct his mistake, the *Tribune* snidely remarked: "And now the *Sun-Leader* is broad minded enough to . . . frankly admit that the story of the killing of the two Union Pacific train robbers was a mistake." "Wonders never cease," concluded the *Tribune.* Regardless of the questionable nature of Tom Horn's claim, Union Pacific Railroad officials apparently concluded that some effort should be made to correct the mistaken notion that the company employed rogue detectives. On 6 February, the *Evening News* of Lincoln, Nebraska, printed a very different version of the Jackson Hole killings. This story, probably inspired by officials at the Union Pacific headquarters in nearby Omaha, asserted that Horn and Tewksbury followed proper procedures. Not only did they take the bodies of their victims—"Chip" Monte and "Tex" Blair—to a nearby village, but they reported the killings to local authorities. Since the shooting "was clearly . . . done in self defense," added the *Evening News,* Horn and Tewksbury were released. The detectives, in this version of the story, also buried the dead men. In spite of the railroad's effort to portray its detectives in a more favorable light, the incident had the adverse effect of further publicizing Horn's name and provoking a public distaste for him that probably helped to seal his fate. After all, the authorities in Laramie and Albany counties still considered him "a person of interest" in connection with the Lewis and Powell murders in 1895. Tom Horn's public references to Ed Tewksbury's presence at these most recent killings was also very indiscreet and could have cost his former partner dearly had an official inquiry into the killings taken place.[20]

As if the Jackson Hole killings were not enough, Tom Horn may have been involved in another set of shootings during his search for the Wilcox train robbers. This second incident did not become public knowledge until the *Denver Times* broke the story at the time of Horn's execution, in November 1903. Like the Blair and Montgomery shootings, details of these latter slayings are very vague. While the *Times* placed these killings "not far from the scene" of the Wilcox train robbery, they probably took place (if at all) in the Red Desert, just north of the Colorado border. The *Times* named the two victims as George Woodruff and Thomas Payne, "well-known" prospectors who had gone missing. Furthermore, a second source existed for this alleged episode. Bob Meldrum, a Carbon County deputy sheriff who occasionally worked with Tom Horn, boasted in a saloon in Dixon, Wyoming, according to writer John Rolfe Burroughs, that he and Horn were involved in a double killing that they did not report to the authorities. The two man hunters, who were searching for train robbers in the Red Desert, according to Burroughs, got on the trail of "two horsemen and shot them down, only to find that they were the wrong men." While Meldrum was no more reliable as a source than Tom Horn, it is intriguing that he specifically referred to *two* innocent victims. Meldrum, who later enjoyed the notoriety of being "Tom Horn's partner," eventually went to prison for another killing.[21]

Tom Horn reportedly went so far as to seek the reward for the Woodruff-Payne shootings, claiming that the victims were train robbers. The *Laramie Republican,* which added additional details to the *Denver Times* story, reported that Union Pacific officials insisted on seeing the bodies. "To convince them that he was telling the truth," according to the *Republican,* Horn took these railroad men "to a point not far from the scene of the robbery." Sure enough, the excavators found two corpses, although they were not the bandits. "Horn swore he shot them both as they came face to face with him in the mountain trail," continued the reporter, "and . . . they had raised their guns to shoot at him." However, no weapons were found with the corpses. "Tom Horn had made a terrible mistake," added the *Republican,* "if he really believed he was killing train robbers." In order to cover his grisly error, "influential friends of the murderer hastened to Cheyenne." These unnamed friends, presumably wealthy cattlemen and, perhaps, railroad officials who had employed Horn, "quickly hushed up" the incident. To ensure that he was not a subject of legal action, the story continues, "Horn waited in the open country until he was assured that he was safe." While this shooting cannot be substantiated, the fact that the newspapers gave the full names of the dead men—completely different from the men killed in Jackson Hole—adds some credibility to the story.[22]

Since his return from Cuba in September 1898, Tom Horn's tendency to boast about his misdeeds had become more pronounced, especially when in his cups, and had the effect of reinforcing public doubts about him. While suspicions of his involvement in the Lewis and Powell murders had been spread largely by word of mouth, newspapers were now openly critical. In recalling the Jackson Hole shootings, Horn discounted this incident as merely a "funny mistake," according to the *Daily Sun-Leader,* and "seemed in no wise concerned that he had murdered two innocent men." (Apparently, Horn expressed no remorse.) Such callous behavior, the *Carbon County Journal* editorialized, "shows a reckless disregard for human life . . . [and] should be rigidly investigated." "If the plan of shooting first and investigating afterwards becomes general [among lawmen] many a poor fellow will be murdered," added this concerned journalist. While it is difficult to discount entirely these reports of murders, neither Tom Horn nor Bob Meldrum could be trusted to tell the truth.[23]

Just as Horn was wrapping up his stint with the Union Pacific at the end of January 1900, the still hunt that he, Charlie Siringo, and other detectives had conducted for the Wilcox robbers began to yield results. Detectives traced Lonnie Logan and Bob Lee from Harlem, Montana, to Cripple Creek, Colorado. On 28 February Pinkerton operatives took Lee into custody without incident. In the meantime, Lonnie Logan was followed to the home of his aunt in Dodson, Missouri. He was killed while attempting to escape. On 17 April, lawmen shot and killed Flat Nose George Currie in northeastern Utah. In May 1900, Bob Lee was tried and convicted of mail robbery in U.S. District Court in Cheyenne and sentenced to ten years in prison.[24]

As more and more newspapers covered Tom Horn's man-hunting activities, more and more misinformation about him circulated. In February 1900, the *Kansas City Star* reported that Horn had recently killed Kid Curry, and his cousin, Bob Lee, in the Hole-in-the-Wall. When this report reached Kid Curry, he angrily accused the Pinkertons of deliberately releasing the story that Tom Horn had killed him. "Them Pinkertons will do anything to get their fee from the Union Pacific by trying to show the Wilcox case closed," he alleged. "Of course, we know they have Tom Horn out shooting people from ambush," continued Curry, "but he ain't come within a hundred miles of catching me. . . . I'd like to get my hands on one of those Pinkerton bastards." (Wild West enthusiasts still enjoy speculating about the outcome of an imaginary confrontation between Tom Horn and Kid Curry. John Rolfe Burroughs asserted that Kid Curry was the only outlaw "who equaled Tom Horn for sheer nerve.")[25]

After leaving Union Pacific employment at the end of January 1900, Horn continued with the Wild Bunch investigation, working the four corners area of Wyoming, Colorado, Idaho, and Utah. He maintained a presence in this lawless region for much of the year, but his primary mission was the search for rustlers; watching for the Wild Bunch riders was secondary. The focus of Horn's attention was Brown's Park, the westernmost precinct of Routt County, Colorado. Neighboring cattle companies suspected the Park's inhabitants not only of cattle theft but of giving aid and comfort to Butch Cassidy and his comrades. Among these suspects were Amos Herbert Bassett and his daughters, Ann and Josephine. Ann Bassett, who was dubbed "Queen Ann" because of her imperious demeanor, was "as handy as a man in the round-up," according to one report. Several Brown's Park cowboys, including Madison M. (Matt) Rash, James (Jim) McNight, Isom Dart (a black man who was born a slave in Arkansas), and Elijah B. "Longhorn" Thompson, were all suspected of rustling.[26]

By the late 1890s, the livestock barons who ran cattle in the vicinity of Brown's Park had responded to the rustler menace by forming the Little Snake River Valley Cattlemen's Association. Among the most aggrieved ranchers was Ora B. Haley. Not only was Haley one of Wyoming's leading citizens, but he was a friend of John C. Coble of the Iron Mountain Cattle Company. In 1896 Haley hired Hiram H. (Hi) Bernard to manage his interests in northwestern (Routt County) Colorado and assigned him the task of leading an upcoming campaign that the cattlemen envisioned against the Brown's Park rustlers. Working through the Little Snake River organization, Haley found others who held equally strong feelings: Charles F. Ayer, whose Bar Ell Seven Ranch was located at Four Mile, in Routt County; the Two Circle Bar of Robert J. and John S. Cary, near Hayden; the Sevens ranch (Jeremiah Pierce and Joseph Reef), on the Yampa River; and, of course, Haley's Two Bar, situated near the village of Maybell. J. Wilson Cary, a son of John Cary, recalled that his father hosted a meeting, presumably in late 1899 or early 1900, to plan their next steps. "I was delegated to collect one hundred dollars each month from the members," J. Wilson Cary informed writer John Rolfe Burroughs, "and turn the money over to Ayer," who had the duty of hiring a detective "to move into Brown's Park and to secure evidence of rustling."[27]

The prime movers in the war on the Brown's Park rustlers met in Ora Haley's office in Denver sometime in early 1900. Present were Hi Bernard, Wilford W. "Wiff" Wilson, Charles Ayer, and John C. Coble. Wilson and Ayer, who loudly "condemned the place as an outlaw hangout," recalled Bernard, singled out Matt Rash and Jim McNight as the rustler leaders. While Coble did not run cattle in Colorado, he "had like grievances in his part of the country" and "offered a solution to the problem that would wipe out the range menace permanently." Coble proposed to "contact a man whom he knew with the Pinkerton Detective Agency," recalled Bernard, "a man that could be relied on to do the job, with no questions asked." The group agreed, formed a committee, and authorized Wiff Wilson, Charles Ayer, and Hi Bernard "to act for the joint interests." Hi Bernard explained Coble's solution:

> Tom Horn was the man chosen by Coble. Horn was not at the meeting, but Coble, acting for him, said that Horn was to be paid $500 for every known cattle thief he killed. Haley was to put up one-half of the money, and Wilson and Ayers [sic] one-half. Wilson and Ayers agreed to handle the financial transaction with Horn. Haley . . . instructed me to furnish Horn with accommodations and saddle horses at the Two Bar ranches.

After the meeting, Haley cautioned Bernard to ensure that he (Haley) could not in any way be associated with "this man Horn." During Horn's murder trial, in 1902, the *Denver Post* hinted darkly at Coble's possible involvement in the Routt County problems. In referring to the cattlemen's use of Tom Horn for "a little reform in Brown's Park," the *Post* described the big ranchers' program as "patterned after the Iron Mountain plan—in other words, assassination." Of course, "the Iron Mountain plan" was presumably the brainchild of Coble.[28]

Using the undercover name of Thomas Hicks, Tom Horn arrived in Brown's Hole about the first of April 1900. He proceeded directly to the ranch of Matt Rash, the suspected rustler king, and asked for a job. At first, Hicks (Horn) deliberately played the part of an inept cowhand, so Rash put him to work as a cook. A few days later, Hicks broke the meanest animals in the remuda, arousing the suspicions of "Queen Ann" Bassett. He talked too much. "His bragging that he had been a great Indian fighter, his boastful, descriptive accounts of the human slaughter he had accomplished single-handed," she continued, "were exceedingly obnoxious." After "several heated arguments" with this fiery little woman, Hicks "removed his carcase [*sic*]." His act did not fool some locals at all; some saw through his alias. William Daniel Tittsworth, a young cowhand (not to be confused with William G. Tittsworth), said the "common talk" was that "Horn was just a cattle detective."[29]

Hicks found various ways to ingratiate himself with some locals. Joe Davenport, another suspect on the detective's list, recalled that Horn offered to buy some of his horses. Another opportunity occurred when Jim McNight and his wife, Josie Bassett McNight, got into a heated divorce proceeding. To prevent McNight from selling their ranch without her consent, Josie obtained a restraining order. When Deputy Sheriff William H. Harris attempted to serve this document on Jim McNight, on the evening of 4 April, a scuffle ensued in which Harris shot and seriously wounded him. The nearest doctor was in Vernal, Utah, and Hicks volunteered to make the forty-five-mile ride. "The report was brought in by Thomas Hicks a range rider," according to a Vernal news dispatch, "who came for the purpose of wiring the wounded man's relatives . . . in Salt Lake City." While Hicks said there was little hope of McNight's recovery, he somehow survived.[30]

Apparently, the Little Snake River cattlemen initially sent Tom Horn into Brown's Park not to assassinate suspected thieves but to gather evidence against them and, if possible, run them out of the country. However, after Horn presented his employers with stark evidence of "the boldest, most outrageous cattle-rustling job I had ever seen," recalled Hi Bernard, the association gave Horn "the go-ahead signal" to kill rustlers but to kill only guilty men. In June 1900, Horn began to post unsigned letters on the doorjambs of suspected thieves, ordering them to "leave Brown's Park within thirty days or suffer the consequences." Another of Horn's ruses was to play the part of a rustler. He allegedly conspired with Charlie Ward, a known petty thief, to pilfer some beeves. Horn then used the stolen cattle as bait, in an effort to entrap Matt Rash and Jim McNight. Ann Bassett, who claimed to have discovered these stolen animals, secretly drove them away into Utah. She later declared that Horn intended to keep the money from the illegal sale and draw his regular pay as well. In another of Horn's schemes, he attempted to provoke a fight between Dart and Rash, hoping that one would kill the other. This ruse failed as well.[31]

While Tom Hicks's erratic comings and goings aroused the suspicions of some Brown's Park residents, one man accidentally stumbled onto evidence of his real intentions. On 6 May 1900, George Banks overheard Hicks, Hi Bernard, and a man known as Mexican Pete talking in a livery stable corral at Craig. They were discussing plans to murder Matt Rash and other suspected cattle thieves. Many years later, Banks put his recollections into a formal affidavit:

> I heard Mr. Bernard say now we have got to get rid of these thieves and he says to Mr. Hicks: you kill Rash and that Negro [Isom Dart] and [Longhorn] Thompson and notify Annie and Elbert Bassett and Joe Davenport to leave the country and you can get your pay any time you want it. And Mr. Bernard says to Mexican Pete, we want you to look after some other certain men, and help us in case Tom fails or gets caught. Mr. Bernard pulled some paper out of his pocket and s[a]ying here is some men we want watched . . . he handed one small sheet of paper to Hicks and one to Pete and said if they don't go carefull [sic] we will wait on them the same way.

Although Banks tried to act as if he had not overheard this conversation, someone made an unsuccessful attempt to kill him a few days later.[32]

Tom Hicks continued to move about Routt County in an unpredictable fashion. On 15 June he was back in Craig, where he had a chance encounter with his old Pinkerton compatriot, Doc Shores, in the Royal Hotel. Horn greeted his friend, and "Doc replied, 'I guess you're Tom Hicks (AKA Tom Horn) for a reason.' With a wry smile, Tom Horn said, 'Yeah, I'm doing a little rat cleaning in Brown's Hole. . . . I'd appreciate your not making a big to-do over seein' me, Doc. It might lead to a little bit of embarrassment and maybe even a bullet in the back. It's kind of a touchy situation.'" As chief of the Denver & Rio Grande Western Railroad's Secret Service, Shores had already heard that Horn was working in Brown's Park, a "fact that . . . put the rustlers on thin ice," as Shores wrote later. Horn changed the subject to the latest rifles and said he carried a brand new 94 Winchester, .30-30 caliber. "Doc, ain't this new smokeless powder somethin?" added Horn. "You can shoot a long way off and that don't make no smoke." This feature was important, he observed, "to men in our line of work." After some reminiscing about their old days together, the two man hunters went their separate ways.[33]

On the way back to Brown's Park, Horn stopped at the Two-Bar ranch, had "some confidential talk" with Hi Bernard and other ranch officials, and then rode off leading several horses. Bernard kept in touch with Horn and occasionally provided him some assistance. Edwin Houghy, a Two-Bar rider at this time, also recalled seeing Bernard more than once "catch up two or three of the best horses at night and ride away leading them. He would come back before morning without the horses and no questions would be asked." Presumably, Bernard was taking the horses for Horn's use. "In a few days we heard that somebody had been killed," continued Houghy, who said they later encountered these animals running wild "as we rounded up [cattle in] the country."[34]

About the first of July, Matt Rash rode to Rock Springs, Wyoming, to attend Fourth of July festivities. On returning to Brown's Park, he stopped briefly at the Bassett ranch and then rode on to his spread at Cold Springs. This was the last time he was seen alive. On Tuesday, 10 July, his badly decomposed body was found in his cabin. A Rock Springs dispatch of 11 July to the *Rocky Mountain News* reported the arrival of Eb Bassett with "the news that Matt Rash, a stock grower and an old timer in Brown's park . . . , was found dead in bed with two gunshot wounds in his body." William Daniel Tittsworth, who was present at the inquest, said it appeared that Rash was eating lunch when the assassin shot him. As Rash struggled to get up from the floor, "the killer shot him in the back." After the shooter departed, Rash managed to reach his bunk and attempted to write something on an envelope by dipping his finger in his own blood. He failed.[35]

Tom Horn was careless in making his getaway. Allen G. Wallihan was a witness to Horn's flight. Wallihan, who kept a roadhouse near Lay, in Routt County, was a Jack-of-all trades: farmer, postmaster, justice of the peace, writer, and wildlife photographer. As postmaster, he had made the acquaintance of Horn, whom he regarded as a very disagreeable person. "He came here several times looking for some boots on the mail," recalled Wallihan, "and when they did not arrive he got mad." As part of Wallihan's efforts to photograph wildlife, he set up a camera for night work. On the evening of 8 July, while Wallihan was checking a camera in a deer blind, he observed a rider "'on a buckskin horse ride to the top of the ridge and stop and look back." He recognized this mysterious rider as Hicks (Horn).

Near Slater, fifty miles north of Craig, Colorado, Horn stopped at Robert McIntosh's spread. Many years later, a McIntosh cowhand recalled that he could tell Horn had "come a long ways." Horn "never said hello, how-de-do, go-to-hell or nothing," added this old cowhand, but went straight to the corral, selected a lively horse, and rode away. "I don't ever want to see a man look at me that way again," the old wrangler remarked. After Horn (Hicks) departed, a fellow puncher remarked, "That sommabix looked like a *real* outlaw."[36]

Rather than ride directly to John Coble's ranch in Wyoming, Tom Horn stopped at Baggs, just inside the Wyoming border on the Little Snake River. About 3:00 A.M., on Sunday, 15 July, he walked into Leroy D. Bailey's Bull Dog Saloon and asked bartender James W. Davis for a drink. The bar was still full of Saturday night drinkers, and Tom Blevins, who observed the stranger's arrival, recalled that he "came walking in straight through everybody—strictly death—and he says to the bartender . . . 'Give me a drink of whiskey.'. . . A feller by the name of [Newton] Kelly . . . his brother, California Red [Edward Kelly], [William M.] Mitt Nichols, and two or three others, all noticed Horn," continued Blevins, "and [Newton] Kelly steps up to the bar and says, 'God damn, I'll just take a drink with you.'" "Hicks gets two or three shots of red eye and he thinks he is a fighting man from Powder River," recalled William D. Tittsworth, the Brown's Park cowboy. Horn took immediate exception to this intruder. "If you drink you'll pay fer it," Hicks blurted out. Suddenly, Newt's brother, Edward, jumped up from a gaming table and shouted "I know every bush in Texas," recalled Tom Blevins, and proceeded to knock Horn "ten feet, face up." As the scuffle turned into a brawl, "Ed grabs both his arms and pins him to the bar; Nute [Newt] outs with his knife and slashes his [Horn's] throat" from his chest up to the right side of his neck. Horn collapsed on the floor from loss of blood.[37]

Fortunately, bystanders stepped in and prevented the Kelly brothers from finishing off the hapless detective. Tom Blevins fetched Dr. Arthur White, who dressed the knife wound and placed him in a local hotel. Deputy Sheriff Bob Meldrum, who happened to be in town, guarded his room. When William D. Tittsworth bumped into Meldrum the day after the fight, the deputy surprised the cowboy with his knowledge of Hicks's background, going so far as "to tell me what a hell-roaring bronc rider Hicks was." A dispatch to the *Rocky Mountain News* reported this encounter, although no connection was made with Tom Horn: "Ed and Newt Kelley of this place got into a fight with John [*sic*] Hicks of Brown's Park here last Sunday. Knives were drawn and a fierce fight ensued. The two brothers cut Hicks in a number of places and his condition is serious; but he will probably recover. No arrests have been made." Had Newt Kelly's knife penetrated Horn's neck a fraction of an inch deeper, the infamous badman would have bled out. Given his gruesome end, perhaps death on a barroom floor would have been merciful.[38]

The injured detective left Baggs as quickly as he could, reportedly stealing a team and wagon, according to Tom Blevins. (One account has Horn hiding outside Baggs using Apache herbal remedies on his wound.) A few days later, Horn stopped at Allen G. Wallihan's roadhouse and said he was going to bathe in mineral waters at Juniper Springs, on the Yampa River. When he could travel, Horn made his way to Ogden, Utah. Although his purpose is not known, he may have been searching for train robbers. In August 1900, he returned to Brown's Park. By this time Horn was no longer seriously trying to maintain his undercover identity, although many of the Park's inhabitants still knew him as Hicks. William D. Tittsworth recalled that by this time "every body suspected this Horn" of the Rash killing. On this second visit to the Park, he stayed with Albert "Speck" Williams, a black man who operated a ferry on the Green River in Brown's Park. In the meantime, Samuel A. Rash, Matt's father, had arrived from Texas to settle his son's estate. When the elder Rash and former Routt County Sheriff Charles W. Neiman, whom the county judge assigned the duty of rounding up Matt Rash's cattle, were riding to Brown's Park, they encountered Tom Hicks on the road. Although Charles Rash did not know it at the time, he was talking with the man who may have murdered his son. When Neiman asked Hicks to assist in rounding up Rash's cattle, Hicks said he could not help at the moment but would join Neiman as soon as possible.[39]

"Queen Ann" Bassett continued to express her suspicions of Tom Hicks openly. In mid-September she and her brother, Elbert, Samuel Rash, David Reavill (a Rock Springs attorney), and Tom Hicks all found themselves traveling together to Hahn's Peak, the Routt County seat. (The purpose of this trip was to settle Ann Bassett's claim against the Rash estate. She claimed that she and Matt Rash were betrothed before his death.) En route, the party stopped at Wallihan's roadhouse in Lay. While Mrs. Wallihan prepared a meal, Ann launched into Hicks, openly accusing him of the murder of Rash. Apparently, Elbert Bassett and Mrs. Wallihan, who despised Horn, took her side. When "Mr. Reavill . . . jokingly said to him [Horn] that Mrs. Wallihan, [and] Anne and Eb Bassett were calling him the murderer of Rash," according to one report, Horn merely shrugged off this accusation, aware that the attorney was only joking.[40]

Apparently, Tom Horn's purpose in returning to Brown's Park was to determine if the Rash slaying had persuaded the rustling fraternity to vacate the valley. When it became evident that these hard cases had not taken the hint, Horn decided on a second "lesson." In preparing for this second killing, Horn spread the rumor that Isom Dart had, in fact, murdered Matt Rash. In one of the many unexplained twists in Horn's conduct as a detective, he filed a formal complaint (26 September 1900) at the county seat against Dart for the theft of one of Jim McNight's horses. Of course, McNight was one of the suspected leaders of the rustlers. Even more puzzling, Horn signed the complaint using his real name, Tom Horn, and listed McNight as a witness to this crime! Since Hicks/Horn's real purpose for being in Brown's Park was known to many inhabitants by late summer, it is possible that he did "go public." There was some indication that Routt County Sheriff

Ethan Allen Farnham may have issued him a temporary deputy sheriff's badge. Edwin Houghy, the Two-Bar employee, recalled that he saw the detective openly talking with officials at the fall 1900 court session in Hahn's Peak.[41]

Coincidentally, Theodore Roosevelt, whom Tom Horn had be-friended in Cuba, was hunting mountain lions in Routt County in September 1900. Harry Ratliff, the local national forest supervisor, de-livered Roosevelt's mail to his hunting camp. One day Ratliff rode into Brown's Park to pick up a stray horse. However, Hi Bernard had already arranged for Tom Horn to recover the animal. "The night I got to the Two Bar ranch," recalled Ratliff, "Tom Horn led the horse in." "Tom and I slept together that night in the Two Bar bunkhouse," said Ratliff, who added that "just two or three days later Isom Dart, the Negro, was found dead." Even though both Roosevelt and Horn had connections to Ratliff, there is no indication that the two met during TR's hunting trip.[42]

On the morning of 3 October 1900, Isom Dart was assassinated by an unknown rifleman. Dart and his partner, John Dempshire, had moved into Jim McNight's recently vacated cabin at Summit Springs. Later, some Brown's Park residents wondered if Jim McNight, rather than Isom Dart, was Horn's intended victim and that the assassin did not know that Dart was occupying Rash's property. Horn had ample mo-tive for shooting the black man, however. Rumors that a mysterious gunman was on the prowl had prompted several local men to hole up with Dart and Dempshire. At sunrise, the occupants strolled out of the cabin to answer the call of nature. The shooter, standing behind a pine tree near the corral, shot Dart twice. He died immediately. Everyone present frantically sought the safety of the cabin and stayed there until darkness fell. William D. Tittsworth, who seemed to be all over this part of the West in the summer of 1900, attended the coroner's inquest and, with Eb and George Bassett and "Speck" Williams (the black fer-ryman), buried Dart.[43]

In making his getaway Tom Horn changed horses at the Hubler Ranch, just outside Brown's Park. Robert Hubler, the young son of the owner, told Tim McCoy, later a noted movie actor, that his father instructed him to "take one our best horses to a spot down in a draw by a creek, tie it up and walk away about a quarter of a mile." After hearing the crack of a rifle, Robert was to fetch the jaded horse left by the mysterious rider. "Damnedest thing," Hubler said, "after about ten minutes, there was a single shot." Back at the spring, Hubler recalled, "I found . . . a different horse, short of breath and heavily lathered."[44]

While the murders of Rash and Dart persuaded a few suspected rustlers to leave, a Rock Springs dispatch of 14 October indicated that "more trouble" was expected. Eb Bassett and his family, as well as Joe Davenport, were given sixty days to leave. After a narrow escape from Tom Horn, Elijah "Longhorn" Thompson left for Utah, where he "bragged that he was the only man Tom Horn ever missed." Joe Davenport, who sought sanctuary in Missouri, recalled that every resident of the Park "was sure that Tom Horn . . . was going to kill him next" When the Bassett family refused to leave, someone left a threatening letter and fired two rifle shots through the window of their house. Ann's brothers tracked the assailant to a point near Baggs, but then lost the trail. Not everyone agreed with Ann Bassett that Tom Horn was responsible for the attempt on her life. Grace McClure, author of a book about the Bassett girls, went so far as to assert that Ann forged the threatening missive that she allegedly received in order prompt Sheriff Farnham to investigate the recent murders "more vigorously."[45]

In keeping with his tendency to talk too much, Tom Horn came close to (inadvertently) confessing to the Brown's Park murders in an interview with George H. Evans, a *Wyoming Tribune* reporter, in November 1900. Addressing Horn as "Colonel," Evans praised the detective for his past services in "running down stage robbers, cattle rustlers and horse thieves" and noted that he had "just returned from a tour through the Wyoming-Utah-Colorado line." In an exhibition of incredible gall, Horn boasted about his recent work in Brown's Park. Although he did not claim credit for deaths of Rash and Dart, Horn declared that "two more notorious rustlers never infested the Rocky Mountain country." Their ranches served as "rendezvous for one of the worst bands of outlaws," said Horn, adding that the Bassett brothers and Joe Davenport fled the Park "as soon as they learned of the death of the two leaders." "Now that Brown's park has been freed of its undesirable residents," Horn assured the reporter, "respectable stockmen will go in there and settle." Given the public outrage at Tom Horn's killing of two innocent men in the Jackson Hole country, such indiscreet remarks could only make him less popular.[46]

Although newspapers avoided any specific accusations, they hinted strongly that Horn was involved in the Brown's Park killings. A Steamboat Springs dispatch to the *Rocky Mountain News* accused the big cattlemen of employing "assassination" in the Park. Although mentioning no names, the writer declared that "some men or organization have employed a Wyoming detective agency to clear out alleged cattle rustlers." Even though some Park residents "go so far as to give the name [in private] of the assassin who killed Rash and Dart," he continued, they lived in great fear and "do not know where the next blow will fall." The *Steamboat Pilot* even went so far as to trace the Routt County cattlemen's decision to use violence to an 1898 meeting of the governors of Colorado, Wyoming, and Utah. The purpose of this conference, which took place in Salt Lake City, was to discuss means "to clean out" the highwaymen and rustlers in the three corners area. They adjourned without adopting any measures at all. While there was no evidence that these state executives specifically gave the cattle companies leave to employ assassination in Brown's Park, the *Pilot* asserted that they "at least encouraged powerful interests . . . to employ a detective to enter that section." "What his instructions were none may know," the story concluded, "but his deadly work speaks for itself." Even the *Wyoming Tribune,* which might be expected to take offense at the allegation that the Brown's Park assassin came from Wyoming, repeated these accusations.[47]

Since territorial and state executives possessed very little authority and few resources with which to fight crime at this time, Ethan Farnham, the sheriff of Routt County, bore the brunt of criticism for the failure of law enforcement in Brown's Park. The *Rocky Mountain News*'s Steamboat Springs correspondent, who went so far as to accuse Farnham of collusion with the person (or persons) involved in the Rash and Dart assassinations, asserted that "the murderer is said to have had a warrant for [the arrest of] Rash and to have gone there with the knowledge of the sheriff." While Sheriff Farnham insisted that he had "not been called upon to protect the citizens of Brown's park," this writer added, "the opinion is general and amounts to almost a conviction that he is perfectly posted on the entire matter." One Cheyenne reporter echoed these accusations and suggested that Sheriff Farnham was "in cahoots" with the mysterious "Wyoming corporation" that was allegedly responsible for the Brown's Park assassinations. An indignant Sheriff Farnham, who declared that he had no information concerning the Rash and Dart murders, blamed the Routt County Board of Commissioners. Farnham alleged that he could not travel to Brown's Park because the commissioners refused to pay his investigative expenses. Furthermore, Farnham was contemptuous of reports of death threats in Brown's Park, characterizing such a story as "a grand stand play." The "supposed" attempt on the life of George Banks—the man who over-heard the conspirators' conversation—was probably "a stray bullet from a chicken hunter," the sheriff remarked dismissively.[48]

As an avid newspaper reader, Tom Horn was surely aware of the intense interest in the Brown's Park troubles, and he must have felt uneasy when the *Daily Leader* announced, in November 1900, that the name of the assassin was known. Furthermore, another report stated that the murderer "openly boasted in Cheyenne" of his exploits. In a clear reference to Horn's November interview, the *Steamboat Pilot* declared that the assassin's assertion "was published in the Denver papers that the 'rustlers' would soon be cleaned out of Brown's Park and it would be a safe place in which to live." Apparently, this newspaper speculation persuaded Horn's employers that he had become a liability, and they decided to send a replacement into Brown's Park. "The second man is in the country now," continued this newsman, but "he is evidently not as good a shot as the other. . . . Twice he has tried and failed." Between the two assassins, "there are said to be seven names on the death list," concluded the *Pilot*. Author Chip Carlson makes the very plausible sug-gestion that this mysterious second hit man was Bob Meldrum.[49]

Tom Horn was allegedly to receive $500 each for the assassinations of Matt Rash and Isom Dart. J. Wilson Carey, manager of the Two Circle Bar ranch in 1900, collected monthly dues from the membership and passed the money on to Charles Ayer, the unofficial treasurer for the "pool" to pay Horn. "I personally know that Horn was paid $500.00 for every rustler he killed," said writer Charles Kelly, who evidently interviewed persons involved. Apparently, the association dragged its feet in paying Horn for the Dart killing, possibly because the target was supposed to be Jim McNight. A note in the Jay Monaghan papers says that "Horn was refused payment for killing Isam [sic] until he became nasty and demanded payment or else." "Queen Ann" Bassett, who, in a most unlikely union, married Hi Bernard after the Brown's Park troubles, declared later that her husband was the payoff man in the Rash and Dart killings. While the love-struck Bernard had attempted to keep his role in the Horn affair from his new bride, this was impossible. She divorced him in 1910. "Horn was not the only one connected with that [Brown's Park] affair that should have been hanged," said Bernard philosophically. "There were several of us [cattlemen] that the country could have gotten along without," he admitted. When Charles Kelly praised Tom Horn's services against rustlers in his popular book *The Outlaw Trail: A History of Butch Cassidy and His Wild Bunch* (1938), Ann Bassett took strong exception. She declared that Kelly "acquits Horn, and thereby lends encouragement to the criminal-minded." "Queen Ann" passed away in 1956 at the age of seventy-nine.[50]

If anyone doubted Tom Horn's guilt, the mouthy detective dispelled such notions by continuing to boast about his misdeeds. Charlie Siringo alleged that Horn described the killings of Rash and Dart to him in great detail in a Denver restaurant shortly after the Brown's Park affair. To provide Horn with an alibi, John Coble arranged for compliant cowhands to swear that the range detective "was seen in Laramie" at the time of the Dart killing, in October 1900. In spite of the vast amount of spleen vented against Tom Horn's name, "there were no more killing bees in Routt County," observed the *Denver Post*.[51]

In the meantime, Butch Cassidy and his followers were very busy. In August 1900, the Kid Curry band robbed a Union Pacific train at Tipton, Wyoming, and Butch Cassidy, the Sundance Kid, and a new Texas recruit, Bill Carver, struck the First National Bank of Winnemucca, Nevada, on 19 September. When Nevada authorities failed to make any progress in this case, George Stuart Nixon, the bank owner, decided to employ a detective. Through Edwin J. Bell, his ranching partner in Laramie, Wyoming, Nixon hired Tom Horn. When Horn traveled to Winnemucca, in February 1901, Nixon came away from their meeting with "a very high opinion" of this frontier sleuth. Although Horn did not know Cassidy personally, he claimed to know friends of the outlaw, including Jack Ryan, a Rawlins saloon owner.[52]

Back in Wyoming, the detective looked into Jack Ryan's movements and found that he had gone to Arizona "to meet Cassidy." A 1901 letter from Tom Horn to Bob Meldrum may relate to Horn's work on the Winnemucca case. Although the date is incomplete, Horn wrote, "I think I am going to need your help to do some work shortly." Whether Horn followed through is not known. Nixon's correspondence with Horn ended abruptly on 29 April 1901. Within a few weeks, Tom Horn was riding the range again for John Coble and the Swan Two-Bar ranch.[53]

Tom Horn's services as a detective were still in demand. In April 1901, Doc Shores, now a Rio Grande Northern Railroad detective, informed James McParland, the Pinkerton representative in Denver, that he wanted Horn for a special assignment. A few months later, J. E. Evary, who resided in the Rattlesnake Mining District, asked the Wyoming Stock Growers Association how to get in touch with Tom Horn. Evary's district was troubled by rustlers. About this same time, Henry Daly, Horn's former packtrain associate, spied the sleuth loitering around the Cheyenne railroad depot. When Daly greeted him, Horn reacted furtively, informing Daly that he "wished to be alone."[54]

CHAPTER 10

"A Man Apart"

Since Tom Horn had assumed the duties of a range detective in Wyoming, he had become well known across the state. While his occupation called for a variety of menacing skills—stealth, intimidation, night riding, and, alas, proficiency with weapons—he believed that lawmen regarded him as a legitimate colleague and that he helped maintain an orderly society. He was a complicated man, far more than just an enforcer. While his talkativeness and boastful nature might be off-putting, persons in frequent contact with him were surprised at his broad range of talents, sense of humor, and demonstrations of loyalty (selective) and compassion (also selective). Horn possessed superior athletic ability, and his skills in horsehair braiding and leatherwork were unusual. In spite of these engaging qualities, however, Tom Horn had few close friendships, condemned by his occupation to remain "a man apart."[1]

The peculiar nature of Horn's duties on the range put a considerable distance between him and the working cowhand. The region between Chugwater and Bosler—the Laramie Plains—"came to be known as Tom Horn's range," according to Henry Melton, who cowboyed there in the late 1890s. "No one seemed to know when he might appear at a place or anything concerning his whereabouts," Melton remarked, since "most of his traveling was done under cover of darkness on horseback." John K. Rollinson, a young employee of the Swan Land and Cattle Company, recalled a frightening encounter with the range detective on a cold and rainy night. Rollinson's horse sensed someone approaching and suddenly a voice called out:

"Hey, Jack!" I shouted back, "Yes, what is it?" I was scared for an instant, and then a rider suddenly appeared beside me, like some ghostly figure. He wore a black slicker, which caused him to be scarcely visible, and the horse was dark in color. "It's me—Tom Horn," was the reply. Then I recognized his voice, and as his horse crowded close to mine I felt the carbine under his left leg, which protruded forward of the saddlebows.

When Rollinson said he thought Horn was asleep, the detective "laughed a low, quiet chuckle" and remarked "that he seldom had a chance to get much sleep," since he always departed "when no one knew he had expected to leave." "Every rustler knew Tom Horn was a night prowler," added Rollinson. Such unpredictable movements "made the rustlers mighty nervous."[2]

Even though it was common knowledge that Horn was a top cowhand and horsebreaker, everyday ranch hands quickly sensed that he was not one of them. While testifying in Horn's murder trial, in October 1902, Duncan Clark, a former manager of the Iron Mountain Ranch, admitted that he had no supervisory authority over the detective's activities. Presumably, that was John Coble's prerogative. When young Robert B. Rogerson went to work for Coble, in 1900, he was struck by the fact that Horn did "nothing"—that is, in the way ranch chores—although he was clearly "a close associate" of the owner. Horn "spent his time just hanging around, drinking," added Rogerson, and not with the common hands. While the detective "was genial and likeable; [and] . . . had an easy-going manner," continued Rogerson, "he never looked at me." In spite of Horn's aloofness, he was "a living legend" in the Iron Mountain region, said Rogerson, who admitted that he had idolized Horn for a time.[3]

Older cowhands were very conscious of the distance that separated the detective from the working hands. In western parlance, his position as a range detective made him an "outside man." Horn "gave the impression of being a sinister, hard-hearted man," recalled James D. Eckel, a cowhand who encountered him in cattle camps on the Little Snake River. "Though he was fairly well liked," continued Eckel, "he did not make as many friends as most fellows with as large an acquaintance as he had." "He always had the best horses . . . in his string," added Eckel, "and would often ride off in the morning and not show up against for a week or two. He generally rode hard, too, and was constantly getting fresh horses." George Shanton, who, with Bud Cowan, associated with Horn on the Iron Mountain Ranch in the mid-1890s, said the detective was always alone and kept his distance. While camping on the range on cold nights, cowboys "always cuddled against the other fellow" around the campfire or slept together under a single tarpaulin for warmth, wrote Shanton, but "never Tom Horn." "He was never a confidant" of the cowhands. It was no accident that when the drovers pulled practical jokes on each other, Horn "was never played with." Horn's isolation was apparent when he faced the hangman's noose in 1903. He asked John Coble to "remember me kindly to all my friends, if I have any besides yourself."[4]

The wranglers could not completely avoid Horn's company. One day Harry N. Robb, who was tending a Swan Company line shack, found Tom Horn there, making himself at home and working a piece of rawhide that Robb "intended for . . . work during the winter." Horn, who "was sitting on one of my box chairs," added the cowhand, "didn't say a word nor look up." After Robb cooked potatoes and biscuits, Horn proceeded to dig right in without asking permission. "Tom seemed right at home sitting . . . by the stove where he could load his plate from the big iron skillet of spuds and reach in the oven for more and more biscuits," recalled Robb, "which he nearly floated in syrup." After eating his fill, the detective sat back and nonchalantly smoked a cigarette. When night came, Horn promptly rolled himself up on the cowhand's bed, although he did leave some room for his host. Apparently, Horn "wasn't very well pleased with my company," Robb continued, as he was "glum" and not very talkative. When the range rider departed, he left a pile of smelly rawhide shavings for Robb to clean up.[5]

In spite of the gulf separating him from the workaday cowboys, Tom Horn's job required that he become familiar with the punchers in his area of responsibility. Since some cowhands were only seasonal employees, cattle company officials considered them potential thieves in their off-seasons. Some uncomfortable moments arose when Horn appeared at the roundup camps. Henry Melton, the Two-Bar herder, recalled that Horn visited their camp on one occasion when William E. (Billy) Powell was present. Billy Powell was the son of Fred Powell, the man whom Horn was suspected of having murdered in 1895. In spite of what must have been an awkward situation for the range detective, recalled Melton, Horn "didn't seem to mind, or show any feeling that it bothered him at all." While many punchers believed Horn "was guilty of murder," said Jim Eckel, the Little Snake River cowboy, "this does not necessarily make a man unpopular in a cow camp." They were a rough-hewn lot themselves.[6]

Intimidation was part of Tom Horn's method of operation. He openly boasted about making sure that potential livestock thieves saw "some signs of me" on the range. Such tactics were his stock in trade. Although Horn was not suspected of having assassinated anyone in Natrona County, local residents said he was often "seen during the evenings in the vicinity of homes of ranchers whom the members of the [Stock Growers] association accused of using a long rope." These marked men "slept in the brush while Horn lurked about." "I generally warn these men [rustlers] three times," Horn informed Fred and Catherine Bell, "and if they don't leave then I have to shoot them." As a *Wyoming Tribune* writer noted after Horn's execution:

> He was by his own statement a man who felt absolutely no compunction in taking human life, and would often tell of adventures which had occurred to him in other days, almost all of which contain[ed] lurid accounts of how he had slain with his own hands enemies who crossed his path. . . . The accuracy of the details of these stories was generally doubted by Horn's hearers, but in the main they served the purpose of the teller, which was to keep all the people of the country in more or less fear of him. It was upon fear that he depended for the success of his peculiar occupation.

Whether true or false, his stories attracted people's attention, and his listeners spread and even exaggerated his wild tales.[7]

On one occasion, Tom Horn took the unusual tack of using persuasion on a man he suspected of throwing "a sticky rope." In an interview with the *Rocky Mountain News,* a woman who cooked for John Coble recalled that Horn had "a whole lot of trouble" with a suspected cattle thief who resided near the Iron Mountain Company ranch at Bosler. After warning the man several times, Horn decided "he was goin' to bring that man home to dinner." The detective even fetched the suspect in Coble's buggy, "though the man was scared to death of him." The two men argued in the bunkhouse, but "they was as quiet as lambs" during dinner, only to resume their squabbling afterward. When Horn began "gatherin' up chips," the cook asked him, "Are you goin' to burn him at the stake?" The detective "just laughed," and using the kindling to warm up branding irons, he forced the man to brand an Iron Mountain cow that Horn and Coble believed this neighbor had originally "worked over." After this humiliation, Horn permitted the man to leave, "crestfallen and madder than a wet hen." When the cook asked the detective if he "could make a good man out of that individual without shootin' him," Horn replied that "it looked like a tough job." After Horn later discovered this "brand artist" selling stolen horses, added the Coble cook, she heard that the suspect "was shot at twice on his place." Recalling this incident in a letter to John Coble in October 1903, Tom Horn maintained that the suspected rustler "offered me five hundred dollars to kill off" the sheep of a neighboring rancher. The cattle thief wanted to "buy the ranch cheap." "So much for the peculiar conditions in the [Iron Mountain] ranching country," concluded the *Rocky Mountain News* writer.[8]

As another means to caution suspected livestock thieves, Tom Horn also gave demonstrations of his marksmanship. In 1899 Hugh McPhee was staying in a Two Bar bunkhouse, when "Horn rode in during a storm":

> While the two men were standing in the door of a house at the ranch, Horn picked up a .30–.30 caliber rifle McPhee had borrowed to shoot at wolves. He asked, "Whose gun is that, kid?" McPhee said he had borrowed the weapon. Horn peered at the front and then the rear sight. He lifted the weapon to his shoulder and indicated a brick on the chimney of a schoolhouse across a small creek, and approximately 250 yards away. Said Horn, "Watch the brick on that chimney." He fired once, and the bullet shattered the brick he had indicated.

Henry Melton, another Two Bar wrangler, recalled assisting Horn during pistol practice at a roundup. While Melton threw "tin cans into the air for him," Horn hit "each one twice before it could come to the ground." Yet Horn was probably no more than an average marksman by frontier standards. James Miller, an Iron Mountain rancher who testified at Horn's murder trial in 1902, recalled passing time with the detective by taking shots at birds. When asked if Horn was "a good shot," Miller replied, "No . . . he missed the buzzard; he missed the bird." "We afterwards were shooting a little twenty two," Miller continued, and "he missed that [target] a time or two; he did hit it part of the time." Horn "was certainly speedy with either a Winchester or a six-shooter—that is, in bringing them into action—," recalled Jim Eckel, "but he was, if anything, not so good a shot as the average cow puncher." By this time, Horn had passed the age of forty and needed reading glasses. To impress potential rustlers, though, he tried to convey the impression that he was still an expert shot.[9]

In spite of the tension that the detective's presence provoked in cattle camps, there were lighter moments. On one occasion, in 1900, Horn caught young John Rollinson in an inadvertent violation of range etiquette. In an effort to get some roping practice, this seventeen year old threw a lariat over the neck of a yearling. When the animal began to buck and cavort around, the novice cowboy lost control of the situation:

> I was just . . . trying to figure out how I was going to get my rope off that steer, when suddenly, apparently from nowhere, a rider halted his horse beside me. I . . . was both surprised and humiliated at getting caught in a fix like that. In a split second my shame turned to fear, and my fear was not a bit lessened at the first words of the stranger. "What the hell is this?," said the mysterious rider, as he viewed the young man with his rope on someone else's beef.

"Mounted on a well-built, rangy gray horse," wrote Rollinson, "he was a fine looking, well-built, clean-cut powerful type, apparently in his late thirties." "Boy, how come you out here roping other folks' cattle?" said the stranger. "Who are you, and where are you from? Speak up—quick!" When Rollinson identified himself, the man said he had heard of him and then "smiled in a more friendly manner" and said, "Well, I'll help you out—this time," as he uncoiled his lariat. After helping Rollinson out of his predicament, the man said, "Now, son . . . take a tip from an old-timer and don't be out roping Two Bar cattle on a Two Bar range." As the stranger rode away, he dropped a bombshell on the youngster: "My name is Tom Horn, and I am a range detective." The two parted company still friends, but with Rollinson "a lot wiser."[10]

That Tom Horn's tactics as a "rustler intimidator" got results went without saying. In his report to Union Pacific officials in January 1900, Horn mentioned that some ranchers (in the Hole-in-the-Wall country, apparently) had just offered him a job. "Cowmen think my being in that country keeps it [rustling] down," he boasted. In seeking employment in Montana two years later, Horn assured Deputy U.S. Marshal Joe LeFors, who was serving as a go-between, that he would guarantee success. "I will get the men sure," wrote Horn, "for I have never yet let a cow thief get away from me unless he just got up a[nd] jumped clean out of the country." John Coble gave Horn a similar recommendation. When sheepmen began to move in on the Iron Mountain Ranch's grazing lands, Coble recommended to his partner, Frank Bosler, that they should hire Tom Horn, who would "straighten them out by merely riding around." At the time, Tom Horn was "straightening out" suspected rustlers in Brown's Park.[11]

Needless to say, the controversial range detective could not count on the hospitality of many small ranchers and homesteaders in his patrol area. While an occasional neighbor of John Coble, such as Mrs. Julia Plaga, always gave Horn "a warm welcome" and "a good meal," the welcome mat was generally withdrawn when the menacing range rider was about. In May 1899, Horn rode up to the ranch of Fred and Catherine Bell near Laramie and informed them that he was in the employ of cattle baron Ora Haley and that he "wanted to put up at the ranch for a while." He assured Catherine Bell that Haley would pay for his stay and that he "would bunk down on the floor anywhere." She reported:

> Mr. Horn remained with us for two or three weeks . . . and was out every night, coming in about our breakfast time. When he arrived at the ranch he would take off a big pistol he had on his hip and two smaller revolvers from pockets in the inside of his coat. He would then lay down on the sofa and sleep all day. Horn then went away and was absent for probably two or three weeks. . . . When he returned he kept in the house very close.

In spite of his protests that he would be no bother, the overbearing detective insisted on regaling the Bells with bloodthirsty tales, boasting that "he had killed lots of people, and that the cattle detective business was all right." He even offered to sell Fred Bell a small spread in the Iron Mountain area that had been owned by a rustler that he had killed! Horn added insult to injury by imposing upon this hapless couple again the following fall.[12]

Charles and Ida Wood, who resided on Bear Creek, in Laramie County, were also reluctant hosts for Tom Horn. As foreman of the Dollar Ranch, Charles Wood, a British immigrant, often had to deal with Horn. Ida Wood was accustomed to feeding her husband's hungry cowboys, but she drew the line at feeding Tom Horn. When the detective was working in the vicinity, "father would come to the house and tell Mother that he must ask Horn in to eat," recalled their daughter, Margaret. However, this cheeky ranch woman, who regarded Horn as an unsavory character, "would retort that she wouldn't have a murderer at her table." "In the end Horn ate," Margaret Wood admitted, "but Father had to serve the meal." A woman of principle, Ida Wood withdrew to her room when Tom Horn was present. Nor was Tom Horn welcome at the ranch of the Woods' neighbor, Samuel and Maggie Gillespie. One day in the fall of 1895, Walter S. Ingham, a family friend, appeared at Maggie's back door with "a very large swarthy tall dark man." When Ingham, the foreman of the John and Dugald Whittaker Ranch ten miles to the south, asked to see the man of the house, Maggie informed him that her husband was away at the moment. Later, she "found out that the dark man was Tom Horn." (Horn's name was in the news at this time in connection with the murders of Billy Lewis and Fred Powell.) Upon encountering Ingham later, an angry Samuel Gillespie asked why he brought Tom Horn to his home when Mrs. Gillespie was alone. "Mr. Ingham was very profuse in his apologies and begged us to believe he did not know who he [Horn] was at the time," she wrote later.[13]

In spite of his bravado, Tom Horn's lone wolf way of life caused him emotional and physical hardship. He periodically sought companionship and relaxation in towns along the Union Pacific, as well as in Denver. Apparently, there were two sides to his personality during such visits, depending on whether he was drinking or not. When sober, he was quiet, inoffensive, and even shy. Peter A. Burman, who became acquainted with Horn at Rock Springs, Wyoming, in 1900, said the detective was not "a mixer or jovial fellow," but "was quiet and only talked when spoken to." Thomas Joseph Cahill (better known as T. Joe) agreed that Horn was "generally a quiet, inoffensive man when in town." Horn was an occasional visitor to the Cahill residence in Cheyenne, but "he would seldom remain for dinner, even when urged to do so." Andrew E. Roedel, Jr., whose father owned a drugstore in Cheyenne, regarded Horn, who was a good customer, as mild mannered and a good friend. Horn was also a frequent customer in the Union Mercantile Company store, where clerk Edwin J. Smalley often served him. Horn always referred to Smalley as "Tommy"; Smalley never knew why. Horn often "borrowed small sums," he recalled, but "always paid it back." One of Horn's favorite Cheyenne hangouts was Enos Laughlin's barber shop at 16th and Capitol streets. Horn was "a nice fellow," recalled Laughlin, and stopped by for "a haircut and shave" every time he came to town.[14]

In his cups, Tom Horn experienced a dramatic personality change. He talked too much for his own good and became boastful and overbearing. Friends and acquaintances noticed that his reliance on whiskey became more noticeable after he returned from Cuba. He may have become more dependent on alcohol as he tried to fight off yellow fever. Ordinarily, Horn "was tight-lipped and distant with people," wrote Dean Krakel, but liquor loosened his tongue. "Tom was lonesome and whiskey made him do and say crazy things," added Krakel. Hugh McPhee, the Two Bar cowpuncher, said that Horn's benders were notorious and could last from seven to fourteen days. After making the rounds of Laramie's saloons with Tom Horn on one occasion, Frank Stone, a fellow Iron Mountain Ranch employee, found him passed out on his hotel room floor. Stone obligingly removed Tom's shoes and clothing and put him to bed.[15]

Even when drinking heavily, Horn normally did not cause trouble. John H. Fullerton, owner of the Inter Ocean Hotel and a friend of Horn, came to the detective's defense at his murder trial in 1902:

> I never saw a kinder hearted man than Tom always showed himself to be. He was the most likeable drunk man that was ever in this house. He was as tractable as a child when he was drinking. A bell boy could always go to him and tap him on the arm and say, "come along, Tom, you need a nap," and Tom would go right along as peaceable as could be. I never saw him ugly as a brutal man is apt to be when he is drinking.

Fullerton did admit that the range rider "brags and tells big stories" when in his cups. William Chapin Deming, editor of the *Wyoming Tribune,* recalled seeing Horn "pretty well loaded with liquor" in the Inter Ocean during the 1901 Thanksgiving season. The playful range rider "amused himself by roping bell boys and guests," recalled Deming."[16]

On one occasion T. Joe Cahill, Tom Horn's best friend in Cheyenne, received an urgent plea from Harry Hynds's bar to put the detective to bed. As a brand-new deputy sheriff, Cahill could not refuse. As he entered Hynds's establishment, Cahill found the drunken detective "flopped sideways up against the bar." "T. Joe! What the hell you doin'?" said the tipsy gunman. "Have a drink with me?" "I said in a half demanding tone," recalled Cahill, 'You're coming with me for some grub and sleep. You've got to get back on the job.'" "I ain't goin' no place until I know where my horse and rifle is!" Horn bristled. When Cahill tried to reassure Horn that his personal items were safe, "Tom stared at me unsteadily, squinting as if trying to focus his eyes so he could study my face. . . . I'll never forget the way he looked." Cahill watched his friend's face change, "eyes cold and the set of his jaw taut as a steel trap." "Suddenly I realized the person before me was not my friend but the other party of a split personality," Cahill said many years later, and "I had my first glimpse of Tom Horn, the killer!" Just as suddenly, Horn's demeanor changed again. "Ya wouldn't try to spoof me, would ya kid?" Horn remarked. Cahill "breathed a sigh of relief" and replied, "Hell no!" Knowing how Horn "felt about his hat," Cahill playfully took it from his head and started toward the door. "'Come on, Tom—if you want this,' I smiled as I waved his new Stetson," whereupon "the notorious Tom Horn followed—meek as a lamb." "For some reason he had taken a liking to me," recalled Cahill, who "never thought of him as anything but a friend." The two would often find a warm place out of the weather and talk for hours. "You wouldn't want to find a more affable and gentlemanly man," Cahill concluded. Horn "never bothered anybody and was rarely mixed up [in brawls] with anybody."[17]

One drinking binge in Denver had near disastrous results for Horn. On Saturday, 28 September 1901, Horn assisted John Kuykendall in the delivery of a train-car load of horses to Denver. These were tough broncs from the ranches of John Coble and his friend Perry Williams, who sent them to Denver for the Festival of Mountain and Plain. After registering at the Windsor Hotel, Horn began to drink and flash a thick roll of bills at various bars. "I'm a detective," he bragged loudly, and "I'm the best shot in the United States or any other goddamn state." On the night of Monday, 30 September, Horn made the mistake of joining a dangerous party of drinkers at the Pennington Saloon: John Corbett, brother of Young Corbett, a nationally known featherweight pugilist, Jack McKenna, Young Corbett's manager, and a third man (a reporter). In the wee hours, a fight broke out between Horn and the rest of the group. According to William McLeod Raine, a Denver journalist who covered the story, Horn began the brawl by throwing "a punch at the smallest of the group," John Corbett. This was exceedingly unwise. Not only did Corbett know how to protect himself, but his companion, McKenna, carried a loaded walking cane. "The gunfighter's blow never landed," added Raine. Within moments, McKenna beat Horn senseless. The detective had never been adept at fisticuffs. Only excessive drinking could account for such recklessness on his part. Initial reports mistakenly placed Young Corbett at the scene. Had he been there, Young Corbett could have killed Tom Horn with his fists[18]

At 5:30 the following morning, the battered range detective was conveyed to St. Luke's Hospital, where Police Surgeon W. L. Davis found that the patient's left jaw was broken in two places. A full facial cast was necessary, which prevented Horn from speaking. He wrote Doctor Davis a note, asking that he be taken to John Coble's room at the Windsor Hotel. Fearing Horn might also have internal injuries, Davis checked the patient back into the hospital. For several days, Horn was believed to be near death, but a news dispatch of 8 October indicated that he was expected to live. Horn had to stay in the hospital for three weeks. A police investigation concluded that the attack "was premeditated . . . for the purpose of robbing Horn," according to the *Denver Post*. John Corbett was arrested but McKenna and the unnamed newspaperman left town. Horn objected to police interference in his case. "He does not want the law to take action against his assailants," said a reporter, "but wishes to avenge his wrongs himself." While the police cautioned Horn against vigilante action, the final disposition of the case is not known. He was released from the hospital on 21 October.[19]

One person whom Tom Horn considered a friend was Harry Hynds. Hynds, the owner of the Capitol Bar in Cheyenne and a respected promoter of the city, left when an anti-saloon and -gambling movement got under way just after the turn of the century. At one time, Horn and Hynds seem to have been business partners. In January 1900, the *Rocky*

Mountains News reported that "Harry P. Hynds, John McDermott and Tom Horn have formed a partnership for engaging in the sheep and wool business." (Apparently, the John McDermott referred to was the former U.S. marshal for Wyoming.) While McDermott informed the *Wyoming Tribune* that he expected to make a good profit, Horn's share in this enterprise is not known. Although raising sheep sounds improbable for a man who had devoted many years to defending cattlemen from the "little woolies," some Wyoming ranchers were overcoming their prejudices and incorporating sheep into their livestock ventures at this time.[20]

The friendship between Tom Horn and Harry Hynds apparently began to go sour shortly after they entered into this reported partnership. Tim McCoy, who became a Capitol Bar regular shortly after Tom Horn's execution, recalled that a rival saloon owner hired the range detective to kill Hynds. But Hynds was fully capable of taking care of himself; he had killed a man in Salt Lake City for becoming intimate with his wife. When Horn entered the Capitol Bar and began to act threateningly—apparently drinking heavily—McCoy reported that Hynds took his assailant's pistol away from him and ordered him out of the bar. Although local newspapers failed to report this incident, a Hynds descendant declared that "a story has been passed down in my family that Tom Horn was one time hired to kill Uncle Harry." For some unknown reason, Horn did not carry out his assignment, this relative continued, and the two men again became "great friends."[21]

Drunk or sober, the notorious range detective was still an impressive-looking man. Horn "stood six feet and two inches," wrote Charlie Siringo, "every inch a physical man." Leonel O'Brien, who wrote for the *Denver Post* under the name Polly Pry, observed Tom Horn up close at the Laramie County sheriff's office shortly after his arrest in 1902 and provided one of the most detailed descriptions of this infamous man:

> He is tall, being six feet one, but he does not look it, as he walks with a forward stoop, with his head thrust out from his broad shoulders and his chin drooping. His body is extraordinarily long and although he weighs 190 pounds he is not fleshy. His feet are small and well shaped but his hands are brutally coarse with thick stubby fingers and long hairs growing clear down to the knuckles. His open shirt collar revealed a breast likewise covered with thick, coarse-looking hair. His head is

well shaped, particularly about the brow, which is broad and well rounded. His hair is dark brown and very thick, the top of his head being quite bare. He has a fine, straight nose, a well shaped chin, a thin, cruel mouth with a cynical sneer lurking about the corners of his lips.

Pry also detected something unusual in his voice, calling it harsh, "with a most peculiar inflection." "It isn't a voice to forget," she added, "nor is it a pleasant one." (Minnie Rietz described Horn's voice very differently. She said it was "soft and drawling," but that he "had a very slight impediment in his speech.")[22]

Friends and acquaintances frequently remarked on Tom Horn's eyes. They were distinctive and disturbing. Pinkerton Operative Doc Shores characterized them as "black, shifty eyes." Hugh M. McPhee, the Swan cowhand, also noted Horn's "beady, black eyes" which "looked right thru [sic] you." Horn had "small black eyes with high cheek bones," according to Henry Melton, "which altogether gave him the appearance of an Indian." Tom Horn had "brown eyes that missed nothing going on around him," said Minnie Rietz, "but yet never appearing watchful—on the contrary, having rather [a] sleepy look most of the time." Allen G. Wallihan, the roadhouse operator in Lay, Colorado, recalled something else that was troublesome about Horn's eyes. He "never looked at you," said Wallihan, and "always looked down." Apparently, this habit offended Augusta Wallihan. "My wife had lived all her life on the frontier and she was not afraid of man, God or the devil," Allan Wallihan wrote, "but she said, 'that man . . . is a bad man.'" Whether his growing eyesight problem had anything to do with the appearance of his eyes is not clear.[23]

In spite of Horn's self-confident demeanor, he was uncomfortable around women. While a friend, J. P. Wallace, dismissed as "silly talk" the allegation that Horn was sometimes "brutal toward women," there was no doubt that he did not hit it off with many women. If he did live with an Apache girl in Arizona, he eventually deserted her. While reports later circulated that he was close to Glendolene Myrtle Kimmell, an Iron Mountain schoolteacher, such stories were so much newspaper fluff. While he was courteous toward females, he informed Henry Melton that "it was bad practice to talk too much before women and little children." "Usually he was quiet to the point of taciturnity, especially if women were present," recalled Minnie Rietz. Yet he took a liking to Minnie and her mother and often entertained them with tales of his exploits in the Apache campaigns. Horn promised Minnie's mother "a basket made from an armadillo shell" that he had seen in Arizona, and he later presented her with such a gift upon returning from the Southwest.[24]

The women with whom Horn kept company were part of the frontier demimonde. Presumably, Horn was referring to such women when he lamented to John Coble from his Cheyenne jail cell in March 1902, "My girls have all left off writing me and my heart is lonely now." Carol L. Bowers, who researched this aspect of Horn's life, found "ample evidence" that he had female friends in "the brothels of Laramie, Cheyenne, and Denver." Several of them wrote appeals to Governor Fenimore Chatterton in November 1903, asking him to commute Horn's death sentence to life imprisonment. One of them called herself, "a lady of Tom Horn."[25]

In the absence of meaningful adult friendships, the range detective exhibited an affinity for children. As a boy on his father's ranch near Gering, Nebraska, Walter Lawyer recalled meeting Tom Horn on a cattle drive. Lawyer never forgot this tall cowhand with "a real interest in kids." Ida Wood, whose mother had refused to feed Tom Horn, said she and her siblings looked forward to his visits. Ida's brother, Robert, remembered fondly how the range rider "used to give us children rock candy" and even permitted them to ride his horse. Minnie Rietz had similar memories of Horn's visits to their ranch. Not only did he permit the children to ride his horse, but he sang with them. Although not a religious man, Horn had "a marked preference for religious songs," she added. On one occasion, Horn and Alfred Cook, sheriff of Albany County, Wyoming, were traveling by train to Denver. During a brief rest stop in Greeley, Colorado, Horn spied a poor family of Russian immigrants on the depot platform. When several of the "ragged, hungry-looking children" asked Horn for help, recalled Cook, "Tom . . . took them to a restaurant and filled them up with a hearty meal." Later, "he took them to a clothing store, and dressed them up with new clothes," added Cook, "and bought each a pair of shoes—as they were bare-footed."[26]

Horn clung to the few people whom he regarded as true friends and was willing to go out of his way to do things for them. When young Otto Plaga assisted Horn in the arrest of Eva Langhoff and her associates in 1893, the detective presented Plaga with a rope from his own outfit. Bud Cowan, Horn's horsebreaking friend, noted that he "had a pair of the prettiest guns I had ever seen." When Cowan "tried to trade him out of one of them," the detective protested that he would never "trade or sell" his handguns, but "if he thought enough of anyone he might give him one, or both." When Cowan was preparing for a trip to Montana sometime later, Tom Horn rode up and talked a few minutes. Before Cowan could leave, Horn tied a package on the cowboy's saddle, calling the item "a kind of remembrance." When Cowan asked what it was, Horn replied, "It's a writing outfit, so you won't forget to write me." The gift was one of Tom Horn's prized revolvers. The two men continued to correspond until Horn's death in 1903. "As a friend, Tom was true blue," said Cowan; "as an enemy, he was deadly."[27]

Horn was always loyal to his employers. Cattlemen who sent Horn on difficult missions, including an occasional assassination, never had to worry that he would betray their names in public. (The fact that he sometimes incriminated himself during alcoholic binges was a different matter.) "John Coble told W. C. Irvine that Horn would never 'squeal,'" wrote Lawrence Woods, "and to the men who hired him, this was his most valuable character trait." "In the end he did not squeal," continued Woods, "and he took whatever knowledge he had of the big cattlemen to his grave with him."[28]

If Tom Horn possessed one talent that truly set him apart from most cowpunchers, it was his horsebreaking ability. He "was a first class broncho twister," said James D. Eckel, "and I have known him to 'uncork' [break] the boys' horses for them, lots of times." Horn was "one of the best horse breakers and cowpunchers I ever worked with," wrote Bud Cowan, who welcomed the help of the range detective in breaking polo ponies for Eastern aficionados. A mutual love of horses brought Tom together with another horse lover, Jack Linscott, a rancher from north of Laramie. "In all other characteristics they were totally opposites," said Minnie Rietz. "Linscott was essentially a town man, loved to wear the finest clothes and jewelry, particularly diamonds. He was talkative, liked women's society and was inclined to be quarrelsome but lacked courage to fight his own battles." Yet Horn genuinely liked the man. When Linscott purchased a horse from one "Frenchy" but failed to pay the agreed-upon price, the owner confronted Linscott in Laramie, whereupon Linscott threw a rock at Frenchy, hitting him in the head. Frenchy chased his attacker down the railroad right-of-way. Tom Horn, who rode up just as this footrace began, naturally took up Linscott's side. He yelled out, "Shall I rope him for you Jack?" Frenchy interjected a counter offer: "By damn, you catch me that feller I gif you five tollar." Seeing the humor of the situation, Tom Horn decided against taking sides. He "tore up the track," according to Minnie Rietz, "circling Linscott, and back around Frenchy, cutting a figure eight, and, laughing heartily." Just how the two resolved their argument is not known.[29]

Tom Horn took any opportunity to demonstrate his abilities with the rope. In August 1901, the *Cheyenne Daily Leader* named him as one of the "noted cowpunchers" who would participate in "the roping and pitching contests" at the forthcoming Frontier Days Celebration. Duncan Clark and Otto Plaga, two of Horn's fellow cowhands from the Coble ranch, were also participants. While Horn, now forty years old, did not fare well in the competition, Henry Melton, another cowhand, recalled that Horn "possessed remarkable skill in handling a lariat." Horn "always carried with him a forty-foot rawhide rope," added Melton, and liked to impress cowhands with what he termed "handy tricks about roping." Alfred Cook, one-time sheriff of Albany County, asserted that "Tom once saved my life by a good throw of his lariat at the right time." Cook, who was apparently in danger of drowning, said he would "never forget" what Horn did for him.

Horsehair braiding and leather working, which Horn learned from the Apaches, remained his favorite pastime. He became an accomplished fashioner of ropes, lariats, hackamores, and other range items. On barns throughout his range, ranchers installed special hooks that Horn used for drying leather strips or for securing one end of his current braiding or weaving project, while he worked from the other. Hugh McPhee, who learned the art of rope making from Horn, praised him as "the best rawhide and leather worker I ever saw." T. Joe Cahill said this craft was literally second nature to Horn, who would "braid in horsehair or rawhide as he talked." Such a craft required strong and dexterous hands.[30]

Tom Horn impressed many people as a man of above-average intelligence, although this is difficult to judge. While his formal education was limited to the elementary grades, Horn continued to make some effort at self-education. He credited army officers in Arizona with providing him books to read, while Robert Pinkerton, who met Tom Horn at the agency's branch office in Denver, observed that he was "inclined to read fairly good books." T. Joe Cahill maintained that Horn "had more breadth" than his occupation indicated. "He was an avid reader and he could discuss national affairs with a high degree of intelligence," continued Cahill. As with so many westerners, "Theodore Roosevelt was his political idol." Horn's fellow cowhands, such as Jim Eckel and Hugh McPhee, were impressed that he could speak Spanish and "quote Shakespeare." Nannie Steele, his nurse in Cheyenne, regarded the detective as "a man of refinement and education." Others, such as an anonymous Brown's Park rancher, considered Horn as merely someone who "put on the airs of a polished gentleman.[31]

One of Horn's fortes was as a teller of tall tales. He cultivated this gift not only for amusement but to reinforce his sinister reputation among potential cattle thieves. Charles Coe, who became a range detective in Wyoming shortly after Horn's death, asserted that he was "a born romancer." Minnie Rietz recalled that when Horn visited her family, she and her siblings "were always teasing him to tell us stories of his work." Henry Melton recalled one Christmas Season at Chugwater when Horn regaled Swan employees with "many stories." (In such situations, Horn did not have to tell the truth.) On this occasion, he told eager listeners about the time five train robbers ambushed him in Colorado. After coming within an eyebrow of losing his life in a fight with the bandits, the resourceful detective finally managed to kill all of them, but not before one outlaw cut him badly. Horn proudly exhibited the scar on his neck. Of course, this tale was a mixture of several experiences—his pursuit of the Cotopaxi train robbers, the alleged killing of two men in Jackson Hole, and his knife fight with the Kelly brothers in Baggs, Wyoming.[32]

Tom Horn "always had one or more good, readable stories to relate when visiting town," recalled one Cheyenne journalist, "and for that reason he was a welcome visitor at the average newspaper office." After the fashion of Buffalo Bill Cody, another frontier romancer, Horn took such opportunities to make himself an expert on many things. In a 1901 interview with George R. Caldwell, chief of the *Rocky Mountain News* Cheyenne bureau, Horn claimed to be an expert on gray wolves, going so far as to claim that cowhands killed a gray wolf near his ranch that "turned the scales at the monstrous weight of 180 pounds." Recently, he reported, a gray wolf had attacked an "entire pack of five dogs" on his premises and "had fairly and disastrously vanquished it." Horn boasted that he trailed the wolf on horseback, "ran him down, roped him, and then killed him." So serious was this wolf menace that he and his neighbors planned "to secure the services of Rattlesnake Jack, the Wyoming wolf slayer in chief." While this story was exaggerated, the Swan Land and Cattle Company and the Laramie [County] Protective Association offered a $20 bounty for each wolf killed.[33]

If Tom Horn was loyal and generous, the question remains, Did he experience remorse for his misdeeds? An anecdote told by Richard R. Mullins, a Wyoming writer, suggests that he had some regrets:

> Horn rode into Casper one afternoon and put up at the Natrona hotel. A double slaying southwest of Casper had been reported. As Horn sat facing the entrance of the hotel [presumably a gunfighter's precaution], he seemed nervous and ill at ease. He indulged in a game of solitaire. Directly, an acquaintance entered the room and started a conversation. Horn admitted that the life [of range detective] was getting [to] him and expressed a desire to leave the country. He further stated that he had got started out on the wrong foot, but that it was too late to change.

While the authenticity of this story is questionable, it is not implausible. In 1900 Horn was forty years old and had very little to show for his efforts.[34]

CHAPTER 11

Train No. 4 to Cheyenne

In mid-July 1901, Tom Horn mounted one of John Coble's prize horses and pointed it in the direction of Iron Mountain. This was to be a routine ride, not unlike his many previous patrols. In subsequent court testimony, Horn declared that Coble had instructed him to see if the sheep of Kelsey P. (Kels) Nickell, a homesteader, were straying onto Iron Mountain Ranch pastures. The detective spent Sunday night, 14 July, at the ranch of Billy Clay, who had a long-standing arrangement with Horn's employers to provide him room and board. On Monday morning, Horn rode to the homestead of James Miller, a near neighbor of Nickell, where he stayed Monday and Tuesday nights. The next morning, 17 July, Horn began the journey back to Bosler.[1]

Violence and contentiousness had been commonplace in the Iron Mountain community for many years, with small farmers and ranchers not only squabbling among themselves but resisting the efforts of big cattlemen to dominate the range. When arsonists torched haystacks on two Iron Mountain ranches in 1897, the *Laramie Republican* reminded readers that this "beautiful mountain vale has been the scene of neighborhood rackets [crimes] without number" and that two of its residents, Fred Powell and William Lewis, "died at the hands of assassins." At the same time, John Coble and other ranchers viewed with alarm the increasing number of sheep on the Iron Mountain range. On one occasion, sheep raisers even hauled Coble and his "anti-woolly" compatriots into court on malicious mischief charges. Hostility toward sheepmen reached a new level when Kels Nickell sold his cattle and contracted with a Denver physician to run 3,000 of the doctor's sheep in the summer of 1900. In July Coble complained to his partner, Frank Bosler, that some of their pastures were "filled with sheep and look wooly." If the sheep growers "attempt to drive or handle our cattle," continued Coble, "I will at once have them arrested." While some cattlemen were "hiring all the six-shooters and badmen they can find," Coble said he desired to recall Tom Horn (who was working in Colorado). Horn would intimidate the sheepmen; as Coble put it, he would "straighten them out by merely riding around."[2]

Personal animosities also played an important part in this struggle for control of the range. For many years, John Coble and Kels Nickell had been at odds. The red-headed and combative Nickell, who had an uncanny ability to offend just about every neighbor, enraged Coble on several levels. In an interview with Polly Pry of the *Denver Post,* a prominent Cheyenne resident gave some background on this rivalry:

> Coble hates Nickell like the devil hates holy water, and because of that, he wants his land. But he never had an excuse to go after him until Nickell brought in all those sheep. . . . You see, they had a row a good while ago [1890] and Nickell gave him a slash that was a long time healing, and Coble isn't a man to forget. He's vindictive to the last degree and never forgets when he has a score to settle. . . . [He] drinks a deal and is ugly, overbearing and dangerous when in his cups. He'll stick by his friends, but his friends must stick by him in everything, and he always carries the whip hand.

In a separate interview with Pry, Mary Nickell confirmed the ongoing hostility between her husband and Coble. "You see, Mr. Coble had used the land we took up for a range," she explained, "and he didn't like it when we fenced it in.'" In regard to the 1890 knifing incident, she recalled that Coble "swore he'd be revenged on Mr. Nickell."[3]

Nickell was also at odds with several neighbors, most especially with James E. Miller. Although they probably could not remember the origins of their quarrel, in early 1900 Nickell and Miller "were principals in an interesting shooting fracas near Iron Mountain," according to the *Wyoming Tribune.* Fortunately, no one was wounded. A few months later,

Nickell charged two of James Miller's sons, Augustus (Gus) and Victor, with fence cutting and trespass. This case, merely "another chapter of the Miller-Nickel [sic] feud," one newsman observed, ended with the Miller boys being found not guilty. Miller began to keep a loaded gun close at all times, and a tragedy soon followed. In August 1900, Miller's shotgun accidentally discharged, killing his son, Frank. The anguished father blamed Nickell for Frank Miller's death. In January 1901, the two men collided in a Cheyenne restaurant. When Miller stabbed Nickell in the shoulder, the latter pulled a pistol, but did not pull the trigger. The following June, Jim Miller accosted Willie Nickell, Kels's fourteen-year-old son, and aimed a gun at the boy's horse. "You cant [sic] tell what he [Miller] will do [next]," moaned a worried Mary Nickell. As in many neighborhood squabbles, relations between the feuding families were not uniformly hostile. While Nickell and Miller were at odds, their womenfolk had the sense to remain good neighbors. When Mary Nickell was giving birth in July 1890, her husband was in the Laramie County Jail for knifing John Coble. Dora Miller, wife of Jim Miller, who resided less than a mile away, helped Mary Nickell give birth.[4]

Since this feud took place in Tom Horn's patrol area, he could not avoid becoming involved. On Thursday, 18 July 1901, Willie Nickell was shot to death about three-quarters of a mile west of his home on the road to the Iron Mountain railroad depot. Kels Nickell had instructed Willie to locate a man who had recently asked his father for work and to try to persuade that man to return. When Willie did not come home on Thursday evening, family members were not unduly alarmed, believing that he had stayed overnight at the station. When Fred Nickell, Willie's younger brother, went out to locate some cows early Friday morning, he stumbled upon the remains of his brother lying near a fence gap. Only then did the Nickells realize that the three gunshots they had heard early the previous morning had resulted in Willie's death.[5]

Kels Nickell immediately sent a messenger to the Laramie County sheriff's office in Cheyenne. Since John P. Shaver, the chief county lawman, was out of town, Deputy Sheriff Peter Warlaumont and Court Stenographer Robert C. Morris left for the murder scene late that same day, 19 July. Conveniently, Thomas C. Murray, the county coroner, District Court Clerk Tunis Joseph Fisher, and County Assessor George Gregory were all on a fishing trip near Iron Mountain. A messenger sought them out and directed them to the crime scene. When Kels Nickell arrived at the fence gap, he "found the body of his son lying face upward," according to the *Rocky Mountain News:*

> His shirt had been torn open at the throat and exposed the hole in the chest where the bullet emerged. Indications point to the fact that after the shooting the murderer came from his hiding place in the rocks and examined his victim, opening the shirt in order to see the wound. The cloth was still crimped where his fingers had clutched it. After being shot young Nickle [*sic*] ran seventy-five yards and fell dead. The two [*sic;* in fact there were three] shots heard at the ranch must have been fired at him as he ran. His face even in death bore an expression of intense alarm.

Local residents were terribly "wrought up over the assassination," said this Denver journalist, who predicted a lynching when the murderer was found.[6]

On Saturday, 20 July, Coroner Murray opened an inquest over Willie Nickell's body in the family home. Jurors included Murray's fishing companions, Fisher and Gregory, with Hiram G. Davidson, a local farmer, rounding out the panel. Only three persons were questioned that day. Fred Nickell and his sister, Catherine, testified as to Willie's movements on the fatal morning of 18 July. Joseph E. Reed, a neighbor, testified that he accompanied Kels Nickell to the nearby school, in order to talk with the teacher, Glendolene Kimmell. Since she boarded with the Miller family, said Reed, Nickell wanted to ask her about the movements of James Miller and his sons the morning of the murder. Obviously, Nickell suspected Jim Miller and one or more of his sons, Gus and Victor. At first, Kimmell, who was aware of the bad feelings between the two families, hesitated to answer. Only after Nickell informed her that Willie had been killed did she reply. After questioning Reed, Coroner Murray adjourned the inquest and announced that the jury would reconvene at the Laramie County Court House in Cheyenne the following Monday. As the county officials prepared to transport Willie Nickell's remains to Cheyenne for autopsy, Kels Nickell suddenly accused Gus Miller of the murder. Deputy Warlaumont arrested the young man and took him to Cheyenne with the other law enforcement officials. Gus Miller was only the first of several suspects in the Willie Nickell case. There was some speculation that John Scroder, a former Nickell sheepherder, "may have put young Nickel[l] out of the way."[7]

Funeral services for Willie Nickell were held in the Methodist Church in Cheyenne on Sunday afternoon, 21 July. The Reverend Benjamin Young, a British immigrant, presided. "The church was crowded to its utmost capacity when the first sweet strains of music opened the services," said the *Daily Leader,* and the coffin was "almost completely hidden by a forest of flowers." After several hymns, the Reverend Young read passages from James Lane Allen's poem "Aftermath," and Henry Wadsworth Longfellow's "The Rainy Day." At the cemetery, Kels Nickell "created a profound sensation" when he "knelt beside the open grave and prayed [to] heaven for strength to slay the murderer of his son." "The excitement over the killing is intense," said one reporter, "and the utmost sympathy is felt for the bereaved parents." The Reverend Young likened the father's dilemma to that of Ajax, the tragic figure from Ancient Greek mythology. Nickell "'had been defying the lightning for years, and when it descended upon his son and upon the life and little ones who remained," observed the minister, "'he felt that he had called it down and his one cry was, 'What can I do?'" A few days later, the Nickells published a "Card of Thanks" for "all those who so kindly assisted us in our late bereavement."[8]

When Coroner Murray opened the inquest the next morning before "a large crowd of morbidly curious people," it was apparent that county officials intended to do more than merely find the cause of death. Given the particularly heinous nature of the crime, they hoped to find a primary murder suspect. While Coroner Murray continued to preside, Walter R. Stoll, the Laramie County district attorney, assumed the primary task of inquisitor. Under Stoll's direction, the inquiry into Willie Nickell's death comprised ten sessions, between 20 July and 15 August, with more than forty witnesses being called. John Apperson, a surveyor who happened to be at the Nickell residence on the day of the murder, drew a diagram of the scene and concluded that the fatal shots had been fired from about 200 feet away. The three physicians who performed the autopsy also testified to the existence of two bullet holes in the body, either one of which could have been fatal. The bullets were from a large caliber weapon, perhaps .38 or .45 caliber. Since Kels Nickell suspected one of the Miller family as the murderer, Walter Stoll's initial line of questioning explored this likelihood. "We have had considerable trouble," admitted Nickell on the witness stand. He went on to say that Jim Miller had chased his son before and even "snapped" his shotgun at him. Stoll then informed the jury that in conversation with Kels Nickell outside the jury room, the latter surmised that the assassin mistook his son for him.[9]

With Kels Nickell still on the stand, the district attorney abruptly shifted his line of questioning from the Nickell-Miller relationship to Tom Horn's presence in the vicinity of the crime. For the remainder of these proceedings, and afterward, Walter Stoll kept Horn's name central to the investigation. Stoll asked Nickell to recall a recent conversation with the range detective. During this meeting, which occurred in a Cheyenne saloon about 1 May 1901, Nickell reported that Horn asked "if I heard of his making any threats against me?" Nickell replied evasively, saying that he had heard "lots of things." A lengthy exchange then followed in regard to threats that Horn had allegedly made against Nickell for introducing sheep on a cattle range. The detective denied making any such threats and recalled that "an understanding" had been reached. When Nickell remarked that he had abided by this agreement, Horn replied, "That is just exactly [what] I thought." "I will tell you," continued the detective, "Tom Horn may be [a] son of a bitch, but he says you have proved to him that you are a man of your word." Horn then raised the subject of a threat he was alleged to have made against Nickell's life because he brought in the sheep. Horn blamed this rumor on Victor Miller—"the damned son of a bitch"—who reportedly said that Nickell "wouldn't last long because Tom Horn was going to kill him as soon as he got in here [with the sheep]." "That son of a bitch don't know Tom Horn," continued the range rider. "Those fellows making talk like that are more in danger of Tom Horn than anybody in the country." Much to Nickell's surprise, Horn assured him that his employers had "no enmity against you for bringing the sheep in here." "We are not afraid of sheepmen going to steal our cattle," said Horn, who assured Nickell that he was in "no danger." Whether Tom Horn was being truthful or merely attempting to allay Nickell's fear of assassination is not known. Nor is the reaction of the jurors known, although they must have been incredulous. After all, John Coble had expressed much anger at the men—especially Kels Nickell—who were introducing sheep into the Iron Mountain country.[10]

The way District Attorney Stoll redirected the questioning from the Millers to the range detective was reported in the *Rocky Mountain News,* which neatly summarized Stoll's strategy: "An attempt is being made to prove that Tom Horn, a detective in the employ of the cattlemen, was the murderer of young Nickel. He was hanging about the vicinity of the Nickel ranch for several days before the killing, apparently watching for somebody, but disappeared the day before the murder and has not since been heard of." In subsequent sessions, Stoll kept Horn's name before the jurors and pointedly asked witnesses if they had heard Horn characterized as "a bad man," or if he was "a hard citizen or a good citizen?" On another occasion, Stoll asked a witness if he had heard the detective's name mentioned in connection with the murder of Billy Lewis and Fred Powell, in 1895. Stoll also asked questions implying that Iron Mountain residents were intimidated by Horn and were thus afraid to talk.[11]

As the inquest continued, Stoll continued to prod jurors for information about Tom Horn's movements just prior to the murder of Willie Nickell. When Horn departed the Miller homestead on 17 July, he informed Mary Miller that he would return the following day. However, he did not return, which left the impression with the jury that he may have killed Willie Nickell and ridden back to Bosler. Glendolene Myrtle Kimmell, the Iron Mountain schoolteacher, testified that she was "strongly attracted by the frontier type." She took the teaching position at Iron Mountain, Kimmell explained, as a means to "meet with the embodiment of that type in its natural environment." On the evening of 15 July 1901, a man rode up to the Miller place "who embodied the characteristics and the code of the old frontiersman." This frontier exemplar was none other than Tom Horn. When Prosecutor Stoll asked her to recall the movements of Jim Miller and his sons, Gus and Victor, on the day of Willie Nickell's death, Kimmell declared that all three ate breakfast at the usual time and were at home when the fatal shots were heard between 7:00 and 8:00 A.M. After listening to the testimony of this "intelligent and interesting witness," the *Daily Leader* concluded that Kimmell "practically exonerates the Miller boys" of the murder of Willie Nickell, while the *Rocky Mountain News* reminded readers that "several witnesses testified as to the presence of Tom Horn in the community just prior to the murder."[12]

At the end of the proceedings on 23 July, Coroner Murray adjourned the jury indefinitely, but subject to recall. Thus far, the evidence submitted had been disappointing, although the Laramie County Board of Commissioners and Governor DeForest Richards each posted a $500 reward. While one newsman believed that "this large sum will result in strenuous efforts being made to apprehend the slayer," Undersheriff James Golden and Deputy Peter Warlaumont found the inhabitants of the Iron Mountain country reluctant to talk. They lived in fear of the big cattle companies and their henchmen, including Tom Horn. When Golden and Warlaumont returned to Cheyenne, they refused to discuss their findings, leading one newspaper to conclude that the officers were "as much at a loss as to where to place the crime as ever." In the meantime, one of the earliest suspects in the Nickell murder case, John H. Scroder, the mysterious flockmaster, had proven an alibi.[13]

As if the brutal assassination of Willie Nickell were not enough, the body of eight-year-old Dee Blair was found on the banks of the Platte River near Casper on 26 July. Young Blair, who had gone fishing on 3 July and simply disappeared, had been killed by a shotgun blast. Although these slayings were unrelated, the *Daily Leader* decried the fact that within a fortnight two young boys had been "foully murdered in the state of Wyoming." When Natrona County lawmen failed to find any tangible clues, one newspaper concluded that the Blair case "has developed into as impenetrable a mystery as the Nickell case." (Indeed, the Blair murder was never solved.)[14]

On Sunday, 4 August, unknown gunmen attempted to kill Kels Nickell while he and his youngest daughter were milking cows in a pasture near the family residence. Although Kels received three gunshot wounds, William P. Mahoney, Nickell's brother-in-law, drove him to a Cheyenne hospital that same day, which saved him. Miraculously, the little girl was uninjured. The assassins apparently knew what time Nickell was in the habit of milking. Nickell informed District Attorney Stoll that he recognized his assailants as James Miller and one of his sons—either Gus or Victor, he was not sure which. To add to the Nickell family's woes, four masked riders attacked his flock a few days later, killing thirty or more animals, and running off his shepherd, an Italian reportedly named Vingenzo Biango. (Locals called him variously Tony or Jim White, suggesting that this was a newspaperman's misspelling of Vincenzo Bianco.) The thoroughly terrified shepherd fled to Cheyenne. While the *Daily Leader* deplored this "dastardly work," a separate rumor held that the sheep killers bribed Bianco to abandon Nickell's flock.[15]

At a brief session of the coroner's jury on Tuesday, 6 August, Prosecutor Stoll, who announced that future proceedings would be held behind closed doors, questioned one John (Jack) Martin, a Laramie City blacksmith and part-time deputy sheriff. Martin had reportedly been in the Iron Mountain country a day or two after the Willie Nickell murder. Unfortunately, the press misconstrued the service of a witness subpoena on Martin for an arrest warrant and erroneously reported that he was a murder suspect. While the prosecutor apparently believed Martin could shed light on Tom Horn's movements around the time of Willie Nickell's murder, this witness turned out to be a friend of the detective and had worked on the Wilcox train robbery case with him in 1899. Much to Stoll's dismay, Martin insisted that Horn was "a very smooth detective" and no "fool." "He don't let everybody see him when he goes out" on a case, added Martin. This witness did qualify his praise of the detective by adding the observation, "when he is sober."[16]

The next day, the coroner's jury met briefly to examine Vincenzo Bianco. Speaking through an interpreter, Bianco informed the jury that unknown persons threatened him a few days before the raid on the Nickell flock. On the day of the raid, the shepherd said that three men appeared—an old man and two boys—and fired some thirty shots at him and his sheep. When he reached Cheyenne, someone he could not identify offered him $500 to leave Wyoming.[17]

While Sheriff John Shaver's deputies did their best in the Nickell cases, their resources were badly stretched, and they needed assistance. Fortunately, U.S. Marshal Frank Hadsell was able to loan them his office deputy, Joseph LeFors. Before joining the marshal's staff, LeFors had served as a range detective in Montana and Wyoming. While there is no evidence that Shaver and LeFors were close friends, the deputy marshal had a reputation as a dogged man hunter who had used his gun when necessary.[18]

In early August, Joe LeFors took up his temporary assignment with the Laramie County sheriff's office, accompanying Deputy Warlaumont and Special Deputies Sandy McNeil and Henry Brown to Iron Mountain. Their purpose was twofold: to investigate the recent attempt on Kels Nickell's life; and to arrest Jim Miller and his sons, Gus and Victor. (Gus Miller had been released earlier.) Kels Nickell had just filed a new complaint against them. After arresting the Millers, the lawmen examined the scene of the attack upon Kels Nickell. In his subsequent testimony before the coroner's jury, on 13 August, LeFors sprang a surprise on the jurors. Contrary to Kels's testimony that two men shot at him, the lawman said he found signs of only one assassin. Not only did LeFors find the hoofprints of one shod horse but this man left a footprint (size 8 or 9). He followed the hoofprints through a gate northeast of the Nickell home (not the gate where Willie was killed) to a point where the tracks entered a road. When District Attorney Stoll, who clearly suspected Tom Horn in the attempt on Kels Nickell's life, asked LeFors the direction that the assailant took on the road, he replied that the assailant rode toward the homes of Joe Reed and Billy Clay, and not toward the residence of Jim Miller. (Clay often provided accommodations for Horn while in the service of the big ranchers.) Before leaving the Iron Mountain area, Warlaumont and LeFors talked with a very frightened Mary Nickell, who was staying alone with her children while her husband was in the hospital. While she insisted that she did not know who attempted to kill her husband, Mary Nickell was certain, according to LeFors, "that everything that happened was because of their sheep." She also admitted that her husband had received an anonymous letter ordering him "to get out of the country with the sheep or suffer the consequences."[19]

Even though he was working for the sheriff's office, Joe LeFors seemed to be acting on his own during this visit. While Deputy Warlaumont was interviewing the Nickell children, LeFors quietly informed Mary Nickell that he would "get the men who had been trying to kill off the family" but told her that he would need her assistance. She would have to restrain her "high tempered" husband when he returned home, as he talked too much, "accusing this one and that one of being the man that was doing the shooting." She and Kels must not, added LeFors, talk to anyone about the case.

The deputy marshal went on (still in private) to insist that he "would investigate and get all the facts" in these cases. Just when "you think I have forgotten my promise," he assured Mary Nickell, "I will be doing my best work." As he and Warlaumont departed, LeFors "cautioned Mrs. Nickell by all means to keep my name from becoming known in the case." The deputy marshal was confident that "not even Peter Warlaumont knew the extent of my talk with Mrs. Nickell regarding the catching of the assassin."[20]

When LeFors returned to Cheyenne, Samuel Corson, chairman of the Laramie County Board of Commissioners, asked to see him privately. They met in U.S. Marshal Hadsell's office on or about 8 August

1901. This was a momentous gathering, not only for Joe LeFors, but even more so for Tom Horn. When Corson asked what evidence had been found at the Nickell ranch, the deputy marshal replied:

> The killing is the result of a sheepmen's and cattlemen's war [for control of the] range and therefore predicated on dollars and cents. Kels P. Nickell has the only sheep between the Iron Mountain country and the U.P.R.R. east-west tracks, a distance of some 30 or 40 miles. This is all open government range. It is not over [cattle] stealing, because Nickell is not and never has been to my knowledge accused of [cattle] stealing.

LeFors concluded that "a few of the major cattlemen" in the Iron Mountain area were responsible for the attempt on Kels Nickell's life.[21]

On 8 August Tom Murray reconvened the coroner's jury, at which time Walter Stoll introduced an assistant, H. Waldo Moore, a former county prosecutor. That the Laramie County commissioners were willing to foot the bill for an assistant prosecutor was another indicator that the public wanted a stop to the violence in the Iron Mountain community. The fact that Moore was a Republican, while Stoll was a Democrat, indicated a bipartisan effort to impose law and order. With Mary McDonald, a Nickell neighbor, on the stand, Walter Stoll took this opportunity to urge the terrified (and close-mouthed) people of Iron Mountain to divulge what they knew about the Nickell cases:

> If they do not tell what they know there will be no safety for anybody or anybody's family or children. One of these days some one may come and kill you, or your husband or your children, and if the neighbors don't tell what they know the murderer will escape. There has been assassination going on for some time and the people of the country [Laramie and Albany counties] are going to see who is doing it. They [counties] have got money to spend and they are going to spend it. . . . It is not [through] any personal desire we are making an investigation; it is simply for the purpose of seeing whether assassins can go unpunished, or whether there is safety to a person's life.

The prosecutor, who threatened to charge anyone who refused to talk as an accessory after-the-fact, returned to this theme when William L.

Clay, an ally of the big ranching interests, took the stand. "You know Mr. Clay we cannot have a civilized community if people are going to be shot from ambush?" To this Clay replied, "I don't suppose you could." "Especially if little boys are going to be shot down?" continued Stoll. "Certainly," Clay answered. (There is no evidence that Clay, who had given Tom Horn aid and comfort for years, changed his allegiance.)[22]

On Friday afternoon, 9 August 1901, the citizens of Cheyenne awaited the arrival of Union Pacific passenger train no. 4 with some trepidation. "Mr. Thomas Horn came in today from the West," said the *Daily Leader*. When his train pulled into the depot at 2:10 P.M., the range detective, still in his "travel stained" riding gear, was greeted by a deputy sheriff, as well as by several friends. Horn, who was responding to a subpoena, went directly to the courthouse, where Walter Stoll immediately put him in the witness chair. Stoll asked pointedly if the detective had any information bearing on the murder of Willie Nickell. Horn admitted that he was in the Iron Mountain region "just prior to the killing of that kid," that he stayed with Jim Miller on the Monday and Tuesday nights prior to Willie's murder, and that he departed on Wednesday morning. When asked if Jim Miller and Kels Nickell were "a source of trouble," he expressed the opinion that they were "the worst kind of people." While Horn admitted to "hereditary bad feeling" between these two men, he pooh-poohed the notion that either one had the courage to shoot the other, or a relative. "I have heard Nick [Kels Nickell] say he was going to do this and do that" to James Miller, Horn remarked, but "it don't amount to a great deal." Horn said he was surprised at the murder of Willie Nickell and went on to say that he "didn't give Miller credit for having [the] stuff in him to do anything of that kind." Furthermore, both Nickell and Miller, who "come here with nothing at all," added Horn, started herds by stealing from John Coble and the Swan Two Bar. In regard to his recent conversation with Kels Nickell concerning the latter's sheep, Horn quoted Nickell as saying "every damned son of a bitch [in the neighborhood] has given me dirt, and I will eat them out of house and home. . . . I will make their asses pop out of the saddle." When Nickell asked for Horn's position on sheep, Horn replied that he "had no feeling about it." Subsequently, Nickell boasted to Horn that he left his sheep "right in Jim Miller's door yard. . . . I wonder how the son-of-a-bitch feels . . . now."[23]

District Attorney Stoll continued to press the conflict between cattlemen and sheepmen in the Iron Mountain region. Tom Horn declared that cattle companies had no objection to a sheepman bringing in sheep, but the livestock interests objected if a cattle raiser suddenly sold his cattle (that is, changed sides) and introduced sheep "for no other reason than to spite the neighbors." Asked if he had heard any cattlemen threaten to drive Kels Nickell's sheep out of the region, Horn replied in the negative. Horn added that he was completely "disinterested" in this matter. (Horn was lying, of course; he was working for cattlemen who were very interested.) Attorney Stoll then asked Horn to recall a quarrel he had with Kels Nickell when the two men attended the grand jury investigation into the murder of William Lewis in 1895. At that time, Nickell confronted Horn in front of the courthouse in Cheyenne and objected to Horn's hunting wild game on his property. When Horn protested that Nickell spoke "in a friendly way" on this occasion, Stoll disagreed and reminded Horn that Nickell ordered the detective not to leave the road when he rode through his property. "No, sir," Horn bristled, "I wouldn't allow fifteen of the worst men in the world to tell me that," and he went on to assert that he had complete freedom "to go where I please." Horn's testimony was an eerie foreshadowing of his time on the witness stand during his murder trial fifteen months later, an occasion on which he also tended to incriminate himself. When he expressed the opinion to the coroner's jury that Jim Miller and Kels Nickells lacked the courage to shoot at each other, Horn eliminated the only other likely suspect in the Willie Nickell murder, Jim Miller. This left only one other likely suspect—Tom Horn.[24]

When the inquest continued on 10 August, Stoll questioned several witnesses in regard to the attack on Kels Nickell on 4 August. Making her second appearance before the coroner's jury, Glendolene Kimmell testified that she could think of nothing in the movements of Jim Miller or his sons that led her to believe any of them committed this attack. The attack took place on a Sunday, when most of the Millers slept late, with the exception of Gus, who had early chores to perform. That day Gus encountered Joe Reid, a neighbor, who informed him that someone shot and wounded Kels Nickell. Kimmell did recall that on this same day Jim Miller spied Vincenzo Bianco with Kels Nickell's sheep on his property and ran the shepherd off at gunpoint.[25]

On 13 August, Diedrick George testified before the coroner's jury that livestock men in the Iron Mountain region had recently established a "protection association." While he made no connection between this new organization and the murder of Willie Nickell, the *Daily Leader* characterized the formation of this "powerful organization" as a disturbing sign of trouble in the area. After two additional persons testified without divulging any important information, the *Daily Leader* concluded that the panel would be forced to rule that the boy came to his death at the "'hands of some person or persons unknown.'" However, Murray reminded the jurors that they were still subject to recall if necessary.[26]

The coroner's inquest gave Tom Horn and Glendolene Kimmell an opportunity to see each other again. Horn greeted her at the railroad station when she answered her second summons. She had also kept Horn informed by letter about testimony before the panel prior to his arrival in Cheyenne. Shortly after the inquest, Horn "was walking along a street in Cheyenne with Miss Kimmel[l] on his arm," the *Denver Times* reported, when an unidentified passerby asked the range detective for a moment of his time. This stranger introduced a second man to him as "Mr. Jones." In turn, he introduced Horn to this stranger as "Mr. Smith." Obviously miffed at this intrusion, the detective remarked, "How wise you fellows are. What's the game?" Obviously enjoying himself, the first man replied, "Why, Tom, don't you know your own brother?" Although obviously taken aback, Horn asked his female companion "to wait for him" on a nearby staircase while he retired to Harry Hynds's bar with his brother. Although the *Times* did not mention the name of the brother, Horn said "his father had given him an awful strapping once and he had run away from home and had not seen his brother for thirty-five years." This unnamed sibling was probably Martin Horn, who reportedly worked in the Union Pacific Railroad shop in Cheyenne in 1901. (Another sibling, an unnamed sister, also reportedly resided in the capital city, although Horn was not aware of her presence.)[27]

In spite of public doubts that the Nickell cases would ever be solved, the Laramie County Board of Commissioners was determined to see these cases through. This three-man body, consisting of Samuel Corson (chair), James B. Boyer, and James M. Newman, played a critical role in maintaining the momentum of the proceedings by providing the sheriff's office with discretionary monies for a lengthy investigation, and by protecting the lawmen from any politically powerful group that might attempt to derail their work. A longtime fixture in Wyoming's legal community, Walter Stoll had at one time or another represented both sides in Wyoming's numerous range disputes. He had actually defended the cattle barons' mercenary band in 1892. In politics, he served as chairman of the Democratic Party's statewide organization. Stoll was considered "a man of signal ability, great force of character . . . [with] a thorough knowledge of the law."[28]

Since Deputy U.S. Marshal Joseph LeFors had already assisted in the early phases of the Nickell investigation, Walter Stoll recommended to the county commissioners that he should be permanently assigned to these cases. In so doing, they ensured that LeFors's name became inextricably tied to that of Tom Horn. Shortly after the deputy marshal returned with Deputy Sheriff Warlaumont's posse from Iron Mountain, LeFors recalled, U.S. Marshal Hadsell approached him about working permanently on the Nickell cases. When LeFors suggested that such an investigation might take some time and would provoke political problems, Hadsell assured him that if he found the murderer of Willie Nickell, "'you can land any position that the State of Wyoming has to offer.'"[29]

To add to the difficulties already apparent in the Nickell cases, Sheriff Shaver passed away on 5 September 1901 after a long illness. The county commissioners were anxious to fill this important position quickly and apparently already had a replacement in mind. This man was Edwin J. Smalley, a Wyoming pioneer and perhaps the first white male baby born in Cheyenne (in 1868). His appointment was surprising, since Smalley was a Republican while Laramie County was largely Democratic. Smalley had run unsuccessfully for sheriff in the last election and was well-liked by a cross-section of the voters. While there was some concern that his lack of law enforcement experience—he was a longtime clerk in a local mercantile store—might work against him, the commissioners persisted. Smalley took the oath of office on 9 September 1901. Since James Golden, Shaver's chief deputy, put up some resistance to this abrupt change, Smalley's first act was to fire Shaver's entire staff. As chief deputy, Smalley selected Richard A. Proctor, a former city policeman. Leslie Snow, formerly assistant county clerk, became a full-time deputy. While these acts prompted some editorializing about Smalley's "good Republican politics," he was determined to proceed with the Nickell investigations.[30]

Since Edwin Smalley was appointed a few weeks after Joe LeFors began his undercover work, there was some doubt that the new sheriff should even be informed of the particulars of this manhunt. When Smalley wrote his recollections in the 1930s, he naturally maintained that he was in the loop from the start and accorded himself an important role in bringing Tom Horn to justice. LeFors, who was also still alive at this time, exploded when he read Smalley's assertions. "*That Is A Lie,*" he declared. "I never at any time conferred [with] or made a report to him concerning the Horn case." District Attorney Stoll "advised me not to tell Smalley I was working on the case," continued LeFors. Yet the district attorney could hardly leave the chief executive officer of the county out of the investigation. Smalley also insisted that Stoll asked him who he believed murdered Willie Nickell. The new sheriff replied without hesitation, "Tom Horn," adding that the only means to pin this crime on Horn was to "get a confession." However, Smalley's assertion in his recollections that he played a part in the decision to employ Joe LeFors as a special investigator is very doubtful, since this appointment was made well before Smalley became sheriff.[31]

That the sheriff's office was aware of the investigation is also confirmed by Leslie Snow, one of Smalley's deputies. Writing in 1946, Snow asserted that Walter Stoll "planned the whole thing" and informed him and Sheriff Smalley of the plan to arrest Horn. The district attorney "called Smalley and I down to his office and told us that the County Commissioners had hired Lefors to work on the Nichols [sic] case," added Snow, "and . . . told us what he wanted done." Stoll also expressed the opinion that Tom Horn's "only weakness" was his garrulousness. If the officers could "get Horn to talk," and thus incriminate himself, said Stoll, they could arrest him. In spite of Edwin Smalley's claim to have had a part in the events leading up to the arrest of Tom Horn, he generously admitted that LeFors was "our main reliance" in the case. Far from recognizing the contributions of "the grocery clerk" sheriff, LeFors insisted ungenerously that he worked only through City Policeman A. D. "Sandy" McNeil when he needed assistance from local officers.[32]

Although Joe LeFors had considerable latitude in conducting his investigation, he later admitted that he served under "the general supervision" of District Attorney Stoll. With a $10,000 contingency fund placed at his disposal by the county commissioners, Stoll did not lack for resources. While there is no record of what LeFors was paid, Thomas C. Allen, who worked undercover for the special investigator, said that the deputy marshal received a lump sum up front. The intent was to prevent Horn's defense attorneys—whoever they might be—from arguing that LeFors was a mere bounty hunter. In spite of the importance of the Willie Nickell case (and the presumably generous fee), LeFors hesitated to accept this appointment. "I knew those Cheyenne politicians were for politics first and justice next," he wrote later. Even his superior, U.S. Marshal Hadsell, a presidential appointee, was a "political boss." However, Hadsell surprised LeFors by urging him to "do your best." Given this encouragement, LeFors informed Commissioner Corson, with typical cockiness, that he "was nearly positive" he could bring in the assassin of Willie Nickell.[33]

"Public feelings were running high" in Laramie County in the fall of 1901, recalled LeFors, and the "demand was strong for justice." The *Laramie Republican* denounced "men who lay in ambush and shoot down other men" and urged Laramie County lawmen to do their utmost "to hunt down . . . the person or persons engaged in the numerous acts of lawlessness in the Iron Mountain district." The fact that no resident of this community would agree to testify against the assassins was a "Black Spot" and "a disgrace," said Edward Slack of the *Daily Leader,* who deplored the "low tone of public morals" and absence of "a proper sense of justice" in this troubled region. The day has "passed when assassins can stalk about the country with impunity," he concluded.[34]

Strong words failed to halt threats and intimidation in the Iron Mountain community. In October 1901, Alfred Axford, who ran a small flock of sheep near Kels Nickell, received an anonymous note ordering him to "take your thievin kids and yore sheap an git out of this cuntry or you . . . wil all be kild." Not only did Axford depart, but the *Daily Leader* reported that other "residents in that vicinity are rapidly reaching a state of terror." Even Kels Nickell, who was known for his stubbornness, removed his family to Cheyenne, leaving unprotected the ranch he had worked for twenty years. Nickell's relatives in Morgan County, Kentucky, who were outraged at these attacks, published an open letter in the *Wyoming Tribune* warning "the hyenas who are seeking the life of Kels P. Nickel[l] and his little boys that they have gone far enough." Nonetheless, Nickell sold his property. While other recipients of menacing notes refused to submit to such intimidation, a writer for the *Daily Leader* expressed the hope "that as soon as Nickel[l] leaves the country the feud will come to an end." Nickell was "very unpopular, as a neighbor," the newsman continued, "to say nothing of his running sheep in a cattle country."[35]

While District Attorney Walter Stoll and the Laramie County coroner's jury had failed to bring about an arrest in the Willie Nickell murder case, the *Denver Republican* observed that these proceedings "left moral certainty in the minds of many that Tom Horn had done the killing." While street talk had pointed toward him in the Lewis and Powell murders five years earlier, newspapers now took the lead, dropping strong hints that Horn was the slayer of Willie Nickell. "Another foul murder has been added to the already long list which disgraces" the Iron Mountain country, wrote a Rawlins editor. "The method followed has in each case been so nearly similar that one is led to believe that they were committed by the same person," he continued, adding that "in each case there has been an apparent attempt [by influential men] to prevent justice from being meted out." While this editor deplored the fact that "the man against whom the finger of suspicion pointed most strongly is allowed to run at large," he went on to observe that there were now healthy signs of new resolve among Laramie County officials. In an obvious dig at these officers for failing to arrest the suspected murderer of Lewis and Powell, he concluded, "It looks as if there really will be an attempt made [this time] to run down the murderer."[36]

If Tom Horn was aware of the intensity of public feeling against him, he kept it to himself. As he faced the gallows two years later, the *Daily Leader* recalled the "bold front" that Horn maintained at the Willie Nickell inquest and "seemed to think that the suspicion connecting him with the murder had been allayed." After these proceedings, he "engaged in protracted carousals" in Cheyenne, continued this journalist, and "had a habit of boasting of his prowess and was prone to claim to have committed every murder of which he had heard." While bystanders discounted such braggadocio, continued this writer, Horn's persistent bragging ultimately "proved his undoing." When he climbed aboard the Union Pacific's Train No. 4 at Bosler on 8 August 1901, in response to the Laramie County coroner's subpoena, he took a fateful step. Much had changed in the last five years. In an unprecedented effort, the Laramie County authorities were not only resolved to bring the suspect before the bar of justice, but to press the case to a conclusion.[37]

In the months immediately following his son's death, Kels Nickell exhibited a strong resolve to fulfill the vow of vengeance that he made over the boy's grave. While Nickell initially believed Jim Miller or one of Miller's sons killed Willie, the grieving father's attention soon turned to Tom Horn. The Reverend Benjamin Young, who talked with Nickell after the murder, said the attempt on his own life convinced Kels that he was wrong. Since Kels Nickell "saw and recognized his assailant," said Young, "from that time on he believed that the same man—Tom Horn—was concerned in both deeds." The minister had another reason for fixing the blame on Horn. On the day of Willie's funeral, a very distraught Jim Miller called on the Reverend Young and asked his advice as to whether he should attend the services. "I am a neighbor of Nick's," said Miller, "and it's no more than right I should [attend]; but—they tell me I'm suspected of—of—that Nick thinks I killed his boy! Now, I want to tell you that while we've had a lot of trouble, Nick and me, I wouldn't do such a thing as that! I've got boys of my own, and while I'm hasty tempered I couldn't do a thing like that." Fearing "a double tragedy" if Miller put in an appearance, Young reluctantly recommended that he "stay away." Nonetheless, two of Miller's daughters attended Willie's funeral.[38]

During the fall of 1901, Kels Nickell began to exhibit fits of erratic behavior that aroused some concern. While friends and associates assumed that he would work within the law to bring his son's murderer to justice, they were surprised when newspapers reported, on 10 October, that he had gone to Denver "for the purpose of killing Tom Horn." At this time, the notorious detective was hospitalized, recovering from the broken jaw he had sustained in a saloon brawl. Even though this report turned out to be "a pipe dream pure and simple," as the *Leader* pointed out, Nickell continued to profess a determination to "bring to justice" the guilty person or persons. This publicity had the effect of keeping Tom Horn's name prominently associated with the murder of Willie Nickell.[39]

In the meantime, Special Detective Joe LeFors was busily gathering evidence of Tom Horn's complicity in the murder. Surprisingly, LeFors and Horn had never met. In his autobiography, as well as in his testimony during Tom Horn's murder trial in 1902, LeFors recalled that he met Horn for the first time in Frank A. Menea's saddlery, in Cheyenne, shortly after the Willie Nickell inquest. The two men "had quite a visit," LeFors testified, mentioning that Horn was "rather inclined to brag." Still on the witness stand, the deputy marshal said that he implied in this conversation that he knew Horn was guilty of the attack on Kels Nickell (and presumably the murder of Willie Nickell).

"I told him his sights must have moved or something [was] wrong with his gun," LeFors asserted, "and asked him how came the old man [Kels Nickell] to get away?" LeFors testified that Horn replied, "It was early in the morning and the sun was—[defense counsel objected and asked that this testimony be stricken, but was overruled] and the sun was not shining on the sights of my gun, or else it would have been different . . . you ought to have saw him run and yell like a Comanche Indian."

Although LeFors may not have been permitted to say so on the witness stand, apparently Tom Horn, who considered LeFors a sympathetic and like-minded individual, made an inadvertent confession of sorts around this time. In a second encounter a few days later during the Frontier Days celebration, LeFors testified, the range detective "asked me what had been found in the investigation of the killing of Willie Nickell before the coroner's jury." When LeFors replied that he didn't know, Horn seemed unconcerned, remarking that a friend who had served on the coroner's jury "will tell me everything." LeFors's testimony suggests that Horn was already concerned about Prosecutor Walter Stoll's interest in him. If Horn was as candid (and self-incriminating) as LeFors indicated, LeFors and Stoll now had evidence to back up their suspicions.[40]

At first, LeFors felt his investigation was moving slowly. The residents of the Iron Mountain community, terrorized by the big cattle companies, refused to talk. To move things along, Policeman Sandy McNeill agreed to inform LeFors when someone from Iron Mountain visited Cheyenne. LeFors would buttonhole the potential informant, hoping he or she was more relaxed when away from home. By this means, LeFors learned that a man named Jim Dixon had delivered food to Tom Horn while Horn was lying in wait for his target on 18 July—the ambush that resulted in the death of Willie Nickell. LeFors may have received some assistance from Jim Miller and his sons. Glendolene Kimmell, the school teacher who initially defended the Millers, turned against them and alleged that they attempted to direct suspicion against Tom Horn. "It's all right to let suspicion fall on Tom Horn," Gus and Victor Miller reportedly said to her. Horn "doesn't care," the brothers insisted, apparently meaning that the detective felt secure under the protection of the cattle companies.[41]

In spite of this slow start, the special investigator and Prosecutor Stoll maintained a good working relationship. LeFors turned in "every scrap of evidence" to Mrs. Charles Kitzmiller, Walter Stoll's secretary, who carefully wrote out "all the Horn case data in alphabetical order." When necessary, the investigator dictated additional findings to her. Walter Stoll also used his discretionary fund to employ additional undercover operatives to assist Joe LeFors. Thomas C. Allen, who had worked with LeFors several years earlier in the Big Horn country, now helped him in Cheyenne. Stoll also hired a female Pinkerton operative who roamed the Iron Mountain country in the guise of a newspaper reporter. Edwin Smalley mentioned this woman in his recollections. Unfortunately, she "did not accomplish much of anything," LeFors had to admit.[42]

In spite of reports that lawmen were working diligently across the state on a variety of criminal cases in 1901, newspapers were generally critical of their slow progress. The Cheyenne Bureau of the *Rocky Mountain News* complained that there was "little doing," especially in the murders of Willie Nickell and Dee Blair. Since Kels Nickell, the primary bone of contention in the Iron Mountain country, had relocated to Cheyenne, this Denver journal opined that Laramie County officers had deliberately slackened their efforts. In regard to the child murder at Casper, this same writer observed sarcastically in October 1901 that "Dee Blair stands in the eye of the law as he did three months ago—'Dead by a visitation of God.'" A *Carbon County Journal* editorial reminded the state's law enforcement officers that they had an obligation "to make people understand that human life is held sacred in the state of Wyoming," and the *Daily Leader* criticized Laramie County Coroner Tom Murray for not convening his jury in the Willie Nickell case for several weeks. "It is not known when the matter will be cleared up," added the editor. On 26 December, the coroner's jury met for the last time and issued the standard verdict in unsolved cases: "the deceased came to his death . . . from a gunshot wound inflicted by a party or parties unknown."[43]

Unbeknownst to these newspapermen, Joe LeFors, Sheriff Edwin Smalley, and other lawmen were quietly at work. In the fall of 1901, George A. Matlock, a shoe shop owner in Laramie, informed Smalley that he had come into possession of a sweater that might belong to Tom Horn and that this garment might tie him to the Nickell case. He said that "not so long after the killing a man resembling Horn left a bundle containing a black [*sic;* the sweater was blue], blood-stained sweater at his shop." The man who left this package failed to return for it. "We

took the sweater as evidence," recalled Smalley. Although its importance was not yet clear, the sweater later played an important part in the
behind-the-scenes investigation of Tom Horn.[44]

District Attorney Stoll, whose first priority remained the Willie Nickell murder, insisted that he must have a solid case against Horn before
going to court. Otherwise Horn's cattlemen friends would certainly
have a battery of clever and gifted attorneys on his side, all working for
a reversal. Since hard evidence was still lacking, LeFors concluded that
he had no recourse but to try to collect it directly from the suspect's
mouth. Tom Horn, known as a garrulous and boastful sort, might unwittingly incriminate himself if LeFors could manipulate him into a
compromising conversation. The special investigator later informed the
Daily Leader that he conceived "the plan to trap Horn into a confession
. . . shortly after the killing of Willie Nickell." "No one else was let
into the secret," he added. "For month after month Lefors [*sic*] worked
on the case without the aid of a single individual," according to the
Daily Leader. In his autobiography, LeFors maintained that he informed
District Attorney Stoll of his plan to manipulate Horn into a confession
only when he had "everything in readiness." (Apparently, this was only
two days before meeting Tom Horn in Cheyenne). The district attorney replied simply, "Fine, I've no suggestions to make." Edwin Smalley, the Laramie County sheriff, presented a contrary story. Smalley
insisted that he and Walter Stoll helped conceive the plot against Horn
early on and then "offered LeFors the job of tricking the dangerous
Tom into a confession." Smalley went on to praise the deputy marshal
for managing to pull off such "a dangerous trick."[45]

In his efforts to ensnare Tom Horn, Joe LeFors needed some pretext
to get closer to him and somehow create a feeling of indebtedness on
the part of the range detective. LeFors assumed that Horn was growing
nervous at the attention he was receiving in the Willie Nickell case and
that both he and his employers believed he should get out of Wyoming,
as he had done after the Lewis and Powell murders in 1895. As a first
step, LeFors arranged through acquaintances for the offer of a stock detective's position in Montana. LeFors rightly assumed that Horn would
be grateful to the deputy marshal and that this would bring the two
closer to one another. LeFors may have made the approach to these
Montana livestock officials or, through a serendipitous series of events,
they may have approached LeFors. In his memoirs, LeFors claimed that

he received a communication from William (Billy) D. Smith, a Montana brand inspector who sought "a detective in good faith." But at the time of Tom Horn's arrest in January 1902, LeFors informed the *Daily Leader* that he "wrote to several acquaintances . . . in Montana stating that he knew of a first class cattle detective for whom he would like to secure a job in that country." Regardless of who initiated the correspondence, LeFors continued to work through both W. G. Preuitt, secretary of the Montana Live Stock Association, and Billy Smith.[46]

An opportunity to take his plan one step further soon came LeFors's way. As he was returning from the delivery of a prisoner to the state penitentiary, in November 1901, he observed George Prentice, Jr., board the train at Bosler, where he had probably visited John Coble. Prentice, a Scotsman, was the son of a former member of the Swan Land and Cattle Company's board of directors. The elder Prentice had sent George, Jr., to Wyoming to learn the cattle business. (While LeFors called Prentice "one of the bosses" of the Iron Mountain Cattle Company, he was more than likely a Swan employee.) The special investigator immediately sensed that Prentice might be unwittingly useful in his plan to inveigle a confession out of Tom Horn. Still assuming that Tom Horn would welcome a position in another state, LeFors now had bait: a letter from Billy Smith, the brand detective, indicating that the Montana Live Stock Association was in the market for a stock detective. If Horn took the job offer, LeFors would be able to get close to him and lure him into a comfortable setting where he might reveal incriminating information relating to the Willie Nickell murder. The tricky part was to invent a scenario compelling enough to ensure that George Prentice, Jr., the unwitting accomplice, would actually see that the news was delivered to Horn.[47]

LeFors came up with a false story guaranteed to alarm Prentice and his livestock associates. "George," LeFors asked Prentice, "what are all the Pinkertons doing around Cheyenne? I saw three there in the last two or three days. I saw them following Tom Horn around. Tom was drinking, and, I understand, talking about the Nickell case. Why don't you get him clear out of the country? Horn is going to get someone in trouble yet with his talk." Prentice fell for the story and began to talk freely about his past association with Horn. He even volunteered that he had served as payoff man for Horn's previous killings, presumably the Lewis and Powell slayings, and turned over the money to him on a train between Cheyenne and Denver. Prentice protested, however, that he did not provide this service in the Willie Nickell murder. Obviously alarmed, he blurted out that "if Horn got to talking too much his employers would have to bump him off." The deputy marshal was overjoyed. "This was the first real information that I could rely on," he recalled. Not only had Prentice confirmed that Horn murdered Billy Lewis and Fred Powell, but the Scotsman had also said (in effect) "that Tom Horn was guilty of the killing of Willie Nickell." When LeFors suggested that Montana "might be a good place to get Horn out of sight for a while," Prentice agreed and said he would see John Coble about releasing Horn from his present contract. Obviously, both Coble and Prentice wanted the stock detective out of Wyoming.[48]

With this important information in hand, LeFors's plan began to come together in the last days of December. "I reasonably knew with all the data I had [that] under the [right] circumstances Horn would talk," he wrote later. While the precise sequence of communications among Horn, LeFors, and the potential Montana employers is difficult to unravel, it appears that Horn first received a verbal offer of the job (possibly through John Coble). While passing through Cheyenne with a cattle shipment destined for Omaha, on 20 December, Horn informed a local newspaper that he planned to proceed directly from Nebraska to his new posting in Billings, Montana. Indeed, he was so certain of this new position that he sent his kit in advance, expecting to follow it later. However, the formal correspondence concerning this job prospect begins with a letter from the Montana Live Stock Association to LeFors, dated 28 December 1901. In this epistle, Billy Smith asked the deputy marshal to recommend "a good man to do some secret [detective] work." LeFors sent this letter to John Coble who, in turn, passed it to Tom Horn. In the meantime, Horn got drunk in Omaha, lost his money, and had to return to Coble's ranch for assistance. On 26 December, as he passed through Cheyenne, he informed the *Daily Leader* that he intended to return briefly to Bosler, after which "the famous cattle detective . . . will leave soon for Billings, Mont."[49]

On New Year's Day 1902, Horn wrote to LeFors, informing him that John Coble had just handed him the 28 December letter containing the Montana job offer. Horn, who desired this position, promised the Montana cattlemen "satisfaction." "I don't care how big or bad his men [rustlers] are, I can handle them," he said confidently. "They can scarcely be any worse than the Brown's Hole Gang," continued Horn, "and I stopped cow stealing there in one summer." Horn also insisted that he could perform his duties "with less expense in the shape of law-yer and witness fees than any man in the business." Assuming that he and LeFors were on the same wavelength, Horn concluded, "Joe you yourself know what my reputation is although we have never been out [in the field] together." Among surviving letters of Tom Horn, this epistle comes close in tone and candor to the detective's correspon-dence with U.S. Marshal William Kidder Meade of Arizona five years earlier (see chapter 8, above).[50]

LeFors wrote to Smith immediately, assuring him of Tom Horn's desire for the position. Within three days, Smith replied to the effect that he expected soon to receive authorization to employ "your man Tom Horn." On 6 January LeFors wired Horn, who responded on the following day thanking him for his good offices. On Friday, 10 January, LeFors received a letter from Horn saying he "would arrive in Chey-enne on Sunday in the forenoon." He would like to visit with LeFors and pick up a railroad pass for the trip to Montana. By this time, LeFors had "everything ready" for the cattle detective's visit. He had chosen U.S. Marshal Hadsell's office as the place for their meeting, although some minor modifications were necessary. When he found the lock on the door connecting the marshal's office with that of the U.S. Court clerk was defective, LeFors summoned locksmith Peter Bergersen to repair it. LeFors also asked Bergersen to trim the bottom of the door to ensure that there was two inches of clearance between the bottom and the door jamb. Bergersen also drilled a peephole in the door. The purpose of these special preparations would soon be obvious.[51]

In the midst of these final preparations, a complication suddenly loomed. For some time, LeFors had been aware of a possible source of information in the form of the wife of an Iron Mountain polo pony raiser. According to LeFors's sources, Tom Horn often visited this man's ranch, which was near the Kels Nickell homestead. The ranch-er's wife, who was "about one-half Spanish," recalled LeFors, lived in Cheyenne while her husband sold ponies in the East. In the meantime, she held trysts with a young cowboy in the back rooms of Cheyenne bars. Believing she had useful information, LeFors plotted to set her up. The female Pinkerton operative, who had just returned from the Iron Mountain area, proved very helpful. Posing as LeFors's wife, she and the investigator frequented bars and drank with the horse breeder's wife (whose name is unknown) and her lover. When the two sleuths finally managed to get this woman alone on the evening of 10 January 1902, they plied her with alcohol—"The Mrs. liked her highballs," LeFors wrote—and loosened her tongue. She "told us that she had carried Horn sandwiches while he was lying in hiding to get a shot" at Kels Nickell. When she finally passed out, the two detectives helped her to her hotel. In a subsequent meeting in her hotel room, she angrily protested LeFors's trick, but he managed to convince her that she would not be called to testify against Horn. Both were armed on this occasion, and LeFors concluded that she "was just about as dangerous as Horn himself."[52]

Feeling more confident now, LeFors finalized his plans for eliciting Horn's confession and laid them before Prosecutor Walter Stoll. LeFors was not fully cognizant of the legal implications of any confession he might obtain and apparently did not plan to have witnesses present. However, the prosecutor realized that any confession that LeFors obtained had to stand up in court. Stoll faced a serious legal dilemma. "It was Stoll, with the keen mind of the prosecutor," observed the *Daily Leader,* "who provided that when this confession was obtained there would be no question about it." The presiding judge must rule the evidence admissible and, equally important, a defense attorney should not be able to discredit it. At this point, Stoll instructed LeFors to have reliable witnesses, in addition to himself, to the conversation. Accordingly, LeFors obtained the services of Deputy Sheriff Leslie Snow and Charles Ohnhaus, the court reporter. LeFors said he arranged for these two men to "hide behind the door in the clerk's office," but Walter Stoll probably demanded that, at the least, Ohnhaus, an accredited court stenographer, should be present. A court would be much more inclined to accept the transcript of a LeFors-Horn chat if a certified court reporter took down the conversation.[53]

"When everything was ripe, which was Saturday, January 11th," said the *Daily Leader,* "LaFors [*sic*] sent a telegram to Horn telling him to come" to Cheyenne and pick up a letter of introduction to his Montana employers. The unsuspecting livestock detective arrived by train that same evening. LeFors met him at the depot. The following morning LeFors met Horn at a local bar. After a few minutes of conversation, "LeFors excused himself to run an errand," recalled Edwin Smalley, "and arranged to meet Horn [later] at the marshal's office." LeFors's purpose was to put his plan in motion by summoning Snow and Ohnhaus to his aid. Onhaus confirmed this fact at Tom Horn's preliminary hearing a few days later. "I was in the clerk's office working," he testified, "and Mr. LeFors told me to come into the marshal's office." Onhaus proceeded to his assigned room adjoining the marshal's suite (and behind Peter Bergersen's specially prepared door), where Deputy Sheriff Snow joined him. "We stayed in there perhaps forty or forty-five minutes," continued the stenographer, "while Joe went for Tom Horn." LeFors had "spread an overcoat down on the floor" of the room adjacent to the marshal's office for warmth, said the *Daily Leader*, "and told Snow and Ohnhaus to listen." Only then, at the very last minute, did he explain his plan. The room Snow and Ohnhaus were secreted in was the marshal's private office, while LeFors and Horn met in the outer office of Chief Deputy Marshal Paul Bailey. In commenting on how "remarkable" it was that the LeFors-Horn conversation took place in the marshal's suite, the *Daily Leader* pointed out that Tom Horn actually requested a private place because he was concerned about being seen talking in public with a law enforcement official. LeFors "suggested they go to his office where they would not be interrupted."[54]

This photograph of Tom Horn was probably taken in Denver about 1891 when he was a Pinkerton operative. Courtesy Arizona Historical Society, Tucson (#30145).

As Pinkerton operatives, Charlie Siringo and Tom Horn became well acquainted. When Horn went to work for the Wyoming cattlemen, Siringo began to hear ominous stories about his former comrade and turned against him. Courtesy Western History Collections, University of Oklahoma (#1776).

After hearing testimony at Tom Horn's robbery trial in Reno, Nevada, in 1891, [Herman?] Ludcke, a "cowboy-artist," was inspired to produce this painting of an imaginary bandit. William Pinkerton of the Pinkerton National Detective Agency was struck by this work and had copies distributed throughout the company. Courtesy Robert G. McCubbin, Santa Fe, N. Mex.

As an employer of Tom Horn, John Cuthbert Coble (1858–1914) of the Iron Mountain Ranch Company played a significant, if not completely understood, part in the range detective's career in Wyoming. Courtesy American Heritage Center, University of Wyoming.

As an employee of the Iron Mountain Ranch Company, located near the Cheyenne and Northern Railroad depot at Iron Mountain, Tom Horn resided in a cabin in the rear of the ranch headquarters. Author photograph.

William Dinwiddie, a *Boston Herald* correspondent, caught Tom Horn (far left) and other packers catching some much-needed sleep at Daiquiri during the Santiago Campaign. Jay Monaghan Collection, Wyles Mss 20, Department of Special Collections, University of California, Santa Barbara.

This photo is captioned "Mule Packers Preparing to Deliver Ammunition to San Juan Hill Battle" (1 July 1898). Since Tom Horn personally led an ammunition train to San Juan Heights on 1 July, this may be his train. Courtesy Cline Library, Northern Arizona University, Flagstaff (AHS.0001.00010).

In 1900 Tom Horn sat for a formal portrait in a Denver studio. The *Denver Republican* maintained that it was "unquestionably the most striking likeness of him yet produced." This image was used as the frontispiece in the *Life of Tom Horn*. Courtesy American Heritage Center, University of Wyoming.

DISTRICT ATTORNEY STOLL QUES-
TIONS KELS NICKELL.

Kelsey (Kels) P. Nickell, a tough former soldier and quarrelsome homesteader, created many enemies in the Iron Mountain community, including John Coble, the manager of the Iron Mountain Ranch Company. Courtesy of the American Heritage Center, University of Wyoming.

The assassination of fourteen-year-old Willie, son of Kels Nickell, in July 1901, proved to be Tom Horn's undoing. Courtesy American Heritage Center, University of Wyoming.

Joseph LeFors, who subtly wangled a confession of murder out of Tom Horn, had much in common with his subject. Both men were cowboys, range detectives, and deputy U.S. marshals. Courtesy American Heritage Center, University of Wyoming.

The notes of court stenographer Charles J. Ohnhaus played a critical part in the range detective's conviction. Courtesy Wyoming State Archives (Biographical Collections, Neg. No. 2741).

The scene of Willie Nickell's murder. (1) The rocks the assassin hid behind. (2) The fence gap where Nickell was shot. (3) Where the boy's body was found. Enhanced photograph by W. G. Walker, 1902.

While newspapers played up the role of schoolteacher Glendolene Myrtle Kimmell as a "love interest" in Tom Horn's last days, their association was probably casual at best. Courtesy American Heritage Center, University of Wyoming.

Although his hairline was receding, Tom Horn's athletic build was still apparent when he was in jail. Here he is shown in the hallway outside his cell that served as his exercise area. Courtesy American Heritage Center, University of Wyoming.

This photograph, taken while Horn was in jail, is probably the last shot of him before his execution. One of his pastimes was fashioning ropes. Courtesy Robert G. McCubbin, Santa Fe, N. Mex.

An alert photographer caught this dramatic moment when Tom Horn was recaptured just after his abortive jail break in August 1903. His captors are escorting the dejected range detective, well aware of his ultimate fate, back to jail. Courtesy Wyoming State Archives, Cheyenne (Meyers, Neg. 625).

As a clerk in a Cheyenne mercantile establishment, Edwin Smalley had known Tom Horn for many years. When Smalley became sheriff in 1901, it became his duty not only to assist with Tom Horn's case but ultimately to preside at his execution. Courtesy American Heritage Center, University of Wyoming.

Tom Horn asked his good friend Thomas Joseph Cahill, a young court clerk and deputy sheriff, to place the noose around his neck. Cahill, shown here (right) in conversation with reformed train robber Bill Carlisle, reluctantly agreed to Horn's request. Courtesy American Heritage Center, University of Wyoming.

Even though Tom Horn's execution took place inside the Laramie County Jail, a large crowd of curious onlookers gathered on the street that cold, blustery 20 November 1903. National guardsmen patrolled the area. Courtesy American Heritage Center, University of Wyoming.

Tom Horn's body was transferred to a local funeral home for a coroner's inquest and embalming. The man standing behind the hearse, with coat over his arm, may be Deputy Sheriff Ed Sperry, who escorted the body to Boulder, Colorado, for burial. Courtesy American Heritage Center, University of Wyoming.

CHAPTER 12

Jailbird

On Sunday morning, 12 January 1902, Joe LeFors met Tom Horn at the Inter Ocean Hotel and led him to the U.S. marshal's office on the second floor in the Commercial Block. LeFors's plan called for engaging his guest in casual conversation to help him relax and, ultimately, to loosen his tongue. Of course, the stock detective was unaware that two witnesses, Deputy Sheriff Leslie Snow and Stenographer Charles J. Ohnhaus, were hiding in the next room. Ohnhaus was recording their conversation in shorthand. To gain Horn's attention, LeFors read a letter that he had written as an introduction to W. G. Preuitt, the Montana Live Stock Association official. This missive recommended Tom Horn as "an able man for the position." When Horn asked what sort of work he could expect, LeFors promised him that his new employers were "good people." "I don't want to be making reports all the time," said Horn. Then he asked if his future employers were "afraid of shooting?" "I shoot too God damn much, I know,'" he admitted without prompting. When LeFors assured him that his future employers "were not afraid of any shooting," Horn went on to boast that he had "never got my employers into any trouble yet over anything I have done." "A man can't be too careful," he added, "because you don't want any God damn officers to know what you are doing."[1]

These remarks—all foolishly volunteered—gave Deputy Marshal LeFors the opportunity he desired to lead Horn into the subject of Willie Nickell's murder:

LEFORS: Tom, I know you are a good man for the place. You are the best man to cover up your trail I ever saw. In the Willie Nickell killing, I could never find your trail, and I pride myself on being a trailer.

HORN: No, God damn; I left no trail. The only way to cover up your trail is to go barefooted.

. . .

LEFORS: I never knew why Willie Nickell was killed. Was it because he was one of the victims named, or was it compulsory?

HORN: I think it was this way: Suppose a man was in the big draw to the right of the gate—you know where it is—the draw that comes into the main creek below Nickell's house where [Kels] Nickell was shot. Well, I suppose a man was in that, and the kid came riding up on him from this way, and suppose the kid started to run for the house, and the fellow headed him off at the gate and killed him to keep him from going to the house and raising a hell of a commotion. That is the way I think it occurred.

LEFORS: Tom, you had your boots on when you ran across there to cut the kid off, didn't you?

HORN: No, I was barefooted.

LEFORS: You didn't run across there barefooted?

HORN: Yes, I did.

LEFORS: How did you get your boots on after cutting your feet?

HORN: I generally have ten days to rest [and heal] after a job of that kind.[2]

Tom Horn changed the conversation to the subject of Glendolene Kimmell, the schoolteacher.

HORN: Joe, do you remember the little girl?

LEFORS: Who do you mean?

HORN: The school marm [sic]. She sure was smooth people. She wrote me a letter as long as the Governor's report, telling me in detail everything asked her [at the coroner's inquest] by Stoll, the prosecuting attorney. Stoll thought I was going to prove an alibi, but I fooled him. I had a man on the outside keeping me in touch before I showed up [to testify] with everything that was going on. I got this letter from the girl the same day I got [the] summons to appear before the coroner's inquest.

LEFORS: Did the school marm tell everything she knew?

HORN: Yes, she did. I wouldn't tell an individual like her anything; not me. She told me to look out for you. She said, "Look out for Joe LeFors. He is not all right." She said, "Look out for him. He is trying to find out something." I said, "What is there in this LeFors matter?" She said "[James] Miller did not like him [LeFors], and Miller said he would kill the son of a bitch if God would spare him long enough." There is nothing to those Millers. They are ignorant old jays [country bumpkins]. They can not even appreciate a good joke. The first time I met the girl was just before the killing of the kid [Willie Nickell]. Everything, you know, dates from the killing of the kid. [Horn could not know how prophetic this observation was.]

LEFORS: How many days was it before the killing of the kid?

HORN: Three or four days, maybe one day. Damned if I want to remember the dates. She was there [at the Millers] at this time, and of course we soon paired ourselves off.[3]

As Joe LeFors plied him with questions, Tom Horn, thinking they were kindred spirits, obligingly answered.

LEFORS: Tom, didn't Jim Dixon carry you grub [in the stake-out that led to Willie Nickell's death]?

HORN: No, by God. No one carried me grub.

LEFORS: Tom, how can a man that weighs 204 pounds go without anything to eat so long?

HORN: Well, I do sometimes. I go for some days without a mouthful. Sometimes, I have a little bacon along.

LEFORS: You must get terrible hungry, Tom.

HORN: Sometimes I get so hungry that I could kill my mother for some grub, but I never quit a job until I get my man.[4]

At this point, LeFors brought up the subject dearest to Tom Horn's heart—weapons. When the deputy marshal asked, "What kind of a gun have you got?" Horn replied that he "used a 30–30 Winchester [rifle]." When LeFors asked if this caliber was as effective as the .30-40 Winchester, Horn replied, "No, but I like to get close to my man . . . the closer the better." When LeFors asked how far away Willie Nickell was when Horn shot the boy, he replied, "about three hundred yards. . . It was the best shot that I ever made and the dirtiest trick I ever done." He admitted that when the boy, who was only wounded by Horn's first shot, began to run, the assassin feared "at one time he would get away." When LeFors asked if he gathered up his spent cartridges (no casings were found at the scene), Horn replied: "You bet your God damn life I did."[5]

Fearing he might be pressing too hard, the deputy marshal suggested they break for lunch. As they were preparing to leave, about 12:15 P.M., Chief Deputy Marshal Paul Bailey entered the office. The three men exchanged greetings, after which LeFors and Horn departed.

> LEFORS: Tom, let us go downstairs and get a drink. [The two men left the office and began to descend the stairs to the street.] I could always see your work clear, but I want you to tell me why you killed that kid. Was it a mistake?
> HORN: Well, Joe, I will tell you all about it when I come back from Montana. It is too new yet.

The two men stopped by Harry Hynds's Capital Bar for a drink, after which LeFors went home for lunch. Ohnhaus and Snow, whose position on the floor was very uncomfortable, left their post as well. Deputy Sheriff Snow withdrew to Hynds's bar, where he saw Horn drinking. After a leisurely lunch break, Snow and Ohnhaus made their way back to Hadsell's office separately. Many years later, John Ohnhaus, father of the stenographer, declared that Horn and LeFors retired to a nearby bar more than once during the day. LeFors "would suggest that they go out for another drink," said John Ohnhaus. This gave his son and Deputy Sheriff Snow additional breaks.[6]

Upon their return to the marshal's office, Tom Horn opened the conversation. "Joe," he said, "we have only been together about fifteen minutes, and I will bet there is some people saying, 'What are those sons of bitches planning now, and who are they going to kill next?'" At this point, the two began to exchange stories about their past shooting exploits. While Ohnhaus did not feel the need to record all these

anecdotes, he noted that Horn regaled LeFors with the story of his killing "a lieutenant in the Mexican army." "I am forty-four years, three
months and twenty-seven days old," said Horn (inaccurately), "and if
I get killed now I have the satisfaction of knowing I have lived about
fifteen ordinary lives." If someone should write the story of his life, he
continued, "It would be the most God damn interesting reading in the
country. . . . The first man I killed, I was only twenty-six years old. He
was a coarse son of a bitch."[7]

The deputy marshal, impatient with such digressions, steered the
stock detective back to further self-incrimination:

> LEFORS: How much did you get for killing these fellows?
> In the Powell and Lewis case, you got six hundred dollars
> apiece. You killed Lewis in the corral with a six-shooter. I
> would like to have seen the expression on his face when you
> shot him.
> HORN: He was the scaredest son of a bitch you ever saw.
> How did you come to know that, Joe?
> LEFORS: I have known everything you have done, Tom, for a
> good many years. I know where you were paid this money.
> HORN: Yes, I was paid this money on the train between
> Cheyenne and Denver.
> LEFORS: Didn't you get two one hundred dollar bills and the
> rest in gold?
> HORN: Yes, and this is where I learned to take care of my
> shells. I left five .45-30 shells [at the murder scene] there after
> I flashed powder in them to make them smell fresh and the
> damn officers never found them.[8]

The deputy marshal then raised the subject of Tom Horn's alleged
"sign"—a stone placed under the head of his victim.

> LEFORS: Why did you put the rock under the kid's head after
> you killed him? That is one of your marks, isn't it?
> HORN: Yes, that is the way I hang out my sign to collect
> money for a job of this kind.
> LEFORS: Did you ever have an agreement drawn up?
> HORN: No, I do all my business through Coble. He is the
> whitest son of a bitch in the country in a job of this kind.

LEFORS: In the Powell and Lewis case did Coble put in toward your pay?

HORN: No, I wouldn't let him. He fed me and furnished
the horses and has done more for me than any man in the
country.[9]

At this point, the special investigator attempted to return to the Willie Nickell murder.

LEFORS: Did you ever have any trouble to collect your
money?

HORN: No, when I do a job of this kind they knew they had
to pay me. I would kill a man if he tried to beat me out of 10
cents that I had earned.

LEFORS: Have you got your money yet for the killing of
[Willie] Nickell?

HORN: I got that before I did the job.

LEFORS: You got $600 for that. Why did you cut the price?

HORN: I got $2,100.

LEFORS: How much is that a man?

HORN: That is for three dead men, and one man shot at five
times. Killing men is my specialty. I look at it as a business
proposition, and I think I have a corner on the market.[10]

Apparently, the two men ended their conversation at this point, as
Charles Ohnhaus's shorthand notes stop here. Since Horn planned to
leave for Montana the following morning, LeFors and other officials
quickly made arrangements to take him into custody. The pressure
was on the stenographer, who worked through the night to transcribe
his notes and prepare a typed copy. A bench warrant for Horn's arrest
was possible only after the transcript was in final form and placed before a judge. Sheriff Edwin Smalley had to be alerted as well, since he
would have to serve the arrest warrant. Walter Stoll "advised me not
to arrest Horn," wrote LeFors, because he was identified with the U.S.
Marshal's Office and not with the sheriff's bailiwick. After the warrant
was obtained the following morning, Monday, 13 January 1902, Sheriff
Smalley and Undersheriff Richard A. Proctor prepared for the arrest.
Smalley recalled that "taking Tom Horn was not a job I would wish off

on one of my deputies." He and Horn had known each for many years, which did not make the chief county lawman's task any easier.[11]

At 11:30 A.M., Sheriff Smalley, accompanied by Undersheriff Proctor, approached the unsuspecting range detective in the lobby of the Inter Ocean Hotel. Horn, sitting on a couch in conversation with Union Pacific Detective Frank Wheeler, was waiting to board a train that would take him to Montana. The approach of the two lawmen did not alarm him. As Smalley walked up to Horn and said "hello," he quickly jerked the detective's pistol from his waistband. This tense moment was over. No one had expected that the infamous cattle detective, whom the public regarded as a dangerous man, could be taken without a fight. Joe LeFors was surprised. Knowing that Edwin Smalley was inexperienced and that Horn might resist arrest, District Attorney Stoll had instructed LeFors "to be near enough to get him if Smalley failed." Accordingly, the deputy marshal slipped into the hotel, but kept himself out of sight. "Horn did not offer the slightest resistance," LeFors recalled. The Cheyenne *Daily Leader*, which appeared late in the day, carried the bold headline: "Tom Horn, Detective, Arrested for Murder. Charged with Killing Willie Nickell on the Morning of July 18, 1901. Sensational Developments Which Occurred This Morning in the Famous Nickell Murder Mystery That Startled and Puzzled the Entire Western Country—A Pistol Taken Away From Horn Before He Had Time to Resist."[12]

It is difficult to believe that Tom Horn was unaware that he was a primary suspect in the Nickell cases. Since the coroner's inquest in the Willie Nickell murder the previous summer, his name had been bandied about as a suspect in the newspapers and by word of mouth. Glendolene Kimmell and others had alerted him that he was in danger. What could he have been thinking? How could he ignore such warnings? Perhaps he was too arrogant to believe he was in serious danger. After all, his cattleman friends had protected him in the past. Nothing had changed, as far as Horn was concerned. Even as the sheriff escorted him to the Laramie County Jail, he made light of his plight and joked with the officers. Within a few days, he would understand that his present situation was no laughing matter.

Upon Horn's arrival at the Laramie County Jail, his home for the remaining twenty-two months of his life, he became a statistic in Smalley's record book:

Name: Tom Horn Address: Bosler, Wyo. Age: 44 [*sic*]
Height: 6'1" Hair: thin brown Eyes: brown
Complexion: dark swarthy
Peculiarities: scar on nose scar on right side of neck left jaw
   out of shape
Charge: murder
Committed: Jan. 13, 1902

Security was an immediate concern. Sheriff Smalley placed him in a cell on the upper level of steel cages, with access only by a set of narrow steel steps. The lawman professed the intention to isolate Horn "from the outside world," according to the *Daily Leader*, "as if he were 1,000 miles from civilization." When the *Leader* asked Horn for a statement, he replied curtly, "There is nothing I care to say."[13]

Until a permanent defense team could be assembled, friends of the prisoner in Cheyenne retained Timothy F. Burke, the U.S. district attorney for Wyoming, to represent Horn. (This federal position was a part-time post, permitting Burke to take other cases.) On Thursday John C. Coble arrived in Cheyenne and went directly to Harry Hynds's Capitol Bar, where he talked with the saloon man about prospective attorneys for Horn. Hynds was high on a promising young attorney, T. Blake Kennedy. He telephoned Kennedy and arranged for him to meet them that evening. When Coble asked Kennedy for recommendations for additional attorneys, he suggested John W. Lacey, a former Wyoming chief justice and successful criminal lawyer. Lacey, who was also Timothy Burke's partner, assumed the leadership of the defense team. Other members were Roderick N. Matson, Gibson Clark, and Edward T. Clark, as well as Kennedy. The next day Kennedy had his first conference with Tom Horn.[14]

Since Horn was practically penniless, John Coble took the lead in establishing a defense fund for his friend. While Horn was "said to have the backing of friends whose aggregate wealth is something like two millions," according to the *Laramie Boomerang*, Coble met with disappointment at every turn. Even William C. Irvine, the president of the Wyoming Live Stock Association and a ringleader of the Johnson County invaders in 1892, refused to contribute. In a fit of pique, Coble insisted that Horn "never killed that boy. . . . He may hang for it," he said angrily to Irvine, "but I want to say to you, whether he does or not, he will never *squeal.*" When even the hardcore "radicals" among the range barons refused to contribute, Coble assumed responsibility for Horn's defense, even though he would have to borrow the money. He turned to Franklin Bosler, Sr., the major stockholder in the Iron Mountain Cattle Company. In recalling this incident, Bosler said that Coble asked him for a $5,000 advance. Bosler complied, although he was not fully aware of how difficult Horn's defense would be and demanded that Coble put up his prize geldings as collateral. On 21 January 1902, Coble turned the money over to Horn's attorneys. Lacey promptly distributed the retainer among his colleagues, giving $2,000 to Burke and Clark, $1000 to Matson and Kennedy, and keeping $2000 for himself. Kennedy, who still had law school bills to pay, recalled that his portion "was the first real money" he had received since setting up his practice. Whether this $5,000 constituted payment in full for defending Tom Horn is not clear.[15]

As Coble went about the business of arranging Horn's defense, newspapermen followed his every move. Coble made no bones about his contempt for them and complained bitterly about "misrepresentation" by the press. Much to his dismay, newspapers made much of a scandal at his ranch. When the wife of Coble's cook, a man named Heley, was rumored to have had an affair with Coble, the cook accused Coble of alienating her affections. (Coble, who was unmarried, had a reputation as a ladies' man.) Whatever the truth of this accusation, the Heleys immediately left his employ.[16]

Even as he stood by Tom Horn, John Coble was upset with his hireling who, in the past, had managed to avoid the law's clutches. According to Alexander (Bob) Coble, brother of the Iron Mountain Ranch boss, John was so angry that he told Horn, "You have got yourself into a hole and now you can get out if you are able to. I won't help you with a cent" (clearly an empty threat). Sometime later, John Coble remarked that "the killing of Willie Nickell was a dastardly crime and I would help to pull the rope to hang the man who murdered the boy. . . . If Horn killed the lad, then he deserves death." In spite of these outbursts, John Coble stood by Horn to the bitter end.[17]

Given the supposed wealth behind Horn's defense, some skeptics doubted that he would even come to trial. If his case did reach the district court, would a jury dare to convict? "Horn knows too much," said the *Rocky Mountain News;* "many prominent men have reason to wish that Horn never comes to trial." As one observer stated bluntly, the arrest of Tom Horn was important only as a prelude to the eventual arrest of prominent people who had backed him in the past. Even Edward Slack of the *Daily Leader* doubted that Tom Horn could be convicted, although he would not say so outright in his newspaper. While Slack desired to see the murderer of Willie Nickell "swing . . . before the grass grows on the Wyoming plains," he was aware that the range barons usually had their way. Since Laramie County officials would now at least have to go through the motions of a trial, Slack took the liberty of lecturing them on how to conduct the state's case. "Our county authorities should leave no stone unturned in the way of investigating and getting at the actual facts of this bloody and awful tragedy," advised Slack, exhorting them to make "no mistakes." The Cheyenne sporting crowd reflected this public uncertainty about the state's ability to win a conviction by offering "even money that he [Horn] is not bound over to the district court at the preliminary hearing."[18]

That District Attorney Walter R. Stoll would direct the prosecution of the Horn case went without saying. However, he was only one man and stood virtually alone against the defendant's high-powered lawyers. In his zeal to see that the alleged murderer of his son was fully prosecuted, Kels Nickell retained attorney H. Waldo Moore to "assist in the prosecution." Stoll did not object to this assistant, although he insisted on having "absolute charge of the case." Walter Stoll might not have been available to prosecute Tom Horn but for a fortuitous turn of events. On the day of Horn's arrest, Stoll took a serious fall from his horse. Fortunately, he escaped with only bad bruises. Had he been incapacitated, some less capable person might have filled his position.[19]

The two sides in the Tom Horn case were scheduled to meet for the first time at a preliminary hearing on 23 January 1902. In spite of the defendant's prominent legal support, the defense was at a serious disadvantage, since the state had maintained a "profound secrecy" about its evidence. Furthermore, the defense team had had very little time to prepare their case. From subsequent events, it appears that Horn was unaware of his perilous position as a consequence of his indiscreet remarks to Joe LeFors, and he did not even think to inform his lawyers early on of the content of these conversations. Given Horn's assumption that he and LeFors were like-minded companions in the cattle detective trade, the *Rocky Mountain News* concluded that Horn believed he was talking with "another bad man and killer." Shortly after his incarceration, Horn asked Sheriff Smalley to summon LeFors. When LeFors arrived, the prisoner said, "I've been arrested." "For what?" asked LeFors. "Killing a kid," he said. "The hell!" responded the lawman and quickly departed. Since Horn made no accusation in this encounter, Smalley concluded that he was still unaware that he was a victim of a trap.[20]

The preliminary hearing began before Justice of the Peace Samuel Becker at 10:00 A.M. on Thursday, 23 January 1902, with sheriff's personnel maintaining tight security. In anticipation of a large crowd, Becker moved the proceedings to the district courtroom on the second floor of the justice complex. Sure enough, eager spectators filled the room, according to one observer, "while others gathered about in groups on the sidewalk and in the corridors." The morning session was taken up with testimony on the circumstances of Willie Nickell's body and the subsequent autopsy. After lunch Joe LeFors, Charles Ohnhaus, and Leslie Snow were called to testify to the defendant's confession of 12 January. So "startling" were these revelations, which included Horn's murder of William Lewis and Fred Powell several years earlier, that some spectators sprang "to their feet in their intense excitement." Even the stoical defendant "lost his customary equanimity," observed the *Daily Leader,* "and could not hide the startled look which crept into his eyes." Not anticipating "a bomb of this nature," continued the *Leader,* "the attorneys for the defense shifted in their seats and leaned forward as the details of the coup d'etat, by which the officers secured the statement of Horn, were slowly . . . brought out." Even though Lacey and Stoll made "quite lengthy arguments" for and against bail, the law required Becker to bind the prisoner over for trial at the forthcoming May district court session. (If a clever defense ploy somehow led to the release of Tom Horn on bail, it was expected that he would quickly depart for Canada or Mexico, never to return.)[21]

The defense's situation appeared hopeless, but John Lacey informed the *Daily Leader* that his client was "guiltless" and he went on to say that the team had a good defense in mind, similar to "what railroad men would call 'a double header.'" The first step would be to establish an alibi for Tom Horn, and the second would be "to take the ground that what is called the confession was simply braggadocio talk." Lacey insisted that Horn's boasting to Joe LeFors was merely for the benefit of "another bad man and killer." The defense attorney also said he had witnesses who would "swear that Horn was intoxicated" when he made the confession and was not responsible for his utterances. As a

final gambit, according to the *Leader,* Lacey intended to try to drag out
the proceedings, calling for a continuance at the May term and another
at the fall term. If he succeeding in delaying Horn's case beyond the fall
term, the defense, with the support of the defendant's cattleman friends,
would then play a political card. Since Walter Stoll's position as district
attorney was elective, continued the *Leader,* "the men who are providing for Horn's defense will use every means to secure" his defeat. With
a person in this key office "who will not care, nor dare, to push the case
against Horn," according to this scenario, the defendant had a good
chance to go free.[22]

Attorneys for both sides began to prepare for the May term. Defense
attorney Kennedy, who drew the duty of going into the countryside
and "looking up evidence and the lie," as he recalled wryly, traveled to
the Coble ranch with the hope of collecting alibi evidence on behalf of
Tom Horn. Early one cold morning in late January, foreman Duncan
Clark led the young city boy "on horseback across the mountain range
through the Sybille country" to the home of Otto Plaga. Plaga, who
said he saw Horn many miles from the Nickell murder scene "at about
the time the killing occurred," gave Kennedy a written affidavit which
the defense considered "very valuable evidence." While the defense
assumed that Horn's confession was the sole basis of the state's case,
Walter Stoll scoffed at such musings and declared that the confession
was only "a drop in the bucket" when compared with his entire arsenal
of evidence. Since Tom Horn resided in Albany County at the time
of the murder of Willie Nickell, Sheriff Alfred Cook assisted Laramie
County officials in the collection of evidence. Likewise, Mortimer N.
Grant, the former Albany County sheriff, also assisted the prosecution.[23]

One piece of evidence that Sheriff Smalley considered very important had turned up in Albany County during the investigation of Tom
Horn's movements. George A. Matlock, the owner of a Laramie shoe
shop, turned in the bloodstained sweater believed to be one that Horn
left at Matlock's shop after killing Willie Nickell. To ensure that Matlock's identification of Tom Horn was correct, Smalley summoned
the shopkeeper to Cheyenne. When Matlock arrived at the jail, probably just prior to the May 1902 term of district court, the sheriff took
him into the exercise area where he could view the prisoners. In this
quasi lineup, Matlock identified Jim McCloud, a robbery suspect, as
the owner of the sweater. "Our spirits sank," recalled Smalley, who
feared the state's "case was beginning to crack at the very outset." But

suddenly, Matlock pointed to another prisoner. "There!" he shouted. "That's the fellow that left the bloody sweater at my place!" and pointed to Tom Horn. A short time later, Undersheriff Dick Proctor took this garment to Horn's cell and asked the prisoner if he would like to have his sweater returned to him. "I sure would," Horn replied agreeably. "It's been a long time since I wore that. I left it over in Laramie City a long time ago." With this admission, another mystifyingly incriminating remark, the authorities were sure they had the right man.[24]

The attorneys on both sides were prepared to go to some lengths to gain the advantage. Since the defense was certain to try to find alibi witnesses from among the range detective's friends in the Iron Mountain community, Walter Stoll was anxious to thwart such an effort. When the prosecutor asked Sheriff Smalley how they might get around an alibi, the lawman proposed a clever stratagem. Smalley suggested that they find a pretext to get "a sworn statement from everybody in that country who could possibly alibi for him." Their plan involved the horse that Tom Horn rode into Laramie to establish his alibi after assassinating Willie Nickell. Smalley proposed to visit Iron Mountain on the pretext of searching for a fictitious horse thief, one John Dunder, who purportedly stole a bay horse (the kind Horn rode) on the day of Willie Nickell's death. In the course of this bogus investigation, the sheriff would issue subpoenas ordering "all the people in the Iron Mountain district to appear in Cheyenne [on a certain date] to testify in the case against this alleged horse thief." Accordingly, Smalley and his deputies served summonses on twenty-two persons, ordering them to appear at Prosecutor Stoll's office on 7 February 1902 to testify in the Dunder case. Stoll used this opportunity to ask questions pertinent to the state's case against Tom Horn: Where had the witness been on 18 July 1901? Had he (or she) seen a man riding a bay horse? Had he seen a stranger in the neighborhood? Each witness to this nonexistent crime had to sign a statement, thereby unwittingly removing himself from the defense's camp. When this maneuver became public, defense attorney John Lacey was outraged and urged all persons summoned in the fictitious case to sue the state "for abuse of process," but nothing came of it. The state "had tied up all possible witnesses for Horn from the Iron Mountain country.[25]

John Lacey and his associates soon retaliated by accusing Stoll and Smalley of irregularities in their use of public monies in the Tom Horn case. It had been their practice to list expenditures under the general heading 'Investigation of Crime" rather than to itemize them as part of the Horn case. In spite of Lacey's efforts to learn more, Walter Stoll simply refused to divulge further details, and the county commissioners backed him up. "The county commissioners knew who received these 'investigation of crime' payments," Smalley recalled, "but they kept the information to themselves." About the same time, the *Denver Post* gave the prosecution an additional boost by reporting that John Coble was attempting to coerce his employees into making false testimony on behalf of Tom Horn. In reporting this "Sensational Charge," the *Post* alleged that Coble went so far as to pressure his foreman, Duncan Clark, who resigned rather than cooperate. Coble indignantly denied these allegations, but the public was not buying his story. Whatever Clark's motive for quitting, the *Post* pointed out, the fact remained he was "Coble's assistant during the years of Horn's supremacy" and knew many dark secrets. (Whatever his motive, Clark established his own ranch after leaving Coble's employ.)[26]

The much-anticipated district court session, which opened on 22 May, turned out to be anticlimactic. Walter Stoll's only direct move against Tom Horn was to charge him formally with the murder of Willie Nickell. In his very next breath, the prosecutor introduced a motion "to quash and set aside the jury list" drawn up earlier for this term. Stoll informed Presiding Judge Richard Scott that many members of the state bar association were concerned that a jury law enacted by the most recent legislative session contained unconstitutional provisions. The most problematic clause authorized the drawing of a jury from among qualified citizens within a five-mile radius of a county seat, rather than from the entire county as provided by the U.S. Constitution. After listening to Stoll, Judge Scott decided to refer the question to the Wyoming Supreme Court. As a result, the entire docket for this court session, including the Horn case, was postponed until 15 September. Defense counsel argued that his client was entitled to a speedy trial, but Scott had no recourse but to deny that plea. Nonetheless, Horn and several other defendants were formally arraigned. Horn pled Not Guilty.[27]

The testimony presented at the preliminary hearing prompted much speculation about Wyoming's range squabbles. The *Saratoga Sun* (Carbon County) saw evidence of "a systematic plan for the assassination of cattle rustlers" but defended such violent tactics as the cattlemen's "only remedy" since "the law afforded them no redress." Others disagreed, noting that the arrest of such a conspicuous player as Tom Horn was a sign of new vigor among the state's lawmen. In complimenting the Laramie County officers for their "magnificent" work in bringing about Horn's arrest, the *Daily Leader* took the opportunity to defend Wyoming from Denver journalists, who had long criticized the state's backwardness. The people of Colorado "should learn a good lesson from the actions of the officers of her sister state," added this journal, which singled out Deputy Marshal Joe LeFors for his "peerless detective work." Frank Murray of the Pinkerton Agency in Denver went so far as to promise to buy LeFors "a drink for doing so well" when the opportunity afforded itself. On the other hand, friends of Tom Horn castigated the deputy marshal as a treacherous sort who used underhanded means to extract the so-called confession.[28]

Both family and friends expressed sympathy for the range detective's plight. At least two relatives—Tom's brother Charles Horn of Boulder, Colorado, and a nephew, Thomas W. Adams—tried to gain access to the prisoner, but Sheriff Smalley refused to permit anyone other than his attorneys to talk with him. Horn was permitted to write and receive letters. Francis Marion (Frank) Ownbey, who worked with Horn on the Cotopaxi train robbery case in 1891, expressed astonishment at the murder charge. "Knowing you as I do, and knowing your ability and sense," he wrote, "I can not believe you would stoop so low as to murder a fourteen-year-old boy for the small sum of five hundred dollars." Although there is no indication that she wrote Tom Horn very often, Glendolene Kimmell, the Iron Mountain schoolteacher, eventually emerged as one of his strongest supporters. Kimmell "is a petite, vivacious piece of femininity, less than five feet in height," said the *Daily Leader,* "but possessing an education extraordinary in a young lady of such an age." After meeting Horn at Jim Miller's ranch, in July 1901, according to this writer, she "became infatuated with him and played quite an important part" in Horn's case. Although she warned Horn to beware of Joe LeFors, he ignored her advice at the time of the inquest, continued the *Leader,* and "he is now languishing in the county jail."[29]

Newspapers continued to dig into Tom Horn's past. The picture was not pretty. The murders of Billy Lewis, Fred Powell, Matt Rash, and Isom Dart were all attributed to him. Should Horn somehow be acquitted in the Willie Nickell case, he could be arrested and tried in Colorado for the latter two killings. Other assassinations were also laid at Tom Horn's door. Catherine Bell, who had provided Horn with room and board in 1899, accused him of robbing her husband of $4,000 and then murdering him. When she confronted Horn, he denied this accusation and maintained that he had seen her husband alive in Rock Springs. While Cheyenne officers "are of the opinion that Tom Horn was responsible for the mysterious disappearance of Fred Bell," said the *Daily Leader* in April 1902, they have "nothing upon which to base an accusation." In time, Catherine Bell reluctantly concluded that her husband might still be alive, but she still believed that Tom Horn knew his whereabouts. A Cheyenne attorney who preferred to remain anonymous attributed the murder of John Blake, a Carbon County sheepherder, to Tom Horn, drawing this conclusion when he defended one Lee Madden, who was charged with the killing. Even though Horn testified in defense of Madden and gave the defendant an alibi, the lawyer concluded that Horn was guilty of the murder. "Poor old Tom Horn," the *Laramie Republican* was moved to remark, "has certainly enough burdens for one man to bear."[30]

Even though he was in jail, Tom Horn was also blamed for the continued feuding in the Iron Mountain region. In May 1902, several small ranchers, among them I. N. Bard, a near neighbor of Kels Nickell, received mysterious letters warning them to sell out and leave. When these homesteaders complained to Laramie County Sheriff Smalley, the lawman responded that he could find "absolutely no cause" for such letters and went on to conclude that such complaints were merely "a ruse to create evidence in favor" of Tom Horn. "If the warning notes continue to be received by ranchmen in that section while Tom Horn is in jail," Smalley continued, "then it would give rise to the belief that Horn was probably not implicated in any way in the sending of the other letters."[31]

It was true that the residents of the Iron Mountain area were a contentious bunch, even without the assistance of the infamous range detective. Their divisions extended even to religious matters. The attacks upon the Nickell family and the continuing threats and intimidation in the community convinced some of the inhabitants of this remote community that they needed "a general place of worship." Previously, any minister who had the courage to preach in the region held services in private residences. When residents in the northern part of the Iron Mountain community suggested that they take up a collection for the erection of a permanent church building, the people in the southern part of town absolutely refused. They regarded people in the northern section as supporters of Tom Horn and contributors to John Coble's defense fund for Horn and refused to be part of what they termed a "killers' church." When the church was finally built, the opposing faction in the south boycotted it. The name "killers' church" stuck for many years.[32]

Tom Horn, who faced several months of incarceration before his trial, had to find ways to pass the time. Even though Sheriff Smalley kept him isolated, permitting only his lawyers to visit, the prisoner somehow preserved an "unruffled equanimity." (The sheriff even forbade visits by representatives of the Salvation Army!) Liberty, said the *Daily Leader,* consisted of exercise in "the corridor of the steel cage, which is but a few feet square." The sheriff even installed a peephole to enable deputies to look in on the prisoner from the outside. "Each day he has taken his regular exercise, read his papers, sung and chatted" with the other prisoners, said the *Rocky Mountain News.* (Horn communicated with other prisoners by shouting to inmates on the floor below his cell.) At times, he even whistled. The prisoner spent much time working with rawhide and horsehair, arts he learned while living with the Apaches. "Many an hour of the day and week have I passed here in jail making rawhide ropes, hair ropes, hackamores, bridles and quirts," he wrote. "Horn is admitted to be the finest maker of hair ropes and leather braid work in the western country," said one reporter, and this pastime "enables him to bear [incarceration] more philosophically." One of his ropes consisted of a staggering 140,000 hairs from cows' tails! In commenting on his confinement in a letter to Duncan Clark, Horn joked, "My only objection to being in jail is that I cant [*sic*] attend church regular."[33]

Sheriff Smalley closely monitored the prisoner's communication with the outside. Horn's letters were mailed through his attorneys, the firm of Matson & Kennedy. In a letter to Charles Irwin, John Coble's foreman, Horn urged him to visit the jail "right away, personally." "If you come in [to Cheyenne]," wrote Matson & Kennedy, "bring Tom's [reading] glasses with you as he wants them." Matson & Kennedy also wrote on Tom's behalf to his brother Charles: "Tom says, 'Tell Charles, that my case is the least bit odd, as the defendant claims that the State has no case and the prosecution claims that they have no law to try

me.'" "Tom wants to hear from you by first mail," this letter continued, but Horn urged that Charles "keep quiet and . . . say nothing to
anyone [about the case] except to Lizzie [Charles's wife]."[34]

Apparently Sheriff Smalley made occasional exceptions to his visitation rule and permitted two of Horn's friends, Jack Rollinson and Sam
Moore, to see him. "We took him some cigars, and . . . two full sacks
of horsehair," recalled Rollinson, who "found Tom in a surprisingly
good humor and frame of mind." Even the sheriff, who characterized
Horn as his "star prisoner," spent time with Horn. The two men, who
had known each other for several years, "smoked pipes and used the
same kind of cut-plug tobacco," recalled Smalley. They smoked, played
cards, and told each other tall tales. The prisoner "was one of the most
entertaining men I ever met," added Smalley, who found Horn's stories
"enthralling." The lawman, of course, hoped the prisoner would slip up
and divulge some incriminating information about the Willie Nickell
murder, but to Smalley's dismay, he "never got a cheep [peep] out of
him about the crime."

It must have been a source of some discomfort to Horn to observe
people on the streets preparing for the annual Frontier Days celebration
in late August. Ordinarily, his name would be listed among the participants, along with his old range compatriots, including Duncan Clark,
Charles Irwin, Hugh McPhee, and Otto Plaga, who signed up for the
various cowboy events. People expressed disappointment that "Tom
Horn will be unable to contribute to this year's celebration in person,"
according to the *Rocky Mountain News*. Even though he would not
be a participant, this writer remarked, Horn's "work will be apparent"
in the presence of his ropes and other paraphernalia employed by the
cowboys.[35]

As the November elections approached, Tom Horn and his attorneys
took a keen interest in certain campaigns, including Walter Stoll's bid
for reelection to the office of district attorney and Edwin Smalley's run
for sheriff. If the popular public prosecutor, a Democrat, was defeated,
John Lacey believed that his client's prospects were improved. Alas, the
early signs were not good. "The public does not desire to see a new
man take hold of the [Horn] case," the *Rocky Mountain News* stated
bluntly, predicting that Stoll would win another term even though the
Republicans were expected to sweep all other local offices in Laramie
County. Edwin Smalley, who sought election to the sheriff's office on

the GOP ticket, had a strong bargaining chip in his arrest of Tom Horn, as the *Daily Leader* pointed out. However, this former grocery clerk experienced an embarrassing moment when his father-in-law, John B. Sloan, threw his hat in the ring for sheriff! This was so unusual that it received widespread newspaper publicity. However, Sloan soon withdrew in favor of another candidate.[36]

In the meantime, the Wyoming State Supreme Court convened on Monday, 18 August, to entertain Prosecutor Walter Stoll's question concerning the constitutionality of the new state jury law. The stickiest point remained the provision that a district court jury could be drawn from persons who resided within a five-mile radius of a county seat rather than from the entire county. Stoll argued that the constitution guaranteed that jurors would always be drawn from the entire "body of the county." However, John Lacey and Timothy Burke, supported by Hugo Donzelman, who had recently returned from a diplomatic post in Austria, argued that Walter Stoll's objection would seldom, if ever, arise. If it did, the defendant could appeal. Surprisingly, Tom Horn's attorneys supported the present law—their reason being that somehow a jury selected from nearer Cheyenne would be more favorable to their client. In outlying precincts, where Horn was known (and feared) as a range detective, jurors were more likely to be against him. Indeed, T. Blake Kennedy said that Lacey's arguments in favor of the jury law were part of the defense's strategy. Rather than overturn the new jury law, the Wyoming Supreme Court ruled it constitutional on 12 September, but with the understanding that district judges would see that in the future jurors were drawn from all eligible persons throughout all counties. Judge Richard Scott, who presided over the First Judicial District, immediately ordered a new jury venire issued for the approaching fall term in Cheyenne. On 24 September, in the presence of attorneys for and against Tom Horn, the names of thirty-six men were drawn and ordered to be present for Horn's trial on 10 October 1902. Looking "slightly pale" from eight months of confinement, Tom Horn appeared before Judge Scott, who ordered him and his attorneys to be ready on 10 October.[37]

Attorneys for both sides were busily completing preparations for the trial. The prosecutor planned to show that Tom Horn made a hasty ride from the Willie Nickell murder site to Laramie, in order to give himself an alibi if it should become necessary. As a means to demonstrate to the court that Horn could have made this thirty-five mile ride in four hours, Stoll had a rider on a good horse duplicate the trip. He made the ride easily, averaging nine miles per hour.

In early September, Stoll, Smalley and surveyor John Apperson traveled to Iron Mountain to serve subpoenas for witnesses and make maps of the murder scene. They found the residents, who recalled Tom Horn's acts of intimidation, still reluctant to cooperate. Sheriff Smalley had sent "deputy after deputy . . . through the [Iron Mountain] country trying to obtain evidence," Walter Stoll later reported, but their efforts were in vain. The prosecutor even dispatched "an agent in disguise" into the frightened community, but without success. As one of the inhabitants exclaimed, "We dare not talk! My God! What will become of us if it gets out if we have told anything?" The *Rocky Mountain News* sympathized with these inhabitants to some degree, noting that many families were tied together through intermarriage and "the smaller ranchmen . . . dependent on the larger ones for work."This unfortunate community lived in fear.[38]

John W. Lacey and the defense team also made their way to the murder scene. "We came to the conclusion that the boy was killed by a shot from a clump of rocks," recalled Kennedy, "which was perhaps thirty yards from the gate." Whether Prosecutor Stoll's subterfuge—the fictitious Dunder case—worked against the defense attorneys' efforts to gather evidence is not clear; Kennedy said nothing about it. However, John Lacey called very few Iron Mountain inhabitants to testify at the trial.

The defense attorneys were also willing to engage in subterfuge. One of Horn's attorneys, identified only as "a man prominent in politics and society," employed a Cheyenne prostitute to extract information from one of the prosecution's witnesses. According to one report, this unidentified man

> stood for two hours in a stuffy and dirty closet, while . . . a scarlet woman attempted to beguile from one of the witnesses . . . what he knew about the attack on Kels Nickell . . . the witness was supplied with beer until he was in a maudlin state of intoxication, but, "I know and you don't know," was all the woman could make him say. When the séance was concluded and the witness had been ejected by the disgusted plotters the attorney

emerged from the closet, his collar and shirt bosom melted by perspiration, and paid the bill.

From his jail cell, Tom Horn also attempted to find additional witnesses on his behalf, without much success.[39]

In spite of the fact that Tom Horn had confessed to the murder of Willie Nickell, his defenders, reflecting the cattlemen's perspective, attempted to excuse his crime. As the *Denver Post* noted, "Horn's friends—and he has many—say that, if it was Horn who shot Willie Nickell, it was a case of self-protection. The boy recognized him as he lay in the bushes, and knowing that the man thus armed was lying in wait for his father, the lad turned back and having his horse and a gun, would have shown fight had Horn given him the chance." While such support for Horn was, in some instances, a result of fear of the man, continued the reporter, the range detective's reputation "has traveled in seven-leagued boots, and the coolness, [and] desperate character of the man has been the dominant setting for the stories being told about him." According to the *Laramie Boomerang,* John Coble and his fellow range barons defended their use of force and terror with the argument that "stealing cattle was so prevalent among smaller ranchmen that a 'rider' [detective] had to be employed with nerve enough to intimidate them." "If the boy was killed by their 'rider,'" according to an unidentified cattleman, "it was a sad mistake." "It was the boy's father who was to have been put out of the way—peaceably, if possible; forcibly if necessary," this same rancher added. A corollary to this argument held that Horn killed Willie Nickell because he was determined to avoid a mistake he had made in the Fred Powell assassination. Powell's nine-year-old son, William, was a witness to his father's murder, but Horn let him live. The "hit man" resolved not to make this mistake twice.[40]

Significant changes had occurred in Wyoming, however, reducing the influence of the cattle barons in the past decade—and with it, the position of range detectives. The population of Wyoming increased from 62,000 in 1890 to 92,000 in 1900, with much of the growth among homesteaders and small ranchers. The economy continued to broaden. Sheep raising expanded, and the exploitation of mineral resources such as coal and oil burgeoned. Better roads and telephone lines tied the state more tightly together. With each year, the cattle barons lost more power. This was apparent in the shrinking membership of the

Wyoming Live Stock Growers Association. Public opinion, once determined by the whims of the big cattlemen, had begun to demand that elected officials be more representative of the people. These changes were felt forcefully in the counties along the Union Pacific Railroad, where communications with the outside world were stronger. This was especially apparent in Laramie County, the "capital county" of Wyoming. The trial of Tom Horn represented an important test of Wyoming's maturity.

Among the outside influences on Wyoming, the Denver press continued to be powerful, especially the *Rocky Mountain News* and the *Denver Post*. The *News* had crusaded for many years on behalf of the common people of Wyoming, and the *Post* was becoming active in reporting on its northern neighbor. One of the *Post*'s most popular and controversial writers was Leonel O'Brien, who wrote under the pen name Polly Pry. While many Wyomingites abhorred her critical articles about their state, she forced readers in Wyoming to consider many difficult issues, among them the Tom Horn case. In a March 1902 article, "Wyoming's Appalling Record of Rustler Assassinations Brought to Light of Day," Pry related the substance of her conversations with Laramie County officials about the present livestock interests and the problems of law enforcement. (While Pry mentioned no names, she apparently talked with Walter Stoll and Sheriff Edwin Smalley, among others.) That "the large stockmen have deliberately retarded the growth of the state," she wrote, went without saying. These heavy-handed tactics, according to Pry's sources, resulted from "the persistence of the professional agitators [the radicals?]" and "the apathy and indifference of the people themselves" that allowed "such crimes as Horn has committed in that county to go unpunished." "However foolish the cattlemen may have acted heretofore as a class," Pry's informants maintained, "the great body of stockmen would not [now] hire it done nor would they give countenance to it today." "As a group, continued Polly Pry, the cattle interests "are as much opposed to hired assassins as any other class of people." Who was to blame, then, if the livestock barons were innocent? The anonymous Laramie County officials asserted that "the principal fault lies with the people living in the [Iron Mountain] neighborhood of these assassinations"—and surprisingly, county authorities themselves who failed to look after "county interests." Had these parties upheld the law, said Pry, "Horn would have been brought to justice long ago."[41]

Polly Pry's unnamed sources bluntly accused the inhabitants of the Iron Mountain community of a want of "intelligence" and (reflecting Walter Stoll's censorious remarks) lacking in "moral courage of their convictions as men and citizens." If only a handful of these people "would open their mouths and tell what they know," continued the reporter, "hired assassination in Wyoming would be a thing of the past, and the bringing in to Wyoming of such men as Horn would be impossible"—a reminder that Tom Horn was an outsider. In assessing what her anonymous sources had told her, Polly Pry stressed the "despotism" of such powerful men as U.S. Senator Francis Warren, who not only discouraged lesser folk from settling in Wyoming, but created "conditions which make it possible for men like Tom Horn to live in a supposedly law abiding community." Whatever their prior abuses, continued Pry, the majority of the Wyoming cattle community had disavowed the few "professional agitators" within their ranks and had abandoned the use of hired assassins such as Tom Horn, men who had no special allegiance to the livestock community and could be employed to murder anyone. Indeed, there was evidence, continued Polly Pry, that Horn himself had been hired to kill men "whose only offense consisted in having some personal difficulty with some one or more" cattlemen. Pry seemed to be suggesting that personal dislike, not cattle rustling, accounted for the death of Willie Nickell, and that John Coble, one of the few remaining "radicals" among the cattle barons, was behind this crime. Pry left the impression that Tom Horn could not expect the backing of a united community of Wyoming cattle barons. He was largely on his own before the bar of justice.[42]

Apparently, the disavowal of Tom Horn and his regulator methods extended throughout the Rocky Mountain cattle community. About the same time as Polly Pry's report appeared, a *Denver Post* headline read: "Stockmen of the Nation Denounce Wyoming's Record of Assassinations. The Methods of Cattle Corporations in Wyoming Will Not Be Tolerated by the Sister States in the Union. Cattlemen Demand Decisive Action and [the] Prosecution of the Tom Horn Case." In what might be termed the "cattlemen's manifesto," the *Post* asserted that western cattlemen were, as a whole, law-abiding and that they disavowed the violence of the past in which as many as 500 persons lost their lives annually in range squabbles. Livestock men now possessed more confidence in the judicial system to protect their property and convict rustlers. If any sentiment existed among them to hire regulators, these diehards were a minority and would soon die out.[43]

In another significant turn of events, John Coble, the longtime manager of the Iron Mountain Land & Cattle Company and one of the primary "agitators" for heavy-handed treatment of the granger element, suddenly lost influence in the region. For some time, Franklin Bosler, who began to invest in the company in 1896, had begun to harbor doubts about Coble's management. In a deposition in a 1904 court battle with John Coble, Bosler said he began to suspect that Coble inflated cattle counts—indeed, he kept two separate sets of books—and that he made excuses for delays when Bosler demanded a hard count. In spite of his doubts, Bosler remained loyal to his old college friend, loaning him $5,000 for Tom Horn's defense against some of Coble's geldings. Now Bosler alleged that Coble attempted to pass off some inferior animals on him. Nor did Bosler realize the extent of his partner's connection with Tom Horn. Only with the increase in publicity about the Horn case, said Bosler, did he become aware of "how Coble actually stood with Horn." "I wanted to server [sic, sever] relations with him," Bosler continued, "but I delayed acting, as I did not wish to embarrass Coble by any further troubles."[44]

Even though Franklin Bosler hesitated to make a formal break with John Coble, news of their disagreement reached the public just as Tom Horn's trial approached in the fall of 1902. While Bosler's desire to dissociate himself from Coble was based primarily on business considerations, newspapers tended to place the Tom Horn scandal at the center of this disagreement. In early October 1902, the *Rocky Mountain News* broke the news of Coble's downfall, even to the extent of Coble's having to "relinquish . . . the signing of checks." "So soon as the [Horn] scandal broke out in unquenchable fury," according to the paper, "Mr. Bosler came all the way from Pennsylvania and personally instituted a new regime." This decisive action broke "the back of the power behind Horn," continued the *News,* noting that no one in the region "believed that Mr. Bosler, the man whose money kept the Bosler-Coble ranches going, was responsible for the policy of which Horn was the central figure."[45]

As John Coble's power began to wane, the wall between Laramie County lawmen and Iron Mountain residents began to break down. "With Horn in jail, Coble shorn of his power, and with a prosecution feared more than either of them," observed the *Denver Post,* the inhabitants of Iron Mountain had "signified their willingness to be subpoenaed for the prosecution." To exploit this welcome opening, Sheriff Smalley began to send deputies into the area even when they had no official business there. Through such "quiet work"—in effect, to "show the flag" of law enforcement—the deputies helped the residents of this remote settlement to recognize the "determination of the state to put the thing [Horn case] through to a finish," said the *Rocky Mountain News.* Times were changing in Wyoming.[46]

After nine months of preparation, the attorneys on both sides of the Horn case predicted "the longest [trial] in the history of the state," according to the *Daily Leader.* Walter Stoll anticipated as much as three weeks simply to select a jury, three weeks to hear testimony, and several days for jury deliberations. While John Lacey was not so pessimistic, he agreed that the entire proceedings could be lengthy. The defendant, who was "ill-looking" after months in confinement, was anxious for the trial to begin. In a surprising move, Lacey filed a motion asking that Laramie County "defray the expenses of bringing witnesses here to testify" for the defense. While this was a common practice in criminal cases involving indigent defendants, Tom Horn was presumed to have many wealthy supporters. The county agreed to pay such expenses, but only for two witnesses. Horn's attorneys requested support for ten, and Judge Scott approved this request. When Tom Horn signed the necessary documents, one reporter noted that he wrote "a neat legible hand."[47]

As both sides put the finishing touches on their cases, there was much public speculation as to their strengths and weaknesses. While the state's case rested heavily upon Tom Horn's confession, Walter Stoll boasted that he had uncovered "new and important evidence" to supplement it. As the *Denver Post* observed, Stoll needed additional "cards"; otherwise the state's case was "more or less circumstantial" if the confession did not fly in court. Significantly, the prosecutor intended, if at all possible, to avoid the subject of Tom Horn's employers. Summoning John Coble and other range barons as witnesses might tend to resurrect "undesirable ghosts" from the earlier range wars, according to the *Post.* Stoll's sole aim was to bring about the conviction of Tom Horn and not to meet the livestock community head on.

Defense counsel Lacey affected a confident public face and protested that he was "not worried." Yet there were signs that the members of the defense team were not so sure of themselves. While Lacey insisted that he would prove an alibi for Tom Horn, he weakened his position in the eyes of some observers by proposing to wait and see what "the prosecution will bring forward" before adopting any additional strategy. While experienced lawyers might not regard this approach as a sign of weakness, the public might.[48]

In spite of Tom Horn's confession, many people did not give Prosecutor Walter Stoll much of a chance. As one Denver newsman observed, he "is only one against eight" of "the best counsel in the state." Laramie County's resources also appeared pitiful when pitted against Wyoming's formidable livestock lobby, and Tom Horn had good reason to believe that he would soon be set free. Nonetheless, the trial promised to be "the biggest sensation the north west has ever had," opined the *Rocky Mountain News*. Only "One Week More," the *Daily Leader* reminded readers on 3 October. By this time the *Denver Post*, which now had its own permanent bureau in Cheyenne, was fully prepared to cover "the most famous trial in the record of Wyoming's criminal courts"—one that would determine which was "the stronger power, the law or the stockmen." The trial of Tom Horn was shaping up to be, in twenty-first-century parlance, a "media event."[49]

CHAPTER 13

The Trial

"He that pleads his own case has a fool for his client."

—English proverb

The justice complex on the corner of Ferguson (present Carey) and Nineteenth streets in Cheyenne was the focus of much attention on Friday, 10 October 1902, as the district court prepared to try the case of the infamous range detective Tom Horn. The red brick building contained not only the courtroom but the jail and the sheriff's office and residence as well. The second-floor courtroom, where Judge Richard H. Scott presided, presented a rustic appearance. The judge

> occupied a swivel chair in an old court-room of high ceiling and flower-papered walls. A tall stove, rusty and tobacco mottled, stood before the bar, its pipe rambling half way across the chamber. On the bench were two Edwardian bronze candelabra for gas lights. The jury box was behind a slender and glistening mahogany rail. Long, green-covered tables stood before the Judge's bench, extending from the jury box on one side to a cottage organ and a blackboard on the other.

Three tables inside the railing were reserved for newspaper reporters—an indication of the widespread interest in the Tom Horn trial.[1]

When the bailiff called for the case of the *State of Wyoming vs. Tom Horn* at 9:00 A.M., the attorneys immediately began jury selection. This process, which was expected to last as long as six weeks, turned out to be very brief. The lawyers asked the usual pro forma questions—have you formed an opinion beforehand? are you opposed to capital punishment? and so forth—but neither side seemed to do so with a sense of conviction. Even John Lacey, the chief defense attorney, made "as little trouble as possible" in jury selection, prompting the *Rocky Mountain News* to conclude erroneously that he and his associates had a "trump up their sleeve." By mid-afternoon the two sides were close to agreement on twelve jurors. While it was the aim of both sides to exclude men who might be detrimental to their respective causes, Edwin Smalley recalled that Prosecutor Stoll had to agree (for some unexplained reason) "to accept a man . . . who was a very close friend of Horn." As a consequence, "the possibility of a hung jury then became one of our problems," added Smalley. The defense had similar concerns. Before the trial began, Tom Horn studied the names on the first jury venire and pointed out to his attorneys the men he believed would be sympathetic. When jury selection was completed, Horn said six jurors were "satisfactory to him." After a mere four hours, a jury of "twelve good men and true" was sworn in. "The panel is a body of representative men," observed the *Rocky Mountain News,* consisting mostly of "ranchmen of good judgment who have formed opinions of greater or less weight from the [news]papers."[2]

This speedy selection was only the first in a series of surprises that defied the predictions of a protracted trial. The attorneys' opening statements, which could be very lengthy, again defied convention. At 3:45 P.M., Prosecutor Stoll took the floor. Referring to maps of the Willie Nickell murder site, he began the state's case with a "short, clear and undramatic statement," said the *Rocky Mountain News,* in language "simple and readily comprehended by the dullest listener." However, Stoll did startle the audience when he declared that, in addition to Tom Horn's confession, the state had two other pieces of incriminating evidence: "a sweater worn by Tom Horn at the time of the killing" of Willie Nickell; and evidence of a second confession that the defendant had made in a Denver saloon. When John Lacey took the floor, he sprang the third surprise of the day by announcing that "the defense would reserve its [opening] statement until the close of the prosecution." Walter Stoll was so taken aback that he asked for an adjournment. Judge Scott complied and ordered everyone to report the following morning at 9:00 A.M. After the dismissal, Lacey, who was obviously miffed that Horn had failed to forewarn him about the sweater and the Denver confession, took his client to a corner for a conference.[3]

On the morning of 11 October, Walter Stoll began the state's case. Much of the initial testimony, as well as maps, photographs and other exhibits, had been presented at the preliminary hearing. Young Fred Nickell "sobbed violently" as he describe how he found the body of his brother, Willie, on 18 July 1901. Mary Nickell, who impressed the audience with her "calm, subdued voice," recalled the threats her family had endured after her husband introduced sheep into the Iron Mountain country. Kels Nickell testified that he and Mary heard the shots that took their son's life but at the time did not associate the gunfire with Willie's demise. Upon finding his son's body, Kels said he found that the assassin had placed a rock under the dead boy's head, a statement that strengthened the legend of Tom Horn's "sign" of his grisly work.[4]

On cross-examination of Kels Nickell, John Lacey revealed an important part of the defense's strategy. As a means to show that someone other than Tom Horn could have been the assassin, Lacey asked Nickell if his son, Willie, had quarreled with anyone in their neighborhood. The witness responded that Willie had clashed with James Miller and his sons, Victor and Augustus (Gus). He attributed these "rows" to youthful emotions. The defense attorney then attempted to connect this feud with the supposition that the assassin had disturbed or rolled over the body. Only a young, inexperienced person (meaning one of the Miller boys) could have committed the murder and moved the body, Lacey declared. The crime must "have been the act of a lad not realizing the full horror of the deed," he continued, and not a professional assassin.[5]

While the prosecution presented witnesses who testified to the size of the fatal bullets, the result was inconclusive since forensic science was in its infancy at the turn of the twentieth century. Nor could much be deduced from the autopsy, since it was not conducted until three days after the murder. No bullets were found in the body. Walter Stoll was on firmer ground when he called Frank C. Erwin to the stand (not to be confused with Frank Irwin, who worked for John Coble). Erwin testified that he encountered Horn on the north side of Laramie about 11:00 A.M., on 18 July, the day Willie Nickell was killed. Horn was riding a large dark bay horse that was "very warm" and "very tired," suggesting that Horn had ridden the animal hard, presumably from the murder scene. Erwin, who knew Horn "slightly," said that the significance of Horn's appearance in Laramie only came to him the following day when he read an account of the murder and remarked "I bet Horn did this." On cross-examination, defense attorney Timothy Burke embarrassed this witness by revealing that Tom Horn had once investigated him on suspicion of cattle theft.[6]

The prosecution then called Charles H. Miller, manager of the Elkhorn Livery Stable in Laramie. Miller testified that Tom Horn brought in a horse on or about 20 July 1901. Miller recalled that when a bystander said to Horn, "Your horse seems tired," the detective replied, "He can't be; he just come in from the ranch." Miller testified that he apprised Albany County Sheriff Alfred Cook of Horn's arrival on a fatigued mount. Alfred W. Reed, a Miller employee, then testified that he saw the defendant ride into Laramie on a bay, which "was sweated up bad and was rode pretty hard." On cross, the defense pointed out that the weather was warm in July and suggested that the twenty-mile ride from Bosler could cause the animal to heat up. With the successful parrying of the testimony of these two prosecution witnesses, the *Daily Leader* concluded, the defense had scored "quite a victory."[7]

On 14 October, Walter Stoll called Mortimer N. Grant, the former Albany County sheriff, who he asserted could "fix the date Horn reached Laramie." This witness had overheard a pertinent conversation between John Wallace, owner of the Elkhorn stables, and others on the evening of 18 July 1901, in which Wallace mentioned the horse Horn had ridden into Laramie on that day. At this point the defense objected on the grounds of hearsay, and Judge Scott sustained the objection and ordered Grant's testimony expunged from the record. Yet Stoll had made his point. When Sheriff Grant testified that he examined a horse that Horn had ridden into Laramie, he did not know what day Horn arrived.[8]

The prosecution then documented Tom Horn's movements in the Horse Creek area just prior to the murder of Willie Nickell through the testimony of Mrs. James (Dora) Miller and three of her children, Eva, Victor and Augustus (Gus). Jim Miller, the father, was not called. Walter Stoll instructed R. C. Morris, the court stenographer, to read Horn's testimony given at the coroner's inquest, on 9 August 1901, in which he admitted to being "in that country during the week of the murder." Defense Counsel Lacey "found a number of flaws in the

record," according to the *Rocky Mountain News,* and demanded that
Morris go back to his original notes for clarification. Whether any further reference was made to this subject is not clear.[9]

In spite of John Lacey's confident demeanor, the proceedings were
"beginning to tell" on Tom Horn, who exhibited various mood swings.
Early in the trial, he appeared "free from care and lounge[d] luxuri-
ously" in a chair immediately behind his counsel. Dressed in "a pink tie
and soft pink shirt," according to one observer, the defendant "placed
his thumbs in his suspenders and broadly winked at one of his friends."
Yet Horn showed an intense interest in the state's witnesses, maintained
a "steady level gaze" at one, and sometimes whispered to his attorneys.
As the days passed, he began to tire and propped his head in his hands or
rested his head on the railing behind his seat. He often twisted his mustache and chewed tobacco "incessantly," according to one observer.
Spectators were amused at the sight of the defendant and the sheriff,
who sat next to him, expectorating into the same spittoon. When bailiffs set up additional tables to accommodate the numerous newspaper
representatives, Horn, whose contempt for the press probably equaled
that of John Coble, smiled at them and then "gave a contemptuous
sneer."[10]

Prosecutor Stoll introduced the bloodstained sweater that the Tom
Horn allegedly left in George A. Matlock's shoe store in Laramie in July
1901. If the state could prove conclusively that this garment belonged
to the defendant, Stoll would score a major victory. Unfortunately,
Matlock upset Walter Stoll's plans. Matlock had positively identified
Horn in the Laramie County Jail. When he occupied the witness chair,
however, he would only say that "a man who resembled Horn" left
the sweater. George Powell, a cobbler in Matlock's store, testified that
he could not be certain of the exact date or the exact identity of this
person who left the bundle. No one came to retrieve the package, so
Powell opened it and found a badly soiled sweater "covered with small
fiber-like stuff which looked like grass roots." It also had stains that appeared to be blood. Powell washed this garment and wore it for about
a month. When the prosecutor asked Powell if he could identify the
man who left the sweater, he responded with a series of circumlocu-
tions: "My belief is that he is the person"; "I would not swear he is
the man"; "I am satisfied he was the man"; and the defendant bore "a
resemblance" to the man. On cross, Powell could remember nothing

distinctive about this person except that he was a big man who walked with a peculiar gait. Powell said he mailed the sweater to Tom Horn in the Laramie County Jail at the suggestion of the Albany County sheriff.[11]

In an effort to strengthen the state's case, Walter Stoll called Lyman Murdock, an employee of John Coble. Murdock recalled seeing a blue sweater tied to Tom Horn's saddle in June 1901. To clarify how the Laramie County sheriff's office came into possession of the sweater, Edwin Smalley testified that George Powell first informed him by letter that he had the sweater. Undersheriff Proctor took the letter to Horn, who read it and admitted the sweater was his. Proctor, who followed his boss on the witness stand, said that when the sweater arrived in the mail, it was addressed to Horn, in care of the sheriff. When Proctor took the garment to Horn's cell, the inmate "said it was his." While the prosecution's evidence may have been inconclusive, this much-discussed sweater helped to form a web of circumstantial evidence supporting the state's contention. The evidence—Horn arrived in Laramie on 18 July; his horse was well lathered; and he left a blood-stained sweater at a shoe store—had an impact upon what the jury came to believe. Whether the prosecution proved these points conclusively did not necessarily matter.[12]

On Wednesday, 15 October, the prosecution called Frank W. Mulock, who testified that he and some drinking buddies talked with Tom Horn during Denver's annual Festival of the Mountain and Plains, in October 1901. (This witness swore that each man had seven drinks.) When Horn boasted that he was a range detective in Wyoming, Mulock suggested that he should try to earn the reward in the Willie Nickell murder case. In reply, Horn blurted out, "I am the main guy in that Nickell case. . . . That was the best God damned shot I ever made in the Nickell case." When Mulock cautioned him against such loud talk, the defendant added, "By God, that is the dirtiest trick I ever done" and went on to say, "There is a lot of people mixed up in it [the Willie Nickell murder] in Cheyenne, and they had better keep their noses out of it." The next morning, Mulock testified, Horn, who had sobered up somewhat, asked him not to divulge anything he said the previous evening. On cross, defense counsel asked Mulock for the precise time of this conversation. Mulock said it occurred before Horn had his jaw broken in a drunken brawl in Denver. When asked if Horn spoke in "a braggadocia [sic] cowboy manner," Mulock replied frankly, "He was braggadocia [sic]." (This word was a tongue twister for all concerned.) Mulock declared that as a consequence of Horn's admissions, he decided to report the conversation to Deputy U.S. Marshal Joe LeFors. Two of Mulock's drinking companions, Roy Campbell and Robert G. Cowsley, also attested to Horn's boastful talk. On cross-examination, Cowsley had to admit that the defendant was very drunk and full of a "drunken cowboy's braggadocio talk."[13]

Since Prosecutor Stoll had revealed Horn's confession at the preliminary hearing, there had been much debate as to the admissibility of this conversation. In an effort to obtain an independent legal opinion, the *Denver Post* asked Edward F. Patrik, a Denver attorney, for his professional point of view. Patrik insisted that "there is no doubt the Horn confession is admissible" and pointed to a similar case, *State of Missouri vs. Brooks,* in which Hugh Brooks, in jail on a murder charge, unwittingly confessed to a policeman who had been planted in his cell. At Brooks's subsequent trial, the judge admitted the confession.[14]

On 15 October, Joseph LeFors took the stand and repeated essentially the same testimony that he gave at the preliminary hearing. Now, however, defense counsel Lacey was better prepared for him. Since the defendant was drinking (or drunk) when he allegedly confessed to LeFors, asserted Lacey, Horn was not responsible for his words. LeFors disagreed, insisting that the range detective "was sober and rational as far as I could tell." Lacey now introduced one of the keystones of his strategy. He asked LeFors if, during their conversations, he and Horn "swapped yarns." From this point on in the trial, the defense aggressively maintained that the two veteran range riders were merely engaged in light conversation and—in spite of the unpleasant subjects of their exchanges—were only "joshing" in an attempt to surpass each other in telling tall tales. In an attempt to weaken Joe LeFors's credibility, John Lacey pointed to his past involvement in "shootings and other disturbances" and characterized him as a "bad man." When Lacey asked if he had killed six men in Texas, LeFors replied emphatically, "'I did not.'" Lacey continued to subject LeFors to a "fierce" grilling, according to the *Denver Post.* All the while Tom Horn kept his "bead-like eyes" riveted on this witness. Eventually LeFors's face "grew flushed" and tears came to his eyes—something of an embarrassment for "the shrewdest and most brilliant detective in the western country." LeFors did not break, but the *Post* concluded that "the defense had the better hand" at the end of LeFors's testimony.[15]

Prosecutor Stoll presented a series of witnesses to reinforce his contention that the defendant's confession was valid. In regard to the defendant's sobriety, Vincent McGuire, E. S. Robinson, Louis M. Hall, Chief Deputy U.S. Marshal Paul Bailey, and Deputy Sheriff Leslie Snow—all of whom saw Horn and LeFors on the day of the confession—testified that Horn appeared sober. (Only one prosecution witness, City Marshal A. D. "Sandy" McNeil, admitted that the defendant had been drinking at all.) In regard to Charles Ohnhaus's transcribing the defendant's confession, Stoll essentially repeated testimony presented at the preliminary hearing. Leslie Snow testified that when LeFors asked for his assistance, he stationed himself behind the door "right next to Bailey's office." Stenographer Ohnhaus lay on the floor beside him. On the witness stand, Ohnhaus declared that he took down verbatim everything LeFors and Horn said (except for stories about killing people). When Stoll asked if Horn was under the influence of alcohol when he made the confession, Ohnhaus testified that on past occasions he had observed Horn when he was drinking and when he was sober. "He was not what you would call an intoxicated man" when he and LeFors were in conversation, Ohnhaus said. "I won't say that he didn't have a drink, one, two or three, perhaps, but I don't think he was drunk."[16]

On cross-examination, John Lacey attempted to discredit Ohnhaus's notes by pointing out that the stenographer admitted on the stand that he "did not take [down] all of the conversation." Ohnhaus continued to insist that he took down everything else that was said, meaning the part in which the defendant incriminated himself. Even though Horn glared at both Snow and Ohnhaus, he failed to intimidate them. As they gave their testimony, the defendant became "nervous and his hands twitched continuously and he moved around in his chair." The importance of Charles Ohnhaus's contribution to the state's case was obvious; without transcription by a person accredited by the courts, the confession would hardly have held up.[17]

In a trial expected to last many weeks, Walter Stoll sprang one of the most astonishing moments upon the court when, at 3:30 P.M., Wednesday, 15 October, he announced that "the state would rest." Since the beginning of testimony four days earlier, prosecution witnesses had passed through the courtroom "with a celerity that made counsel gleeful," according to one observer. When Stoll concluded, he had called only 55 witnesses from a prospective list of 150. It was no accident that the clever prosecutor concluded the state's case "with the dramatic climax of the reading of Ohnhaus's original notes." The *Daily Leader* praised Stoll for presenting a very strong case but detected "a missing link" in the state's evidence. Stoll had no one to "swear that he saw the fatal bullet . . . enter the body of Willie Nickell"—what we now call a smoking gun. But the district attorney had the next best thing. Tom Horn had confessed to at least six men: Joe LeFors, Charles Ohnhaus, Leslie Snow (in Cheyenne), and, in Denver, to Frank Mulock and his two drinking companions. Furthermore, the defendant had admitted to Sheriff Smalley and Undersheriff Proctor that the blood-stained sweater was his. "Tom Horn was like the famous parrot," observed the *Leader*; he "talked too much."[18]

Not everyone agreed with this assessment. A "prominent lawyer" who preferred to remain anonymous pointed out that some prosecution witnesses failed to fulfill Stoll's expectations. The prosecutor "'always sees more in a witness's statement previous to going on the stand," this unnamed attorney concluded. For instance, Frank Mulock "refused to tell the story Stoll expected of him," he continued, and the state's witnesses from the Iron Mountain district were "habitually reticent" on the stand. Even though the defense had not yet presented its side, some spectators continued to believe that the jury would disagree and that a second trial was likely. On the evening of 15 October, an unidentified "junior member" of the defense team expressed the opinion to a *Rocky Mountain News* correspondent that should the jury disagree, there would be no new trial. "The county will spend no more money," he said confidently, "and there is no more money for the defense."[19]

With spectators eager for more surprises, John Lacey began the defense the next morning. He immediately attacked the legitimacy of the defendant's confession and proposed to prove an alibi for his client. (Since there is no indication that the defense presented an argument against the admissibility of the confession, Lacey must have assumed that that this battle was lost already.) The defense presented several witnesses who had seen Tom Horn drinking on Sunday, 12 January 1902, the day of his confession. Grover Reis, a hotel bellboy, said Horn was "about half shot," while Al Leslie, a bartender, said that Horn was drinking beer and whiskey and talking loudly, "like any other drunken man would talk." Bartender Frank Kerrigan, who saw Horn about 4:00 A.M., said the defendant had already had six drinks. Kerrigan maintained that Horn was not drunk and did not stagger at all. While the use of "evidence of booze and braggadoccio [sic] from men [witnesses] who might be called experts on jags [drunks]" was very repugnant, observed J. Emerson Smith of the *Denver Post,* John Lacey was driven to this tactic. He hoped to convince the jury that Horn was so tipsy when LeFors put leading questions to him that he "was befuddled from the effects of dissipation" and that he made these incriminating remarks "in a spirit of braggadocio."[20]

Defense counsel devoted much of its first day to demonstrating that the bullets that killed Willie Nickell were not fired from Tom Horn's .30-30 rifle. The trial transcript on this subject filled 120 pages. To support his contention that the fatal bullets were larger than a .30 caliber, defense counsel called, among others, two physicians, George P. Johnston and John H. Conway, who had assisted with the autopsy of Willie Nickell, and both asserted that the fatal cartridge was "a large caliber bullet," probably about the size of a .45 caliber. On cross, Prosecutor Stoll prompted "a lively tilt" with numerous questions about differences in the size of the entrance and the exit wounds, as well as what effects decomposition could have had on the wounds. The result of Stoll's grilling was to muddle the subject beyond all recognition, prompting the *Daily Leader* to observe, "It seems to us that according to the importance given to the bullet testimony . . . the defendant's life is suspended by an almost imperceptible difference between the testimony of doctors about a small orifice which . . . did the business for poor Willie Nickell." At the conclusion of their testimony, these expert witnesses had to "admit that there are so many varying and modifying conditions that no one can speak with certainty about the matter in dispute." At one point the spectators, and even the defendant, laughed out loud. "It is such scenes as these that make a mockery of justice," remarked the *Leader.*[21]

John Lacey's next focus was on the position of the victim's body when it was found near the gate, a topic that had also been raised by the prosecution. The presence of coagulated blood and embedded gravel on Willie Nickell's vest indicated that the assassin may have turned the body over after shooting the boy. Dr. George Johnston testified that while the blood could have oozed three or four hours after the boy was shot, it could clot in three to seven minutes. In order for gravel to adhere to the deceased's body, ten or twelve hours would be required. In the defense's opinion, no professional assassin would linger at the murder scene. (The aim of the defense was to demonstrate that an amateur shot Willie Nickell, meaning a local person—Jim Miller or one of his sons—and not Tom Horn.) In countering the defense's expert, Prosecutor Stoll adopted the unusual tactic of emphasizing the legitimacy of the observations of everyday human beings and using the expert witnesses as foils. In regard to the examination of Willie Nickell's clothing, Stoll asked Dr. William Lewis: "There would be nothing about the condition of the clothes of the body that would require any special . . . expert knowledge, but rather the appearance could be accounted for by our own common experience in daily life?" The physician replied, "I should think so." "It is a fact sometimes that physicians, although scientific men, also take into consideration those facts which they meet with in every day life?" Again, Lewis replied, "Oh, yes."[22]

On Friday, 17 October, the defense team challenged the testimony of Frank Mulock and his two associates in regard to Tom Horn's second, or Denver, confession. Unfortunately for John Lacey, Tom Horn had muddied the waters two days earlier when he found an opportunity to talk to a *Rocky Mountain News* reporter. Horn was in a Denver hospital with a broken jaw suffered in a bar fight at the time of this alleged confession, he insisted, so "how could I be in the saloon where they said I talked too much?" Regardless of Horn's faux pas, Mulock was a vulnerable prosecution witness, well known to Denver police as a gambler and con man. Lacey specifically questioned Mulock's assertion that Horn made this confession during Denver's annual Festival of the Mountain and Plains, which took place 1–3 October 1901. On the witness stand, Denver Police Surgeon W. L. Davis testified that he treated the defendant's broken jaw on Monday 30 September 1901. The next day, Tuesday, Davis applied a plaster cast to the patient's face, which prevented him from talking. He "had to write everything he told me." On Wednesday, Davis placed Horn in St. Luke's Hospital, where he remained until 21 October. The defense called Robert D. Stockton, a Denver hotel keeper and deputy sheriff, who testified that Mulock had been mixed up in "many disreputable things" in Denver and that his reputation for telling the truth "is very bad." The defense also questioned the date that Mulock said Horn's confession took place. Walter Stoll did not seem concerned about the reliability of these defense witnesses, since Horn's drunken boasts were well known. Furthermore, as the *Rocky Mountain News* pointed out, these Denver witnesses may have "made a mistake in the date of their conversation with Horn." (Horn's second confession took place on Sunday evening, 29 September, when he was in a saloon and had not yet been injured.)[23]

While these proceedings were under way, John C. Coble was at work on the outside gathering additional evidence on behalf of his friend. On 15 October, Coble traveled to Denver, where he hired a private investigator to assist him in this search. The two men visited Police Surgeon Davis's office, police headquarters, and St. Luke's Hospital, among other places. At police headquarters, Coble was permitted "to see the blotter" for the period when Tom Horn was in town at the time of his confession to Frank Mulock. Coble, who left Denver "in a very happy frame of mind," attended Horn's trial on 17 October. His mood changed abruptly when rumors began to circulate that he "paid for evidence" on behalf of Tom Horn. Coble heatedly denied such allegations.[24]

As the defense's case unfolded, John Lacey and his associates were especially sanguine about their attack on the validity of Tom Horn's confession to Joe LeFors. If the jury was receptive to the defense's assertion that the defendant had been drinking when he confessed, the state's case was greatly weakened. On 16 October, an unnamed lawyer—evidently not a trial participant—expressed the opinion to the *Rocky Mountain News* that Tom Horn would be soon be out "on bail, pending a new trial." "You newspaper people can pack your grips ready to catch a train back to Denver Monday [20 October] or Tuesday noon," he added confidently. The prospects of "the notorious Tom Horn being out on bail was so startling" to this reporter that he asked J. A. Van Orsdel, the state attorney general, if such a scenario was possible. If the jury disagreed, Van Orsdel had to admit that such an eventuality was possible, although at the "discretion of the court."[25]

The defense continued to attack each piece of the state's case. In regard to the prosecution's assertion that Tom Horn made a hard four-hour "alibi ride" to Laramie after murdering Willie Nickell, the defense maintained that the defendant did not arrive in that city until two days later. John A. Wallace, part owner of the Elkhorn Livery Stable in Laramie, "was positive he had heard of the killing of Willie Nickell" before Horn stabled a horse at his livery. Wallace's stable book revealed that

Horn left his animal at the Elkhorn 1–7 July and 20–30 July 1901. Willard S. Carpenter, an employee of John C. Coble at this time, testified that the range detective arrived at the Iron Mountain ranch on 20 July.[26]

When the defense called Duncan Clark, John Coble's former foreman, spectators "brightened up and watched with expectant faces to what might happen." They were tired of testimony about bullets and such, observed the *Daily Leader*. Clark had reportedly left the foreman's position when Coble attempted to coerce him, and other employees, into providing Tom Horn with a false alibi. However, Clark insisted that he had had nothing to do with the range detective and had "never paid much attention" to his movements. As foreman, Clark only supervised the common cowhands. Clark did admit that he saw Horn in Laramie on 20 July, two days after Willie Nickell's death. In regard to Pacer, the horse Horn allegedly rode into Laramie, Clark testified that this horse was fat and "would sweat considerably" if Horn rode him hard. In regard to the defendant's alleged blue sweater, Clark declared, "the only kind I ever seen him with was a Dun sweater," that is, the color of "a buckskin horse."[27]

One of the surprising facts to emerge during the trial was that lawmen in Laramie and Albany counties suspected Tom Horn's involvement in the murder of Willie Nickell very early and began to look into his movements during the coroner's inquest in July and August 1901. This would indicate that Joe LeFors, who was vague in his autobiography as to the source of his initial suspicions of Horn, knew where to start his investigation from the outset. Albany County Sheriff Cook testified that shortly after the death of Willie Nickell he investigated the time of Horn's arrival in Laramie and made a copy of the brand on the defendant's horse. (Apparently Frank Erwin, who observed Horn's arrival in Laramie on 18 July, supplied the information that spurred Cook's inquiry.) However, Cook had to admit that when he encountered Horn in Laramie on 21 July and asked the defendant what day he arrived, Horn said he rode into town the previous day.[28]

In spite of defense counsel's public show of optimism, John Lacey and his colleagues had to resort to desperate tactics in Tom Horn's defense. They belittled and scoffed at the state's accusations at every opportunity. Prosecutor Stoll inadvertently provided an opening when he asserted that the defendant had gone barefoot at the murder scene in order to leave no boot prints. Timothy Burke, one of the defense attorneys who visited the murder scene, testified that the area was so rocky and rough that "it would be utterly impossible" to go barefoot there. The assassin would have lacerated his feet "very badly," remarked Burke, who presented some rock samples as evidence. T. Blake Kennedy then took the stand to present essentially the same testimony. To reinforce the point, defense counsel summoned Frank Stone, a Coble employee and friend of Tom Horn. Stone shared a room with the defendant at a Laramie hotel on the night of 21 July 1901. Horn was "pretty well intoxicated," said this witness, who not only had to help the range detective to his room, but removed his shoes and clothing. Stone saw no cuts or abrasions on Horn's feet. In regard to the blue sweater, Stone declared that he had only seen Horn wearing a buckskin sweater.[29]

On Friday afternoon, 17 October, the defense called its most important witness, Otto Plaga. A twenty-four-year-old cowboy, Plaga was well acquainted with Tom Horn, having assisted him in the arrest of Eva Langhoff and her compatriots for cattle theft in 1893. Plaga testified that about 8:00 A.M., on 18 July 1901—the day Willie Nickell was killed—he was "gathering cattle and prospecting" about eight miles from his residence when he spied the defendant on horseback. Plaga was very specific as to the location: an area known locally as Marble Top, between the Middle and Main Sybille creeks. He estimated this point to be about twenty-five miles from the murder scene, meaning that the defendant could not have committed the murder. Horn was riding his favorite horse, Cap, at "an easy trot." Plaga was about 150 yards away and did not hail the range detective. When asked if Tom Horn saw Plaga, the witness had to reply, "No." When Plaga returned to his residence later in the day, he informed his stepfather, Raymond Hencke, that he had seen Horn that morning.[30]

Prosecutor Walter Stoll subjected Plaga to a strenuous cross-examination. He was able to call attention to the slightest inconsistencies in Plaga's story by comparing his statements to his earlier deposition, in which he had stated that he was prospecting when he spied Horn. "You said nothing about hunting calves," Stoll reminded the witness pointedly. "I can't answer," replied Plaga. Nor could Plaga show on a map where he had seen the range detective. When asked if he had been "friendly with Horn for a long time," Plaga answered affirmatively. When asked what clothing Horn had worn on 18 July, Plaga said the defendant had on "a light stripped [sic] shirt and a vest," with a light gray felt hat. When asked why he had not hailed Horn, Plaga said he had thought the detective was searching for rustlers and did not want to be disturbed. When Stoll finished, John Lacey asked Plaga to explain his apparent secretiveness. Plaga said he had wanted to keep his prospecting site to himself until he filed a claim. When the prosecutor resumed his cross-examination and again questioned Plaga's failure to announce himself to Horn, the witness explained that the stock detective was such a common sight on the range that he had not made a particular "impression" at that time. Plaga fixed the date of his observation as 18 July because the mailman delivered the post the following Saturday (20 July) and informed Plaga and his stepfather, Raymond Hencke, of the Nickell murder. It was at this time, Plaga testified, that he reminded his stepfather that he had seen Horn earlier, on 18 July.[31]

Defense counsel called Raymond Hencke to the stand. Hencke, who "spoke with a decided German accent," said he had known Tom Horn about eight years. He informed the court that Otto Plaga, his stepson, left the ranch about 6:00 A.M., on 18 July 1901 to search for cattle. When Plaga returned to the ranch, Hencke said his stepson told him that he saw Horn "spooking around," in other words, looking for signs of rustling. On cross, the prosecutor asked Hencke how many days elapsed between the time Plaga said he saw the defendant and when the subject of "Tom Horn and the Nickell boy" came up again. Hencke replied that the arrival of Peter Warlaumont, the Laramie County deputy sheriff, in their neighborhood about two weeks after the murder prompted Plaga to inform Hencke of his sighting of Tom Horn. Hencke testified the he asked Otto Plaga at this time, "how came they to accuse Tom if you seen Tom that day[?]" When Stoll asked Hencke why he failed to inform Warlaumont of Plaga's encounter with Tom Horn on 18 July, the witness replied, "He didn't ask me." Nor did Hencke think to take the initiative and inform the lawman of his stepson's observation of Horn's movements. (Had Hencke informed Warlaumont, the Plaga-Hencke alibi for Tom Horn would have been more credible.) Oscar Coldick (Colditz), an employee of Hencke, testified that Otto Plaga had worked on the range on 18 July.[32]

While John Lacey considered Otto Plaga's testimony absolutely critical to the defense of Tom Horn, it was unfortunate that only Plaga could place the defendant somewhere else on the day of the murder. A long-standing maxim in the legal profession maintains that "one witness is no witness," while a complementary truism holds that "if a fact is fully proved by two witnesses it is as good as if proved by a hundred." In the absence of an additional witness who could place Horn elsewhere at the time of the murder of Willie Nickell, Raymond Hencke's assertion that Otto Plaga said he had seen Tom Horn was only hearsay. On cross, Walter Stoll vigorously attacked Plaga's credibility, since Plaga, as well as his younger brother, Albin, were known to look up to Horn as a hero. Not only were they "would-be imitators of the notorious cattle detective," according to one newsman, but Otto Plaga "openly allied himself with Horn" from the time of his arrest. If Plaga was willing to lie for the defendant, his loyalty was terribly misplaced. In one of the strangest ironies in this case, Horn, testifying at the coroner's inquest in August 1902, had occasion to comment on Otto Plaga's reputation for untruthfulness. He was "just about as unreliable," testified Horn, as the two feudists, Kels Nickell and Jim Miller. Had Walter Stoll recalled this contemptuous remark for the benefit of the trial jury, the prosecutor could have embarrassed the defense even more. (Both sides exhibited many signs of haphazard preparations for the trial; this was just one of them.)[33]

Defense counsel continued to try to show that persons other than the defendant desired to do Willie Nickell and his family harm. However, when John Lacey asked Andrew F. Whitman to testify to the prevalence of personal feuds in the Iron Mountain region, the prosecution objected to this line of questioning as immaterial, and Judge Scott sustained the objection. This decision "shut out a large amount of testimony," observed the *Daily Leader,* "which would have tended to prove . . . that there were other people who not only had an opportunity to commit the murder, but a motive for it." In an interview with the *Rocky Mountain News,* John Lacey tried to put a positive spin on this setback by asserting that Scott's decision removed from "the defense's shoulders the task of proving upon someone else a motive for the murder." "In either case the defense stood to win," Lacey asserted, attempting to turn a setback into a victory.[34]

When Judge Scott cut short Andrew Whitman's testimony, the defense had no choice but to proceed to its next witness, none other than Tom Horn. The defendant was determined to testify, feeling confident that he had the ability to sway the jury. A few days earlier, a *Rocky Mountain News* writer had an opportunity to ask him "how he felt" about his case. Horn replied enthusiastically, "Good!" "Now comes the chance I have been waiting for all along," he continued, "a chance to be heard myself." This was certainly the most critical moment in the trial, since the naïve and arrogant defendant would be subjected to cross-examination. One newsman rightly predicted the worst for Tom Horn. "The 'professional killer' is in a state of nervous weakness on account of months of suspense and confinement," observed this writer. Hence "a breaking down under cross examination would seem to be inevitable." When the defendant took the stand at 4:00 P.M., Friday, 17 October, John Lacey pointedly remarked that the purpose of the defendant's testimony was to explain away the confession to Joe LeFors. Horn proceeded to describe his movements from Sunday, 14 July 1901, through 17 July when he left Jim Miller's homestead. "I do not keep track of the dates or days," the defendant explained, "and I never would have kept track of these [days] if I had not been arrested." Horn said he rode a "very dark brown or black" horse branded CAP and carried a .30-30 Winchester rifle and field glasses. When asked if he had a sweater, Horn replied (very improbably) that he "never had a sweater," not even a coat.[35]

In describing his movements on the day he left Jim Miller's homestead (17 July 1901) the defendant said he crossed the South Chugwater Creek "below Nickell's ranch" and at no time came close to "this gate [where] Willie Nickell was killed." Horn crossed Sybille Creek near John Brae's ranch in order to examine other pastures in the neighborhood of his employer, the Iron Mountain Ranch Company. On the night of the 17th, he examined several pastures along Sybille Creek to surprise any would-be rustlers. He camped on "a little branch that puts into the Sabylle [sic, Sybille]" and, on the morning of the 18th (the day Willie Nickell was killed) he continued up this stream toward its headwaters. Since he had no "particular place to go" nor any particular schedule, the defendant explained, he spent much of the day in the vicinity of Marble Top (where Otto Plaga said he saw the detective). Horn camped out again that night (18 July) at the headwaters of the Sibylle. Since this was "very rough" country, Horn rode at what he called "a job trot," following no straight line. "I naturally go all over the country," he continued, "or else would not know what was going on." The following night the range rider slept out again and arrived at the Coble ranch about noon on Saturday, 20 July. Horn did not talk to anyone until he arrived at the Iron Mountain Ranch. He insisted that he rode only one horse, Cap. Later in the day, Horn rode John Coble's personal horse, Pacer, to Laramie, to keep an appointment. This animal, which "had a little touch of the wild" in him, the defendant explained, "wanted to go [run] and I didn't care to disappoint him." This would explain why Pacer was well lathered at the stable in Laramie.[36]

In regard to the defendant's conversation—not a confession, according to the defense—with Deputy U.S. Marshal Joe LeFors on Sunday, 12 January 1902, John Lacey instructed him to "just explain to the jury what it was that you and Lafors [sic] were doing, when you had that talk . . . that was over heard by Les Snow and Charlie Ohnhaus." "We were just joshing one another," said Horn, "throw[ing] boquets [sic] at one another." When Lacey asked, "What intention if any did you have in any way in the world to seriously admit that you had killed Willie Nickell?" Horn replied, "I never had anything to do with the killing of Willie Nickell; I never had any cause to kill him. And I never killed him. He [LeFors] was joshing me about it and I did not object. . . . There was nothing serious about the talk at all." The conversation "was all a josh all the way through," he insisted, and Horn maintained that he made no effort at "concealment" in talking with the lawman. Had Snow and Ohnhaus been present in the room with them rather than lurking in the adjacent room, he said, "I don't think that would have made any difference."[37]

In recalling these courtroom moments years later, T. Blake Kennedy asserted that the defense attorneys believed they had made "a pretty good case" that Tom Horn's remarks to LeFors "was just a braggadocio talking." In regard to Ohnhaus's transcript, the defense not only asserted that it was incomplete but insisted that the stenographer "had been directed" to avoid taking down (or had deleted) the names of prominent persons mentioned by Horn. Kennedy said he recommended that Tom Horn should testify by name to all the men with whom he had any business connections. His fellow attorneys rejected this suggestion, but Kennedy believed that such an exposé would have a very unsettling effect on the cattle barons. (Given Tom Horn's loyalty to his employers, he would probably have vetoed this suggestion.)[38]

Defense counsel followed with efforts to counter other prosecution testimony. In regard to the second, or Denver, confession, the defendant denied it outright. At that time, Horn insisted, he was in St. Luke's

Hospital with a broken jaw and could not "communicate with anybody except by writing." When Lacey asked if he left a blood-stained sweater at Matlock's store in Laramie, the defendant replied, "I never saw it before," and accused Laramie County lawmen of "jobbing" (framing) him. (In spite of the defendant's refusal to acknowledge the sweater, Sheriff Smalley and Undersheriff Proctor insisted that the prisoner admitted to them in jail that the garment was his.) When asked if he was in Laramie on 18 July 1901, Horn insisted that he did not arrive until two days later. At this point, a few minutes before 5:00 P.M., on Friday, 17 October, the court adjourned until the following day.[39]

For a fleeting moment, Horn and his attorneys could feel good about their case. In a mere fifty minutes, Horn had explained away (to his own satisfaction, at least) the various accusations of the prosecution. Even the *Daily Leader* agreed that the defendant presented a "convincing story." However, when Horn faced Prosecutor Walter Stoll's cross-examination the following morning, his fortunes changed dramatically and proceeded downhill until his execution thirteen months later. The prosecutor began by asking Horn if his "method of detecting the stealing of stock resulted in no necessity for . . . trials by a jury, witnesses in court, attorney's fees or anything of that kind." "Ordinarily not," responded the defendant frankly. To drive home to the jury the prosecution's point that in his capacity as a range detective Horn routinely bypassed the judicial system, Walter Stoll referred to the defendant's letter of 1 January 1902 to Deputy Marshal LeFors, in which he boasted that he suppressed livestock theft in Brown's Park "in one summer." Stoll went on to ask Horn if he meant that he employed legitimate methods—such as cooperating with county lawmen—or did this letter "refer to the well known fact that there were two men killed . . . while you were there?" When defense counsel objected to the prosecution's implication that the defendant had something to do with "men being killed," the bench sustained the objection.[40]

The wily prosecutor was not through with this line of questioning. He merely rephrased his question and asked what Horn meant by his remark about preventing livestock theft in Brown's Park? Horn glanced at John Lacey, who nodded his assent and said out loud, "Finish your answer." Horn then launched into a bizarre explanation in which he criticized stock detectives as a group of unprincipled loafers and scam artists who took their employers' money but performed no meaningful

services. Far from employing such underhanded methods, Horn assured
the court, he was an energetic and principled man who "remained continuously in the country" until he caught the thieves. "I associate myself
so directly with [the affected] neighborhood," he explained, "that . . .
if they steal I will catch them in the act." After catching a thief in the
act, the defendant added that the pilferer "gets out of it the best way
he can." The prosecutor then asked the defendant to explain another
sentence from his letter to LeFors: "I don't care how big or bad his men
are, or how many, I can handle them." Rustlers' threats "never cut
any figure with me," he added. When Stoll asked Horn if his work as
a detective was "always of the character you have described," the range
rider replied, "I think Mr. LeFors understood it that way." (Horn's ar-
rogance apparently knew no bounds. To exalt his place in a trade that
was highly questionable from the start showed terrible judgment.)[41]

Tom Horn betrayed a keen awareness of his reputation as a stock
detective on the witness stand, but to his disadvantage with the jury. In
an incredibly muddled fashion, he tried to explain: "A man like myself
must be very careful, or the numerous reports that are following a m[a]
n with the reputation I have gained . . . with the reputation I have I
know it necessitates my being extremely careful all the time; and I am
naturally careful to protect the interest of the people I work for." In
spite of such bravado, Horn was apparently vaguely aware that to attempt to defend his methods while under cross-examination was risky.
(One wonders to what degree John Lacey prepared his client for the
prosecutor's questions.) Furthermore, Horn violated a fundamental rule
in court testimony—to volunteer nothing. In response to one of the
prosecutor's questions, Horn insisted on giving a more detailed explanation, believing the jury would understand and be more sympathetic.
The more he talked, the more vulnerable he became; the more vulnerable he made himself by talking too much, the more the jury (and
spectators) saw that he was capable of killing for money. Thanks to his
propensity to boast and let his big ego run away with him, Horn thoroughly incriminated himself.[42]

The prosecutor returned to the subject of the detective's methods in
the field by referring to another sentence from Horn's letter to LeFors:
"I never yet let a cow thief get away from me unless he just jumped
up and got clear of the country." The prosecutor then asked Horn if
his "business was that of arresting the man." "I did not," the defendant

replied, going on to explain that no thief could "remain in the country without my being present." (Since his days in Arizona, Tom Horn had tried to affect educated speech, but he often ended up in a confused muddle of words.) To drive home the point that Horn did not arrest suspects (but disposed of them in some extralegal way), Stoll asked the defendant if he had arrested anyone other than the Langhoff gang in the Iron Mountain region. He answered bluntly, "No." To explain or justify his methods as a range detective, Horn distinguished between a freshly settled country and a more established community. "In a new country it would be necessary to arrest some of them," said Horn, but as soon as word spread that the livestock detective was present, "the stealing stops itself." To counter the prosecutor's implication that he employed illegal means, Tom Horn explained that his "preliminary experience [in the Langhoff case] weaned me" from the use of the courts. From that time on—the Langhoff trial, in January 1894—"I had more faith in getting [repossessing] the calf than in courts," he continued. While this last remark elicited a laugh from the spectators, the attempt at humor was ill-timed. The clumsy defendant even went so far as to admit that after his disappointment in the Langhoff case, a deputy sheriff's badge was "not necessary in a case of that kind."[43]

Prosecutor Stoll then asked the defendant to explain his reason for visiting Jim Miller's ranch just prior to the murder of Willie Nickell. "Was it to see whether somebody had stolen calves," he asked, "or was it to ride in among the people there and inspire terror by your presence?" Ignoring the clever way the prosecution planted the idea of inspiring terror in the minds of the jurors, Horn replied that since "Mr. Nickell had moved a bunch of sheep into that country," he wanted to ensure that the sheep were not "trespassing on any ground belonging to Mr. Coble." Horn declared that he had no particular reason for staying with the Millers over any other family except that the Miller place was at the "extreme" edge of his patrol area. In regard to Horn's movements before and after the murder of Willie Nickell, the prosecutor made much of the discrepancy between Horn's testimony during the coroner's inquest that his mission was to see if Kels Nickell's sheep were trespassing on Coble pastures and his statement later that he was searching for unbranded calves. In another contradiction, Horn said at the inquest that, on Wednesday, 17 July 1901, he was eight or nine miles away from the Nickell residence, but he testified at the trial that he was only three or four miles away. Horn objected, insisting that the stenographic record from the coroner's inquest was inaccurate. "The fact that I was associated with it [the Nickell murder] in the minds of some people at least before I was arrested," continued Horn, "has certainly had a tendency to refresh my mind on the subject." Nevertheless, he failed to convey a very clear recollection of these July days. When the defendant insisted that he did not meet a single person on his ride from the Miller place to Coble's ranch, nor on his subsequent trip to Laramie, the prosecutor reacted with obvious incredulity.[44]

A story later circulated that Tom Horn made a particularly self-incriminating remark on the witness stand in regard to the time necessary for a good horseman to ride from the Nickell murder site to Laramie. According to this story Horn said that "he thought a good man and horse" could make this ride in four hours. If the defendant did volunteer this information on the witness stand, he was playing into the hands of the prosecution's assertion that Horn rode rapidly from the murder site to Laramie in order to establish an alibi. Far from helping his own case, Tom Horn was testifying for the prosecution! However, there is no indication in the trial transcript that Horn made such an admission. Many years later, T. Blake Kennedy asserted that the defendant's actual remark concerned the time required to ride from the Nickell place, not to Laramie, but to the point on Marble Top where Otto Plaga allegedly saw Horn. Yet Kennedy concluded that Horn's "passion for 'braggadocio'" on this occasion hurt their case. One of the defendant's biggest faux pas was in inadvertently contradicting Otto Plaga's alibi for him. While Plaga said he saw Horn about 8:00 on the morning of the murder, the stock detective informed the court that he did not reach Plaga's vicinity until late in the day.[45]

The prosecutor exposed other aspects of Tom Horn's character that were detrimental to the range detective's case. In regard to the Denver confession, Stoll asked the defendant if he was sober enough at that time "to remember whether you had these conversations?" "I remember everything that occurred to me in my life," Horn replied confidently. (If Horn truly remembered everything he said, a juror might conclude that he was fully aware of his confession to Joe LeFors.) In regard to Horn's boast to LeFors that he had "paired off" with Glendolene Kimmell—implying that he had had sex with her—the *Rocky Mountain News* observed that John Lacey had obviously cautioned the defendant "to correct the damaging impression he had made by his former slurs upon women." When Stoll "pointedly asked for this lady's name," added the *News,* Horn "assumed a sheepish, cunning smile that was too knowing for the occasion." "Well, I talked most with the school teacher, Miss Kimmell," the defendant replied with some reluctance, and "with a twinkle of his black eyes and a grin that would have made Miss Kimmell turn state's evidence on the spot."[46]

Walter Stoll's remorseless examination of Tom Horn's confession, which occupied an entire afternoon, "was a frightful ordeal," observed the *Daily Leader.* It left him "perceptibly restless." To a *Rocky Mountain News* reporter, the most surprising result of this grilling was that the defendant "made no attempt to deny" his statements to Joe LeFors. However, Horn's insistence that his words were merely lighthearted banter—even though the subject was man killing—was difficult for onlookers to swallow. By placing Tom Horn in the witness chair, John Lacey was taking a great risk. In so doing, he defied one of the most hallowed tenets of his profession: "He that pleads his own case has a fool for a client." Certainly, Tom Horn fulfilled this expectation.[47]

The members of the defense team were well aware of the risk, given Tom Horn's big ego and tendency to brag. In November 1903, Joe LeFors declared that Edward T. Clark, one of Horn's attorneys, said he "was opposed to Horn's going on the stand and testifying, but that Lacey and Burke insisted upon it." Clark believed "Horn had got just what he deserved," according to LeFors. Edward Slack of the *Daily Leader* agreed and concluded that the defendant, noted for talkativeness, failed "to appreciate the delicacy of his situation" and was "an easy mark for the prosecution." In spite of the attempts of his attorneys "to restrain" him on the witness stand, Horn indiscreetly "slopped over," continued Slack, "telling all that was necessary and a great deal more." The defendant should learn "to keep his mouth closed," the *Leader* editor concluded in understatement. The *Denver Post* pointed out that Horn, in an incredibly damaging moment, failed to provide testimony that supported Otto Plaga's alibi for him, noting that Horn "would not say that he saw Plaga or was at the point named by him at the time." Did this omission result from the defendant's dull-wittedness or from lack of proper coaching by defense counsel?

Although Horn insisted on taking the witness stand, Lacey and his associates did not have to give their consent. They were probably driven to do so by desperation. Since Judge Scott had admitted Horn's confession into evidence, they faced an uphill (perhaps impossible) task from the outset. They were prompted to gamble, and lost. Even if the defendant had been inebriated when he made his incriminating admissions to Joe LeFors, jurors would find it hard to believe that he was so addled as to be unaware of his statements. An old adage (attributed to the cowboy artist Charles Russell) holds that "If you want to get to know a man, get him drunk." The defendant insisted, after all, that even when drinking, "I remember everything that occurred to me in my life."[48]

Newspapers were divided on the decision to place Horn on the stand. One reporter believed that the defendant "showed the advantages of rather more than the average mentality" during his testimony. Not only did Horn present "rational accounts of his doings and whereabouts" in the days around the Willie Nickell murder, said the *Salt Lake Tribune,* but John Lacey clearly stole the prosecution's thunder "by taking up the confession piecemeal and having Horn acknowledge the whole thing, laughing it off as so much cowboy josh." In spite of Stoll's fearsome cross-examination, continued this account, Horn "stood the terrible ordeal . . . without a sign of breaking down." The *Rocky Mountain News* noted that "so long as Horn was serious and apparently ingenuous, he made the best of impressions." But he "made the mistake of lapsing into a humorous vein," continued the *News,* "and immediately lost ground." A murder trial "is too grave a one for jesting."[49]

As the trial continued, Tom Horn began to betray signs of stress. Early in the trial, the defendant "laughed heartily" at some testimony. However, he "quailed" when Joe LeFors testified, said W. H. Emmons of the *Denver Post,* and no longer evinced his usual "supreme confidence and nerve" after Walter Stoll's grilling. When Stoll drew from the defendant the fact that "his business was 'man killing,'" continued Emmons, Horn "was a very different person." Emmons and fellow journalist J. Emerson Smith both scoffed when Horn testified that he had never killed a man. "This man, the pride of whose life had been to be pointed out as the notorious killer . . . [and] hired wolf of the cattle barons of Wyoming," they remarked, "pleaded earnestly . . . that he was only a miserable braggart." For Tom Horn to be acquitted, these *Post* writers pointed out, the jurors would not only have to believe that "he is one of the most remarkable liars ever known," but that he "is the victim of an unparalleled mania to tell lies about committing murders."

In summing up defense counsel's overall strategy, these reporters asserted that John Lacey's "defense of Horn is really that telling stories of murder is as necessary to him as opium is to the opium fiend and that he couldn't help it [bragging]."[50]

This trial was not only an ordeal for the defendant but for Kels Nickell and his family. The elder Nickell exhibited remarkably eccentric behavior throughout the proceedings, going so far as to assault two prospective jurors. However, Judge Scott demonstrated a generous disposition toward the grieving father and permitted him to sit in on the trial even though he was called as a witness. When the prosecutor read aloud the "part of the confession where Horn told LeFors that he had received $2,100 for three deaths and shooting five times at Kels Nickell," a *Rocky Mountain News* reporter noted that Nickell's "eyes were fixed upon the prisoner . . . [and] the fingers of one hand opening and closing spasmodically." When Horn took the witness stand, Nickell stepped inside the bar and occupied Horn's chair in order to be "face to face with Horn." When Sheriff Smalley and his deputies suddenly realized that the angry man might try to kill the defendant, a bailiff quickly escorted Nickell to a far corner of the courtroom.[51]

On Monday morning, 20 October 1902, John Lacey surprised the court by abruptly announcing, "'The defense rests, your honor.'" The remarkably short duration of the defense of the infamous range detective was indeed astounding. The fact that Lacey could find only one (alleged) alibi witness for the defendant was a telling point. Perhaps the defense attorneys realized that they lacked the evidence for a long trial and thought it was best to conclude their case quickly, thus giving the jury less time to contemplate the evidence. In the absence of any other telling evidence, Lacey staked everything on the testimony of Tom Horn.[52]

Later this same morning, Walter Stoll began the final phase of the trial, the state's rebuttal. The prosecutor recalled Joe LeFors in order to give him an opportunity to refute Tom Horn's allegation that LeFors proposed that they jointly frame a third party for the Willie Nickell murder and split the reward. When John Lacey objected to the admissibility of this testimony, he set off "one of the most fiercely contested [battles] of the trial," said the *Daily Leader,* noting that if Horn lied about this conversation, "the inference was that Horn had lied about other matters." After Judge Scott ordered the jury from the courtroom, the debate continued until Scott ruled in favor of the prosecution. (Apparently, LeFors remained in the witness chair during this verbal confrontation.) Continuing his testimony, LeFors denied that "any such conversation" ever took place. Walter Stoll then asked LeFors to recall any conversations he had had with the defendant before Horn's arrest on 12 January 1902. In reply LeFors said he had two conversations with Horn in which he expressed curiosity about the investigation into the attempt on Kels Nickell's life. Suddenly, LeFors dropped a bombshell among the spectators. In effect, he accused the defendant of making another confession during their second conversation, having tricked Horn into incriminating himself much as he did in January 1902. At this point Lacey objected, arguing that LeFors's testimony had "no connection" with the present case. When Judge Scott overruled, LeFors testified that Horn admitted taking shots at Kels Nickell and remarked, "You ought to have saw him run and yell like a Comanche Indian." In spite of defense counsel's repeated objections, Judge Scott ordered LeFors to continue his testimony. When the prosecutor asked whether there was "any indication either in the tone of voice, manner or otherwise of the defendant, as to his statements relating to the Willie Nickell killing, being a josh or joke?" LeFors replied, "It was perfectly sincere."[53]

The state then introduced six witnesses for the purpose of undermining the reputation of Otto Plaga, who provided Tom Horn with an alibi. "If Plaga's testimony could be broken down," as the *Daily Leader* remarked, "the case of the defense would be materially weakened." While this testimony worked to the prosecution's benefit overall, defense counsel contested it in "another fierce legal battle," according to the *Leader*. On the question of the date of Tom Horn's arrival in Laramie—18 July or 20 July 1901—additional evidence was given by Justice of the Peace Mortimer N. Grant and City Marshal Ernest B. Davies, both of Laramie. Both testified that they were present in Grant's office on 6 October 1901 when Frank Stone, an employee of John Coble, asserted that he had seen Tom Horn in Laramie on 19 July. Stone reported that he and Horn had drinks that same evening. Stone had earlier testified that the defendant did not arrive in Laramie until the following day. Davies testified that he not only heard Stone say he drank with the defendant on 19 July but also saw Horn with his own eyes in Laramie that day. This statement impeached the testimony of Frank Stone. All efforts by defense attorney Timothy Burke to undermine the credibility of the prosecution's witnesses failed. When Prosecutor Stoll resumed his questioning, Davies explained his theory that while John Coble had sent Frank Stone to Laramie "to prove an alibi" for Tom Horn, Stone lost his nerve and hesitated to go through with the plot. Unfortunately, Davies admitted, he did not realize the full implications of this incident at the time. A last-ditch effort of defense counsel to prove that Stone was drunk when he appeared before Justice of the Peace Grant also failed.[54]

The bench then gave defense counsel an opportunity to present its surrebuttal (the plaintiff's reply to the state's rebuttal). To counter the prosecution's attack upon Otto Plaga, John Lacey presented ten witnesses, all of whom testified to Plaga's "truth and veracity": Thornton Biggs, foreman for Ora Haley, testified that Otto Plaga's reputation was "good"; Sam Moore, a detective for the Swan Land and Cattle Company (Tom Horn's former employer) echoed this sentiment; William Clay, the Iron Mountain rancher who permitted Tom Horn to bunk at his ranch, had heard nothing "against his [Plaga's] character"; Duncan Clark presented similar statements. In rebuttal Prosecutor Stoll, who obviously took no stock in these witnesses, pointed out that all of them had some connection with the region where Tom Horn plied his trade.[55]

At 2:20 P.M., Monday, 20 October 1902, this widely publicized trial, which some attorneys had predicted would last four to six weeks, was over with only eight days of testimony! How could this be? "The closing of the evidence in the Horn case was a surprise to most people," observed one Cheyenne newsman in understatement, "as it was expected several days more would be consumed before the case went to the jury."[56]

CHAPTER 14

The Verdict

Trials were a popular form of entertainment on the frontier, and the Tom Horn trial gratified the audience's expectations in spite of its brevity. Cheyenne "is filling up," said a Cheyenne dispatch to the *Denver Republican* on 7 October 1902. By the opening day of the trial, only three days away, this paper predicted, "there will be several hundred outsiders in Cheyenne either to take part in the trial or to witness the proceedings." Numerous newspaper representatives had already arrived, some of them from the East. The city was already "assuming a gala appearance," observed the *Denver Post,* "as if a festival . . . was about to be rung up." Hotels soon filled up, while saloons and gambling dens ran at full tilt. "Bets of $50 and $100 are being made at even money that Horn will not hang," said one journalist. Since Tom Horn was believed to know many dark secrets about the cattle barons, street talk held that they "were sprouting goose flesh as big as oranges," recalled Andrew Roedel, whose druggist father was a friend of the range detective. Would Horn talk to save his life? No one knew.[1]

When the proceedings began on 10 October, bailiffs had their hands full with more than a hundred witnesses and a room overflowing with spectators. This scene "could not be duplicated in any other court room in the country," according to J. Emerson Smith of the *Denver Post.* Cowboys, who were "very much in evidence," wrote Smith, were dressed in typical range garb—"soft flannel shirts, the boots, gay neck cloths and sombreros—while others sported fresh store bought clothing." So many women and children were present, said one observer, that they pressed "the men back into the standing room against the wall." While Smith believed many females attended merely out of "morbid curiosity," a *Daily Leader* newsman credited them with being "the most attentive and interested spectators." Some women who attended every day—dubbed "trial fiends" by newsmen—took only brief lunch breaks in order to reclaim their seats for the afternoon session. When "a well-featured woman with a small sombrero hat and veil" took a seat beside John Coble, Tom Horn's good friend, the place was suddenly abuzz. As events transpired, they were not acquainted. "Not far from Coble sat three young people who did nothing but watch and chew gum," Smith continued. In the absence of any vacant seats, a mother with two grown daughters perched precariously on a window sill. Some women exhibited "undisguised aversion and hate" for Tom Horn. "The fear of Horn still lingers," continued J. Emerson Smith, and "the man's personality and the dark story behind him truly overshadows the entire county." When the prosecution presented "the blood-stained shirt" of Willie Nickell, said this correspondent, "the mothers in the court room fairly blazed."[2]

The presence of children was cause for some concern. Many youngsters considered Tom Horn "a true western hero," observed the *Denver Post*'s W. H. Emmons, even more important than dime novel subjects like Jesse James and Cole Younger. One headline captured this concern: "Courtroom Crowded by Morbid Youngsters Eager to Worship the Killer." A few eager children even wormed their way inside the railing that separated the spectators from court officers. Since some of the evidence presented contained expletives—Tom Horn's confession being the most explicit—the children were exposed to "the vilest oaths." On the witness stand, Horn had to admit, "'I use profanity in a general way.'" When Prosecutor Stoll read parts of Horn's confession aloud, one correspondent observed that the wide-eyed children "enjoyed it as much as a Dead-Eye Dick novel." This unwholesome spectacle finally persuaded Judge Scott "to clear the court room of children."[3]

The presence of many strangers in the courtroom caused Sheriff Edwin Smalley concern. He watched them closely, not knowing what to expect. Smalley had cause for worry. Horn was an object of curiosity to strangers, but he also had supporters from outlying ranches. Many were "young men who have known the livestock detective for years . . . and who regard him as a hero," according to one newsman. These ranch hands "know little of life outside of the range," he continued, and often "lose sight of commandments of the laws." These young cowhands, who were "loud spoken in their conviction that Horn is guiltless," added this observer, objected so openly to the testimony of a prosecution witness on one occasion that "the bailiff had to rap for order."[4]

In such a boisterous atmosphere, safeguarding the witnesses and jury was one of the sheriff's primary duties. While Smalley tried to ensure their "physical comfort," the court instructed him to attempt to close "every loophole of leakage." Witnesses "for the defense are kept in one dwelling," one observer noted, "while those for the prosecution are quartered in another." Even though Judge Scott ordered "the jury to keep to themselves and not to discuss the case with any one," the sheriff found it well nigh impossible to completely sequester them, especially when they took their meals at the Inter Ocean Hotel restaurant. Nor was he always able to control the atmosphere in the courtroom. Reporters and newspaper artists crowded the floor. Additional tables were necessary to accommodate them. After the jurors complained about the artists' intrusions, Judge Scott ejected all artists. Correspondents were permitted to remain. The October weather also posed a problem. On cold days, "the big stove in the center of the court room was red hot," said one reporter; on warm days, windows had to be opened, thus exposing the proceedings to outside noise. When a nearby store caught on fire, the "great bell on the fire house tower rang twenty-four—two and four twice—crashing through the gray afternoon," reported the *Denver Post*. A fire would ordinarily draw a crowd, but not on this occasion. All eyes remained fixed on John Lacey, who was holding forth at that moment.[5]

Much to the dismay of his attorneys, Tom Horn's conduct in the courtroom seriously hurt his case. While Horn had a haircut and was neatly dressed, he was much too nonchalant for such a grim event. He slouched in his chair, fingered his suspenders, and smiled at acquaintances among the spectators. On one occasion, a "pleasant smile" even crossed the defendant's face at an inopportune time during the testimony. On another, he laughed out loud at a witness's remarks. When the judge gave the jury permission to attend church services, the defendant, who had little use for religion, "lay back . . . and laughed silently."

As one observer noted, everything that took place in the courtroom was too important for such cavalier behavior[6]

In addition to the defendant, two other individuals associated with Tom Horn's case were subjects of considerable interest. Although John Coble seldom attended, he attracted much attention when present. On one occasion, he was seated in the front row, sporting a red bow tie—when the sun's rays fell across his brow illuminating "the bald spot on his head." On another visit, a bailiff had to remove a revolver from Coble's coat pocket. When Coble did not attend, which was most of the time, his foreman, Charles Irwin, served as his representative. Glendolene Myrtle Kimmell, Tom Horn's alleged girl friend, also attracted attention—by her absence. While she testified on behalf of Jim Miller and his sons at the Willie Nickell inquest, street talk held that she would appear at Tom Horn's trial as a prosecution witness. This was an unwelcome surprise for the defense attorneys. The defendant's crude remark in his confession about "pairing off" with Kimmell was said to have discouraged her from testifying on his behalf. Prosecutor Stoll made an effort to find her and arrange for her testimony. (One newspaper alleged that the schoolteacher "was discovered" in a Denver saloon. There was no truth to this report.) Stoll eventually located her in Kansas City, Missouri, but she did not testify. The reason is not clear.[7]

Outside the courtroom, witnesses and other interested parties tried to find ways to pass the time. Fortunately, Edward "Doc" Moore, a Sybille Creek rancher, had his fiddle. While the attorneys held sway in the courtroom, Moore fiddled while the crowd danced away their woes. Doc's fiddle was "the best thing yet for us fellows that's got to stay outside here," said one grateful bystander. When persons inside the courtroom were observed tapping their feet to Moore's music, a bailiff had to close the window. When someone asked Doc Moore if he knew Tom Horn, he admitted that he had only "heard of him."[8]

Although public interest in the trial remained strong, attendance began to decline as the proceedings wore on. "A majority of the witnesses . . . have left the city," said the *Daily Leader* on 15 October. Even Mrs. Addie Whitely, the most ardent of the trial fiends, was conspicuously absent one day. However, attendance began to pick up again when the attorneys began their final arguments.

Kels Nickell, who attended every session in spite of the demands of his night watchman's job with the Union Pacific, continued on his unpredictable way. On the night of 14 October, he assaulted defense witness Andrew Whitman, whom Nickell accused of having hosted a meeting in the Iron Mountain community ten years earlier "to decide whether or not Nickell should be put out of the way." When Whitman made the mistake of walking across railroad property, Nickell used his billy club on the unfortunate man. "I tried to break his neck," Nickell admitted excitedly. "That's what I wanted to do, but he dodged and ran."[9]

Even after testimony concluded on Monday, 20 October, Tom Horn had many more uncomfortable moments to look forward to. On the following day, Judge Scott began his instructions to the jury—including thirteen points for the state and fifteen for the defense. (Since the number 13 had been conspicuous in Tom Horn's case, the fact that Scott presented thirteen instructions for the prosecution was not lost on superstitious spectators.) The possible findings included first or second degree murder, said Judge Scott, as well as acquittal. He then instructed the panel as to "what must be taken into consideration to prove Horn guilty of either degree of murder." "The testimony of the defendant was to be considered just as any other witness's testimony," said Scott. "The confession was mentioned," according to one reporter, "and reasons given for [its] truthfulness and corroboration." In section 11 the judge discussed the defendant's alibi and outlined "the conditions to prove an alibi." He explained the legal facts of burden of proof and what constituted reasonable doubt. Judge Scott's instructions, which consumed thirty-five minutes, included "all the red tape of legal documents," according to this same observer.[10]

The summations of the prosecution and defense were extremely important, as in all criminal trials. Each attorney had the opportunity to fit the pieces of evidence together from the point of view of his side, synthesize the evidence, and present a clear picture of guilt or innocence as the case might be. Since the summations also gave the attorneys an opportunity to exercise their speaking abilities, the lawyer with the greatest oratorical skills might lose a case during the presentation of testimony, but win it back during summation. The opportunities afforded by the summation could constitute a retrial of the accused. In the Tom Horn trial, a *Rocky Mountain News* correspondent concluded that, far from relying upon the testimony of witnesses, both the prosecution and the defense would "depend largely on the address to the jury" to plead their respective cases. (If this was true, neither side had much confidence in its evidence as presented.)[11]

Walter Stoll, who was noted for his oratorical flights, began the state's final argument at 11:00 A.M., on Tuesday, 21 October. With the exception of a brief lunch break, he spoke until 5:30 that afternoon. After setting the stage for the murder of Willie Nickell, which had so shocked "the moral sense of the community," he went on to impress upon the jurors that they were "as essential . . . as the judge, the prosecuting attorney or the sheriff" in this case. He reminded the panel that since "Wyoming has been afflicted for years with a series of assassinations," the citizenry feared that the murder of Willie Nickell, "another private assassination," represented a continuation of this reprehensible practice. Such crimes "retard the development of the state," added the prosecutor, and they must be punished. In this particular case, Stoll said pointedly, "facts and circumstances pointed in a certain direction, and Tom Horn was arrested as the result."[12]

Stoll then began to outline various aspects of the case from the prosecution's point of view:

> What was Horn doing in the vicinity of the Nickell house? He was not there at the time of the shooting, so he says. At 7 o'clock on that day [18 July 1901] he claims to have been a long way off. But he did go to Nickell's. Why, he testified at the coroner's inquest, and not very clearly, but now he knows many things. He has had time to go over the records, and he knows the light to be thrown on his every action, because of his interest in it.[13]

The prosecutor continued to point out contradictions between the defendant's testimony at the coroner's inquest and his most recent testimony. The *Daily Leader* gave the following account of his speech:

> Horn said he was following up his employer's interest in looking after calves. Horn's employers, said Stoll, were the Bosler people and not the Two-Bar concern, and why was he not attending to his business? He took a distinct route, a very narrow compass, to Nickell's ranch. His object was to get to Kels Nickell's. The season was short and he said he had to look after the

calves. Then why did he stay in Laramie ten days if time was so
valuable? Ten days is a long time when your employers' calves
are being stolen. I say there was an object other than looking
after calves. He said he had to look after the sheep. Whose
sheep? Kels Nickell's.[14]

After the lunch break, Walter Stoll continued his review of Tom
Horn's movements just prior to the murder. According to the *Rocky
Mountain News*,

He stated Horn was at the Colcord place at about the time
Apperson, Nickell and Mahoney were there, and that if any
significance were to be attached to it, it was that he [Horn] was
near Nickell['s], [but] that at the inquest Horn said he was on
the divide, at the head of the chug [Chugwater Creek], and not
on the stream, in refutation of his and [Otto] Plaga's statements
that he was near Fitzmorris' place on Thursday [18 July 1901].
. . . In this case, you are at liberty to disregard the defendant's
testimony, but you may give it what weight you think it carries.
When we consider the route he took we must think he wanted
to be near Kels P. Nickell, and that calves had nothing to do
with it.

The prosecutor pointedly attacked Otto Plaga's alibi for the defendant
and reminded the jurors that "the alibi statements come from sources
that are friendly to Horn." Stoll "scorched" Plaga's testimony, according to the *Rocky Mountain News*. Using the map entered into evidence,
the prosecutor "measured the distance from Nickell's gate to Marble
Top," the place where Plaga allegedly saw Tom Horn. Stoll "found it
to be thirteen miles, not twenty-five, as testified to by Plaga." He declared that this distance "could easily be ridden between the time of the
killing [7:00 A.M.] and the hour when Plaga saw Horn. In other words,
the alibi was not an alibi, in the state's estimation.[15]

The district attorney also addressed the defendant's confession to
Deputy Marshal LeFors:

Usually doubt is thrown on a confession, because a witness
speaks from recollection, but . . . this could have no aspersions

cast upon it, because it was taken in shorthand. Its genuineness was admitted by the defense. We read of confessions every day. They are almost always made under the influence of liquor, which seems to prompt the consciences of the murderers. Secret murders are brought to light by Almighty God.

In reviewing the confession, the prosecutor delivered a "terrible arraignment of the defendant," according to the *Daily Leader:*

> Little by little he showed why Horn was telling the truth; how he professed to know nothing regarding the circumstances surrounding the murder and yet went on to give the details of the awful crime which fitted with extraordinary nicety into the facts surrounding the murder as brought by witnesses. "I do not profess to know all of the working of the unseen laws of nature," said the able prosecutor in his brilliant per-oration [*sic*]. . . . "There is some unseen, unknown force in human nature that invariably brings to light, through confessions, crimes which could never become known in other ways. . . . It was this force which, operating in a way which only the Almighty God can explain, that compelled the man that stood in that big draw at the right of the gate, when he was speaking to Joe Lefors, to confess the murder of the boy whose blood was upon his hands."[16]

Stoll went on to explain "Why Horn Told the Truth":

> No other man upon the face of the world could have described that crime as did the one who confessed to Joe Lefors. No one but he could have known that the man who fired the fatal shots was 300 yards away, as by actual measurement, the big draw in which Horn said he was stationed, was just 10 feet less than 300 yards from the gate where the boy was killed. No one but Horn could have known that the boy ran back towards the gate; no one but he could have known that a rock was placed under the lad's head; no one but the guilty man could have known that the lad was "cut off at the gate," as it was not until afterwards that it came out that a pool of blood was discovered at that

point showing where the boy was first struck by the bullets. No one but Tom Horn could have known that it was "just before the killing of the kid that I met the school teacher [at] Miller's."

When the prosecutor finally closed his five-hour summation at 4:45 P.M., he did so with "a burst of eloquence." "Something always impels an assassin to confess," he remarked; "in this case it was the voice of Willie Nickell, striving to tell his father who had brutally slain him." After listening to Walter Stoll's summation, the *Daily Leader* concluded that this "masterpiece of forensic oratory" actually added new significance to the state's case. Regardless of the decision that the jury might reach, continued this writer, Walter Stoll was a "faithful" public servant whose "meager salary" was a poor reward for his efforts.[17]

Defense attorney Timothy F. Burke was scheduled to follow Prosecutor Stoll on Wednesday, 22 October, but he was unable to appear until later that morning. Assistant prosecutor Clyde M. Watts, the next person in the rotation, spoke instead. Watts, who reminded the jury that the state's case "rests upon the confession of Tom Horn," spoke "of the remarkableness of the fact that Horn, when he did confess to the crime, would do so to a man [Joe LeFors] whom Horn believed was like himself." If the defendant "lied to Joe Lefors, as he admits he did," continued Watts, "then is it not a reasonable presumption that he would lie on the witness stand with his life hanging in the balance?" Watts also clarified the state's position on the date of Tom Horn's confession to Frank Mulock and two other "creditable witnesses" in Denver, even though the defense denied that it ever occurred. Watts argued that Horn made this confession "in the week before" the Festival of the Mountain and Plain, that is, on the evening of 29 September 1901. This was correct; Horn's jaw was broken the following evening, so he could not have confessed any later.[18]

Horace Waldo Moore, Jr., whom Kels Nickell retained at his own expense to assist the prosecution, summarized the state's case in a thirty-minute address. The most notable aspects of Moore's remarks, said the *Rocky Mountain News,* were his melodramatic "flights of oratory" in which he painted "a graphic picture of [Kels] Nickell's pretty little home nestling amidst the rocks and pines in that [Iron Mountain] wilderness, [and] how the murdered lad was a product of this home." Tom Horn, the assassin, disrupted this bucolic scene by snuffing out "the life of the innocent boy." One listener concluded that Moore was using this opportunity to run for Walter Stoll's position of county prosecutor.[19]

Just after 10 A.M., Timothy Burke began the defense's summation by reminding the jurors that at the outset of this trial they promised to require "strong" circumstantial evidence before they would convict. Burke, who was also an accomplished "pulpit orator," admonished the jury to remember that "it is better that 100 guilty men escape" than to convict on insufficient evidence. Nor had the state shown motive. Hate is "the mother of murders," he declared, and Tom Horn had no reason "to hate that boy." This constituted "reasonable doubt No. 1," he said. In challenging the authenticity of the Denver confession, Timothy Burke went so far as to define the term for the jury: "Confession is an unloading of sin from a sick mind and is not braggadocio." Confession "is done seriously," Burke continued, "with the desire of having the identity of the criminal to be known." Tom Horn's alleged confession did not match these conditions. Burke also pointed out "the language alleged to have been used by Horn in his Denver statements is identical with that used by him in his statements to Lefors" and accused Mulock of taking "the words from newspaper reports." In Burke's estimation, Mulock and his two compatriots were totally unreliable, the prosecution having "raked the slums of Denver" to find them. The state's recourse to perjured testimony constituted "reasonable doubt No. 2," said Burke.[20]

In regard to the defendant's confession to LeFors, Burke reminded the jurors that the defense had presented numerous witnesses who testified that Tom Horn was "half shot" at this time. "Are you going to take his life because he talked when drunk," asked Burke? In "impassioned" tones, Burke characterized the confession as a pack of "yarns," in which each man tried to spin "the biggest yarn." The fact that stenographer Charles Ohnhaus refrained from recording their tales "indicates the men were simply telling yarns," added Burke. In an effort to tweak the heartstrings of the jurors, Burke urged them, as they arrived at a decision, to "think of the old mother four score years and ten waiting in her New York home for the defendant to come back." (Mary Horn, who had never lived in New York, was in her eighties and lived in British Columbia.) In regard to the state's evidence concerning the site where Willie Nickell was killed, Burke argued that the draw, in which Tom Horn was said to have concealed himself, had a 120 foot precipice.

If the assassin was positioned on this high point, he could hardly cut off his victim's escape. Furthermore, Horn liked to "get close" to his victim, and this ledge was 300 yards from the fence gap. If Horn was barefooted at the murder scene, his feet showed no signs of it a few days later. If Tom Horn rode into Laramie four hours after the murder, on 18 July 1901, he could not have waited around for three hours (the time for blood to coagulate on Willie Nickell's body) before turning him over. It was absurd to think that Horn would leave an incriminating piece of evidence such as a blood-stained sweater in a Laramie shoe store. In regard to the alibi provided by Otto Plaga, Burke asserted that when Horn "says he did not see Plaga on the morning of the murder," such an admission "is evidence of innocence."[21]

At 4:05 P.M. Chief Defense Counsel John Lacey began his summation. He spoke until adjournment one hour later and continued for three hours the following morning. Although "not an eloquent orator in the general acceptance of the term," said the *Daily Leader*, Lacey delivered "keen, incisive statements that have . . . as great an effect in influencing opinions of men" as "flights of oratory" (such as Walter Stoll delivered). Lacey reminded the jury that the defense was not required to prove Tom Horn innocent, but that "the state must prove him guilty beyond a reasonable doubt and to a moral certainty." In regard to the defendant's confession to Joe LeFors, Lacey argued that "a confession must be supplemented by a perfect chain of circumstantial evidence, perfect in every link." Any "flaw in the chain must necessarily give rise to the creation of a reasonable doubt," he continued.

Continuing on the matter of the confession, Lacey "showed how the counsel for the state used the wrong words in quoting Horn's supposition as to the way the boy was killed" and insisted that this error "makes a material difference." "Horn, as shown by his evidence, said the big draw in which he assumed the man [assassin] was secreted was north of the gate when in fact in going to Iron Mountain Willie Nickell went south." "This shows the supposition of Horn's did not fit the facts," Lacey remarked. (It was no surprise when, suddenly, a voice rang out from the audience. "'There is only one draw there," shouted Kels Nickell, who disagreed with defense counsel.) In concluding his analysis of the confession, Lacey remarked pointedly, "The prosecution had a keen, bright man [LeFors] trying to trap a half-drunken friend." (Of course, Horn and LeFors were not friends.) Furthermore, Lacey

insisted that "Horn didn't state new facts" in his confession. The fact
that the imprint of a rifle butt was found near the murder scene but not
in the draw contradicted Tom Horn's assertion that the killer waited in
a draw. "This assumption does not conform to the material facts in the
case," continued Lacey, "and must give rise to a reasonable doubt." In
commenting on the Denver confession, Lacey used this opportunity to
take a jab at Walter Stoll: "I did not suppose such a stout counsel would
claim anything for the Denver testimony."[22]

The chief defense counsel attempted to insinuate into his summation
a portion of the defense's argument that Judge Scott forbade during
the trial. Since "the court had shut him off when he tried to introduce" pertinent testimony as to feuding between neighbors in the Iron
Mountain community, remarked Lacey, "consequently it was not in-
cumbent upon the defense to prove who committed the crime." At this
point, the chief defense counsel "played one of its best trump cards,"
according to the *Daily Leader,* arguing that footprints found near Willie
Nickell's body were "of a size between 6 and 7." The defendant's feet
did not fit these prints. In an especially bold statement, Lacey implied
that one witness in the trial—he did not provide a name—"wore shoes
of this size." As the *Leader* was quick to point out, Lacey implied that
"he meant Victor Miller." Lacey pooh-poohed the state's expert witnesses who argued that the bullets that killed Willie Nickell were the
same size (.30 caliber) as Tom Horn's rifle. Even if this were true, Lacey
pointed out, many Iron Mountain residents possessed such weapons.
Furthermore, the evidence showed that the lethal bullets were "leaden
bullets fired by black powder." Horn's rifle fired the newer smokeless
powder cartridges. In regard to the blue sweater, Lacey observed the
"the two shoemakers at Laramie couldn't say positively that it was Horn
who left the sweater." Given the divergence of views as to whether the
defendant arrived in Laramie on the 18th or 20th, John Lacey could ask
if the jury did not have a reasonable doubt as to the prosecution's assertion. In regard to Otto Plaga's alibi for the defendant, Lacey pointed
out the while five witnesses said his reputation was bad, ten men had
declared that "his reputation for veracity was good."

In reviewing Lacey's summation, the *Rocky Mountain News* was struck
by his manner of delivery. Lacey "would drawl out in the most biting
sarcasm, 'and the state asks you to hang a man on that evidence?'" He
would refer snidely to the "fine tooth comb process of the state." A

Daily Leader reporter was so impressed that he believed that the chief defense counsel "practically established the fact that Tom Horn could not commit the crime." One spectator was moved to exclaim after Lacey's summation, "Ain't he the queen of the bunch?"[23]

At 2:00 P.M., on 23 October, Walter Stoll took the floor and began the state's closing argument, a refutation of the defense's summation. Stoll expressed sympathy for the jurors, who were very tired by this time, and reminded them that they were sitting in judgment in a case that transcended the murder of Willie Nickell. "The people of this county have a right to demand that a stop be put to the epidemic of crime which has stalked abroad in our community," he declared. In an oblique reflection of his concern that one (unnamed) juror might try to bring about a hung jury, Stoll urged that "if a majority of you are in favor of a conviction the opinion of the majority should not be changed by the opinion of the minority." "There are but three material allegations . . . which must be proved beyond a reasonable doubt," he asserted: "Willie Nickell was killed; the crime took place in Laramie County; and the defendant committed that murder." In regard to Tom Horn's movements on the day of the murder of Willie Nickell, the prosecutor insisted that it made no difference to him if Tom Horn appeared at the Bosler ranch on 20 July. If Horn did so, it was after he had made his alibi ride into Laramie two days earlier, on 18 July 1901. Concerning Horn's confession to LeFors, the prosecutor remarked: "God pity this country . . . when the word of a criminal on trial for his life is taken before that of an officer." "This defendant has an interest to testify falsely," the prosecutor argued, "and you can't knock down the testimony of the sheriff with his story."[24]

While the prosecutor had the floor, the ever-vigilant Kels Nickell made another unannounced intrusion. When Stoll picked up Willie Nickell's bloody shirt and fumbled in an attempt to find the bullet holes, the anguished father stepped forward, grabbed the garment, and shouted, "'I'll find them for you.'" While the spectators still sympathized with the Nickell family, this latest outburst made a bad impression. Mary Nickell, who had quietly endured just as much anguish and heartbreak as her husband, attempted to turn away from this display. "The whole community is much relieved that the trial is so near an end and the tension eased," observed one correspondent, probably understating the case.[25]

Resuming control of the floor, the prosecutor spoke until adjournment. The following morning, Friday, 24 October, he proceeded to deny the defense's contention that the state had no eyewitness testimony and was relying purely on circumstantial evidence. "There was an eye witness to the crime [Horn] and that eye witness confessed every detail of the awful deed to Joe Lefors," the prosecutor asserted; only "an eye witness could have told every incident surrounding the murder of that young boy with such startling accuracy and correctness." In regard to the footprints found at the murder scene (and the absence of cuts on Tom Horn's feet), the prosecutor made a new and novel suggestion— the defendant wore "stockings or moccasins." In reference to defense's charge that the state failed to show motive for the murder, Stoll gave the jury a hypothetical example: "If a man tried to kill B [Kels Nickell], and in the pursuance of his purpose kills C [Willie Nickell], he is just as guilty as if he had killed B [Kels Nickell]." The shots that killed Willie Nickell could only have been fired by "an expert at the game," he continued, that is, an experienced assassin. The motive for this crime was money, Stoll declared, and Tom Horn admitted that he received $2,100 for killing three men and firing five times at a fourth. The prosecutor suggested that "Powell, Lewis and Willie Nickell were the dead men and Kels Nickell [was] the man shot at five times." "Does not this give a glimpse of the character of the man?" he asked the jury.[26]

In concluding his final statement, Walter Stoll again soared into oratorical flight in an effort to inspire the jury to do its duty:

> Gentlemen of the jury, the oath which you have taken, and that oath which is registered before the throne of eternal justice and in the minds of your fellow citizens, simply requires you to do your duty; and that duty we submit requires at your hands a verdict of murder in the first degree. Do not worry, gentlemen, about embrueing [sic] your hands in human blood. You are supposed to live in a community of law and order, and the laws are to be enforced or the community had better elapse into barbarism. . . . Do not think for a minute, gentlemen, that you can escape the consequences of not doing your duty. Duty fulfilled remains with us for all time as a consolation; duty violated remains with us for all time as a remorse. Our conscience appeals to us and will not be stilled. There is no ocean wide

enough to enable us to flee from it; there is no mountain high enough to shut it [duty] out from our mental vision. . . . It will go with you as you leave this jury box, and it will remain with you during the balance of your lives. . . . Gentlemen, the people of this county and the officers of this county, at vast expense and under great and overwhelming difficulties, have done their duty. It now remains for you to do yours.

With this final "burst of eloquence," Walter Stoll concluded his ten-hour summation at 11:25 A.M. "The sublimity of his masterly per-oration crept into the hearts of his hearers," according to one newsman, and "tears and breathless silence" pervaded the courtroom. "The Horn case is his masterpiece," declared the *Daily Leader*. (The gist of the prosecution's case, according to a Cheyenne dispatch writer, was that "Horn, in the pay of certain large cattle owners, killed the Nickell boy in an effort to frighten his father and cause him to leave the country.")[27]

The fate of Tom Horn was in the hands of the jury. "Amid hushed silence, Judge Scott gave the jury a few final instructions," and the panel prepared to withdraw to the jury room on the third floor. The defendant and the attorneys searched for some hint as to their intentions, but the jurymen's "impassive faces threw no light on their possible verdict." The four days taken up with the final summations had been excruciating for Tom Horn, noted the *Daily Leader;* the defendant's emotions were "plainly written" in his courtroom demeanor. For much of the time, he "sat low down in his chair, with his head on his hand and eyes fixed on the speaker." "When pleas are being made in his behalf and his innocence is being asserted his emotional nature reflects the elation he feels," continued the *Leader,* but "when he is being arraigned . . . as a criminal of an extraordinary type his elation gives way to melancholy and despair."[28]

The final summations played a critical part—perhaps *the* critical part—in the trial. But as the *Daily Leader* observed, the case boiled down to one brutal fact: "Upon Tom Horn's veracity rests his fate." If the jury believed his confession to LeFors, it would convict; if the panel did not believe him, Horn would be acquitted. The evidence for this conclusion was in "the fierce battle" the attorneys waged over his confession. "Every word uttered in the confession is discussed, interpreted and construed according to interests of the speaker." There was a third possibility. If the jurors could not agree, the *Daily Leader* noted, "the jury and not the accused will hang."[29]

It was apparent that the defendant feared Walter Stoll's "wonderful power in swaying a jury," said the *Rocky Mountain News,* and that the prosecutor's summation was "more dangerous than the evidence." "I am not . . . afraid of the evidence," Horn was heard to say, "so much as Stoll." Evidently, many people believed that even if Tom Horn was innocent, Walter Stoll possessed the ability to persuade twelve men good and true against their collective wishes to convict the accused! "The greatest criminal case ever tried in the state of Wyoming [has] reached its crisis," observed the *Daily Leader,* "and now with anxious face, Tom Horn, the man who has gained a notoriety that extends from the New England pines to the Golden Gate, awaits his fate." "On one side [lies] the ignominious death of a murderer" confronted him, "and on the other, life and liberty, the privilege to ride once more over the limitless prairies on his favorite horse Cap." Bill Barrow of the *Douglas Budget* had no doubt that Tom Horn would be acquitted. Barrow concluded that the labors of everyone involved in the prosecution of the infamous range detective were in vain. "It's a weary, weary, and I fear useless grind," Barrow lamented. "Five of the best lawyers in the state are defending him, and although there is little doubt of his guilt I predict the worst that can happen to him is a 'hung' jury or an acquittal. . . . He'll get justice some day, let us hope—but probably not in this world."[30]

After a brief period of deliberation, the jury retired to the Inter Ocean Hotel for lunch and returned to its room. No decision had been reached by 4:00 P.M., and many people saw this as a sign of "final disagreement." Twenty minutes later, Hiram Yoder, the jury foreman, announced from the door of the jury room: "We have arrived at a verdict." "Like wildfire the news spread," said one reporter, "and within ten minutes people were flocking to the court house from all directions." At 4:32 P.M., the foreman led the panel to the jury box. In the midst of a "dead silence," wrote the *Leader,* Tom Horn took his seat and anxiously "scrutinized the face of each juryman."[31]

Judge Scott proceeded with the prescribed protocol for this moment:

> At 4:35 Judge Scott ordered the roll call, and then said:
> "Gentlemen of the jury, have you arrived at a verdict?"
> "We have, your honor," replied the foreman, H. W. Yoder.

"Give me the verdict, if you please."

Amidst breathless silence, so profound the dropping of a pin could have been heard in the courtroom, the bailiff took the small piece of paper upon which was written the words that to Tom Horn meant life or death.

Judge Scott read it with a perfectly impassive face and passed it to Clerk Fisher.

"Read it aloud, if you please, Mr. Clerk," said the judge.

Clerk Fisher slowly opened the verdict and began to read. "We, the jury, empaneled in the above entitled case, do find the defendant, Tom Horn, guilty of murder in the first degree, as charged in the information."

Even as the prospects of death on the scaffold confronted him, said the *Daily Leader,* "the defendant for whose life the brightest attorneys in the state have been battling for two weeks sat unmoved with his impassive face." As Sheriff Edwin Smalley escorted Horn from the courtroom, the stock detective obviously believed in his ultimate freedom. He "even smiled to a friend." So confident were Horn and his attorneys that Timothy F. Burke had carried a message from the defendant to Deputy Marshal Joe LeFors asking "that when the jury acquitted him not to allow [Kels] Nickell or anyone [else] to harm him." "Mr. Burke, you can tell Tom Horn for me that I hold no personal grievance or malice against him," LeFors replied. As events transpired, there was no need for worry.[32]

The reactions of the attorneys involved were predictable. Prosecutor Walter Stoll, who had complained of anxiety and sleepless nights during the trial, was at home fast asleep when the verdict came in. When he received word of the jury's decision, he expressed much satisfaction. In a written statement, the prosecutor again reminded the public that such crimes as assassination were "detrimental to the development of a state." Not only did property values decline, but "the worst of it all is that they [crimes] have a tendency to lower the moral character of the community . . . and to degrade the people of this locality," and citizens in the affected area "become cowards." Horn's attorneys tried to show no emotion, but they were "bewildered" at the guilty verdict. "They had fought a hard fight and had placed seemingly insuperable obstacles in the path of the prosecution," observed the *Rocky Mountain News,* "but they had lost." The verdict "was a surprise and a distasteful one," admitted John Lacey, "but we must grin and bear it. . . . We are not beaten yet, and will undoubtedly appeal it on error."[33]

Back in his cell, Tom Horn maintained a defiant façade. "I'm not a dead man yet," he exclaimed on the Sunday morning following the verdict. As good Catholics entered St. Mary's cathedral across the street from Horn's cell window, the convicted man entertained these worshipers with "a high, tenor whistle [to] the rollicking strains of 'Good-bye, My Honey, I'm Gone.'" His whistle "was as light, airy and unbroken as that of a darky on a Mississippi levee," according to one listener. When the prisoner persisted with this shrill distraction beyond a reasonable length of time, this reporter concluded that Horn was attempting to defy the public's "conception of the condition of the condemned man's mind." Horn continued to eat "heartily three times a day," resumed his rope making, and made jokes "through the bars with the minor criminals in the corridor below." "Either Tom Horn has a strain of humor which the shadow of the gallows cannot subdue," one reporter remarked, "[or] else life, even his own, is of such slight importance to him that he does not care when it is at stake."[34]

While the jury's decision prompted some surprise and created some controversy (which continues to this day), the makeup of the panel revealed no peculiarities for that day and place. Hiram Warren Yoder, the jury foreman, was born in Indiana in 1862. After studying medicine at Drake College (but not graduating), Yoder moved his family to Wyoming in 1887. He was a longtime employee of the Swan Land and Cattle Company, Tom Horn's sometime employer. In 1902 he operated a pharmacy in Torrington and served as school principal. He was ranching at Lakeview when he was called to serve on the jury. Yoder "was a remarkably strong character and a leader of men," according to the *Torrington Telegram*.[35]

Frank F. Sinon was born in Vermont and settled in Wyoming in 1886. Sinon homesteaded in western Laramie County, tried ranching near Pine Bluffs, and ran the Becker Hotel in Cheyenne. At the time of trial, Sinon was foreman of the White ranch on Little Horse Creek.[36]

Homer Payne was born in Washburn, Illinois, in 1876, and arrived in Wyoming in 1892, where he went to work for the Swan Land and Cattle Company's Two Bar Ranch. He was still so employed at the time of trial. Of all the jurors, Payne, who resided at Wheatland, was

considered the closest to Tom Horn and was expected to be the hold-
out who would hang the jury.[37]

Charles H. Tolson, the only African American on the jury, was born
in Missouri in 1863. He settled in Cheyenne in 1879, where he served
as head waiter at the Inter Ocean Hotel and later took up the carpet
business. Tolson and his wife, Mary, as well as other family members,
were instrumental in establishing the Colored Baptist Church of Cheyenne. At the time of the trial, Tolson was a porter and bootblack at the
Union Pacific Depot.[38]

Charles Stamm was born on a farm near Fort Howard, Wisconsin, in 1868. At the time of the trial, Stamm owned a small ranch at
Wheatland.[39]

Orien V. Sebern (Seburn) was a small stock raiser on a 160-acre
homestead fifteen miles east of Lakeview. Born in Iowa, in 1855, Sebern and his wife, Lois, had three children.[40]

Howard W. Thomas was born in Iowa, in 1861. He resided at La
Grange, where he farmed and raised a small herd of cattle. Thomas and
his wife had three children.[41]

Ebbie C. Metcalf was born in Minnesota and was thirty-four years
of age. Metcalf, a blacksmith, resided with a brother and a sister in
Wheatland.[42]

Amos Sarbaugh also lived in Wheatland. He was born in Ohio and
was forty-three years of age at the time the trial. Sarbaugh was foreman
of the Two Bar Ranch, one of the Swan Land and Cattle Company's
spreads. He and his wife, Ada, had one child.[43]

James E. Barnes was born in England in 1857 and immigrated to
Wyoming at the age of twenty-six. He was a butcher in Cheyenne at
the time of the trial. He and his wife, Sarah, had three children.[44]

George H. Wrightman (Wightman) was born in Kansas in 1861. He
and his wife, Ruth, had four children. In 1900 George Wrightman was
a real estate dealer in Cheyenne, but also operated a small ranch at
Uva.[45]

Thomas R. Babbitt was ranching at La Grange at the time of the
trial.[46]

The conviction of Tom Horn prompted much speculation as to
what transpired in the jury room. Newspaper reports and subsequent
affidavits of several jurymen revealed that six ballots were required for a
decision. In the jurors' first ballot, which took place just before lunch,

the vote was eight to four for murder in the first degree. In this vote, foreman Hiram Yoder cast his ballot for acquittal, but he allegedly did so merely "for the effect of it." Homer Payne, the cowboy friend of Tom Horn, Howard Thomas, and possibly Frank F. Sinon and Charles Stamm held back. As a compromise, Thomas suggested a verdict of murder in the second degree. This was ignored. In the second ballot, which took place immediately after lunch, the vote was nine to three for conviction. Hiram Yoder made the ninth man. The jurors then decided to reexamine Judge Scott's instructions. By the fifth ballot, according to Charles Tolson, the African American juror, the vote was ten for murder in the first degree and two for acquittal. The two holdouts were Payne and Thomas. After these two men withdrew to a corner and discussed the matter, they then suggested another ballot. "Thereupon the sixth ballot was taken resulting in twelve votes being cast for murder in the first degree," according to a subsequent affidavit of Tolson. Thomas's affidavit included a handwritten note: "and thereupon juror Thomas remarked, 'Gentlemen, do not think that we are not men.'" Tolson concluded his affidavit by saying that at no time "during the entire discussion of the matter" did Homer Payne say that "he voted as he did by reason of any [coercive] remarks . . . being made by any [outside] third person."[47]

One wonders what the silent majority of the panel were thinking and why they were for conviction from the outset. One person who might be expected to hold out for acquittal was Amos Sarbaugh, the longtime Two-Bar foreman. Indeed, all the jurymen from Wheatland might be expected to have some acquaintance with Tom Horn, since this village was a neighbor of the Swan Land and Cattle Company, whose cowboys were frequent visitors. Homer Payne, who was bothered most at sitting in judgment over a friend, reportedly said later "that he had known Horn for a long time and felt sorry for him but . . . thought he was guilty and had to do it [vote for conviction]." In conversation with newspaperman J. Emerson Smith, Payne reiterated his discomfiture and asked the newsman, "But what could I do? The question was too hard to be dodged." In the end Payne answered his own question by saying, "I did my duty." Since at least eight jurors stood for conviction at the beginning of the deliberations, some part of the state's case must have been convincing from the start. Frank Sinon probably spoke for many of them when he told the *Rocky Mountain News* that "the confession was what determined Horn's guilt." This single fact, he added, "swung the jury." Another (unnamed) juror expressed the opinion that "when Horn told his story on the stand he signed his own death sentence." "His story was too palpably false to be believed," added this juryman.[48]

Some Horn partisans felt that the jurors were impatient and did not take sufficient time to deliberate. They alleged that Frank Sinon, a newlywed, was anxious to return to his bride, while Homer Payne resented having to postpone his wedding in order to answer the call to jury duty. A few days after the jury rendered its decision, George Milne, a Swan Land and Cattle Company employee, bluntly asserted that the panel "was mostly composed of ignorant men." John Lacey "appealed to their intelligence," according to Milne, and "Stoll to their ignorance"—hence the unjust conviction of Tom Horn. Charles Coe, a stock detective who later wrote in Horn's defense, alleged that "the jury was composed [primarily] of small ranchers or their employees" and could in no wise weigh the evidence objectively. Coe maintained that while Horn recovered stolen cattle for the big cattlemen, he had actually helped nesters and small ranchers by reclaiming their pilfered livestock at the same time. Some of the persons whom the range detective helped in this way, asserted Coe, later served on the jury that convicted him. Coe obviously considered the jurors who could be classified as townspeople—"a porter, a blacksmith, and a butcher"— equally incompetent. While Walter Stoll admitted that the jury consisted primarily of small ranchers, he interpreted their willingness to serve in such a controversial case as a sign of bravery. In spite of the fact that the defendant was the employee and friend of the big cattlemen, Stoll was impressed that they "had no hesitation in convicting Horn."[49]

The cost of Tom Horn's trial has long been a subject of discussion. While figures for Laramie County's expense were soon available, figures for the expenses of the defense varied greatly. "Sixty-six witnesses were paid . . . , eleven days each, counting the two Sundays, at $2 per day and mileage," according to the *Rocky Mountain News*. On average, each witness earned $22 in fees and $15 in mileage with the total court expenditure amounting to $2,600. (Walter Stoll's annual salary as prosecuting attorney was only $1,500.) Samuel Corson, chairman of the Laramie County Board of Commissioners placed the total cost to the county at about $10,000, although other estimates went much higher. Estimates for the defense were more problematic, the only certainty being that the defendant was practically penniless. "At the time of Horn's arrest he had but 5 cents on his person and was known to possess no property," according to the *Laramie Republican*. While the $5,000 that Frank Bosler and John Coble put down for a retainer in January 1902 is documented, very little is known about subsequent expenses. (Many years later, Judge Ewing Kerr of Cheyenne declared that Mrs. John [Elise] Coble "showed me a cancelled check for ten thousand dollars" payable to John W. Lacey "as his first payment." Kerr's memory may have failed him in this instance, and Elise Coble could have been showing him the original $5,000 retainer.) Since Coble expected Horn to be acquitted, he probably believed all expenses would end at this point. One of the defense attorneys (unnamed) reported at the end of the trial in October 1902 that the defense fund was exhausted. However, the only documented contribution made after the trial was in November 1902, when Coble presented John Lacey with an additional $600. In the absence of information, speculation abounds. In spite of rumors that some cattle barons contributed to Tom Horn's defense, any such contributions by no means covered all the defense's expenses. Just what Lacey and his colleagues charged for their services from the end of the trial to Horn's execution is not known. Furthermore, the makeup of the defense team changed after the trial. While the *Denver Republican* said that Horn's supporters pooled about $40,000, the total cost was probably closer to $20,000 for the full two years of defense expenses. However, this is mere speculation.[50]

In spite of the efforts of John Lacey and his associates to defend an essentially undefendable client, they have been the recipients of much criticism. Historian Dean Krakel, who wrote the first serious analysis of the Tom Horn trial, compiled a list of the defense's failures. In spite of "the best legal counsel money could buy in Wyoming," Krakel declared that Lacey and his colleagues failed to plausibly rebut Horn's confession to Joe LeFors. Furthermore, not only was Lacey's argument that the confession was mere "josh" ineffectual, but he also failed to call important witnesses such as John Coble and Glendolene Kimmell. In spite of strong suspicions of Tom Horn's past wrongdoings in Wyoming, Krakel pointed out that the defendant had stood on the side of law and order and had amassed an impressive record in the Apache campaigns and in Cuba. William McLeod Raine, the Denver journalist and writer of popular westerns, argued that Horn would have been foolish to destroy a lifetime of work as a civilian scout and lawman by murdering a boy. Why, asked Raine, did defense counsel fail to produce a new set of such affidavits to replace those submitted on Horn's behalf during his robbery trial in Reno? While Tom Horn's overall record indicated that he was a patriotic American, Raine concluded that he bore the brunt of Wyoming's wrath at the cattle barons' many past wrongdoings. In Raine's estimation, Tom Horn was a scapegoat for the crimes of the cattle barons, who were apparently out of reach of the law.[51]

The defense attorneys also failed to present a sound alibi for their client. According to Dean Krakel, the sole alibi witness, Otto Plaga, was "a well-known 'yarn spinner.'" In this regard, Krakel might have recalled the maxim "One witness is no witness." A second alibi witness would have solidified the defense's case. Ironically, there may have been just such a person. On the day after the jury returned its verdict, John S. Gavitt, a Sybille Creek miner, informed the *Rocky Mountain News* that "he had seen Horn on the Sybille at a time that made it impossible for the latter to have killed Willie Nickell." Apparently, John Lacey had been informed of Gavitt's potential value and asked him to testify. One of John Coble's missions on his visit to Denver during Horn's trial was apparently to locate Gavitt, but he failed to find him. Fearing that "the enemies of Horn would do him injury," Gavitt demanded a $50,000 indemnity bond. Horn's attorneys refused to provide the bond and did not have him subpoenaed. The Gavitt story, one of many unsubstantiated reports about the Tom Horn case, may be a canard.[52]

The defense attorneys may have had difficulty getting beyond the notion that his confession was true. If so, they labored under an overwhelming burden. According to Lacey's friend William R. Coe (not to be confused with Charles H. Coe), the chief defense counsel admitted that "he felt Horn was guilty." While T. Blake Kennedy believed Horn was innocent of the Nickell murder, he had little good to say about the range detective. Recalling Tom Horn's remark "killing men is my specialty . . . [and] I think I have a corner on this market," Kennedy mused, "One is prone to adopt a philosophy that, technicalities aside, the world is better off without [such] a man." In talking with Dean Krakel about the trial, a prominent (but unnamed) Denver attorney who had studied the Horn trial also believed "Horn killed Willie Nickell deliberately." In spite of defense counsel's efforts to put on an optimistic public face during the trial, they had no idea whether the jury would buy the "joshing" argument. Lacey had to gamble that the jury would be swayed by this improbable theory. Tom Horn had undermined his own case with indiscreet remarks in public and his behavior on the witness stand. As many observers noted, Tom Horn talked himself into a noose.[53]

Since returning from Cuba in 1898, Tom Horn exhibited what may have been signs that he was becoming mentally unstable. Shortly after the trial, James D. Eckel, who had ridden with the detective on the Little Snake River range, expressed that opinion. "I have known Tom Horn for years, ridden with him and camped with him," Eckel remarked. "Personally, I believe he is crazy." While Horn was generally easy "to get along with" in cattle camps, continued this cowhand, "he would have spells when he wouldn't say a word to anyone for a day or two." He would then "take spells and ride, apparently without any object, over the country without food or rest for two or three days." If Horn was mentally unstable, Eckel continued, he "would rather see Tom Horn in an insane asylum than to see him hanged." Since the range detective still had "strong hopes" that the cattle barons would find a way to save him, Eckel believed Horn's attorneys would "play his insanity as a last card."[54]

A few days after the guilty verdict was rendered, a *Daily Leader* reporter raised the subject of Horn's mental state with John Lacey. When this newsman observed that there had been "hints" that Horn "is partially insane," Lacey (surprisingly) agreed. "Tom Horn has not been of sound mind . . . since he returned from Cuba," Lacey remarked. While the defense attorney did not consider his client insane, Lacey said that Horn's mind "is certainly effected [sic]," presumably by the severe case of fever that the defendant suffered in the Santiago Campaign. Lacey went on to argue that Horn's illness accounted for his confession and asserted that his mind was "in that state where he would admit the commission of any crime imputed to him." In preparing the case, "we asked him questions regarding . . . matters of importance," Lacey added, "but though he denied these, they were later proven to be true." "If he had been of sound mind he would have told us these things and benefited his case," Lacey added, in an obvious effort to explain the defense's failure to anticipate these adverse developments. One might ask the question, If Horn's mind was not sound, why permit him to take the witness stand at all? Any defendant on the witness stand was in a risky position; an emotionally unstable one in such a vulnerable position invited disaster. Indeed, Tom Horn's indiscreet statements on the stand seem to be those of a person oblivious to everything around him.[55]

That Tom Horn's state of mind in 1902 qualified him for a plea of innocence by reason of mental defect might not be so farfetched. Since he entered military service in 1881, he had operated largely outside the bounds of established society, even by frontier standards. He had provided powerful institutions, both government and private corporations, with services that were outside societal norms"—services that called for working alone in the mountains and deserts of the American West and in Mexico. Since his subsequent career as a range detective also placed him outside the pale of respectable society—as an "outside man," even most cowhands merely tolerated him—a feeling of alienation on Horn's part would not be surprising. He was a misfit and not fit company for polite society. Operating as such a loner, Horn could easily have become somewhat delusional. Given his obsessive hatred for thieves, he may have believed that his irrational feelings were within the bounds of convention.

In spite of his past support from the powerful range barons, Tom Horn stood largely alone before the Wyoming court. Even the small coterie of vocal supporters at the trial could not be relied upon for anything beyond verbal encouragement. "Not one prominent cattleman . . . evinced . . . any interest in the case," according to a reporter for the *Denver Post*. "John C. Coble and Ora Haley, the names of Horn's former employers, and those heard often in connection with Horn," continued this writer, "have not been here. . . . The members of the Stock Growers association have not been interviewed on the case, simply because they have nothing to say." In spite of Prosecutor Stoll's public boast prior to the trial that the state would go beyond the conviction of the "tool," he quickly forgot this promise, although just how the livestock barons avoided prosecution is still something of a mystery. Not even John Coble was called to the stand. "Feeling against the men who hired Horn is higher than that against Horn himself," said the *Rocky Mountain News* shortly after the trial. "The people feel that weak and degenerate as he is," continued the reporter, the range detective "is not nearly so reprehensible as his employers." Since the Lewis and Powell assassinations in 1895, John Coble's name was routinely associated with that of Tom Horn, prompting the *Denver Post* to characterize them as a team engaged in nefarious undertakings. It is easy to conclude that public officials such as Walter Stoll did not want to tackle these wealthy barons—better to let Tom Horn be the cattlemen's sacrificial lamb.[56]

Not only did the big cattlemen leave Tom Horn to his fate, but another powerful organization that might have provided him assistance, the Pinkerton National Detective Agency, remained silent. In a letter to William Pinkerton in January 1906, Pinkerton's brother, Robert, admitted that "I have always been sort of sore at myself that I did not look a little more thoroughly into Tom Horn's case. . . . I have an idea he might have been innocent." At the time of Horn's arrest, however, "Our managers . . . believed that Horn was guilty," Pinkerton continued, "and recommended to me that we offer him no assistance." Presumably, Pinkerton was referring to James McParland, superintendent of the agency's western operations, and perhaps, John Fraser, head of the Denver office at the time of Horn's execution. Although William Pinkerton's reply to Robert's letter has not been found, he was less sympathetic than his brother to Tom Horn's case. In an interview with the *San Francisco Call* on the day of Horn's execution, in November 1903, William Pinkerton praised the range detective as a brave and "game" man, but deplored his "methods of getting rid of objectionable characters." "Drink was his ruin," concluded William Pinkerton. "Had he abstained from liquor," he added, "Tom Horn would have lived to enjoy a reputation that few men can boast of."[57]

According to Edward Slack, perhaps the most influential editor in Wyoming, judicial authorities had done their job. Horn's conviction had vindicated Wyoming and its court system, particularly officials of Laramie County. Slack, who was always sensitive not only to the opinions of the cattle lobby but to outside criticism, observed in the *Daily Leader:*

> We notice a disposition on the part of some of the outside newspapers to charge the killing of Willie Nickell upon the stockmen. . . . The Leader . . . has no hesitation in saying that the charge is unfounded. And we do this after a full and careful investigation of all the circumstances leading up to the crime and what has since transpired. It cannot be truthfully said that the stockmen or cattlemen contributed to the defense of Tom Horn. Neither were they previously asked to subscribe to a fund for killing anybody.

While Slack admitted that in the past the cattlemen took the law into their own hands, "It is serving no good purpose to rake up the dead past." He was content to "let bygones be bygones." Slack stoutly maintained that "the prosecution of Tom Horn was not aimed at anything beyond the assassination of Willie Nickell." By so stating, Slack was letting Prosecutor Walter Stoll, and the men who had employed Tom Horn, off the hook.[58]

CHAPTER 15

Fight for Freedom

While Tom Horn marked time in the Laramie County Jail, defense and state's attorneys continued to match wits in various judicial venues in their efforts to save his life, or take it, as the case might be. In the meantime, Sheriff Edwin Smalley had the increasingly unpleasant job of keeping Tom Horn locked up. Horn had been "a model prisoner" prior to his trial, recalled Smalley, but he turned desperate after his conviction. "Sentencing Tom Horn to be hanged," Smalley observed, "was not hanging him." Since Horn was believed to know secrets of the range barons, the sheriff believed they would employ any means, "from bribery to tearing down the jail," to liberate him. When Kels Nickell, who had appointed himself to the job of keeping track of Horn and his case, spotted several strangers in Cheyenne shortly after Horn was convicted, he declared that he was "'going to keep an eye'" on them. Even though Sheriff Smalley made light of such alarmism, he still took the precaution of reinforcing the jail windows with iron grating.[1]

Sheriff Smalley faced other problems associated with his infamous prisoner. "Should he get off by hook or crook," one newsman wondered, what might happen on the streets of Cheyenne. Would Joe LeFors or Kels Nickell be waiting for an opportunity to "get the first drop" on him? John Coble, who continued to work on behalf of Horn, was Smalley's most immediate problem. A few days after the trial, he hired two female detectives from Denver to gather new evidence in support of Horn's appeal. However, one of these female sleuths was "notorious in half a dozen towns of this region," according to the *Rocky Mountain News,* and "their work was so raw and their plans so apparent" that the sheriff ordered them out of town. "This is not the first time that Horn's people have attempted the use of siren influence to obtain information," added the *News.* A few nights later, Halloween mischief-makers gave the sheriff another jangle by hanging both Tom Horn and John C. Coble in effigy. Apparently, one figure sufficed for both men. "On its breast was a huge white placard bearing the inscription, 'Horn and Coble,'" the *Daily Leader* reported.[2]

Horn and his attorneys were keenly interested in the county elections, which were scheduled for 4 November. Should the present county commissioners, district attorney, and sheriff be ousted, the winners might be more sympathetic to an appeal. The race for district attorney was the most important. Walter Stoll, who was seeking reelection on the Democratic ticket, had increased his political capital significantly through "the Horn matter," according to the *Rocky Mountain News.* Although Horace Waldo Moore, Stoll's former colleague in the prosecution of Horn, opposed him, Cheyenne gamblers offered odds that Stoll "will receive more majority than Moore does votes." Likewise, Edwin Smalley, who was running for sheriff, had the advantage of his connection with the Horn case. When the polls opened, the condemned man could observe activity at a voting booth across the street from his cell. The results were extremely disappointing to Tom Horn, as the incumbents won by sizable majorities. While the Iron Mountain community was about equally divided between pro- and anti-Horn voters, the countywide vote "showed how thoroughly the people . . . are standing behind Mr. Stoll in his investigation of conditions which made Tom Horn's work possible," observed the *Rocky Mountain News,* noting that the vote also reflected the public perception that "the price of the recent conviction [of Horn] was money well spent."[3]

On 8 November John Lacey and Timothy Burke presented Judge Richard Scott (also reelected) with Tom Horn's appeal for a new trial. Walter Stoll represented the state. Speaking for the defense, Burke outlined twenty-three arguments, supported by numerous affidavits from persons willing to speak on behalf of their client, some of which defense counsel had presented at the recent trial. Among new arguments, Burke also asserted that public opinion at the time of the trial was so hostile to Horn that he could not get a fair hearing. Two witnesses, Greta

Rhode and J. Emerson Smith (the latter a reporter), stated in depositions that "the jury . . . was coerced into arriving at a verdict of guilty
by remarks made within the hearing of the jury" when they took their
meals at the Inter Ocean Hotel, and Burke went so far as to characterize "the statements of Stoll in his [closing] arguments" as a form of
coercion. Homer L. Payne, a member of the jury at Tom Horn's trial,
now took the side of the defense, stating that while he "was convinced
in his own mind of Horn's innocence" during the jury's deliberations,
his fellow jurors "told him that if he voted for acquittal it would be said
that he was bribed," so he changed his vote to one "for conviction."
(Lacey had found Glendolene Kimmell in Kansas City, Missouri, and
persuaded her to make an affidavit on behalf of the defendant, but it did
not arrive in time to be presented.)[4]

Prosecutor Stoll was well prepared with affidavits to counter the defense's request for a new trial. Charles H. Tolson and James E. Barnes,
jurors in Horn's trial, denied that they coerced Payne. Two bailiffs who
escorted the jurors to the Inter Ocean Hotel for their meals declared
that the jurors were not compromised at the Inter Ocean. Stoll also presented arguments of "a technical nature" concerning "the admissibility
or inadmissibility of evidence," according to the *Leader*. After Judge
Scott gave defense counsel an opportunity to reply to Stoll's counter-
arguments, he retired to take their arguments under advisement. The
following day, 12 November, Scott announced that he could find no
just cause to grant a new trial and overruled the defense's motion. The
Wyoming Criminal Code provided that a case such as Tom Horn's
would go directly to the highest state tribunal regardless, so the defendant still had means of redress.[5]

Judge Scott still had one very "painful and disagreeable" duty to perform during these proceedings: passing sentence on Tom Horn. "The
defendant may stand up," declared the bench. "Amid breathless silence
Tom Horn arose from his chair, took a step forward, and then with his
hands clasped behind his back and his body perfectly erect, awaited . . .
the words spoken by the judge," wrote the *Daily Leader*. With "a voice
which slightly trembled," Judge Scott asked the defendant, "Is there
anything you have to say why sentence should not be pronounced
upon you?" "'I do not think I have, sir,' was the reply, uttered in calm,
measured tones." At this point, Judge Scott pronounced the dreaded
sentence: "It is ordered, adjudged and decreed that you, Tom Horn, be

... confined until the 9th day of January, 1903, on which day, between the hours of 9 o'clock in the forenoon and 3 o'clock in the afternoon, you will be taken by the sheriff of Laramie county to a place prepared by him, and there hanged by the neck until you are dead." Although the prisoner betrayed no immediate emotion, he departed the court-room so quickly that he left his embarrassed escorts, Sheriff Smalley and Undersheriff Proctor, standing alone. When they finally found Horn at the door to the sheriff's office, "he turned and said with a smile, 'The door is locked against me.'"[6]

The defense attorneys immediately began to prepare an appeal to the Wyoming Supreme Court. "The battle for the life of the defendant will not stop for a minute," John Lacey informed the *Daily Leader*. This process required a mass of documents, including a bill of exceptions, followed by a petition in error, all of which was supported by a complete copy of the trial transcript, and any other pertinent records from the district court. Once this paper work was assembled, the defense had sixty days to file its brief, after which the state had forty days to file its brief. "This time may be extended upon application," continued the *Leader*, "so that it will be at least four months before the case is ready for argument." After the attorneys argued their respective cases, the court could take as many as sixty days before rendering a decision. Should the three justices rule in favor of the defendant, he would receive a new trial; if the decision went against him, Judge Scott would be called upon to set a new execution date. In order for this protracted judicial procedure to be fulfilled, the high court had to grant Tom Horn a stay of execution.[7]

With the threat of the hangman's noose temporarily removed for as much as eight months, the defendant cheered up. He "spoke smilingly to his attorneys," laughed at a remark by Edwin Smalley, and "executed a jig step" as he left the courtroom. Defense counsel expressed appreciation at this opportunity to strengthen Horn's case and believed that this hiatus would enable "public feeling" against him to subside. On the last day of the year, Timothy Burke formally presented the petition in error (a legal document) to the State Supreme Court in order to get their appeal under way. This document put forth "the single ground that the district court erred in overruling the plaintiff's [previous] bill of exceptions." The new bill of exceptions eventually presented to the Supreme Court contained more than "1,000 pages and a wagon load of exhibits," according to one observer. In turn, the justices—Chief Justice Samuel T. Corn, and Justices Jesse Knight and Charles N. Potter—then issued "an indefinite stay of execution" (separate from Judge Scott's), in order to give both sides an opportunity to prepare arguments.[8]

In spite of his apparently easygoing attitude, Tom Horn was bitterly disappointed at the outcome of his trial. From this time on, he demonstrated the characteristics of a hardened criminal, and he lost his "star prisoner" status at Sheriff Smalley's jail. When Homer Dietrick, a young accused forger, "broke down and sobbed" in his cell, according to the *Rocky Mountain News,* Horn "jeered" at this unfortunate youth, calling him "a 'big baby,' 'calf,' and 'coward.'" Such callous behavior won Horn no friends and prompted widespread "disgust and indignation." Public resentment was further increased when the *Wyoming Tribune,* in Cheyenne, broke the story a few days later of a plot to break the notorious range detective out of jail. Thomas P. Herr, who had just completed a term in the Laramie County Jail for stealing a saddle, approached the *Tribune's* William Chapin Deming with a deal. Herr would turn over letters secretly exchanged between Horn and John Coble if Deming agreed to provide railway fare to get Herr safely out of the state. According to Herr, while working for the Iron Mountain Ranch Company, John Coble and his foreman, Charles Irwin, persuaded him to join in a conspiracy to free Tom Horn. This plan called for planting Herr in the Laramie County Jail to communicate with Horn. According to Herr, Coble arranged for him to deliberately steal a saddle in Laramie County; hence Herr's sixty-day stay in the Cheyenne jail. The first part of the plan worked, as jail records show that a T. P. Herr was incarcerated from 17 November 1902 to 21 January 1903. Tom Horn passed him notes written on toilet tissue, which Herr concealed in his clothing as he left the jail. In one missive, Horn suggested that his friends on the outside should blow a hole in the jail wall and leave food and a horse for his escape.[9]

When Herr began to fear that Coble would have him killed after he finished his jail term, he decided to divulge the conspiracy to the *Wyoming Tribune.* Editor Deming paid Herr's railroad fare to Ogden and then "splashed" details of the plot on the front page of the paper. While Horn's friends tried to dismiss the jailbreak scheme as "a good joke," the fact that Thomas Herr had in his possession letters in Tom Horn's own handwriting persuaded Prosecutor Stoll and Sheriff Smalley that a plot existed. The Herr incident had several important consequences, all of which redounded against Horn. His "desire to escape is taken as a still further proof of his guilt," said the *Rocky Mountain News*, "and popular opinion now is that his chances to avoid hanging are about one in a hundred." To further exacerbate public feeling, Thomas Herr informed an Ogden newspaper that before Horn's arrest—while Herr was still employed at Coble's ranch—he had overheard Charles Irwin and Tom Horn discussing a plan to kill Kels Nickell. Horn said he would do it for $1,000.[10]

In spite of the close association of John Coble with Tom Horn, and the public assumption that they constituted some sort of nefarious team, there was never any indication among Wyoming lawmen that they suspected Coble of personally pulling the trigger in either the murder of Willie Nickell or the attempt on Kels Nickell's life. As farfetched as this scenario may seem, it was not impossible. While Coble made no bones about his hatred for the nester element, it was generally believed that wealthy range barons did not stoop to the level of murder. They hired such deeds done. Yet Coble, a highly emotional and self-righteous man, had harbored an intense hatred for Kels Nickell since the latter's assault upon him in 1890. Frederick Perry Williams, an Albany County rancher and close friend of Coble, recalled that after the murder of Willie Nickell, Coble had stunned him by admitting in a letter, "Perry, I killed the boy." Apparently, Coble had to tell someone to ease his conscience.[11]

Not knowing what to do with this incriminating letter, Williams tucked it away in his desk drawer, where it was destroyed in a fire in 1913. But Williams could not keep this dark secret to himself. He told the story to his brother, Frank, who passed it down through his family. In 2012 Roy W. Lilley, a grandson of Perry Williams, related it to D. Claudia Williams of the American Heritage Center at the University of Wyoming. Lilley went so far as to speculate that not only was John Coble capable of such a crime—although he killed Willie Nickell by mistake—but that he and, possibly, his foreman, Duncan Clark were the two men who attempted to kill Kels Nickell a few days after Willie Nickell's death. Williams, of course, may have misinterpreted Coble, who may have meant not that he shot Willie Nickell himself but that he hired the killer.[12]

Only a few days after Thomas Herr divulged John Coble's plan to liberate Tom Horn, a story broke about a more subtle attempt to free him. On 7 February 1903, the *Daily Leader* announced that Representative John Nolan had introduced a bill in the Wyoming legislature to abolish capital punishment. While this bill did not mention the Horn case, reporters covering the statehouse saw it as a devious means by the cattle companies to prevent Tom Horn from hanging. It was alleged that "when the sentence of death was thus suspended by the [Nolan] bill," continued the *Leader,* "Tom Horn could not even be re-sentenced to life imprisonment since that would constitute double jeopardy. The judiciary committee, which recommended this bill to the assembly, was chaired by none other than Representative Roderick Matson, one of Tom Horn's attorneys. Edward Slack, outraged at this ploy, went so far as to suggest that the committee members were attempting "to circumvent the Almighty with their schemes to keep Tom Horn among us." If the attorneys on the judiciary committee were honest, he said, they should have offered amendments to the bill exempting their clients who presently faced the death penalty.[13]

Even though Tom Horn had occupied a jail cell for more than a year, his name was still associated with violent incidents in the ongoing struggle for control of Wyoming's grazing lands. On 2 February 1903, Benjamin B. Minnick, a sheep raiser near Basin, in Big Horn County, was murdered and two hundred of his sheep destroyed. In reporting this event, newspapers expressed the fear that the conditions that spawned the murderous deeds of Tom Horn in the southern counties were being duplicated in the north country. "This is not the first time an enemy of the cattle barons, whether engaged in the sheep industry or [cattle] 'rustling' has met his death at the hands of hired assassins in northern Wyoming," the *Daily Leader* observed, "and cattlemen frankly admit that they have detectives at work." "Catch the man who murdered Ben Minnick," said an unnamed eyewitness, "and you will have a second Tom Horn trial on your hands." When Big Horn County lawmen arrested James "Driftwood Jim" McCloud for the Minnick murder, they lacked a secure jail to hold him and transferred this "second Tom Horn" to the Laramie County Jail, where "the first" Tom Horn was imprisoned.[14]

Meanwhile, attorneys for and against Tom Horn continued to gather evidence while the Wyoming Supreme Court studied the mass of documents comprising Horn's appeal. In March 1903, John Lacey was busily compiling additional documents to support of Horn's appeal. While the deadline for the submission of this brief was 1 April, Lacey said he intended "to prolong the case" up to the final day allowed. "The brief will be quite a voluminous document," said the *Daily Leader,* "setting forth the legal propositions in support of the seventy grounds of error alleged in the petition." Prosecutor Walter Stoll had sixty days to reply to this brief, but in late April the district court granted him an additional thirty days. Since defense counsel's intention was to use all the time allowed, the high court was not expected to entertain Horn's appeal until the fall.[15]

Various persons associated with Horn continued to make the news. In December 1902, Deputy U.S. Marshal Joe LeFors made a daring arrest of a Shoshone Indian charged with "assault to kill" a white schoolteacher on the Wind River Reservation. A few months later, LeFors announced that he had accepted a position as ranch manager in Nicaragua. Before departing, he signed a waiver of the $1,000 reward in the Willie Nickell case in favor of his superior, U.S. Marshal Frank Hadsell. As LeFors left for Nicaragua, rumors circulated that either Tom Horn's friends drove him out of the country or they paid him to leave. Kels Nickell also made the news when he decided to visit his old home at Iron Mountain in defiance of threats against his life if he should return. Harry J. Windsor, a staunch friend of Tom Horn and John Coble, suggested that Nickell should be lynched if he dared to return. Apparently, Nickell's visit took place without incident, and he was soon back in Cheyenne, where he was hauled into court the next month to stand trial for an earlier assault charge.[16]

With each passing day, Tom Horn grew more desperate to escape. To do so he would require the assistance of fellow prisoners. Since most of them were serving short terms for minor crimes, recalled Edwin Smalley, "they had nothing to do with his plans." Only one inmate, P. D. Shepardson, who faced manslaughter charges, agreed to help Horn, but he was transferred to the state penitentiary before the plot could reach fruition. When "Driftwood Jim" McCloud, the "second Tom Horn," arrived at the Laramie County lockup, tensions began to mount immediately. Sheriff Smalley's fear that this new inmate would add substance to Tom Horn's escape plans was well founded. At 8:40 A.M., on Sunday, 9 August 1903, while many residents of Cheyenne were in church, Horn and McCloud overpowered Undersheriff Richard A. Proctor, who was alone at the jail, and forced him to open the weapons safe.

Although Proctor fought back, the two prisoners beat him badly, and the deputy was lucky to escape with his life. Fortunately, Deputy Sheriff Leslie Snow happened along. "I opened the office door and Macleod [sic] stood there with my 30-40 [rifle] and said stick em up Snow." The deputy quickly slammed the door and began to fire warning shots into the air. Then he found a telephone and alerted the sheriff. As Smalley ran toward the jail, he spied McCloud mounting the lawman's horse. Editor E. A. Slack, who happened to be in the street, shouted excitedly, "Two men just escaped! There's one now!" He pointed at McCloud. Smalley took a shot at him and unhorsed the escapee. When McCloud got to his feet, he pointed his rifle at the hapless sheriff, whose revolver was empty. "It was my lucky day," Smalley remarked, since "his gun jammed." Although McCloud took cover in a nearby barn, he soon gave up. This "second Tom Horn" surrendered without a fight.[17]

Horn, now deserted by his comrade, had his hands full with the plucky Undersheriff Proctor. After opening the weapons safe, Proctor grabbed a pistol and attempted to turn it on Horn. Horn took the weapon away from him, pointed it at the hapless undersheriff and squeezed the trigger. It would not fire. It was a newfangled Browning Model 1900 semiautomatic pistol, which differed radically from the revolvers that Horn knew. This weapon had a safety latch that had to be switched off before firing. (Proctor, who was a quick thinker, cleverly switched on the safety as the prisoner took the pistol from him.) Ironically, Tom Horn, who took great pride in his knowledge of guns, had failed to keep up with the latest weapons technology. Since McCloud had deserted him, Horn ran out the rear door and fled on foot down the alley behind the justice complex. By this time the town was thoroughly aroused by Deputy Snow's shots, and Leona Bruner at the central telephone switchboard alerted acquaintances across the city. Worshipers also swarmed out of nearby churches. T. Joe Cahill, Tom Horn's good friend, was passing the collection plate in his church when he heard the hue and cry. Dropping the plate, Cahill ran into the street and, much to his astonishment, nearly collided with Tom Horn, who was "loping along," gun in hand. Horn "was nervy enough to say 'Howdy!'" recalled Cahill, and to add, "You stay out of it, T. Joe!" As Horn emerged from an alley near the intersection of Twentieth and Capitol streets, he passed the automobiles of the wealthier churchgoers who had parked along the sidewalks.[18]

Nearby, O. A. Aldrich (Oelrich), who operated a portable merry-go-round, spied the escapee and opened fire with a .38 caliber revolver. His first shot grazed Tom Horn's scalp and momentarily stunned him. A second shot went wild and barely missed Mrs. Bert Millyard and her three-year-old daughter, Erna, who were watching the excitement from a nearby window. As Aldrich caught up with the dazed fugitive, who had fallen to the ground, Horn pointed his pistol and made another futile effort to pull the trigger, failing again to flip the safety latch. Out of cartridges, Aldrich began to hit Horn on the head. "At Aldrich's heels went a growing pack of citizenry," recalled newspaperman John Thompson, who had also just emerged from church. When Policemen Otto Ahrens and Lou Stone arrived on the scene, Tom Horn said meekly, "I give up." As the posse took custody of the chastened fugitive, a photographer captured the scene as Tom Horn, towering over his captors, walked dejectedly back to jail. It was his last moment of freedom. As the prisoner neared the jail, Deputy Sheriff Snow rode up, and in a fit of rage, began to hit Horn over the head with a rifle butt. Had not Stone interfered, Snow would have inflicted a severe injury. Stone received a broken arm for his trouble. Many years later, Snow admitted he had "never been proud" of this act, but blamed it on "impetuous youth." When Kels Nickell tried to incite a lynch mob against Horn and McCloud, who was also back in custody, Sheriff Smalley threatened to arrest Nickell and place him in Tom Horn's cell if he did not calm down.[19]

Tom Horn's attempted jailbreak prompted much speculation. One theory held that Horn's friends deliberately planted McCloud in the Laramie County Jail "for the express purpose of assisting Horn to escape," although the *Rocky Mountain News* asserted that the two prisoners "depended solely on luck to get away." Whatever their plan, the two amateurish badmen made the mistake of frittering away ten minutes in their struggle with Undersheriff Proctor to gain access to the gun safe. Furthermore, Horn's attempt to kill Proctor "plainly show[ed] a pure brute instinct for . . . the taking of human life," observed the *Wheatland World*, whose editor was acquainted with Horn. "There was a time when Horn was considered in a better light than this." The transformation of the range detective's image, which began with the assassinations of Billy Lewis and Fred Powell in 1895, was completed on 9 August 1903. Sheriff Smalley was now more security conscious than ever. "Nothing short of an armed attack," according to one observer, could penetrate the jail's defenses.[20]

Whether or not Horn's attempted jailbreak was abetted by the Iron Mountain Ranch Company, the publicity reflected adversely upon John Coble. These were bad times for him, since Franklin Bosler, now fully aware of his partner's connection with Horn, was still intent on a complete break with Coble. As the fortunes of Tom Horn continued to decline, so did the future prospects of John Coble, although the latter's problems were primarily business related. As the final dissolution of the company drew nearer, Coble's correspondence with Bosler became testier. In reply to Bosler's request in June 1903 that Coble "sign the power of attorney for transfer of stock" in the company, Coble complained that the "tone" of his letters was becoming "contemptible." "I had hoped Frank that we could close up our business affairs pleasantly," wrote Coble, expressing his "earnest wish" that the dissolution should end on a cordial note. Bosler made one move toward severance right in the midst of Tom Horn's abortive jailbreak when he ordered new letterhead that did not feature Coble's name as manager. "I explained my desire to you and wish to keep from the public our private business affairs," he wrote, "and just now there is great excitement in Cheyenne over the attempted escape of Tom Horn and another convict." Too add to Coble's dismay, newsmen were asking him for details about the breakup. Coble, who despised the press, "politely told them that it was none of their business."[21]

On Thursday, 20 August 1903, Chief Justice S. T. Corn and Justices C. N. Potter and Jesse Knight convened to entertain Tom Horn's plea for a new trial. John Lacey, Timothy Burke, Roderick N. Matson, and T. Blake Kennedy represented the defendant. Wyoming Attorney General Josiah A. Van Orsdel represented the state, with Walter Stoll assisting. With the appeal coming hard on the heels of their client's abortive jailbreak, the defense attorneys were in a difficult situation. Burke began the defense's case by enumerating errors in Tom Horn's trial, in October 1902: the verdict was contrary to the evidence and was contrary to the law. Burke attacked the confession to Joe LeFors which, he asserted, was "the only evidence which in any way tended to establish the guilt of Horn." This confession was "mere coarse josh," he continued, and "told in a contest between he and [Joe] Lefors in the telling of tall yarns at a time when Horn was intoxicated." Furthermore, not only did Judge Scott fail to inform the jury "that confessions are a doubtful species of evidence," but the bench erred "in refusing to the defendant the right to prove that others [the Miller boys] had connection with the crime."[22]

The following morning, Walter Stoll opened for the state. The prosecutor first raised the subject of Tom Horn's motive for killing Willie Nickell. Stoll reminded the high court that the defense had characterized as "illogical" the prosecution's argument that Horn killed Willie Nickell to prevent the boy from "'raising a hell of a commotion'" at the fence gap. Stoll declared that Horn shot Willie Nickell "because he had experience of this nature before," and he reminded the justices of an incident at the fall 1895 court session in Cheyenne when "the little son of Powell, seeing Horn, exclaimed, 'There is the man who killed papa.'" In order to avoid "repetition of this occurrence," continued Stoll, Tom Horn "killed the Nickell boy to keep him from telling on him." John W. Lacey then followed with the defense's closing argument, after which the three justices announced that they would take up the case immediately. They were well aware that the public was impatient with the law that permitted a condemned person twelve months to appeal the death sentence, and a recent rash of lynchings in Wyoming reinforced the justices' resolve to work doubly hard on the Horn case.[23]

Tom Horn's family had followed his case closely and awaited the decision of the Wyoming Supreme Court with much concern. On 9 August, Tom Adams, the condemned man's nephew, wrote Attorney General Van Orsdel asking if he thought his uncle's appeal would be approved. Van Orsdel, who frankly admitted that his task was to oppose a new trial, said that it was "very doubtful." In reply to a letter from Nannie Adams, the prisoner's sister in Granger, Missouri, Van Orsdel assured her that the State of Wyoming wanted no innocent man to hang, but he went on to point out that her brother's case was "a very serious one." However, he asserted, "this matter is entirely with the court."[24]

As the Supreme Court session approached, the prevailing feeling in the public was that the justices would rule against Tom Horn. In part, such thinking was based on the conduct of county and state officials throughout the adjudication of Horn's case. Furthermore, the high court had recently denied the appeal of another convicted murderer, James Keffer, and Acting Governor Fenimore Chatterton also denied a plea for commutation of sentence. Keffer was hanged in Lander, Wyoming, on 25 September 1903. When the high court convened on Thursday, 1 October, "the court room was crowded with spectators," reported the *Daily Leader,* among them Kels Nickell. "Vindictive by nature, he has clung with tiger-like fierceness at the heels of the county authorities throughout the history of the case."[25]

The reading aloud of the court's decision took a full two hours. Justice Potter concluded, "We fail to find . . . that Horn did not receive a fair and impartial trial and that the evidence does not sustain the verdict." At this point, Potter announced, "It now becomes our painful duty to fix a date for the carrying out of the sentence imposed by the trial court. . . . We, therefore, fix Friday, November 20th, of the year 1903, on which date the judgment of the court below will be carried into effect." "The decision in the Tom Horn case seems to meet with general satisfaction all over the city," observed the *Daily Leader.* It was now the defense attorneys' task to convey the high court's decision to Tom Horn. "Well, we have lost," one of them told Horn. "Has the date been set?" asked Horn. "Yes, it is November 20th," was the reply. The prisoner "turned slightly paler, took two or three deep breaths," according to the *Daily Leader,* "and then said, with a tinge of bitterness in his voice: 'All right, but, by God, they are hanging an innocent man.'"[26]

Under the law, the defendant still had thirty days to file for a rehearing in the high court. As Horn now realized that most legal avenues were exhausted, he began to write letters of appeal to persons interested in his case. "You and I and Snow and La Fors and Stoll all know that you changed your stenographic notes," Horn declared in a personal letter to stenographer Charles Ohnhaus. These changes were made "at the instigation of some one," continued Horn, "from what was actually said, to what you wanted me to say." "You are a young man not yet in the prime of life," wrote Horn. "Do you want to go through life knowing, as you do, that your perjured testimony took away my life?" On 12 October, he wrote Billy Loomis, an acquaintance of Frank Mulock in Denver, asking that he try to persuade Mulock to make an affidavit admitting that Walter Stoll and Joe LeFors had bribed him to lie on the stand. A few days later, Horn wrote directly to Frank Mulock. "If you done as you did [lied] at the instigation of the prosecuting attorney and deputy United States marshal," said Horn, "THEY AND NOT YOU ARE

RESPONSIBLE [Horn's emphasis]." "You can open your mouth and save my life," added the desperate prisoner. In a letter to John Coble, Horn insisted that he could not have made the attempt on Kels Nickell's life on 4 August 1901, because he was a hundred miles from the scene of the shooting. Horn said he saw a good friend, Jack Linscott, at this same time and was preparing to write him in Rock River.[27]

Since his trial in October 1902, Tom Horn had worked sporadically on an autobiography that covered his life from boyhood in Scotland County, Missouri, to his arrival in Wyoming in 1892. He now tried hastily to complete the manuscript, which comprised "four large note books of about 125 or 150 pages each . . . written in a clear, legible hand," according to the *Daily Leader*. The author devoted the lion's share of these pages to his experiences in the Apache campaigns of the 1880s, with Tom Horn at the heart of each battle or campaign—first as an understudy to Chief of Scouts Al Sieber and finally as Sieber's replacement. As the grand climax of his story, Tom Horn singlehandedly brought about the surrender of Geronimo in 1886. He mentioned his activities in the Pleasant Valley War and as a Pinkerton operative only briefly. In spite of Horn's boastfulness, embellishments, and even outright lies, he produced a rousing tale, told in *Police Gazette* fashion. The *Daily Leader* commented that it "shows that Horn not only has a remarkable army record but during his lifetime met many great men and was on terms of close friendship with them" and that he "performed . . . many brave deeds, which entitle him to recognition by the government." (The question remains, How could Horn's attorneys fail to bring this record out at his trial?) Timothy Burke, who was apparently the first person to read the manuscript, also complimented his client on his storytelling ability. Horn informed John Coble that he could publish it and possibly recover some of his expenses in the stock detective's defense.[28]

Throughout October, the public expected Tom Horn's attorneys to take advantage of the thirty-day appeal process permitted after the Supreme Court's rejection of the bill of exceptions. Yet a new appeal was not forthcoming, which led the *Daily Leader* to note on 31 October that midnight of the previous day "was the last day" for this motion. The only possible avenue of appeal remaining was Acting Governor Fenimore Chatterton, the Wyoming secretary of state who was serving out the unexpired term of Governor DeForest Richards. Richards had died in April. Chatterton, however, was unlikely to be sympathetic to an appeal. Unless he found "gross irregularities . . . [or] a strong doubt as to the guilt of a condemned man," Chatterton declared, "the courts were in a better position to understand the nature of the testimony and the justness of a conviction than he."[29]

Rumors that Tom Horn's friends were plotting another jail delivery continued to spread. One report held that his friends—presumably, the big cattlemen—in Brown's Park, Colorado, were working on his behalf, while another version had Butch Cassidy, whom the detective had once pursued, planning to liberate the condemned man. Taking no chances, Sheriff Smalley obtained three rapid-fire guns from nearby Fort D. A. Russell and placed them at strategic places inside the jail. The most effective means to discourage an attack on the jail, Smalley insisted, was "to make the failure of the attack almost certain." When the irrepressible Kels Nickell asked Smalley to permit him to stay in the jail in order "to assist in repelling an attack," the lawman bluntly refused. Since the jail was to be the site for Tom Horn's execution, the sheriff contracted with James P. Julien, a local carpenter and architect, to erect the scaffold inside the jail, adjoining the condemned man's cell. Tom Horn could walk a few feet from his cell to the scaffold. While the standard gallows required the executioner to cut a rope or jerked a prop from under the trapdoor, Julien's plan called for the flow of water into a pan that tripped the lever under the platform. In this way, the condemned man was said to "hang himself," and Sheriff Smalley could rationalize that human hands did not bring about the death of the victim.[30]

In the midst of these preparations, two persons closely associated with Tom Horn's case, Glendolene Kimmell and Joseph LeFors, appeared unexpectedly in Cheyenne. Horn's alleged sweetheart arrived on 30 October amidst rumors that she had sworn an affidavit for the defense, and that Lacey and Burke considered her statement as perhaps the most important in their case. (She had already made one affidavit asserting that Horn did not kill Willie Nickell.) The unexpected appearance of Joe LeFors, who was supposed to be hospitalized with a fever in Central America, created "a decided sensation," said the *Laramie Republican*. LeFors had already quietly informed U.S. Marshal Frank Hadsell that he was returning to defend himself against allegations of wrongdoing in the Tom Horn case.[31]

On Saturday, 31 October 1903, Acting Governor Chatterton opened the hearings into Tom Horn's latest appeal in the executive office in the capitol building. Present were attorneys Lacey, Burke, and Kennedy for the defense, and Attorney General Van Orsdel, representing the state, as well as Glendolene Kimmell, John C. Coble, Harry Windsor (a friend of Coble and Horn), and, of course, Kels Nickell. The entire appeal package consisted of Horn's signed letter of appeal, together with fifty pages of affidavits and a complete copy (400 pages) of the Willie Nickell coroner's inquest. The defense attorneys insisted the transcript of Horn's trial showed prejudice against their client; hence, Timothy Burke's assertion that the transcript of the Nickell inquest was fairer to Horn and thus was "the best history of this crime which can be obtained." In what the *Daily Leader* dubbed "The Affidavit War," the defendant was playing "his last card in his lengthy game with death." In a pointed editorial, William E. Chaplin of the *Laramie Republican* reminded the acting governor that "the eyes of the people" were upon him. "If he fails in the performance of his full duty, as judged by the great public mind," continued Chaplin, "then upon him the odium will fall."[32]

In a personal letter to the governor, Tom Horn "solemnly" averred that he did not know who murdered Willie Nickell, but, he continued, "I am informed that affidavits have been procured from different persons by my attorneys indicating that another has confessed to the crime." The prisoner concluded by asking for a reprieve and the substitution of life in prison for the death sentence. The basic argument of the defense continued to be that someone other than Tom Horn murdered Willie Nickell. For the entire afternoon, Burke read aloud numerous affidavits that the defense believed spoke directly to the innocence of the defendant. Frank Mulock, who apparently responded to Horn's personal appeal, changed his testimony. Mulock stated that he had since discovered that the man he thought was Tom Horn turned out to be a person "who greatly resembles him." In regard to the attempt on Kels Nickell's life on 4 August 1901, Peter Warlaumont, the former Laramie County deputy sheriff, deposed that Kels Nickell informed him that he recognized his assailants as James E. Miller and one of his sons. Lillie C. Graham, an Iron Mountain resident, deposed that "she heard James Miller, after his son had been accidentally shot, swear to avenge his son's death." Other affiants alleged that they heard Victor Miller confess to the murder of Willie Nickell. According to

E. W. (Ollie) Whitman, Victor Miller informed him that "my father wanted me to kill him; because we are always having trouble together, always fighting." The defense later submitted the affidavit of William Fitzmorris, an Iron Mountain resident, who deposed that a few days before Willie Nickell was killed, Victor Miller informed him that "'if that damned kid (Willie Nickell) bothered him he would kill him."[33]

While still in Missouri, Glendolene Kimmell made a fifteen-page affidavit in defense of Tom Horn, on 13 October 1903. This was "a sensational and lurid" statement, according to one newspaper. In this document, she abandoned her earlier defense of the Millers and asserted that both Victor and his father "confessed to this [murder] to her on four different occasions." In concluding her statement, Kimmell made "a theoretical defense of Tom Horn," according to the *Daily Leader*. She subscribed to the defense's description of Horn's confession as "josh" and applied this same term to his admission that he killed Billy Lewis and Fred Powell in 1895. She then asserted that there was a big difference between Horn's "manner and talk when drunk and sober." (In other words, he was a blowhard.) She now maintained that she was "actuated solely by the desire of saving the life and liberty of an innocent man—Tom Horn." Edward Slack, impressed with the irony of this development, headlined one article, "Horn's Fate Hangs on Woman's Word." After leaving Wyoming to avoid testifying at Horn's trial, he noted, she reappears "at the eleventh hour . . . and astounds all by her marvelous tale."[34]

The defense's affidavits then addressed Deputy U.S. Marshal Joe LeFors's investigation leading to the arrest of Tom Horn. Attorney Edward T. Clark, who had served on Horn's defense team, deposed that LeFors had complained bitterly in his presence that Walter Stoll had delayed payment of the reward money due him in the Horn case. Clark reported that LeFors said "Stoll had better be careful how he treated him, as Stoll knew that Lefors had knowledge of evidence which would clear Tom Horn." Jack Martin, the Laramie City blacksmith who had already testified in the Horn case, accused LeFors of accepting a $500 bribe from Jim Miller to cease investigating the Miller family in regard to the Willie Nickell murder. Martin also deposed that LeFors suggested that Martin "go in [with him] and cinch Horn," in order to earn the $1,000 reward. Martin asserted that he informed Albany County Sheriff Cook and Deputy Yund of this conversation. Even John Coble made an affidavit for the defense. He attested to his "great personal friendship" for Tom Horn, which explained "why he has taken such an interest in the trial." Otherwise, Coble declared that not only did he know "nothing at all" regarding the murder of Willie Nickell, but he had "not offered any reward for any testimony in the case."[35]

With the completion of the defense's presentation, Governor Chatterton announced that he would "take the case under advisement" and give the prosecution an opportunity to study these statements. However, Glendolene Kimmell continued to be a matter of concern for the governor, as well as for the county authorities. At the close of the afternoon session, Chatterton called her into his office and questioned her about her affidavit. In his recollections, written many years later, Chatterton said she was a devious person with an agenda. Her purpose was not only "to obtain commutation of Horn's sentence to life imprisonment," but, at the same time, to "later free Victor Miller of her charge that he had confessed to her." In an effort to learn more, the governor obtained "the original letters she had written Coble and the [defense] attorneys"—a move that reportedly caused "consternation" among them. Kimmell, who obviously detested the governor, accused him of nosing around in her "private affairs." Newspapers were also puzzled by her behavior. "If she knew what she says she does why in Sam Hill has she remained silent so long?" asked the *Saratoga Sun*. On 3 November, District Attorney Walter Stoll cleared the atmosphere by charging Kimmell with giving perjured testimony before the coroner's jury in August 1901. John C. Coble, Edward T. Clark, and John H. Fullerton provided her bond of $2000.[36]

On 4 November, John Lacey and Timothy Burke submitted additional defense affidavits to the governor. Albert W. Bristol, Jr., an Iron Mountain resident, deposed that he had a conversation with either Victor or Augustus (Gus) Miller (he did not know them well enough to tell them apart) about the time of Tom Horn's trial, in October 1902. One of the brothers answered, "No, Tom Horn never killed the boy; I happen to know who killed the boy." In regard to Jack Martin's accusation that Joe LeFors accepted a bribe from Jim Miller, Alfred Cook, sheriff of Albany County, deposed that Martin informed him of the deputy marshal's proposal to join him in framing Tom Horn. While Cook admitted that Martin was known for telling "imaginary stories," the sheriff did not believe he would "swear falsely." Deputy Sheriff Charles Yund attested to the content of Alfred Cook's affidavit.[37]

During the hiatus in the governor's hearing, newspapers continued to cover the Tom Horn case copiously. On 4 November the Wyoming Supreme Court directed Laramie County District Court Clerk T. Joe Fisher to deliver to the sheriff of Laramie County a certified copy of the death sentence. Fisher delivered the death warrant to Sheriff Smalley the next day. "The court orders that the sentence . . . be carried out November 20, between 9 o'clock in the morning and 4 o'clock in the afternoon," reported the *Daily Leader*. At the same time, the sheriff received a letter to Horn from Bob Meldrum, Tom Horn's old sidekick. "If the worst comes to the worst, YOU WILL NEVER HANG," wrote Meldrum, "as I know of a way that will get you out of that." Needless to say, this threatening missive put the Laramie County authorities "on their guard," observed the *Denver Post*.[38]

To add to the excitement, a report circulated that Victor Miller had confessed to the murder of Willie Nickell. To get to the bottom of the matter, Governor Chatterton ordered the sheriff to bring the Miller family to his office. Upon arriving at the Miller ranch, the lawmen learned that Charles Irwin and Neal Clark, two Coble cowhands, had tried to pressure Victor into confessing to the murder. Although very frightened, the young man insisted on talking to the governor. On the morning of the 5 November, Victor Miller and his parents appeared before the governor. (A bodyguard was assigned to accompany Victor Miller when he walked the streets.) After questioning the Millers about Willie Nickell's death, as well as their recent encounter with Irwin and Clark, Chatterton concluded the boy was not guilty. "As I was a lawyer of analytical ability," he later wrote confidently, "I knew how to search for and get the truth from these people." The Millers also insisted that Glendolene Kimmell's assertion that Victor Miller confessed to her was "absolutely false."[39]

When the governor reconvened the hearings on Thursday, 12 November, Walter Stoll presented the state's affidavits. Mary Simpson, a Laramie restaurant owner, added weight to the state's assertion that Tom Horn arrived in the Albany County seat on 18 July 1901, the day Willie Nickell was assassinated. She knew that "Tom Horn came into her restaurant for supper [on the 19th]," said Simpson, because she remembered that the Laramie newspapers carried a story of the Nickell killing that day. James Daugherty, also a resident of Laramie City, declared that he saw the defendant there on 18, 19, and 20 July. An affidavit by Stephen Frazier supported Daugherty's claim. Van L. Gifford's

(Guilford's) deposition addressed the matter of the ownership of the blue sweater. Possibly two weeks prior to the death of Willie Nickell, this affiant declared that he was in Max L. Meyer's mercantile store in Laramie when Tom Horn came in and asked for "a dark sweater that people would not recognize when they saw it." Since Meyer did not have such a sweater in stock, he had to special-order one. During Horn's trial, in October 1902, Meyer informed Gifford that the prosecution had found "that sweater" and that Meyer "told affiant that he had secured a sweater for Horn from Marks' [store], a dark sweater." This revelation created another "sensation" in the already sensational proceedings, according to one reporter. Stoll added to the excitement by announcing that he had had the bloody sweater analyzed by a noted expert at Rush Medical College in Chicago, who found that the stain was human blood.[40]

The resourceful prosecutor continued to respond methodically to each defense affidavit. In reply to Frank Mulock's assertion that he had mistakenly identified another man as Tom Horn, Stoll "produced letters written by Mulock after the conviction of Horn congratulating him [Stoll] on his victory." In response to the defense's allegation that Jim Miller paid Joe LeFors a $500 bribe from a certain amount of money in his (Miller's) possession, the prosecutor "produced vouchers from business men accounting for every cent" as legitimate expenditures. In a lengthy affidavit, Joseph LeFors denied Jack Martin's allegations and declared that everything the blacksmith said was "absolutely and unqualifiedly false." In response to Edward Clark's accusation that LeFors had threatened Walter Stoll if he did not receive the reward, LeFors denied that he made any such threat. Far from it—the deputy marshal admitted that the Laramie County Commissioners were correct in refusing to pay the reward until the state supreme court ruled on Tom Horn's appeal. The state then introduced several affidavits that criticized Jack Martin's reputation for truthfulness, alleging that he posed as a badman and member of an outlaw band. At this point, Governor Chatterton permitted the defense attorneys to submit seven affidavits in support of Jack Martin's reputation as a truthful individual. At least two of these—from Ora Haley and E. J. Bell—were statements from the most influential cattlemen in southern Wyoming and former employers of Tom Horn.[41]

The prosecutor continued to present affidavits relentlessly. Charles Fletcher declared that "he saw Tom Horn fire the shots that killed Willie

Nickell." Fletcher had to admit, however, that he could not testify at Tom Horn's trial because "he then was serving a term in the Colorado penitentiary for rustling." Christopher Lund deposed that "he saw Horn near the scene of the murder a short time after the killing, and talked to him." (The prosecution neglected to explain why Lund did not testify at Horn's trial.) In regard to Glendolene Kimmell's affidavit, Walter Stoll referred to his official letter book to demonstrate the "extraordinary efforts he made to secure the presence of the girl" at Tom Horn's trial. He "did not dwell at much length upon [her] testimony," remarked the *Laramie Republican,* "but left it for the governor to infer that her evidence had no weight as being perjured." William B. Ross, an attorney, deposed that while Tom Horn's trial was under way Walter Stoll sent him to Kansas City, Missouri, with instructions to try to persuade Glendolene Kimmell to return to Cheyenne and testify. She refused. "At no time did Miss Kimmell intimate to affiant that she knew who did the killing or that Victor Miller did the killing," Ross asserted.[42]

In a separate deposition, Victor Miller denied that there was any truth in Glendolene Kimmell's affidavit, and he denied absolutely that he confessed to Bristol. In response to the defense's efforts to establish an alibi for Tom Horn on the day of the Willie Nickell slaying, Walter Stoll first reviewed the facts in detail (over the objections of Lacey and Burke) and then presented the affidavit of Clarence D. Houck (which must have confused everyone in the house). Houck averred that Alexander Sellars [Sellers], a Sybille rancher, informed him that John C. Coble had asked Sellars to convey a letter to Timothy Burke in Cheyenne. Upon receiving this missive, Burke permitted Sellars to read it. Sellars told Houck that Coble's letter said that Sellars "would testify that Horn stayed at his [Sellar's] ranch on Wednesday night, July 17, 1902 [*sic*; 1901], and did not leave until noon the next day." While Sellars admitted that Horn did not stay with him, he informed Lacey and Burke that he would not testify to this fact. In response to Sellars's allegations, both Lacey and Burke made affidavits denying the Sybille rancher's accusations. In regard to Otto Plaga's alibi for Tom Horn on the day Willie Nickell was killed, Walter Stoll declared that he now had evidence that Plaga had seen the assassin only a few miles from the infamous fence gap and that Horn "'was riding like h——'" at the time. At this point, Prosecutor Walter Stoll rested the state's case.[43]

The defense then assumed the floor with additional counter affidavits. Charles Irwin and Neal Clark affirmed that "they told the Millers that Victor should not confess to the murder if he did not commit it." Gaines M. Allen, a Denver resident, deposed that he was an acquaintance of Robert Cousley (Cowsley), who supported Frank Mulock's assertion that Horn confessed to them. Allen declared that Cousely admitted that "he was going into a scheme to make some money out of the Horn case" when he agreed to testify. When Allen criticized Frank Mulock to his face for "jobbing" Horn, Mulock allegedly replied, "It was easy money." Mulock admitted to Allen that he did not know the cattle detective and "never saw Horn until he attended the trial." In an effort to bolster the sagging reputation of Glendolene Kimmell, the defense presented several affidavits of persons in Missouri who attested to her "good character." At this point, the prosecution and defense presented their final arguments, after which Governor Chatterton took all presentations under advisement.[44]

The reaction of Governor Chatterton, as well as of the public, to these many statements in the Affidavit War was mixed at best. Of the many depositions, the state's documents were probably more reliable overall. Yet many people questioned "the reliability of the evidence," said the *Laramie Boomerang.* As an indication of defense counsel's lack of confidence in its own statements, Lacey and Burke had reportedly asked several "influential women" to approach Governor Chatterton with a last-minute appeal. Nor did Prosecutor Stoll escape criticism. When it was pointed out that the evidence contained in several of the state's affidavits was in his possession during Tom Horn's trial and should have been submitted at that time, Stoll replied that "the witnesses were afraid to testify against Horn for fear some calamity would overtake them." In an unusually blunt editorial, Edward Slack of the *Daily Leader* attacked the various attorneys' resort to affidavits as "a cheap thing." "The courts do not recognize them as evidence in a case on trial," this editor asserted, and "the lawyer usually writes them and says what he thinks ought to be said to make his point." This "war of affidavits" was, concluded Slack, "a battle royal with paper wads."[45]

Nor were editorialists optimistic about Tom Horn's appeal. At best the defense's affidavits muddied the waters by presenting "evidence tending to show that a young boy [Victor Miller], not yet out of his teens, was guilty," according to the *Daily Leader.* "If true, Tom Horn has suffered all of the horrors of long imprisonment, the trial and the imposition of the death penalty" without justification. If these defense affiants were truthful, Joe LeFors "came into open court and swore away the life of an innocent man," all for $500. The irrepressible Kels Nickell attended the affidavit hearings and "frequently interrupted" the testimony. On one occasion, when Timothy Burke presented evidence that pointed to Victor Miller as the murderer of Willie Nickell, the excitable father blurted out, "Victor Miller did not kill my boy." "'Who did?' demanded Mr. Burke. 'Tom Horn,' was the instant response."[46]

As the Tom Horn case continued to gain nationwide publicity, kooks and cranks entered the fray. An anonymous resident of Kansas City, Missouri, confessed on his deathbed to the murder of Willie Nickell. On 4 November, Frank D. Hines, a Denver clairvoyant, sent Governor Chatterton copies of a "Psychometric test and Psychic message." Hines declared that he had received a visitation the previous night from the person who murdered Willie Nickell. The murderer is "a dark complected youth . . . , age 22, height five feet seven and one-fourth inches, weight one hundred and forty-four pounds." A skeptical *Daily Leader* correspondent pointed out that this specter bore a strong "resemblance to Victor Miller."[47]

At 4:00 P.M., on Saturday, 14 November 1903, Governor Chatterton dispatched copies of his formal opinion to the attorneys for each side. In this document Chatterton said he failed to find any "extenuating circumstances" in Tom Horn's case. In regard to the defense's allegation that Tom Horn's confession had been "doctored," the governor declared that to determine the truth of this accusation he "obtained the original [Ohnhaus] stenographic notes." With the assistance of his secretary, Jesse Knight, Jr., who could read shorthand, the governor "checked each character with the evidence given at the trial." "Every stenographic sign checked with the evidence; there was nothing left out," added the executive, "and there even were no interlineations." In regard to Tom Horn's assertion that his confession was mere "josh," the governor asserted that he could contradict neither the trial jury's conclusion that the defendant's statements were true nor the judgment of the state supreme court. Concerning the Denver confession, Chatterton concluded that the defense's affidavits were "not worthy of consideration." The governor went on to deplore the attack on Deputy U.S. Marshal LeFors, but added that even with the deputy marshal's testimony withdrawn from the case, "there still remains sufficient evidence to warrant a conviction."[48]

In regard to Glendolene Kimmell's affidavits, the governor declared that if her assertions were truthful, the defense should have presented "the facts . . . to the court rather than to me." As to the veracity of her statements, Chatterton maintained that Kimmel's assertions as to Horn's innocence were based upon "theories" and not facts or observations. In the governor's mind, she "was willing to present 'theories'" to save the condemned man, "intending after the commutation of Horn's sentence, to exonerate Victor Miller of the imputation cast upon him by her affidavit." (The governor detected an element of "conspiracy" in this matter; the *Daily Leader* of 15 November 1903 accused Kimmell of a "double cross.") In justifying his decision, Chatterton observed that "none of the matters presented to me in support of the application would be competent evidence in the trial court on behalf of Tom Horn."[49]

It was a difficult decision for Chatterton, a practicing attorney personally opposed to capital punishment, and his refusal to take action in Tom Horn's case created some controversy. The controversy persists to this day. Admittedly, Fenimore Chatterton confronted a complex situation and was undoubtedly torn between the humane thing (commutation to life imprisonment) and upholding the courts' decisions. Even though he was an "accidental" governor—having assumed the office of the deceased DeForest Richards—he desired to be his own person. Chatterton "is demonstrating that he has a mind of his own," said the *Laramie Republican,* "and is not likely to be smothered by any amount of affidavits from either side." As an experienced lawyer, the executive "is very thorough and never takes snap judgment in anything."[50]

Chatterton may have had other considerations in mind. As a longtime Wyoming resident familiar with the power of the cattlemen's lobby, he was aware of his political vulnerability. At the same time, he would almost certainly throw his hat in the ring at the next election. "Had he refused to permit the hanging," said the *Rocky Mountain News,* "he would have committed political suicide." (In the event, he was literally in a no-win situation.) While visiting Denver a few days later, Chatterton informed the *Rocky Mountain News* that the Tom Horn case was "definitely settled." Given the *News*'s long crusade against the Wyoming cattlemen's lobby and the state's crime problems, this journal gave the harried state executive a sympathetic ear. "Perhaps no other man in the United States has had more arduous duties with which to contend in the past few days," wrote the reporter, who noted that Glendolene Kimmell's perjury case "was the cause of many appeals to the governor." Chatterton expressed sympathy for Kimmell in spite her efforts "to exculpate Victor Miller" and obtain the release of Tom Horn. "It was a clear case of attempted self-sacrifice in order to save Horn's life," continued the governor, "and for that reason there is some sympathy for her." However, Chatterton insisted that she must stand trial for perjury. In a sensational revelation, the executive declared that he had "become cognizant of a plot to rescue Tom Horn." If he had commuted the condemned man's sentence to life imprisonment, this would necessitate moving the prisoner to the state penitentiary in Rawlins. According to his information, Horn's friends planned to stop the train, liberate the prisoner, and spirit him out of the country by a relay of fast horses.[51]

After nearly two years of determined and costly efforts, John W. Lacey and his defense team had to admit defeat. As Lacey said to the *Daily Leader,* "further efforts on their part would be useless." Timothy Burke, who had assumed a larger role in the defense, insisted that they "did not miss a point in the defense of the prisoner." While last-minute appeals could always be presented to the governor, he was not likely to be receptive. The only options left for Tom Horn were extreme ones: escape or suicide. "Bearing in mind the verdict of the jury in the case and the penalty imposed by the judge," Edward Slack concluded, "Governor Chatterton's decision could not have been otherwise." The executive's decision was "a blow to anarchy," continued Slack, in a reference to Wyoming's lawless past. When it is "understood in Wyoming that the courts are competent to punish the crime of murder," he continued, "there will be an end to lynching by mobs." In reflecting upon Tom Horn's downfall, this veteran newspaperman observed, "The fact is Tom Horn really convicted himself by his indiscretion before arrest; by his testimony and bearing in presence of the jury, and last by his bold attempt to escape, during which he attempted to kill the jailer." In these few words the *Daily Leader* editor summed up Tom Horn's case for all time.[52]

CHAPTER 16

Deathwatch

When Sheriff Edwin Smalley received word on Saturday, 14 November 1903, of Governor Fenimore Chatterton's refusal to act in Tom Horn's case, the lawman had only six days to finalize the arrangements for the execution. When Undersheriff Richard Proctor informed the prisoner on 15 November "that he must prepare for death," Horn received the news with what the *Daily Leader* called "the grim stolidity of a savage." After reading the executive's decision in the newspaper, the prisoner then "calmly turned to the other news features." "I'm not afraid to die," he remarked; "I'm ready any time now." To the reporter's astonishment, Horn began to calculate "the number of minutes he would have to live." He was even "able to joke and laugh, [and] . . . utterly conceal the conflict that must be occurring in his soul." But when Sheriff Smalley began to read the death warrant, the condemned man's face "took on an ashen hue," and "a great welt seemed to come up on the right side of his throat and there throbbed spasmodically." After regaining his composure, Horn "affected a smile, [and] thanked the officers for their kindness."[1]

With the deathwatch now in place, deputy sheriffs maintained a round-the-clock vigil that the *Daily Leader* described as a guard hovering "near the Spartan prisoner like a Nemesis." George Proctor, the twenty-year-old son of the undersheriff, had the onerous duty of watching the prisoner throughout the night. Visitors were generally turned away. When William Pinkerton, passing through en route to

California, asked to talk with the prisoner, the guards informed him that "no one was allowed to visit." Pinkerton left his former employee some cigars.[2]

Even though Tom Horn's attorneys had exhausted all avenues of appeal, he still clung to the hope of a last-minute miracle. "'There is no more chance of my hanging than there is of the governor's,'" Horn boasted. Naturally, such talk simply intensified Sheriff Smalley's fears of a jailbreak, and on the evening of 18 November the governor ordered National Guard units around the justice complex. Rumors circulated that the troops had orders to kill Tom Horn first if anyone tried to break him out, but Chatterton "positively denied" this report. As if this hysteria had not gone far enough, the adjutant general of the Colorado National Guard, Sherman Bell, got the erroneous notion that an insurrection loomed in Cheyenne and offered to send an additional regiment. While this offer was refused, Sheriff Smalley did accept the assistance of detectives from the Denver police force, as well as deputy sheriffs from outlying counties in Wyoming. With this extra manpower in addition to his own deputies, the sheriff was able to man two twelve-hour shifts. Undersheriff Proctor took charge of the night watch, while Tom Castle, an old friend of the sheriff, supervised the daytime guard. Such extraordinary security measures prompted some deputies to accuse their boss of "over playing his hand." Although some people believed Joe LeFors had used an underhanded method to obtain Horn's confession, and expressed outrage at such an action, Deputies Tom Castle and Dick Proctor rightly "doubted [that] the range hands" would risk a bloodbath to liberate him. As a final precaution, Smalley had a rope strung up around the justice complex to prevent people from getting too close to the jail. The national guardsmen formed a picket line behind the rope. Electric lights illuminated the jail and its environs at night.[3]

Nonetheless, rumors of a last minute jail delivery abounded, "bordering on hysteria," recalled John Charles Thompson of the *Wyoming Tribune.* Virginia Haldeman Jones, a schoolteacher, recalled that people had visions of "a great clan of masked riders" riding pell-mell into Cheyenne and rescuing the infamous range detective. Any pedestrian who wandered near the justice complex, especially at night, said the *Daily Leader,* was "brought to a standstill by the stentorian command of a militiaman." Guards armed with shotguns covered each window. On Thursday, 19 November, the day before the scheduled execution, Karl

Karnotsky (Knotsky), who had just been released from the county jail, caused a stir when he reported that someone had smuggled a message to Tom Horn informing him that he would be freed that evening. After Horn reportedly passed this information to "Driftwood Jim" McCloud, who had participated in the abortive August breakout, McCloud spread the word to other inmates. The deputy sheriffs had already concluded that something was in the wind when they found a message—"keep your nerve"—scratched in the snow outside the jail. To further arouse Sheriff Smalley's anxiety, gamblers in Denver and Cheyenne were wagering up to one hundred dollars "that Horn would never be hanged," according to one report. Among the gambling parlors where such bets were laid was that of Harry Hynds, Tom Horn's good friend.[4]

As execution day approached, James Julien rushed to complete the scaffold, which adjoined the condemned man's cell. The prisoner would have to walk only a few steps directly from his cell to the platform. After Julien's carpenters finished the scaffold on Thursday afternoon, the 19th, Undersheriff Proctor fashioned the noose and began to test the mechanism. To spare Horn the burden of witnessing this unsettling spectacle, a piece of canvas was suspended between the prisoner and the scaffold. However, T. Joe Cahill, who was present, recalled that Horn objected, exclaiming, "What in hell's going on out there?" When Cahill replied that they we were testing the gallows, Horn remarked, "That's good, but I think I'm the most interested bird in the world, and I want to see what you are doing." The canvas was removed, "and Tom stood there with his hands on the bars and watched us," recalled Cahill. No doubt the sheriff, who had never presided at a hanging, had visions of something going wrong as it had at the execution of train robber Thomas "Black Jack" Ketchum, in Clayton, New Mexico, the previous year. Sheriff Salome Garcia had failed take into account the fact that the victim had put on sixty extra pounds while languishing in prison. When his body dropped through the trapdoor, the noose decapitated Ketchum.[5]

To avoid making this mistake, Smalley's deputies tested the drop by using sacks of sand of various weights. Since the lawmen believed Horn weighed about 180 pounds, they adopted what they assumed to be the appropriate sack. (Why the lawmen did not weigh Horn is unclear. While in confinement, Horn lost 50 pounds, and therefore weighed only 150–60 pounds.) The situation at the jail was very eerie, recalled

Edwin Smalley, since Horn could plainly hear the water draining into the pan and hear the sack "hurtle through the trap door and snap at the end of the rope." When the condemned man "hears the sounds incident to the building of the gallows" and does not lose his nerve, observed the *Rocky Mountain News,* "there is no probability that he will not meet death like a man." The *News* also noted that the ordeal inflicted upon Horn was much "more severe than that of the majority of murderers." Newsman John Charles Thompson, who also witnessed these tests, agreed, opining that "a more barbaric ordeal for the condemned man could hardly have been arranged." The actual execution was almost anticlimactic.[6]

By law, Sheriff Smalley could invite as many as thirty people to witness the execution, six of them the prisoner's guests. In addition to asking his counterparts in other counties to attend, Smalley invited County Commissioner Corson, several newspapermen, and a few personal friends. A press table was set up within "full view of everything," according to the *Denver Republican.* Apparently, Tom Horn did not use his full allotment of invitations, although he invited Charles and Frank Irwin (Big Charlie and Little Frank, to their friends), both employees of John Coble, as well as T. Joe Cahill. No doubt Horn also asked John Coble to attend, but he refused. Of his defense attorneys, Horn asked only T. Blake Kennedy to witness the proceedings, but he declined as well. Among the personal friends whom Sheriff Smalley invited was Devine (Vine) Carley, a Union Pacific brakeman. Carley's invitation read simply: "You are requested to be present at the legal execution of Tom Horn which will occur Friday morning at ten o'clock, November 20, 1903, at Laramie County Jail."[7]

As execution day drew near, Sheriff Smalley informed T. Joe Cahill that Tom Horn had a favor to ask. When Cahill arrived at Horn's cell, he was taken aback at his friend's words: "T. Joe, this is funny; well, it may be funny to you but it isn't funny to me, but a jury and Judge Scott said I was guilty of the murder of Willie Nickells [*sic*]. . . . It looks like I will have to take the job [hang] on the 20th, and I want you to do the job." Horn had a particular reason for this request. "There is a certain deputy—a s-o-b that I don't want in the place," he explained. Instead, "I want you to fix me up and give me the works." Cahill, who had just recently married, would have preferred to avoid such a grim task, but he reluctantly agreed to Horn's request. "Tom, that's an unusual chore to ask anyone to do," he said, "but if that's what you want I will try to get the job done." (The "certain deputy" to whom the prisoner objected was either Dick Proctor or Leslie Snow.)[8]

Friends of Tom Horn still hoped that Governor Chatterton could be persuaded at the last minute to relent. Jack Rollinson, who had worked the range with Horn, recalled that he and his fellow hands expected "up to the very last" either a new trial or a commutation of sentence. Some encouragement came from the fact that several persons who had sworn affidavits against Horn had since withdrawn their statements. Charles Irwin was also actively seeking signatures for a petition to present to Chatterton, and John Coble was also reportedly working behind the scenes. Various individual appeals continued to reach out to the governor. One epistle, signed by an unlettered "lady of Tom Horn," said, "I[t] seam like thair is another punishment besides hangs." Another anonymous female, signing her letter "J," urged Chatterton to "be wise, not otherwise." A letter postmarked Denver pleaded, "Dont hang Tom Horn because someone else ought to hang." While "Horn is a peculiar character," wrote J. H. Packard of Denver, "I feel sure he would not murder a child." T. D. McKown, a physician in Cripple Creek, Colorado, pointed out that Horn had "given some years of his life . . . in defense of country," and was also "kind to animals"; such a person could not commit so heinous a crime.

On 19 November an anonymous person wrote: "I killed Willie Nickell. Tell them I do not want to see an innocent man hung. I will confess if they will not hang me." Another man, signing himself "A Cowboy," who claimed to know Tom Horn personally, denied that the range detective killed Willie Nickell. Horn, he said, had merely served as a go-between and had hired another man to commit the crime. Should Horn be executed, this writer said threateningly to the governor, "I don't give a penny for your life." Horn's friends had reportedly even recruited a New York eye specialist who would show that the stock detective had a severe eye ailment and "could not see the distance at which he is said to have shot" Willie Nickell. (It was true that Horn had to wear reading glasses, but whether this condition affected his shooting ability is not known.) The *Denver Times* rightly attributed these last-minute efforts to "the broad-hatted friends of Horn who frequent the saloons and public places." Governor Chatterton merely filed them away.[9]

In a last-ditch effort to obtain a commutation, Timothy Burke, Charles Irwin (and possibly John C. Coble) approached Governor Chatterton the afternoon before the hanging with the argument that "mistakes of a serious nature" existed in some of the affidavits recently presented to him. When a reporter asked the executive at the conclusion of this conference if he agreed to issue a commutation, Chatterton replied bluntly, "No, sir. You may state that no respite will be granted Tom Horn. He will hang to-morrow." As this was the final bid of the Lacey-Burke team on behalf of their client, it is unfortunate that details of what passed at this meeting were not revealed. While the executive did give Irwin permission to visit Horn, Sheriff Smalley refused him entry. Apparently, Chatterton received one last appellant late in the day—an emissary of the cattlemen. "Governor, there is a hundred thousand dollar fund ready to defeat any political ambition you have," this anonymous stockman said threateningly, "if you do not commute the sentence." Chatterton ejected this man from his office. The governor later maintained that he received no threats on his life, but a Cheyenne dispatch to the *Chicago Chronicle* reported that an unnamed writer in Denver warned him that his life was in danger if he did not commute Horn's sentence.[10]

The days immediately preceding the execution were very stressful for Glendolene Kimmell, although Sheriff Smalley permitted her to stay at the Inter Ocean Hotel under house arrest. On 16 November, Kimmell appeared before Justice of the Peace Trump, where she firmly protested her innocence. To avoid any additional adverse public criticism while Tom Horn's execution was pending, Prosecutor Stoll wisely obtained a postponement of her case until after the hanging. In an effort to correct public misconceptions about her connection with Tom Horn, Timothy Burke explained that this "is not a love story or anything but an honest effort on the part of a young woman to do what she thinks is right." As for Kimmell changing her testimony in favor of Tom Horn, Burke maintained that the officials who took her deposition "tangled up the statements." The *Denver Times* explained the many contradictory statements attributed to her by saying she was merely a flighty female who believed "that she heard Victor Miller and his father confess." When Kimmell appeared in the hotel restaurant on the day of the hanging, she admitted that she had passed "an extremely nervous night." She refused to give an interview, but she confessed that she believed Horn was "doomed." Nonetheless, Glendolene Kimmell had her admirers. "This remarkable little woman will meet the terrors of her coming [perjury] trial," declared William Chaplin of the *Laramie Republican,* "with the same calm demeanor and unruffled composure" with which "Horn faced his jury and judge."[11]

By this time, Tom Horn's family had also lost all hope. On the day before the execution, Horn received letters from two of his sisters, Nancy Adams, in Granger, Missouri, and Bertha (Alice) Loney, who resided in Elgin, British Columbia. "If it is God's will that you should be martyred for another's crime," Bertha remarked, "we must learn to say, 'Thy will be done.'" She also conveyed the sad news that their brother Austin (Oss) had recently died on a seal-hunting expedition in the Bering Sea. Nancy, who believed Tom was a victim of a conspiracy, urged him to make a last-minute appeal to President Theodore Roosevelt, according to the *Denver Republican,* pointing out his "meritorious service in campaigns against the Indians and also as a scout and packmaster" in the war with Spain. When the *Denver Republican* asked Charles Horn if his family was keeping Mary Ann Horn in the dark about her son's fate, he replied, "nonsense." She was eighty-four years old and "hale and hearty," and she knew all about Tom's fate, added Charles, although "It is pretty hard on the old lady."[12]

As darkness approached on the evening of the 19th, the residents of Cheyenne were "in the grip of an attack of 'jitters,'" recalled *Wyoming Tribune* reporter John Charles Thompson. One unconfirmed report held that "600 cowboys were massing fourteen miles north of town ready for a dash [on the jail]." While Sheriff Smalley had the good sense to discount the wildest of these reports, he took the additional precaution of arranging for the ringing of the fire bells as a means to broadcast the news of any such attempt. As the evening dragged on, national guardsmen with fixed bayonets confronted curious early birds who crowded the rope around the jail. When a soldier threatened one unfortunate spectator, Burke Bartholomew, the poor man "suffered a hemorrhage and was removed to the hospital." "If Cheyenne stood over a tremendous infernal machine that would blow the entire city into kingdom come," said the *Denver Times,* "the situation would not be more tense." In the event, however, everyone's fears proved baseless; the many visitors in the city, including Tom Horn's supposed cowboy supporters, voluntarily "retired to their beds shortly before midnight," according to the *Denver Republican.*[13]

At the last minute, Edwin Smalley relaxed visitation rules to allow ministers to talk with Tom Horn, even though the condemned man expressed "no religious sentiment or belief," according to the *Rocky Mountain News*. When someone asked if he desired spiritual consolation, he replied, "I don't know, and guess I never will." Yet he liked the Reverend John Watson, an Episcopal minister, and asked that he visit. "It won't do any harm," Horn remarked, "and may help me." When the Reverend Watson, whom John Charles Thompson described as an "eccentric preacher," said that the prisoner had "professed his belief" in God, the public assumed that Horn also confessed to the murder of Willie Nickell. Both assumptions turned out to be premature. While Horn "denied that he ever confessed," according to a Cheyenne dispatch to the *San Francisco Chronicle,* he reportedly admitted to "his spiritual advisers [that] he had been guilty of [other] crimes." Even so, he protested that he never "willfully" committed a crime. Horn may have considered himself a Christian, after a fashion. In a letter to John Coble some months earlier, he recalled an instance when the two men were involved in a train wreck and somehow survived unharmed. "You can't hurt a Christian," he concluded.[14]

The night before the execution was a long one for all the occupants of the jail. Although the prisoner appeared to accept his fate philosophically, he was occasionally irascible, swearing at a deputy who arrived late with his breakfast. The mortuary attendants made a racket as they delivered his casket, and Horn commented, "That's the wooden overcoat, but I guess I won't need it." Upon hearing this remark, the shaky guards went on extra alert, anticipating the long-expected jail delivery at any moment. Throughout the night, "a guard with ready gun stood over his couch with instructions to apply the 'law of the trail' in case of attack—to kill the prisoner rather than see him rescued." As the evening wore on, Horn wrote letters and carried on "an animated conversation with the death watch [George Proctor]," reported the *Denver Republican.* Eventually, "Horn went to sleep at once and soundly," recalled Edwin Smalley, while "the rest of us . . . sat up in the jail office throughout the night." This long evening was especially difficult for the sheriff, who had come to admire the victim. As Julien and his assistants were putting the finishing touches on the scaffold, the noise seemed to bother Driftwood Jim McCloud and the other prisoners more than Tom Horn. When the deputies tested the rope for a second time, Horn asked McCloud—in a bit of what can truly be termed gallows humor

—"[Did you] hear anything go 'ka-chunk!?'" When McCloud became emotional and rambled on—"Ain't it terrible, Tom?"—Horn told him to shut up.[15]

As Smalley and his deputies began to stir early on Friday, 20 November 1903, they found the condemned man, not surprisingly, in a foul mood. "He uttered oaths and seemed to have discarded the religious sentiment which he so suddenly expressed last night," said the *Rocky Mountain News*. Yet T. Joe Cahill recalled that Horn "seemed perfectly reconciled" to his fate. After washing up, Horn ate a modest meal of "sliced oranges, two pieces of toast, and a cup of coffee," wrote Edwin Smalley. He requested a Bible and magazines, read for a while, and "wrote farewell notes to relatives and friends." Surprisingly, Horn wrote an apology to Undersheriff Dick Proctor for his attack upon the lawman the previous August.[16]

Since Tom's brother, Charles Horn, resided in Boulder, Colorado, he felt some pressure to attend the execution but declined the invitation, pleading that his presence "would only complicate matters." "The officers there might think I went to assist in the talked-of rescue," he added, "and I know nothing of it." Charles did agree to assume responsibility for his brother's body. "With all his faults Tom is my brother," he told a reporter. He arranged for Boulder County Undersheriff Ed Sperry to serve as the family's agent at the hanging and escort the body to Boulder. Through Sperry, Charles Horn sent his doomed brother a touching message. "Tell him that while I have the greatest respect for him as a brother, and have the same feeling for him as a brother that I have always had . . . I could not endure the execution. . . . There is nothing that I could possibly do for him."[17]

Even though 20 November 1903 was cold and blustery in Cheyenne, with snow on the ground, a large crowd gathered outside the justice complex. The town came to a near standstill, recalled John Charles Thompson, and a "'Roman Holiday' spirit was in the air." People came from all directions to be present "when the trap falls," one newsman observed. National guardsmen formed an "unbroken line from corner to corner of the courthouse square," reported the *Denver Republican*. Among the spectators was Tom Horn's friend Hugh M. McPhee, who, with his wife, drove to the scene in their new automobile. Although this was a school day, many children played hooky. In defiance of orders to remain behind the rope, some managed to slip through the cordon of soldiers and press up to the jail windows, recalled Edwin

Smalley, "straining curious eyes, trying to see through the barred windows . . . where the gallows stood." Children who grudgingly attended school that day still tried to participate vicariously in this macabre event. Author Agnes Spring Wright, who was a fourth grader in 1903, wrote that one imaginative schoolmate "managed to tie a paper doll on a string to an electric light cord." "All eyes were on that dangling paper doll as the hands of the clock neared" execution time, she wrote.[18]

Among the men at the rope fence that day was Joe LeFors, the man many people believed responsible for Tom Horn's appointment with death. LeFors, who still carried the badges of a deputy sheriff and deputy U.S. marshal, was angered by allegations that he fled to Central America because he feared death at the hands of Tom Horn's friends. Even though Sheriff Smalley urged LeFors to stay in the background, recalled Tom Castle, "Joe refused and calmly strolled along the rope barricade, nodding to acquaintances on the other side of the rope." While some cowboys "jeered and dared him to draw," continued Castle, "Joe only said, 'I did my duty.'" "It really took guts," concluded Castle, "since he was not carrying a gun."[19]

At 9:00 A.M., Sheriff Smalley permitted Tom Horn to have one last visitor, John C. Coble. It was an awkward moment, and Coble could hardly speak: "Well, John," said Horn, "I'm glad you came." "Tom—" Coble's voice failed him. When he recovered his composure he said: "I'm sorry, Tom, but die like the man I know you to be. Tom, fate's against you. You must die." At this point, Coble "choked and wipe[d] away a tear." After thanking his former employer, Tom Horn assured him, "I'll die all right, John. Don't worry about that. I am not afraid John. John, John, I'm not afraid. Say good-by to all the boys. . . . Keep your nerve, John, for I'll keep mine. You know Tom Horn." "Tom, I can't stay to see it. I've done all I can. Some day the truth may be known, but I don't know. They are hanging an innocent man. I've gone to the end of every string and can't do anything [more]." In a breach of death watch security, Smalley unlocked Horn's cell and permitted the two men to shake hands without the impediment of the cell bars. "Good-bye, John," said Horn. "Coble murmured a faint 'Good-bye,' and walked away." As he departed the jail, Coble protested out loud that he had "stood by Tom" while the prisoner's "alleged friends have deserted him." After doing "all I could to save the law from hanging an innocent man," he protested, "I now give up, I can do no more." True to his word, Coble did not remain for the hanging.[20]

By this time, as men with invitations began to gather in the court clerk's office, across the hall from the sheriff's suite, a potentially explosive situation loomed. Charlie and Frank Irwin, good friends of the man about to hang, were outraged when Kels Nickell walked into the room. Nickell, who was not invited, was convinced that the sheriff had conspired with the cattle barons to hang a substitute—"a friendless tramp"—in place of Horn. Nickell resolved to thwart any such "put up job." "You've been given ten thousand dollars to let Horn out," Nickell said accusingly to Sheriff Smalley. "I demand that you let me be a witness at the execution to prevent such a thing." The sheriff escorted Nickell out of the building. "You won't see this hanging," he said. John Charles Thompson, who feared shooting might erupt, was relieved when the sheriff kicked Nickell out.[21]

Apparently Sheriff Smalley deliberately delayed the execution, which was scheduled for 9:00 A.M., to permit John Coble to make one final appeal to Governor Chatterton. When Coble and Charlie Irwin failed in this attempt, Smalley began to prepare the prisoner for his final moments. The time was about 10:55 A.M. Visitors had to enter by way of the aisle in front of Tom Horn's cell. "He watched them curiously," recalled Smalley, and nodded to persons he recognized. As a group of county sheriffs walked past his cell, Horn remarked to Richard Proctor, "Dick: that's a mighty sick looking lot of sheriffs." After the visitors took their places, Smalley entered Horn's cell and instructed him to get ready. The condemned man, who put on "slippers, dark trousers, a red and black shirt with a turn-down collar, and a light leather vest," recalled John Charles Thompson, puffed on a cigar. He then laid it down and prepared to follow a "visibly nervous" Sheriff Smalley and Deputy Snow from his cell. After surveying the crowd and detecting no threatening moves, Smalley nodded to Tom Castle and Dick Proctor to follow with the prisoner. "I was shaking," Castle admitted. When the procession, led by the Reverend Rafter, the Episcopal minister, reached the platform, they looked down at the Irwin brothers, who were standing at the foot of the stairway that led to the platform. The brothers had to stretch their necks in order see their friend as he mounted the scaffold. On the gallows platform, Dick Proctor gave the rope a tug and opened a red bag containing straps for binding the victim's arms and legs. Proctor laid the straps across the railing.[22]

When they received the go-ahead from Sheriff Smalley, Reverend Rafter led Horn and his guards onto the scaffold platform. Undersheriff

Proctor then informed the visitors that Charles and Frank Irwin would sing a song, "Life Is like a Mountain Railroad," requested by Tom Horn. From their places at the foot of the scaffold, the brothers began to sing. It was "a remarkable scene," wrote a *Denver Republican* reporter, as "the two old friends . . . filled the jail with the odd, wild notes of an odd, wild song" in two-part harmony. "It was their farewell greeting to their 'pard of the plains.'" Suddenly the sun broke through the overcast sky and "sunshine played around the man." Just as the Irwins finished, "the clouds came out and the jail was again dark and gloomy."[23]

As the condemned man walked onto the platform, Proctor signaled Tom Castle to join him. Still anticipating that someone might take a shot at Sheriff Smalley, Proctor wanted to get Castle out of the line of fire. (The most current rumor held that a rescue attempt would take place "when the Irwin brothers reached the first chorus" of their song.) "Would you like to say anything?" the sheriff asked Horn? Horn declined, and at this point, Dick Proctor summoned Frank and Charles Irwin up onto the platform. By prearrangement, Sheriff Smalley had agreed to permit them to say good-bye and to ask Horn publicly if he had confessed that he murdered Willie Nickell. (Charles Irwin believed that, being a good friend, if he pointedly asked Horn as he faced the noose, the range detective would tell the truth.) As the brothers mounted the platform, Castle recalled, they were the only composed persons present. Charles Irwin said:

> "Good-bye, Tom. You can only die once!"
> "Good-bye, Charley," answered Horn in a strong voice.
> "Tom, I want to ask you a question. Did you make a confession to this murder to a minister, as reported in the *Denver Times?*"
> "No, sir, I did not."
> "That is true, Tom?"
> "It is, Charley."
> "Good-bye," the men exclaimed together as they shook hands.

After the brothers left the platform, they, too, refused to witness the death of their friend and withdrew to the sheriff's office.[24]

Even though Tom Horn did not want Undersheriff Dick Proctor involved, Sheriff Smalley intended all along for him to play a key role. While Horn wanted Cahill to tie the leather straps around his legs and arms, the young man fumbled with them, and Proctor helped with this task. When Horn observed Cahill's shakes, he said, "What's the matter, Joe? Ain't losing your nerve are you?" (Cahill recalled that "old Tom . . . looked down and said to me: 'T. Joe, isn't that the scaredest bunch of s-o-b's you ever saw?'" referring to the spectators below.) As the process was taking longer than Proctor intended, he tried to speed it up. "Joe, I hear you're married now," said Horn. "Yes," replied Cahill. "Well, treat her right and I hope you live happily." Proctor then knelt down and began to fit the straps around Horn's legs. "Make 'em tight," said Horn, "I don't want to kick." Horn looked at the sheriff and remarked, "You look as though you were worried and had lost considerable flesh." "I have," Smalley replied, "and you look thin, too, Tom." "Yes, I have fallen off about 50 pounds. I have worried some." "I have also worried," replied Smalley. Observing that both Smalley and Cahill were very nervous, recalled Tom Castle, Horn remarked, "Don't be nervous boys, you're only doing your duty." When the leg straps prevented him from stepping on the trapdoor, Horn said "I'll have to have a hand to get on that thing." Smalley placed the noose around Horn's neck, and Tom remarked that it "pinches a little." The lawman "straightened it."[25]

As the onlookers bowed their heads and the Reverend Rafter prayed, Tom Horn "looked straight ahead. When "Proctor placed the black cap over Horn's head," said the *Denver Republican,* the prisoner voluntarily adjusted his head "as to assist the officer and at the same time closing his eyes." Even though he hated Proctor, observed this newsman, "the last face he looked at and the one that he has seen more than all others in the last 2 years" was the undersheriff. As Proctor tightened the drawstring, he asked Horn, "Are you ready, Tom?" "Yes," replied Horn. Smalley and Cahill picked up Horn bodily and placed him on the trap door. The time was 11:07 A.M. "There was a clicking noise as Horn's weight bore down on the collapsible post and operated the [water] valve," according to the *Denver Republican,* "and the sound of running water filled the jail." As the faint splashing of the water disturbed the silence, Tom Horn uttered his last words to the two officers holding him on the trapdoor: "You are not getting nervous, are you, boys?" For a few seconds, the sheriff feared the trap mechanism had malfunctioned, and "Horn was seen to clench his fists tight, [and] move his head back slightly so as to bring the noose to bear tighter on the throat." "Suddenly, there was silence, as "the sound of running water ceased," continued the *Republican* reporter; "the silence was distressing and many heads turned away." "Finally at the end of thirty-one seconds, which seemed like so many hours," the reporter observed, "there was a cracking sound as if a bolt had suddenly shot into a socket, and almost before the spectators were aware of it, the body dropped through the opening." Horn's body "turned slightly and then hung still." (Dick Proctor had boasted to John Charles Thompson that he designed the noose so that Horn's body would take a half-turn so that his back would be to the spectators.) The time was 11:08 A.M.[26]

Below the scaffold, Doctors John H. Conway and George P. Johnston awaited the grim moment when Tom Horn's body plunged downward. According to official protocol, each physician was required to "take a wrist of the dangling man and follow his pulse until life is extinct." After sixteen minutes, they pronounced the infamous range detective dead. As a hearse transferred the corpse to William Gleason's Funeral Parlor for embalming and preparation for the journey to Boulder, Colorado, a crowd of curiosity seekers tagged along, hoping Sheriff Smalley would permit them to see the body. He did not, allowing only "a few close friends of Horn" to view the body. At the funeral home, Coroner Thomas Murray empaneled a jury to rule as to the cause of death. "We, the jury," read the ruling, "do find that the deceased Tom Horn, came to his death by hanging, said hanging having been inflicted by the sheriff of Laramie County in the execution of a sentence of death. John F. Barron, Foreman." William Chaplin of the *Laramie Republican* remarked that Murray must have had "a very dull year" when he would investigate the death of a man who died on the gallows (forgetting that the law required a coroner's inquest over persons who had been executed, just as in any other death). Coroner Murray, who had been a part of the Willie Nickell case from the beginning, was heard to remark with much satisfaction, "Now I close the case."[27]

Immediately after Tom Horn was pronounced dead under the scaffold, Sheriff Smalley ordered all visitors from the jail area. Newspaper reporters required no such encouragement since they were anxious to file their stories. Griffin Cochran, a reporter for the *Wyoming Tribune,* left as quickly as he could in order to assist Editor William Chapin Deming with an extra. As John Charles Thompson, Cochran's colleague, left the jail "at a high lope," he collided with Kels Nickell, "who had contrived to get through the police line." "'Is the s-o-b dead?' he asked? 'Yes,' I replied, and loped on—I had an extra to get out." Fortunately, Sheriff Smalley had the wisdom to permit Kels Nickell to view Horn's remains at the funeral parlor, in order to allay any suspicions that imaginary conspirators hanged a substitute. When Nickell tried to congratulate the officer for "a good job" and tried to shake the lawman's hand, Smalley "told him to go to hell." "The long weary months had been hard on me," Smalley later explained in his own defense. He regretted his gruff treatment of the aggrieved father, who had been through an equally torturous period.[28]

In spite of the fact that a coroner's jury confirmed the death of Tom Horn, a rumor quickly spread, according to the *Laramie Boomerang,* "that by some mysterious legerdemain the county authorities had substituted a dummy for the real man." In spite of the efforts of the *Daily Leader* to quash such "foolish rumors," this wild story was "given credence by a considerable number of Cheyennites." Yet the examination of Tom Horn's remains revealed that Sheriff Smalley had narrowly avoided an even greater embarrassment, one that could have placed him in the unenviable category of New Mexico Sheriff Salome Garcia, who botched the hanging of Black Jack Ketchum in 1901. "The neck was broken and the ends of the spinal column pulled apart," said the *Daily Leader.* Had the condemned man "dropped a foot farther it is believed the shock would have torn his head off." "As it was, the weight on the end of the rope when the jerk of the fall came was equivalent to nearly 1,000 pounds." Like his colleague to the south, Smalley had failed to take into account the very opposite of the circumstance that resulted in Black Jack's decapitation. Tom Horn had lost about fifty pounds during his long imprisonment. Nonetheless, Sheriff Edwin Smalley now hastened to complete his last official act in the Tom Horn case—affixing his signature ("official return") to the death warrant and filing it with the district court clerk. "The clerk will enter the return of the warrant in the record," said the *Daily Leader,* "and the case will then be closed for all time."[29]

From his office in the capitol building, an anxious Governor Fenimore Chatterton was much relieved when his representative at the jail telephoned him "when the drop fell." Since Tom Horn had not confessed to the murder of Willie Nickell (and many people believed he would at the last moment), the dead range detective was still cause for some concern. Yet, the fact that Horn "made no direct denials of the

Nickell murder when the question was put to him," Chatterton wrote later, confirmed his guilt. The governor received much public applause for his steadfast attitude in the Horn case. In spite of "the great pressure brought to bear by Horn's friends," observed William Reid of the *Rawlins Journal,* he was willing to endanger "his own political aspirations" in order to see justice done. The stubborn executive showed backbone, concluded Reid. Echoing these sentiments, the *Wyoming Tribune* complimented Chatterton for the "masterly manner" in which he managed the Horn case. Nonetheless, Chatterton's political enemies succeeded in thwarting his effort to win the gubernatorial nomination in the forthcoming campaign.[30]

Sheriff Edwin Smalley, Prosecutor Walter Stoll, the county commissioners, and other Laramie County officials all received plaudits for their work in the Horn case. "The execution was conducted with the regularity of clockwork," the *Daily Leader* observed, "and was perfect from a hangman's standpoint." Even Joe LeFors, who had no love for Smalley, had to admit that the sheriff and his deputies performed "their duties well in the face of the enormous political influence brought to bear in Horn's favor." Needless to say, Smalley and his subordinates "express deep relief to have their troublesome prisoner off their hands," said the *Rocky Mountain News,* and "for the first time in months" they could leave the office door unguarded. Although Samuel Corson and the county commissioners were less visible, Edward Slack of the *Daily Leader* praised them "for the steadfast manner" in which they assisted the prosecutor and sheriff. While the commissioners regretted "the unusual expense to the county" in the Horn case, Slack added, "it was only as a last resort that they consented to raise the levy." "There are some things of more consequence than money," concluded Slack, and "the people of this county are fortunate in having such an able and discreet board of commissioners in a crisis we have been passing through."[31]

The significance of the execution of the notorious range detective transcended the victim. As William Chaplin of the *Laramie Republican* observed, "The people of Wyoming have risen above the methods of the anarchists [vigilantes] and proved their ability to enforce the laws against murder." "Hereafter in Wyoming the occupation of the assassin who kills for hire will be gone," he asserted. "No man nor set of men will henceforth dare to conspire against the life of any citizen," added Chaplin, "because he is suspected of cattle-stealing or other violations of the laws of the state." In "the staining of one's hands with . . . the blood of a criminal, the man who hires an assassin does himself equal harm." The execution of Tom Horn should prompt the men behind this hired assassin to beware that "through their courts the people of Wyoming have spoken," Chaplin concluded.

Yet Chaplin had to admit that hired assassins such as Tom Horn might have continued their nefarious activities "had not a mistake been made and a boy killed instead of a man." Edwin Smalley agreed with this assessment, remarking that he doubted "if there ever would have been a Tom Horn case, if it had been Kels Nickell, rather than his young son, who was killed."[32]

Since the trial of the controversial range detective had received widespread publicity, his execution received commensurate attention. Newspapers across the land carried lengthy descriptions of this grisly proceeding. Such descriptions took the place of respectful obituaries. A *San Francisco Chronicle* headline announced "Tom Horn Pays the Penalty"; in the *Los Angeles Times* "Horn Laughs at Death." The *Washington Post,* referring to the Irwin brothers' song at the gallows, declared that the victim was "Hanged with Some Unusual Features." The *Chicago Daily Tribune* said simply, "Tom Horn Is Executed: No Attempt to Rescue Him." The *New York Times* reported "'Tom' Horn Dies Coolly." While these various columns were labeled as "special dispatches" from Cheyenne, they merely contained standard fare, including many errors about Tom Horn's life.[33]

The Tom Horn case continued to arouse varied emotions. When Jack Rollinson, the range detective's friend, and Hiram Yoder, the jury foreman at Horn's trial, traveled together to Cheyenne a short time after the hanging, Rollinson said openly in a local bar that Tom Horn was not guilty. "I had two fights in town with fellows who said, 'served him right,'" recalled Rollinson. "I feel that that man who was such a wonderful Indian scout, such a fine mountain man, and good cowman," he continued, "could not deceive anyone who believed in him." Like other cowhands on the Laramie Plains, Rollinson "expected up to the very last that he would be set free." The inmates at the Laramie County Jail were also disturbed, not only over the death of one of their own, but by Tom Horn's ghost! "Ghostly Sounds Disturb Prisoners in County Jail and Suggest Phantom Hanging," said the *Daily Leader,* which added that no prisoner wanted "to live in a dead man's quarters."

The speculation was that Jim McCloud—"the most desperate character now in the jail"—would be the next occupant of the "death cell."[34]

Tom Horn's family still faced the duty of interment. While John Coble offered to bury Tom at the Bosler ranch, Charles Horn insisted on interment in Boulder. Even so, Coble paid for all the burial expenses including "a copper lined oak casket, trimmed in white satin and silver" that could be "hermetically sealed." "On the cover is a large plate of solid silver," according to the *Rocky Mountain News,* "bearing the simple inscription: 'At Rest.'" (This casket reportedly cost $700.) As Deputy Sheriff Ed Sperry, the Horn family's representative at the hanging, had the remains loaded onto an express car at the Cheyenne depot, a potentially explosive situation loomed. Not only were John Coble and the Irwin brothers among the "morbid crowd" of onlookers, but Joe LeFors inexplicably put in an appearance. These men were bitter enemies, noted a *Denver Times* reporter who was there, and "every one had a brace of six shooters under his arms." Fortunately, this confrontation was only a staring match.[35]

When Sperry arrived in Boulder with Horn's body, several hundred people were gathered at the depot. As representatives of W. F. Buchheit's mortuary took charge of the remains, a crowd of curious spectators made an unsuccessful request to view the body. Charles Horn intended to limit the visitation to family members and a few friends, but the press of interested persons was so great that he reluctantly opened the casket. "For several hours this morning up to noon there was a constant stream of people," observed the *Denver Republican.* They wanted to get a look at the man "who in his lifetime had created such a stir and who for the last few weeks has perhaps been talked of more than any other man in the West." These visitors, "with hats off, took their look at the body silently, made no remarks, and left the room as quietly and respectfully." Many viewers were probably disappointed, since Tom Horn looked very "ordinary," according to the *Republican,* and "no one would have believed that this man had confessed that he made killing of men a business." While Horn's face was "somewhat discolored" and his "neck also showed the marks of the hangman's rope," the undertakers had applied "a white powder . . . to the bloodshot parts." When the Denver reporter pointedly referred to "the morbid curiosity of the people of Boulder" in his article, the editor of the *Boulder Daily Camera* took umbrage at this supposed slur and asserted that his community had "no more than its share" of inquisitive citizens. It was apparent that this former scout and range detective was becoming an even more notable celebrity in death.[36]

In spite of their curiosity, the good citizens of Boulder did not feel compelled to make a church available for Tom Horn's funeral service. The last rites were performed in Buchheit's Funeral Home on 22 November 1903. Edith Rheaume—the future wife of Jack Ganzhorn, and an old Arizona friend of Tom Horn—agreed to sing. When "the regular orthodox churches of Boulder refused to have anything to do with the funeral," she recalled, Edward G. Lane, pastor of the First Baptist Church, agreed to preside. With a large but "respectful crowd" gathered outside the mortuary, the Reverend Lane delivered a short message emphasizing "the hope in the hereafter." An old spiritual, "How Good Has Jesus Been to Me," was also sung, apparently by the future Mrs. Jack Ganzhorn. A large crowd accompanied the hearse to the Pioneer's Cemetery. "We buried Tom with all due respect that relatives could show," Charles Horn informed John Coble. "We had the largest funeral that was ever in this town," Charles continued, and "everybody showed due courtesy [with hat off] to the hearse. . . . There must have been anyhow 2500 people at the funeral."[37]

Given his brother's notoriety, Charles Horn expected circus promoters to want to display his body in some ghoulish sideshow. Such promoters might even try to steal the body. At the suggestion of attorney Timothy Burke, Charles placed a guard at his brother's grave site. Burke had demonstrated some sensitivity to the feelings of the Horn family, and Charles Horn expressed his appreciation in a letter to John Coble. Burke "is an old friend of ours and Tom's," wrote Charles, "and never falls down on anything." Just as Charles Horn predicted, a stranger appeared at his door shortly after the funeral service and offered $500 for the body of his brother! Had not his wife restrained him, the angry brother would have thrashed the promoter.[38]

Meanwhile, Glendolene Kimmell, who had suffered what might be termed "collateral damage" as a result of her association with the Tom Horn case, remained under house arrest at the Inter Ocean Hotel on perjury charges. Although not romantically involved with Horn, she still regretted his death. Maids reported sounds of sobbing coming from her room during the execution. "Perhaps no one passed through the ordeal [of Horn's execution] with more anguish of heart than she," concluded the *Denver Times*. To add to her discomfiture, from her room Kimmell could see Tom Horn's casket being loaded on the train. She sought to have her trial moved to a less prejudiced community, but she need not have worried since Prosecutor Walter Stoll dropped her case on 16 December 1903. While Stoll cited a legal technicality as his justification, it was obvious that he wanted to clear the court calendar of every Tom Horn–related matter. He was happy to be rid of this "dwarfish little woman."[39]

While Kimmell's relationship with Tom Horn was (and remains) the subject of much speculation (and salacious gossip), they had very little time together. Aside from two days at the Miller ranch, in July 1901, and a similar amount of time during the Willie Nickell inquest, their association was, as the *Denver Times* remarked, at best "platonic".

Yet this "enigmatic figure," according to historian Carol L. Bowers, deserves recognition beyond her connection with Tom Horn. By having only a brief and perhaps accidental "association with the notorious stock detective," observed Bowers, she became "an object of public scrutiny." Bowers asserts that Kimmell was an early example of a woman attempting to break out of the traditional mold that a patriarchal frontier society imposed. "An intense, complex woman, Glendolene Kimmell resisted the submissive role for women prescribed by late Victorian society," writes Bowers. "Her assertiveness and unswerving personal resolve empowered her to resist attempts to silence her as an advocate of Horn."[40]

In a parting shot, Kimmell filed an affidavit in the district court alleging that her statement in support of Tom Horn was truthful. As she boarded a train to depart Wyoming, on 18 December, Kimmell informed a *Rocky Mountain News* reporter that "her arrest was simply one of the cards played in the great legal battle to convict Tom Horn— nothing else." When asked if the range detective was guilty of the Willie Nickell murder, she replied, "No, Tom Horn was not guilty of the murder of Willie Nickell. . . . I told only the truth when I said in my affidavit that Victor Miller and his father had confessed to me that Victor killed . . . [Willie Nickell]." She stoutly maintained that she had "no reason to declare that Horn was innocent, as all those stories regarding our affection for each other were myths—nothing else." "Our relations were merely platonic," she went on. Tom "was a good friend who brightened many lonely hours on that ranch by his conversation, for he was an interesting talker." As Kimmell departed for Missouri, she declared that she was going to try to recover from "the awful strain of this affair" and return to teaching.[41]

Unlike Glendolene Kimmell, who could leave Wyoming, John Coble was constrained to remain in the state. Not only did he have to live with many bitter memories, but his name would be forever associated with Tom Horn's. After saying his farewells to Horn on execution day and leaving the jail, according to the *Daily Leader,* Coble "was so overcome [by grief] that he had to be supported [by friends] as he walked . . . to his hotel." Coble was also unwell at this time. En route to his ranch, he had to stop for rest at a hotel in Laramie. At this same time, Franklin Bosler was completing the dissolution of their partnership. By now Bosler was fully cognizant of Coble's close association with Tom Horn. A few months later, in 1904, Coble sued Bosler, arguing that Bosler was not giving him a proper share of resources from the breakup of the Iron Mountain Land and Cattle Company. In the resulting legal wrangling, which not only publicized their internal feuding but further tied Coble's name to Tom Horn, Coble won a settlement of more than $16,000.[42]

That Coble continued to stand by Tom Horn's memory was apparent in his efforts to get Horn's autobiography into print. In December 1903, Coble began negotiations with the *New York Herald* to publish the manuscript. In spite of reports that "a tidy sum" was involved, this arrangement fell through. The following month, Coble arranged for publication with the Denver firm of Louthan & Jackson Book & Stationery Printing Company. While Coble served as chief editor and decided what part of Horn's writings should be included, the actual preparation of the manuscript was the work of Glendolene Kimmell. Kimmell, who had taken a stenographer's position in Denver, welcomed this opportunity. Hattie Louthan, daughter of the publisher, Overton E. Louthan, and a prominent member of Denver's literary circle, also assisted. To strengthen the manuscript, Coble and Kimmell sought additional information from Horn's Arizona friends, among them Edwin Tewksbury and Al Sieber. Tewksbury did not respond, but Sieber's recollections were included in an appendix. With the inclusion of Sieber's letter, dated 7 April, Kimmell's lengthy memoir, and Coble's "Closing Word," the entire corpus went to press. With considerable advance publicity, the book appeared on 20 or 21 April 1904—*Life of Tom Horn,*

Government Scout and Interpreter, Written by Himself, Together with His Letters and Statements by His Friends: A Vindication. Five thousand copies were printed, all in paper covers but for 120 in hardback. Paper copies sold for fifty cents; hardbacks for $1.25.[43]

In a final statement included in the *Life of Tom Horn,* John Coble extolled the virtues of the man he knew so well:

> The story is done. Close the pages that tell of fighting our country's foes, of secret service, of Cuban campaigning, of zeal, of faithfulness, of fearlessness. Unwritten always must remain the record of Tom Horn's bravery, loyalty, generosity, and the countless kindly acts which marked his pathway through life. I am proud to say that he was my friend, always faithful and just. When can I hope to see such another! And no man ever walked more bravely to his death.

Coble was adamant as to the unjust conviction of his friend and blamed the newspapers for Horn's problems. "I am convinced, and I re-assert it to be true, that Tom Horn was guiltless of the crime for which he died."[44]

In spite of his many problems, John Coble attempted to get on with his life. In March 1904, at the age of fifty-six, he married Elise Towson of Laramie. The association of Coble's name with that of Tom Horn even intruded into his wedding. In announcing the nuptials, the *Buffalo Bulletin* could not refrain from mentioning Coble's association with Tom Horn and elevating their friendship by association with Greek mythology: "John C. Coble, the well-known cattleman, and fidus Achates of Tom Horn," reported the *Bulletin,* was married recently. (Achates was the faithful companion of Aeneas.)

Unfortunately, the indebtedness that Coble incurred from the Tom Horn trial continued to beset him. Fellow ranchers who had promised to contribute to Horn's defense failed to come through. In January 1905, the *Daily Leader* headlined a story "Tom Horn's Employers Said To Be Quarrelling." "Tom Horn's body lies mouldering in the grave," the story continued, "but the influences which sent him on his murderous missions . . . have fallen out over . . . how much each is to contribute. . . . Two prominent cattlemen . . . both of whom were frequently mentioned in connection with the 'Horn syndicate,' are said to have indicated that the syndicate has gone to pieces on the rock of expenses." One rancher said he had "washed his hands of the Horn affair." Another stockman expressed the fear that "if the present quarrel continues," documents that could reveal details of this "Horn syndicate" might be made public. If this should happen, the newspaper predicted, "some of the mysteries of the Horn case may be explained." Sadly, no such exposé occurred.[45]

John Coble's ultimate demise was a tragic one. After the dissolution of the Iron Mountain Ranch Company, Coble tried various ranching efforts on his own, eventually ending up in Nevada. By now deeply despondent, he confided to friends that he contemplated suicide. After begging Franklin Bosler for some sort of employment, he shot himself to death in a hotel in Elko, Nevada, on 4 December 1914. In an obituary, the *Cheyenne State Leader* accorded John Coble two distinctions: first, as manager of one of the largest ranches in Wyoming; and second, as an implacable enemy of rustlers. "In company with other cattlemen Coble determined to do away with 'rustling' in Wyoming," the writer remarked, "and to that end Tom Horn, a noted Arizona gunman, was employed to hunt down the cattle thieves." Just before Coble took his own life, he wrote his wife, Elise, "Believe me, I am yours to the end, lovingly."[46]

Joseph LeFors, the other major figure in Tom Horn's life, continued to serve in various law enforcement capacities for two more decades. While he was regarded as brave and hardworking, many people could not forgive him for his method of extracting the confession of Tom Horn. "One could argue over who was the more unprincipled—Tom Horn or Joe LeFors," wrote Chip Carlson. In the end, Carlson had to select LeFors as the more honorable by "a slim margin." In Carlson's opinion, the violent times in which these men flourished often pressured them to put "ends before means." In spite of the many enemies that LeFors made, he lived a long life, and like Tom Horn, wrote about his experiences. He died in Buffalo, Wyoming, on 1 October 1940.[47]

While LeFors never doubted Tom Horn's guilt, his investigation of the range detective set in motion a controversy as to the frontier sleuth's guilt or innocence that continues to this day. Surprisingly, some persons who might be expected to defend Horn believed him guilty of the murder of Willie Nickell. Horn "was tried by a court of law, the verdict was guilty, and we hung him!" T. Joe Cahill informed writer Dean Krakel. Among Horn's attorneys, John W. Lacey apparently believed him guilty; T. Blake Kennedy believed him innocent of the Nickell murder but believed he had killed others for money. "Doc" Shores, who was in a good position to learn about Tom Horn's misdeeds, asserted that Horn had admitted privately to shooting Willie Nickell on the mistaken notion that his target was Kels Nickell. In a letter to Jay Monaghan, Horn's biographer, Shores declared that "the man . . . who paid Horn the money for killing Mat[t] Rash and Isam [sic] Dart" informed him that Tom Horn admitted the Willie Nickell killing. Dr. George P. Johnston, who testified at Tom Horn's trial, informed Dean Krakel in 1954 that he believed Horn "was railroaded by the jury." Others who knew Tom Horn or were familiar with his case believed Horn innocent—among them newspaperman William M. Raine, Charles Camp, owner of the famous cutting horse, Muggins, that Horn trained, and Charles H. Coe, a range detective in Wyoming after Horn's death.[48]

Tom Horn's friends in Arizona were equally incredulous at his tragic demise. George H. Kelly, editor of the *Arizona Bulletin* in Solomonville, declared that Horn's execution "was cause of some regret" since he "had the good will and respect of all who knew him." Thomas N. Wills, who worked cattle with Horn in the 1880s, insisted that Horn was "a quiet, peaceable man" and incapable of "a willful murder." Graham County pioneers informed Lorenzo D. Walters, a popular Arizona writer, that Horn was always "a square shooter" and insisted that he was "railroaded to the scaffold." Among Horn's Arizona friends, Burt and Horace Dunlap were perhaps most disturbed at his death on the scaffold. Burt had gone to great lengths to gather depositions for Horn's defense against robbery charges in Nevada in 1891. Horace Dunlap, who devoted much time to gathering material about Tom Horn, summed up his defense in the *Arizona Historical Review* (1938). Even Geronimo, the Chiricahua medicine man, expressed surprise at the former scout's demise. When Charles Ackenhausen, who was acquainted with both the old Apache warrior and Tom Horn, asked the old shaman what he thought about Horn's execution," Geronimo replied that "he did not believe him guilty."[49]

Some writers have accorded Tom Horn a significance beyond the simple matter of his guilt or innocence. Shortly after Horn's arrest in 1902, a *Denver Republican* editorialist connected his case with the ongoing controversy and bloodshed surrounding "the public land question." This writer asserted that the Horn case brought this festering issue "to the front as never before." "On the land laws of the United States are blamed hundreds of deaths throughout the west very year," the writer remarked, citing a figure as high as 500 annually. Newspapers dismissed such deaths as merely personal squabbles, he continued, but they were "really crimes committed in the struggle that is constantly going on over the grass on the public range." While these encounters take place "between big cattlemen and settlers, between cattlemen and sheepmen, and lately between sheepmen and between cattlemen," continued the editorialist, the law says "that all have equal privileges on them." In an effort "to prevent open clashing as far as is possible," he added (in an oblique reference to the Tom Horn case), the large cattle companies have resorted to "hired murder."[50]

Richard Maxwell Brown of the University of Oregon, a leading student of violence in the American West, places such frontier figures as Tom Horn in the context of what he calls "The Western Civil War of Incorporation" (WCWI). "At the core of the WCWI," writes Brown, "was the conservative, consolidating authority of capital that was, according to the scholar Alan Trachtenberg, incorporating America into a tightly controlled social and economic order during the late nineteenth century." Of the forty-two violent episodes that Brown includes in "the Western Civil War of Incorporation" between 1850 and 1919, Tom Horn participated in at least two of them—the Pleasant Valley War, in Arizona, and the struggle for the Wyoming grasslands. In "the combat of homesteaders against the incorporating forces of land wealth and power," according to Brown, hired gunmen served as "the point men." They fell into two groups, "incorporation gunfighters," who hired out to wealthy individuals or companies, and "resister gunfighters," who fought for the granger element. In the struggle for Wyoming's grazing lands, according to Brown, Tom Horn fitted into the former category. In the "resister" category, such men as Nate Champion and Nick Ray, who were victims of the cattlemen's invasion of Johnson County, Wyoming, in 1892, were on the homesteaders' side. However, Tom Horn does not fit snugly into Brown's scheme of things in the Pleasant Valley War, where he joined the anti-incorporating Tewksbury faction against the Graham group. This was only logical, since Ed Tewksbury, whom Brown also categorizes as a "resister gunfighter," and Tom Horn were close friends.[51]

Biographer Jay Monaghan notes that Horn placed himself at the service of powerful interest groups in the West:

> Tom Horn was universally praised when the United States hired him to kill red men—to exterminate one civilization to make room for another. His obloquy arose when he used his talents to exterminate one class of white men to make room for another class, called "substantial property owners." It is easy enough to understand how a man of Tom Horn's mentality might turn from the first kind of assassination to the second kind; how he might become famous as a killer for a great group of people like the United States and infamous as a killer for a smaller group of capitalists.[52]

Some writers characterize Tom Horn as a victim in the Willie Nickell murder case, asserting that he was a dupe of the Wyoming cattle barons, who used him and then sacrificed him. Others believe he fell prey to a conspiratorial clique of politicians. Yet recklessness was apparent in Tom Horn's conduct for much of his short life. This unsettling side of Horn appeared as early as his time with the Texas cattle drives and as a railroad hired gun at Leadville. Even though his services in the 1880s to the U.S. Army were formally sanctioned, he was immersed in intensely violent, no-holds-barred campaigns in which women and children were sometimes victims. Although Horn's involvement in the Pleasant Valley War is shrouded in mystery, there are indications that he participated in some of its violent episodes, including the lynching of three men. Even as an operative for the Pinkerton National Detective Agency, he was twice tried for robbery. Two of his fellow Pinkertons, Doc Shores and Charlie Siringo, also observed disturbing traits in his personality that might help explain his later murderous deeds. While Tom Horn enjoyed some protection from the Wyoming cattle companies, in the 1890s, the degree of shelter that the cattle barons could provide him began to erode late in this decade. As he grew more vulnerable to the law, many citizens of Wyoming saw him as a public danger (in present-day parlance, a loose cannon). Neither the Laramie County authorities nor the public at large would stand for any further highhandedness from the controversial detective. His insistence upon remaining in the neighborhood of his suspected killings as though nothing untoward had happened—a fact the newspapers noted in the

Lewis and Powell assassinations—eventually caught up with him. His arrogant disregard for the law, reinforced by protracted drinking bouts and intolerable braggadocio, was too much even for the often easygoing frontier law enforcement officials. The murder of fourteen-year-old Willie Nickell was the last nail in Tom Horn's coffin. That he was capable of such a callous deed—even if Willie Nickell was not his intended victim—was evident in the tell tale pattern of violence in his many years on the frontier.

Epilogue

No sooner did Laramie County authorities pronounce Tom Horn dead than the legend of the infamous range detective began to emerge. It has proven extraordinarily durable and continues to grow. The same issue of the *Cheyenne Daily Leader* that reported Sheriff Edwin Smalley's return of the death warrant to the district court clerk also mentioned that there were still "persons in the city who profess to believe that Tom Horn was not hanged." Perhaps reflecting the attitudes characteristic of the Populist era, these skeptics asserted "that a dummy was dropped through the trap in his place." Tom Horn, in death, was already entering the ranks of a small, exclusive circle of frontier characters, including Jesse James and Billy the Kid, whom Americans did not want to die. Somehow, myths of their miraculous escape from death at the hands of supposed oppressive, rapacious corporations and government officials gave comfort to many average citizens who considered themselves underdogs in the harsh struggle for survival in the West.[1]

Since Tom Horn walked onto the gallows platform in Cheyenne in November 1903, an immense body of material—books, articles, tales, relics, movies, and so forth—has arisen to add to his legend. The origins of Horn's legendary persona, however, go back almost twenty years before his hanging. Horn's association with Capt. Emmet Crawford's ill-fated Sonoran campaign, in 1885–86, is a good starting place. The fact that Horn was wounded during the fight in which his commander received a mortal wound at the hands of Mexican militiamen gave the young chief of scouts free publicity. In reporting Crawford's death, newspapers also broadcast Horn's name. William Edwardy, the roving correspondent who had ridden with Horn in the Geronimo campaign, also assisted in spreading the scout's reputation. In May 1890, Edwardy published "A Young Scout," a lengthy piece that praised Horn's accomplishments. Already well known in southeastern Arizona for being "full of himself," Horn seized on this dramatic moment and throughout the remainder of his life regaled anyone who would listen with his version of these events in Mexico. Horn's skill as a performer in cowboy tournaments (now known as rodeos) also spread his name, as newspapers such as the *New York Police Gazette* and *Philadelphia Times* reported his exploits. As a teller of tall tales, Tom Horn continued to add to his own reputation for the rest of his life.[2]

The events surrounding his arrest, trial, and execution were the most widespread part of his legend. The dramatic newspaper coverage, typical of the "yellow press" of that day, went far beyond merely reporting the facts and made the name of Tom Horn a household word. As the *Colorado Springs Telegraph* observed during Horn's trial in October 1902, it appeared that each Denver newspaper was trying "to out-yellow the other" in covering these proceedings. "Enough was testified, gossiped, and written in the trial's two weeks," asserted Dean Krakel many years later, "to forever engrain Tom Horn and Willie Nickell into the lore and legend of Wyoming." Horn promoted his own legend very effectively in the highly embellished autobiography *Life of Tom Horn: Government Scout and Interpreter,* which he wrote in jail. Published posthumously in 1904, this book is still in print and widely read.[3]

Fiction writers had already begun to contribute to the Tom Horn legend before his execution in 1903. In August 1894, John Heard, Jr., the mining engineer and member of the eastern syndicate that purchased Horn's Ore Hanna Mine in 1890, treated Horn as a heroic character in a story, "The Killing of the Captain," for *Cosmopolitan Magazine.* Heard wove a fictional love triangle around the events of the Crawford expedition, beginning the story in a village in southern Arizona where a young vaquero, Santanta, is wooing the beautiful Orejana. But she loves another—a handsome army captain (Emmet Crawford). The scene shifts to Captain Crawford and his Apache scouts, culminating in the tragic clash with Mexican militiamen in the Sierra Madre. While

Heard fails to mention Tom Horn by name, he still figures prominently in the story as "the big interpreter" who attempts to hail the attacking Mexicans and alert them to their error.[4]

When Lieutenant Marion Maus, who succeeds to Crawford's command, is taken hostage by the Mexicans, "the big interpreter" devises a ploy to get his own hostages. When the Chihuahuans demand mules to carry their dead and wounded away, Horn suggests that they send two men to the American camp, in order to fetch the animals. The Chihuahuans unwittingly walk into Horn's trap and are taken hostage. Heard's piece is interesting for its account of Horn's counterhostage maneuver. While this episode was not mentioned in either the American or Mexican records, Horn emphasized it in his autobiography.[5]

Stewart Edward White, a popular writer of short stories, wrote a series of stories collectively entitled "Arizona Nights" for *McClure's Magazine,* in 1906. In one installment, "Uncle Jim's Yarn, the Indian Story," Uncle Jim Fox recalls an encounter with a party of the U.S. Army's Apache scouts at his ranch in southeastern Arizona. The scouts mistake him for a notorious Mexican outlaw named Maria who rode with the renegade Apaches. They seize Uncle Jim, take him to their camp, and are just about to roast him over a fire when he is miraculously saved. "The first man I saw sitting at that [camp] fire," recalls Uncle Jim, "was Lieutenant Price of the United States Army, and by him was Tom Horn."[6]

Tom Horn also appeared in Forrestine Hooker's novel *When Geronimo Rode* (1924). Forrestine Hooker was the daughter of Captain Charles Cooper, who served in the campaigns against Geronimo. In May 1886, Forrestine, "Birdie" to her family, married Edwin R. Hooker, the son of Henry C. Hooker, owner of the sprawling Sierra Bonita Ranch near Fort Grant. In *When Geronimo Rode,* she has Emmet Crawford stopping at the Sierra Bonita en route to Mexico. When someone cautions Crawford that he cannot trust his Apache scouts, he insists that he is "reasonably certain" of their reliability. "Still, no one can ever tell. No white man will ever understand the Apaches' peculiar racial code. Tom Horn, whom I have known for a long time, is going to act as interpreter and also chief of scouts. His influence is remarkable. I guess he understands the Apaches as well as any man in this section." If Forrestine Hooker did not know Horn personally, she certainly knew of him.[7]

After his death, Tom Horn assumed a prominent place in both fiction and nonfiction accounts of range disputes in the Rocky Mountain West. In "The Last War for the Cattle Range" (*Outing Magazine,* 1905), popular writer Arthur Chapman not only placed Horn in the cattlemen's invasion of Johnson County but asserted that his "method of assassination" in subsequent years was very similar to that employed in 1892. In July 1907, John L. Cowan, a contemporary of Chapman who wrote widely on western subjects, published "Wars of the Range," describing several flare-ups on grazing lands. In such fracases, Cowan observed, the man "quickest with his gun is regarded as having proved incontestably his superior right" to the land. The best illustration of . . . this species of frontier justice," he declared, "is supplied by the case of Tom Horn." In 1910 John Lloyd (pseud. Jacque Lloyd Morgan) published *The Invaders: A Story of the "Hole-in-the-Wall" Country,* a love story set during the Johnson County War, in 1892. Horn appears as the assassin of Orley "Ranger" Jones. Interestingly, the author portrays him as a ladies' man.[8]

Charles A. Siringo, Tom Horn's old Pinkerton comrade, also helped keep his name alive in literature. In *A Cowboy Detective* (1912), Siringo recalled episodes in which he worked with Horn. However, the Pinkerton National Detective Agency successfully sued the author, forcing him to remove some incidents and fictionalize some names in the book. For instance, Pinkerton was changed to Dickensen, and Tom Horn became Tim Corn. In *Two Evil Isms: Pinkertonism and Anarchism* (1915), an exposé of his former employer, Siringo was much more critical of Horn, alleging that the Pinkerton Agency hired him as a "cowboy detective" because Siringo would not do the dirty work—meaning assassination—that the agency demanded. As an indication of his hostility toward Horn, the author included a photograph of Tom Horn as part of the frontispiece, in a montage of other noted criminals. The caption referred to Horn as "the Pinkerton detective hung in Cheyenne, Wyoming, for murdering men at six hundred dollars each."[9]

Horn's popularity took off with the remarkable growth of Wild West literature in the 1920s and 1930s. Since that time, the legend of Tom Horn has flourished. Although Horn did not rate a full-length biography as soon as other frontier notables—Billy the Kid, for example, in Walter Noble Burns's *The Saga of Billy the Kid* (1926) and Wyatt Earp in Stuart N. Lake's *Wyatt Earp: Frontier Marshal* (1931)—he became a stock item for article- and chapter-length pieces. This treatment installed him in the pantheon of frontier personalities, and an almost constant flow of fictional and factual treatments of his life has continued. Because most writers have relied heavily on the *Life of Tom Horn, Government Scout and Interpreter* for his Arizona years, this literature is rife with misinformation.[10]

Among writers who helped reintroduce Tom Horn into Wild West literature after World War I, Arthur Chapman, a Denver newspaperman and freelance writer, played an important part. In October 1925, Chapman's "Wyoming's Death Rider," published in *The Frontier,* a Doubleday pulp magazine, stimulated a new interest in the infamous range detective. Charles Siringo also continued to spread Horn's name. In *Riata and Spurs: The Story of a Lifetime Spent in the Saddle as Cowboy and Ranger* (1927), Siringo inserted material directly from Horn's autobiography into a second printing after the Pinkerton National Detective Agency succeeded in having the first printing suppressed. Other writers, including Lorenzo D. Walters (*Tombstone's Yesterdays,* 1928), Dane Coolidge (*Fighting Men of the West,* 1932), and Eugene Cunningham (*Triggernometry,* 1934) included chapter-length treatments of Tom Horn in larger works. All were heavily dependent upon Horn's autobiography and on legends about his Wyoming days. Coolidge, a popular western novelist, took great liberties with his subject. As Walter S. Campbell (Stanley Vestal) slyly noted in his *Book Lover's Southwest,* "occasionally his [Coolidge's] fictional habits get the better of his historical intention." Such inaccuracies were spread even further when *Fighting Men of the West* went into an Armed Services Edition in World War II and a paperback edition in 1952. Benjamin "Stookie" Allen, a popular writer and illustrator, added a new dimension to Horn in *Men of Daring* (1933). Taking his cue from Dane Coolidge's unreliable version of Horn's life, Allen, told the story in comic-book fashion, with drawings depicting various stages in the infamous range detective's career.[11]

As this stream of inaccurate treatments of Tom Horn's life appeared in the 1920s and 1930s, men who had some personal knowledge of the facts of the famous scout's life, including Charles B. Gatewood, Jr., began to try to set record straight. The son of First Lieutenant Charles B. Gatewood, Sr., the officer responsible for Geronimo's final surrender, the younger Gatewood was also a professional soldier. When he retired at the end of World War I, he devoted the remainder of his life to gaining recognition for his father's part in Geronimo's surrender. When Gatewood read Arthur Chapman's piece in 1925, he responded with a letter of protest to the editor. Soon, the younger Gatewood began a regular correspondence with old Arizona pioneers and veterans of the Apache campaigns. He also began to ransack army archives for documents concerning these campaigns. As he attempted to set the record straight and give his father his due, one of Gatewood's primary targets was the *Life of Tom Horn: Government Scout and Interpreter,* which he saw as having an insidious influence on the historical record. Gatewood and his many correspondents—what might be called the Gatewood circle— included numerous persons who had worked with, or had known, Tom Horn, among them Anton Mazzanovich, James C. Hancock, and Henry Daly. Writers such as Earl Brininstool and Cody Blake were also members of the circle.[12]

Perhaps Owen Payne White's article "Talking Boy," which appeared in *Collier's Weekly* in early 1932, did the most to galvanize the members of the Gatewood circle into action. Unlike other writings about the notable scout, an article in a widely read mainstream magazine brought the name of Tom Horn to a truly national audience. White drew his uncritical account of Tom Horn's activities in the Apache wars almost exclusively from Horn's autobiography, which slighted the professional soldiers' role in the Geronimo campaign and presented the civilian faction's version of these events. Gatewood and his circle deluged *Collier's Weekly* with protests and demanded that both the magazine and Owen White apologize for such bad history. While neither the magazine editor nor White took these protests seriously, the Gatewood circle stimulated interest in the pioneer history of southern Arizona. In the early 1930s, newspapers in Tombstone and Bisbee, Arizona, and elsewhere, reprinted letters and articles generated by the circle. In their effort to correct the bad history promoted by Tom Horn's autobiography, Gatewood and his correspondents made a helpful contribution by unearthing new facts about this controversial figure.[13]

In spite of the attention that writers gave Tom Horn in the 1920s and 1930s, he did not rate a full-length biography for many years. In the estimation of Wild West enthusiasts, Horn failed to measure up to the standards of gun wielders such as Wyatt Earp and Billy the Kid, who fought in stand-up shootouts with their enemies. Tom Horn had the reputation of a bushwhacker and back shooter—not considered manly behavior even by the crudest frontier standards. In frontier mythology, a murderer's technique was as important as the taking of human life.

Richard R. Mullins made one of the first efforts to tell the complete story of Tom Horn. In 1930, Mullins wrote "The Inside Story of the Life and Death of Tom Horn," which was serialized in the *Denver Post* in twenty installments. Unfortunately, Mullins's account depended almost exclusively upon the *Life of Tom Horn* and a cursory review of his activities in Wyoming. In 1946 Jay Monaghan presented the first full-length biography, *Last of the Bad Men: The Legend of Tom Horn,* which is still in print. He neglected to include source notes and, as historian Dan Thrapp pointed out, "he had a tendency to fictionalize for the sake of readability." Since Monaghan (rightly) portrayed Tom Horn as a tool of the cattle companies, partisans of the Wyoming range barons detected in the book a taint of New Deal leftist hostility toward big corporations.[14]

In 1954 Dean F. Krakel published *The Saga of Tom Horn: The Story of a Cattlemen's War,* which consisted largely of lengthy reprints of select testimony from Horn's trial. While the author's aim was to correct "a farrago of Tom Horn misinformation," the protests of descendants of some persons mentioned in the book obliged Krakel to delete some passages. Eventually, the book went into print and remains an important contribution to the authentic Tom Horn story. In 1964 Krakel also provided an introduction to the first reprint edition of the *Life of Tom Horn: Government Scout and Interpreter* (University of Oklahoma Press). There would be many more.[15]

While Krakel's volume was tied up in a lawsuit, Ivan Lee Kuykendall published *Ghost Riders of the Mogollon,* which purported to be a history of the Pleasant Valley War. As a resident of the valley, Kuykendall admitted that he "had to piece actual facts together with legendary facts" and, occasionally, included "semi-fiction." Indeed it is essentially a work of fiction and decidedly partisan. Kuykendall characterized Gila County Sheriff Glenn Reynolds as a crooked and corrupt lawman and portrayed his deputy, Tom Horn, as the manager of a bordello in Globe, Arizona! Descendants of Glenn Reynolds, with the support of Pleasant Valley pioneers, brought a libel suit against the publisher, the Naylor Company of San Antonio, Texas. Only 200 copies reached the marketplace. Admittedly, some citizens of Gila County did, indeed, regard Glenn Reynolds as a "killer" sheriff, since he reportedly led the vigilantes in Tonto Basin. This taint rubbed off on his deputies, including Tom Horn.[16]

Since the 1950s, several biographies of Tom Horn have appeared. The quality of these volumes has been very uneven. In 1961 Gene Caesar published *Rifle for Rent: A Dramatic True Story of One of the Most Colorful Figures of the Untamed Southwest.* This volume, a part of Monarch Books' Americana and Western Series, included some imagined dialogue. Lauran Paine's *Tom Horn: Man of the West,* which first appeared in London in 1962, is readable but "somewhat fictionalized," according to bibliographer Donald M. Powell. Like Caesar's volume, it lacks documentation. Johan P. Bakker's *Tracking Tom Horn* (1994) added little new material to the story. Doyce B. Nunis, Jr.'s *The Life of Tom Horn Revisited* (1992) represented a serious departure from past treatments. Essentially an expansion of Nunis's introduction and afterword to the Lakeside Press reprint of *Life of Tom Horn* (1987), it is a refreshingly sober and critical evaluation of Tom Horn's life. While Nunis admitted he was "fascinated with Tom Horn," he rightly concluded that the range detective had "some profound psychological problems" and was "a pathological liar."[17]

Several publications by Chip Carlson also represented improvements in telling the Tom Horn story. Carlson, who served as the publicity agent for the Cheyenne Frontier Days, published *Tom Horn: "Killing Men Is My Specialty . . ."* in 1991 and a revised and enlarged biography, *Tom Horn: Blood on the Moon,* in 2001. In 1995, Carlson also edited and annotated the autobiography of Joe LeFors—*Joe LeFors: "I Slickered Tom Horn"; The History of the Texas Cowboy Turned Montana-Wyoming Lawman, A Sequel.* Carlson uncovered new material on Tom Horn and brought his subject into sharper relief. In addition, living in Wyoming placed him close to the source of the Tom Horn controversy. From his research, Carlson concluded that Horn did not kill Willie Nickell. Current rumor holds that it will eventually be revealed that someone other than Tom Horn murdered the boy. Carlson agreed, however, that Tom Horn was guilty of earlier murders in the service of the cattle barons.[18]

Sketches of Tom Horn's life appear in numerous encyclopedias, most of them focusing on the American West. The quality of these entries varies greatly. Many are filled with errors and tend to merely enlarge the legend of Tom Horn—who would have been gratified to know that he rated entries in two of the most highly regarded reference works on American history. William James Ghent, a well-known early-twentieth-century newspaperman and author, penned the biography of Horn for the *Dictionary of American Biography* (DAB). While Ghent admitted that "much controversy" surrounded Horn's demise, he concluded by saying that Horn's friends regarded him "as a man of unfailing good nature, courteous, considerate, generous, and thoroughly honest," not to mention innocent of the Nickell murder. (The DAB also included a biography of Al Sieber, Tom Horn's mentor.) The DAB's successor, *American National Biography* (ANB), also included a sketch of Tom Horn. The ANB entry for Horn, written by Robert L. Gale, is by far the most objective and reliable such encyclopedia entry.[19]

Many western writers have written fiction about Tom Horn. In 1948 MacKinlay Kantor published *Wicked Water.* While Kantor changed Horn's name to Buster Crow, the setting and circumstances in this novel clearly refer to the infamous stock detective's Wyoming experiences. Kantor exaggerated the vicious nature of his protagonist, having him kill no fewer than seventy-two men. Reviewer William M. Raine reminded readers that Horn "was not the complete monster depicted by Kantor. . . . Tom Horn was a complex personality, possibly even a schismatic personality." One of the contributions of fiction writers to the factual Tom Horn story has been the effort to illuminate the enigmatic character of this killer-for-hire.[20]

In 1975, Will Henry (a pseudonym of Henry Wilson Allen) published *I, Tom Horn.* Henry stayed close to the facts of Horn's life and added the premise that the "lost" latter part of *Life of Tom Horn: Government Scout and Interpreter*—it never existed—had been providentially found. Critics quickly concluded that *I, Tom Horn* would become a classic in western fiction. Historian Dale L. Walker commented, "Will Henry has honored what is known of Horn's life, taken that and what is not known and created a novel so vivid, so filled with life, humor, ironies, poetry and melancholy, that it cannot be forgotten." In a Western Writers of America survey, this work was voted "one of the 26 greatest western novels of all time." Henry believed this novel was probably his best. Robert L. Gale, a student of Will Henry's works, strongly disagreed, asserting that Henry had merely succeeded in making "a credible hero out of history's thug."[21]

Novels that feature Tom Horn or include him as a supporting character continue to appear. In 1984, Andrew J. Fenady published *Claws of the Eagle: A Novel of Tom Horn and the Apache Kid.* Fenady, who wrote television and movie westerns, cast Tom Horn and the Apache Kid as understudies to the famous civilian scout Al Sieber in the pursuit of Geronimo. Horn and the Kid were the "claws" of Sieber, the "eagle". In the novel, after the deportation of Geronimo, Horn and the Kid have a falling out, leading to Horn's pursuit of the Kid. A more recent effort to treat Tom Horn in fiction is Jon Chandler's *Wyoming Wind: A Novel of Tom Horn* (2002). Magazines and anthologies continue to reproduce parts of Horn's autobiography. One of Horn's recent appearances is in Stephen Brennan's *The Greatest Cowboy Stories Ever Told* (2004), in which the editor places an excerpt from the *Life of Tom Horn* alongside the writings of such notable authors as Frederic Remington, Eugene Manlove Rhodes, Charlie Siringo, and Larry McMurtry.[22]

Tom Horn became a favorite in pulps and comics as well. In September 1948, *Western Killers* featured him in an article, "Murder Is My Business." The publisher characterized this issue accurately as one of "extreme violence." A 1951 Avon comic book, *Geronimo and His Apache Murderers,* gave Chief of Scouts Horn a prominent place (with Lt. Charles Gatewood).[23]

The Tom Horn legend also encompasses poetry and song. In 1934, while researching his biography of Butch Cassidy, *The Outlaw Trail,* Charles Kelly interviewed Albert Williams, an African American pioneer in Brown's Park. Williams, known locally as "Speck," operated a ferry on the Green River in the 1890s and early 1900s and was acquainted with Tom Horn. Much to Kelly's surprise, Williams sang a ballad that he had composed about Tom Horn's memorable visit in 1900. This ballad consisted "of twenty verses telling the story of the death of Matt Rash and Isom Dart," but naturally from "the rustler's angle." In 1966, folklorist Olive W. Burt was surprised to hear a Wyoming informant, Samuel Weymouth, sing a song, "Tom Horn." As a ten-year-old, Weymouth accompanied his father to Cheyenne on the day of Tom Horn's execution. Unfortunately, only the lyrics, and not the music, are known:

> Tom Horn! Tom Horn!
> He killed Willie Nickell, so now he has to die
> He killed Willie Nickell so he's got to swing high.[24]

The story of Tom Horn can also be found in poetry. Diana Kouris, another resident of the Brown's Park area, preserved the memory of Tom

Horn and other Brown's Park bad men in a prose poem: "Night shadows remind Brown's Park of hired gun Tom Horn and his deeds; of Butch Cassidy and the other outlaws slipping through the pasture gate at the Park live to catch fresh horses." Perhaps the most recent effort to treat Tom Horn in verse comes from the poet Rawdon Tomlinson. In *Geronimo after Kas-ki-yeh* (2007), Tomlinson has Tom Horn in the Laramie County Jail reflecting on his past.[25]

Hollywood latched onto the Tom Horn legend early. Horn became a stock character in radio, television, and moving pictures. The first movie ever shown in Cheyenne ran in May 1902, while Tom Horn was in jail. Little did he know that he would soon be the subject of numerous films. In a strange twist to the Tom Horn story, Charles Burton Irwin, who sang at the range detective's hanging, teamed up with Otis H. Thayer in 1912 to form the Cheyenne Feature Film Company. Thayer was a professional entertainer from Chicago who first visited Cheyenne in 1904, when the memory of Tom Horn was very fresh. T. Blake Kennedy, one of Tom Horn's attorneys, served as the film company's attorney. One of their first productions was *Roundup on the Y-6 Ranch,* which included footage from an early Cheyenne Frontier Days cowboy tournament. Two years later, in 1914, Thayer, who, in the meantime had established the Colorado Motion Picture Company, produced *Pirates of the Plains.* According to one authority, this movie "has some major parallels to the Tom Horn story including a long rifle shot [by an assassin], [and] a courtroom scene." In keeping with the Tom Horn legend, however, the script has the hero escaping the gallows in the end. Unfortunately, the name of the actor who played the Tom Horn character is not known. Charles Irwin went on to produce a Wild West show.[26]

Allan Radbourne, a British authority on the Apache wars and western film, has compiled a list of actors who portrayed Tom Horn in Hollywood and on television. Among them are Barry Sullivan (*Bad Men of Tombstone,* 1949), George Montgomery (*Dakota Lil,* 1950), Macdonald Carey (*Hannah Lee,* a 3-D movie of MacKinlay Kantor's *Wicked Water,* 1953, featuring a fictitious street duel between Buster Crow [Tom Horn] and a lawman), Louis Jean Heydt (an episode of the television series *Stories of the Century,* 1954), John Ireland (*Fort Utah,* 1967, in which a character named Tom Horn is "the man from nowhere"), David Carradine (*Mr. Horn,* made for television, 1979), and Steve McQueen (*Tom Horn,* 1980). As Radbourne has observed, script writers have substituted other names for Tom Horn when he is portrayed unsympathetically. When his role is more positive, Horn's name is used. One of the most unsympathetic portrayals of a Tom Horn–like character is in the Arthur Penn production *The Missouri Breaks* (1976). The main character, a regulator in the Tom Horn mold, is given the name Robert E. Lee Clayton. Marlon Brando plays an especially malevolent and twisted Clayton.[27]

One of the more ambitious efforts to tell Horn's story on film was *Mr. Horn,* televised in 1979, a CBS special production. The script was written by William Goldman, better known for his work on *Butch Cassidy and the Sundance Kid.* Two veteran actors headed the cast. David Carradine, a member of a distinguished show business family, had the title role. Richard Widmark played Al Sieber, the veteran scout and Tom Horn's mentor in the Apache wars.

A somewhat more successful effort to tell Horn's story on the screen was Steve McQueen's *Tom Horn,* released in 1980. McQueen not only played the part of Horn, but produced the film through his Solar Productions. The McQueen version focused on the last four years of Horn's life. Reviewers criticized the script as well as McQueen's portrayal of the controversial detective. Perhaps the keenest critics were residents of Wyoming, where the film first previewed. They expected more. Phil Roberts and Bill Barton, two members of the Wyoming State Archives staff, were especially critical. They were mystified that after three summers of research in Wyoming, representatives of Solar Productions revealed little understanding of the conditions in which Tom Horn flourished. According to Roberts, "virtually everyone disagreed on the way it was presented," especially the portrayal of Horn as a dim-witted "stumblebum," when the detective was "a fairly intelligent man who had picked up some style and panache over the years." As Larry Caldwell, another reviewer, pointed out, Horn was not "congenitally dimwitted," as McQueen portrayed him, but "was literate enough to write a good autobiography." (In fairness to Steve McQueen, he made the film when he was suffering from the cancer that would soon kill him.)[28]

Overall, the script stressed "the idea that during the latter part of his life, Horn had become a mythical figure—a symbol for the Old West that was ending—and, that, like the West, Horn had to be tamed." Newspaperman Kirk Knox found McQueen's portrayal "appealing."

With an excellent performance by veteran actor Richard Farnsworth as John Coble, the film captured the grittiness and brutality of the no-holds-barred range war between the cattle barons and the rustler element. Solar Productions staged an aggressive publicity campaign. They went so far as to ask Rodney Guthrie, a retired Wyoming Supreme Court justice, and Randall A. Wagner, director of the Wyoming Travel Commission, to urge Wyoming Governor Ed Herschler to issue a posthumous pardon for Tom Horn. Both men refused, and Governor Herschler remained unmoved. "Tom Horn will have to walk into my office to get my pardon," he declared. Disappointed with the film's performance, Warner Brothers eventually turned it over to the cable market. In "Tom Horn: Dialectics of Power and Violence in the Old West," which appeared in the *Journal of Popular Culture* in 1988, Stephen Prince characterized *Tom Horn* as "the last great Western." This film, said Prince, "like the best Westerns, offers a studied and nuanced presentation of an evolution of violence, in particular, of a movement away from personalized codes of violence, and toward the practice of a bureaucratic form of violence in which no-one is held responsible." Another academic, Nina Rosenstand, an instructor in ethics at San Diego Mesa College, has used the McQueen movie in her textbook *The Moral of the Story: An Introduction to Ethics*. With examples from the screenplay, Rosenstand puts provocative questions to students. Was Tom Horn brave in keeping silent about his employers? What did Glendolene Kimmell mean by saying that Horn was "crushed between two civilizations, the old and the new?"[29]

There were other spin-offs from Steve McQueen's portrayal of Tom Horn. When the actor's personal possessions were auctioned off after his death in 1980, the chaps that he wore in *Tom Horn* brought $14,000. A presentation copy of the movie script sold for $30,000.[30]

Radio and television helped spread the Tom Horn legend. In 1941, Bert Fireman, a popular Arizona historian, featured the story of the range detective in his *Arizona Crossroads* series on the Arizona Broadcasting System. While the content of his script, "Tom Horn, Good Man and Bad Man," was standard fare, Fireman concluded that Horn's dilemma was that he "couldn't adapt himself to the new order in the West." When television entered American households in the 1950s, similar programs were common. One popular weekly western series was *Stories of the Century,* in which actor Jim Davis played Matt Clark, a railroad detective who (with actress Peggy Castle) encountered an infamous frontier character in each episode. In one such adventure in 1954, Louis Jean Heydt portrayed Tom Horn. Michael Hinn played Horn in "The Last Bugle" for *Zane Grey Theater* (1956). Les Johnson took up the role in "Tom Horn," a *Tales of Wells Fargo* episode in 1957. Greg Palmer did likewise in "Perilous Cargo," in *Death Valley Days* (1952). No doubt there were others.[31]

Relics are often part of frontier legends, and many are associated with Tom Horn. Numerous examples of his horsehair braiding and leatherwork—quirts, ropes, and the like—are still exhibited in museums. Horn even gave his name to a rope, the Tom Horn, according to Ramon F. Adams. The fact that he fashioned ropes while awaiting hanging in Cheyenne gave rise to the erroneous tale that he "spent his last months . . . weaving the rope that would be used to hang him."[32]

Since weapons played such a prominent part in Tom Horn's life, pistols and rifles that he is thought to have owned are highly valued collectibles today. According to tradition, Sheriff Edwin Smalley took from Horn a Colt model 1878 double-action .45 caliber revolver, with holster, when he arrested the stock detective in January 1902. This weapon is in the possession of the Texas Ranger Hall of Fame Museum in Waco, Texas. Even before Horn's execution, James A. Scott, a Laramie County rancher, placed one of Horn's revolvers, a .38 caliber Smith and Wesson, on exhibit in a Denver hardware store. In noting that seven notches were cut into the butt, the *Denver Times* made a futile effort to make them fit the pattern of Horn's alleged assassinations, theorizing that since "two of these notches are joined together," this peculiar marking referred to "a double death"—possibly the assassinations of Matt Rash and Isom Dart. A separate, shorter notch, "is supposed to represent a boy," added the *Times,* obviously referring to Willie Nickell. The *Denver Republican,* which reported eight notches instead of seven, offered a different interpretation. "On each side of the butt are carved four notches," the reporter observed, and "these are of different sizes and two of them are connected. . . . It is said that the two joined notches, one being smaller than the other, meant the killing of a man and a boy at the same time." In the process of burglarizing this store sometime later, a pair of thieves lifted this pistol. Upon their arrest, they admitted that they thought if they had "the gun of the great outlaw" in their possession, according to the *Republican,* "their careers might equal his." Later on, several guns and a saddle belonging to Tom Horn were displayed in Denver, according to A. L. Johnson, who, as a boy, was excited to get an opportunity to view these relics.[33]

That such a notorious gunman as Tom Horn carried only a small .38 caliber pistol rather than the hefty .45 Colt revolver proved unsettling to many frontier aficionados. Like many frontiersmen, Horn favored this lighter pistol because it could be "easily concealed" under a man's shirt—a "cheater"—rather than lugged in a leather belt and holster. Phil Spangenberger, a student of frontier weaponry, opined that late in Horn's life the gunman carried a .45 double- action Model 1878 Colt revolver in a full-flap holster. "Horn was apparently more concerned with protecting the gun than a fast draw," according to Spangenberger. Whatever Horn's preferred armaments, he did not conform to the expectations of the pulp and Hollywood script writers, who invariably placed in the hands of their heroes a single-action .45 Colt revolver and a Winchester rifle of the same caliber (thus enabling them to carry only one size of cartridge).[34]

Tom Horn's preferred weapon was a rifle, and he carried several different long guns during his career. One rifle said to have belonged to Horn is inscribed, "Presented to Tom Horn by His Friend, John Coble." Whether this is an authentic presentation piece is not known. Another rifle that purportedly belonged to Horn is in the Buffalo Bill Cody Museum in Cody, Wyoming. In *Famous Firearms of the Old West,* Hal Herring discusses twelve weapons that, in his opinion, "shaped our history." In addition to guns used by Buffalo Bill Cody, James Butler "Wild Bill" Hickok, and Geronimo, Herring singles out Tom Horn's .30-30 Winchester Model 1894 for attention. This rifle fired the new high-velocity smokeless cartridge. Horn gave this shoulder weapon to his good friend Charles B. Irwin a few days before his execution. It is reportedly still in the family's possession.[35]

Other relics associated with Tom Horn include the handcuffs and ankle bracelets allegedly used to secure him for his walks from the jail to the courtroom. In January 1904 the *Denver Republican* reported these items in the possession of Michael Geary, a guard at the Arapahoe County Jail in Denver. As a publicity stunt, "a committee of city and county officers" locked them on a showman and escape artist named Cunning, who styled himself as the Handcuff King. Cunning reportedly freed himself within "a few seconds." Since Geary was vague about how he obtained these items, the *Daily Leader* pooh-poohed this report, adding that the prisoner did not wear "handcuffs or ankle irons during his incarceration."[36]

As Tom Horn was quick to admit, horses were among his most valued possessions. Even though he was unsuccessful in establishing his own ranch, he always tried to run a small herd of horses. If not, he used the horses of his employers on the Wyoming range. He was believed to have ridden one of John Coble's big powerful animals called Cap from the scene of the Willie Nickell murder to Laramie in order to establish an alibi. A story circulated after Horn's death that Charles Jarvis, not John Coble, actually owned this animal and that Horn (using his prerogative as a range detective) deliberately took the horse from Jarvis's pasture as he rode to the murder scene. Cap was gentle and was trained not to flinch at rifle fire. Alice Cornelius, a granddaughter of Charles Jarvis, said that Horn did, indeed, ride Cap from the murder site and that he drove the horse so furiously that the animal was permanently "broken" by the hard ride. Jarvis sold the unfortunate animal to an itinerant horse buyer who, in turn, sold the worn-out Cap to a soap factory. One of the most famous Wyoming bucking horses, Steamboat, was a product of John Coble's stables. Whether Horn had any connection with this animal is not known. However, his rifle, presently in the Buffalo Bill Museum in Cody, Wyoming, was used to dispatch Steamboat when the animal had to be put down in 1914. One version of the Tom Horn legend has him still alive and serving a prison sentence at this time. Horn was temporarily released from his prison cell, so this story goes, to dispatch this famous animal! After the range detective's execution, another bucking horse gained much fame in Wyoming. This horse was called Tom Horn.[37]

Various geographic features were also associated with the legend of Tom Horn. Near Baggs, Wyoming, where Horn was seriously injured in a knife fight, legend has it that he and Bob Meldrum erected a rock fortress on the Seven-Mile Ranch and took refuge there from nosy lawmen. George L. Erhard, writing for the *Rock Springs Rocket* in 1928, said that a cave on the property of Nicholas Krappe was used by Tom Horn as a sanctuary after his killings. Horn even scratched his name, and the year, 1890, on the cave wall. Of course, Horn was not in Wyoming at this time. More recently, a separate inscription attributed to the range detective was found on a cliff face near Billings, Montana. This one, which reads "Tom Horn, 1894," may actually be authentic.[38]

Like the graves of many notable gunmen, Tom Horn's gravesite in the Pioneers' Cemetery, in Boulder, Colorado, is a pilgrimage site. (The present writer and his wife, Ruth, dutifully made this pilgrimage to Boulder.) Directions posted at the cemetery gate lead the visitor to the old scout's monument which, unfortunately, carries the erroneous birth date of 1861. Horn was born in 1860. Among the persons who paid Horn's gravesite many visits was T. Joe Cahill, Horn's good friend and the man who assisted with his hanging. Among Cahill's duties as a promoter of Cheyenne Frontier Days was to escort interested persons to Horn's grave. On one trip, Cahill was called upon to lead "a troupe of Indians" to Boulder.[39]

Horn is even famous overseas, especially among the English, who are among the most fervent students of western Americana. Among these aficionados of Tom Horn is Roy Lacey of Portsmouth, England. Lacey has adopted the stage name Tom Horn. He and his wife, Belle, avidly promote the infamous frontiersman's name in Wild West shows at theme parks and on television.[40]

As noted earlier, one of the most persistent myths about Horn is that he miraculously avoided the hangman's noose. In March 1947, the *Denver Post* summarized this story:

> Through connivance of big cattlemen, the body carried from the jail on that hanging day and buried in the Boulder, Colo., cemetery, was that of a tramp. . . . Horn himself was smuggled, alive, out of the building and away. Torrents of words and gallons of printer's ink have not yet stilled the story. Time and again, newspapermen and others are told, "Why, Tom's alive and kicking, living right now in Chugwater"—or Sundance, or Big Piney, [or] any old place.

The legendary stock detective "still lives, a white-haired old skeleton of a man, scared of his own shadow," according to William Walker, who was acquainted with Horn. In 1936, William Asa "Dad" Bennitt, an old cowhand who also knew Horn, insisted that the former range rider was "living in South America!" When this tale was mentioned in a television documentary in December 2009, historian Paul Hutton, who served as one of the "talking heads," received a telephone call from an informant who insisted that some people (but not him) still believed Horn did not die on the gallows. A black man was hanged in place of

Tom Horn, who was permitted to return to Texas and live out his life in obscurity.[41]

No sooner had Tom Horn died on the gallows than reports of his ghost began to circulate. Cowhands in the Iron Mountain region reported sightings of Horn's apparition, as if he was condemned by his misdeeds to ride his old range forever. (Willie Nickell's ghost has also allegedly been seen.) Even though Tom Horn exhibited no overt signs of remorse for his crimes, tales were told that while alive he was bothered by previous malevolent acts. Archie Baird Gibbs, who worked for the Swan Land and Cattle Company during World War I, said that an old-time cowhand informed him that Horn had nightmares about his killings. Horn "would scream and rail about his victims" in his sleep, this unnamed wrangler asserted. William Walker, who believed Horn escaped the gallows, declared that as an old man Horn could still see "the shadow of unarmed men and little boys, [whom he] shot in the back." Indeed, the infamous range rider's legend grew so menacing that mothers used his name when children misbehaved: "Hush, or Tom Horn will get you!"[42]

As in many legends, superstitions occupy an important place. For instance, newspapers noted that Fridays the 13ths were prominent in Horn's last days. "To the superstitious mind," observed the *Daily Leader,* things appeared "ominous for the notorious prisoner." Graphology, the pseudoscience of handwriting analysis, also played a part in this legend. In an effort to determine Horn's character "scientifically," Charles Coe, the Wyoming range detective who stoutly defended Tom Horn, presented Louise Rice, a noted graphologist, with samples of Tom Horn's handwriting. The range detective was "affectionate, loyal, and kind-hearted," she concluded, and "the hanging of such a man was unjust." In response to the Hollywood films about Tom Horn, in 1979–80, Horn's handwriting was subjected to an "extensive examination." Marion Huseas, writing for the *Guernsey Gazette* (Wyoming), declared that this most recent analysis revealed "a sensitive man who was highly emotional; a man who acted on impulse, sometimes violently, and with little provocation." While Horn was an "intelligent person and a quick learner," continued Huseas, he "was an unhappy, discontented man" who harbored much "resentment" and "was easily hurt." "Horn had a conscience and knew right from wrong," continued this analyst, but his "urge to inflict injury was difficult to restrain."[43]

The City of Cheyenne has also capitalized upon its association with Tom Horn. One Sunday morning just prior to Horn's execution, Frank Benton, who was taking a herd by train to Omaha, made a short stopover in Cheyenne. When Benton asked someone to name the main features of Cheyenne," this person replied, "Tom Horn and Senator [Francis] Warren." When Benton asked, "What were they noted for?" the informant replied without hesitation, "Tom Horn was noted for killing people that took things that didn't belong to them and then blowing his horn about it afterwards, and Senator Warren was noted for building wire fences on government land and taking everything in sight."[44]

For many years, Tom Horn's name played an important part in the annual Cheyenne Frontier Days Celebration. In 1917 the *Cheyenne State Leader* noted that three close friends of Tom Horn—T. Joe Cahill and Charles and Frank Irwin—would play an important part in the festivities. Cahill "always wore a big grin and waved his Stetson as he pranced his horse up and down the street," recalled Dean Krakel, who witnessed the parade as a child in the 1930s. "Each year the parade had a float portraying the hanging of Tom Horn."[45]

The building where Deputy U.S. Marshal Joe LeFors obtained the confession of Tom Horn is still standing in Cheyenne. The U.S. Marshal's suite of offices on the second floor of the Concord Block has recently been restored and the room where the LeFors-Horn conversation took place is open to tourists. Significantly, the structure has been renamed the Tom Horn Building. In selecting the "Top Ten True Western Towns of the Year" in 2007, the editors of *True West* magazine ranked Cheyenne as Number 4. Of course, one reason for this selection is the inextricable tie between Tom Horn and the city. In September 1991, author Chip Carlson initiated another promotional activity in Cheyenne, the "Tom Horn Kick & Growl," a play on a remark Horn made while testifying at his murder trial. This celebration includes a tour of various places associated with Horn's career, including the Willie Nickell murder site. Tom Horn T-shirts, featuring a photograph of Horn in his jail cell, are available, as are Tom Horn greeting cards. Even a tote bag with a photograph of Horn's nemesis Joe LeFors is for sale.[46]

In September 1993, Carlson was responsible for staging a retrial of Tom Horn in the Wyoming State Museum. Joseph Moch, a Michigan attorney who admired Tom Horn, defended the stock detective. Robert Skar, the attorney for Hot Springs County, Wyoming, served as prosecutor. C. Stuart Brown, a retired Wyoming Supreme Court justice, presided. Skar probably realized that the deck was stacked against the prosecution. In accordance with present-day judicial practice, the presiding judge would almost certainly rule that the confession obtained by Joe LeFors was inadmissible as evidence. He did. Brown agreed with defense attorney Moch that since Charles Ohnhaus, the stenographer who took down the original conversation, had failed to record the entire exchange between Tom Horn and Joseph LeFors, it was not admissible. Furthermore, Moch singled out the person posing as Joseph LeFors as the primary enemy of the defense and gave this man a thorough grilling. "Legal observers of the retrial agreed that Moch's relentless cross questioning of LeFors, [and] his continuing challenges to the marshal's reputation and reliability," said one observer, "probably had assured that the jurors would find Horn not guilty." On Friday, 17 September 1993, the "jury" acquitted Tom Horn of the charge of murdering Willie Nickell. With this vindication, Tom Horn partisans took the next logical step: an appeal to Wyoming Governor Mike Sullivan for a posthumous pardon. To add to the drama, Amnesty International endorsed this request. "Evidence suggests that Horn's conviction was secured on the basis of a coerced confession and questionable evidence," according to this organization's brochure. Governor Sullivan refused to pardon Tom Horn.[47]

The retrial was widely publicized and attracted capacity crowds in the courtroom. The *Economist* labeled the proceedings "Tom Horn's second chance," and characterized the event as "a proper trial," adding that new evidence was presented. However, this highly regarded journal repeated the erroneous notion that Tom Horn fashioned the rope used in his execution.

While descendants of Tom Horn might gain some comfort in the belated mock acquittal of their controversial ancestor, this does not mean that he was truly innocent of the murder of Willie Nickell. To take the entire case out of historical context and restage the proceedings ninety years later could hardly guarantee impartiality. The fact remained that the basis for the prosecution's case was the confession obtained by Joseph LeFors and that a jury of Horn's peers found him guilty of murder. Just because a "judge" in 1993 threw it out does not mean Charles Ohnhaus's transcript of his conversation with LeFors did not reflect accurately the words that passed between the two men in January 1902. In the matter of the assertion that Tom Horn had been drinking when he made these admissions—probably true—it is a fact that alcohol can not only confuse the mind but can loosen inhibitions and cause a person to (perhaps unwittingly) tell the truth. During Tom Horn's trial, in October 1902, the defense counsel was unable to undermine the character of stenographer Ohnhaus.[48]

As the retrial of Tom Horn indicated, the legend of this infamous frontier personality continues to flourish. In 1901, one hundred years after the murder of Willie Nickell, *True West* recognized this centennial with an article by Chip Carlson, Tom Horn's biographer, who laid out the case for someone other than the range detective being the assassin. Of course, the identity of that someone else remains a mystery. And while western writers would prefer to elevate Horn to the top rung of frontier gun wielders—along with Wyatt Earp, Billy the Kid, and others—a question mark still shadows Horn's reputation. In spite of his services as a civilian scout and packer in the 1880s and 1890s, his legend contains enough negative characteristics to mar his reputation. In this regard, Horn is comparable to train robber "Black Jack" Ketchum, who also exhibited certain personality traits that persuaded even his lawless companions to shun him. As a writer for the *Denver Post* observed in 1947, in spite of having a reputation as a "professional murderer," Tom Horn's "ghost still rides on." In spite of Tom Horn's many accomplishments, the shadow that still hangs over his memory will never be completely erased.[49]

Notes

ABBREVIATIONS

AHC   American Heritage Center, University of Wyoming, Laramie
AHS   Arizona Historical Society
CHS   Colorado Historical Society, Denver
DFB   Dan L. Thrapp, ed. and anno., *Dateline Fort Bowie: Charles Fletcher Lummis Reports on an Apache War* (Norman: University of Oklahoma, 1979).
DL   *Cheyenne Daily Leader*
DP   *Denver Post*
DR   *Denver Republican*
DT   *Denver Times*
JMP   Monaghan Papers, William Wyles Collection, University of California, Santa Barbara
LBGC   Letter Books of George Crook, 2 volumes, Rutherford B. Hayes Presidential Library, Freemont, Ohio
LC   Library of Congress, Washington, D.C.
LOTH   Tom Horn, *Life of Tom Horn* (Norman: University of Oklahoma Press, 1964).
MR   *Memphis (Missouri)Reveille*
NA   National Archives
OAG   Letters Received, Office of the Adjutant General of the Army, Records of the U.S. Army Continental Command, National Archives
OQG   Records of the Office of the Quartermaster General, National Archives
RG   Record Group
RMN   *Rocky Mountain News* (Denver)
WSA   Wyoming State Archives, Cheyenne

PREFACE AND ACKNOWLEDGMENTS

1. For Edwin Smalley's arrest of Tom Horn, see *Cheyenne Daily Leader*, 13 January 1902; Shields, "Edwin J. Smalley."

CHAPTER 1

1. Much has been written about Tom Horn, but it is not always reliable. For the most recent biography, see Carlson, *Tom Horn*. Nunis, *Life of Tom Horn* takes a more a critical look at Horn. Monaghan, *Last of the Bad Men* is still useful. For Horn family genealogy, see Day, *Short Family History*. Rice, *History of Scotland County,* 207–209, 328–30, 425, contains some helpful information. See N. Will to the Bobbs-Merrill Company, 13 September 1946, enc. in Rosemary (a Bobbs-Merrill employee) to Monaghan, 27 September 1946, JMP. While the relationship of N. Will to the Horn family is not known, he seems to have had some knowledge about the family background. See also *DL*, 19 August 1903; and *RMN*, 8 May 1904. Hartman, a common name in the Horn genealogy, was spelled variously as "Hardtman" or "Hardman."

2. Day, *Short Family History*, 1; *RMN*, 8 May 1904. A rumor persisted after the death of Tom Horn, Jr., that the Horn lineage contained Indian blood, although there is no evidence for this. Mary Ann Miller's name is sometimes listed as "Maryam Maricha" rather than "Mary Ann."

3. See Carlson, *Blood on the Moon*, 22–24, for Thomas Horn, Sr.'s financial problems in Ohio.

4. *Memphis (Missouri) Conservative*, 13 February 1879, for recollections of Etna's boom years.

5. Day, *Short Family History*, 1–2.

6. *RMN*, 8 May 1904; *MR*, 3 September 1874. See *MR* 28 May 1885 for partnership with Purmort.

7. Much that has been written about Tom Horn is based upon his autobiography (*Life of Tom Horn*, 1904). Horn devoted most of this volume to the Apache wars in Arizona in the 1880s. He was generally present at the events he mentions, but made many wild and unsubstantiated claims as to his contributions. Yet his recollections cannot be totally ignored, and he sometimes inadvertently or unconsciously made useful statements. Unless otherwise noted, the present writer cites the University of Oklahoma Press edition of *Life of Tom Horn* (1964), which has an introduction by Dean Krakel (hereafter *LOTH*). Although lacking annotations, this is a complete reprint including the appendices. For some analysis of Horn's autobiography, see Ball, "That 'Miserable Book.'" *LOTH*, 4, 8, for Horn's recollections of his father.

8. Carlson, *Blood on the Moon*, 22.

9. *History of Lewis, Clark, Knox and Scotland Counties,* 1178. For Thomas Horn, Sr.'s, various activities, see *Memphis Conservative*, 29 February 1872; *MR*, 10 September 1874, 2 July 1885, 29 July 1886.

10. *LOTH*, 3; Carlson, *Blood on the Moon*, 28.

11. *LOTH*, 3. For the Campbellites, see Lamar, *New Encyclopedia of the American West,* 306–307, s.v. "Disciples of Christ."

12. *LOTH*, 3.

13. Ibid., 5–6.

14. Ibid., 6.

15.*DP*, 11 October 1902.

16. *LOTH*, 5–6.

17. *DT*, 19 August 1903.

18. *LOTH*, 5.

19. *Memphis Conservative,* 21 November 1872; *DT*, 19 August 1903.

20. *RMN*, 8 May 1904; Whitehead, letter to editor, 58–59.

21. *LOTH*, 6–7.

22. *DT*, 19 August 1903; *LOTH*, 6–7.

23. *LOTH*, 7–8.

24. Ibid.

25. *MR*, 1 June 1876, 12 July 1877; *Memphis Conservative*, 2 August 1877, 5 February, 4 March 1880.

26. *MR*, 3, 10 December 1874.

27. Monaghan, *Last of the Bad Men*, 24.

28. *LOTH*, 8–9.

29. *RMN*, 8 May 1904.

30. *LOTH*, 8–10; *Laramie Boomerang*, 21 August 1903.

31. *LOTH*, 10. Newton, Kansas, was a division headquarters, 1871–1879.

32. *DT*, 19 August 1903.

33. Monaghan, *Last of the Bad Men*, 42–43; *Newton Kansan*, 22 March, 10 May 1877; *Hutchinson News-Herald*, 13 April 1952, repr. in Dewey, *Legends of the Wheat Country*, 111–13; *Hutchinson News*, 18 December 1977, Harvey County Historical Society clippings, vol. 3, Kansas Historical Society, Topeka.

34. Dewey, *Legends of the Wheat Country*, 11–13; *Harvey County News*, 24 January 1878; Monaghan, *Last of the Bad Men*, 43. The Blades family was very large, see *Newton Kansan*, 14 October 1875, 3 May 1877.

35. Day, *Short Family History*, 3; *Burrton Telephone*, 16 August, 13 September 1879, 21 February, 27 March, 11 September 1880, 7, 11 February, 20 March 1881; *Newton Kansan*, 11 July 1878, 29 March, 3 July, 4 September 1879, 1 April 1880; *Burrton Monitor*, 10 June, 14 October 1881.

36. Monaghan, *Last of the Bad Men*, 33–41; Paul Frison, *Apache Slave*, 32–33. Thomas Joseph Cahill, who became a good friend of Tom Horn in Cheyenne, Wyoming, recalled that his father met Horn in Dodge City in the 1870s (Leslie Gregory MSS, Clara Woody Collection, series 2, AHS).

37. Monaghan, *Last of the Bad Men*, 40–41.

38. *MR*, 8 January 1880.

39. *MR*, 8 May 1880; *Burrton Telephone*, 14 February, 3 April, 8, 22, 29 May 1880; Monaghan, *Last of the Bad Men*, 44.

40. Dewey, *Legends of the Wheat Country*, 111–13.

41. Monaghan, *Last of the Bad Men*, 44–47; *MR*, 8 April 1880. Some uncertainty exists as to Tom Horn's movements in 1880. There were two persons named Tom Horn listed in the 1880 Census for Leadville, both about the same age and from Missouri (*Tenth Census*, U.S. Bureau of the Census, NA roll 90). The 1880 Census for Scotland County, Missouri, also listed him residing there with his parents. Perhaps, our Tom Horn made a hasty visit back to Missouri and then returned to Colorado, or his parents gave his name to the census taker as a precaution (ibid., roll 736). For Tom Horn, see also *Leadville City Directory* for 1880, 195, and *Directory* for 1881, 163.

42. *Leadville Democrat*, 9 July 1880, for Fowler's discovery; *MR*, 17 November 1881, for Fowler's death; Monaghan, *Last of the Bad Men*, 49.

43. Monaghan, *Last of the Bad Men*, 50; "Reminisce with Leora Peters," *Platte County (Wyoming) Record-Times,* 28 July 1967; for "Munson's Chunk," see Clara Woody Collection, AHS, series 4, box 15.

44. Drago, *Legend Makers*, 194; Thatcher, "One Night in Las Vegas"; and Rasch's letter to the editor ridiculing such an unsubstantiated tale. Four men named Murray were listed

in the 1880 census for New Mexico Territory. However, no evidence has been found that they were connected with mail contracts at the time (*Tenth Census*, U.S. Bureau of the Census, NA, rolls 802–804). Horn could have failed to recall the mail contractor's name correctly. There were a J. R. Miner (Federal Register, 1882, 439–40) and a George V. Meserole involved in such contracts (*Letters from the Postmaster General . . . , October 15, 1880, and March 10, 1881*). *LOTH*, 11. See Barnes, *Arizona Place Names*, 333–34, for Beaverhead Crossing.

45. Daly to Gatewood, 17 July 1925, Gatewood Collection, AHS, roll 9. A J. W. Payne was hired as a teamster at Whipple Barracks on 1 October 1883 (Report of Persons and Articles . . . , Whipple Barracks, February 1884, OQG, NA, box 584). Payne continued in service at Whipple Barracks as a messenger and corral master and became a clerk on 1 October 1885 (Report of Persons and Articles . . . , Whipple Barracks, October 1885, OQG, box 590). For the possible association of Tom Horn and Frank Stilwell, see Young, *Cochise County Cowboy War*, 66. Tom Horn's omission of the years 1876–81 from *LOTH* is puzzling. Perhaps, he was trying to hide some indiscretion, such as the alleged shooting in Texas, and chose to place himself in Arizona Territory from the time he left Missouri. Horn's friends in Arizona were certain that he did not arrive there before 1881 or 1882. An alternative, but unlikely, scenario is that Tom Horn made two trips to Arizona Territory, first around 1876, and again in 1881. Perhaps the most telling evidence that Horn did not arrive until 1881 is in the organization of his autobiography, where his narrative of the Apache wars begins with the Cibecue uprising, which took place in August 1881 (although Horn was not present at this encounter).

46. Frazier, *Forts of the Old West*, 14, for Fort Verde. Garrison, "John Hance" 4–11; *LOTH*, 11–12; Corbusier, *Verde to San Carlos*, 262–63, for some recollections of the Hance brothers. J. P. Wallace, who was familiar with Horn's activities in Arizona in the 1880s, recalled that Horn was "a mule herder at Camp Verde" (Wallace to Bobbs-Merrill Company, 25 October 1946, JMP).

47. Griffith, *Mickey Free*, 77. While not always a reliable source, Griffith maintained that he gathered stories about Horn from old Apache scouts at Fort Apache. *Weekly Arizona Miner*, 17 March 1882, for Dan Thorne's advertisement. For Horn's initial employment, see Report of Persons and Articles . . . , Whipple Barracks, OQG, box 544. For Willcox, see Scott, *Forgotten Valor*.

48. Thrapp, *Conquest of Apacheria*, for background on the Apache struggles; Ogle, *Federal Control*, 86–178. For San Carlos, see Bret-Harte, "San Carlos Indian Reservation."

49. Collins, *Apache Nightmare*, for detailed coverage. Report of Persons and Articles . . . , Whipple Depot, OQM, boxes 544, 555, 546, 547.

50. Thrapp, *Al Sieber*, for the standard treatment; *LOTH*, 12.

51. "Statement from Al Sieber," 7 April 1904, in *LOTH*, 269–71. Report of Persons and Articles . . . , Whipple Depot, OQG, box 558.

52. Daly to Gatewood, 17 July 1925, Gatewood Collection, AHS, roll 9. Deposition of James Cook, 5 February 1884, Exhibit H, in Report of George R. Milburn, U.S. Special Indian Agent, to Hiram Price, Commissioner of Indian Affairs, 16 February 1884, enc. in Robert T. Lincoln, Secretary of War, to Henry M. Teller, Secretary of Interior, 21 January [*sic*; February] 1884, Letters Received, Bureau of Indian Affairs, NA, box 177. Williamson, "Story of Oskay De No Tah," 78–83. See *Weekly Arizona Miner*, 2 September 1881, for Long Jim Cook. Allan Radbourne, e-mail messages to author, 20, 24 June 2007.

53. Report of Persons and Articles . . . , Whipple Depot, OQG, boxes 557, 558, show Cook's train "transferred Jany. 9, 1882, to 1st Lieut. Frederick von Schrader, 12 Inf., AAQM, in the field," and then to 2nd Lieut. Millard Fillmore Waltz, 12th Infty, Acting

Asst. QM, Fort McDowell, ibid., box 559 (for Jan., Feb., May, June, July, Aug. 1882. Waltz's report for March 1882 is in box 560; his report for April 1882 was not found.) The monthly post returns for various army installations occasionally listed the names of civilian employees, although regulations did not require them. The Fort McDowell returns for March–September 1882 provide the names of Long Jim Cook's train, including Tom Horn (*Returns from U.S. Military Posts*, Records of the Adjutant General's Office, NA, roll 669). Tom Horn possibly left the pack train for the period, 1–18 July, since he was given a new contract, dated 19 July 1882. Cook's train remained on Lieutenant Waltz's roster through 31 August 1881.

54. Essin, *Shavetails and Bell Sharps*, for the standard work on the subject. Arnold, "Mule" 35–50; Cruse, *Apache Days*, 54–55; Betzinez, *I Fought with Geronimo*, 57; Daly, "Following the Bell," 111–17.

55. Essin, *Shavetails and Bell Sharps*, 89–121. For pack train personnel and duties, see Daly, *Manual of Pack Transportation*, 153–60. Daly knew Tom Horn well and worked with him on several campaigns. Ward, "A Trip to the Cavalry Camps," 109–14.

56. Collins, *Apache Nightmare*, 110, for Packmaster Cook serving temporarily as a scout.

57. *LOTH*, 11; Monaghan, *Last of the Bad Men*, 44.

CHAPTER 2

1. For Horn's army employment in 1881–82, see chap. 1.

2. Thrapp, *Conquest of Apacheria*, 231–38; *LOTH*, 44–46; Shapard, *Chief Loco*, 152–55; Connell, "Draft on Apaches," unpub. MS, AHS, 179–230. Connell was chief clerk of the reservation and an eyewitness. The author is also indebted to Allan Radbourne for his thoughts on Tom Horn's description of Loco's breakout, Radbourne to author, 10 June 2006.

3. *LOTH*, 44–46. See *Arizona Weekly Star*, 27 April 1882, for the theft of Ming's horses.

4. *LOTH*, 46–47; Connell, "Draft on Apaches."

5. Thrapp, *Conquest of Apacheria*, 238–50; "Statement from Al Sieber," *LOTH*, 269–71.

6. Dunlay, *Wolves for the Blue Soldiers*, 165–86; Sieber's "Statement," *LOTH*, 269–71; Daly, "Scouts, Good and Bad," 24–25, 66, 68–70.

7. Barnes, *Apaches and Longhorns*, 71; Williamson, "Al Sieber," 6, Dan R. Williamson Papers, AHS, box 2. See also Williamson, "Al Sieber," 60–76. Shipp, "Captain Crawford's Last Expedition," 343–61; *DFB*, 124; Daly, "Scouts, Good and Bad," 68.

8. *LOTH*, 12–13.

9. Ibid., 57–64; Shapard, *Chief Loco*, 162–63; Thrapp, *Al Sieber*, 229–34. The wounded soldier was a Private Miller, but there is no indication that Tom Horn had a part in the rescue.

10. Thrapp, *Conquest of Apacheria*, 248–50.

11. Thrapp, *Al Sieber*, 227n6; *DR*, 18 April 1898.

12. King, *Arizona Charlie*, 20–21.

13. *LOTH*, 70–71, 80–84; Thrapp, *Al Sieber*, 244–57; King, *Arizona Charlie*, 19–21; Northern Gila County Historical Society, *Rim Country History*, 70, 154–55; Platten to Williamson, 15 October 1930, Dan R. Williamson Papers, AHS. Platten was a soldier in the relief party.

14. Thrapp, *Al Sieber*, 245–57; *LOTH*, 84–89. For Dan Ming and the Apache volunteers, see *Arizona Silver Belt*, 6 July 1882, and Bret-Harte, "San Carlos Indian Reservation," 669–72.

15. Thrapp, *Al Sieber*, 245–57; Morgan, "Big Dry Wash," 21–28.

16. *LOTH*, 84–86; Morgan, "Big Dry Wash," 21–28; Cruse, *Apache Days*, 158–69. Cruse was part of one of the flanking parties. Thrapp, *Al Sieber*, 245–57. Barnes, "Apaches' Last Stand," 36–59, maintained that Horn was not involved in the battle, but remained with the pack train.

17. Thrapp, *Al Sieber*, 255–57.

18. *LOTH*, 94–99; Monaghan, *Last of the Bad Men*, 201; Dunlap to Williamson, 5 February 1931, Williamson Papers, AHS, box 1, for Charles Willcox's recollections.

19. Thrapp, *Conquest of Apacheria*, 255–61; Davis, *Truth About Geronimo*, 38–39.

20. Davis, *Truth About Geronimo*, 41; Cruse, *Apache Days and After*, 54–55; Thrapp, *Dictionary of Frontier Biography*, 2:1011–12, s.v. "Thomas Moore"; Crook, *Autobiography*, 245; *Los Angeles Times*, 28 April 1886, repr. in *DFB*, 124–28. Report of Persons and Articles . . . , San Carlos, October 1882, OQG, box 561. Britton Davis later erroneously characterized Horn's claim to have been at San Carlos as "trash" (Davis, *The Truth About Geronimo*, 196–97).

21. Daly to Gatewood, 17 July 1925, Gatewood Collection, AHS, roll 9; Radbourne, *Mickey Free*, for the best treatment of Free.

22. Ganzhorn, *I've Killed Men*, 13–14. Jack Ganzhorn was the son of William Ganzhorn. Mazzanovich, "Truth About Tom Horn," in *Brewery Gulch Gazette*, 12 May 1933, Mazzanovich Collection, AHS; *Arizona Silver Belt*, 1 January 1881. See Bailey, *Henry Clay Hooker*, 73–75, for Norton and Stewart.

23. *LOTH*, 42. For contracts, see Exhibit A (Matthew F. Shaw) and Exhibit E (Eugene O. Shaw), in Report of George R. Milburn, U.S. Special Indian Agent, to Hiram Price, Commissioner of Indian Affairs, 16 February 1884, enc. in Robert T. Lincoln, Secretary of War, to Henry M. Teller, Secretary of Interior, 21 January 1884, Letters Received, Bureau of Indian Affairs, NA, box 177. See also Shaw's testimony, Record of Court of Inquiry in the Case of Cpt. Emmet Crawford, box 3721. Shaw, who testified on 7 May 1884, declared that he began as "agent for the beef contractor" in April 1883. Anderson, "Eugene and Matthew Shaw," 319–54; Bret-Harte, "San Carlos Indian Reservation," 1:156–57. See the recollections of Ming, Jones, and the Dunlap brothers contained in depositions that they provided in support of Tom Horn when, as a Pinkerton operative, he was tried for robbery in Reno, Nevada, in 1891 (*State of Nevada vs. Thomas H. Horn*, case no. 2832, 1891, Special Collections Department, University of Nevada, Reno). For the Dunlap's ranch, see Bailey, *Henry Clay Hooker*, 98. Tom Horn erroneously dated his work as herd foreman to 1879 (*LOTH*, 42).

24. *LOTH*, 42. For Clark's recollections, see *Arizona Bulletin*, 27 November 1903.

25. Elliott, "Indian Reservation," 91–102.

26. Davis, *Truth About Geronimo*, 42.

27. Hanchett, Jr., *They Shot Billy Today*, 99–106, for John Rhodes. McCarthy to Brininstool, 28 March 1933, enc. in Brininstool to Gatewood, 28 March 1933, Gatewood Collection, AHS, roll 4. Bailey, *"We'll All Wear Silk Hats,"* 52, for the Murphy brothers.

28. Baber, *Longest Rope*, 108–110, for Walker's recollections of Tom Horn. See also Baber, *Injun Summer*, 134–43. *LOTH*, 42. By "on the prod," Horn meant that the Apaches were "fighting mad" (Adams, *Western Words,* 210).

29. Davis, *Truth About Geronimo*, 42–43. The *Arizona Silver Belt*, 5 July 1884, which reported Shaw's expulsion, said that he "was the accredited agent of William Griffith," who probably had a contract with Tully and Ochoa.

30. Thrapp, *Conquest of Apacheria*, 267–77; *LOTH*, 108–11; Davis, *Truth About Geronimo*, 38–39; Bourke, *Apache Campaign*. See Thrapp, *General Crook*, for the standard treatment.

31. Bourke, *Apache Campaign*, 57. *LOTH*, 269–71 (for Sieber's statement), 112–37 (for Horn's description of the expedition). Donald McCarthy, a miner who became acquainted with Horn at San Carlos, also recalled that Horn accompanied the 1883 expedition (McCarthy to Brininstool, 28 March 1933, enc. in Brininstool to Charles B. Gatewood, Jr., 27 October 1941, Gatewood Collection, AHS, roll 4). Thrapp, *General Crook*, 128, says that "If Tom Horn accompanied the expedition, he did so as an ordinary packer."

32. *LOTH*, 112. Charles B. Gatewood, Jr., rejected the suggestion that Sieber personally paid Horn, since the chief of scout's monthly income of $125 "could hardly have enabled him to employ Horn out of his own pocket" ("Memorandum to *Collier's*," 10 March 1933, Gatewood Collection, AHS, roll 4). Yet if Horn really desired to accompany Sieber as his "assistant," wages of perhaps $25–50 per month might have been sufficient inducement.

33. Bourke, *Apache Campaign*, 57–73; Fiebeger, "General Crook's Campaign," in Carroll, *Papers*, 193–201; *LOTH*, 114–15; "With Crook in the Sierra Madre," repr. in Cozzens, *Eyewitnesses to the Indian Wars*, 1:355. See Goodwin, "Experiences of an Indian Scout," 56, for Rope's recollection of the peaches.

34. Randall, "Crook's Apaches," *Albuquerque Daily Democrat*, 21 June 1883; "Bourke's Diary," in Cozzens, *Struggle for Apacheria*, 360–63 (10 May), 363–64 (11 May), 377–78 (20 May). Bourke, *Apache Campaign*, 84–95. *LOTH*, 114–17 (for Horn's claim), 268–71 (for Sieber's recollections). For Horn's boast, see *DR*, 18 April 1898. Thrapp, *Conquest of Apacheria*, 289nn15–16, also discounts Horn's claim that he was an interpreter. Bigelow, *On the Bloody Trail*, 214.

35. *LOTH*, 118–35; Thrapp, *Al Sieber*, 281n15; Goodwin, "Experiences of an Indian Scout," 31–73. Thrapp, *General Crook*, 155–65, for Crook's negotiations with the hostiles.

36. *LOTH*, 136–37; Mazzanovich, "Truth about Tom Horn," clipping, *Brewery Gulch Gazette*, 12 May 1933, Mazzanovich Collection, AHS. Thrapp, *Conquest of Apacheria*, 293–94, for the confiscation of Geronimo's livestock.

37. *LOTH*, 136; Thrapp, *General Crook*, 167–72.

38. Thrapp, *Conquest of Apacheria*, 295–302; Bret-Harte, "Conflict at San Carlos, 27–44.

39. *LOTH*, 137–41.

40. Ming recalled that Horn worked at various jobs on the reservation from 1884 to 1886 (Deposition of Daniel Ming, *State of Nevada v. Thomas Horn*, 1891, case 2832, University of Nevada, Reno); *LOTH*, 138; Wilcox to Commissioner of Indian Affairs Hiram Price, 11 August 1884, Letters Received, Bureau of Indian Affairs, NA, box 203. On the employees list for 1884, Horn is listed as storekeeper, but then this word is marked out and asst. farmer inserted (Records of Agency Employees, 1853–1909, 13:85–86). For Matthew F. Shaw's deposition, see "Exhibit A" in the Report of George R. Milburn, U.S. Special Indian Agent, to Hiram Price, Commissioner of Indian Affairs, 16 February 1884, enc. in Lincoln to Secretary of Interior, 21 January 1884, Letters Received, Bureau of Indian Affairs, NA, box 177.

41. Ford to Price, 26 March 1885, Letters Received, Bureau of Indian Affairs, NA, box 234. Ford to Price, 24 January 1885, ibid., box 225. Winnerick became assistant farmer (Bret-Harte, "The San Carlos Indian Reservation," 2:794–97).

42. Debo, *Geronimo*, 222–23; Davis, *Truth About Geronimo*, 48–50, 141. *Arizona Silver Belt*, 10 May 1884, for the tizwin party. Thrapp, *Al Sieber*, 266–67; Williamson, "Al Sieber, Famous Scout," 60–76.

43. Daly to Gatewood, 17 July 1925, Gatewood Collection, AHS, roll 9; *LOTH*, 100–101.

44. *LOTH*, 12–14; Sweeney, *From Cochise to Geronimo*, 212–13. Captain Francis E. Pierce referred to an incident that could possibly be the centipede episode. "A party commenced the manufacture of *tiswin* on one occasion," wrote Pierce, "but it was stopped before they had an opportunity to drink any of it by the prompt and decisive action of a scout who happened to be in camp on a visit." However, Pierce said nothing about an Apache being killed. Instead, "the offenders were brought to trial."(Captain F. E. Pierce, 1st Infantry, Cmdg. Post and Acting Indian Agent, San Carlos, to Captain Cyrus S. Roberts, 17th Infantry, A. A. D. C., 11 September 1885, LBGC, Appendix N). While downplaying Sieber's rougher side, Dan Thrapp admitted he could be "utterly ruthless." Thrapp also admitted that Emmet Crawford did not always do things "according to the book" when policing the reservation (Thrapp, *Al Sieber*, 173).

45. Siringo, *Two Evil Isms*, 47–48; Monaghan, *Last of the Bad Men*, 74.

46. *LOTH*, 20–21; Thrapp, *Encyclopedia of Frontier Biography*, 3:1128–29, s.v. "Pedro." Kraft, *Lt. Charles Gatewood*, 70–73, for Pedro's ear horn.

47. Griffith, *Mickey Free*, 78–80. In Will Henry's biographical novel, *I, Tom Horn*, 112–17, the author has Horn living with a Yaqui girl named Nopal. Irvin Van Enwyck, e-mail to author, 2 February 2005. See Goodwin and Goodwin, *Apache Diaries*, for an effort to locate "Lost Ones" in the 1920s and 1930s. McCarthy to Owen P. White, 1 April 1933, enc. in Earl A. Brininstool to Charles B. Gatewood, Jr., 27 October 1941, Gatewood Collections, AHS, roll 4. *LOTH*, 18–19.

48. *LOTH*, 18–19; Griffith, *Mickey Free*, 77–80; Irvin Van Enwyck, e-mail to the author, 2 February 2005; Daly, "Scouts Good and Bad," 25.

49. *LOTH*, 25; Chapman, "Tom Horn," 69–76, for Horn's use of herbal medicine.

50. See White, "Remarks on the Article, 'Talking Boy,'" enc. in Gatewood to president, *Collier's*, 11 March 1933, Gatewood Collection, AHS, roll 8. Army officers insisted that interpreters have "credentials" and be "accredited." *LOTH*, 12–13; Daly to Gatewood, 17 July 1925, Gatewood Collection, AHS, roll 9. Long Jim Cook, who later denied that Horn could speak Spanish well enough to interpret, was in error (Cook to Gatewood, 30 March 1933, AHS, roll 8).

51. McCarthy to Brininstool, 28 March 1933, enc. in Brininstool to Gatewood, 27 October 1941, Gatewood Collection, AHS, roll 4. Mazzanovich, "Truth About Tom Horn," clipping, *Brewery Gulch Gazette*, 12 May 1933, Mazzanovich Collection, AHS. "Sieber's Statement," in *LOTH*, 269–71.

52. Thaddeus (Bud) Ming to Will C. Barnes, 6 March 1931, Barnes Collections, AHS, box 4. Bud Ming, a son of Dan Ming, wrote his reply on the bottom of Barnes's letter of 5 March 1931 and returned it. See Hadley, *Environmental Change* for geographic setting and early settlement. *LOTH*, 20; Bret-Harte, "San Carlos Indian Reservation," 2: 739–40 and 785, for stolen animals sold on the reservation. Horn to "Dear Father and Mother," *MR*, 4 March 1886. In a letter of 1 March 1904 to Ed Tewksbury, Glendolene Kimmell said that Horn had made two attempts to start a ranch in Arizona (copy courtesy of Richard Pierce, Phoenix, Arizona). The *New York Times*, 18 July 1881, reported a stolen Mexican herd sold at San Carlos.

53. *LOTH*, 202–204, 213–14, and 222, for Horn's other mining activities. Ridgway, *Mount Graham Profiles*, 2: 58–59, 164–65. Milt Rhea, retired police chief, Safford, Arizona, 9 December 2000, informed the author that Horn's Ore Hanna mine is still recognizable. *Weekly Arizona Star*, 26 July 1888, for John P. Harr and the Dunlap brothers in the Aravaipa Mining District. *Great Register of Graham County*, entry 505, for John P. Harr. For Wid Childress, see Meadows to Willson, 7 June 1959, Roscoe Willson Collection, Arizona

Historical Foundation, Arizona State University, Tempe, Tom Horn folder. Hadley, *Environmental Change*, 99–133, for early mining ventures.

54. *LOTH*, 25–28, for Horn's alleged Tombstone adventure. Carmony, *Apache Days*, 23, for the story that Al Sieber suggested the name of Tombstone. Thrapp, *Al Sieber*, 210. For Schieffelin's recollections, see Underhill, "The Tombstone Discovery," 37–76, which makes no mention of Sieber.

55. Donald F. McCarthy to Owen P. White, 1 April 1933, enc. in Earl A. Brininstool to Charles B. Gatewood, Jr., 27 October 1941, Gatewood Collection, AHS, roll 4.

CHAPTER 3

1. Horn to "Dear Father and Mother," 20 February 1886, *MR*, 4 March 1886.

2. Thrapp, *Conquest of Apacheria*, 303–15, for the breakout. To add confusion to the Tom Horn story, a second Tom Horn served as a civilian scout in the 1876 Sioux campaign. Horn to "Dear Father and Mother," *MR*, 4 March 1886. Horn's ranching partner may have been Billy Harrison, his sidekick in the pack train.

3. For a list of pack trains, see Dan R. Williamson Papers, AHS, box 2. "Statement from Al Sieber," *LOTH*, 268–71. For Tom Horn's description of this campaign, see *LOTH*, 164–69. Cruse, *Apache Days*, 220–21, declared he never heard of Tom Horn until late 1885. Edward Arhelger Papers, AHS. Griffith, *Mickey Free*, 125–28, for Horn and Spike. Griffith claimed that he interviewed Mickey Free's family (219n3).

4. Nickell, "Tom Horn in Arizona," 15–22, says Tom Horn arrived at Crook's base camp with a pack train led by Al Sieber. Thrapp, *Conquest of Apacheria*, 324. See *Army-Navy Journal*, 11 July 1885, for Tom Moore. Fort Bowie Post Returns, July 1885, *Returns from U.S. Military Posts, 1800–1916*, Records of the Adjutant General's Office, NA, roll 130, for list of packers. *LOTH*, 165–66.

5. Davis, *Truth About Geronimo*, 154–56, 166–69; *LOTH*, 166. Horn is very confused, saying that Sieber did not accompany this foray. *Army-Navy Journal*, 22 August, 5 September 1885.

6. *Army-Navy Journal*, 4 July 1885; Davis, *Truth About Geronimo*, 166–69; Thrapp, *Conquest of Apacheria*, 324–27 and 328n1.

7. Daly, "Geronimo Campaign"; Davis, *Truth About Geronimo*, 174–92; Crawford to Crook, 30 Aug 1885, *Letters Received by the Office of the Adjutant General of the Army, Main Series*, Records of the Adjutant General's Office, NA, roll 184; Davis to Adjutant General, Department of Arizona, 15 September 1886, Report of Brigadier General George Crook for 1886, LBCG, appendix H, 1:42–46.

8. "Sieber's Statement," *LOTH*, 269–71.

9. Edward Arhelger Papers, AHS; Crawford to Crook, 30 Aug 1885, Letters Received by the Office of the Adjutant General, NA, roll 184; Davis to Adjutant General, Department of Arizona, 15 September 1886, Report of Brigadier General George Crook for 1886, LBGC, appendix H, 1:42–46.

10. *LOTH*, 166–69.

11. Corbusier, *Verde to San Carlos*, 263n1. Corbusier was unsure whether this encounter with Horn took place in 1875 during his first tour of duty in Arizona or on his second in 1885.

12. Shipp, "Captain Crawford's Last Expedition." Altshuler, *Cavalry Yellow and Army Blue*, s.v. "Marion Perry Maus" (225), and "William Ewen Shipp" (301); Dunlap, "Tom

Horn," 73–85; Daly, "Geronimo Campaign," 79–80. In *LOTH*, 169–70, the author confuses these preparations with activities of the following summer, 1886.

13. Report of Persons and Articles . . . , Fort Bowie, October 1886, OQG, box 590. The
names of civilian employees, including Tom Horn, were also listed on the Fort Bowie Post
Returns, October 1885, *Returns from U.S. Military Posts, 1800–1916*, Office of the Adjutant,
NA, roll 130. Lane, *Chasing Geronimo*, 27, 5 May 1886. Apparently, Allsop had earlier been
fired on a previous campaign and then rehired *(Arizona Weekly Star*, 5 November 1885).

14. *LOTH*, 166; Daly to Gatewood, 17 July 1925, Gatewood Collection, AHS, roll 9;
Daly, "Geronimo Campaign," 43, 78–79; "Sieber's Statement," *LOTH*, 269–71; *Prescott
Courier*, 2 October 1885.

15. Thomas N. Wills Papers, AHS; Shipp, "Captain Crawford's Last Expedition,"
343–61.

16. Altshuler, *Cavalry Yellow and Infantry Blue*, s.v. "Maus" (225), "Faison" (126–27),
"Shipp" (301); Geene, *Nez Perce Summer*, 150, 259–62, 284, 300–323; "Conqueror of
Nana," 205, for Nelson Miles's applause of Maus in the Nez Perce Campaign. *DFB*, 69.
There is some confusion as to this Harrison's first name. Possibly, his full name was William
Thomas Harrison, but he appears to be the Billy Harrison who was Tom Horn's friend.

17. Shipp, "Captain Crawford's Last Expedition," 343–61. Sam Noche was highly regarded by American army officers *(DFB*, 63n1).

18. *LOTH*, 170. Since Sieber was a "senior" chief of scouts when other civilian scouts
were present, Tom Horn was apparently "senior" to William Harrison (Thrapp, *Conquest
of Apacheria*, 334–39). Much of the material for this chapter is taken from, U.S. Congress,
"Killing of Captain Crawford." See, Torres to Palomares, 21 March 1886, 664, enc. depositions of C. Leivas, Prefect, District of Moctezuma, ibid., 660–61, and V. Arvizu, Granados,
Sonora, 27 December 1885, 661. For a summation of the Crawford incident, see "Brief Review of the Circumstances Connected with the Killing of Captain Emmit [sic] Crawford,"
22 (typescript), John G. Bourke Papers, Nebraska State Historical Society.

19. Shipp, "Captain Crawford's Last Expedition," 343–61.

20. Daly, "Scouts Good and Bad," 24–25, 66–70.

21. Daly, "Geronimo Campaign"; Shipp, "Captain Crawford's Last Expedition," 343–61.

22. Maus to Roberts, 8 April 1886, LBGC, vol. 1, appendix I. Maus also wrote a more
detailed account for Miles, *Personal Recollections,* 450–71. San José de Teópare was situated
forty miles southeast of Nácori Chico, on a tributary of the Rio Aros. According to Hatfield, *Chasing Shadows*, 163n21, "It is near the Chihuahua border and the Devil's Backbone,
the roughest part of the Sierra Madre." *LOTH*, 183; Sweeney, *From Cochise to Geronimo*,
494–97.

23. See Maus's narrative in Miles, *Personal Recollections*, 450–71; Maus to Roberts, 21
January 1886, LBGC.

24. *LOTH*, 171–80.

25. Maus to Roberts, 21 January 1886, LBGC, vol. 1, appendix K.

26. Shipp, "Captain Crawford's Last Expedition," 343–61; *LOTH*, 183.

27. In addition to previous sources cited, see Nalty and Strobridge, "Captain Emmet
Crawford," 30–40; Shelley Bowen Hatfield, "The Death of Emmet Crawford," 131–48.
For Charles Lummis's reports to the *Los Angeles Times*, see *DFB*, 162–84; "Reminiscences
of Harvey Nashkín," Grenville Goodwin Notebooks, Arizona State Museum, Phoenix,
series A, vol. 3 (copy courtesy Allan Radbourne). For Maus's report of the Crawford Incident, with depositions by Tom Horn and other participants, see Maus to Captain Cyrus
Swan Roberts, Asst. Adj. Gen., Dept. of Arizona, 27 January 1886, enc. in Annual Report

of Brigadier-General Crook, 1886, LBGC, vol. 1, appendix L. Marion Maus provided additional details to the *San Francisco Chronicle*, 11 July 1886.

28. *LOTH*, 184–85; Statement of 2nd Class Hospital Steward Frank J. Nemeck [Nemick], Feb. 23, 1886, exhibit F, in Maus to Roberts, 23 February 1886, LBGC, 1:68–69. Statement of Horn, 23 February 1886, ibid., 1:66–67, exhibit D; Horn's statement to Lummis, in *DFB*, 181–83.

29. Cpt. Cyrus Roberts, George Crook's aide, instructed Maus to "make a careful and full report" of the 11 January encounter, to include "statements . . . obtained from people belonging to your command." "Strengthen your report by certificates of the officers and [civilian] employes [sic] of your command . . . ," continued Roberts, as "this is a matter of the greatest importance" (Roberts to Maus, 19 February 1886, Letters Sent, Department of Arizona, 1886, Records of U.S. Army Continental Commands, NA, 19:234). Statement of Capt. Santa Ana Perez, 1886, U.S. Congress, *"Killing of Captain Crawford,"* 601–603 (13 Feb.), 606–607 (23 Feb.), and 650–51 (2 May). See Crook's interview with Charles F. Lummis, 16 May 1886, in *DFB*, 184. There is some confusion as to who commanded the Chihuahuan militiamen. The governor of Chihuahua authorized Santa Ana Perez, a second lieutenant, to raise the company of 150 men. Apparently, Mauricio Corredor, who is referred to as a major, commanded only the scouts.

30. Maus to Roberts, 23 February 1886, LBGC, 1:68–69; Maus interview with Lummis, in *DFB*, 263–70; *LOTH*, 184–85.

31. Maus to Roberts, 23 February 1886, LBGC, 1:58–63; *DFB*, 164 for the map.

32. Shipp's statement to Lummis, in *DFB*, 179–83; Horn's statement, ibid., 181–85.

33. *LOTH*, 185; Shipp, "Captain Crawford's Last Expedition," 343–61. Horn's statement to Lummis in *DFB*, 181–83; "Reminiscences of Harvey Nashkín," Grenville Goodwin Notebooks, Arizona State Library.

34. *LOTH*, 184.

35. Maus's statement to Lummis, *DFB*, 163–70; Shipp, "Captain Crawford's Last Expedition," 343–61; Statement of Thomas Horn, 23 February 1886, LBGC, 1:66–67; Maus to Roberts, 23 February 1886, ibid., 1:58–63; *LOTH*, 185–88. *"Nan-t-an tle-ha-des-aadn"* translates as "Leader Who Leaves with Them at Night," or "Leader Who Leaves Between Them (i.e., with persons on both sides of him) At Night." The author is indebted to Keith Basso for this translation.

36. Statement of Thomas Horn, 23 Feburary 1886, LBGC, 1:66–67; *LOTH*, 188; "Reminiscences of Harvey Nashkín," Grenville Goodwin Notebooks, Arizona State Library.

37. *LOTH*, 186–87; Statement of William Harrison, 25 January 1886, LBGC, 1:67–68;

38. Statement of Thomas Horn, 23 February 1886, LBGC, 1:66–67; Horn statement to Lummis, *DFB*, 181–83.

39. Maus to Roberts, 23 February 1886, LBGC, 1:58–63; Maus statement to Lummis, *DFB*, 163–70. Horn interview with Lummis, ibid., 181–83. Statement of Thomas Horn, 23 February 1886, LBGC, 1: 66–67.

40. *LOTH*, 186; Davis statement to Lummis, *DFB*, 183–84.

41. *LOTH*, 189; Horn's statement to Lummis, *DFB*, 181–83, and Maus statement to Lummis, ibid., 163–70.

42. *LOTH*, 189–91; Statement of Francisco Araiza, 17 February 1886, and of Estevan Vidal, 15 February 1886, U.S. Congress, "Killing of Captain Crawford," 635; Jesus Maria Romero, 25 April 1886, ibid., 647; Maus's statement to Lummis, *DFB*, 163–70, Horn statement, ibid., 181–83; Davis statement, ibid., 183–84. See LBGC, 1:63–64, exhibit A, for Perez's note.

43. Maus statement to Lummis, *DFB*, 163–70; Statement of Sgt. Concepcion Aguirre, 23 February 1886, LBGC, 1:69–70, exhibit G. Aguirre signed his name with an "X" and Tom Horn added his signature as witness.

44. Statement of Sgt. Concepcion Aguirre, 23 February 1886, LBGC, appendix G, 1:69–70; Maus to Roberts, 23 February 1886, ibid., 58–63; Statement of Thomas Horn, 23 February 1886,ibid., 66–67. In January 1902, Horn informed Deputy U.S. Marshal Joseph LeFors, in Cheyenne, Wyoming, that "The first man I ever killed, was when I was only twenty-six years old. He was a coarse son of a bitch" (Carlson, *Tom Horn*, 209–10). Reminiscences of Harvey Nashkín, Grenville Goodwin Notebooks, Arizona State Museum.

45. Deposition of Sgt. Concepcion Aguirre, 23 February 1886, LBGC, 1:69–70; Maus report, 58–64; *LOTH*, 191–92; Maus statement to Lummis, *DFB*, 163–70. Maus to Roberts, 23 February 1886, U.S. Congress, "Killing of Captain Crawford," 576–80; *San Francisco Chronicle*, 11 July 1886, for interview with Maus.

46. Maus statement to Lummis, *DFB*, 163–70; Maus to Roberts, 23 February 1886, "Killing of Captain Crawford," 576–80; *San Francisco Chronicle*, 11 July 1886.

47. *LOTH*, 190–93; Heard, Jr., "Killing of the Captain," 440–50. Edwardy, "Border Troubles," a correspondent who accompanied Maj. Henry Lawton in the pursuit of Geronimo in the summer of 1886, also made this assertion. Shipp and Welsh, "Our Indian Scouts," refuted Edwardy's accusation.

48. Griffith, *Mickey Free*, 132–35, 136n12; Ward, "A Trip to the Cavalry Camps," 109–14, for Apaches gambling. The author is indebted to Allan Radbourne for Chi-kis-in's name from the scouts' muster roll for the Crawford expedition.

49. Maus to Roberts, 23 February 1886, LBGC, 1:58–63; Daly ("The Geronimo Campaign," 83–84) fashioned a travois to carry Captain Crawford. Crook to Sheridan, 27 January 1886, Letters Received by the Office of the Adjutant General, Main Series, NA, roll 181. *Arizona Silver Belt*, 30 January 1886; *LOTH*, 194.

50. Maus to Roberts, 8 April 1886, LBGC, 1:47–54. See Maus's narrative in Miles, *Personal Recollections*, 465, who said they went unarmed.

51. *LOTH*, 195.

52. Ibid.; Deposition of Casimirio Grajeda, 30 March 1886, U.S. Congress, "Killing of Captain Crawford," 681–82.

53. Deposition of Cristobal Valenica, 23 January 1886, ibid., 662–63.

54. *LOTH*, 195–96; Shipp, "Captain Crawford's Last Expedition," 5:343–61; deposition of Luis Gomez and Emilio Kosterlitsky, 28 January 1886, U.S. Congress, "Killing of Captain Crawford," 688, 685–86; Maus's statement to Lummis, *DFB*, 163–70. Horn said he later became "intimately" acquainted with Kosterlitsky (*LOTH*, 93).

55. Maus to Roberts, 8 April 1886, 1:47–54; Davis to Terrasas, 30 Jan 1886, LBGC, 1:41.

56. Deposition of Shipp, 20 January 1886, LBGC, 1:64–66, exhibit C. Depositions of Santa Ana Perez and Fermin Chavez, 13 February 1886, U.S. Congress, "Killing of Captain Crawford," 601–603, 625. Clipping, Chihuahua City, Mexico, quoted in *St. Louis Globe-Democrat*, 17 February 1886.

CHAPTER 4

1. Cyrus S. Roberts, Captain, 17th Infantry, A. A. D. C., to Maus, 19 February 1886, Letters Received, Department of Arizona, 1886, Records of U.S. Army Continental Commands, NA, 19:234–35; *LOTH*, 159.

2. Bourke Diary, 1872–96, University of New Mexico,83:126–27; Cleary to Mazzanovich, 13 April 1929, Will C. Barnes Collection, AHS, Tom Horn file, box 18.

3. *MR*, 4 March 1886. While Horn's letter is dated, Sonora, Mexico, 20 February, he probably mailed it on his visit to Fort Bowie.

4. Bourke Diary, 22 April 1889, vols. 94–95 (28 March–23 June 1889), 18.

5. Report of Brigadier-General George Crook, Department of Arizona, 10 April 1886, Annual Report of the Secretary of War for 1886, copy in LBGC, 1:147–81; U.S. Congress, "Killing of Captain Crawford,"570–691, 724–31, for American and Mexican reports. See ibid., 574 for Jackson's letter and 585 for Morgan's letter. See also Deposition of Santa Ana (Santanta) Perez, ibid., 601–603; Apolinar Zapien and Ramon Chavarria, ibid., 638–39; Barie to De Palomares, 11 April 1886, ibid., 690–91. See *New York Times*, 4 Feb 1886, for a reprint of Perez's letter; *DFB*, 51–52, for Diaz's speech. See ibid., 6 May 1886, 123, for Lummis's comments about the report.

6. Daly, "The Geronimo Campaign," 19:92–93 for Geronimo's arrival; *LOTH*, 198.

7. Record of a Conference Held March 25th and 27th, 1886, between General Crook and the Hostile Chiricahua Chiefs, Exhibit M, 72–79, Report of Brigadier-General George Crook, 10 April 1886, LBGC, 1:79; *LOTH*, 198–99. On 25 and 26 March 1886, Fly took nineteen images, numbered 170–188. In number 175, entitled "General Crook, Staff, Interpreters, and Packers," Horn is kneeling in the front row, fifth from the left, with his left arm on the knee of Marion Maus (sitting). In number 184, "Scouts Under Lieut. Maus," Fly has the Apache scouts standing along the edge of an arroyo. Chief of Scouts Horn, wearing the same white shirt, is resting on a rock in the upper right of the frame (Van Orden, *Geronimo's Surrender*, 5).

8. *LOTH*, 200–201; Thrapp, *Conquest of Apacheria*, 334–47, 346–47n47; *DFB*, 34–35, 50; Rynning, *Gun Notches*, 67–69.

9. Thrapp, *Al Sieber*, 313; Daly, "The Geronimo Campaign," 19:252–53; Daly to Mrs. John [Elise] Coble, 5 June 1924, Crime and Criminals, Tom Horn, WSA. Daly recalled that Horn was part of this chase. Elise Coble was the widow of John C. Coble, who had employed Tom Horn as a range detective in Wyoming.

10. Maus to Adjutant General, letter missing, but received 3 July 1891, Records of the Adjutant General's Office, NA, file no. 10951–1891, with endorsements. Since Maus could not receive a medal for fighting the forces of a friendly (Mexican) nation, his citation placed him in New Mexico Territory (Lang, et al, *Medal of Honor Recipients, 1863–1994*, 1:286).

11. Thrapp, *Conquest of Apacheria*, 348–50. *DFB*, 52–58, 66–70; Miles, *Personal Recollections*; *LOTH*, 166, 201.

12. Daly, "Geronimo Campaign," 43:255–56; Lane, *Chasing Geronimo*, 26. Wood did not mention Horn, but said Andrew Ames and James Allsop were guides when the expedition departed Fort Huachuca. *Los Angeles Times*, 9 May 1886, repr. in *DFB*, 159–61. Radbourne, "Geronimo's Last Raid into Arizona," 22–29; Gale, "Lebo in Pursuit," 11–24; Gale, "Hatfield Under Fire," 447–68; *LOTH*, 201.

13. *LOTH*, 201–204.

14. Report of Persons and Articles . . . , Fort Bowie, Nov. 1885, OQG, NA, box 483. Fort Bowie Post Returns, Returns from U.S. Military Posts, Records of the Adjutant General's Office, NA, roll 130, also listed Horn as superintendent of trains. William A. Thompson, Captain, Acting Assistant Adjutant General, Fort Bowie, Arizona, to James Wade, Major, Commanding Fort Apache, 11 May 1886, OAG, 1886, 20:475–76; Thompson to Miles, 23 May 1886, ibid., 20:550–51. See *LOTH*, 203–204, for his absurd claim that the army made two separate appeals for his return to work. Lane, *Chasing Geronimo*, 33–34,

130n9, suggested that Horn may have been recalled to replace an Apache scout named Chimney, who had deserted Lawton's command.

15. Neall to Thompson, 18 June 1886, Gatewood Collection, AHS, roll 1; Thompson to Lawton, 18 June 1886, Henry Lawton Papers, LC, Washington, D.C., box 1. Dapray to Royall, 17 June 1886, ibid., box 1. General Miles directed that William Edwardy be employed as a packer and sent to Lawton. *LOTH*, 204.

16. *San Francisco Chronicle*, 13 July 1886.

17. *Las Vegas Democrat* (New Mexico), 7 June 1890. Edwardy, who established this newspaper in May 1890, featured Tom Horn in several articles about the Geronimo campaign.

18. *San Francisco Chronicle,* 13 July 1886.

19. Lane, *Chasing Geronimo*, 57, entry for 22 June 1886. Lawton to Thompson, 26 June, Lawton to Mame (wife), 21 June 1886, Lawton Papers, LC, box 1. Lawton wrote letters daily to his wife, but rather than mail them individually, he assembled them into one larger letter. His letter of 21 June to Mame is included with a letter of 24 June.

20. *LOTH*, 204. The Fort Huachuca post returns reported the theft of "3 public horses—Capt Lawton, 4 Cav, responsible, stolen from detail at Bacauchi, Mexico, June 21, 1886" (Returns From U.S. Military Posts, Records of the Adjutant General's Office, October 1886, roll 490).

21. Lawton to Thompson, 2 July 1886, Lawton Papers, LC, box 1; Lane, *Chasing Geronimo*, 59, entry for 24 June 1886; McCallum, *Leonard Wood*, 32.

22. Lane, *Chasing Geronimo*, 50–54; Bailey, *White Apache*, 125–34.

23. Ganzhorn, *I've Killed Men*, 46; Gray, *All Roads Led to Tombstone*, 88; *LOTH*, 147–52, 208–209, for Slaughter's hospitality.

24. *Conquest of Apacheria*, 353. See also Eve Ball, *Indeh*, 106–14. Charles B. Gatwood, Jr., who became an ardent crusader for recognition of his father's work in the Geronimo Campaign, gathered a large collection of pertinent documents (Gatewood Collection, AHS, 9 rolls). Wratten, "George Wratten, Friend of the Apaches," in Sonnichsen, *Geronimo*, 91–106. *LOTH*, 206.

25. Kraft, *Gatewood and Geronimo*, 138–39; Bailey, *Devil Has Foreclosed*, 2:232. Parsons rode out to White's ranch on the evening of 13 July and returned to Tombstone four days later. Fort Bowie Post Returns, 31 July 1886, Records of the Adjutant General's Office, NA, roll 130. Bailey, *"We'll All Wear Silk Hats"*, for Theodore White. Royall to Thompson, 16 July 1886, Letters and Telegrams Sent, Fort Huachuca, Arizona, Records of U.S. Army Continental Commands, NA, 5:179–80. Daly, "Geronimo Campaign," 19:260–61.

26. Daily "Geronimo Campaign," 19:260–61; Daly, "Capture of Geronimo," 30, 42–45.

27. Lane, *Chasing Geronimo*, 82–83, entry for 2 August 1886.

28. Ibid., 88–92, entries for 3–6 August 1886.

29. Lane, *Chasing Geronimo*, 94, entry for 11 August 1886. Miles, *Personal Recollections*, 506–17, for another version of Leonard Wood's recollections of these events. *LOTH*, 204–205.

30. Lane, *Chasing Geronimo*, 94–99, entries for 12, 13, 15 August 1886.

31. Ibid., 97–99, entries for 17, 19 August 1886.

32. Kraft, *Gatewood and Geronimo*, 152–53. Lane, *Chasing Geronimo*, 99–100, entry for 22 August 1886; Bourke Diary, 94:14–18, entry for 20 April 1889. In his diary for 5 August 1885, Leonard Wood noted: "Was with Capt. L.[awton] until quite late. (Alcohol versus Capt. L.) Capt. L. 2d best" (Diaries of Leonard Wood, LC, box 1). Lawrence R. Jerome, a private in Lawton's 4th Cavalry detachment, also recalled that Horn was present at this time. Stout, Jr., "Soldiering and Suffering," 154–69). Daly, "Capture of Geronimo," 45, also says Gatewood took Horn with him when the lieutenant left Lawton's camp for Fronteras.

33. Kraft, *Gatewood and Geronimo*, 154; Kraft, *Lt. Charles Gatewood*, 131. See Brown to Brininstool, 5 April 1921, enc. in Brininstool to Gatewood, Jr., 13 July 1925, Gatewood Collection, AHS, roll 9, for the composition of Lieutenant Gatewood's party at Geronimo's camp.

34. Bourke Diary, 91:72–77, entry for 20 April 1889. For Lawton getting lost, see Kraft, *Gatewood and Geronimo*, 155.

35. *LOTH*, 205–207; Nickell, "Tom Horn in Arizona," 15–22, rightly observed, "Here again, all his good work [as a scout] has been clouded by [a] ridiculous tale."

36. *LOTH*, 207.

37. Kraft, *Lt. Charles Gatewood*, 132–33.

38. *San Francisco Chronicle*, 5 September 1886. Edwardy's dispatch was dated, Fort Bowie, 4 September. See Wratten's recollections ("An Interview with Geronimo and His Guardian, Mr. G. M. Wratten," Gatewood Collection, AHS, roll 2).

39. *San Francisco Chronicle*, 5 September 1886. Some question exists as to the exact date of this meeting. The best evidence, as Kraft has assembled it, shows that it took place on 25 August (*Gatewood and Geronimo*, 254n14). Stout, "Soldiering and Suffering," 154–69.

40. Robert A. Brown, Colonel, Fort Des Moines, Iowa, to Earl A. Brininstool, Los Angeles, California, 5 April 1921, Gatewood Collection, AHS, roll 9. Brown to Hagedorn, 22 April 1929, Hagedorn Papers, LC, box 4. Wellman, "Death of General Brown," *Kansas City Times*, 7 October 1937, for an appreciation of Robert A. Brown's services.

41. Kraft, *Gatewood and Geronimo*, 162–66.

42. Ibid., 166–67; Kraft, *Lt. Charles Gatewood*, 143–44.

43. Kraft, *Lt. Charles Gatewood*, 138 for Gatewood's explanation of his use of interpreters. Utley, *Geronimo*, 209.

44. Leonard Wood's narrative in, Miles, *Personal Recollections*, 511–12; Lane, *Chasing Geronimo*, 104–107, entry for 28 August 1886; Kraft, *Gatewood and Geronimo*, 175–78; Utley, *Geronimo*, 214–15.

45. Kraft, *Gatewood and Geronimo*, 184–85; Lane, *Chasing Geronimo*, 108–109, entry for 31 August 1886; Mazzanovich, *Trailing Geronimo*, 268–69. While not a party to this conspiracy, Lieutenant Robert A. Brown overheard soldiers talking about it (Brown to Hermann Hagedorn, 22 April 1929, Hagedorn Papers, LC, box 4). Utley, *Geronimo*, 215–17.

46. Faulk, *Geronimo Campaign*, 139–45, for this exchange between Lawton and Miles. Porter, *Paper Medicine Man*, 253–54.

47. Bourke Diary, 94:14–18, entry for 18 April 1889; Porter, *Paper Medicine Man*, 253–54. Kraft, *Gatewood and Geronimo*, 183–85, 259n57.

48. Kraft, *Lt. Charles Gatewood*, 152–53.

49. *LOTH*, 211; *San Francisco Chronicle*, 11 September 1886; For the unofficial citizens' escort, see Serven, "Recollections of Geronimo's Final Surrender," 225–31.

50. For Dunn's story, see *Bisbee Daily Review*, 25 February 1909. The author is indebted to Ed Sweeney for a copy of this item.

51. *Bisbee Daily Review*, 25 February 1909.

52. *LOTH*, 211; Griffith, *Mickey Free*, 157.

53. Beaumont to Acting Assistant Adjutant General, 16 September 1886, Letters, Endorsements and Telegrams Sent, 1865–94, Fort Bowie, Arizona. See enclosures, Baldwin to Beaumont, 13 September, and Budd to Beaumont, 14 September 1886, Thompson to Miles, 13 September 1886, Baldwin to Acting Assistant Adjutant General, 15 September 1886, all in Letters Received, Fort Bowie, U.S. Army Continental Commands, NA, box 7.

54. John A. Dapray, Second Lieutenant, Acting Assistant Adjutant General, Department of Arizona, to Commanding Officer, Fort Bowie, 23 October 1886, Letters Sent, U.S.

Army Continental Commands, NA, 1886. The author is indebted to Allan Radbourne for a copy of this letter. See the Leonard Wood Diaries, LC, box 1, 30 October 1886–30 January 1887, for his Mexican reconnaissance. Hagedorn, *Leonard Wood*, 1:106–108; Report of Persons and Articles . . . , Fort Bowie, September 1886, OQG, box 600.

55. Griffith, *Mickey Free*, 146; *LOTH*, 212.

56. McCarthy to White, 1 April 1933, enc. in Brininstool to Gatewood, Jr., 27 October 1941, Gatewood Collection, AHS, roll 4; Brown to Brininstool, 5 April 1921, enc. in, Brininstool to Gatewood, 13 July 1925, ibid., roll 9. Kraft, *Gatewood and Geronimo*, 201; Daly, "Capture of Geronimo," 44; Nickell, "Tom Horn in Arizona," 15–22.

CHAPTER 5

1. *LOTH*, 202, 212. See obituary for Horace Dunlap, Horace E. Dunlap Papers, AHS. Ming, "Biographical Sketch," 23, Ming Family Papers, AHS, box 1. See depositions of Dan Ming, Elias Jones, and Burt Dunlap, *State of Nevada v. Thomas H. Horn* (1891), University of Nevada, Reno, Case 2832, for their recollections of Horn. Dunlap, "Tom Horn," 73–85.

2. *Weekly Arizona Star*, 26 July 1888. *Great Register for Graham County, 1886*, entry 505, listed John P. Harr, age 41, U.S. Citizen, residing in Aravaipa Canyon. Graham County Historical Society, "Tom Horn," in *Mt. Graham Profiles* 2:164–65; *Weekly Arizona Star*, 26 January 1888. For Wid Childress, see Meadows to Willson, 7 June 1959, Willson Collection, Arizona Historical Foundation, Arizona State University, Tempe, Tom Horn folder. Clipping, *Eastern Arizona Courier*, n.d., ibid. The author is grateful to Milton Rhea, retired police chief of Safford, Arizona, for information about Tom Horn's mine (author conversation with Rhea, 9 December 2000).

3. The literature concerning the Pleasant Valley War is extensive, but see Dedera, *Little War of Our Own*. Forrest, *Arizona's Dark and Bloody Ground* is a pioneer work but still useful. Hanchett, Jr., *They Shot Billy Today*, 1–53, for background on the makeup of the two factions. Roberts, "Graham-Tewksbury Feud," in Larmar, *New Encyclopedia of the American West*, 441–42.

4. *LOTH*, 213; Dunlap, "Tom Horn," 83; Hanchett, *They Shot Billy Today*, 1–53.

5. For William C. Colcord's recollections, see Colcord to Barnes, 19 June 1931, Barnes Collection, AHS, box 1. See depositions of Dan Ming, Elias Jones, and Burt Dunlap, *State of Nevada v. Thomas H. Horn*, University of Nevada.

6. Nickell, "Tom Horn in Arizona," 15–22. Horn was probably referring to the death of Mauricio Corredor in Sonora. Dunlap, "Tom Horn," 73–85; Forrest, *Arizona's Dark and Bloody Ground*, 342n4, for Walter Tewksbury's recollections. Colcord to Barnes, 19 June 1931, Barnes Collection, AHS, box 1.

7. Dunlap, "Tom Horn," 73–85; Dunlap to Kitt, 29 August 1934, Dunlap Papers, AHS. For background on county sheriffs, see Ball, *Desert Lawmen*. Horn may have being serving as George Shute's deputy as early as March 1888 (Clardy, *Sometimes the Blues*, 153–63). Forrest to Gregory, 4 September 1930, Gregory Collection, AHS; Colcord to Barnes, 19 June 1931, Barnes Collection, AHS, box 1. *DT*, 1 November 1902. Clipping, *RMN*, quoted in *Laramie Boomerang*, 5 October 1902, Tom Horn Biographical File, AHC. For John Henry Thompson, see Parley P. Greer, justice of the peace, Globe, Arizona to Barnes, 9 June 1931, copy in Dan Williamson Papers, AHS, box 1.

8. For J. V. Brighton, see Edwards, "Killing of Ike Clanton," 27–31. Carlock, *Hashknife*, 129–30.

9. Colcord to Barnes, 19 June 1931, Barnes Papers, AHS, box 1.

10. Dedera, *Little War of Our Own*, 184–88; Willson, *Pioneer Cattlemen of Arizona*, 1:21, for sketch of Ellison. Meadows to Willson, 7 June 1959, Roscoe Willson Collection, Arizona Historical Foundation, Arizona State University, Tempe; Fish, "History of Arizona," (unpub. MS, 1906), Joseph Fish Papers, AHS, 690. See also Colcord to Barnes, 19 June 1931, Barnes Collection, AHS, box 1. Woody to Thrapp, 13 March 1969, Thrapp Collection, Nita Stewart Haley Library, Midland, Texas. *LOTH*, 213.

11. Leonard Wood Diaries, LC, box 1, entry for 31 August 1888. Rhodes was shot in a saloon brawl (*Arizona Silver Belt*, 3 May 1888, quoted in Leslie Gregory MSS, in Clara T. Woody Papers, AHS, series 2, box 7).

12. *Hoof and Horn*, 15 November 1888; King, *Arizona Charlie*; Baxter, "Ropers and Rangers"; *Arizona Silver Belt*, 6, 13 July 1889; Woody and Schwartz, *Globe, Arizona*, 4. Contemporary newspapers often added an "e" to Tom Horn's name.

13. Walker and Bufkin, *Historical Atlas of Arizona*, map 32. Williamson to Barnes, 19 June 1931, Barnes Collection, AHS, box 1; *LOTH*, 217.Tom Horn was evidently referring to this enlargement of Gila County when he recalled that as a deputy sheriff he received responsibility for "a new county." Greer to Williamson, 9 June 1931, Williamson Papers, AHS, box 1; *LOTH*, 213.

14. *Arizona Daily Gazette*, 18–22 October; *Phoenix Daily Herald*, 14–22 October 1889; *Daily Star*, 11 March 1890; *Daily Citizen*, 12 March 1890.

15. Baxter, "Ropers and Rangers," 315–48; clipping, *New York National Police Gazette*, 10 December 1892, repr. in King, *Arizona Charlie*, 92; *Philadelphia Times*, 27 January 1895.

16. For Apache Kid, see de la Garza, *Apache Kid*; *LOTH*, 213–14. One of the deserters, Vacasheviejo, admitted to the theft of a horse in Aravaipa Canyon, probably Horn's mount (McKanna, Jr., *White Justice in Arizona*, 84–85).

17. *LOTH*, 218–22.

18. Dunlap, "Tom Horn," 73–85; *MR*, 4 March 1886; *Arizona Bulletin*, 27 November 1903, for Clark's recollections; Will [perhaps Thomas N. Wills], to The Bobbs-Merrill Company, 13 September 1946, enc. in Rosemary [perhaps a secretary] to Monaghan, 27 September 1946, JMP. For Horn's big ears, see Siringo, *Cowboy Detective*, 233.

19. Frank Murphy, quoted in Coe, *Juggling a Rope*, 91–93; Meadows to Willson, 7 June 1959, Willson Collection, Arizona Historical Foundation, Arizona State University, Tempe, Tom Horn folder, for the Childress story.

20. McCarthy to Brininstool, 28 March 1933, enc. in Brininstool to Gatewood, Jr., Gatewood Collection, AHS, roll 4; *Arizona Bulletin*, 27 November 1903.

21. Clipping, *Eastern Arizona Courier*, n.d., Ridgway Collection, Hayden Library, Arizona State University, Tempe; Tom Horn Biographical File, Arizona Historical Foundation, Arizona State University, Tempe. Coffee-throwing story from Karen Williams, Graham County Historical Society, Safford, Arizona.

22. Depositions of Barnes, 28 July 1891, and Dunlap, 2 July 1891, *State of Nevada v. Tom Horn*, University of Nevada, Reno. Horn to Shores, 5 March 1896, Shores Papers, Western History Collections, Denver Public Library, box 1. Shores, "A Story of the Stealing of Twenty Four Head of Horses," ibid. See also Rockwell, *Memoirs of a Lawman*, 258–76, for a slightly different version. Dunlap, "Tom Horn" 73–85; *Southwestern Stockman*, qtd. in *Arizona Daily Citizen*, 27 January 1890. On 23 January 1890, a Gunnison dispatch to *RMN*, 24 January 1890, reported Shores's capture of the fugitives.

23. Rockwell, *Memoirs of a Lawman,* 273–74; *LOTH*, 222; Shores, "Story of the Stealing" (see previous note); Pinkerton to Pinkerton, 19 January 1906, qtd. in Horan, *Pinkertons*, 381–83. See also William Pinkerton's recollections (clipping, *San Francisco Call*, 21 November 1903, courtesy of Allan Radbourne).

24. Deposition of Dunlap, 22 July 1891, *State of Nevada v. Tom Horn*, University of Nevada. For Ming's recollections, see Graham County Historical Society, "Tom Horn," in *Mt. Graham Profiles*, 2:164–65. *Valley Bulletin*, 18, 25 April 1890. For the Ore Hanna sale, see *Arizona Weekly Citizen* (Tucson), 1 Februarly 1890. For W. J. Parks's comments, see *Mohave County Miner* (Kingman, Ariz.), 23 February 1901.

25. Morn, *"Eye That Never Sleeps"*; *New York World* editorial reprinted in *DL*, 26 August 1892, for criticism of the Pinkertons' strike-breaking practices.

26. Morn, *"Eye That Never Sleeps,"* 55–59; Lamar, *Charlie Siringo's West*, 139; Thorp, "Cowboy Charlie Siringo," 32–33, 59–62. See also *Omaha Evening Bee*, 16 October 1899, for Thorp's comments about Siringo.

27. For Thomas Horn, Sr.'s, legal difficulties, see Carlson, *Tom Horn*, 261–62. For genealogical background, see Day, *Short Family History*, 25; *Denver City Directory*, 1891, 714–15.

28. "Report of Opr [Operative] T H Horn on the Lake Labish Train Wrecking Operation, Reno, Nevada, Thursday, 9 April 1891," copy in *State of Nevada v. Tom Horn*, University of Nevada. See also Testimony of Horn, 1 October 1891.

29. *Daily Nevada State Journal*, 10, 11, 12, 16, 19, 21, 23 April 1891.

30. Telling, "Coolidge and Thoreau," 210–23; "In the Early Days at Coolidge," 399–400.

31. Dunlap, "Tom Horn," 73–85; deposition of Nelson Miles, 23 June 1891, *State of Nevada v. Tom Horn*. Maxon's deposition is lost.

32. *Daily Nevada State Journal*, 11, 12, 15, 16 July 1891; Shores, "Cotopaxi Train Robbery," Cyrus W. Shores Collection, Western History Collections, Denver Public Library, 28. For more of Shores's recollections, see also Shores to Monaghan, [?] September 1930, JMP, and *DP*, 19 November 1927.

33. Harry Ball, "'Audacious and Best Executed,'" 18–27; Miller, "McCoy Gang," 22–25, 68–72; *RMN*, 3 August, 1 September 1891.

34. *DR*, 1, 2, 3 September 1891; *RMN*, 3 September 1891; Rockwell, *Memoirs of a Lawman*, 277–323. See also Shores, "Cotopaxi Train Robbery," 11–12.

35. McDonald, "Memoirs," McDonald Papers, Center for Southwest Research, University of New Mexico, Albuquerque, 618–26.

36. Shores, "Cotopaxi Train Robbery," 12; *DR*, 7 September; *Colorado Chieftain*, 10 September 1891.

37. *Daily Nevada State Journal*, 17, 22, 26, 29, 30 September 1891. *State of Nevada v. Tom Horn*, University of Nevada.

38. *Daily Nevada State Journal*, 1 October 1891.

39. Ibid., 1 October; *San Francisco Chronicle*, 1 October 1891.

40. *Daily Nevada State Journal*, 2 October 1891.

41. *Ibid.*, 2 October 1891; *San Francisco Chronicle*, 2 October 1891.

42. *San Francisco Chronicle*, 3 October 1891; *Daily Nevada State Journal*, 21 November 1903. For Pinkerton's mention of Shercliffe, see *Toronto Sunday World*, 28 March 1915. The author is grateful to Art Sowin and Bob McCubbin for this news item.

43. Siringo, *Two Evils Isms*, 45–46; Peavy, *Charles A. Siringo*, 16–18; *Arizona Silver Belt*, 17 October 1891; *Graham County Bulletin*, 16 October 1891.

44. *Toronto Sunday World*, 38 March 1915.

45. Shores, "Cotopaxi Train Robbery," 14–16; Rockwell, *Memoirs of a Lawman*, 301–302. See also Shores to Monaghan, [?] September 1930, JMP.

46. Shores, "Cotopaxi Train Robbery," 13; Shores to Monaghan, [?] September 1930, JMP; Rockwell, *Memoirs of a Lawman*, 302–303; Ownbey to Horn, 24 January 1902, in *LOTH*, 226–27.

47. Shores, "Cotopaxi Train Robbery," 16–17; Miller, "McCoy Gang," 68–72, reported that Horn also borrowed a horse at Cotopaxi.

48. Shores, "Cotopaxi Train Robbery," 17–18; Rockwell, *Memoirs of a Lawman,* 309. Shores to Monaghan, [?] September 1930, JMP; *DR,* quoted in *Gunnison Tribune,* 7 November 1891.

49. Shores, "Cotopaxi Train Robbery," 19–21; Rockwell, *Memoirs of a Lawman,* 316. Elsewhere, Shores called the farm owner, Woods.

50. Shores, "Cotopaxi Train Robbery," 21–23; *Fort Worth Gazette,* 29 October 1891.

51. *LOTH,* 223; *DT,* 2 November 1891; *DR,* quoted in *Gunnison Tribune,* 7 November 1891.

52. *DR,* quoted in *Gunnison Tribune,* 7 November 1891.

53. *Colorado Sun,* 3 November 1891; Shores, "Cotopaxi Train Robbery," 25–27.

54. *DT,* 24, 25, 31 December 1891; *Colorado Sun,* 1 January 1892; *RMN,* 4, 9 January 1892. *DR,* 4 January 1892, for an interview with James McParland in which he apparently made available Tom Horn's report of the capture of Joseph McCoy. *LOTH,* 224.

55. *United States v. Robert Eldridge, alias Thomas R. Watson, alias Peg Leg Watson, Burt O. Curtis, alias David Breckenridge,* U.S. District Court, Colorado Civil and Criminal and Cases, 1876–1911, Record Group 21, National Archives Branch, Denver, Colorado, box 28, cases 883, 884, 885; *DR,* 14, 15, 17 January 1892; *RMN,* 13, 14, 15, 31 January 1892, 12 September 1894, *New York Times,* 13, 15, 16 January 1892; Ball, "'Audacious and Best Executed,'" 18–27.

56. Pinkerton to Pinkerton, 19 January 1906, quoted in Horan, *Pinkertons,* 381–83.

57. For Jim King's observations, see Tittsworth, *Outskirt Episodes,* 221–22; Peplow, Jr., *History of Arizona,* 1:609.

CHAPTER 6

1. *LOTH,* 225; Siringo, *Cowboy Detective,* 135–91, for Siringo in the Coeur d'Alene strike.

2. For the frontier cattle industry, see Osgood, *Day of the Cattleman* and Dale, *Range Cattle Industry.* For the Wyoming range wars, see Davis, *Wyoming Range War* and Smith, *War on Powder River.* See also Penrose, *Rustler Business.* Emmons, "Moreton Frewen," 155–74. Hufsmith, *Wyoming Lynching;* DeArment, *Alias Frank Canton.* Many years later Tom Horn's name was associated with these Johnson County murders, but he was occupied with other (Pinkerton) duties at this time ("Testimony of Charles Franklin Basch," 11 May 1935, Basch Biographical File, AHC). *RMN,* 4, 6, 8,10 December 1891.

3. Monaghan, *Last of the Bad Men,* 146.

4. Ibid., 146; Sieberts to Robinson 2 June 1945, Benjamin C. Ash Papers, South Dakota Historical Resource Center, Pierre; Sandoz, *Cattlemen,* 348–59. Sandoz, who had the erroneous notion that the Pinkertons had fired Horn prior to the Johnson County War, asserted that the Wyoming cattlemen not only hired him to recruit gunmen, but "to lead the force he gathered." The recruitment aspect of the mercenary party has not been fully researched, but see *San Francisco Chronicle,* 17 April 1892. See also O'Neal, *Johnson County,* 97–105, for the Texas connection. *RMN,* 2 April 1892.

5. Smith, *War on Powder River,* 196–219. Burroughs, *Guardian of the Grasslands,* 91n21, says Alexander C. (Bob) Coble—the brother of John Coble, who later employed Tom Horn as a range detective—was this messenger. This is uncertain. Murray, *Army on the Powder River,* 40–44.

6. Baber, *Longest Rope*, 108–110, 116–17; Chapman, "Last War for the Cattle Range," 668–75; Irvine to Penrose, 11 February 1914, Charles Penrose Papers, AHC, box 1. *Wyoming State Tribune*, 20 November 1903; Shores to Monaghan, 13/14 September 1930, JMP; *RMN*, 15 April 1892; Clipping, 19 April 1892, Wyoming Stock Growers Association Scrapbook, Wyoming Stock Growers Association Papers, AHC, 155.

7. For the newspaper debate, see *Daily Sun* and *DL* for April–May 1892; *Frank Leslie's Weekly*, 2 June 1892; *Standard-Union*, qtd in, *Chicago Daily Tribune*, 17 June 1892. See also ibid., 3 May 1892. Clover, *On Special Assignment*. Clover covered the cattlemen's invasion for a Chicago newspaper. *Daily Boomerang*, quoted in *Carbon County Journal*, 27 August 1892. *RMN*, 10, 15, 19 April 1892; Smith, *War on Powder River*, 260–61; O'Neal, *Johnson County War*, 181–84; *Progressive Men*, 450–52 (for Amos Barber), 27–29 (for Carey).

8. For Rankin, see Gorzalka, *Wyoming's Territorial Sheriffs*, 145, 171–78; *RMN*, 25 September 1890. Rankin was appointed U.S. marshal on 22 September 1890. Riner to Miller, 3 August 1892, Letters Received, Department of Justice, NA, year file 6316–1892. A microfilm copy of this file, "Johnson County War, U.S. Marshals," is available in WSA. The full title of the injunction case is *Henry A. Blair, the Western Union Beef Company, Wyoming Cattle Ranch Company, Limited, and the Ogalalla Land and Cattle Company, Complainants v. O. H. Flagg, alias Jack Flagg, Martin A. Tisdale, alias Al Allison, et al.* See also Smith, *War on Powder River*, 254. Jack Flagg, a Buffalo newspaper editor and spokesman for the Johnson County 'nesters,' was a victim of a scathing propaganda attack by the cattlemen.

9. Joseph Rankin's actions during the summer of 1892 came under examination (Frank B. Crossthwait, Department of Justice Examiner, to Attorney General William H. H. Miller, 2 November 1892, Department of Justice, NA, Year File 10517–1892, copy in WSA, Cheyenne.) For the vulnerability of ranch foremen in Johnson County, see *New York Commercial Advertiser*, 19 April 1892.

10. Raymond Thorp, Secretary-Chief Inspector, Wyoming Stock Growers Association, to Charles Kelly, 10 October 1939, Kelly Papers, University of Utah. Rankin to Miller, 31 October 1892, enc. in Crossthwait to Miller, 2 November 1892, "Report on U.S. Marshal Rankin," Department of Justice, NA, year file 10517; *Daily Sun*, 21 May 1892.

11. For the Wellman assassination, see Brayer, *Range Murder*, 6–10; Brown, "Truth Failed to Hide" 54–56; Brock, "Murder of George Wellman," 5–10; *RMN*, 11 May 1892. For the latest assessment of the Wellman case, see Davis, *Wyoming Range War*, 218–20.

12. *Cheyenne Daily Sun*, 21 May 1892; Crossthwait Report, 2 November 1892, Dept. of Justice, year file 10517-1892, NA. At the time of Tom Horn's trial for murder, in 1902, Johnson County residents made the connection with Tom Hale. Chapman, "Last War for the Cattle Range," 668–75, also made this connection. Davis, *Wyoming Range War*, 219–20.

13. *Buffalo Bulletin*, 12, 19 May 1892; clipping, [20?] May 1892, copy in Wyoming Stock Growers Association Papers, AHC, box 208; Hawthorne, "Conflict and Conspiracy," 12–17; Rankin to Miller, 21 June 1892, Letters Received, Department of Justice, NA, year file 6316–1892, copy in "Johnson County War, U.S. Marshals," WSA.

14. *RMN*, 22 May 1892; *Cheyenne Daily Sun*, 21 May 1892; Rankin to Miller, 21 June, and Fowler, U.S. District Attorney, to Miller, 27 June 1892, 1892, Letters Received, Department of Justice, NA, year file 6316–1892.

15. Burritt to Stoll, 15 June 1892, Correspondence of Charles H. Burritt, Wyoming Stock Growers Association Papers, AHC, box 208; *Cheyenne Daily Sun*, 27 April 1892, for names of Red Sash Gang; Davis, *Wyoming Range War*, 219–20.

16. James J. Van Horn, Colonel, 8th Infantry Commanding Ft. McKinney, to Assistant Adjutant General, Letters Sent, Department of the Platte, 21 May 1892, U.S. Army,

Continental Commands, NA, copies in WSA, roll 3, 37–38. O'Neal, *Johnson County War*, 179–80. See also Fowler, U.S. District Attorney, to Miller, 27 June 1892, Letters Received, Department of Justice, NA, year file 6316–1892, copy in "Johnson County, U.S. Marshals," WSA; *RMN*, 22 May 1892.

17. Thom, "Lawless Element of Gun Fighters," *Buffalo Bulletin*, 18 August 1960, for reprint of articles concerning Black Henry's escapade. *RMN*, 22 May 1892.

18. *RMN*, 22 May 1892.

19. El Comancho, "Come Listen with Me," 279.

20. Riner to Miller, 3 August 1892, Letters Received, Department of Justice, NA, year file 6316–1892, for the judge's discussion of the various injunctions. Fort Robinson Post Returns, Nebraska, June 1892, Returns from U.S. Military Posts, Records of the Adjutant General's Office, NA, roll 1029; *Chicago Daily Tribune*, 8, 11 June 1892; Schubert, "Suggs Affray," 57–68.

21. *Chicago Daily Tribune*, 11, 13 June 1892; *Buffalo Bulletin*, 9 June 1892; Burritt to Stoll, 15 June 1892, Burritt Correspondence, copies in Wyoming Stock Growers Association Papers, AHC, box 208.

22. *Chicago Daily Tribune*, 13 June 1892; clipping, 7 July 1892, Amos Barber Scrapbook, AHC, 394; Rankin to Miller, 31 October 1892, "Johnson County War," Attorney General's Documents, Department of Justice, NA, file 29763–1892; Burritt to Rankin, 22 July 1892, quoted in ibid; Telegram, Rankin to Miller, 20 June 1890, Letters Received, Department of Justice, NA. Miller to Rankin, 1 July 1892, Letters Sent by the Department of Justice, NA, roll 23, 47–49. Thrapp, *Encyclopedia of Frontier Biography*, s.v. "Baptiste (Little Bat) Garnier," (2:538–39), "Frank Grouard," (2:592–93).

23. Rankin to Miller, 20 June, 31 October, 1892, Miller to Rankin, 1 July 1892, "Johnson County War," Letters Received, Department of Justice, NA, file 29763–1892, copy in Wyo. State Archives, 1 roll; Burritt to Rankin, 22 July 1892, Instructions to U.S. Attorneys and Marshals, Department of Justice, NA, roll 23, 47–49.

24. *RMN*, 27 July 1892. See Agnes Wright Spring's note cards on the Wellman murder, AHC; *Carbon County Journal*, 6 August 1892; clipping, [13] August, 1892, Amos Barber Scrapbook, AHC, 240. Telegram, Fowler to Miller, 29 July 1892, Department of Justice, NA, year file 6316–1892.

25. Fowler to Miller, 27 June 1892, Department of Justice, NA, year file 6316–1892; *DL*, 30 July 1892; Clipping, *Denver News*, 11 August 1892, Wyoming Stock Growers Association Papers, AHC, box 208. For Rankin's appointments of deputies, see Stumpf, "United States Marshals and Deputies of Wyoming, 1869–1978," WSA, Cheyenne, 45.

26. *Rocky Mountain News*, 11 August 1892, 165–66; clipping, 12 August 1892, Wyoming Stock Growers Association Papers, AHC, 169–70. See also clipping, 26 August 1892, Amos Barber Scrapbook, AHC, 243.

27. Harrison to Miller, 30 July 1892, Department of Justice, NA, year file 6316-1892; Rankin to Miller, 4 September 1892, ibid., year file 3616–1892; *Carbon County Journal*, 6 August 1892, reporting a Buffalo dispatch of 3 August; *Buffalo Bulletin*, 18 August 1960; *Cheyenne Daily Sun*, 2 September 1892.

28. Rankin to Miller, 4 September 1892, Department of Justice, NA, year file 3616-1892. *RMN*, 19 November 1893. Deputy Marshal James Huff had been accused of cattle theft. *Buffalo Bulletin*, 25, 30 August 1892; clipping, 27 August 1892, Amos Barber Scrapbook, AHC, 243; *Buffalo Voice*, quoted in *Carbon County Journal*, 10 September 1892.

29. Clippings, 17, 21 September 1892, Amos Barber Scrapbook, AHC, 243–44.

30. Rankin to Miller, 31 October 1892, enc. in Crossthwait to Miller, 2 November 1892, "Crossthwait Report," Department of Justice, NA, year file 10517–1892, 24.

31. *Buffalo Bulletin*, 20, 27 October 1892. See Moses's recollections, "Capture of 'Hank' Smith," March 1943, unpub. MS, Wyoming Stock Growers Association Papers, AHC, box 208; G. E. Lemmon, "Hank Smith forerunner of the Johnson County War," 17 April 1934, unpub. MS, 2, in ibid.; *Cheyenne Daily Sun*, 10, 18 March, 1 April 1893; Spring, *Seventy Years*, 242.

32. Frye, *Atlas of Wyoming Outlaws*, 138, for Horn's reappointment as a deputy marshal in July 1893.

33. *Buffalo Bulletin*, 4 May 1893; Carlson, *Tom Horn*, 50, for Horn's release from witness duty. *DL*, 10 March 1893, for Cruse's (Crewes's) surrender. *Cheyenne Daily Sun*, 22 November 1893. For Ed Starr, see Hegne, *Border Outlaws*, 36–40.

34. *LOTH*, 225; Siringo, *Riata and Spurs*, 240; Horn to Shores, 5 March 1896, Shores Collection, Denver Public Library, box 1; Shores, "Story of the Stealing," unpub. MS, 12, ibid. Shores to Monaghan, 13/14 September 1930, JMP.

35. Clipping, *San Francisco Call*, 21 November 1903, courtesy of Allan Radbourne; *LOTH*, 225. An alternative explanation is that the Pinkertons kept him on the payroll until 1894, but assigned him to the Swan Land and Cattle Company.

36. Horn to Shores, 5 March 1896, Shores Collection, Denver Public Library, box 1.

37. *LOTH*, 225; Woods, *Alex Swan*, 133–36; Woods, *John Clay, Jr.*, 133–36; Clay, *My Life*, for his recollections; *DL*, 3 April 1894.

38. Rockwell, *Memoirs of a Lawman*, 274–76; Clay, *My Life*, 145.

39. *State of Wyoming v. Tom Horn* (Murder), 10–24 October 1902, copy in WSA. For Horn's testimony, see 595–608, 611–701, 710a.

40. Coroner's Inquest in the Matter of the Killing of William Nickells [sic], 406, 20, 22–23 July, 6, 8–10, 13, 15 August 1901, copy in WSA. Horn testified 9 August 1901, 283–98. See also testimony of William Clay, 205–13.

41. Clay, *Fate of a Cattle Rustler* (pamphlet, 1910), reprinted in *My Life on the Range*, 290–303.

42. Woods, *Alex Swan*, 31n26, 158n9; Langhoff, *Tom Horn*; Carroll, "Tom Horn" 34–44, repr. in Langhoff, *Tom Horn*, 29–55. See also, Dugan, *Tales Never Told*, 193–202, for the Langhoff case. Clippings, 10, 12 August 1893, Wyoming Stock Growers Association Papers, AHC, box 208; *New York Commercial Advertiser*, 10 August 1892, repr. of a Cheyenne dispatch of 10 August; *Cheyenne Daily Sun*, 10, 13, 14 August 1892; *DL*, 14 August 1892; Minnie Rietz, Works Projects Administration interview, 1 December 1938, WSA; *Daily Boomerang*, 15 November 1893, for Horn's explanation of his investigative methods.

43. *Daily Boomerang*, 15 November 1893; Rosentreter, "My Cowboy Experiences," 221–33. See Rietz, Works Projects Administration interview, WSA, for her recollections of Otto Plaga's remarks.

44. *DL*, 14 November 1893; Carroll, "Tom Horn," 34–44; *Cheyenne Daily Sun*, 14 November 1893; Clay, *My Life*, 290–303.

45. See complaint, warrant, and brands introduced in district court, 4 Dec 1893, signed James M. Fenwick, clerk, District Court, copy in Tom Horn vertical file, WSA; Langhoff, *Tom Horn*, 71, appendix A; *Daily Boomerang*, 14, 15, 16 November 1893. Upon her release on her own recognizance, Eva Langhoff was rearrested for an unrelated offense, "obtaining money under false pretense." She was again released (*Buffalo Bulletin*, 30 Nov 1893). Louis Bath, Eva Langhoff's lover, posted a one-thousand-dollar bond and was released, while William Taylor and James Cleve (each under five-hundred-dollar bonds) were unable to make bail. Cleve finally made bail at the end of the month.

46. *Laramie Republican*, qtd. in *Cheyenne Daily Sun*, 15, 18 November 1893.

47. Ibid., 18 November 1893; *Daily Sun-Leader*, 24 August 1897.

48. Camp, *Muggins*, 8–9; Coe, *Juggling a Rope*, 114; Clay to McNaughton, 28 November 1928, John Clay File, WSA.

49. Cowan, *Range Rider*, 225–27. Cowan placed this incident in 1895, but it probably took place in 1894. Frison, *Apache Slave*, 32–33, for Wells's recollections. There is some indication that Horn may have extended this patrol into Montana. Recently, an inscription— "Tom Horn, 1894"—was found on a sandstone ledge near Billings. The author is indebted to Mr. and Ms. Ron Cooper for this information (conversation at the annual meeting of the Western Outlaw-Lawman Association, Cheyenne, July 2007).

50. *Wheatland World*, 16, 30 November 1894, repr. in *Wheatland Times*, 10 August 1933; Cowan, *Range Rider*, 227.

CHAPTER 7

1. *Wyoming State Tribune*, 20 November 1903.

2. Carroll, "Tom Horn," 34–44; Monaghan, *Last of the Bad Men*, 154–55; Irvine to Penrose, 22 February 1914, Penrose Papers, AHC, box 1. See also, Penrose, *Rustler Business*, 55–56.

3. Burroughs, *Where the Old West Stayed Young*, 204; Irvine to Penrose, 22 February 1914, Penrose Papers, AHC, box 1.

4. Thorp to Kelly, 10 October 1939, Charles Kelly Papers, University of Utah Library, Salt Lake City; clipping, *DP*, 23 March 1947, Subject Files, Johnson County War, AHC. Larson, *History of Wyoming*, 372–74; Krakel, *Saga of Tom Horn*, 5–6.

5. Krakel, *Saga of Tom Horn*, 5–6; Irvine to Penrose, 22 February 1914, Penrose Papers, AHC; Thorp to Charles Kelly, 10 October 1939, Kelly Papers, University of Utah. A list of so-called "radicals" has not been compiled. However, some Englishmen were reportedly supporters of extreme measures. John Coghill, who ranched with his brother, Windsor Coghill and Sir Horace Plunkett in the Big Horn Basin, was "a very staunch friend and accomplice of Tom Horn," according to Charles Wells (Frison, *Apache Slave*, 32).

6. Irvine to Penrose, 22 February 1914, Penrose Papers, AHC, box 1.

7. Ibid.; see also Penrose, *Rustler Business*, 55–56; Walker, "Wyoming's Fourth Governor," 99–130; Clipping, *Buffalo Voice*, quoted in *Daily Boomerang*, 30 September 1895, Tom Horn Biographical File, AHC.

8. Very little attention has been devoted to Coble in spite of his close association with Tom Horn, but see *Progressive Men*, 57–58; Woods, *Wyoming's Big Horn Basin*, 83, 105; Burroughs, *Guardian of the Grasslands*, 91, 183–84, 261; *RMN*, 12 October 1902, for the extent of the Iron Mountain Ranch Company. For the community of Iron Mountain, see Urbanek, *Wyoming Place Names*, 104. Ruhl, "War for the Pastures," 272–76.

9. *RMN*, 2 September 1892, 25 January 1902; *DP*, 2 March, 15 October 1902; Clay, *My Life*, 72–73; Pauly, *Last of the Rogersons*, 66–67, for Bob Coble's scolding of his brother. Spring, *Seventy Years*, 68, 252; *DT* quoted in *Buffalo Bulletin*, 4 April 1895.

10. Coble to Bosler, 15 July; Coble and Lawrence to Bosler, 17 July 1896, Bosler Family Papers, AHC, box 112. See Coble to Bosler, 22 August, and Lawrence to Bosler, 15 April 1898, in ibid., box 115.

11. *RMN*, 2 September 1892, for one of Coble's law suits. See also *RMN*, 19 November 1895; Lawrence to Bosler, 18 May 1898, Bosler Family Papers, AHC, box 115.

12. Nickell, "Family Tom Horn Destroyed," 23–25, copy in Tom Horn Vertical File, WSA; Nickell, "Who Were Tom Horn's Victims?" 22–38; *RMN*, 11 October 1902; Field,

History of Cheyenne, Wyoming, 2:361, with a photograph of Kels and Mary Nickell. *DP*, 7, 11 October 1902. Helper, "Smashing," 4–9, 93–97.

13. Helper, "Smashing," 5. According to the *Oxford English Dictionary*, Paris green is "a vivid light green pigment composed of aceto-arsenite of copper." *DL*, 24 July 1890; *Daily Boomerang*, 24 July 1890; *Cheyenne Daily Sun*, 26 July 1890.

14. *DL*, 5, 7 September, 11 December 1890.

15. Nickell, "Family Tom Horn Destroyed," 23–25; *RMN*, 11 October 1902; *DP*, 7 October 1902.

16. *DP*, 11 October 1902; John Coble recalled his association with Tom Horn in an affidavit on the latter's behalf (*DL*, 1 November 1903). Horn to Coble, 17 November 1903, in *LOTH*, 240–41; *RMN*, 26 October 1902. See also Krakel, "Was Tom Horn Two Men?" 12–17, 52–56.

17. Burroughs, *Guardian of the Grasslands*, 174.

18. Clay, *My Life*, 292; McParland to Shores, 26 July 1897, Cyrus W. Shores Collection, Denver Public Library.

19. *Daily Boomerang*, 9, 16, 27 September 1895; *RMN*, 27 April 1894, 7 October 1895; *Daily Sun-Leader*, 5 August 1895; Dugan, *Tales Never Told*, 202–208; *Cheyenne Daily Sun*, 30 November 1893; *Laramie Republican*, 16 January 1894.

20. *RMN*, 4, 5 August 1895; *Daily Boomerang*, 6, 8 August 1895; Carlson, *Tom Horn*, 69–71; Laramie County Coroner's Record, WSA, 3 August 1895, A:51; clipping, *DP*, 11 October 1902, Leslie Snow Collection, AHC.

21. See Wilkerson Biographical Collection, WSA, for a sketch of Fredendall, who was sheriff 3 January 1893–4 January 1897. *Cheyenne Daily Sun*, qtd. in *Daily Boomerang*, 7 August 1895; *Cheyenne Daily Sun*, 27 October 1892, 1, 6 January 1893. Dugan, *Tales Never Told*, 207; *RMN*, 6 August, 20 October 1895; *Carbon County Journal*, 10 August 1895.

22. *RMN*, 12 October 1902; Dugan, *Tales Never Told*, 209–15. See also Dugan, *Making of Legends*, 184–212; clipping, *Green River Independent*, 20 November 1952, Tom Horn Biographical File, AHC, for Dean Krakel's interview with Ross.

23. *RMN*, 10, 11, 17 September 1895; *Daily Boomerang*, 11, 25 September 1895; *DP*, 11 October 1902; Dugan, *Tales Never Told*, 211–12.

24. *DP*, 11 October 1902; *RMN*, 17 September 1895; *Daily Boomerang*, 25 September 1895; *Daily Sun-Leader*, 5 October 1895.

25. *DP*, 11 October 1902; *RMN*, 21 September, 2 October 1895; *Daily Boomerang*, 24, 25 September 1895.

26. For Mary Powell's recollections, see Tom Horn vertical file, WSA, 8.

27. *RMN*, 17, 18 September, 4 October 1895. See the issue of 23 January 1899, for reference to "The Hub of the West," and 25 January 1902, for the claim that the *News* broke the "invasion" story. Woods, *Wyoming's Big Horn Basin*, 131. George Caldwell served as bureau chief until November 1903 (*DL*, 18 November 1903).

28. *Daily Boomerang*, 25, 27, 28 September, 3 October 1895; *RMN*, 25 September 1895.

29. *Daily Boomerang*, 2, 4 October 1895; *RMN*, 5 October 1895. While the Cheyenne bureau of the *News* wrote its story on the 4th, it did not appear until the following day. The *Daily Sun-Leader* of the 5th also carried the Billy Powell story.

30. *RMN*, 5, 7 October 1895; clipping, Thompson, "In Old Wyoming," *Wyoming State Tribune*, 3 March 1940, Tom Horn Biographical File, AHC.

31. Coroner's Inquest in the Matter of the Killing of William Nickells [sic], copy in WSA, 26–45, 22 July 1901. For Horn's testimony, see 283–98, for Kels Nickell's testimony, 26–45.

32. *Daily Boomerang*, 7 October 1895.

33. *Cheyenne Daily Tribune*, quoted in *Daily Boomerang*, 3 October 1895; *Cheyenne Daily Sun*, qtd. in ibid., 7 October 1895; see also, *Daily Boomerang*, 4 October 1895; Irvine to Penrose, 22 Feb 1914, Penrose Papers, AHC, box 1.

34. *RMN*, 9, 10, 11 October 1895.

35. Ibid., 13, 14 October 1895; *DL*, 3, 14 October 1895.

36. *State v. Horn*, 694–95, for Horn's testimony in regard to the Lewis case. Prosecutor Walter Stoll, who was questioning Horn, remarked when "you were examined" before the grand jury in 1895. Horn may have been one of the witnesses only "cursorily" examined (Coroner's Inquest, Horn Testimony, 9 August 1901, 283–98). *RMN*, 14 October 1895. For background on the Whitakers (Whittakers), see Beard, *Wyoming*, 173–75.

37. *RMN*, 14, 15 October 1895; *DR*, 21 November 1903; *Laramie Republican*, 20 November 1903.

38. *RMN*, 20 October 1895; *Daily Boomerang*, 23 October 1895.

39. *RMN*, 15, 20 October 1902; *Daily Boomerang*, 23 October 1895.

40. Irvine to Penrose, 22 February 1914, Penrose Papers, AHC, box 1. For the conversation between Horn and LeFors, see LeFors, *Wyoming Peace Officer*, 144. Shores to Monaghan, [13?] September 1930, JMP.

41. *DT*, 20 November 1902; Cowan, letter to the editor, *The Frontier*, April 1926, clipping in Gatewood Collection, AHS, roll 2. Cowan's letter was in response to Chapman, "Tom Horn—Wyoming's Death Rider," 69–76, copy in ibid., roll 1.

42. Cowan, letter to the editor, *The Frontier*, April 1926, clipping in Gatewood Collection (AHS), roll 2.

43. Cowan, *Range Rider*, 226–27; *Daily Boomerang*, 7 October 1895; Shanton, letter to the editor, *The Frontier*, October 1925, clipping in Gatewood Collection, AHS, roll 1. "Rimrockers" refers to "a horse agile enough to climb steep hills and travel over rocks and rough country (Adams, *Western Words*, 251).

44. Cowan, *Range Rider*, 227–28; *DL*, 20 November 1902, for a subsequent report on Horn's involvement in the Lewis and Powell murders. See also *RMN*, 29 November 1902.

45. LeFors, *Wyoming Peace Officer*, 137–44. George Prentice, Jr., was a Scotsman and son of an investor in the Swan Land and Cattle Company.

46. Carlson, *Blood on the Moon*, 72; Dugan, *Tales Never Told*, 212–13.

47. Irvine to Penrose, 22 February 1914, Penrose Papers, AHC, box 1.

48. *Wyoming Tribune*, 16 December 1896; *DT*, quoted in *Daily Sun Leader*, 10 February 1897.

49. McParland to Shores, 26 July 1897, Shores Collection, Denver Public Library, box 1.

50. *RMN*, 22 October 1895, 12 October 1902; Thompson, "Hanging of Tom Horn," 111–29; *DP*, 28 November 1895; Nickell, "Tom Horn in Arizona," 15–22.

CHAPTER 8

1. *Graham County Bulletin*, 20 December 1895; Horn to Shores, 5 March 1896, Shores Collection, Denver Public Library, box 1; *Sulphur Valley News*, 27 March 1896.

2. Horn to Shores, 5 March 1896, Shores Collection, Denver Public Library; Porter to Horn, 16 January 1896, Henry Miller Porter Papers, CHS, Denver, Letter Book 14; Hoover, "Denverite [C. W. Shores] Says He Has Proof that Tom Horn Confessed," *DP*, 15 April 1928.

3. *Graham County Bulletin*, 27 March 1896, 29 January 1897.

4. Hatfield, *Chasing Shadows*, 114–23; Hayes, *Apache Vengeance*, 113–68. Official material concerning the 1896 campaign is found in OAG, boxes 206, 207. See especially two briefs on the border troubles: "Raids from across the Mexican border by renegade Indians into Arizona," 15 May 1896, 7; and "A Plan for the Capture of Renegade Indians, 'Kid,' 'Massai,' and Followers," 20 May 1896, 2, both from OAG, file 36966. Sumner to Wheaton, 27 April 1896, quoted in "Raids From Cross the Mexican Border by Renegade Indians into Arizona," 15 May 1896, OAG. See also, Britt Wilson, "Soldiers v. Apaches," 24–30. Copies of documents from Wilson. See also an anonymously written article, "Campaigning in Arizona and New Mexico, 1895–[9]6," 25–28. Tanner and Tanner, Jr., "Arizona's 1896 Apache Campaign," 1, 10–15. The "hot pursuit" convention had been renewed in November 1892 because of Apache Kid's raids (*RMN* 1892), but had since expired.

5. Telegrams, Sumner to Volkmar, 25 April; Volkmar to Sumner, 27 April; and Sumner to Wheaton, 4 May; enc. in Wheaton to Ruggles, 8 May 1896, OAG, file 37131.

6. Wheaton to Ruggles, 8 May 1896, OAG, file 37131; Telegram, Sumner to Volkmar, 12 May, enc. in Volkmar to Ruggles, 12 May 1896, OAG, file 36697. See also, "Plan for the capture of renegade Indians, 'Kid,' 'Massai' and followers," 20 May 1896, ibid.

7. Howe to Stewart, 14 April, enc. in Stewart to Ruggles, 29 April 1896, OAG, file 36697.

8. See Miles's 2nd endorsement, Miles to Lamont, 18 May; 3th endorsement, Lamont to Miles, 22 May; 4th endorsement, Miles to Lamont, 23 May 1896, OAG, file 36697.

9. See 4th endorsement, Nelson Miles, 23 May 1896, OAG, file 36697; Volkmar to Ruggles, May 1896, quoted in "A plan for the capture of renegade Indians, 'Kid,' 'Massai' and followers," 20 May 1896, OAG, files 36697, 37131; Volkmar to Sumner, 24, 25 May 1896, Letters Received, Fort Grant, U.S. Army Continental Commands, NA, box 14; *Sulphur Valley News*, 2 June 1896. Archie McIntosh, a scout for George Crook in the 1870s, also submitted a proposal (McIntosh to Miles, 21 June 1896, copy enc. in Acting Secretary of War to Secretary of State, 1 September 1896, Letters Received, AGO, file 41026). Reports of Persons and Articles, Fort Grant, 1896, OQG, box 682, files 1896–156, 1896–307.

10. *Tombstone Epitaph*, 3, 10, 17, 24 May 1896; *Arizona Silver Belt*, 28 May 1896. See the recollections of William H. Eckhorst, a packer with Rice's detachment (Eckhorst to Williamson, 31 December 1939, Williamson Papers, AHS, box 2). John Slaughter and his wife raised this Apache girl (Erwin, *Southwest of John Horton Slaughter*, 301–308).

11. Report of Brigadier General Frank Wheaton, 30 September 1896, in *Annual Report of the Secretary of War, 1896*, House Document No. 2 (1896–97), 2:141–53; *Sulphur Valley News*, 16 June 1896.

12. *Annual Report of the Secretary of War, 1896*, 2:142–44. Nicholson to Adjutant, 25 July 1896, OAG.

13. *Sulphur Valley News*, 4 August, 1 September 1896; Tanner and Tanner, Jr., *Last of the Old-Time Outlaws*, 50–52.

14. *Sulphur Valley News*, 1 September 1896.

15. "Report of Tom Horn," 4 September 1896, OAG, box 14.

16. Sumner to Volkmar, 18 September, Volkmar to Sumner, 2 November 1896, OAG, box 14. See also Volkmar to Sumner, 23 September 1896, 1st endorsement to above letter. Report of Persons and Articles . . . , Fort Grant, September 1896, OQG, box 682, file 1896–307, shows Horn received thirty dollars for 1–12 September and forty-five dollars for 13–30 September. *Sulphur Valley News*, 22 September 1896; Ganzhorn, *I've Killed Men*, 80.

17. Tanner and Tanner, *Last of the Old-Time Outlaws*, 44–54. Tanner, Jr., to the author, 16 January 2001; Horn to Meade, 7 November 1896, Ball, "'No Cure, No Pay,'" 200–202.

18. *Arizona Silver Belt*, 21 May, 18 June 1896, 8 July 1897, 21 April 1898; *Tombstone Prospector*, 10 September 1896; *Arizona Bulletin*, 17 June, 2 December 1898, explained the procedure for "segregating" the coal fields from the reservation. Walker and Bufkin, *Historical Atlas of Arizona*, map 44, for the survey. *Sulphur Valley News*, 16 June, 22 September 1896; *Graham County Bulletin*, 26 February, 16 July 1897.

19. Thaddeus (Bud) Ming, son of Dan Ming, said that Horn worked at the family ranch into 1898 (Ming to Dan L. Thrapp, 30 March 1960, Thrapp Collection, Nita Stewart Haley Memorial Library, Midland, Texas, Al Sieber folder). For the War with Spain, see Cosmas, *An Army for Empire*. For the call for packers, see *Arizona Daily Citizen*, 22 April 1898; *Arizona Daily Star*, 20, 27 April 1898; *DR*, 22, 27 April 1898. Atwood to Ludington, 15 April 1898, OQG, file 74279.

20. *Casper Derrick,* 28 April 1898; *DR*, 18 April 1898.

21. See Glendolene Kimmell's statement in *LOTH*, 246–58; *RMN*, 24 September 1898; *DT*, 23 April 1898; *Cheyenne Tribune*, qtd. in *Laramie Boomerang*, 26 April 1898; Daly to Mrs. John Coble, 5 June 1924, Crime and Criminals, Tom Horn, WSa.

22. Coble to Bosler, 20 May 1898, Bosler Family Collection, AHC, box 115; Report of Persons and Articles . . . , Jefferson Barracks, Missouri, to Major J. W. Pope, Quartermaster, Tampa, Fla., 27 April, 1898, General Correspondence, OQG, box 700A. Daly to Mrs. Coble, 5 June 1924, Crime and Criminals, Tom Horn, WSA; *St. Louis Globe-Democrat*, 25 April 1898.

23. Report of Persons and Articles . . . , Tampa, Florida, April 1898, General Correspondence, OQG, box 698. Report of Captain John B. Bellinger, Asstant Quartermaster, Tampa, May 1898, ibid.; Report of Lieutenant Colonel Joshua W. Jacobs, Chief Quartermaster, Santiago, Cuba, June–July 1898, ibid. The latter two reports are in oversized volumes ("Large Reports"). *RMN*, 24 September 1898. See unid. clipping, 15 March 1911, Appointment, Commission, and Personal Branch File of Archibald A. Cabaniss, Records of the Adjutant General's Office, NA, 1780s–1917, for Cabaniss's military career. Among the packers whom Horn met at Tampa Bay was Joseph P. Cahill. Cahill was the uncle of Thomas Joseph Cahill who became a good friend of Horn in Wyoming (clipping, *Wyoming State Tribune-Eagle*, 14–15 June 1967, Biographical Files, Tom Horn, AHC).

24. Miley, *In Cuba with Shafter*, 22–36; Essin, *Shavetails and Bell Sharps*, 125. For a list of pack trains see Humphrey, Chief Quartermaster, *Expedition to Santiago de Cuba*, 8, 19–29. Report of Persons and Articles . . . , Santiago, Cuba, June–July 1898, OQG, "Oversize" volumes; Daly to Mrs Coble, 5 June 1924, Crime and Criminals, Tom Horn, WSA. Coston, *Spanish-American War Volunteer*, 30–32, for Daly's activities.

25. Trask, *War with Spain*, 213–16; Humphrey, *Expedition to Santiago de Cuba*, 9–10; unid. clipping, 15 March 1911, Appointment, Commission and Personal Branch Files, Records of the Adjutant General's Office, NA, "Archibald Atkinson Cabaniss"; Dunlap, "Chief of Scouts," 73–85; "Miss Kimmell's Statement," *LOTH*, 246–66.

26. Humphrey, "Quartermaster's Department," in Society of Santiago de Cuba, *Santiago Campaign*, 195–206; Willson, "Several Living Arizonans Remember," 45–47; Rynning, *Gun Notches*, 157; "Kimmell's Statement," *LOTH*, 246–58; *Army and Navy Journal*, 16 July 1898; Miley, *With Shafter*, 69–70.

27. Miley, *With Shafter*, 69–70; Humphrey, *Expedition to Santiago de Cuba*, 10–12; clipping, Kirk Knox, "Saga of Tom Horn," *Wyoming State Tribune*, 18 November 1954, Tom Horn Biographical File, AHC. Anton Mazzanovich recalled an instance in the Cibicue campaign, in 1882, when a packer "began ringing the bell, and the mules on the opposite [Gila] bank at once plunged into the stream and swam across" (Mazzanovich, *Trailing*

Geronimo, 127). Shafter, "Capture of Santiago de Cuba"; McClernand, "Santiago Campaign," Society of Santiago de Cuba, *Santiago Campaign*, 3–44. See the *Army-Navy Journal*, 27 August 1898, for Marcotte's observations.

28. Shafter to Adjutant General, 23 June 1898, reprinted in Center of Military History, *Correspondence Relating to the War with Spain*, 1:53–54; *DR*, 26 September 1898.

29. Monaghan, *Last of the Bad Men*, 164–65, for Horn's encounter with Wood. Quartermaster records indicate that Horn had already been promoted to corps chief packer on 14 June.

30. *St. Louis Globe-Democrat*, 24 June 1898; *Boston Herald*, 8 July 1898; Miley, *With Shafter*, 84; Dunlap, "Tom Horn," 73–85; Cabaniss to Shafter, 28 June 1898, Letters Received, Records of U.S. Army Overseas Operations and Commands, 5th Army Corps, May–August 1898, NA, box 2.

31. Miley, *With Shafter*, 79–80; *Army and Navy Journal*, 16 July 1898. See George O'Toole, *Spanish War*, 280–81, quoting Davis's description of the *camino real*. Trask, *War With Spain*, 219–20.

32. *St. Louis Globe-Democrat*, 25 June 1898; *Boston Herald*, 8 July 1898; Whitney, "Santiago Campaign," 803–18; *Boston Herald*, 25 June, 8 July 1898; Harris, "Cavalrymen at Guasimas," in Staff Correspondents in the Field, *Chicago Record's War Stories*, 64–70; *DR*, 24 Sep 1898, for Horn's recollections. Wheeler, *Santiago Campaign*, 243.

33. Sargent, *Campaign of Santiago de Cuba*, 2:87; *St. Louis Globe-Democrat*, 14 July 1898; Miley, *With Shafter*, 84–85; Bisbee, *Through Four American Wars*, 246; Twitchell, *Allen*, 90–92; Shafter, "Capture of Santiago De Cuba"; Wheeler, *Santiago Campaign*, 196–97. See also Shafter to Wheeler, 25 June 1898, repr. in ibid., 245–48.

34. Sargent, *Campaign of Santiago de Cuba*, 2:87–88.

35. *Boston Herald*, 29 June 1898; Rynning, *Gun Notches*, 179; *RMN*, 24 September 1898.

36. "Kimmell's Statement," *LOTH*, 246–66.

37. Hemment, *Cannon and Camera*, 124–29.

38. Cunningham, *Triggernometry*, 360–61, for Maus quote.

39. "Kimmell's Statement," *LOTH*, 246–66; *DR*, 24 September 1898, for Horn's recollections. *DT*, 23 September 1898; Bacon, *Seventy-First at San Juan* for a defense of the Seventy-first. See report of a special correspondent of the *Herald*, repr. in Wheeler, *Santiago Campaign*, 85–86.

40. *DT*, 23 September 1898.

41. Shafter to Alger, 9 July 1898, Center for Military History, *Correspondence Relating to the War with Spain*, 1:113. "Address of Major General William R. Shafter," in *Santiago Campaign*, 246–63. Wheeler, *Santiago Campaign*, 46–47; *RMN*, 24 September 1898; unid. clipping, 15 March 1911, Appointment, Commission, and Personal Branch Files, Office of the Adjutant General, NA, "Archibald Atkinson Cabaniss"; Prentice, "Rough Riders"; *St. Louis Post Dispatch*, 17 July 1898.

42. Remington, "With the Fifth Corps," 963–72; Whitney, "The Santiago Campaign," 303–18; *Natrona County Tribune*, 13 July 1899, for Clark's observations.

43. *RMN*, 24 September 1898; *Sun-Leader*, 29 October 1898.

44. Unid. clipping, 15 March 1911, Appointment, Commission, and Personal Branch Files, Office of the Adjutant General, NA, "Archibald Atkinson Cabaniss"; Rosenfeld, 138–39; *DR*, 26 September 1898.

45. Sweeter to Mills, repr. in *Arizona Bulletin*, 19 August 1898. Apparently, Sweeter, who was earning $50 monthly as a packer 1st class, hoped to get promoted to cargador. *DR*, 26 September 1898, for Horn's complaint about quinine. Cabaniss to Shafter, 27 July 1898,

Register of Letters and Telegrams Received, Records of the U.S. Army Overseas Operations and Commands, 1898–1942, 5th Army Corps, NA, 1:1477.

46. Raine, *Famous Sheriffs*, 81–82. See Butler's advertisement, *Daily Boomerang*, 13 September 1898.

47. *RMN*, 24 September 1898.

48. Report of Persons and Articles . . . , Santiago, Cuba, September 1898, OQG. For William Pinkerton's recollections, see clipping, *San Francisco Call*, 21 November 1903 (copy courtesy of Allan Radbourne). Monaghan, *Last of the Bad Men*, 156; *DT*, 23 September 1898.

49. *DT*, 23 September 1898; Horn to Quartermaster General, 30 September 1898, and endorsements, OQG, Documents File, 1890–1914, box 384, files 120468 and 120599.

50. *RMN*, 24 September 1898; *DR*, 24, 26, 27 September 1898.

51. Coble to Bosler, 20 May 1898, Bosler Family Collection, AHC, box 115; *DR*, 24 September 1898; *New York World*, 2 September, reprinted in *Omaha World-Herald*, 3 September 1898.

52. *Denver Evening Post,* 17 April 1899.

53. *DR*, 24 September 1898; Shafter, "Capture of Santiago De Cuba," 612–30.

CHAPTER 9

1. *DR*, 27 September 1898, 21 November 1903; *DT*, 20 November 1903. *Wyoming State Tribune*, 18 November 1954, for Hugh McPhee's recollections. Carlson, *Tom Horn,* 90, for John L. Jordan's recollections. Shields, "Life of Nannie Clay Steele," 93–103. *Cheyenne City Directory, 1905–1906*, listed Nannie Steele (widow of John R. Steele), residence 2016 Maxwell Street; *Sun-Leader,* 26, 29 October 1898.

2. *Cheyenne Sun-Leader*, repr. in *Daily Boomerang*, 5 October 1898; Horn to Ludington, 5 October; Schreiner to Horn, 22 October 1898; Maus to Ludington, 28 February 1899, OQG, Documents File, 1890–1914, box 384; *RMN*, 17 February, 17 July, 21, 29 August 1899; *DL*, 18, 24, 27 February, 4, 9, 11, 21 March 1899.

3. For Horn's residence at Bosler, see "Miss Kimmell's Statement," in *LOTH* 246–66; *DL*, 24, 31 March, 9, 16 May 1899.

4. For George Currie, see Dullenty, "George Currie," 4–7. The literature on Butch Cassidy and his associates is extensive, but see Patterson, *Butch Cassidy*. Ernst, *Harvey Logan*. Mokler, *History of Natrona County,*318–26, for a useful older account of the Wilcox robbery. See also the official report of the Union Pacific special agent (Armstrong, "Wilcox Train Robbery, June 2, 1899," Roy C. Armstrong File, WSA). LeFors, *Wyoming Peace Officer,*109–15, for his recollections of the Wilcox train robbery case. Hanson, *Powder River Country,*453–56, for Brock's personal recollections. For Billy Speck, see Works Projects Administration Interviews, WSA, interview no. 1999.

5. For the still-hunt procedure, see Ball, *United States Marshals,* 204–205.

6. *Salt Lake Herald*, 20, 25 June 1899; *Weekly and Semi-Weekly Boomerang*, 5 March 1900; *RMN*, 1 July 1899. Telegram, Hadsell to Griggs, 9 June 1899, Letters Received, Department of Justice, NA, year file 16434–1898, box 1112, for the Wilcox robbery. See also Hadsell to Griggs, 7 July 1899, in ibid. Griggs to Hadsell, 13 July 1899, Instructions to U.S. Attorneys and Marshals, NA roll 127, 423.

7. Siringo, *Cowboy Detective,*305–24; *Globe Times*, qtd. in *Arizona Bulletin* (Solomonville), 21 July 1899, for Tewksbury's invitation. Leslie E. Gregory Papers, in Clara Woody Collection, AHS, series 2, box 7; *RMN*, 14, 15 July 1899, "Wyoming Department," for hotel registrants.

8. Patterson, *Butch Cassidy*, 148–49; Ernst, *Harvey Logan*, 34–35; Siringo, *Cowboy Detective*, 305–24; *Globe Times*, qtd. in *Arizona Bulletin*, 22 September 1899. Dispatch from Cheyenne, 28 January, in *RMN*, 29 January 1900.

9. Speck, Works Projects Administration interview, WSA. See Wheelwright's recollections in Kelly, *Outlaw Trail*, 329–36; Condit, "Hole-in-the-Wall," 191–212.

10. Hanson, *Powder River Country*, 427–28; James F. Dillinger, interview by Robert Everett, director, Jim Gatchell Museum, and the author, Buffalo, Wyoming, 16 June 2005, for the Ghent story.

11. *Omaha World-Herald*, 17 August 1899; *Globe Times*, qtd. in *Arizona Bulletin*, 22 September 1899; *RMN*, 19 August 1899.

12. *RMN*, 19 August 1899; Waller, *Last of the Great*, 113; *Omaha World Herald*, 17, 19 August 1899.

13. *RMN*, 30 January 1900. Forty miles west of the village of Jackson Hole would have placed these killings in Idaho.

14. *Globe Times*, qtd. in *Arizona Bulletin*, 22 September 1899. For Williamson's recollections, see Gregory, "Tom Horn," unpub. ms., copy in Clara T. Woody Papers, AHS, series 2, box 7. See also Woody's notes of the Anderson interview, ibid., series 4, box 13, as well as her, "Tewksbury Version" *Arizona Record*, 11 May 1950, Clip Books, AHS.

15. Siringo, *Cowboy Detective*, 305–37; *Buffalo Bulletin*, 1 February 1900. Catherine Bell recalled Horn's movements in connection with her suspicions that the stock detective murdered her husband, Fred Bell (DL, 9 April, 29 October 1902). Carr to Canton, 12 December 1899, qtd. in DeArment, *Alias Frank Canton* 353n16.

16. Horn to Harris, 15 January 1900, enc. in Murray to Hadsell, 7 June 1900, vertical files, Tom Horn, WSA. Speck interview, Works Projects Administration interview, WSA, no. 1999.

17. Horn to Harris, 15 January 1900, vertical files, Tom Horn, WSA. See *Buffalo Bulletin*, 18 January 1900, for Horn's interview with the Casper newspaperman. The authorities may have been confused when they asserted that "Harvey Ray" was an alias of Harvey Logan. The real Harvey Ray was a schoolmate of George Currie at Huless, Wyoming, and later ran with Currie's rustling band. For Speck's personal account of his alleged complicity in the escape of the train robbers, see Beard, *Wyoming*, 313–15.

18. DL, 29, 30 January 1900. See a Cheyenne dispatch, dated 29 January, qtd. in *Buffalo Bulletin*, 1 Feb 1900. *Wyoming Daily Tribune*, 27 January 1900; *RMN*, 29 January 1900.

19. *RMN*, 29 January 1900; DL, 2 February 1900.

20. *Wyoming Daily Tribune*, 27 January, 3 February 1900; *RMN*, 29 January 1900; Brown, *Coyotes and Canaries*, 41–45. Deming became editor of the *Tribune* in 1901 (Spring, *William Chapin Deming*, 87–97). *Lincoln Evening News*, 6 February 1900. Gregory, "Tom Horn," Woody Collection, AHS, series 2, box 7, for Tewksbury's concern about his association with Horn.

21. DT, 19 November 1903; Carlson, *Tom Horn*, 100–104; Ernst, "Friends of the Pinkertons," 34–36. Burroughs, *Where the Old West Stayed*, 300; Patterson, *Historical Atlas*, 201–202. See also DL, 20 December 1902, 11 November 1903, for Meldrum references.

22. *Laramie Republican*, 20 November 1903; DL, 21 November 1903.

23. DL, 21 November 1903; *Carbon County Journal*, 10 February 1900; Carlson, *Tom Horn*, 98, 104.

24. Ernst, *Harvey Logan*, 34–36; Frye, *Atlas of Wyoming Outlaws*, 215, for Bob Lee.

25. Burroughs, *Where the Old West Stayed Young*, 299.

26. Ibid., 10–22, 31–34, 159; DeJournette, *One Hundred Years*; Dunham, *Flaming Gorge Country*, 373–77; Tittsworth, *Outskirt Episodes*; Kouris, *Romantic and Notorious*; McClure,

Bassett Women, 3–46; *RMN,* 12 August 1900; Carlson, *Tom Horn,*118–20. Dart's first name has been spelled variously—"Isam," "Isom," "Isham."

27. *DP,* 12 Aug 1911; *RMN,* qtd. in Patterson, *Historical Atlas,* 35. See also, *RMN,* 5, 7, 18 March 1898, for governors conference. See also *RMN,* 27 February 1900. Burroughs, *Where the Old West Stayed Young,* 136–45, 199–200. See Cary to Burroughs, 9 April 1959, qtd. in ibid., 203–204. *DL,* 27 January 1899. For Ora Haley, see Stone, *History of Colorado,* 4:12–13. In 1917 Hiram Bernard told his story, entitled "Confidentially Told," to Frank Willis, CHS. For a convenient reprint of Bernard's recollections, see Carlson, *Joe LeFors,* 186–215. "E. V. Houghy Account," Craig, Colorado, December 1937, Civil Works Administration Interviews, CHS, Pamphlet Books, 140–43; Houghy's recollections are reprinted in McClure, *Bassett Women,* 85–86.

28. "Confidentially Told," in Carlson, *Joe LeFors,* 204–205; Burroughs, *Where the Old West Stayed Young,* 203–204.

29. "Confidentially Told," in Carlson, *Joe LeFors,* 187–215. Willis, "'Queen Ann' of Brown's Park," 58–76; Goodnough, "Tom Horn," *Rock Springs Miner,* 6 March 1936, copy in Tom Horn Biographical File, AHC. *Moffat County Stockman,* qtd. in *DP,* 12 Aug 1911. Tittsworth, *Outskirt Episodes,* 206–207. See Tittsworth's recollections, *Craig Empire-Courier,* n.d., repr. in Carlson, *Blood on the Moon,* 115, 127–32. Although uncertain, William Daniel Tittsworth may have been a son of William G. Tittsworth.

30. Goodnough, "Tom Horn," *Rock Springs Miner,* 6 March 1936, Tom Horn Biographical File, AHC, for Davenport's recollections. *Salt Lake Herald,* 6 April 1900; *Craig Courier,* 14 April 1900, qtd. in McClure, *The Bassett Women,* 67–73; *RMN,* 6, 12, 17 April 1900.

31. "Confidentially Told," in Carlson, *Joe LeFors,* 205; Willis, "'Queen Ann,' of Brown's Park," 58–76; Tittsworth, *Outskirt Episodes,* 179–89, 206–207.

32. See the affidavit in George Banks Collection, AHC; Thompson, "Tom Horn's Accusers," 26–29.

33. Carr, "A Chance Meeting," 8–9. Shores related the story of this meeting to Earl Pankey, a young lawman in Salida, Colorado. In turn, Pankey passed it on to Carr.

34. "E. V. Houghy Account," CHS; Willis, "'Queen Ann,' of Brown's Park," 58–76.

35. *RMN,* 12 July 1900; see also clippings, *Rock Springs Miner,* 12 July 1900, 6 March 1936, Tom Horn Biographical File, AHC. William Daniel Tittsworth's Recollections, in Carlson, *Blood on the Moon,* 127–30. *RMN,* 12 July 1900; Burroughs, *Where the Old West Stayed Young,* 207; *DP,* 12 August 1911. Clipping, *DP,* 11 October 1902, Leslie Snow Collection, AHC.

36. See "A. G. Wallihan's Account," December 1936, Civil Works Administration Interviews, CHS, Pamphlet Books, 136–48; Burroughs, *Where the Old West Stayed Young,* 207–208; Monaghan, *Last of the Bad Men,* 189–90.

37. Tom Horn's fight with the Kelly brothers became legendary. William Daniel Tittsworth, qtd. in Carlson, *Tom Horn,*115; "Tom Blevins's Account of Tom Horn," Youghal, Colorado, December 1938, Civil Works Administration Interviews, CHS, Pamphlet Books, 144–47. *RMN,* 20 July 1900, 8, 15 August 1903. Burroughs, *Where the Old West Stayed Young,* 211, 214, for Tom Vernon. Burch, "Tom Horn's Visit on Snake River," Works Projects Administration Subject Files, WSA, interview 604, 8 June 1937.

38. See Tittsworth's recollections, in Carlson, *Tom Horn,* 115; Monaghan, *Last of the Bad Men,* 179–83; *RMN,* 20 July 1900.

39. "Tom Blevins's Account of Tom Horn," Civil Works Administration Interview 604, CHS; *DR,* 21 November 1903; Chapman, "Tom Horn," 69–76; Wallihan's recollections, in Carlson, *Joe LeFors,* 182–83; Tittsworth, *Outskirt Episodes,* 214; Burroughs, *Where the Old West Stayed Young,* 208, 222–23; Kelly, "The 'Speckled Nigger' [Albert Williams],"

unpub. ms., Kelly Papers, Special Collections, Marriott Library, University of Utah, Salt Lake City. See Kelly's shorter treatment (*The Outlaw Trail,* 320–28). *RMN,* 12 August 1900.

40. *RMN,* 19 August, 26 September 1900; Goodnough, "Tom Horn," *Rock Springs Miner,* 6 March 1936; Willis,"'Queen Ann' of Brown's Park," 58–76; Burroughs, *Where the Old West Stayed Young,* 210, and repr. of Horn's complaint, 212–13.

41. Willis, "'Queen Ann' of Brown's Park," 58–76; Burroughs, *Where the Old West Stayed Young,* 210, and Horn's complaint, 212–13. "E. V. Houghy Account," CHS, Pamphlet Books, 140–43.

42. Burroughs, *Where the Old West Stayed Young,* 209–10; see also Fradkin, *Sagebrush Country,* 202–203.

43. Tittsworth, *Outskirt Episodes,* 214; Goodnough, "Tom Horn," *Rock Springs Miner,* 6 March 1936, Tom Horn Biographical File, AHC. See William D. Tittsworth's recollections in Carlson, *Blood on the Moon,* 130–31; Kelly, "The 'Speckled Nigger,'" Kelly papers, University of Utah.

44. McCoy, *Tim McCoy Remembers the West,* 74–75.

45. *RMN,* 15 October 1900; Wallihan's recollections in Carlson, *Joe LeFors,* 182–83; DeJournett, *One Hundred Years,* 44–46; Kelly, "The 'Speckled Nigger,'" Kelly Papers, University of Utah; *RMN,* 15 October 1900; *Craig Courier,* 20 October 1900, qtd. in McClure, *Bassett Women,* 84–86; *DP,* 20 December 1900; Willis, "'Queen Ann' of Brown's Park," 58–76; "Confidentially Told," in Carlson, *Joe LeFors,* 208.

46. *Wyoming Tribune,* 18 November, 22 December 1900; *RMN,* 19 November 1900.

47. *RMN,* 22 December 1900; *Steamboat Pilot,* 5 December 1900, qtd. in Carlson, *Blood on the Moon,* 122; clipping, *Wyoming Tribune,* 23 December 1900; *DL,* 25 December 1900.

48. *RMN,* 22 December 1900, 5 January 1901; *Steamboat Pilot,* 5 December 1900; *DL,* 25 December 1900.

49. *DL,* 22 November 1900; Brown, *Coyotes and Canaries,* 160–63, for Meldrum. William G. Tittsworth said that a detective named Clous Caseburg was in Brown's Park at this same time. Caseburg, who is otherwise unknown, may have been Tittsworth's effort to conceal this person's real name (*Outskirt Episodes,* 212). Carlson, *Blood on the Moon,* 110.

50. Kelly, Review of *Life of Tom Horn,* 93–94; undated note, JMP. Burroughs, *Where the Old West Stayed Young,* 215, for facsimile of Ann Bassett's article. Kelly, *Outlaw Trail,* 231–33, 300; Willis, "'Queen Ann' of Brown's Park," 58–76; McClure, *Bassett Women,* 87–96. A retired bawdy house operator in Rock Springs maintained that Tal Nelson, a friend of Hi Bernard, betrayed the latter to Ann Bassett ("Unidentified Correspondent" to Charles Kelly, n.d., Kelly Papers, University of Utah.) "Confidentially Told," qtd. in Carlson, *Joe LeFors,* 201–208.

51. Monaghan, *Last of the Bad Men,* 1900; Siringo, *Two Evil Isms,* 46–47.

52. Patterson, *Butch Cassidy,* 161–72; Ernst, *Sundance Kid,* 109–20; Ernst, "George S. Nixon," 43–48; Nixon to Gentsch, 9 December 1900; Nixon to Fraser, 21 February, 1901, Nixon Papers, Nevada Historical Society, Reno. The author is indebted to Chip Carlson for copies of the Nixon letters.

53. Nixon to Fraser, 4 March 1901, Nixon Papers, Nevada Historical Society; Horn to Meldrum, 25 [month ?] 1901, copy in Carlson, *Tom Horn,* 102.

54. McParland to Shores, 30 April 1901, Shores Collection, Denver Public Library, box 1; Evary to Smith, 7 December 1901, copy in Tom Horn Biographical File, AHC; Daly to Mrs. Coble, 5 June 1924, copy in Crime and Criminals, Tom Horn, WSA.

CHAPTER 10

1. See chapter 6 for duties of the range detective.

2. Melton, "Henry Melton's Recollections of Tom Horn," 1939, Tom Horn Biographical File, WSA, Cheyenne; Rollinson, *Pony Trails*, 148–49.

3. *State of Wyoming v. Tom Horn (Murder)*, copy in WSA, 710, testimony of Duncan Clark, 148–52; Nell Pauly, *Last of the Rogersons*, 54–66.

4. *DP*, 26 January 1903, for the Eckel interview. Shanton, letter to the editor, *The Frontier*, October 1925, 172–73, copy in Charles B. Gatewood Collection, AHS, roll 1. Horn to Coble, 17 November 1903, *LOTH*, 240–41. According to Richard R. Mullins, Horn "appreciated a good joke" and entered "into the pranks of his cowboy friends" (Mullins, "The Inside Story of the Life and Death of Tom Horn," *DP*, 23 November 1903). For the range detective as an "outside man," see Grover, *Diamondfield Jack*, 24.

5. Clipping, *Laramie Republican Boomerang*, 1 October 1952, Tom Horn Biographical File, AHC.

6. "Henry Melton's Recollections of Tom Horn," Tom Horn Biographical File, AHC; *DP*, 26 January 1903.

7. Mokler, *History of Natrona County*, 332–34; *DL*, 29 October 1902; *Wyoming Tribune*, 20 November 1903.

8. *RMN*, 13 October 1902; Horn to Coble, 9 October 1903, in *LOTH*, 234–35.

9. Clipping, Kirk Knox, "Saga of Tom Horn Is No Legend," *Wyoming State Tribune*, 18 November 1954, Tom Horn Biographical File, AHC. "Henry Melton's Recollections of Tom Horn," AHC. *Coroner's Inquest in the Matter of the Killing of William Nickells*, WSA, testimony of James Miller, 98–120; *DP*, 26 January 1903, for James Eckel's comments.

10. Rollinson, *Pony*, 95–97.

11. Horn to LeFors, 7 January 1902, repr. in, Joe LeFors, *Wyoming Peace Officer*, 191–92; Horn to Edmund C. Harris, U. P. Railroad Co., 15 January 1900, enc. in Frank Murray, Assistant Superintendent, Pinkerton National Detective Agency, Denver, to Frank Hadsell, U.S. Marshal, 7 June 1900, Frank Hadsell Collection, WSA, roll 2; Coble to Bosler, 16 July 1900, a copy of this letter was found inserted in Agnes Wright Spring's copy of *Wyoming Peace Officer*.

12. Minnie A. Rietz Interview, Works Projects Administration Interview 229, 1 December 1938, WSA, for Julia Plaga's hospitality; *DL*, 9 April 1902, for Catherine Bell's recollections.

13. Wood, "The 'Old Dollar Ranch,'" in Johnson, *Trails, Rails and Travails*, 185–93; Gillespie, "My Early Day Ranch Experiences," in Burns, Gillespie, and Richardson, *Wyoming's Pioneer Ranches*, 223–28.

14. See the recollections of Peter A. Burman (1944), repr. in Carlson, *Blood on the Moon*, 110; Hanes, "Colorful Figures and Days," unid. clipping, ca. 1958, Knox, "Saga of Tom Horn," *Wyoming State Tribune Eagle*, 14–15 June 1967, and Roedel, review of Krakel, *Saga of Tom Horn*, all in *Wyoming State Tribune*, 16 February 1958, copies in Tom Horn Biographical File, AHC. Helper, "Smashing the West's Murdering Horseman," 4–9, 93–97; Blanchard, "Tom Horn's Barber," clipping, *The Eagle*, 22 June 1956, Tom Horn Biographical File, AHC.

15. Knox, "Saga of Tom Horn Is No Legend," *Wyoming State Tribune*, 18 November 1954; *State of Wyoming v. Tom Horn*, testimony of Frank Stone, 562–68; Krakel, "Was Tom Horn Two Men?" 12–17, 52–56.

16. *RMN*, 17 October 1902, for Fullerton's remarks; Spring, *William Chapin Deming*, 98.

17. Cahill, "I Hanged My Friend," *DP Empire Magazine*, [1958], copy in Crime and Criminals, Tom Horn, WSA.

18. *RMN*, 27 January, 6, 10 October 1901; *DT*, 7 October 1901; Raine, *Famous Sheriffs*, 80–91; Fowler, *Timber Line*, 116. For the sources of the horses, see Lilley, interview with D. Claudia Thompson, Wellington, CO, 10 July 2012, AHC.

19. *DL*, 2, 7, 8, 9, 14 October, 1 November 1901; *RMN*, 6, 17 October 1901. See Testimony of W. L. Davis, *State of Wyoming v. Tom Horn*, 528–34; Raine, *Famous Sheriffs*, 80–91.

20. *RMN*, 31 January 1900; *Wyoming Tribune*, 30 January, 6, 25 February 1900; *Sun-Leader*, 2 October 1897.

21. McCoy, *Tim McCoy Remembers the West*, 75–77. *Buffalo Bulletin*, 11 June 1896, for the Salt Lake City shooting incident. See Chip Carlson's webpage, http://www.tom-horn.com/forum/.

22. *DP*, 2 March 1902; Siringo, *Two Evil Isms*, 46; "Henry Melton's Recollections of Tom Horn," 1939, Tom Horn Biographical File, AHC; Minnie Rietz, Works Projects Administration Interview 229, 1 December 1938, WSA.

23. Rockwell, *Memoirs of a Lawman*, 261; Knox, "Saga of Tom Horn Is No Legend," *Wyoming State Tribune*, 18 November 1954, copy in Tom Horn Biographical File, AHC. Melton, "Henry Melton's Recollections of Tom Horn," 25 January 1939, WSA, 7; Matson and Kennedy, to Charles [Horn], 29 May 1902, T. Blake Kennedy Papers, WSA, box 2, for Horn's reading glasses. "A. G. Wallihan's Account, Lay, Colorado," Civil Works Administration Interviews, CHS, Denver, December 1936, Pamphlet Books, 136–39; James D. Eckel considered Horn's eyes "shifty" and did not believe the detective trustworthy (*DP*, 26 January 1903).

24. Bowers, "School Bells and Winchesters," 14–32; Horn to Coble, 1 March 1902, in *LOTH*, 228–29; Minnie Rietz Interview, 1 December 1938, WSA; Glen L. Melton, "Henry Melton's Recollections of Tom Horn," 25 Jan 1939, WSA, 7; Wallace to Bobbs-Merrill, 25 October 1946, JMP.

25. See Bowers, "School Bells and Winchesters," 14–32, for letters from Horn's girlfriends.

26. Lawyer, "Uncle Clyde Rode with Tom Horn," 22–24, 26; Wood, "The 'Old Dollar Ranch,'" in Johnson, *Trails, Rails and Travails*, 185–93; Minnie Rietz interview, Works Projects Administration interview 229, WSA. For Alfred Cook, see "Miss Kimmell's Statement," *LOTH*, 246–66. Sam Moore, who had served as a Swan Land and Cattle Company foreman, was Kimmell's informant. Raine, *Famous Sheriffs*, 80–91, also recounts this story.

27. Cowan, *Range Rider*, 235–37.

28. Woods, *John Clay*, 136.

29. *DP*, 26 January 1903, for Eckel interview; Minnie Rietz interview, WSA; Camp, *Muggins the Cow Horse*. While awaiting the hangman's noose, Horn mentioned Jack Linscott to John Coble (Horn to Coble, 31 October 1903, *LOTH*, 238–39).

30. *DL*, 28, 29, 30 August, 2 September 1901; *Laramie Republican*, 5 September 1901. Subsequently, Horn was erroneously credited with taking "all around honors" in the 1901 Frontier Days celebration. Rollinson, *Pony Trails*, 149; Melton, "Henry Melton's Recollections of Tom Horn," 25 January 1939, WSA, 7; "Miss Kimmell's Statement," *LOTH*, 246–66, for Sheriff Cook's recollection. Kirk Knox, "Saga of Tom Horn Is No Legend," *Wyoming State Tribune*, 18 November 1954; Cahill, "I Hanged My Friend, Tom Horn,"

clipping *DP Empire Magazine*, 2 March 1902, copy in Crime and Criminals, Tom Horn, WSA.

31. Cahill, "I Hanged My Friend," *DP*, 2 March 1902; *Cheyenne Daily Sun*, 18 November 1893; Shields, "Nannie Clay Steele," 93–103; Kirk Knox, "Saga of Tom Horn Is No Legend," *Wyoming State Tribune*, 18 November 1954; *DP*, 26 January 1903, for James Eckel interview; Pinkerton to Pinkerton, 19 January 1906, qtd. in Horan, *Pinkertons*, 381–83.

32. Coe, *Juggling a Rope*, 98; Melton, "Henry Melton's Recollections of Tom Horn," 25 January 1939, copy in WSA; Minnie Rietz, Works Projects Administration interview WSA, 1 December 1938.

33. *RMN*, 19 February, 26 March 1900; Clipping, *Cheyenne State Leader*, June 1917, Tom Horn Biographical File, AHC.

34. Mullins, "The Inside Story," *DP*, 23 November–12 December 1930.

CHAPTER 11

1. "Coroner's Inquest in the Matter of the Killing of William Nickells [sic], 20 July–15 August 1901," Laramie County, Wyoming, 405, copy in WSA. See testimony of Kels P. Nickell, 26–45 and Tom Horn, 283–298 (hereafter cited as Nickell Inquest).

2. Krakel, *Saga of Tom Horn*, 13–14; *RMN*, 12 August 1900, 21 February 1901; *Cheyenne Daily Sun*, 26, 27 February 1895; *Daily Sun-Leader*, 25, 28 June, 2 July 1895, 6 October 1897; *Laramie Republican*, 13 September 1897; Coble to Bosler, 16 July 1900, copy in Carlson, *Tom Horn*, 114.

3. *DP*, 2 March 1902; *DL*, 24 July 1890.

4. *Wyoming Tribune*, 22 April 1900; *DP*, 2 March 1902. A few months earlier, Nickell fired on two trespassers. *RMN*, 27, 29 March, 24 August 1900, 6 January, 28 May, 11 July, 6 August 1901; Nickell to "My Dear Daughter," 9 June 1901, copy courtesy of Chip Carlson. This letter is written on letterhead of "K. P. Nickell, Dealer in Live Stock." *DL*, 7 September 1890.

5. Carlson, *Tom Horn*, 143–45.

6. *DL*, 19, 20 July 1901; *RMN*, 20, 21 November 1901.

7. Nickell Inquest, testimony of Fred Nickell, 2–3; Joseph E. Reed, 2–3; and Catherine Nickell, 3. *DL*, 22 July 1901.

8. *DL*, 22, 31 July 1901. See also the issue of 6 November 1902, for Young's recollections of the funeral.

9. *DL*, 22 July 1901. The coroner's jury met 18, 20, 22, 23 July, 6, 8, 9, 10, 13, 15 August 1901. Nickell Inquest, testimony of Doctor Amos W. Barber, 7; Doctor John H. Conway, 7; Doctor George P. Johnston, 7–9; John A. B. Apperson, 7–9; 45, Kels Nickell, 26–45. *DL*, 22 July 1901.

10. Nickell Inquest, testimony of Kels Nickell, 26–45.

11. *RMN*, 23 July 1901. Nickell Inquest, testimony of William Eckert, 224–33.

12. Nickell Inquest, testimony of Augustus (Gus) Miller, 45–68; William Edwards, 384–87; Glendolene Kimmell, 80–97. See also Kimmell's statement in *LOTH*, 246–66. *DL*, 23 July 1901; *RMN*, 24 July 1901; Bowers, "School Bells and Winchesters," 14–32.

13. *DL*, 23, 24, 29, 30 July, 1 August 1901; *RMN*, 25, 30 July 1901. For a copy of the county commissioners' proclamation of the Laramie County portion of the reward, see vertical files, Tom Horn, WSA.

14. *RMN*, 7, 30 July 1901; 29 July, 4 August 1901; *DL*, 29 July, 5 August 1901; Mokler, *History of Natrona County*, 285–86.

15. *DL*, 5, 6 August 1901; *RMN*, 5, 6, 7 August 1901.

16. *RMN*, 7 August 1901; Nickell Inquest, testimony of John Martin, 143–48; see *DL*, 5 August 1901, for Martin's remarks.

17. Nickells Inquest, testimony of Vingenjo Biango, 148–56; *RMN*, 8 August, 11 October 1901.

18. LeFors, *Wyoming Peace Officer*, 130–31. For useful commentary on Joe LeFors's autobiography, see Carlson, *Joe LeFors*. Krakel, "Was Tom Horn Two Men?" 12–17, 52–56.

19. *DL*, 6, 7 August 1901; Nickell Inquest, testimony of Joseph LeFors, 402–405. Kels Nickell also changed his mind about the number of assailants and ultimately fingered Tom Horn. LeFors, *Wyoming Peace Officer*, 131–34.

20. LeFors, *Wyoming Peace Officer*, 131–33.

21. Ibid., 134. LeFors misspelled Corson as "Carson" in his recollections. *DL*, 8 August 1901.

22. *DL*, 8 August 1901; Nickell Inquest, testimony of Mrs. Mary McDonald, 193–205; William L. Clay, 205–13.

23. *DL*, 9 August 1901; *RMN*, 9 August 1901; Nickell Inquest, testimony of Tom Horn, 283–98.

24. Nickell Inquest, testimony of Tom Horn, 283–98.

25. *DL*, 10 August 1901; Nickell Inquest, testimony of Glendolene Kimmell, 355–74.

26. Nickell Inquest, testimony of Diedrick George, 389–95; *DL*, 13, 15 August 1901; *RMN*, 14 August 1901.

27. *DT*, 23 October 1902; Monaghan, *Last of the Bad Men*, 204.

28. *Progressive Men*, 333–34, for Samuel Corson. See also Bartlett, *History of Wyoming*, 2:198–201; *RMN*, 14 October 1902; O'Neal, *Johnson County War*, 216; *Buffalo Bulletin*, 25 April 1895.

29. LeFors, *Wyoming Peace Officer*, 134–35. LeFors insisted that he was already "under a moral obligation" to Mary Nickell to find her son's killer. Writing more than thirty years after these events, LeFors suffered memory lapses. Yet, his account of the Nickell investigations remains important, even though he refused to tell all. Fortunately, newspapers and other contemporary sources provide some correctives.

30. *DL*, 6, 7, 9, 10 September 1901, 24 October 1902; *RMN*, 6, 7, 9, 10 September 1901. For a sketch of Smalley, see *Progressive Men*, 416. See also LeFors's correspondence with Agnes Wright Spring, Joe LeFors Biographical File, AHC. This exchange took place in 1934–36. Several letters are undated or are fragments of letters. *Carbon County Journal*, 14 September 1901.

31. LeFors, *Wyoming Peace Officer*, 146. See the fragment of a letter, LeFors to Agnes Wright Spring, [September 1935?], LeFors Biographical File, AHC. Spring, *Near the Greats*, 79–83; Helper, "Smashing the West's Murdering Horseman," 4–9, 93–97. See also Shields, "Edwin J. Smalley," 58–72. *DL*, 16 April 1902. Smalley probably secretly deputized LeFors, although newspapers did not report that LeFors carried a deputy sheriff's badge until later.

32. Snow to Monaghan, [?] September 1946, JMP; Smalley, "Smashing the West's Murdering Horseman," 9; LeFors, *Wyoming Peace Officer*, 135–36.

33. Allen, letter to the editor, *True West*, January–February 1964. *State of Wyoming v. Tom Horn (Murder)*, WSA, Cheyenne, testimony of Joseph LeFors, 704–12; Affadavit of Joseph LeFors, 6 November 1903, Tom Horn Vertical File, WSA, 5. LeFors, *Wyoming Peace Officer*, 135.

34. LeFors, *Wyoming Peace Officer*, 135; *Laramie Republican*, repr. in *DL*, 7, 8, 10 August 1901.

35. *DL*, 6, 13, 26 September, 11 October 1901; *RMN*, 6, 27 September, 16 October 1901. Ruhl, "War for the Pastures," 272–76, for a firsthand recollection of the fear and intimidation in the Iron Mountain community. *Wyoming Tribune*, qtd. in *RMN*, 28 August 1901. Allan Cisco, who signed this open letter for the Kentucky branch of the Nickell family, was probably a relative by marriage to Kels Nickell (Nickell, "Who Were Tom Horn's Victims?" 22–38).

36. *DR*, [20?] November 1903, clipping, Dawson Scrapbook, CHS, 18:157; *Carbon County Journal*, 27 July 1901.

37. *DL*, 21 November 1903.

38. *RMN*, 10 October 1901; *DL*, 6 November 1902, for Reverend Young's recollections.

39. *DL*, 10 October 1901.

40. See Tom Horn's testimony, 17, 18 October 1902, 595–608, 611–701, testimony of Joe LeFors, 304–25, 704–12, *State of Wyoming v. Tom Horn*, WSA. LeFors, *Wyoming Peace Officer*, 136. Menea (also spelled Meanea) was widely known for his saddles (Brown, *Coyotes and Canaries*, 50–54). *DL*, 25 January 1902.

41. Ruhl, "War for the Pastures," 272–76; *DL*, 25 January 1901. For mention of Jim Dixon, see the reprint of Tom Horn's confession in *DL*, 23 January 1902. Affidavit of Glendolene M. Kimmell, 13 October 1903, repr. in Carlson, *Joe LeFors*, 238–50. See also Kimmell's statement, *LOTH*, 246–66.

42. LeFors, *Wyoming Peace Officer*, 137; Affidavit of Joseph LeFors, 6 November 1903, Vertical File, Tom Horn, WSA; *DL*, 24 September 1903. Kitzmiller was apparently secretary for several attorneys. Allen letter to the editor, 4, 58.

43. *DL*, 3 October, 27 December 1901; *RMN*, 31 October 1901; *DP*, 7 October 1902. *Carbon County Journal*, 2 November 1901.

44. Smalley, "Smashing the West's Murdering Horseman," 8.

45. *DL*, 25 January, 27 October 1902; LeFors, *Wyoming Peace Officer*, 139; Smalley, "Smashing the West's Murderous Horseman," 8.

46. LeFors, *Wyoming Peace Officer*, 138. See LeFors to Spring, n.d., qtd. in Carlson, *Joe LeFors*, 236; *DL*, 25 January 1902, 20 November 1903.

47. Two federal prisoners were delivered to the penitentiary in November, George W. Allen, on the 9th, and Albert Phillips, on the 30th (Frye, *Atlas of Wyoming Outlaws*, 233). For George Prentice, Jr., see Woods, *John Clay, Jr.*, 154, 160; and *Alex Swan*, 109, 146, 175. LeFors to Spring, [January 1935?], Joe LeFors Biographical File, AHC. LeFors also suggested to Agnes Wright Spring that Prentice might have been "running stock" with the Coble-Bosler outfit (LeFors to Spring, 24 May 1935, Joe LeFors Biographical Files, AHC). See also Carlson, *Joe LeFors*, 227.

48. LeFors, *Wyoming Peace Officer*, 137–38.

49. LeFors to Spring, n.d., qtd. in Carlson, *Joe LeFors*, 236; *DL*, 21, 26 December 1901, 14 February 1902. This correspondence is reprinted in LeFors, *Wyoming Peace Officer*, 187–92. Writing from his jail cell in March 1902, Horn asked John Coble to make inquiries in Montana about his "saddle, bed and valise" (Horn to Coble, 1 March 1902, in *LOTH*, 228–29). Glendolene Kimmell recalled this embarrassing episode in ibid., 246–66. In his subsequent testimony at his murder trial, Horn said he met Joe LeFors during his brief stopover in Cheyenne (*State of Wyoming v. Tom Horn*, 690–93).

50. Horn to LeFors, 1 January 1902, repr. in LeFors, *Wyoming Peace Officer*, 190–91. See chap. 8 for Horn's letter to Meade.

51. LeFors, *Wyoming Peace Officer*, 138–39. Some confusion exists as to the office where Snow and Ohnhaus secreted themselves. Ohnhaus said it was Marshal Hadsell's private office, while LeFors said it was the office of the U.S. District Court Clerk.

52. LeFors, *Wyoming Peace Officer*, 136–40; Kittredge and Krauzer, "Marshal Joe LeFors," 36–45, mistakenly put Glendolene Kimmell in the place of the horse raiser's unfaithful wife.

53. *DL*, 27 October 1902.

54. LeFors, *Wyoming Peace Officer*, 138–39; *DL*, 23, 24, 25 January, 16 October 1902. See *DL*, 24 January 1902, for the first complete newspaper reprint of the testimony of Joe LeFors, Leslie Snow and Charles J. Ohnhaus taken in the preliminary hearing on Thursday, 23 January. See Carlson, *Blood on the Moon*, 205–10 for a reprint of a part of this exchange.

CHAPTER 12

1. See *DL*, 24 January 1902, for the first published transcription of the LeFors-Horn conversations. This first official transcription became available when Charles Ohnhaus read his notes into evidence while on the witness stand in Tom Horn's trial, in October 1902 (*State of Wyoming v. Tom Horn*, copy in WSA, 335a, 335–44, 739). Ohnhaus's testimony is also included (with expletives deleted) in *State of Wyoming v. Tom Horn*, copy in WSA; see esp. 708–709. Ohnhaus's original shorthand notes are presently in private hands.

2. *DL*, 24 January 1902.

3. Ibid.

4. Ibid.

5. Ibid.

6. Ibid.; Bailey later testified to his visit to the marshal's office (*State of Wyoming v. Tom Horn*, copy in WSA, 324a and 325a); see also *DL*, 16 October 1902, for reference to Bailey. Ohnhaus, "Early Settler," 10-page typescript, WSA.

7. *DL*, 24 January 1902. Presumably, Horn was referring to Mauricio Corredor, the Chihuahuan milita officer, who was killed by Apache scouts in Mexico, in January 1886. At that time, Horn denied that he killed Corredor. Army officers credited Dutchy, an Apache scout, with this deed.

8. *DL*, 24 January 1902. If Horn is to be believed, he planted these spent cartridges in the vicinity of the murder, in order to divert suspicion. He used a .30-30 caliber rifle.

9. *DL*, 24 January 1902. In testimony before the coroner's jury, John Apperson said he saw "a stone about two inches in diameter" that he believed the assassin deliberately "placed under the side of his [Willie's] head." This may be the first documented mention of Horn's alleged practice of placing a rock under the head of his victims.

10. *DL*, 24 January 1902.

11. LeFors, *Wyoming Peace Officer*, 145; Helper, "Smashing the West's Murderous Horseman," 94.

12. LeFors recalled that a third officer, City Policeman Sandy McNeil, accompanied the sheriff and Proctor (LeFors, *Wyoming Peace Officer*, 145). See also LeFors to Spring, [January 1935?], Joe LeFors Biographical File, AHC.

13. Prison Calendar, Laramie County Sheriff's Office, copy in Crime and Criminals, Tom Horn, WSA; *DL*, 13, 14, 15 January 1902.

14. Kennedy, "Memoirs," Kennedy Papers (unpub. MS), AHC, 1:202–204; *DL*, 15, 16, 18 January 1902; *Laramie Daily Boomerang*, 16 January 1902. For John Lacey, see *Progressive*

Men, 24–25. Clipping, *Wyoming State Tribune Eagle*, 14–15 June 1967, Tom Horn Biographical File, AHC. See *RMN*, 29 April 1901, for Edward T. Clark.

15. Irvine to Penrose, 22 Feb 1914, Charles B. Penrose Papers, AHC, box 1; *RMN*, 18 January 1902; Monaghan, *Last of the Bad Men*, 16; Burroughs, *Guardian of the Grassdlands*, 91; *Laramie Daily Boomerang*, 15 January 1902. For Fanklin Bosler's loan, see his affidavit presented as evidence in a law suit with John Coble, in 1904–1905 (Bosler Family Collection, AHC, box 73). "Affidavit of John W. Lacy [sic] acknowledging receipt from Tom Horn, through the hands of John C. Coble, of the sum of Five Thousand ($5,000.00) Dollars," 21 January 1902, Crime and Criminals, Tom Horn, WSA; Kennedy, "Memoirs," 1:204.

16. *DL*, 17 January 1902.

17. *RMN*, 26 October 1902; *DL*, 8 October 1903.

18. *RMN*, 15, 22 January 1902; *DL*, 15 January 1902.

19. *DL*, 14, 18 January 1902; *DR*, 21 January 1902; Carlson, *Tom Horn*, 217–18, for Walter Stoll.

20. *DL*, 20, 22 January 1902; Smalley, "Smashing the West's Murderous Horseman," 94; *RMN*, 25 January 1902.

21. *DL*, 23, 24 January 1902; unid. clipping, [24?] January 1902, copy in Pinkerton Papers, LC, box 116; Ohnhaus, "Early Settler in Cheyenne," WSA.

22. *DL*, 13 March, 20 May 1902; *RMN*, 28, 29 January, 20 May, 7 August 1902.

23. Kennedy, "Memoirs," AHC, 1:205–206; *RMN*, 7 February 1902; *DL*, 13 February 1902. Otto Plaga visited Coble a few days later, although this may have been purely innocent. See Grant's testimony in regard to his assistance in the Horn case (*State of Wyoming v. Tom Horn*, copy in WSA, 722–24). *DL*, 1, 8, 27 May 1902.

24. Smalley, "Smashing the West's Murdering Horseman," 94.

25. Ibid.; *DL*, 7 February 1902; *RMN*, 8, 10 February 1902.

26. Smalley, "Smashing the West's Murdering Horseman," 94; *DP*, 11, 12 March 1902; *DL*, 11, 13 March 1902, quoting the *DP*.

27. *DL*, 22, 24, 26, 27 May 1902, 14 June 1902. For Walter Stoll's information (filed 21 May 1902) and his motion to quash the jury list (26 May), see the collection of documents related to the Tom Horn case, WSA.

28. *Saratoga Sun*, quoted in *DL*, 3 February 1902; *DL*, 14, 25 January, 3, 14 February 1902; Murray to Hadsell, 29 January 1902, Frank Hadsell Collection, WSA, roll 1.

29. Ownbey to Horn, 24 Jan 1902, reprinted in *LOTH*, 226–27; *DL*, 25, 27 January, 29 March, 30 October 1902; *RMN*, 7 March 1902; *DT*, 1 November 1902.

30. *DL*, 31 January, 3, 20 February, 10 March, 9, 24 April 1902, 9 October 1903; *DP*, 8 March 1902; *Laramie Republican*, quoted in *DL*, 12 April 1902; *DL*, 9 October 1903. While this unnamed attorney's facts concerning Tom Horn may have been accurate, he was mistaken in placing this case in 1891. Horn was not in Wyoming at the time. *Laramie Republican*, quoted in *DL*, 12 April 1902. *Blood on the Moon*, 127. Chip Carlson says Horn may have killed a man named Walker on the Red Desert, in 1900, but this could refer to the double murder that Bob Meldrum claimed he and the range detective committed about this time.

31. *DL*, 22, 23 May 1902; *RMN*, 23, 25 May, 8 June 1902.

32. *RMN*, 13, 14 Oct 1902; *DL*, 7 Feb 1902.

33. *DL*, 14, 29 January, 5, 10 March, 13 June 1902; *RMN*, 29 May, 10, 26 October 1902. See issue of 21 November 1903, for the peep hole. *LOTH*, 25; Snow to Monaghan, September 1946, JMP.

34. Two letters, Matson and Kennedy to Irwin, and Matson and Kennedy to Charles Horn, 29 May 1902, Kennedy Papers, WSA, box 2.

35. Rollinson, *Pony Trails in Wyoming*, 191–93; Smalley, "Smashing the West's Murdering Horseman," 94; *DL*, 26, 28 August 1903.

36. *RMN*, 7 August 1902; *DL*, 11 September, 17 October, 18 December 1901, 4, 7 June, 14 August, 24 October 1902; *Progressive Men*, 416.

37. *DL*, 12, 13, 15, 16, 18, 20 August, 12 September 1902; *RMN*, 21 August, 15, 16, 24 September 1902; Kennedy, "Memoirs," 1:207; *DT*, 24 September 1902.

38. *DR*, 15, 16 October 1902; *DL*, 2, 8, 11 September 1902; *RMN*, 5, 22 October 1902; unid. clipping, October 1902, vertical file, Tom Horn, WSA; *DP*, 7 October 1902.

39. *RMN*, 27 October 1902; Ferguson to Matson and Kennedy, 2 October 1902, T. Blake Kennedy Papers, WSA, AHC, box 2.

40. *DP*, 7 October 1902.

41. Ibid., 2 March 1902.

42. *DP*, 2, 7 March 1902.

43. Ibid., 7 March 1902; *DL*, 12 February 1902.

44. See the deposition of Franklin Bosler, (1904/5), Bosler Family Collection, AHC, box 73.

45. *RMN*, 5 October 1902.

46. *DP*, 7 October 1902; *RMN*, 25 September, 6, 10 October 1902; *DL*, 16, 23, 27 September 1902.

47. *DL*, 23, 27, 30 September, 1, 3 October 1902; *DP*, 7 October 1902. See the motion and affidavit of Tom Horn asking that the county pay expenses of his witnesses, filed 30 September 1902 (*State of Wyoming v. Tom Horn*, WSA).

48. *DP*, 7, 12 October 1902.

49. *DP*, 7 October 1902; *RMN*, 25 September, 7 October 1902; *DL*, 23 September, 7, 13 October 1902.

CHAPTER 13

1. *DR*, 7 October 1902; Fowler, *Timber Line*, 184; Field, *History of Cheyenne*, 2:39, for the justice complex.

2. *RMN*, 7, 11 October 1902; *DP*, 7, 9 October 1902; *DL*, 9 October 1902; Kennedy, "Memoirs," (MS), Kennedy Papers, AHC, 1:207–208. *State of Wyoming v. Tom Horn*, copy in WSA, 739, for the trial transcript, and Tom Horn's appeal of his conviction, and subsequent legal actions on his behalf.

3. *RMN*, 9, 10, 11 October 1902.

4. *State of Wyoming v. Tom Horn*, 1–45, for preliminary testimony. See 62, for Fred Nickell, 46–51, for Mary Nickell, 51–62, for Kels Nickell. *DP*, 12 October 1902. Although Horn boasted to Joe LeFlors that placing a rock under the head of his victim was his "sign" of the successful completion of an assassination, there is no evidence that he employed this practic in previous killings.

5. Testimony of Kels Nickell, *State of Wyoming v. Tom Horn*, 51–62; *DP*, 12 October 1902.

6. *State of Wyoming v. Tom Horn*, 96–102, for Peter Bergesen (Bergersen), 102–107 and 115–16, for Doctor H. J. Maynard, 107–114, for Doctor L. P. Desmond, 116–43, for Doctor M. C. Barkwell. Doctor Amos Barber did not testify at the trial. However, his expert testimony presented at the coroner's inquest was read into the trial record (*RMN*, 12 October 1902). See also *State of Wyoming v. Tom Horn*, 88–95, for T. F. Cook; 75–82, for Coroner Thomas J. Murray; 63–75, for Apperson; 230–46, for Frank C. Erwin.

7. *State of Wyoming v. Tom Horn*, 247–49, for Charles H. Miller; *DL*, 13 October 1902.

8. *State of Wyoming v. Tom Horn*, 266, 283 for Mortimer N. Grant. See 283 for Judge Scott's decision. *DL*, 15 October 1902.

9. *State of Wyoming v. Tom Horn*, 183–91, for Victor Miller; 192–99, for Augustus Miller; 202–204, for Mary Nickell (recalled); 204–208, for Mrs. James (Dora) Miller; 208–211, for Eva Miller; 211–19, for John M. Bray; 219–29, for Robert C. Morris. See *RMN*, 15 October 1902, for commentary on errors enumerated by defense counsel.

10. *DP*, 12 October: *DL*, 13 October 1902.

11. *DL*, 13 October 1902; *State of Wyoming v. Tom Horn*, 267–72, for George A. Matlock; 272–77, for Powell.

12. *State of Wyoming v. Tom Horn*, 296–98, for Lyman Murdock; 300–302, for Edwin J. Smalley; 302–303, for Richard A. Proctor. Joe LeFors's later assertion that the sweater played no part in the state's case is erroneous (LeFors to Agnes Wright Spring, [1935 ?], copy in Joe LeFors Biographical File, AHC.

13. *State of Wyoming v. Tom Horn*, 284–89, for Frank W. Mulock; 278–82, for Campbell; and 290–96, for Cowsley; *RMN*, 13, 16 October 1902.

14. *DP*, 16 October 1902.

15. *State of Wyoming v. Tom Horn*, 304–25, for LeFors; *DP*, 16 October 1902; *DL*, 15 October 1902.

16. *State of Wyoming v. Tom Horn*, 318a, for A. D. McNeil; 319a–320a, for McGwire (McGuire); 320a–322a, for Robinson; 322a–324a, for Hall; 324a–325, for Bailey. See 325–34, for Snow; 335a, 335–44, for Ohnhaus. Some pages of testimony were apparently left out in the preparation of the original trial transcript, but later inserted with numbers followed by a letter of the alphabet.

17. *State of Wyoming v. Tom Horn*, 342, for Ohnhaus; *DP*, 16 October 1902; Ohnhaus, "Early Settler in Cheyenne," WSA, 1937, 10 (typescript). While John Ohnhaus, father of the stenographer, admitted that the "confession was obtained in a most peculiar manner," he asserted that his son's shorthand notes were "the most important testimony" at Tom Horn's trial.

18. *State of Wyoming v. Tom Horn*, 344, for Stoll's announcement; *DL*, 15, 16 October 1902.

19. *RMN*, 16 October 1902.

20. *State of Wyoming v. Tom Horn*, 400–401, for Reis; 401–404, for Leslie; 404–405, for Nelson; 405–408, for Kerrigan; 408–409, for Fullerton. *DL*, 16 October 1902; *DP*, 7, 16 October 1902.

21. *State of Wyoming v. Tom Horn*, 441–79, for Lewis; 511–28, for Burgess; 409–41, for Johnston; 479–511, for Conway. *RMN*, 17 October 1902; *DL*, 16 October 1902.

22. *State of Wyoming v. Tom Horn*, 409–41, 547–50 (recall) for Johnston; 479–511, 581–82 (recall), for Lewis.

23. *RMN*, 16, 17, 19 October 1902; *State of Wyoming v. Tom Horn*, 528–34, for Davis; 608–11 for Stockton.

24. *RMN*, 19 October 1902; *DL*, 17 October 1902. *LOTH*, 272–74, for Coble's denial that he paid for evidence.

25. *RMN*, 17 October 1902.

26. *State of Wyoming v. Tom Horn*, 534–42, 708a–709a, for Wallace; 542–47, for Carpenter.

27. Ibid., 550–56, for Clark; *RMN*, 18 October 1902; *DL*, 14 October 1902.

28. *State of Wyoming v. Tom Horn*, 556–59, for Cook; *DL*, 17 October 1902.

29. *State of Wyoming v. Tom Horn*, 559–61, for Burke; 561, for Kennedy; 562–68, for Stone. *RMN*, 18 October 1902.

30. *State of Wyoming v. Tom Horn*, 568–81, for Plaga.

31. Ibid.; *RMN* 18 October 1902.

32. *State of Wyoming v. Tom Horn*, 582–88, for Hencke; 588–93, for Coldick; *RMN*, 18 October 1902.

33. Attributed to Mr. Justice Buller, *Judgment in Calliard vs. Vaughan*, 1798 (Mencken, *New Dictionary of Quotations*, 1311). Unid. clipping, October 1902, vertical files, Tom Horn, WSA. "Coroner's Inquest in the Matter of the Killing of William Nickells [sic]," 405, copy in WSA. See 283–98, for Horn's testimony.

34. *State of Wyoming v. Tom Horn*, 594, for Whitman; *DL*, 17 October 1902; *RMN*, 18 Oct 1902.

35. *RMN*, 16 October 1902; unid. clipping, October 1902, vertical files, Tom Horn, WSA. *State of Wyoming v. Tom Horn*, 595–608, 602a–609a, for Horn's responses to the defense's questions.

36. Ibid., 596–605a.

37. Ibid., 605.

38. Interview with T. Blake Kennedy, clippings, *Wyoming State Tribune-Eagle*, 14, 15 June 1967, Tom Horn Biographical File, AHC.

39. *State of Wyoming v. Tom Horn*, 605–608.

40. *DL*, 18 October 1902; *State of Wyoming v. Tom Horn*, 612–701, for cross examination of Horn.

41. *State of Wyoming v. Tom Horn*. See 612 for reference to Horn's presence in Brown's Park.

42. Ibid., 612–13, 672.

43. Ibid., 614–20.

44. Ibid., 621–63; see 650–53, for specific remarks; *DL*, 18 October 1902.

45. *State of Wyoming v. Tom Horn*, 623–63; Kennedy, "Memoirs," AHC, 1:207.

46. *State of Wyoming v. Tom Horn*, 667–68, 681–83; *RMN*, 19 October 1902.

47. *DL*, 18 October 1902; *RMN*, 18 October 1902.

48. *State of Wyoming v. Tom Horn*, 671–75, 688–93, for Horn's implied admission. Affidavit of Joe LeFors, 6 November 1903, copy in vertical files, Tom Horn, WSA.

49. *State of Wyoming v. Tom Horn*, 612, 667–68; *Salt Lake Tribune*, 21 November 1903; *RMN*, 18, 19 October 1902; unid. clipping, 18 October 1902, Leslie Snow Collection, AHC.

50. *DP*, 16, 19 October; *DL*, 18 October 1902.

51. *RMN*, 19 October 1902.

52. *State of Wyoming v. Tom Horn*, 703; *RMN*, 21 October 1902.

53. *State of Wyoming v. Tom Horn*, 704–712, for LeFors; *DL*, 20 October 1902.

54. *State of Wyoming v. Tom Horn*, 713–15 (for Granville W. Faulkner), 715–16 (for Charles H. Edwards), 716–17 (for Hiram G. Davidson), 717 (for Thomas G. Moore), 718 (for Richard Fitzmorris), 718–19 (James McArthur), 720–22 (for Davies), 722–24, (for Grant). *DL*, 20 October 1902.

55. *State of Wyoming v. Tom Horn*, 724–25 (for Biggs 725–26 (for Henry Mudd), 726–27 (for Ed Hofmann), 727–29 (for Fred Hofmann), 729–30 (for Sam Moore), 730–33 (for Frank Perry Williams), 733–35 (for William Clay), 735–36 (for Ferguson), 735–36 (for Reed), 736–37 (for Duncan Clark). *DL*, 20 October 1902.

56. *State of Wyoming v. Tom Horn*, 737; *DL*, 21 October 1902.

CHAPTER 14

1. *DR*, 7 October 1902; *DP*, 7 October 1902; Roedel, review of *Saga of Tom Horn* in *Wyoming Tribune*, 16 February 1958, copy in Tom Horn Biographical File, AHC.

2. *DL*, 14 October 1902; *DP*, 15 October 1902. See ibid., 16 October 1902 for illustrations of women present.

3. *DP*, 19 October 1902; *RMN*, 19 October 1902.

4. Helper, "Smashing the West's Murdering Horseman," 4–9, 93–97; *DL*, 14, 15 October 1902; *DP*, 7, 12 October 1902.

5. *DP*, 12 October 1902; *DL*, 13, 17 October 1902.

6. *DP*, 12 October 1902.

7. *DL*, 13, 26 October 1902; *RMN*, 26 September 1902.

8. Ibid., 16 October 1902; *DL*, 14 October 1902.

9. *DL*, 15, 22, 23 October 1902; *DP*, 16, 23 October 1902.

10. *RMN*, 16, 22 October 1902; *DL*, 22 October 1902. For a copy of Judge Scott's instructions to the jury, see the collection of trial documents in *State of Wyoming v. Tom Horn*, WSA.

11. *RMN*, 22 October 1902; *DL*, 21 October 1902.

12. *DL*, 22 October 1902.

13. Ibid.

14. Ibid.

15. *RMN*, 22 October 1902.

16. Ibid; *DL*, 22 October 1902.

17. *DL*, 22 October 1902.

18. Ibid.

19. *RMN*, 23 October 1902; *DL* 22 October 1902.

20. *RMN*, 23 October 1902.

21. Ibid.; *DL* 22 October 1902.

22. *DL*, 22, 23 October 1902; *RMN*, 24 October 1902.

23. *DL*, 23 October 1902; *RMN*, 24 October 1902.

24. *DL*, 23, 24 October 1902; *RMN*, 24 October 1902.

25. *RMN*, 24 October 1902.

26. *DL*, 24 October 1902; *RMN*, 25 October 1902.

27. *DL*, 24 October 1902; *RMN*, 25 October 1902; *Cheyenne Dispatch,* 24 October 1902, to *Wichita Daily Eagle,* 25 October 1902.

28. *DL*, 22, 23 October 1902; *RMN*, 23 October 1902.

29. *RMN*, 23 October 1902; *DL*, 22, 23 October 1902.

30. *DL*, 21, 23, 24 October 1902; *Douglas Budget*, reprinted in *DL*, 24 October 1902.

31. *DL*, 24, 25 October 1902.

32. *DL*, 25 October 1902; LeFors, *Wyoming Peace Officer*, 145.

33. *DL*, 25 October 1902; *RMN*, 24, 25 October 1902.

34. *DL*, 27 October 1902.

35. For a list of the jurors and their occupations, see *RMN*, 11 October 1902, and *DL*, 10, 25 October 1902. Clipping, *Torrington Telegram*, 16 July 1925, Crime and Criminals, Tom Horn, WSA. For Yoder, see Downing, *Stories of the North Platte Valley*, 25.

36. Johnson, *Trails, Rails and Travails*, 64–65.

37. Obituary of Homer Payne, clipping, *Casper Tribune Herald*, 8 May 1944, WSA.

38. For Tolson, see Works Projects Administration, biography 961, 8 July 1936, WSA.

39. *RMN*, 11 October 1902.

40. Ibid.

41. Ibid.

42. Ibid.

43. Ibid.

44. Ibid.

45. Ibid.

46. Ibid.

47. *DP*, qtd. in *DL*, 27 October 1902. See Payne's affidavit, 30 Oct 1902, in Tom Horn's appeal in a supplemental motion for a new trial, filed 3 November 1902, *State of Wyoming v. Tom Horn*. Affidavit of James E. Barnes, 7 November 1902, in ibid.

48. *RMN*, 26 October 1902; affidavit of George S. Walker, 8 Nov 1902; affidavit of J. Emerson Smith, 7 November 1902; Counter Affidavits as to Supplemental Motion for New Trial, WSA; *RMN*, 25 October 1902; *DP*, qtd. in *DL*, 27 October 1902; *DL*, 25 October 1902.

49. *RMN*, 26 October, 17 November 1902. Coe, *Juggling A Rope*, 106; *DL*, 23, 24, 25, 27 October 1902.

50. *RMN*, 21, 25 October 1902; *DL*, 7, 10 November 1902. Two clippings, *Wyoming State Tribune*, 3 March 1940, and *Laramie Republican and Boomerang* (Second Annual Vacation Edition), 5 June 1954, Tom Horn Biographical File, AHC; *RMN*, 25 October 1902; *Laramie Republican*, 20 November 1903; *DR*, 21 November 1903; Joe LeFors estimated the expense at $200,000 (*Wyoming Peace Officer*, 146). See Chip Carlson, *Tom Horn*, 331, for Kerr's recollections.

51. Krakel, "Introduction," *LOTH*, xii–xiii. See also, Krakel, "Was Tom Horn Two Men?" 12–17, 52–56. Raine, *Famous Sheriffs*, 87n1.

52. *RMN*, 25 October 1902.

53. Krakel, "Was Tom Horn Two Men?" 54; Kennedy, "Memoirs," AHC, 1:210–11; *DL*, 16 October 1902.

54. *DP*, 26 January 1903.

55. *DL*, 30 October 1902.

56. *RMN*, 26, 28 October 1902; *DP*, 12 October 1902.

57. Pinkerton to Pinkerton, 19 January 1906, qtd. in Horan, *Pinkertons*, 391–83. Clipping, *San Francisco Call*, 21 November 1903, courtesy of Allan Radbourne.

58. *DL*, 25, 27 October 1902; *RMN*, 26 October 1902.

CHAPTER 15

1. Smalley, "Smashing the West's Murdering Horseman," 4–9, 93–97; *RMN*, 26, 27, 28 October 1902.

2. Smalley, "Smashing the West's Murdering Horseman," 95; *RMN*, 26, 27 October 1902.

3. *DL*, 27, 31 October, 7, 22 November 1902; *RMN*, 30 October, 3, 4, 5, 7 November 1902.

4. *DL*, 8 November 1902. For a copy of the motion for a new trial, filed 27 October 1902, 47, and subsequent submissions surrounding this motion, see *State of Wyoming v. Tom Horn*, copy in WSA. Affidavits of Greta Rohde and J. Emerson Smith, both dated 3 November, Homer L. Payne, 30 October 1902, Supplemental Motion for New Trial, 7 in ibid.; *DL*, 7, 8 November 1902. A copy Glendolene Kimmell's, affidavit, dated 10 November 1902, is in vertical files, Tom Horn, WSA.

5. Affidavits of Charles H. Tolson, James E. Barnes, John H. Rees, George A. Proctor, and J. Emerson Smith, all dated 7 November 1902, Counter Affidavits as to Supplemental Motion for New Trial, 8 November 1902, in *State of Wyoming v. Tom Horn*, WSA; *DL*, 8, 12 November 1902.

6. *DL*, 8, 12, 13, 18 November 1902.

7. *DL*, 17 November 1902.

8. *DL*, 17 November, 2, 17, 18 December 1902; *RMN*, 14, 16 November 1902; *DL*, 17 December 1902. Preparation of a copy of the trial transcript cost the defense $1,450.

9. *DL*, 10, 22 January 1903; *RMN*, 12, 22 January 1903; Thompson, "Hanging of Tom Horn," 111–29. Clipping, *Laramie Boomerang*, 22 January 1903, Tom Horn Biographical File, AHC. Carlson, *Tom Horn*, 288–89. Thomas P. Herr is referred to as Hubert Herr and Frank Herr in the newspapers.

10. *RMN*, 22, 23, 24, 26 January, 20 November 1903; Smalley, "Smashing the West's Murdering Horseman," 95; Clipping, *Ogden Standard*, 22 January 1903, Tom Horn Biographical File, AHC.

11. Roy W. Lilley, interview with D. Claudia Thompson, Wellington, CO, 10 July 2012, Roy W. Lilley Oral History Collection, AHC. The author is indebted to Thompson for a copy of this interview.

12. Ibid.

13. *DL*, 7, 9, 10 February 1903; Carlson, *Tom Horn*, 288–89.

14. *DL*, 3, 14, 20 February, 20 April, 27 May, 20, 23 July, 31 October 1903; *RMN*, 20 February 1903.

15. *DL*, 7, 20 March 1903.

16. LeFors, *Wyoming Peace Officer*, 146–56; *DL*, 27 October, 18 December 1902, 7 May, 8 June, 8 October, 1 November, 3 December 1903; *RMN*, 3, 13 December 1902; *Buffalo Bulletin*, 18, 25 June 1903. See also LeFors's waiver and related documents, vertical files, Tom Horn, WSA.

17. *RMN*, 2 August 1903. See the issue of 10 August for a diagram of the Laramie County Jail. See also Farlow, *Wind River Adventures*, 117, for background on McCloud. Snow to Monaghan, [?] September 1946, JMP; Smalley, "Smashing the West's Murdering Horseman," 96–97.

18. Carlson, *Tom Horn*, 288–95. Doctor George P. Johnston informed Dean Krakel that Tom Horn used his (Johnston's) pistol in his escape (Krakel, "Was Tom Horn Two Men?" 12–17, 52–56). Field, *History of Cheyenne*, 2:225; Gregory, "Tom Horn," Clara T. Woody Collection, series 2, AHS, box 7, 30, for Cahill's recollections.

19. Field, *History of Cheyenne*, 2:331; Smalley, "Smashing the West's Murdering Horseman," 96–97; Monaghan, *Last of the Bad Men*, 229; Thompson, "Hanging of Tom Horn," 111–29; Snow to Monaghan, September 1946, JMP. *Carbon County Journal*, 16 January 1904; *RMN*, 12 August 1903.

20. John Charles Thompson, the *Wyoming Tribune* reporter, gave a different version of Horn's escape attempt. Thompson declared that a pistol was smuggled into his cell by a female member of a prominent cattleman's family. This weapon once belonged to Doctor George Johnston, who had traded it to John Coble. Johnston informed Thompson that when he next saw this gun "it lay at Horn's feet in the street" when he was recaptured (Thompson, "The Hanging of Tom Horn," 111–29). Snow to Monaghan, [?] September 1946, JMP; *Wheatland World*, qtd. in *DL*, 15 August 1903.

21. Coble to Bosler, 29 June, 12 August 1903, Bosler Family Papers, AHC, box 115.

22. *DL*, 20 August 1903; *RMN*, 22 August 1903.

23. *DL*, 21, 22, 30 August 1903; *RMN*, 23, 30 August 1903.

24. Van Orsdel to Adams, Fort Bayard, New Mexico, 15 August 1903, WSA, box 3, book 3, 417; Orsdel to Adams, 25 August 1903, Attorney General, *Horn v. State*, ibid., 423.

25. *DL*, 20 August, 8, 17, 18, 22, 23, 25, 26, 30 September, 1 October 1903.

26. For the complete text of this decision, see Attorney General, *Horn v. State, WSA*; *DL*, 1, 11, 13 October 1903.

27. *DL*, 25, 28, 31 October 1903; Horn to Ohnhaus, 3 October, in *LOTH*, 231–33; Horn to Coble, 31 October 1903, in ibid., 238–39; Horn to Mullock, 20 October 1903, reprinted in *DL*, 21 October 1903. The name of the addressee was not included in the first printing, but reported later.

28. Ball, "That 'Miserable Book'" 323–48; *DL*, 29 October 1903.

29. *DL*, 3, 31 October 1903.

30. *DL*, 8, 17, 23, 24 October 1903; Krakel, *Saga of Tom Horn*, 219–20.

31. Unid. clipping, Denver, Colorado, 31 October 1903, Tom Horn File, Pinkerton National Detective Agency Papers, LC, Washington, D.C., box 116. There is some uncertainty as to the number of affidavits that Kimmell made. One is dated 10 November 1902 (copy in vertical files, Tom Horn, WSA); another is dated, 13 October 1903, Jackson County, Missouri (see the copy in Carlson, *Joe LeFors*, 238–50); *Laramie Republican*, 2, 3 November 1903; *RMN*, 11 October 1903.

32. *Laramie Republican*, 2 November 1903; *Wyoming State Tribune*, qtd. in ibid., 5 November 1903; *DL*, 25, 30, 31 October, 1, 5 November 1903.

33. *DL*, 1, 8, 13 November 1903.

34. Affidavit of Glendolene Myrtle Kimmell, 10 November 1903, repr. in Carlson, *Joe LeFors*, 238–50; *DL*, 1 November 1903.

35. Affidavit of E. T. Clark, 26 October 1903, copy in vertical files, Tom Horn, WSA; *DL*, 1 November 1903, for Martin, Cook, Yund, and Coble.

36. *DL*, 1, 3, 4 November 1903; "Miss Kimmell's Statement," in *LOTH*, 246–66; *Laramie Republican*, 4 November 1903; *Saratoga Sun*, qtd. in ibid., 9 November 1903.

37. *DL*, 5 November 1903. Affidavit of Albert W. Bristol, Jr., 2 November 1903, affidavit of Alfred Cook, 3 November 1903, vertical files, Tom Horn, WSA.

38. *DL*, 5, 6 November 1903; *DP*, 10 November 1903.

39. *Laramie Republican*, 5 November 1903; *DL*, 6 November 1903; Chatterton, *Yesterday's Wyoming*, 84; clipping, *Wyoming State Tribune*, 5 November 1903, Tom Horn Biographical File, AHC.

40. See *RMN*, 13 November and *DL*, 13 November 1903; *Laramie Republican*, 13 November 1903.

41. *RMN*, 13 November 1903; *DL*, 13 November 1903. For a copy of Joe LeFors's affidavit, dated 6 November 1903, see vertical files, Tom Horn, WSA, 5.

42. *DL*, 13 November 1903; *Laramie Republican*, 13 November 1903.

43. *DL*, 13 November 1903; *Laramie Republican*, 13 November 1903, for Plaga's alleged remark.

44. *DL*, 13 November 1903; *RMN*, 13, 14, 15 November 1903.

45. Clipping, *Laramie Boomerang*, 3 November 1903, Tom Horn Biographical File, AHC. *Evanston Press*, qtd. in *DL*, 10 November 1903. See also *DL*, 5 November 1903; *DT*, 12 November, qtd. in *Laramie Republican*, 13 November 1903.

46. *DL*, 1, 13 November 1903; clippings, *Laramie Boomerang* and *Evanston Press*, qtd. in *DL*, 10 November 1903; unid. clipping, Pinkerton Papers, LC, box 116. Clipping, *Laramie Boomerang*, 3 November 1903, Tom Horn Biographical File, AHC; *RMN*, 13 November 1903.

47. Hines to Chatterton, 4 November 1903, vertical files, Tom Horn, WSA; *DL*, 15 November 1903.

48. *DL*, 15 November and *RMN*, 15 November 1903, for the summation of Chatterton's decision.

49. *DL*, 15 November 1903.

50. *Laramie Republican*, 5 November 1903.

51. *RMN*, 15, 17 November 1903; Chatterton, *Yesterday's Wyoming*, 83.

52. *RMN*, 15 November 1903; *DL*, 18 November 1903; Krakel, "Was Tom Horn Two Men?" 12–17, 52–56.

CHAPTER 16

1. *DL*, 17 November 1903; *RMN*, 16 November 1903; Horn to Coble, 17 November 1903, in *LOTH*, 240–41.

2. *DL*, 17 November 1903; *Laramie Republican*, 14 November 1903; *RMN*, 16 November 1903. Clipping, *San Francisco Call*, 21 November 1903, copy courtesy of Allan Radbourne.

3. *DL*, 18, 25 November 1903; Brown, *Coyotes and Canaries*, 206–209, for Edwin Taylor, who commanded the national guardsmen at the jail. Chatterton, *Yesterday's Wyoming*, 86–87. Tom Castle interviewed by Roy C. Armstrong, "Hanging Tom Horn, Nov. 20, 1903," 4, WSA. For Samuel Corson see Spring, *William Chapin Deming*, 121.

4. Thompson, "Hanging of Tom Horn," 111–29; Jones, "Fifty Years Ago," 22–40; *DL*, 19 November 1903; *RMN*, 19 November 1903; clipping, *Chicago Chronicle*, 20 November 1903, Tom Horn file, Pinkerton National Detective Agency Papers, LC, box 116; Chatterton, *Yesterday's Wyoming*, 86.

5. *New York Times*, 5 October 1903; *RMN*, 19 November 1903; *DL*, 8, 17 October 1903; Cahill to "Dear Friend," in Wright, *Pardners*, xi–xii. Smalley, "Smashing the West's Murdering Horseman," 4–9, 93–97. Tom Castle interview, WSA. Burton, *Deadliest Outlaws*, 290–304, for the latest assessment of the Black Jack Ketchum hanging.

6. *DL*, 20 November 1903; *RMN*, 19, 20 November 1903; Thompson, "Hanging Tom Horn," 123–24.

7. *DL*, 18 November 1903; *RMN*, 20 November 1903; *DR*, 20 November 1903; Smalley to Carley, 15 November 1903, copy in Crime and Criminals, Tom Horn, WSA. Kennedy, "Memoirs," AHC, 1:210; *Laramie Republican*, 17 November 1903.

8. Cahill to "Dear Friend," in Wright, *Pardners*, xi–xii.; *DL*, 1 April 1902, for Cahill's marriage.

9. *DL*, 17, 18, 19 November 1903; Rollinson, *Pony Trails*, 198–99, 206–207; *RMN*, 19 November 1903. "M. L. W." to Chatterton, 12 November, and Anonymous to Chatterton, 14 November 1903, repr. in *RMN*, 17 November 1903. Packard to Chatterton, 16 November 1903, and McKown to Chatterton, 18 November 1903, copies in vertical files, Tom Horn, WSA. Anonymous to Smalley, 17 November 1903, in *DL*, 19 November 1903; "A Cowboy" to Chatterton, [?] November 1903, in *RMN*, 26 November 1903. See also *DT*, 19 November 1903.

10. *RMN*, 19 November 1903; Chatterton, *Yesterday's Wyoming*, 82–83; Clipping, *Chicago Chronicle*, 20 November 1903, in Horn File, Pinkerton Papers, LC, box 116.

11. *DT*, 19 November 1903; *Laramie Republican*, 17 November 1903; Bowers, "School Bells and Winchesters," 14–32.

12. Loney to Horn, 15 November, and Adams to Horn, 16 November 1903, repr. in *DL*, 20 November 1903; *DR*, 20, 21 November 1903.

13. Thompson, "Hanging of Tom Horn," 120; *RMN*, 20 November 1903; *DR*, 20, 21 November 1903; *DT*, 19 November 1903.

14. *DT*, 19 November 1903; *DP*, 20 November 1903; Helper and Smalley, "Smashing the West's Murdering Horseman," 96; *DL*, 18 November 1903; *RMN*, 20 November 1903; Thompson, "Hanging of Tom Horn," 120–21; *DL*, 18 November 1903. While Sheriff Smalley permitted representatives of several denominations to visit Tom Horn, the lawman inexplicably denied a Pentecostal delegation permission to pray with the prisoner. *San Francisco Chronicle*, 21 November 1903; Horn to Coble, 1 March 1902, in *LOTH*, 228–29.

15. Smalley, "Smashing the West's Murdering Horseman," 96–97; *RMN*, 20 November 1903; *DR*, 21 November 1903; *DT*, 20 November 1903; *DL*, 20 November 1903.

16. *RMN*, 20 November 1903; *DR*, 21 November 1903; Smalley, "Smashing the West's Murdering Horseman," 96–97; T. Cahill to "Dear Friend," in Wright, *Pardners*, xi–xii.

17. *DR*, 20 November 1903.

18. Thompson, "Hanging of Tom Horn," 121; *DR*, 21 November 1903; Knox, "Saga of Tom Horn," clipping, *Wyoming Tribune*, 18 November 1954, Tom Horn Biographical File, AHC; Spring, *Near the Greats*, 79–83.

19. Knox, "Saga of Tom Horn," clipping, *Wyoming Tribune*, 18 November 1954, Tom Horn Biographical File, AHC.

20. For reports of this conversation, see *DT*, 20 November and *Laramie Boomerang*, 22 November 1903.

21. Smalley, "Smashing the West's Murdering Horseman," 96–97; Thompson, "Hanging Tom Horn," 121.

22. Ibid.; *DL*, 21 November 1903; Smalley, "Smashing the West's Murdering Horseman," 4–9, 93–97.

23. Spring, *William Chapin Deming*, 101; *DR*, 21 November 1903; Field, *History of Cheyenne*, 2:311–12, for background on Charles Irwin's family.

24. Thompson, "Hanging of Tom Horn"; Castle Interview, WSA; *DR*, 21 November 1903.

25. Cahill to "Dear Friend," in Wright, *Pardners*, xi–xii; Castle Interview, WSA; Smalley, "Smashing the West's Murdering Horseman," 96–97.

26. *DR*, 21 November 1903; Thompson, "Hanging Tom Horn," 123–24.

27. Smalley, "Smashing the West's Murdering Horseman," 97; Dean Krakel, "Was Tom Horn Two Men?" 12–17, 52–56; *DL*, 20 November 1903; *DR*, 21 November 1903; *Laramie Boomerang*, 24 November 1903; *Laramie Republican*, 25 November 1903.

28. Smalley, "Smashing the West's Murdering Horseman," 97; Spring, *William Chapin Deming*, 96–97; Thompson, "Hanging Tom Horn," 128.

29. *Laramie Boomerang*, 24 November 1903; *Laramie Republican*, 25 November 1903; *DL*, 20, 22, 25 November 1903; *RMN*, 22 November 1903.

30. Chatterton, *Yesterday's Wyoming*, 77–87; *RMN*, 22 November 1903; *Rawlins Journal*, qtd. in *Laramie Republican*, 24 November 1903; clipping, *Wyoming Tribune*, 20 November 1903, copy in Crime and Criminals, Tom Horn, WSA.

31. *DL*, 20 November 1903; *RMN*, 21 November 1903; *DL*, 21 November 1903; LeFors, *Wyoming Peace Officer*, 146.

32. *Laramie Republican*, 20 November 1903; clipping, *Wyoming Tribune*, 20 November 1903, copy in Crime and Criminals, Tom Horn, WSA; *RMN*, 21 November 1903; Thompson, "Image of Tom Horn," 1–11; Smalley, "Smashing the West's Murdering Horseman," 97.

33. *San Francisco Chronicle*, 21 November; *Los Angeles Times*, 21 November; *Washington Post*, 21 November; *Chicago Daily Tribune*, 21 November; *New York Times*, 21 November 1903.

34. Rollinson, *Pony Trails*, 198–99, 206–207; *Wyoming Tribune*, 24 November 1903; *RMN*, 22 November 1903; *DL*, 5 December 1903.

35. *DT*, 18, 21 November 1903. See Coble's "Closing Word," in *LOTH*, 272–74. *RMN*, 21 November 1903; *Boulder Daily Camera*, 21 November 1903; *DR*, 22 November 1903.

36. *DR*, 22, 23 November 1903; *Daily Camera*, 21 November 1903.

37. Ganzhorn, *I've Killed Men*, 87; *Daily Camera*, 21, 23 November 1903; *DR*, 22 November 1903; *RMN*, 9 December 1903; Horn to Coble, 27 November 1903, in *LOTH*, 244–45.

38. Horn to Coble, 27 November 1903, in *LOTH*, 244–45; *DL*, 22 November 1903; Ball, "Tom Horn: Rogue Frontiersman."

39. *DT*, 21 November 1903; *Laramie Republican*, 30 November 1903; *Wyoming Tribune*, 25 November 1903; *RMN*, 26 November, 9, 17 December 1903; *DL*, 17 December 1903.

40. *DT*, 21 November 1903; *DL*, 28 November, 18, 19, 23 December 1903; *RMN*, 30 November 1903; "Miss Kimmell's Statement," in *LOTH*, 246–66; Bowers, "School Bells and Winchesters," 14–32. Bowers concluded that Laramie County officials may have deliberately misplaced or destroyed some documents relating to Glendolene Kimmell, although such records often disappear through negligence and accident.

41. *RMN*, 18, 19 December 1903.

42. *DL*, 5, 24 December 1903; *Laramie Republican*, 27 November 1903; *Laramie Boomerang*, 24 May 1904. For the case of *Coble v. Bosler*, see the Bosler Family Papers, AHC, boxes 73, 118.

43. Horn to Coble, 17 November 1903, in *LOTH*, 240–41; *DL*, 18 December 1903; *DT*, 28 October 1903; *DP*, 14 April 1904; Ball, "That 'Miserable Book'" 323–48; Kimmell to Tewksbury, 1 March 1904. The author is indebted to Richard A. Pierce of Phoenix, Arizona, for a copy of this letter. Pierce to Ball, 1 June 2001, e-mail, author's files. "Statement from Al Sieber," Roosevelt, Arizona, 7 March 1904, in *LOTH*, 269–71; *Denver City Directory*, 1903, for Louthan Printing Company. In 2008 Old West Books advertised a first edition, hard cover of the *Life of Tom Horn, Government Scout and Interpreter* for $1,250.00 (oldwestbooks@earthlink.net).

44. *LOTH*, 272–74.

45. *Buffalo Bulletin*, 17 March 1904; Carlson, *Tom Horn*, 311–12; clipping, Thompson, "In Old Wyoming," *DL*, 31 January 1905, qtd. in *Wyoming State Tribune*, 26 February 1941, Tom Horn Biographical Files, AHC; Thrapp, *Encyclopedia of Frontier Biography*, 1:289, s.v. John C. Coble.

46. *Wyoming State Leader*, 5 December 1914 (obituary).

47. Carlson, *Joe LeFors*, 6; McCoy, *Tim McCoy Remembers*, 235. Thrapp, *Encyclopedia of Frontier Biography*, 2:838–39, s.v. Joe LeFors.

48. Krakel, "Was Tom Horn Two Men?" 12–17, 52–56; Cahill, "I Hanged My Friend," *DP Empire Magazine*, [1958?], copy in Crime and Criminals, Tom Horn, WSA. Shores to Monaghan, [?] September 1930, JMP. Shores said essentially the same thing in two interviews with the *DP*, 19 November 1927, 15 April 1928. Shores refused to name his informant. Raine, *Famous Sheriffs*, 80; Camp, *Muggins*, 8–10. Coe, *Juggling a Rope*, 98–101, 105–107, 111.

49. *Arizona Bulletin*, 27 November 1903; unid. clipping, Cheyenne, Wyoming, [1908], qtd. in Walters, *Tombstone's Yesterdays*, 45–46; Dunlap, "Tom Horn," 73–85. Horace Dunlap died in Liberal, Kansas, in 1937 (Horace E. Dunlap papers, AHS); clipping, *Worland Grit*, 5 April 1934, Tom Horn Biographical File, AHC. Ackenhausen, who eventually

settled in Wyoming, asserted that Tom Horn once visited Geronimo at Fort Sill. There is no evidence of such a visit.

50. *DR*, qtd. in *DL*, 12 February 1902.

51. For Brown's thesis, see Gottesman and Brown, *Violence in America*, 3:441–43, s.v., "Western War of Incorporation"; Brown, *No Duty to Retreat*, 189n13. Trachtman, *Gunfighters*, 198.

52. Monaghan, *Last of the Bad Men*, 17, 179.

EPILOGUE

1. *DL*, 25 November 1903.

2. *Las Vegas Democrat*, 31 May 1890; *New York National Police Gazette*, 10 December 1892; *Philadelphia Times*, 27 January 1895.

3. *Colorado Springs Telegraph*, qtd. in *DL*, 22 October 1903; Krakel, "Was Tom Horn Two Men?" 12–17, 52–56; *LOTH*.

4. Heard, "Killing of the Captain," 440–50. See "Rambler," 438, for a sketch of Heard.

5. Heard, "Killing of the Captain," 440–50.

6. White, *Arizona Nights*," 292–96; Alter, *Stewart Edward White*, 26–29.

7. Hooker, *When Geronimo Rode*, 84; Carmony, "Critical Essay," 41–45. See also Hooker, *Child of the Fighting Tenth*.

8. Lloyd, *Invaders*; Chapman, "Last War for the Cattle Range"; John L. Cowan, "Wars of the Range."

9. Siringo, *Cowboy Detective*; Siringo, *Two Evils Isms*.

10. Burns, *Saga of Billy the Kid*; Lake, *Wyatt Earp*.

11. Siringo, *Riata and Spurs*, 219–43; Walters, *Tombstone's Yesterdays*; Coolidge, *Fighting Men of the West*; Campbell, *Book Lover's Southwest*, 68; Cunningham, *Triggernometry*, 350–89. Allen, *Men of Daring*. For further criticism of writings about Tom Horn, see Adams, *Six-Guns and Saddle Leather*, 148–49 (for Coolidge), 10 (for Allen).

12. Ball, "Tom Horn and the 'Talking Boy' Controversy," 333–56. See Elise Coble's advertisement of Horn's autobiography for sale (*Arizona Historical Review* 2 [July 1929]:9). Chapman, "Tom Horn," 69–76, copy in Charles B. Gatewood Collection, AHC, roll 1. See Gatewood's letter to the editor, 11 April 1926, copy in Gatewood Collection, roll 7.

13. White, "Talking Boy," 18, 38–40. See also, Ball, "Tom Horn and the 'Talking Boy' Controversy," 333–56.

14. Mullins, "Inside Story," *DP*, 23 November–12 December 1930; Monaghan, *Last of the Bad Men*; Thrapp, *Encyclopedia of Frontier Biography*, 2:997–98, s.v. "James Jay Monaghan IV."

15. Krakel, *Saga of Tom Horn*; "Introduction," *LOTH*, vii–xiii.

16. Kuykendall, *Ghost Riders of the Mogollon*, vii–viii; Adams, *Six-Guns and Saddle Leather*, 377. In 2009 the Hermitage Book Shop, in Denver, offered this book for sale for $2,500.

17. Caesar, *Rifle for Rent*. This was an expanded version of Caesar's previous publication in *True, The Man's Magazine*, February 1961. Paine, *Tom Horn*; Adams, *Six-Guns and Saddle Leather*, 490, for Paine; Bakker, *Tracking Tom Horn*; Nunis, *The Life of Tom Horn Revisted*, 6.

18. Carlson, *Tom Horn: 'Killing Men,'* Tom Horn, and Joe LeFors.

19. Waldman, *Who Was Who in Native American History*, 156; Nash, *Encyclopedia of World Crime*, 2:1619–20; McLoughlin, *Wild and Woolly*, 235–37; *Dictionary of American Biography*, 5:230; *American National Biography*, 11:208–10.

20. Kantor, *Wicked Water*; Raine, "Tom Horn," clipping, *DP*, 23 January 1949, Tom Horn Biographical File, AHC; Blatt, "Wicked Water," 24 September 2006, http://tom -horn.com/forum/; Tuska and Piekarski, *Encyclopedia of Frontier and Western Fiction*, s.v. MacKinlay Kantor.

21. Henry, *I, Tom Horn*; Walker, "Henry's 'I, Tom Horn,'" *RMN*, 3 December 1989; "Emmett Harrington, Fine Books," catalogue 16, 2000, 54–55, for reference to the Western Writers of America poll; Tuska, *The American West:*, 301–302.

22. Fenady, *Claws of the Eagle*. This novel was later reissued under the title, *Tom Horn and the Apache Kid*. Chandler, *Wyoming Wind*; Brennan, *Greatest Cowboy Stories*, 157–66.

23. "Murder Is My Business," *Western Killers*, no. 60 (September 1948), available at Lone Star: Comics, Games, Gifts (http://mycomicshop.com); *Geronimo and His Apache Murderers* (New York: Avon, 1951). The author is indebted to William M. Clements, Professor of Folklore at Arkansas State University, for these items.

24. Kelly, *Outlaw Trail*, 306–16; Burt, "We Sing of Murder," 1–8.

25. Kouris, *Brown's Park*, 282; Tomlinson, *Geronimo After Kas-ke-yeh*, 59–60.

26. *DL*, 30 May 1902; Hall, "1913 Tom Horn Movie," 13 September 2002, http://read thewest1.community.everyone.net. Huey, *In Search of Hollywood*, 78. See http://www.silent movies.com/homthayter/tomhorn.htm.

27. Allan Radbourne, e-mail to author, 9 April 2007; Billy Blatt, "Wicked Water," 8 February 2006, http://tom-horn.com/forum/.

28. Boyer, "'Just-Couldn't-Miss' Just Doesn't Make It," clipping, *DP*, Tom Horn Biographical File, AHC; Bensen, *Mr. Horn*.

29. Clipping, *Casper Tribune*, 31 October 1979; Willon, "Tom Horn Movie Not Fact," clipping, *Eagle* [ca. 1979], both in Crime and Criminals, Tom Horn, WSA; clipping, *Casper Star*, 31 October 1979, Tom Horn Biographical Files, AHC. Prince, "Tom Horn: Dialectics of Power and Violence in the Old West," 119–29; Rosenstand, *Moral of the Story*, 545–49.

30. Saar, "Tom Horn Hits the Auction Block," 18.

31. Fireman, "Tom Horn, Good Man, Bad Man," *Arizona Crossroads*, Arizona Broadcasting System, aired 21 April 1941, 8:30 P.M., Fireman Collection, Arizona Historical Foundation, Arizona State University, 12-page typescript. Allan Radbourne, e-mail to author, 9 April 2007.

32. Adams, *Western Words*, 326; Pryor, *Outlaws and Gunslingers*, 182.

33. O'Neal, "A Rope for Tom Horn," in Knowles and Lansdale, *The West That Was*, 307–309. See 309 for a photograph of Horn's revolver and holster. *DT*, qtd. in *DL*, 10 March 1903; *DR*, [?] January 1904, qtd. in Thompson, "In Old Wyoming," *Wyoming State Tribune*, 4 May 1944, Tom Horn Biographical File, AHC; Johnson, "Walker Castle and Its Setting," 234–36. Johnson, a retired railroad man, related this recollection to a gathering at Walker Castle, 22 May 1949. *DL*, 27 January 1904.

34. *DR*, January 1904, qtd. in Thompson, "In Old Wyoming," *Wyoming State Tribune*, 4 May 1944, and clipping, *Rock River Review*, 8 April 1926, all in Tom Horn Biographical File, AHC; Spangenberger, "Blazing Their Way Into History," 27–34.

35. Herring, *Famous Firearms of the Old*, 120–36; Lauterborn, review of *Famous Firearms of the Old West*, 72, 75. See Newlin, letter to the editor, *Wild West*, August 2003, 8, for exchange with Johnny Boggs concerning Tom Horn's preferred rifle.

36. *DR*, qtd. in *DL*, 27 January 1904.

37. Clipping, *Laramie Daily Boomerang*, 22 August 1965, Crime and Criminals, Tom Horn, WSA, for Alice Cornelius's recollections. Howe, "Steamboat—King of the Buckers," 20–21, 45. The author is indebted to John Davis, a highly regarded Wyoming historian, for information about the horse, "Tom Horn."

38. Works Projects Administration, *Wyoming: A Guide*, 242, for Horn's "rock fortress." Clipping, *Lovell Chronicle*, 14 June 1928, Tom Horn Biographical File, AHC.

39. Clipping, *Wyoming State Tribune-Eagle*, 14, 15 June 1967, Tom Horn Biographical File, AHC; Cahill to "Dear Friend," in Wright, *Pardners*, xi–xii.

40. Author correspondence with Roy Lacey (Tom Horn).

41. Clipping, *DP*, 23 March 1947, Subject Files, Johnson County War, AHC; Baber, *Longest Rope*, 284; Bennitt, Works Projects Administration interview no. 578, WSA, 8; Paul Hutton, Department of History, University of New Mexico, to the author, 9 December 2009, copy in author's files.

42. Gibbs, "People of the Laramie Plains," 45, 56; Clipping, *Wyoming State Tribune*, 16 February 1958, Tom Horn Biographical File, AHC; Baber, *Longest Rope*, 284.

43. *DL*, 15 October 1902, 11 November 1903; Coe, *Juggling a Rope*, 111; Huseas, "Jekyll or Hyde?" clipping, *Guernsey Gazette*, 26 April 1976, Tom Horn Biographical File, AHC.

44. Benton, *Cowboy Life on the Sidetrack*, 9–11, 77.

45. Clipping, *Wyoming State Leader*, [?] June 1917, Tom Horn Biographical File, AHC; Krakel, "Introduction," *LOTH*, vii–xiii.

46. "Top Ten True Western Towns," *True West*, 26–31, 34–37, 40; "Update on the Downtown Cheyenne Fire," 24 September 2006, http://tom-horn.com/forum/; Chip Carlson, e-mail to author, 16 April 2001. See flyer, "Tom Horn Kick and Growl," copy in Dan L. Thrapp Collection, Nita Stewart Haley Memorial Library, Midland, Texas. For T-shirts, see http://cafepress.com.

47. *RMN*, 6, 17, 18 September 1993; clipping, *Arizona Republican*, 14 September 1993, and *Arizona Republic*, 14 September 1993, both in Clip Books, AHS; unid. clippings, 17, 18 September 1993, Crime and Criminals, Tom Horn, WSA; Carlson, *Tom Horn*, 308–309.

48. *Economist*, 25 September 1993; see chap. 15.

49. Carlson, "Caught in the Crossfire," 23–27; clipping, *DP*, 23 March 1947, Subject Files, Tom Horn, AHC.

Bibliography

PRIMARY SOURCES

United States Government Documents

Annual Reports of the Secretary of War 1881–86, 1896, 1898.
Federal Register, 1882.
National Archives, Washington, D.C.
    Record Group 20: U.S. Bureau of the Census.
        Tenth Census of the United States (1880). Microcopy T9.
        Twelfth Census of the United States (1900). Microcopy T623.
        Thirteenth Census of the United States (1910). Microcopy T624.
    Record Group 28: Post Office Department.
        Records of Appointment of Postmasters, 1832–30 September 1971. Microcopy M841.
    Record Group 60: Department of Justice.
        Letters Received. Department of Justice. Year files 6316–1892, 9396–1892, 10517–1892, 29763–1892, 1643–1898. Microfilm copy. Wyoming State Library and Archives, Cheyenne.
        Letters Sent by the Department of Justice: Instructions to U.S. Attorneys and Marshals, 1867–1904. Microcopy 701.
    Record Group 75: Records of the Bureau of Indian Affairs.
        Letters Received. Bureau of Indians Affairs. 1884.
        Letters Received by the Office of Indian Affairs, 1824–1881. Microcopy M234.
        Record of Agency Employees, 1853–1909. San Carlos, Arizona, 1884.
        Reports of Inspections of the Field Jurisdictions of the Office of Indian Affairs, 1873–1900. Microcopy 1070.
        Special Files of the Office of Indian Affairs, 1807–1904. Microcopy 574.
    Record Group 92: Records of the Office of the Quartermaster General.
        General Correspondence. Office of the Quartermaster General. 1817–1922.
        Office of the Quartermaster General. Document file 1890–1914.
        Reports of Persons and Articles Employed and Hired. Arizona, 1881–86, 1896, 1898.
        Subject and Name Card Index to Personnel of the Quartermaster Department
    Record Group 94: Records of the Adjutant General's Office, 1780s–1917.
        Appointment, Commission and Personal Branch Files.

Letters Received by the Office of the Adjutant General. Box 207. Document file 36697–1896.

Letters Received by the Office of the Adjutant General, Main Series, 1881–1889. Microcopy 689. Rolls 36–39, 96–97, 173–184.

Returns from U.S. Military Posts, 1800–1916. Microcopy M617.

Record Group 153: Records of the office of the Judge Advocate General. Army Court Martial Files. 1809–1894.

Record of Court of Inquiry in the Case of Captain Emmet Crawford, 3rd Cavalry, 21 April 1884–14 July 1884. Whipple Barracks, Arizona, RR 440.

Record Group 393: Records of U.S. Army Continental Commands, 1821–1920

Letters and Telegrams Received. Fort Grant, Arizona. 1873–1905.

Letters, Endorsements, and Telegrams Sent. Fort Bowie, Arizona. 1865–94.

Letters Received. Department of Arizona, 1886.

Letters Received. Fort Bowie, Arizona. 1886.

Letters Sent. Department of Arizona, 1886.

Letters Sent. Department of the Platte. 1892. Copies in Wyoming State Archives.

Letters Sent. Fort Bowie, Arizona. November 1873–October 1894 (Including District of Bowie, 1886–1887). Microfilm copy. University of Arizona Library.

Registers of Letters and Telegrams Received. Fort Huachuca, Arizona, 1885–86.

Record Group 395: Records of the U.S. Army Overseas Operations and Commands, 1898–1942, 5th Army Corps.

Letters Received. May–August 1898.

Orders Received. Chief Quartermaster. 1898.

Quartermaster Letters Received. April 19–May 20, 1898.

Quartermaster Letters Sent. April–May, 1898.

Register of Letters and Telegrams Received. 5th Army Corps. May–October 1898.

U.S. Congress

House. "Killing of Captain Crawford." Papers Relating to the Foreign Relations of the United States, 1886 to 1887. 49th Congress, 2nd session, 1887. Executive document 1. Serial 2460. Volume 1. 570–691, 724–31.

House. Letters from the Postmaster General, Transmitting a Report of the Offers Received under the Advertisement of October 15, 1880, and March 10, 1881, for the Carrying of the Mails. . . . 47th Congress, 1st session. Executive document 226. Serial 2033.

Senate. Letter from the Secretary of War, Transmitting, in Response to Resolution of February 11, 1887, Correspondence with General Miles Relative to the Surrender of Geronimo. 49th Congress, 2nd session, 1887. Executive document 117. Serial 2449.

Senate. Report of the Commission Appointed by the President to Investigate the Conduct of the War Department in the War with Spain. 56th Congress, 1st session, 1900. Executive document 221. Serial 3859–3866.

Archival Collections

American Heritage Center, University of Wyoming, Laramie

George Banks Collection

Amos Barber Scrapbook

Charles F. Bash Biographical File

E. W. Bennett Family Papers, 1883–1933

Biographical Files: Charles F. Bash; John C. Coble; Tom Horn; John A. Tisdale

Bosler Family Papers, 1864–1930

J. Elmer Brock Papers

T. Blake Kennedy Collection

Joseph LeFors Collection

Roy W. Lilley Interview

Charles Bingham Penrose Papers

Leslie Snow Collection

Agnes Wright Spring Collection

Subject Files: Johnson County War

Wyoming Stock Growers Association Collection

Arizona Department of Library and Archives, Phoenix

Leslie E. Gregory Papers. Works Projects Administration.

Arizona Historical Foundation, Hayden Library, Arizona State University, Tempe

Roscoe Willson Collection

Biographical Files: Tom Horn

Bert Fireman. "Tom Horn, Good Man and Bad Man." "Arizona Crossroads." Arizona
Broadcasting System. 21 April 1951. Script.

Arizona Historical Society, Tucson

Arizona Clip Books

Edward Arhelger Papers

Arizona Law Enforcement Collection

Will C. Barnes Collection

Charles T. Connell Papers

Dunlap Family Papers

Fish, Joseph. "History of Arizona." Unpublished manuscript. 1906.

Flake, Osmer D. "Some Reminiscences of the Pleasant Valley War and Causes That Led
Up to It." In Levi S. Udall Collection.

Charles B. Gatewood, Jr., Collection

Hazelton, Drusilla. "The Tonto Basin's Early Settlers." Unpublished manuscript.

John Plesent Gray Papers

Leslie E. Gregory Collection

Anton Mazzanovich Collection

Ming, Marcus A. S. "Biographical Sketch of Daniel Huston Ming." Ming Family Papers.
1888–1951.

Frank E. Murphy Biographical File

Dan R. Williamson Papers

Thomas N. Wills Papers

Clara Woody Collection

Arizona State University, Tempe, Hayden Library, Special Collections Department

H. Ryder Ridgway Collection

Colorado State History Society, Denver

Anna B. Bassett Vertical File

Boulder City Directory, 1895

Civil Works Administration Pamphlet Files: Tom Blevins; A. G. Wallihan; E. V. Houghy

Colorado State Business Directory, 1890, 1904

Dawson Scrapbooks

Denver City Directory, 1891, 1903

Hoy, J. S. "The History of Brown's Park." Unpublished manuscript.

Leadville City Directory, 1880, 1881

Henry Miller Porter Papers
Denver Public Library, Western History Collections
    Cyrus W. "Doc" Shores Collection
Harold B. Lee Library, Brigham Young University, Salt Lake City
    Charles Kelly Papers (Xerox copy)
Jim Gatchell Museum, Buffalo, Wyoming
    James F. Dillinger Interview
Kansas State Historical Society, Topeka
    Clippings Files
    Kansas Tract Books. Volume 97. Roll 352.
Library of Congress (Washington, D.C.)
    Hermann Hagedorn Papers
    Henry Lawton Papers
    Nelson A. Miles Family Papers
    Pinkerton National Detective Agency Papers
    Leonard Wood Diaries
Nebraska State Historical Society, Lincoln
    John Gregory Bourke Papers
Nita Stewart Haley Memorial Library and History Center, Midland, Texas
    Dan L. Thrapp Collection
Rutherford B. Hayes Presidential Library, Fremont, Ohio
    Letter Books of George Crook
Salem Public Library, Oregon
    Lake Labish Train Wreck (Xerox copy)
Sharlot Hall Museum, Prescott
    Roscoe G. Willson Scrapbooks
South Dakota Historical Resource Center, Pierre
    Benjamin C. Ash Papers
University of Arizona Library, Tucson
    Anton Mazzanovich Collection. Special Collections Department.
University of California Library, Santa Barbara, Special Collections Department
    Jay Monaghan Papers, William Wyles Collection
University of Nevada, Reno, Special Collections Department,
    State of Nevada v. Thomas Horn. Case 2832. 1891. (Xerox copy)
University of New Mexico, Albuquerque, Zimmermann Library, Center for Southwest
    Studies
    John Gregory Bourke Diary (photostatic copy)
    Angus McDonald Papers
University of Utah, Salt Lake City
    Charles Kelly Papers (Xerox copies)
Wyoming State Archives and Library, Cheyenne
    Roy T. Armstrong Papers
    Attorney General. *Horn v. State.* Letterpress Books.
    Frank A. Hadsell Collection
    Horn v. State, 12 Wyo. 80, 73 Pac. 705 (Wyo. 1903).
    John Clay, Jr., File
    Coroner's Inquest. In the Matter of the Killing of William Nickells [*sic*]. 20 July–15 August 1901.

Crime and Criminals: Tom Horn
"Johnson County War"
T. Blake Kennedy Collection
Laramie County Clerk of Court. Criminal Docket 4–58. *State of Wyoming v. Tom Horn.*
"Law Enforcement Officers, Sheriffs, Marshals, et al."
Glenn L. Melton. "Henry Melton's Recollections of Tom Horn."
McPherren, Ida. "Livestock Industry—Rustling." Works Projects Administration files.
Millyard, Mrs. B. H. As told to H. Ridgely. "The Re-Capture of Tom Horn in 1902."
Ohnhaus, John. "Early Settler in Cheyenne."
Potter, Charles N., comp. *Cases Decided in the Supreme Court of Wyoming from August 3, 1901, to April 25, 1904.* Volume 12.
Stumpf, George R. "United States Marshals and Deputies of Wyoming, 1869–1978."
Vertical Files, Tom Horn
Wilkerson Biographical Collection
Works Projects Administration Subject, Biographical Files, and Interviews
    William Asa "Dad" Bennitt. 29 June 1936.
    Hiram Burch
    Carbon County—Crime and Criminals
    Ed Kassahn Interview
    G. E. Lemmon, Sam Moses—Deputy U.S. Marshall [sic] and Detective, 1891–1892.
    Mary Powell
    Mrs. Minnie A. Rietz
    Sackett, Charline. "Bill Speck."
    Charles H. Tolson

Newspapers

Albuquerque Daily Democrat, 21 June 1883
Apache Review (St. Johns), 30 May–26 December 1888
Arizona Daily Democrat (Prescott), 21 June 1883
Arizona Daily Gazette (Phoenix), 15 October 1889–11 March 1890
Arizona Daily Star (Tucson), 15 April–14 August 1884, 6 February–16 May 1886, 14 May 1889–11 May 1890
Arizona Silver Belt (Globe), 7 February 1879–31 December 1882, 1 January 1884–15 November 1890, 8 July 1897–12 May 1898
Arizona Weekly Star, 1 January 1880–31 December 1889
Army and Navy Journal, 6 August 1881–23 October 1886, 18 May 1889–7 June 1890, 2 April–5 November 1898, 17 April, 3 July 1909, 18 March, 1 April 1911
Boston Herald, 15 April–20 September 1898
Boulder Daily Camera (Colorado), 14 September 1969
Buffalo Bulletin (Wyoming), 1 October 1891–16 May 1905
Burrton Monitor (Kansas), 20 May 1881–6 January 1882
Burrton Telephone (Kansas), 2 November 1878–22 April 1881
Carbon County Journal (Rawlins, Wyoming), 8 October 1891, 2 April–5 November 1892, 6 January–22 December 1894, 10 August–28 December 1895, 1 January–30 April 1898, 1 July–9 December 1899, 3–16 June 1900, 5 January–28 December 1901, 3 January 1903, 16 January–6 May 1904
Casper Derrick, 28 April 1898.

Cheyenne Daily Leader and *Sun-Leader*, 14 July 1891–31 December 1895, 1 January–31 December 1897, 1 January 1899–23 April 1904, 14 January–28 February 1905, 5 December 1914

Cheyenne Daily Sun, 10 July 1891–28 February 1895

Chicago Daily Tribune, 3 May–9 October 1892, 21 November 1903

Colorado Chieftain (Pueblo), 10 September 1891

Colorado Sun (Denver), 1 November 1891–24 April 1892

Commercial Advertiser (New York), 10 April–15 September 1892

Daily Boomerang (Laramie, Wyoming), 14–17 November 1893, 2 August–23 October 1895, 1 April–15 May, 7 September–6 October 1898, 22 January 1900–6 April 1904, 13 January 1941

Daily Citizen (Tucson), 23 May 1885–24 September 1886, 2 May 1889–30 June 1890

Daily Epitaph (Tombstone, Arizona), 14 May 1889–8 February 1890, 3 May–16 August 1896, 10 April–29 May 1898

Daily Nevada State Journal (Reno), 8 April–31 October 1891

Dawes County Journal (Chadron, Nebraska), 9 June 1899–1 June 1900

Denver Evening Post, 17 April 1899.

Denver Post (Colorado), 1 July–31 December 1895, 18 April–9 September 1898, 2–30 March, 7–19 October 1902, 26 January 1903, 1–30 April 1904, 12 August 1911, 19 May 1919, 15 April 1928, 23 November–12 December 1930, 27 November 1932, 8 February 1953

Denver Republican (Colorado), 22 January 1890, 1 September 1891–17 January 1902, 15 April–27 September 1898, 28 September–27 October 1902, 19 November–22 November 1903

Denver Times (Colorado), 16 July 1891–2 May 1892, 23 April–23 September 1898, 30 January 1900, 7 October 1901, 24 September–20 November 1902, 19 August 1903–18 April 1904

Fort Worth Gazette (Texas), 29 October 1891

Frank Leslie's Weekly, 2 June 1892

Gunnison Tribune (Colorado), 7 November 1891

Harvey County News (Newton, Kansas), 3 January 1878–12 June 1879

Hoof and Horn (Prescott, Arizona), 1885–1889

Hutchinson News (Kansas), 19 November 1903

Kansas City Times (Missouri), 7 October 1937

Laramie Boomerang (Wyoming), 14–17 November 1893, 5 August–23 October 1895, 1 April–6 October 1898, 30 August–25 September 1900, 1901–1904, 1941

Laramie Republican (Wyoming), 1 November–31 December 1895, 1–30 April, 1 September–29 December 1897, 1 July–30 November 1898, January–May 1900, 2–25 November 1903

Laramie Republican (Wyoming), 13 October–3 November 1892, 2 January 1894–30 April 1894, 9–10 November 1903

Las Vegas Democrat (New Mexico, weekly), 10 May–1 November 1890

Leadville Democrat (Colorado), 9 July 1880

Lincoln Evening News (Nebraska), 6 February 1900

Los Angeles Times, 21 November 1903

Memphis Conservative (Missouri), 26 February 1869–21 July 1881

Memphis Reveille (Missouri), 9 September 1865–6 October 1904

Mohave County Miner (Kingman, Arizona), 23 February 1901

Morning Oregonian (Salem), 1 November 1890–15 May 1891

Natrona County Tribune (Casper, Wyoming), 13 July 1899

Newton Kansan, 5, 12 November 1891

New York Commercial Advertiser, 19 April 1892

New York Herald, 6 June–22 September 1886

New York National Police Gazette, 10 December 1892

New York Times, 16 February 1879–21 November 1903 (by index)

New York World, 16 January–28 February 1902

Omaha Daily Bee (Nebraska), 1 December 1897–30 September 1898, 22 December 1899–
    10 March 1900

Omaha Evening Bee (Nebraska), 1 June–9 November 1899

Omaha World Herald (Nebraska), 1 April–30 September 1898

Philadelphia Times (Pennsylvania), 27 January 1895

Phoenix Herald (Arizona), 18–22 October 1888, 14 October–2 December 1889

Prescott Courier (Arizona), 27 May 1882, 14 January–30 December 1887

Rocky Mountain News (Denver), 1 January–27 September 1890, 31 July 1891–1 December
    1894, 1 January 1896–31 January 1903, 30 April 1904

Salt Lake Herald (Utah), 1 January 1898–1 March 1900

Salt Lake Tribune (Utah), 1 November 1898–28 February 1899

San Francisco Chronicle (California), 9 December 1882, 22 June–23 October 1886, 21 No-
    vember 1903

Semi-Weekly Standard (Ogden, Utah), 1 April–29 July 1893

Southwestern Stockman (Willcox, Arizona), 3 January–31 October 1885, 11 May 1889–17 May
    1890

St. Louis Globe-Democrat (Missouri), 20 January–30 April 1886, 3 April–30 September 1898

St. Louis Post Dispatch (Missouri), 15 April–31 July 1898

Sulphur Valley News (Willcox, Arizona), 12 May–22 September 1896

Tombstone Daily Epitaph (Arizona), 14 May 1889–8 February 1890, 1894–1898

Tombstone Prospector (Arizona), 27 June–1 October 1896

Toronto Sunday World (Canada), 28 March 1915

Valley Bulletin, Graham County Bulletin, and *Arizona Bulletin* (Solomonville), 1889–1904

Washington Post, 21 November 1903

Weekly Journal-Miner (Prescott, Arizona), 26 August 1881–9 June 1882, 1 January 1889–
    31 December 1890

Wheatland Times (Wyoming, Souvenir Edition), 10 August 1933

Winners of the West (St. Joseph, Missouri), 1924–1944

Wyoming Daily Tribune (Cheyenne), 16 February, 7 June 1896, 27 January–22 April 1900,
    20, 24 November 1903, 23, 30 April 1904

Books

Baber, Daisy F. As told by Bill Walker. *Injun Summer: An Old Cowhand Rides the Ghost
    Trails.* Caldwell, ID: Caxton Press, 1952.

————. *The Longest Rope: The Truth about the Johnson County Cattle War.* Caldwell, ID:
    Caxton Printers, 1953.

Bacon, Alexander S. *The Seventy-First at San Juan: A Brochure.* 2nd edition. New York:
    Cortlandt Press, 1902.

Bailey, Lynn R., ed. *The Devil Has Foreclosed: The Private Journal of George Whitwell Parsons.*
    Vol. 2, *The Concluding Arizona Years, 1882–87.* Tucson: Westernlore Press, 1997.

Ball, Eve. *Indeh: An Apache Odyssey*. Norman: University of Oklahoma, 1967.

Barnes, Will C. *Apaches and Longhorns: The Reminiscences of Will C. Barnes*. Edited by Frank C. Lockwood. Tucson: University of Arizona, 1982. First published 1941.

Benton, Frank. *Cowboy Life on the Sidetrack*. Denver: Western Stories Syndicate, 1903.

Betzinez, Jason. *I Fought with Geronimo*. Harrisburg, PA: Stackpole, 1959.

Bigelow, John Jr. *On the Bloody Trail of Geronimo*. Edited by Arthur Woodward. Los Angeles: Westernlore Press, 1968.

Bisbee, William H. *Through Four American Wars*. Boston: Meador, 1931.

Bourke, John Gregory. *An Apache Campaign in the Sierra Madre: An Account of the Expedition in Pursuit of Hostile Chiricahua Apaches in the Spring of 1883*. New York: Charles Scribner's Sons, 1958. First published 1886.

Carlson, Chip, ed. *Joe LeFors, "I Slickered Tom Horn": The History of the Texas Cowboy Turned Montana-Wyoming Lawman, A Sequel*. Cheyenne, WY: Beartooth Corral, 1995.

Carmony, Neil B., ed. *Apache Days and Tombstone Nights: John Clum's Autobiography, 1877–1887*. Silver City, NM: High Lonesome Press, 1997.

Carroll, John M., ed. *The Papers of the Order of Indian Wars*. Fort Collins, CO: Old Army Press, 1975.

Center of Military History, United States Army. *Correspondence Relating to the War with Spain, Including the Insurrection in the Philippine Islands and the China Relief Expedition, April 15, 1898, to July 30, 1902*. 2 vols. Washington, D.C.: Center of Military History, 1993. First published 1902.

Chatterton, Fenimore. *Yesterday's Wyoming: The Intimate Memoirs of Fenimore Chatterton, Territorial Citizen, Governor and Statesman*. Aurora, CO: Powder River, 1957.

Chicago Record's War Stories. Chicago: The Record, 1898.

Clardy, Susan, ed. *Sometimes the Blues: The Letters and Diaries of Frank Hammon, a Lonely Frontiersman in Globe and Phoenix, 1882–1889*. Tucson: Arizona Historical Society, 2007.

Clay, John. *My Life on the Range*. Norman: University of Oklahoma Press, 1962. First published 1924.

Clover, Samuel T. *On Special Assignment*. Boston: Lothrop, 1903.

Corbusier, William T. *Verde to San Carlos: Recollections of a Famous Army Surgeon and His Observant Family on the Western Frontier, 1869–1886*. Tucson: Dale Stuart, 1968.

Coston, William H. *The Spanish-American War Volunteer*. 2nd rev. ed. Freeport, NY: Books for Libraries, 1971. First published 1899.

Cowan, Robert Ellsworth. *Range Rider*. Garden City, NJ: Doubleday, Doran, 1930.

Cozzens, Peter, ed. *The Struggle for Apacheria*. Vol. 1 of *Eyewitnesses to the Indian Wars, 1865–1890*. 4 Vols. Mechanicsburg, PA: Stackpole Books, 2001.

Crook, George. *General George Crook: His Autobiography*. Edited and annotated by Martin F. Schmitt and Joseph C. Porter. Norman: University of Oklahoma, 1986. First published 1946.

Cruse, Thomas. *Apache Days and After*. Lincoln: University of Nebraska Press, 1987. First published 1941.

Davis, Britton. *The Truth about Geronimo*. Edited by Milo M. Quaife. Lincoln: University of Nebraska Press, 1976. First published 1929.

Downing, C. V., as told to Sharon Smith. *Stories of the North Platte Valley*. N.p., 1971.

El Comancho [Walter Shelley Phillips]. *The Old Timer's Tale*. Chicago: Canterbury Press, 1929.

Farlow, Edward T. *Wind River Adventures: My Life in Frontier Wyoming*. Glendo, WY: High Plains Press, 1998.

Frison, Paul, ed. *The Apache Slave: "Life of Charles Wells."* Worland, WY: privately printed, 1969.

Ganzhorn, Jack. *I've Killed Men: An Epic of Early Arizona.* New York: Devin-Adair, 1959. First published London: Robert Hale, 1940.

Goodwin, Grenville, and Neil Goodwin. *The Apache Diaries: A Father-Son Journey.* Lincoln: University of Nebraska Press, 2000.

Gray, John Plesent. *When All Roads Led to Tombstone: A Memoir.* Edited by W. Lane Rogers. Boise, ID: Tamarack Books, 1998.

Hanson, Margaret Brock, ed. *Powder River Country: The Papers of J. Elmer Brock.* Cheyenne: Frontier Printing, 1981.

Hemment, John C. *Cannon and Camera: Sea and Land Battles of the Spanish-American War in Cuba, Camp Life, and the Return of the Soldiers.* New York: D. Appleton, 1898.

Hooker, Forrestine. *Child of the Fighting Tenth: On the Frontier with the Buffalo Soldiers.* Edited by Steve Wilson. New York: Oxford University, 2003.

Horn, Tom. *Life of Tom Horn: Government Scout and Interpreter. Written by Himself, Together with His Letters and Statements by His Friends. A Vindication.* Denver: Louthan Book Company (for John C. Coble), 1904.

———. *Life of Tom Horn: Government Scout and Interpreter. Written by Himself, Together with His Letters and Statements by His Friends. A Vindication.* Introduction by Dean Krakel. Western Frontier Library Series 26. Norman: University of Oklahoma, 1964.

———. *Life of Tom Horn: Government Scout and Interpreter. Written by Himself, Together with His Letters and Statements by His Friends. A Vindication.* Edited and annotated by Doyce B. Nunis, Jr. Chicago: R. R. Donnelley and Sons, Lakeside Press Classics, 1967.

———. *Life of Tom Horn: Government Scout and Interpreter. Written by Himself, Together with His Letters and Statements by His Friends. A Vindication.* Introduction by John Greenway. Rio Grande Classics. Glorieta, NM: Rio Grande Press, 1976.

———. *Life of Tom Horn: Government Scout and Interpreter. Written by Himself, Together with His Letters and Statements by His Friends. A Vindication.* Introduction by James D. Horan. New York: Jinglebob Press, 1977.

———. *Life of Tom Horn: Government Scout and Interpreter. Written by Himself, Together with His Letters and Statements by His Friends. A Vindication.* Facsimile edition. Provo, UT: Triton Press, 1988.

———. *Life of Tom Horn: Government Scout and Interpreter. Written by Himself, Together with His Letters and Statements by His Friends. A Vindication.* Temecula, CA: Reprint Services, 1991.

———. *Life of Tom Horn: Government Scout and Interpreter. Written by Himself, Together with His Letters and Statements by His Friends. A Vindication.* Santa Barbara, CA: Narrative Press, 2001.

Humphrey, Charles F. *Expedition to Santiago de Cuba, Under the Command of Major General William R. Shafter, U. S. V.* Washington, D.C.: War Department, 1898.

Kraft, Louis. *Gatewood and Geronimo* (Albuquerque: University of New Mexico Press, 2000).

———, ed. *Lt. Charles Gatewood and His Apache Wars Memoirs.* Lincoln: University of Nebraska Press, 2005.

Lane, Jack C., ed. *Chasing Geronimo: The Journal of Leonard Wood, May–September, 1886.* Albuquerque: University of New Mexico Press, 1970.

LeFors, Joe. *Wyoming Peace Officer: An Autobiography.* Edited by Agnes Wright Spring. Laramie, WY: Laramie Printers, 1953.

Letters from Old Friends and Members of the Wyoming Stock Growers Association. Cheyenne, WY: S. A. Bristol, 1923.

Mazzanovich, Anton. *Trailing Geronimo.* 3rd edition. Hollywood, CA: printed by the author, 1931.

McCoy, Tim. *Tim McCoy Remembers the West: An Autobiography.* With the assistance of Ronald McCoy. Garden City, NY: Doubleday, 1977.

Miles, Nelson A. *Personal Recollections and Observations of General Nelson A. Miles.* Chicago: Werner, 1896.

Miley, John D. *In Cuba with Shafter.* New York: Charles Scribner's Sons, 1899.

Pauly, Nell, ed. *The Last of the Rogersons: 95 Years of Colorado Pioneer History—Horse, Cattle and Sheep Lore, Memoirs of Robert (Bob) Rogerson.* N.p.: n.d.

Penrose, Charles B. *The Rustler Business.* Edited by Keith S. Rider. Douglas, WY: Douglas Budget, n.d.

Rockwell, Wilson, ed. *Memoirs of a Lawman* [Cyrus W. Shores]. Denver: Sage Books, 1962.

Rollinson, John K. *Pony Trails in Wyoming: Hoofprints of a Cowboy and U.S. Ranger.* Edited by Earl A. Brininstool. Lincoln: University of Nebraska Press, 1988. First published Caldwell, ID: Caxton, 1941.

Rynning, Thomas H. *Gun Notches: The Life Story of a Cowboy-Soldier.* New York: A. L. Burt, 1931.

Scott, Robert G., ed. *Forgotten Valor: The Memoirs, Journals and Civil War Letters of Orlando B. Willcox.* Kent, OH: Kent State University Press, 1999.

Siringo, Charles A. *A Cowboy Detective: A True Story of Twenty-Two Years with a World-Famous Detective Agency.* Introduction by Frank Morn. Lincoln: University of Nebraska Press, 1988. First published 1912.

———. *Riata and Spurs: The Story of a Lifetime Spent in the Saddle as Cowboy and Detective.* Boston: Houghton Mifflin, 1927.

———. *Two Evil Isms: Pinkertonism and Anarchism.* Chicago: printed by the author, 1915. Facsimile of the first edition. Austin, TX: Steck-Vaughn, 1967.

Society of Santiago de Cuba. *The Santiago Campaign: Reminiscences of the Operations for the Capture of Santiago de Cuba in the Spanish-American War, June and July, 1898.* Richmond, VA: Williams Printing, 1927.

Spring, Agnes Wright. *Near the Greats.* Frederick, CO: Platte 'N Press, 1981.

Tittsworth, William G. *Outskirt Episodes.* Foreword by Chuck Parsons. Green River, WY: Sweetwater County Historical Museum, 2006. First published Avoca, IA: printed by the author, 1927.

Wheeler, Joseph. *The Santiago Campaign, 1898.* Port Washington, NY: Kennikat, n.d. First published 1898.

Wright, Edgar. *Pardners.* Foreword by T. Joe Cahill. New York: Vantage Press, 1958.

Articles

Allen, Thomas C. Letter to the Editor. *True West* 11 (January–February 1964): 4, 58.

Byars, Charles, ed. "Gatewood Reports to His Wife from Geronimo's Camp." *Journal of Arizona History* 7 (Summer 1966): 76–81.

Daly, Henry W. "The Capture of Geronimo." *American Legion Monthly* 8 (June 1930): 30, 42–45.

———. "Following the Bell." *The American Veteran.* (February 1928): 111–17.

——. "The Geronimo Campaign." *Journal of the United States Cavalry Association* 19 (July 1908): 68–103; 20 (October 1908): 247–62.

——. "Scouts, Good and Bad." *American Legion Monthly* 6 (August 1928): 24–25, 66, 68–70.

El Comancho [Walter Shelley Phillips]. "Come, Listen in with Me." *Outdoor Life* (April 1926): 279.

Elliott, Charles P. "The Geronimo Campaign of 1885–6." *Journal of the United States Cavalry Association* 21 (September 1910): 211–36.

——. "An Indian Reservation under General George Crook." *Military Affairs* 12 (Summer 1948): 91–102.

Gatewood, Jr., Charles B., comp. "Lieut. Chas. B. Gatewood, 6th U.S. Cavalry, and the Surrender of Geronimo." *Arizona Historical Review* 4 (April 1931): 29–44.

Goodwin, Grenville, ed. "Experiences of an Indian Scout: Excerpts from the Life of John Rope." *Arizona Historical Review* 7 (January 1936): 31–68, (April 1936): 31–73.

Hanna, Robert. "With Crawford in Mexico." *Arizona Historical Review* 6 (April 1935): 56–65.

Helper, Morris, as told by Edwin J. Smalley. "Smashing the West's Murdering Horseman." *Famous Detective Cases* 1 (August 1935): 4–9, 93–97.

Jones, Virginia H. "Fifty Years Ago." *Annals of Wyoming* 25 (January 1953): 22–40.

McClernand, E. J. "The Santiago Campaign." *Infantry Journal* 21 (September 1922): 280–302.

Morgan, George H. "The Fight at the Big Dry Wash in the Mogollon Mountains, Arizona, July 17, 1882, with Renegade Apache Scouts from the San Carlos Indian Reservation." *Proceedings of the Annual Meeting of the Order of Indian Wars of the United States* (February 24, 1940): 21–28.

Pettit, James S. "Apache Campaign Notes—'86." *Journal of the Military Service Institution of the United States* 7 (1886): 331–38.

Prentice, Royal A. "The Rough Riders." *New Mexico Historical Review.* Pts. 1 and 2. 26 (October 1951): 261–76; 27 (January 1952): 29–50.

Remington, Frederic. "With the Fifth Corps." *Harper's New Monthly Magazine.* 97 (October 1898): 963–72.

Rosentreter, G. W. "My Cowboy Experiences in the 1890's." *Annals of Wyoming* 37 (October 1965): 221–33.

Serven, James E. "Recollections of Geronimo's Final Surrender." *The Smoke Signal* (Tucson Corral of Westerners), no. 31 (Spring 1974): 225–31.

Shafter, William H. "The Capture of Santiago De Cuba." *Century Illustrated Monthly*, n. s., 35 (February 1899): 612–30.

Shipp, William E. "Captain Crawford's Last Expedition." *Journal of the United States Cavalry Association* 5 (December 1892): 343–61.

Stout, Joe A., Jr., ed. "Soldiering and Suffering in the Geronimo Campaign: Reminiscences of Lawrence R. Jerome." *Journal of the West* 11 (January 1972): 154–69.

Ward, C. H. "A Trip to the Cavalry Camps in Southern Arizona." *Cosmopolitan* 2 (1887): 109–14.

Whitney, Caspar. "The Santiago Campaign." *Harper's New Monthly* 97 (October 1898): 803–18.

Williamson, Dan R. "Story of Oskay De No Tah: 'The Flying Fighter.'" *Arizona Historical Review* 3 (October 1930): 78–83.

Willis, Ann Bassett. "'Queen Ann' of Brown's Park." *Colorado Magazine* 29 (April 1952): 81–98; 30 (January 1953): 58–76.

SECONDARY SOURCES

Books, Dissertations, and Film Scripts

Allen, [Benjamin] Stookie. *Men of Daring*. New York: Cupples and Leon, 1933.

Alter, Judy. *Stewart Edward White*. Boise, ID: Boise State University Press, 1975.

Bailey, Lynn R. *Henry Clay Hooker and the Sierra Bonita*. Tucson: Westernlore Press, 1998.

———. *"We'll All Wear Silk Hats": The Erie and Chiricahua Cattle Companies and the Rise of Corporate Ranching in the Sulphur Springs Valley of Arizona, 1883–1909*. Tucson: Westernlore Press, 1994.

———. *White Apache: The Life and Times of Zebina Nathaniel Streeter*. Tucson: Westernlore Press, 2010.

Bakker, Johan P. *Tracking Tom Horn*. Union Lake, MI: Talking Boy, 1994.

Ball, Larry D. *Desert Lawmen: The High Sheriffs of New Mexico and Arizona, 1846–1912*. Albuquerque: University of New Mexico Press, 1992.

———. "Tom Horn: Rogue Frontiersman." Chapter 4 of Richard W. Etulain and Glenda Riley, eds., *With Badges and Bullets: Lawmen and Outlaws in the Old West*, 70–86. Golden, CO: Fulcrum, 1999.

———. *The United States Marshals of New Mexico and Arizona Territories, 1846–1912*. Albuquerque: University of New Mexico Press, 1978.

Bartlett, Ichabod S., ed. *History of Wyoming*. 4 vols. Chicago, IL: S. J. Clarke, 1918–19.

Bensen, D. R. *Mr. Horn*. New York: Dell, 1978.

Birkhead, Frances B., ed. *Wyoming: From Territorial Days to the Present*. Chicago: American Historical Society, 1933.

Brayer, Herbert O. *Range Murder: The Red Sash Gang Dry-Gulched Deputy United States Marshal George Wellman*. Evanston, IL: Branding Iron Press, 1955.

Brennan, Stephen. *The Greatest Cowboy Stories Ever Told: Incredible Tales of the Western Frontier*. Guilford, CT: Lyons Press, 2004.

Bret-Harte, John. "The San Carlos Indian Reservation, 1872–1886: An Administrative History." 2 vols. PhD diss., University of Arizona, 1972.

Brown, Larry K. *Coyotes and Canaries: Characters Who Made the West Wild . . . and Wonderful!* Glendo, WY: High Plains Press, 2002.

Brown, Richard Maxwell. *No Duty to Retreat: Violence and Values in American History and Society*. New York: Oxford University Press, 1991.

Burns, Robert Homer, Andrew Springs Gillespie, and Willing Gay Richardson. *Wyoming's Pioneer Ranches*. Laramie, WY: Top-of-the-World Press, 1955.

Burns, Walter Noble. *The Saga of Billy the Kid*. Garden City, NY: Doubleday and Page, 1926.

Burroughs, John Rolfe. *Guardian of the Grasslands: The First Hundred Years of the Wyoming Stock Growers Association*. Cheyenne, WY: Pioneer Printing and Stationery, 1971.

———. *Where the Old West Stayed Young*. New York: William Morrow, 1962.

Burton, Jeffrey. *The Deadliest Outlaws*. N.p.: Palomino Books, 2006.

Caesar, Gene. *Rifle for Rent*. Derby, CT: Monarch Books, 1963.

Camp, Charles. *Muggins the Cow Horse*. Denver: Welch-Haffner, 1928.

Carlock, Robert H. *The Hashknife: The Early Days of the Aztec Land and Cattle Company, Limited*. Tucson: Westernlore, 1994.

Carlson, Chip. *Tom Horn, Blood on the Moon: Dark History of the Murderous Cattle Detective.* Glendo, WY: High Plains Press, 2001.

———. *Tom Horn: "Killing Men Is My Specialty . . .": The Definitive History of the Notorious Wyoming Stock Detective.* Cheyenne, WY: Beartooth Corral, 1991.

Chandler, Jon. *Wyoming Wind: A Novel of Tom Horn.* New York: Dorchester, 2002.

Coe, Charles H. *Juggling A Rope: Lariat Roping and Spinning Knots and Splices, Also the Truth about Tom Horn, "King of the Cowboys."* Pendleton, OR: Hamley, 1927.

Collins, Charles. *Apache Nightmare: The Battle of Cibicue Creek.* Norman: University of Oklahoma Press, 1999.

———. *The Great Escape: The Apache Outbreak of 1881.* Tucson: Westernlore Press, 1994.

Coolidge, Dane. *Fighting Men of the West.* New York: E. P. Dutton, 1932.

Cosmas, Graham. *Army for Empire.* Columbia, MO: University of Missouri Press, 1971.

Coutant, Charles G. *History of Wyoming (and the Far West), Embracing an Account of the Spanish, Canadian and American Explorations.* 2 volumes. New York: Argonaut Press, 1966. First published 1919.

Cunningham, Eugene. *Triggernometry: A Gallery of Gunfighters.* Caldwell, ID: Caxton Printers, 1958. First published New York: Press of the Pioneers, 1934.

Dale, Edward Everett. *The Range Cattle Industry: Ranching on the Great Plains from 1865 to 1925.* Norman: University of Oklahoma Press, 1960.

Daly, Henry W. *Manual of Pack Transportation.* Geneva: Long Riders' Guild Press, n.d. First published 1908.

Davis, John W. *Wyoming Range War: The Infamous Invasion of Johnson County.* Norman: University of Oklahoma Press, 2010.

Day, Mike. *A Short Family History of Tom Horn, His Parents and Siblings.* Wichita: privately printed, 2004.

DeArment, Robert K. *Alias Frank Canton.* Norman: University of Oklahoma Press, 1996.

Debo, Angie. *Geronimo: The Man, His Time, His Place.* Norman: University of Oklahoma Press, 1989. First published 1976.

Dedera, Don. *A Little War of Our Own: The Pleasant Valley Feud Revisited.* Flagstaff: Northland Press, 1988.

DeJournette, Dick and Dawn. *One Hundred Years of Brown's Park and Diamond Mountain.* Vernal, UT: DeJournette Enterprises, 1996.

De la Garza, Phyllis. *The Apache Kid.* Tucson: Westernlore Press, 1995.

Dewey, Ernest. *Legends of the Wheat Country.* N.p.: privately printed, n.d.

Drago, Harry Sinclair. *The Legend Makers.* New York: Dodd, Mead, 1975.

Dugan, Mark. *The Making of Legends: More True Stories of Frontier America.* Athens, Ohio: Swallow Press, 1997.

———. *Tales Never Told around the Campfire: True Stories of Frontier America.* Athens, Ohio: Swallow Press, 1992.

Dunham, Dick, and Vivian Dunham. *Flaming Gorge: A History of Daggett County, Utah.* Manila, Utah: Daggett County Lion's Club, 1977.

Dunlay, Thomas W. *Wolves for the Blue Soldiers: Indian Scouts and Auxillaries with the United States Army, 1860–91.* Lincoln: University of Nebraska Press, 1982.

Ernst, Donna B. *Harvey Logan: Wildest of the Wild Bunch.* Kearny, NB: Morris, 2003.

———. *The Sundance Kid: The Life of Harry Alonzo Longabaugh.* Norman: University of Oklahoma Press, 2009.

Erwin, Allen A. *The Southwest of John Horton Slaughter, 1841–1922: Pioneer Cattleman and Trail-Driver of Texas, the Pecos, and Arizona and Sheriff of Tombstone.* Glendale, CA: Arthur H. Clark,1965.

Essin, Emmett M. *Shavetails and Bell Sharps: The History of the U.S. Army Mule.* Lincoln: University of Nebraska Press, 1997.

Faulk, Odie B. *The Geronimo Campaign.* New York: Oxford University Press, 1969.

Fenady, Andrew J. *Claws of the Eagle: A Novel of Tom Horn and the Apache Kid.* New York: Walkerand, 1984.

Field, Sharon Lass, ed. *History of Cheyenne, Wyoming.* 2 vols. Dallas: Curtis Media, 1989.

Forrest, Earle R. *Arizona's Dark and Bloody Ground.* Revised and enlarged. Caldwell, ID: Caxton Printers, 1959. First published Caldwell, ID: Caxton, 1936.

Fowler, Gene. *Timber Line: A Story of Bonfils and Tammen.* New York: Covici-Friede, 1933.

Fradkin, Philip L. *Sagebrush Country: Land and the American West.* Tucson: University of Arizona Press, 1989.

Frye, Elnora L. *Atlas of Wyoming Outlaws at the Territorial Penitentiary.* Cheyenne: Wyoming Territorial Prison, 1990.

Gorzalka, Ann. *Wyoming's Territorial Sheriffs.* Glendo, WY: High Plains Press, 1998.

Greene, Jerome A. *Nez Perce Summer, 1877: The U.S. Army and the Nee-Me-Poo Crisis.* Helena: Montana Historical Society Press, 2000.

Griffith, A. Kinney. *Mickey Free: Manhunter.* Caldwell, ID: Caxton Printers, 1969.

Grover, David H. *Diamondfield Jack: A Study in Frontier Justice.* Reno: University of Nevada Press, 1968.

Hadley, Diana. *Environmental Change in Aravaipa, 1870–1970: An Ethnological Survey.* Cultural Resource Series 7, Phoenix: Arizona State Office of the Bureau of Land Management, September 1991.

Hagedorn, Herman. *Leonard Wood: A Biography.* 2 vols. New York: Harper and Brothers, 1931.

Hanchett, Leland J., Jr. *They Shot Billy Today: The Families of Arizona's Pleasant Valley War.* Phoenix: Pine Rim, 2006.

Hatfield, Shelley Bowen. *Chasing Shadows: Apaches and Yaquis Along the United States-Mexico Border; 1876–1911.* Albuquerque: University of New Mexico Press, 1998.

Hayes, Jess G. *Apache Vengeance: True Story of Apache Kid.* Albuquerque: University of New Mexico Press, 1954.

Hegne, Barbara M. *Border Outlaws of Montana, North Dakota and Canada.* Eagle Point, OR: printed by the author, 1993.

Henry, Will. *I, Tom Horn: Last Will and Testament of the Old West.* Philadelphia: J. B. Lippincott, 1975.

Herring, Hal. *Famous Firearms of the Old West.* Guilford, CT: Globe Pequot, 2008.

History of Lewis, Clark, Knox and Scotland Counties, Missouri. Chicago: Goodspeed, 1887.

Hooker, Forrestine C. *When Geronimo Rode.* New York: Doubleday, Page, 1924.

Horan, James D. *The Pinkertons: The Detective Dynasty That Made History.* New York: Crown, 1967.

Huey, William R. *In Search of Hollywood, Wyoming: 1894—The Silent Years—1929.* N.p.: printed by the author, 1985.

Hufsmith, George W. *The Wyoming Lynching of Cattle Kate, 1889.* Glendo, WY: High Plains Press, 1993.

Johnson, Elizabeth W., comp. and ed. *Trails, Rails and Travails.* Cheyenne: Frontier Printing, 1988.

Kantor, Mackinlay. *Wicked Water: An American Primitive.* New York: Random House, 1949. First published 1948.

Kelly, Charles. *The Outlaw Trail: A History of Butch Cassidy and His Wild Bunch.* Revised and enlarged. New York: Devin-Adair, 1959. First published 1938.

King, Jean Beach. *Arizona Charlie: A Legendary Cowboy, Klondike Stampeder, and Wild West Showman*. Phoenix: Heritage, 1989.

Knowles, Thomas W., and Joe R. Lansdale, eds. *The West That Was*. New York: Wings Books, 1993.

Kouris, Diana Allen. *The Romantic and Notorious History of Brown's Park*. Greybull, WY: Wolverine Gallery, 1998.

Krakel, Dean. F. *The Saga of Tom Horn: The Story of a Cattlemen's War, with Personal Narratives, Newspaper Accounts and Official Documents and Testimonies*. Laramie, WY: printed by the author, 1954.

Kuykendall, Ivan Lee. *Ghost Riders of the Mogollon*. San Antonio, TX: Naylor, 1954.

Lake, Stuart N. *Wyatt Earp: Frontier Marshal*. New York: Houghton Mifflin, 1931.

Lamar, Howard R. *Charlie Siringo's West: An Interpretive Biography*. Albuquerque: University of New Mexico Press, 2005.

Langhoff, Dever Babb. *Tom Horn and the "Langhoff Gang" of Wyoming*. Cedro, NM: privately printed, 1993.

Larson, Thomas A. *History of Wyoming*. Lincoln: University of Nebraska Press, 1965.

Lloyd, John [Jacques Lloyd Morgan]. *The Invaders: A Story of the "Hole-in-the-Wall" Country*. New York: R. F. Fenno, 1910.

Look, Al. *Unforgettable Characters of Western Colorado*. Boulder, CO: Pruett Press, 1966.

McCallum, Jack. *Leonard Wood: Rough Rider, Surgeon, Architect of American Imperialism*. New York: New York University Press, 2006.

McClure, Grace. *The Bassett Women*. Athens, OH: Swallow Press, 1985.

McKanna, Clare V., Jr. *White Justice in Arizona: Apache Murder Trials in the Nineteenth Century*. Lubbock: Texas Tech University Press, 2005.

Mokler, Alfred James. *History of Natrona County, Wyoming, 1888–1922*. Chicago: R. R. Donnelley and Sons, 1923.

Monaghan, Jay. *Last of the Bad Men: The Legend of Tom Horn*. Introduction by Larry D. Ball. Lincoln: University of Nebraska Press, 1997. First published Indianapolis: Bobbs-Merrill, 1946.

Morn, Frank. *"The Eye That Never Sleeps": A History of the Pinkerton National Detective Agency*. Bloomington: University of Indiana Press, 1982.

Murray, Robert A. *The Army on the Powder River*. Fort Collins, CO: Old Army Press, 1972.

Northern Gila County Historical Society, comps. *Rim Country History*. Payson, AZ: Rim Country Printery, 1984.

Nunis, Doyce B., Jr. *The Life of Tom Horn Revisited*. Los Angeles: The Westerners, Los Angeles Corral, 1992.

Ogle, Ralph H. *Federal Control of the Western Apaches, 1848–1886*. Albuquerque: University of New Mexico Press, 1970. First published 1940.

O'Neal, Bill. *The Johnson County War*. Austin: Eakin, 2004.

Osgood, Ernest Staples. *The Day of the Cattleman*. Chicago: University of Chicago Press, 1954.

O'Toole, G. J. A. *The Spanish War: An American Epic—1898*. New York: W. W. Norton, 1984.

Paine, Lauran. *Tom Horn: Man of the West*. Barre, MA: Barre, 1963. First published London: John Long, 1962.

Patterson, Richard. *Butch Cassidy: A Biography*. Lincoln: University of Nebraska Press, 1998.

Peavy, Charles D. *Charles A. Siringo: A Texas Picaro*. Southwest Writers Series, vol. 3. Austin, TX: Steck-Vaughn, 1967.

Peplow, Edward H. Jr. *History of Arizona*. 3 vols. New York: Lewis Historical, 1958.

Porter, Joseph C. *Paper Medicine Man: John Gregory Bourke and His American West.* Norman: University of Oklahoma Press, 1986.

Progressive Men of the State of Wyoming. Chicago: A. W. Bowen, 1903.

Radbourne, Allan. *Mickey Free: Apache Captive, Interpreter, and Indian Scout.* Tucson: Arizona Historical Society, 2005.

Raine, William M. *Famous Sheriffs and Western Outlaws.* New York: Home Library, 1944.

Rice, Mabel Wildman. *History of Scotland County, 1830–1971* [Missouri]. Memphis, MO: Scotland and Clark County Weeklies, 1973.

Rosenfeld, Harvey. *Diary of a Dirty Little War: The Spanish-American War of 1898.* Westport, CT: Praeger, 2000.

Rosenstand, Nina. *The Moral of the Story: An Introduction to Ethics.* 5th edition. New York: McGraw-Hill, 2005.

Sandoz, Mari. *The Cattlemen: From the Rio Grande Across the Far Marias.* New York: Hastings House, 1958.

Sargent, Herbert H. *The Campaign of Santiago de Cuba.* 3 vols. Chicago: A. C. McClurg, 1914.

Shapard, Bud. *Chief Loco: Apache Peacemaker.* Norman: University of Oklahoma Press, 2010.

Smith, Helena Huntington. *The War on Powder River: The History of an Insurrection.* New York: McGraw-Hill, 1966.

Sonnichsen, Charles Leland, ed. *Geronimo and the End of the Apache Wars.* Lincoln: University of Nebraska Press, 1986.

Spring, Agnes Wright. *Seventy Years: A Panoramic History of the Wyoming Stock Growers Association, Interwoven with Data Relative to the Cattle Industry in Wyoming.* Cheyenne: Wyoming Stock Growers Association, 1942.

———. *William Chapin Deming: Pioneer Publisher, and State and Federal Official, A Biography.* Glendale, CA: Arthur H. Clark, 1944.

Sweeney, Edwin R. *From Cochise to Geronimo: The Chiricahua Apaches, 1874–1886.* Norman: University of Oklahoma Press, 2010.

Tanner, Karen Holliday and John D. Tanner, Jr. *Last of the Old-Time Outlaws: The George West Musgrave Story.* Norman: University of Oklahoma Press, 2002.

Thrapp, Dan L. *Al Sieber, Chief of Scouts.* Norman: University of Oklahoma Press, 1964.

———. *The Conquest of Apacheria.* Norman: University of Oklahoma Press, 1967.

———. *Dateline Fort Bowie: Charles Fletcher Lummis Reports on an Apache War.* Norman: University of Oklahoma Press, 1979.

———. *General Crook and the Sierra Madre Adventure.* Norman: University of Oklahoma Press, 1972.

Tomlinson, Rawdon. *Geronimo after Kas-ki-yeh: Poems.* Baton Rouge: Louisiana State University Press, 2007.

Trachtman, Paul. *The Gunfighters.* Alexandria, VA: Time-Life Books, 1974.

Trask, David F. *The War with Spain in 1898.* New York: Macmillan, 1981.

Tuska, Jon, ed. *The American West: Masters of Western Fiction.* New York: Galahad Books, 1982.

Twitchell, Heath. *Allen: The Biography of an Army Officer, 1859–1930.* New Brunswick: Rutgers University Press, 1974.

Utley, Robert M. *Geronimo.* New Haven: Yale University Press, 2012.

Van Orden, Jay. *Geronimo's Surrender: The 1886 C. S. Fly Photographs.* Museum Monograph 8. Tucson: Arizona Historical Society, 1991.

Waller, Brown. *Last of the Great Western Train Robbers.* Cranbury, NJ: A. S. Barnes, 1968.

Walters, Lorenzo D. *Tombstone's Yesterdays.* Tucson: Acme Printing, 1928.

Willson, Roscoe G. *Pioneer Cattlemen of Arizona*. 2 vols. Phoenix: McGrew Commercial Printery, 1951–56.

Woods, Lawrence M. *Alex Swan and the Swan Companies*. Norman, OK: Arthur H. Clark, 2006.

———. *John Clay, Jr.: Commission Man, Banker and Rancher*. Spokane, WA: Arthur H. Clark, 2001.

———. *Wyoming's Big Horn Basin to 1901: A Late Frontier*. Spokane, WA: Arthur H. Clark, 1997.

Woody, Clara T. and Milton L. Schwartz. *Globe, Arizona: Early Times in a Little World of Copper and Cattle*. Tucson: Arizona Historical Society, 1977.

Works Projects Administration. *Wyoming: A Guide to Its History and People*. New York: Oxford University Press, 1941.

Wyoming Stock Growers Association. *Letters from Old Friends and Members of the Wyoming Stock Growers Association*. Cheyenne: S. A. Bristol, 1923.

Young, Roy B. *Cochise County Cowboy War: A Cast of Characters*. Apache, OK: Young and Sons, 1999.

Zachariae, Barbara. *Pleasant Valley Days: Young, Arizona*. Young, AZ: Pleasant Valley Historical Society, 1991.

Articles

Anderson, Mike. "Eugene and Matthew Shaw: The Last of Pima County's Frontier Sheriffs." *Journal of Arizona History* 38 (Winter 1997): 319–54.

Arnold, Watson C. "The Mule: The Worker That 'Can't Get No Respect.'" *Southwestern Historical Quarterly* 112 (July 2008): 35–50.

Ball, Larry D. "'Audacious and Best Executed': Tom Horn and Colorado's Cotopaxi Train Robbery." *Colorado Heritage* (Autumn 2000): 18–27.

———, ed. "'No Cure, No Pay': A Tom Horn Letter." *Journal of Arizona History* 8 (Autumn 1967): 200–202.

———. "That 'Miserable Book': *Life of Tom Horn, Government Scout and Interpreter*." *Journal of Arizona History* 48 (Winter 2007): 323–48.

———. "Tom Horn: Rogue Frontiersman," In *With Badges and Bullets: Lawmen and Outlaws in the Old West*. Edited by Richard W. Etulain and Glenda Riley. Golden, CO: Fulcrum, 1999.

———. "Tom Horn and the 'Talking Boy' Controversy." *Journal of Arizona History* 45 (Winter 2004): 333–56.

———. "The Two Tom Horns." *Journal of the Wild West History Association* 5 (August 2012): 10–20.

Barnes, Will C. "The Apaches' Last Stand in Arizona." *Arizona Historical Review* 3 (January 1931): 36–59.

Baxter, John O. "Roper and Rangers: Cowboy Tournaments and Steer Roping Contests in Territorial Arizona." *Journal of Arizona History* 46 (Winter 2005): 315–48.

Bowers, Carol L. "School Bells and Winchesters: The Sad Saga of Glendolene Myrtle Kimmell." *Annals of Wyoming* 73 (Winter 2001): 14–32.

Bret-Harte, John. "Conflict at San Carlos: The Military-Civilian Struggle for Control, 1882–1885." *Arizona and the West* 15 (Spring 1973): 27–44.

Brock, J. Elmer. "The Murder of George Wellman." *Denver Westerners Brand Book* 9 (March 1953): 5–10.

Brown, Larry K. "Truth Failed to Hide in a Tin." *True West* 50 (October 2003): 54–56.

Burt, Olive W. "We Sing of Murder." *Bits and Pieces* (Newcastle, WY) 2 (1966): 1–8.

"Campaigning in Arizona and New Mexico, 1895–[9]6." *Journal of the United States Cavalry Association* 10, no. 36 (1897): 25–28.

Carlson, Chip. "Caught in the Crossfire: The Murder of Willie Nickell." *True West* 48 (July 2001): 23–27.

Carmony, Neil B. "A Critical Essay by Neil B. Carmony Regarding *An Arizona Vendetta: The Truth About Wyatt Earp–And Some Others* by Forrestine C. Hooker." *Quarterly of the National Association for Outlaw and Lawman History* (NOLA) 24 (October–December 2000): 41–5.

Carr, Dalton. "A Chance Meeting." *Frontier Magazine* (Craig, CO) (September 1994): 8–9.

Carroll, Murray L. "Tom Horn and the Langhoff Gang." *Annals of Wyoming* 64 (Spring 1992): 34–44.

Chapman, Arthur. "The Last War for the Cattle Range." *Outing Magazine* 46 (September 1905): 668–75.

———. "Tom Horn, Wyoming's Death Rider." *The Frontier* 2 (October 1925): 69–76.

Condit, Thelma Gatchell. "The Hole-in-the-Wall." *Annals of Wyoming* 31 (April 1959): 53–75; (July 1959): 191–212.

"The Conqueror of Nana." *The Illustrated American* 17 (16 February 1895): 205.

Cowan, John L. "Wars of the Range." *Evening Star* (Washington, D.C.) Sunday Magazine (7 July 1907), 3–4, 17.

DeArment, Robert K. "Wyoming Range Detectives." *Old West* 30 (Fall 1993): 14–21.

Dullenty, Jim. "George Currie and the Curry Brothers." *Quarterly of the Outlaw-Lawman Association* 5 (October 1979): 4–7.

Dunlap, Horace E. "Tom Horn, Chief of Scouts." *Arizona Historical Review* 2 (April 1929): 73–85.

Edwards, Harold L. "The Killing of Ike Clanton." *Quarterly of the National Outlaw and Lawman Association* 16 (July–September 1992): 27–29, 31.

Edwardy, William M. "Border Troubles." *Harper's Weekly* 32 (18 August 1888): 611.

Emmons, David M. "Moreton Frewen and the Populist Revolt." *Annals of Wyoming* 35 (October 1963): 155–74.

Ernst, Donna B. "Friends of the Pinkertons." *Quarterly of the National Association for Outlaw and Lawman History* 19 (April–June 1995): 34–36.

———. "George S. Nixon: More than One Run-in with Outlaws." *Journal of the Western Outlaw-Lawman History Association* (WOLA) 10 (Summer 2001): 43–48.

———. "The Wilcox Train Robbery." *Wild West* (June 1999): 34–40.

"The Fifty Most Important Historical Photos of the Old West." *True West* 50 (January 2003): 39–44, 46–48, 51, 53–59.

Gale, Jack C. "Hatfield under Fire, May 15, 1886: An Episode of the Geronimo Campaign." *Journal of Arizona History* 18 (1977): 447–68.

———. "Lebo in Pursuit." *Journal of Arizona History* 21 (1980): 11–24.

Garrison, L. "John Hance, Guide, Trail Builder, Miner and Windjammer of the Grand Canyon," *Arizona Highways* 25 (June 1949): 4–11.

Gibbs, Archie Baird. "People of the Laramie Plains." *Old West* 4 (Winter 1967): 45, 56.

Graham County Historical Society. "Tom Horn." In *Mt. Graham Profiles*. Volume 2 (1988): 164–65.

Greene, Jerome A. "The Crawford Affair: International Implications of the Geronimo Campaign." *Journal of the West* 11 (January 1972): 143–53.

Hatfield, Shelley Bowen. "The Death of Emmet Crawford: Who Was to Blame?" *Journal of Arizona History* 29 (Summer 1988): 131–48.

Hawthorne, Roger. "Conflict and Conspiracy. Events Leading to the Johnson County War of 1892: The Lynching of Tom Waggoner." *True West* 31 (June 1984): 12–17.

Heard, John, Jr. "The Killing of the Captain." *Cosmopolitan Magazine* 17 (August 1894): 440–50.

Howe, Sam. "Steamboat–King of the Buckers!" *True West* 5 (January–February 1958): 20–21, 45.

"In the Early Days at Coolidge [New Mexico]." *Santa Fe Employes' Magazine* 2 (May 1908): 399–400.

"John Heard, Jr., with Portrait," *The Book Buyer* 12 (1895–96): 438.

Johnson, A. L. "Walker Castle and Its Setting." *Colorado Magazine* 27 (July 1950): 234–36.

Kelly, Charles. Review of *Life of Tom Horn, Government Scout and Interpreter*. Edited by Dean Krakel. Norman: University of Oklahoma Press, 1964. *Utah Historical Quarterly*. 33 (1965): 93–94.

Kittredge, William and Steven M. Krauzer. "Marshal Joe LeFors v. Killer Tom Horn. *American West* 22 (November–December 1985): 36–45.

Krakel, Dean. "Was Tom Horn Two Men?" *True West* 17 (January–February 1970): 12–17, 52–56.

Lauterborn, Dave. Review of *Famous Firearms of the Old West,* by Hal Herring. *Wild West* 22 (June 2009): 72, 75.

Lawyer, William. "Uncle Clyde Rode with Tom Horn." *Old West,* 13 (Winter 1976): 22–24, 26.

Miller, Victor W. "The McCoy Gang." *Old West* 6 (Summer 1970): 22–25, 68–72.

Mullins, Richard R. "The Inside Story of the Life and Death of Tom Horn," *Denver Post,* 23 November–12 December 1930.

Nalty, Bernard C., and Truman R. Strobridge. "Captain Emmet Crawford, Commander of Apache Scouts, 1882–1886." *Arizona and the West* 6 (Spring 1964): 30–40.

Nickell, Dennie. "Tom Horn in Arizona or—Who Killed Old Man Blevins." *Quarterly of the National Association and Center for Outlaw and Lawman History* 14, nos. 3 and 4 (1990): 15–22.

———, ed. "Who Were Tom Horn's Victims?" *Yesterday in Wyoming* (October–November, 1977): 22–38.

Peters, Leora. "Reminisce with Leora Peters." *Platte County Record-Times,* 28 July 1967.

Prince, Stephen. "Tom Horn: Dialectics of Power and Violence in the Old West." *Journal of Popular Culture* 22 (Winter 1988): 119–29.

Rasch, Philip J. Letter to the editor. *True West* 3 (November–December 1955): 46.

Ruhl, Win. "The War for the Pastures." *Out West* 20 (March 1904): 272–76.

Saar, Megan. "Tom Horn Hits the Auction Block." *True West* 54 (March 2007): 18.

Schubert, Frank N. "The Suggs Affray: The Black Cavalry in the Johnson County War." *Western Historical Quarterly* 5 (January 1973): 57–68.

Shields, Alice M. "Edwin J. Smalley: One of Cheyenne's First Native Sons." *Annals of Wyoming* 13 (January 1941): 58–72.

———. "The Life of Nannie Clay Steele." *Annals of Wyoming* 13 (April 1941): 93–103.

Shipp, William E. and Herbert Walsh. "Our Indian Scouts." *Harper's Weekly* 32 (October 1888): 811.

Spangenberger, Phil. "Blazing Their Way into History." *True West* 51 (January–February 2003): 27–34.

Tanner, Karen Holliday, and John D. Tanner, Jr. "Arizona's 1896 Apache Campaign," *Tombstone Epitaph* (October 2001): 1, 10–15.

Telling, Irving. "Coolidge and Thoreau: Forgotten Frontier Towns." *New Mexico Historical Review* 29 (July 1954): 210–23.

Thatcher, H. F. "One Night in Last Vegas." *True West* 2 (July–August 1955): 25–26, 28.

Thompson, D. Claudia. "The Image of Tom Horn." *Annals of Wyoming* 77 (Spring 2005): 2–11.

———. "Tom Horn's Accusers." *Annals of Wyoming* 77 (Summer 2005): 26–29.

Thompson, John Charles. "The Hanging of Tom Horn." *Denver Westerners Brand Book* 13 (1957): 111–29. First published in mimeograph form, 1 (1945).

Thorp, Raymond W. "Cowboy Charlie Siringo." *True West* 12 (January–February 1965): 32–33, 59–62.

"Top Ten True Western Towns of the Year." *True West* 54 (January–February 2007): 26–31, 34–37, 40.

Van Orden, Jay. "C. S. Fly at Cañon De Los Embudos: American Indians as Enemy in the Field, a Photographic First." *Journal of Arizona History* 30 (Autumn 1989): 319–46.

Walker, Tacetta. "Wyoming Fourth Governor, William A. Richards." *Annals of Wyoming* 20 (July 1948): 99–130.

White, Owen P. "Talking Boy." *Collier's* (February 18, 1933): 18, 38–40.

White, Stewart Edward. "Arizona Nights: Uncle Jim's Yarn, the Indian Story." *McClure's Magazine* 26 (January 1906): 292–96.

Whitehead, Eva Horn. Letter to the editor. *True West* 8 (November–December 1960): 58–59.

Williamson, Dan R. "Al Sieber, Famous Scout of the Southwest." *Arizona Historical Review* 3 (January 1931): 60–76.

Willson, Roscoe. "Several Living Arizonans Remember Scout Tom Horn." *The Stockman Magazine* 28 (March 1961): 45–57.

Wilson, Britt W. "Soldiers v. Apaches: One Last Time." *Wild West* (October 2001): 24–30.

Reference Books

Adams, Ramon F., ed. and comp. *Six-Guns and Saddle Leather: A Bibliography of Books and Pamphlets on Western Outlaws and Gunmen*, revised and enlarged. Norman: University of Oklahoma, 1969.

Adams, Ramon F., comp. *Western Words: A Dictionary of the American West*. Revised edition. Norman: University of Oklahoma, 1968.

Altshuler, Constance Wynn. *Cavalry Yellow and Infantry Blue: Army Officers in Arizona Between 1851 and 1886*. Tucson: Arizona Historical Society, 1991.

American National Biography. 24 vols. New York: Oxford University Press, 1999–2002.

Barnes, Will C. *Arizona Place Names*. Revised and enlarged by Byrd H. Granger. Tucson: University of Arizona, 1960.

Campbell, Walter S. [Stanley Vestal]. *The Book Lover's Guide to the Southwest: A Guide to Good Reading*. Norman: University of Oklahoma, 1955.

Cheyenne City Directory. 1905, 1906.

Denver City Directory. 1891, 1903.

Dictionary of American Biography. 10 vols. and supp. New York: Charles Scribner's Sons, 1929–36.

Frazier, Robert W. *Forts of the Old West*. Norman: University of Oklahoma Press, 1972.

Frye, Eleanor, comp. *Atlas of Wyoming Outlaws*. New York: Facts on File, 1995.

Gottesman, Ronald, and Richard Maxwell Brown, eds. *Violence in America: An Encyclopedia*. 3 vols. New York: Charles Scribner's Sons, 1999.

Great Register of Graham County, Territory of Arizona, 1886.

Lamar, Howard R., ed. *New Encyclopedia of the American West*. Revised and enlarged. New Haven: Yale University Press, 1998.

Leadville City Directory. 1880, 1881.

Luttrell, Estelle. *Newspapers and Periodicals of Arizona, 1859–1911*. University of Arizona Bulletin 15. Tucson: University of Arizona Press, July 1949.

McLoughlin, Denis. *Wild and Woolly: An Encyclopedia of the Old West*. Garden City, NY: Doubleday, 1975.

Mencken, Henry L., comp. *A New Dictionary of Quotations on Historical Principles*. New York: Alfred Knopf, 1962.

Nash, Jay Robert, ed., *Encyclopedia of World Crime: Criminal Justice, Criminology, and Law Enforcement*. 6 vols. New York: Crime Books, 1990.

Patterson, Richard, ed. and comp. *Historical Atlas of the Outlaw West*. Boulder, CO: Johnson Books, 1985.

Thrapp, Dan L, ed. and comp. *Encyclopedia of Frontier Biography*. 4 vols. Glendale, CA, and Spokane, WA: Arthur H. Clark, 1988–93.

Tuska, Jon, and Vicki Piekarski, eds. *Encyclopedia of Frontier and Western Fiction*. New York: McGraw-Hill, 1983.

Urbanek, Mae, comp. *Wyoming Place Names*. Missoula: Mountain Press, 1988.

Waldman, Carl, comp. *Who Was Who in Native American History: Indians and Non-Indians Through 1900*. New York: Facts on File, 1990.

Walker, Henry P., and Don Bufkin. *Historical Atlas of Arizona*. Norman: University of Oklahoma Press, 1979.

Wentworth, Harold, and Stuart B. Flexner, comps. *Dictionary of American Slang*. New York: Thomas Y. Crowell, 1967.

Index

Aravaipa Canyon (Ariz.), 44–45, 32, 98, 109, 111, 116–20, 191, 198
Aravaipa Mine (Ariz.), 110
Arhelger, Ed, 48, 50
Arizona, 19–21, 25, 30, 37, 43, 51, 55, 68, 75, 77, 86, 98, 112, 158, 192–93, 199, 208, 213–14, 220, 223, 242, 257, 428, 437, 440; Geronimo's surrender in, 91, 93, 96; military commanders of, 19, 76–77; Rough Riders of, 203; rustling in, 30, 113; Tom Horn in, 8, 16–17, 21, 44–45, 70, 72–73, 83, 109, 120, 129, 139, 191–92, 199, 201, 215, 256, 259, 349, 432; Tom Horn's reputation in, 46–47, 117, 128, 130, 135, 431, 436
Arizona Bulletin (Solomonville), 199, 431
Arizona Crossroads (radio show), 447
"Arizona Nights" (White), 437
Arizona Silver Belt (Globe), 115, 130, 195
Arizona Star (Tucson), 52, 110, 115
Army and Navy Journal, 204
Aros (Haros) River (Mexico), 55–57, 84
Atchison, Topeka and Santa Fe Railroad, 11–12, 15
Atlantic and Pacific Railroad, 124
Atwood, Edwin Byron, 200, 214
Averill, Nathan King, 195
Axford, Alfred, 278
Ayer, Charles F., 231, 241

Babbitt, Thomas, 374
Bad Men of Tombstone (film), 445
Baggs, Wyo., 235–36, 239, 260, 450
Bailey, Leroy D., 235
Bailey, Paul, 288, 306, 336
Baird, John A., 179, 183
Baker, Etherton P., 188
Bakker, Johan P., 442
Baldwin, Theodore A., 97
Baldwin, William H., 195
Banks, George, 233, 241
Barber, Amos W., 142–43
Bard, I. N., 318
Barnes, James E., 374, 385
Barnes, Sarah, 374
Barnes, Will C., 26, 113
Barron, John F., 421
Barrow, Bill, 371

Bartholomew, Burke, 414
Barton, Bill, 446
Bassett, Amos Herbert, 230, 234, 239
Bassett, Ann, 230, 232–34, 237, 239, 241–42, 488n50
Bassett, Elbert ("Eb"), 233–34, 237–39
Bassett, George, 238
Bassett, Josephine ("Josie"), 230, 232
Bates Hole, Wyo., 179, 182–83, 187–89
Bath, Louis, 162–63, 478n45
Bavispe River (Mexico), 36, 70, 89–90, 196
Beauford, Clay. *See* Bridwell, Welford C.
Beaumont, Eugene Beauharnais, 97
Becker, Samuel, 313
Bell, Catherine, 224–25, 247, 250, 318
Bell, Edwin J., 242, 402
Bell, Fred, 224–25, 247, 250–51, 318
Bell, Sherman, 409
Bellinger, John, 202
Bender (Chiricahua Apache), 61
Benjamin, Everett E., 78
Bennitt, William Asa ("Dad"), 451
Benson, Harry C., 79
Benton, Frank, 453
Bergersen, Peter, 286, 288
Bergstein, Henry, 127
Bernard, Hiram H. ("Hi"), 231–34, 238, 241–42, 488n50
Besias, Antonio, *104*
Betzinez, Jason, 20
Bianco, Vingenzo, 269–70, 274
Big Dry Wash, Battle of, 29–30
Biggs, Thornton, 355
Big Horn Basin (Wyo.), 164, 168, 219, 282, 389, 479n5
Billy the Kid, 16, 435, 439–40, 455
Birchfield, William P. ("Billy"), 192
Blades, John W., 12
Blair, Dee, 269, 282
Blair, Henry, 144, 228
Blair, Tommy, *104*
Blake, Cody, 440
Blake, John, 318
Blattner, Elizabeth ("Lizzie"). *See* Horn, Elizabeth ("Lizzie"; Blattner)
Blevins, Martin ("Old Man"), 110–11
Blevins, Tom, 235–36
Bolser, Frank, 263